Germans and the
Revolution of 1848–1849

New German-American Studies
Neue Deutsch-Amerikanische Studien

Don Heinrich Tolzmann
General Editor

Vol. 18

PETER LANG
New York · Washington, D.C./Baltimore · Boston
Bern · Frankfurt am Main · Berlin · Vienna · Paris

Justine Davis Randers-Pehrson

Germans and the Revolution of 1848–1849

PETER LANG
New York · Washington, D.C./Baltimore · Boston
Bern · Frankfurt am Main · Berlin · Vienna · Paris

Library of Congress Cataloging-in-Publication Data

Randers-Pehrson, Justine Davis.
Germans and the revolution of 1848–1849 / Justine Davis Randers-Pehrson.
p. cm. — (New German-American studies/
Neue deutsch-amerikanische Studien; vol. 18)
Includes bibliographical references and index.
1. Germany—History—Revolution, 1848–1849. 2. Germany—Social
conditions—19th century. 3. German Americans—History—19th century.
4. Refugees, Political—United States—History—19th century. I. Title.
II. Series: New German-American studies; vol. 18.
DD207.R36   943'.076—dc21   98-29251
ISBN 0-8204-4118-X
ISSN 1043-5808

Die Deutsche Bibliothek-CIP-Einheitsaufnahme

Randers-Pehrson, Justine Davis:
Germans and the revolution of 1848–1849 / Justine Davis Randers-Pehrson.
–New York; Washington, D.C./Baltimore; Boston; Bern;
Frankfurt am Main; Berlin; Vienna; Paris: Lang.
(New German-American studies; Vol. 18)
ISBN 0-8204-4118-X

Interior illustrations courtesy of Glenn Randers-Pehrson

The paper in this book meets the guidelines for permanence and durability
of the Committee on Production Guidelines for Book Longevity
of the Council of Library Resources.

© 1999 Peter Lang Publishing, Inc., New York

Printed in the United States of America

For the known living descendants of Anton Joseph Kilp and Franziska Engert, his wife. This book was written with love, because they are all my descendants too.

Glenn Randers-Pehrson
    Justine Davis Randers-Pehrson Garrett
            Zackary Miles Garrett
    Laura Mabel Randers-Pehrson Knoops
    Emily Elizabeth Randers-Pehrson
    Christopher Brady Randers-Pehrson
Gerhard Randers-Pehrson
    Michael Nils Randers-Pehrson
    Timothy Ralph Randers-Pehrson
Sigrid Elizabeth Randers-Pehrson Smith
    Catherine Boyer Smith Noxon
    Tamara Pehrson Smith Carmel

Special warm thanks are due to Glenn for his generous use of his time in preparation of the illustrations for this book.

Contents

For the Sake of a Great-Grandfather
Anton Joseph Kilp 1819–1876

Records in the US Archives relate to the military service of my maternal great-grandfather, Anton Joseph Kilp. Examining them, I reach the conclusion that his life and times are worth closer investigation. From what can be gleaned from these dry emotionless pages, it appears that this was a man whose life was touched by a number of events and issues that were stirring the world in 1848 and 1849. It seems clear that Anton Kilp must have been affected somehow by the revolutions that swept over all Europe at that time. Otherwise, how explain the statement written by his son that he came to America in 1849 because of "false denunciations"?

In post-revolutionary Germany, the hunt for suspects went on for months, even years. As just one horrifying example, take the statistical study on eight hundred and sixty-nine persons who were examined in 1849 by the Dresden city court. These were only a fraction of the nine to twelve thousand individuals who underwent investigation in Saxony in that year alone.

Maybe the air in Europe smelled of defeat then, but the bloodshed and sorrow had not resulted in total failure. The revolutions had nevertheless transformed Europe, breaking feudal bonds, liberating the individual, freeing the peasants of Austria and Hungary, and giving direction to nationalist movements in Italy and Germany, to say nothing of the social movement set going by Marx's *Communist Manifesto*.

The refugees were too close to their failure to see its potential victories, but they still perhaps had some shreds of optimism. A rapid scanning of the pages of Boatner's Civil War dictionary reveals the fact that many of them rushed to the Union colors as soon as the Civil

War broke out, no doubt with the notion that they might yet usefully serve a liberal cause. Some joined the Union army at the very start of the war, while many more responded to the call for volunteers that was voted by the U.S. Senate and House and signed by President Lincoln on 22 July 1861. The bill authorized 500,000 troops, to be enlisted for a three-year term.

Anton Kilp was editing a newspaper in Davenport, Iowa, when the war broke out, yet he was commissioned a 1ˢᵗ Lieutenant of the Engineer Corps on 24 September 1861. Like many of the refugees, some of whom worked as carpenters or hotel-keepers, or ran small business enterprises, Anton Kilp was an educated man, an engineer and apparently something of a scholar. He arrived in New York in April or May 1849 with his companion Franziska Engert (both of them Bavarians), and they immediately traveled to Peru, Illinois, where he bought a small farm. In other words, he must have been one of those immigrants jokingly nicknamed "Latin farmers", said to be pondering the weighty ideas of Kant and Fichte while they labored in their fields.

It is curious to consider the two emerging societies that Anton Kilp lived in. Bavaria had undergone many dislocations and transfers of territory in the wake of the French Revolution and the dictatorial period of Napoleon's "patronage". There is a hint of the general feeling of the newness of political arrangements in the notation in the hand of Anton Kilp's wife in her little cookbook, where she wrote "Franziska Engert of Kloster Ebrach, 1846, in Upper Franconia." Presumably she did not yet view herself as a Bavarian. For that matter, Kloster Ebrach was no longer a *Kloster* [monastery] because it had been secularized in 1803.

Contrast that with the situation in the United States. Almost all territory west of the Mississippi had been added after the Mexican War of 1845, and the West had become joltingly attractive with the discovery of gold in California. The Bavarian problem had been complicated by the weight of centuries of conflicting traditions and religious belief, whereas problems in the United States may have been compounded by the very rawness of the new country, barely sixty years old, with no traditions to speak of.

It is tempting to think that disheartened liberals arriving on our shores may have thought that here the air was fresher and less polluted by a long past, and that something might be done that would bring positive results. Away from the surveillance and censorship of official Germany, away from a land where supposedly representative bodies could do little more than debate, the open prairies of the West must have seemed like the virgin soil of another planet.

Reconstruction of Anton Kilp's life and career in Bavaria is largely a matter of guesswork. His father was the chief forester of the *Graf* von Schönborn, whose administrative seat was at Pommersfelden, not far from Bamberg. Upon the death of the father, the Kilp family moved to Bamberg, where Anton and his brother Franz Peter went through the local *Gymnasium*. After three and a half years as a volunteer in the Bavarian army, Anton joined the railway service, which at the time was in its infancy. The first line on the European continent was built in 1835, running from Nürnberg to Fürth in Bavaria.

Railroad design was so new that those engaged in it were feeling their way along, improvizing. In Bavaria, they used *Katasterkarten* [maps intended for use in tax collection] as a basis for plotting future railway lines. The only dependable guide for their work was an English-language text, but they found that the tax maps were a helpful base on which to trace newly surveyed lines, grade crossings and so on.

Railroads captured popular imagination in a way that can well be compared to the public hysteria over aircraft at the time of Charles A. Lindbergh. People wrote feverishly about snorting dragons and quoted Goethe and Hegel and went to the stations in throngs to witness arrivals and departures. They composed odes to locomotives and laughed at the comedian who said that he knew all about steam but he'd have to talk to a horse-trader to find out how the engine got its horsepower.

Everyone had an opinion about this novel means of transportation. The king of Prussia was bored by the idea. What was so great, he wanted to know, about saving an hour or two in going from Berlin to Potsdam? The tsar of Russia was worried. Filth now lying below the surface will come to the top, he declared morosely. Goethe thought that if the railroads had the effect that Berlin would become the sole cultural center, as opposed to Germany's many courts and capital cities, there might be a resulting stale uniformity that would be most unfortunate. Karl Marx observed that whereas philosophical systems were developed in men's brains, it was the hands of labor that would create the new network, implying that intellectuals and labor could cooperate in the coming revolution. There were others who were every bit as earnest about the spread of ideas across frontiers as Al Gore is today on the subject of his information highway.

Anton Kilp had planned to resign from the railway service and return to the army, where presumably his eight years of experience with the railroads would qualify him for officer rank, but something sinister happened. Ironically, it was only after a long ocean journey and years of hard struggle that he became an officer—in a bitter civil war in a foreign land. He had fled precipitately to the United States, accompanied by Franziska Engert, whom he married immediately upon their arrival in New York City. Had something prevented their marriage in Bavaria? Mixed marriages were frowned on: she was a Catholic, he a free-thinker.

There are few tangible remains, aside from a handful of yellowed photographs and an extremely blackened tintype of Anton and Franziska and their four children, presumably made about 1866. There is his sword in its dented scabbard, his small magnifier that he used in topographical work, some handsome Civil War campaign maps made by him, from the collection of General William Tecumseh Sherman (now in the Library of Congress), and a much spattered cookbook, printed in 1844, that belonged to Franziska.

I have written this book in honor of my ancestors, with the thought that many American descendants of Forty-Eighters may want to mark the one hundred and fiftieth anniversary of the revolution by considering the factors that sent their own ancestors across the Atlantic to these shores.

Justine Davis Randers-Pehrson
Reston, Virginia   December 1997

The tensions of prerevolutionary society were not expressed once and for all in the spring of 1848, nor did the revolution as mass movement come to an end then. . . . Any interpretation that cannot explain this . . . period of conflict and crisis . . . and understand its roots in prerevolutionary society is simply incomplete.

Jonathan Sperber

Chapter 1

The Stagnant Society:
Sovereigns, Nobles, and Bureaucrats

To the average European of 1848, the word "revolution" was laden with horrifying images of the dripping blade of the guillotine. The great French Revolution was still too recent for comfort. The very thought of it evoked such vivid memories of ugly tumbrels carrying haggard victims and of impassive gory heads impaled on pikes that even the years of Napoleonic warfare and dictatorship had not diminished the terror. It is odd therefore to consider that in 1848, when revolutionists once again took up arms in Paris, the citizens of major continental centers everywhere went into action, building barricades.

Revolutions are not spontaneous eruptions. There has to be an existing balance, and something that upsets it. The triggering mechanism is rarely anything so simple and distinct as popular dislike of the ruler. The crucial element is more plausibly an economic disturbance, some trouble that touches the pocketbook and empties the cupboard. In 1846 and 1847, near-famine raged in many parts of Europe because of poor grain harvests, and the potato blight pushed peasant families to the verge of starvation. The agricultural crisis spilled over into the cities, where reduced purchasing power caused shutdowns and failure of small businesses. Consequently, there was unemployment on such a scale in the major European cities that more than half the work force was out on the streets.

If France alone had undergone crop failures and an old style cyclical economic depression in 1847, Europe might have been spared its wave of revolutions, but social conditions had become shaky everywhere because of dislocations introduced by new industry, especially metallurgy and railroad development, as well as textile manufacture where steam-powered machinery was adopted early. There were novel interactions between financiers and entrepreneurs. In their turn, small businessmen and the workers were in difficulty, struggling with problems brought on by the abandonment of the old guild system and by a sudden spurt in population that enlarged the ranks of the laborers who were hunting for employment. Moreover, these same new conditions had made the nations interdependent, not only in their search for raw materials but also in their urgent need for funds. While reformers like Marx and Engels were calling for an international network of the laboring classes, the depression of 1847 was impressively demonstrating the fact that another powerful network was already coming into being—the web of great financial houses and enterprises that some day would evolve into multinational corporations. Large-scale operations, notably railroad building, had already absorbed such vast sums that the major banking houses and national treasuries had been drawn into the crisis and were approaching desperation.

The resulting problem was novel but not easily understood or managed. Any dislocation in one capital almost immediately caused repercussions elsewhere because various ventures had become inextricably interlocked.[1] Swiss businessmen began writing to James Rothschild in Paris early in 1847, calling attention to the drastic drop in the value of railway stock and asking if this might not portend grave consequences for the whole European financial market. By the end of 1847 it was clear that the trouble was indeed serious, and of alarming magnitude. Well-established firms in Vienna, Milan, Antwerp, Frankfurt, and London were bankrupt. Half the blast-furnaces in England were shut down, and many cotton mills were idle there. Even as far away as New York, the major banking house of Prim, Ward was stopping its payments.

Not only was cash scarce. Credit was approaching the vanishing point, a situation that was causing acute anxiety at industrial centers such as Le Havre, Rouen, Nantes, and Lyon. People were even looking doubtfully at the Rothschilds, those giants who seemed to hold the world in the hollow of their hands, engineering state bond issues all the way from Russia to Haiti.

In 1848, industrialists and financiers comprised the controlling upper level of French society. The aristocrats had lost much of their power by that time. Especially since the advent of Louis-Philippe, it was the upper *bourgeoisie* that was looked on with suspicion. The distrust had been fanned by agitators who, in the spirit of Marx and Engels, wanted the people to unite in the overthrow of the middle class. They were listened to by many French artisans because their proposals were deliberately tailored to the problems of the workers. Alexis de Tocqueville recognized the significance of the change. The working classes, he observed, were gradually forming opinions destined not only to upset this or that law, ministry, or even form of government. They were destined to upset society itself.[2]

Such in brief was the situation in France that threatened to engulf all Europe. On the right bank of the Rhine, in Germany, and elsewhere on the continent, the soil where radical reformers hoped that the seeds of revolution might flourish was startlingly infertile. In many ways, the prospect was far from promising.

Germany was the collective name for an assemblage of kingdoms, duchies, free cities and ecclesiastical principalities that was not in control of its own destiny. Its very existence was bound into the fate of all Europe. It was an emergent industrial society that was trying to put down roots through the hard barren striated crust of a feudalism that covered soil that rested on the fossils of a barbarized Roman civilization, which in its turn overlay the antagonistic remains of pre-Roman groupings. Even now, Germans refer to each other as Burgundians or Swabians, so long is their memory of the past.

Ever since the Thirty Years' War dragged itself to its weary conclusion, the odd congeries of German states had been "Europe's hollow center".[3] By the terms of the treaties of Westphalia (1648) the contending powers had recognized an impasse and established not so much a peace as a mechanism for maintaining an uneasy balance, with "hollow" Germany as the fulcrum. No country or sovereign had won the Thirty Years' War, and thereafter no country or sovereign would be able to gain the mastery of Europe. The various elements responsible for this uneasy peace could shift positions as circumstances required, since it had been provided that the states of the Holy Roman Empire could make or alter alliances at will, while at the same time they were guarantors of the conglomeration of states known collectively as Germany. If, for example, the Habsburgs seemed to threaten Germany, Prussia and France would come to the rescue, but if France and Prussia appeared to threaten, the German Electors could throw their support to the Habsburgs. Within Germany itself, the same balance could be sustained by action on the part of the Habsburgs, or Sweden, or France, or England, or Russia against any principality or minor state that appeared to be too ambitious in the matter of territory and influence.

This strange mechanism had rocked along fairly efficiently until the advent of Napoleon, who upset the status quo all over the continent. The Napoleonic disturbance was temporary, to be sure. The Congress of Vienna (1815) presumably had set the old mechanism going again, but its chief result within Germany was a shift in the nature of the precarious balance. The reform-minded Wilhelm von Humboldt called the new creation (the *Deutscher Bund*—German Confederation) a monster because, he protested, the whole well-being of the new confederation rested on an unconstitutional arrangement in which Berlin and Vienna would agree on policy before it was presented to the supposed governing body, the *Bundestag* [Confederation Diet] at Frankfurt. The system prevailed because each of the two major powers had fairly limited objectives. Austria wanted to secure herself against any liberal or nationalist movement and to retain influence over the smaller states, whereas Prussia aimed at a cautious blockade of Austrian primacy: Berlin wanted to strengthen the confederation and gain certain advantages by means of a Prussian customs union.

The equilibrium was not so much a balance of power among states as a reluctant solidarity of conservative power intended to stabilize the world against the subversive force of potential revolution. England, Russia, Prussia, Austria and later even France were joined to constitute an uneasy front. The shift was no doubt basic to the resistance of most small German states to socio-economic development or political change.

Contemplation of the map of Germany as it was constituted in the early years of the Nineteenth Century and the thought of the various conflicting elements that made up the beginning of the Industrial Revolution, rather presents a puzzle. Why would a *revolution* result in 1848, and not pure anarchy? Altogether, this once comparatively backward sluggish land of nobles in fancy castles, of peasants dutifully working for their lords, and craftsmen supervising their handful of journeymen and apprentices, had been called upon to cope with most of the strains that we of a thoroughly industrialized civilization find difficult to handle.

Within the span of just one lifetime, the Germans had to reorganize their lives somehow around new territorial arrangements, new forms of large-scale manufacture with their accompanying threat to the centuries-old ways of handicraft, along with the awesome spectacle of steam-powered transportation on land and water, and an alarming population explosion. Add to this the stress generated by the spread of ideas eddying out from the French Revolution and the regime imposed upon them by Napoleon. New social classes—new ideas about collective and individual rights—ideas about suffrage and the protection of industry—a new view of the little German states as potentially a nation—new demands on old resources with contradictory claims on usage rights.

Superficially it might appear that a new kingdom like Bavaria could have contained the various pressures by fixing attention on one salient issue, namely the need to integrate newly-acquired lands into a unit that would solidify the changed political arrangement despite the lack of dynastic loyalties and shared traditions. A useful mechanism in such a case would be a constitution, a legal code that could be decreed by the sovereign. That in fact was the guiding idea of the Bavarian minister Montgelas, who devised a constitution that was issued under the hand of King Maximilian I Joseph in 1808.—Montgelas believed that a patchwork realm like Bavaria could only be seamed together smoothly by such means. If European conditions had been relatively steady, this might have been a workable solution throughout Germany, but these were not ordinary times. An Industrial Revolution was brewing. With everything on the boil at once, open revolt must have seemed to many Germans to be inevitable, especially in crowded urban centers.

The *Düsseldorfer Zeitung* of 3 September 1843 editorialized on the destructive nature of the multiplicity of small German states, noting that the struggle to satisfy the demands of separate interests of all those governments led to such a tangle that no post could be hurried and no mailing charge reduced without special conventions, and that railroad planning was more or less at a standstill because of the determination of each state to keep the railroad in question within its own boundaries as long as possible.

Despite this gloom, thirty-nine states were an improvement. Before the advent of Napoleon (i.e., after the French Revolution) there had been no less than three hundred and sixty states, including free cities and ecclesiastical principalities. By the settlement of 1803, one hundred and twelve of these mini-states disappeared and church properties were secularized. Bavaria became a kingdom in terms of the treaty of Pressburg on 26 December 1805, when the Holy Roman Empire flickered to an end. In the following year, sixteen principalities as well as Westphalia and the new grand duchy of Warsaw joined in a shaky confederation known as the *Rheinbund*, but this short-lived organization did little to unify the Germans. Next came the Congress of Vienna, 1815. Of its many complex provisions, one of the more lasting was the establishment of the *Deutscher Bund,* a diplomatic league that was more a meeting-ground for princes than a representative body.

With its headquarters, the *Bundestag,* at Frankfurt am Main, the confederation witnessed the struggles of the Austrian and Prussian members, each of whom had a clear ambition to be central in all matters of European power. Earnest reformers like Carl Theodor Welcker thought wistfully that the confederation might one day add some sort of elected parliament that could meet alongside the existing *Bundestag,* as a basis for conversion to a national government. As early as 1831, Welcker had in fact ventured, in a session of the Baden *Landtag* [provincial assembly], to propose the establishment of what he called a *Volkshaus* that would represent the people, but since the presidency of council meetings at Frankfurt was reserved for the Austrian representative, this was not much more than a daydream.

The implications of the inordinate multiplicity of German states can best be understood by thinking for a few moments of one small segment of Germany, the Thuringian states just to the north of Bavaria. There were the territories of the Ernstine line of the Wettin family (Saxe-Weimar, Saxe-Gotha, Saxe-Meiningen, Saxe-Hildburghausen, and Saxe-Coburg). There were lands belonging to the senior branch of the Reuss family (Reuss-Greiz), and those of the junior branches (Reuss-Lobenstein, Reuss-Schleiz, and Reuss-Ebersdorf.) That was not all. There were two principalities known as Schwarzburg-Rudolstadt and Schwarzburg-Sondershausen. Eleven little states. In the long-distance view from another century, the one faint landmark is the fact that Goethe was once summoned to the court of Karl August of Saxe-Weimar, but this small detail is not enough to bring the blurry picture into focus.

"The small state system was the true historical fate of Germany in the 19th Century—it cried for revolution, and revolution alone could remedy the situation." So wrote the historian, Veit Valentin.[4] Just how insoluble the fatal question of small states could be is plainly illustrated in the report of the French ambassador to Saxony, written from Dresden in November 1848, the year of revolution—the year that was supposed to have produced solutions for Germany's problems.[5] He was referring specifically to the little Thuringian states as an example.

He pointed out that if all the Thuringian states were assigned to Saxony, the ruling grand duke of Weimar would surely object, with strong support on the part of Russia. If the states were to be grouped around Weimar, two dukes—those of Coburg and Meiningen—would certainly refuse, with the backing of England. If there were to be some kind of special league set up among the minor princes, with a revolving directorate, there would be too many rivalries and the whole system would rapidly disintegrate. The ambassador dismissed the notion of a Thuringian republic out of hand as unworkable. There remained, he suggested, only annexation (mediatizing) of the little Thuringian states by their most powerful neighbor. A stupefying jumble of internal rivalries and foreign influences, in other words.

In his own discussion of the small state problem, Veit Valentin described the little kingdoms and duchies as "dwarf states, splinter states, private properties that had become states" and lamented that the *great darkness of sovereignty* of the many lordlings had poisoned German freedom. Whereas in the Empire, there was one figure who stood above all the highnesses, very reverends, and lordships, above princely, ducal and other graces, whose stature made all the rest small, even majesty itself had been cheapened. "Even the highness of an archduke is called royal."

All too true. In those wee Graustarkian realms, the emphasis was on etiquette and elaborate forms of address. It was even customary to back out of the royal presence, bowing respectfully. This was no place for wit or initiative or democratic reform. In these dwarf kingdoms, there must have been enacted many a scene not unlike the comic royal audience of Fabrice, the hero of Stendhal's *Chartreuse de Parme*.

Indeed, the subject in one of those miniature states must have understood that his fate was in the hands of the ruler, who regarded the realm as his personal property. Take the case of little Oldenburg. A neutral territory during the Thirty Years' War, Oldenburg was taken over jointly by King Christian V of Denmark and the duke of Holstein-Göttorp when the hereditary ruler died without issue. A subsequent pact handed Oldenburg over to the royal Danish house. King Charles VII gave it to Paul of Holstein-Göttorp (a grand duke of Russia) in exchange for certain rights over Schleswig and Holstein (this occurred in 1773). Grand Duke Paul turned Oldenburg over to his cousin Friedrich August, bishop of Lübeck, who had it made into a duchy in 1777. When the bishopric was secularized (1803), it became a hereditary principality that the bishop gave to his nephew Peter Friedrich Ludwig, along with Oldenburg. Napoleon took possession of the duchy in 1810, joining it to northern Hannover, the Hanseatic cities and

part of the duchy of Berg (he was strengthening his continental blockade). Tsar Alexander I attempted at that point to negotiate some kind
of indemnity for his kinsman, Grand Duke Peter Friedrich Ludwig,
and the failure of this move is thought to have had something to do
with the resumption of hostilities between Russia and France in 1812.
At the conclusion of the war of liberation, Oldenburg was restored to
the grand duke, whose heirs were not forced out until 1918.

Oldenburg, tiny and ineffectual as it was, was a model for other
small German principalities, which—in the wry words of E. J.
Hobsbawm—had the main international function of providing good
breeding stock for the royal houses of Europe.[6] The Oldenburg house
was connected by blood lines with the royal houses of England and
Scotland (Stuart and Hanover), Sweden, Denmark and Norway, France
(both Bourbon and Orléans), Greece and Russia.(by virtue of the marriage of Karl Friedrich of Schleswig-Holstein-Göttorp to Anne, daughter of Peter the Great). Not all the highnesses were great and powerful, like those of the illustrious houses—Habsburg, Hohenzollern,
Saxe-Coburg-Gotha, and Hannover, although there was enough inter-
marriage to make the German royals into an enormous cousinship.

Many rulers were financially pinched and grasped at any opportunity to help them keep up appearances. One way to do this was open
to any sovereign whose territory had the good fortune to be on a river
or a major trade route. Such a person exacted customs duties from all
who passed by or through his land. One of the most conspicuous
struggles of the early decades of the century had to do with customs
and tolls. In the dawn of the industrial age, it was unthinkable that
such barriers could exist. Toll was clearly a survival from the middle
ages, and petty monarchs clung to it for their own survival.

> Der König und der Bischof teilen sich Burg und Stadt und Stift und Dom.
> Mehr Zölle sind am Rhein als Meilen.[7] [King and bishop between them
> divide fortress and city, church foundation and cathedral. The Rhine has more
> tolls than miles.]

In spite of all their dignities, court etiquette, retainers, lavishly uniformed ministers and ambassadors, not all the thirty-nine states were
centers of culture and enlightenment. Most of the scientists and philosophers had gravitated to the great universities like those of Berlin
and Göttingen. The lives of these conspicuously well-educated men
give a false impression because most of them traveled on invitation
from one university to another to take prestigious chairs, or enjoyed
the patronage of powerful princes.

A less prominent man would live out his days within the boundaries of his own little duchy or kingdom. Travel in those times required not only money and leisure but also privilege, in the sense that one usually had to have special official permission to leave one principality in order to establish oneself in another little realm. At the artisan level, there were the traditional years of wandering as a journeyman, but once accepted by a guild, the worker found himself just as thoroughly hemmed in by the confining bonds of community custom and exclusiveness as any monk would be within the walls of a monastery. The artisan quickly learned to be suspicious of outsiders and to have as little contact with them as possible.

At this distance, it looks obvious that a primary problem that the Germans needed to solve was the matter of national unity. After all, the French had accomplished that fairly well. There they had a unitary legal and administrative system, and their spreading system of public education was promoting a national language.

Germany should have made herself into a nation. Easy enough to say. But in those days Germans were not quite clear about this in their own minds. Which ought to come first? Loyalty to a united Germany, or loyalty to one's own endangered class? As far as that goes, what about some deeply ingrained loyalty to one's own exclusive little town, or one's native patch of a duchy or kingdom? It is true that ethnically at least, there were few of the divisions that were so conspicuous in Austria-Hungary with its large Slavic population, but in Germany itself there was sharp cleavage between Catholic and Protestant regions, and even the German language was not a true binding force. (Not so long before, the king of Prussia, Friedrich *der Grosse*, had habitually spoken and written French most of the time.) Besides, local dialects were distinct and even incomprehensible to German-speakers from different areas.

Twenty-five of the small states of the German confederation were constitutional monarchies, usually with a legislative arrangement that in most cases was bicameral. Bavaria had such a system, but Prussia did not. There would be an upper house where membership was hereditary for the most part (nobles, high-ranking clergy), whereas members of the lower house, the *Landtag*, were "elected" according to various complex processes that weighted it with top echelon bureaucrats and other state officials, including university professors. There was not much freedom of expression in a lower house because if a member spoke up too insistently in favor of some measure that was repugnant to the sovereign, the upshot more often than not was loss of the *Landtag* seat as well as one's professional post.

Germans had little opportunity to become acquainted and to discover what ideas and problems they shared in the midst of the strange diversity of their small states. They had little or no experience in political participation because public organizations were closely supervised everywhere, and a leader who appeared to be too hot-headed could be promptly arrested or exiled. Not much relief from the oppression of surveillance and censorship could be expected from the local parliaments. Most had been based on cautious provisions of new constitutions like Bavaria's (a product of the Napoleonic era), and they were not much more than advisory bodies at best. The Bavarian *Landtag* was dismissed in 1838 because the election had returned too many Protestants (one third of all delegates) and a new election was called to straighten this out. Further, the aristocratic upper house, the chamber of the *Reichsräte,* kept its debates secret. Whatever was reported in the newspapers omitted the names of the speakers.[8] Moreover, initiation of legislation, control of state finances and of the army remained in the hands of the sovereign. In any case, parliaments existed only in the free cities and in the states of south Germany. There were none in Prussia or in the Habsburg Empire.

In this top-heavy class structure, the absolute rulers, the sovereigns, were so far above all the rest that Germans in general seem to have accepted them, not even thinking of challenging them. As soon challenge Wagner's dragon Fafnir, indolent in his cavern, guarding the Ring: *Ich lieg' und besitze. Lass mich schlafen.* [I lie here, possessing. Let me sleep] To challenge one of those rulers would mean challenging others who might respond with armed force to any undesirable attack, in recognition of marital or blood ties.

Just below the sovereigns were ranged the various social orders known as *Stände. Stand* is troublesome because it has no precise equivalent in English. Reputable multilingual dictionaries sometimes present a variety of possible translations, including rank, class, status, station, order, caste, or estate. The word derives from the Latin, and suggests something immutable.[9] It ought not to be translated as "class", if it is admitted that social mobility is a historical phenomenon that was familiar even in the days of Rome's greatness, and that the makeup of a given class at a given historical moment is largely derived from common economic interests. *Stand* has an aura of privilege, and is much more rigid.

Members of the high aristocracy were men whose ideas and impulses could have a serious effect on the life of their subjects because these nobles (about eighty in number throughout Germany) were in fact petty rulers interposed between the sovereign and the rank and file of his subjects. Many of the *Standesherren* had been hereditary nobles of the Empire before 1806, and as mediatized nobility they had been accorded special privileges by the provisions of the founding document of the confederation.[10] Their privileges usually included a seat in the upper house of the provincial assembly, jurisdiction in local courts and the right to collect taxes. The taxes were in addition to taxes collected by the state. These men were in effect rulers.

Bavaria offered a spectacular example of the powerful high aristocracy. Not far from Bamberg was the stupendous *Schloss* Weissenstein at Pommersfelden, which seems to have been an administrative seat of the Schönborn nobles. This castle dominated the landscape in all its magnificence of huge vistas and courtyards and English-style gardens and presented clear evidence of the staggering wealth of the family. The Schönborns were no petty provincial upstarts. Kenneth Clark does not hesitate to rank those who flourished in the 18th century right up with the Medici as art patrons. Their great architect Johann Balthasar Neumann (1687–1753) had a hand in the design of *Schloss* Weissenstein at the edge of the Steigerwald. There is a wonderful portrait of the superbly uniformed Neumann painted conspicuously by none other than Tiepolo on the great ceiling of the episcopal *Residenz* at Würzburg, celebrating Neumann as architect of the edifice. (A Schönborn built that sumptuous palace too, as bishop of Würzburg.)[11]

Monumental construction did not wholly absorb the attention of the Schönborns, especially that of Friedrich Karl von Schönborn, archbishop of Bamberg and Würzburg who died in 1746. He was undeniably a benevolent despot, clearly an "enlightened man", who exemplified in his restlessly energetic life both benevolence and patriotism. Obviously he viewed himself as the leading citizen, teacher and advocate of his subjects—a genuine *Landesvater*.[12] He was also something of an anachronism—a Janus in his feudal approach to growing social and industrial problems that remained stubbornly in place in the next century. In general he was destined to fail because Germany was stagnant.

Bishop Friedrich Karl made strenuous efforts in many innovative ways to improve the lot of his people, often anticipating the proposals of latter-day economists like Friedrich List, to whom is attributed much of the Nineteenth-Century attention to railroads and the development of the *Zollverein* [customs union]. Friedrich Karl's thoughts focused on trade networks, new industrial developments, improved transportation, reform of the confused monetary system and a simplification of customs arrangements.

The original impetus for all this vigorous episcopal effort came from the steadily increasing demands from the state for funds to sustain military undertakings. Even an archbishop had to maintain fortresses within his domain (e.g. Bamberg, Vorchheim, Kronach), replacing antequated walls with modern bastions and installing more efficient artillery. Taxes had to be raised. Bishop Friedrich Karl differed from his predecessors as well as from most of his contemporaries because the need to increase the tax burden of his people caused him to think about public welfare.

Almost a century before the economist Friedrich List, the bishop was worrying about the enormous multiplicity of toll houses along any given trade route. He reorganized the system within his own territory so effectively that there was a substantial gain not only in collected fees but also in general efficiency for the traveler. Who else in Bishop Friedrich Karl's day grasped the concept of **time** as an economic factor? He set up a single toll-collecting point with minor stations that were responsible only for inspection. The point he selected was Kitzingen rather than his residential city. Kitzingen was located on the Main, right at the point where the river began to be navigable for deep-draught vessels. The bishop had the river dredged in order to eliminate sandbars, and established loading cranes and warehouses. He saw to it that a fleet of cargo ships moved on a precise schedule, and he advertized this in a "patent" issued shortly before his death.

In forest regions the sale of wood was of prime importance, with the result that profiteers tended to take so much from the area known as the Steigerwald [13] that there were severe winter shortages of fuel in Würzburg, whereas at Bamberg, so close to heavy woodland, the problem was different. There people set themselves up as independent entrepreneurs, seriously overcut the forests of first-quality wood, and floated it via Main and Rhine to Netherlands shipbuilders. Bishop Friedrich Karl intervened in a spirit of what today would be called environmental protectionism. He decreed that wood had to be collected and stored in warehouses at Würzburg, in order to protect the people, who were to be assured of an adequate supply at a fair price. In Bamberg, the forest wardens were told that they must prevent excessive cutting. There was to be no more floating of logs downstream to other states, no matter how profitable that might be for certain individuals.

On the whole, the bishop's flock seems to have shown little initiative and was sluggish in response to his efforts. If energetic industrial leaders were to be found, they usually had to be brought in from other countries where there was better technical education, and where there was more aptitude for vigorous action. This was probably true all over Germany at the time, but it seems to have been especially so in the Bamberg-Würzburg area. Karl Wild, from whose study this account was taken, suggests that the church was to blame.[14] It was still a power that ruled over the people, and the spirit of enterprise was sharply suppressed. Tradespeople were apathetic, always expecting to have suggestions and directives, leadership and orders come from above. This same apathy seems to have survived into the decades just prior to the revolution of 1848.

To resume the discussion of social orders in Nineteenth-Century Germany, below the privileged high aristocracy was the caste made up of diplomats, high governmental administrators, and top-ranking military men. These aristocrats effectively blocked the advance of competent intellectuals from the middle class. At the court of king Friedrich Wilhelm IV in Prussia, they closed ranks around the monarch, who trusted them as his most valued councillors and friends. During the 1848 revolution, they candidly referred to themselves as his Majesty's *Kamarilla*. It was they who encouraged the foggy-brained ruler in his stubborn absolutism.

Eduard Gans of Berlin described Prussia back in 1830 as "a guardianship state".[15] The definition would seem to imply that the citizens were incapable, like minors, of handling their own affairs, but such a patronizing attitude was hardly justified. As the industrialist Gustav von Mevissen (1815–1899) was to point out, "The Prussian Crown, as long as Prussia existed, had been supported by the available intelligence. So long as this intelligence was concentrated and represented by the bureaucracy, the Crown never called on any [other] estate . . . but the times have moved forward and intelligence that was to be found primarily in the bureaucracy is today outside it."[16]

At still another level were the members of the *Kleinadel*, the lower aristocracy. As landowners and proprietors of large estates, this group truly controlled the life of the rural people after the church had been secularized and lost its throttle hold. In East Prussia especially, non-noble newcomers among these landlords had been able to buy up small plots from serfs who were unable to meet the requirement that they pay for their land or work off their indebtedness, and had thus accumulated enormous estates that were used in industrial-scale cultivation of grain for shipment abroad. Unlike the lords of large estates in most of the German lands, the new landowners lived on their latifundia, applying "modern" methods of agriculture and evolving into a capitalist class. They experimented with crop rotation and diversification as well as with new fertilizing techniques, using crushed marl, calcium sulfate or lime, for example.[17]

Moreover, they were making contact with shippers who freighted their rye to merchants as far away as the Rhineland. With their primitive "agribusiness", they were erecting factories for production of beet sugar, or distilleries for production of liquor from the potato crop. A few were even putting out cautious feelers:—perhaps there might be fruitful cooperation, they thought, with upper middle class merchants. The intrusion of disturbing interlopers among the old established nobility was responsible for serious tensions that found expression in impassioned debate on the relationship of the old and new elites. If old-style dominance [Herrschaft] was to be maintained, what was to be done about the new entrepreneurial landowners? Could these upstarts be excluded from the halls of power? Friedrich Wilhelm IV stoutly believed that nobility implied land ownership, but his close friend Christian Karl Bunsen was reminding him that "A commercial class, in control of the new wealth, will gradually monopolize the noble estates."[18]

Notes

1   Bertrand Gille, *Histoire de la maison Rothschild*, 2:7–45.

2   George Rudé, *The Crowd in History*, pp. 165–167.

3   Mack Walker, *German Home Towns*, pp. 24–26.

4   Veit Valentin, *Geschichte der deutschen Revolution von 1848–1849*, 2:229.

5   Hellmut Kretzschmar and Horst Schlechte, editors, *Französische und sächsische Gesandtschaftsberichte aus Dresden und Paris 1848–1849*, p. 212.

6   Norman F. Cantor and Samuel Berner, editors, *The Modern Era; 1815 to the Present*, p. 28.

7   Edwin J. Clapp, *The Navigable Rhine*, p. 6.

8   Valentin, 1:112–113.

9   Robert M. Berdahl, *The Politics of the Prussian Nobility*, pp. 11–12.

10 Mediatized nobility. If a lesser state was annexed by another, the nobles of the lesser state retained their titles and usually some of their seigneurial rights.

11 Hanns Hubert Hofmann, "Pommersfelden," in Karl Bosl, *Handbuch der historischen Stätte Deutschlands*, 7:559; Kenneth Clark, *Civilisation*, pp. 228–229. An article in the *Washington Post*, 31 December 1995, signed by Benjamin Forgey, nominates the Würzburg *Residenz* for recognition as "the greatest building of the millennium".

12 Manfred Agethen, *Geheimbund und Utopie; Illuminatien, Freimauerer und deutsche Späterklärung*, p. 27. Similar comment about the prince-bishops of Cologne and Mainz.

13 Siegfried Bachmann, *Die Landstände des Hochstifts Bamberg*, pp. 54, 105. The Steigerwald appears as a district reserved for nobles in Franconia as early as the mid-16th Century. Rudolf Albart, *Rundwanderungen Steigerwald*; Hildegard Weiss, *Stadt- und Landkreis Bamberg*.

14 Karl Wild, *Staat und Wirtschaft in den Bistümern Würzburg und Bamberg*. pp. 134–186.

15 Reinhart Koselleck, *Preussen zwischen Reform und Revolution*, p. 380.

16 Ibid.

17 Erich Jordan, *Die Entstehung der konservativen Partei und die preussischen Agrarverhältnisse von 1848*, pp. 10-17.

18 Cited by Berdahl, p. 329.

Chapter 2

The Middle and Lower Classes

Although the upper levels of German society were stagnant in the early years of the Nineteenth Century, this was not true of the strata below the sovereigns, *Standesherren*, aristocracy and the upper ranks of officialdom. Reaction to new or latent forces that were moving across Europe was responsible for unusual population shifts, new demands for economic and political power, and even for physical living space and such basic requirements as food, shelter and employment. On the land and in urban centers, there were flux and uncertainty and conflicting cross-currents, brought on in part by the delayed effect of the great French revolution and of the train of events that followed the Napoleonic conquests, territorial domination, and defeat. In rural Germany, the most disturbing problems resulted from the reformers' abolition of serfdom. In growing urban communities on the other hand, not only advances of technology and industry were having their effect, but also there were problems springing from the reformers' action in loosening the grip of the guilds. In this complex state of affairs, few generalizations hold true all across Germany or even across a given level of society. Interaction was extending not only from one social group to another, but likewise across lines that once clearly separated rural and urban populations.

There was a rising urban middle class in the early decades of the Nineteenth Century, but on the threshold of the industrial era Germany remained essentially rural. Cities were growing, yet at the mid-century, seventy percent of the entire German population continued to live on the land or in small villages. If in those early decades there was actually a recognizable upper middle class among the rural people, its members would have been found predominantly among the local *Honoratioren*, and class distinctions were blurry.

Honoratioren cannot be construed as a title. It was an ambiguous term, applied to persons of recognized substance, education, and fields of responsibility (physicians, public health officers, judges, head bailiffs, managers or chief foresters of noble estates and so on). The closest approximation, if the word is to be translated, might be "notables". Not celebrities, but solid people whom everyone knew and whose professional competence was respected.[1] In Austria at least, the *Honoratioren* comprised a group distinct enough to be singled out officially for census purposes.[2] Though certainly not of the nobility, the *Honoratior* enjoyed certain privileges such as exemption from military service.

Carl Schurz, the German revolutionist who was to make his mark in the United States as Union general, Senator from Missouri, and US Secretary of the Interior, left a lively account of this youthful adventures in his native Germany that sheds a strong light on the doings of a prosperous rural household. He lived as a small child in the home of his grandfather, a tenant at the manor of the *Graf* von Wolf-Metternich, whose stately mansion was in the Rhineland.[3] "I was born in a castle," his autobiography begins. The grandfather was a *Halfen*, an old designation surviving from earlier times for a farmer who would have handed over half his harvest to the lord of the manor, but who in the years of Schurz's boyhood paid cash rent. He has been described as a peasant, but the passage in Schurz's work that is cited does not state it so precisely.[4] The general tenor of his remarks seems to put the *Halfen* close to the *Honoratioren*. He comments that although relationships with the manor people were friendly and relaxed, one had to be aware of obvious class differences.

Even though he was a well-to-do man, Schurz's grandfather deliberately avoided unwonted display by going about on social visits in a two-wheeled chaise rather than in four-wheeled vehicle, which would have been considered to be presumptuous. Similarly, his wife wore pretty hoods but never a city-style bonnet.[5] The lord of the manor regularly invited Schurz's grandfather to go along on his festive hunts, but when the grandfather organized a hunt of his own, word trickled back by some underground route that the manor people were uneasy and expressing doubts about this. The cleavage between *Bürger* and lower class was much sharper in urban settings than it was in the country, because in the city those who prospered tended to become social climbers and adopted stiffer manners, whereas in rural settings it was much more relaxed, and there was a *Mittleschicht* of fairly well educated tenants and parsonage families.[6] All the same, though the grandfather may have been a peasant in the technical sense, it appears that the peasant class must itself have had clear gradations. When the grandfather drove off in his two-wheeled chaise in order to pay social calls on his friends, it was other men of the *Halfen* rank whom he visited, certainly not farmhands or tenant farmers at the miserable level of *Zwergwirtschaft* [literally dwarf economy].

A clue relating to striations in middle-class or peasant life lies in material on established pay scales based on data for the year 1834.[7] A man who served as *Oberförster* [chief forester] on a noble's estate customarily received a salary of about 1400 florins, plus an allowance of 134 florins for food staples, as well as a supplement according to the size of the forest area he administered (between 300 and 500 florins). In addition, he was entitled to a house allowance of about 120 florins with 5 acres [6 *Tagwerk*: a Bavarian land unit] for his own use and up to 20 cords of firewood per year. (Firewood was so expensive that 20 cords would have cost about 250 florins on the market).[8] Estimates for general income levels indicate that the average German household at that time had a total income ranging between 300 and 600 florins, most around 300 florins a year. These figures lead to the conclusion that the family of an *Oberförster* was probably ranked among the *Honoratioren*, situated comfortably in the upper middle class. This might also have applied to the Schurz family, where the grandfather was a *Halfen* and one of his sons was manager of a large peat operation belonging to the *Graf*.

In Schurz's recollections, the grandfather, a powerfully-built man, directed his field hands and worked with them at times. At harvest time, he was symbolically astride one of the four horses teamed in tandem that pulled the lead cart. The grandmother hovered in the background, directing the cooks and superintending preparation of meals for the field hands, all of them seated along a table in a separate room, using wooden spoons and cutting up meat with their own pocketknives. The grandmother served her own family in their private living room-dining room. She busied herself superintending the young girls who brought in their spinning wheels in the evening, the wheels whirring, and everyone singing.

In an old-fashioned household of this sort, husband and wife had clearly delineated responsibilities, all aimed at the well-being of the self-contained *ganzes Haus*. This complex "economy" was described in sets of multi-volume encyclopedias known as *Hausväterliteratur*.

These exhaustive works embodied the whole proto-industrial operation.[9] In essence, it was a partnership in which both husband and wife were producers. The woman's responsibilities were extensive, encompassing a strange variety of activities. Such, for example, were the cultivation of flax, brewing, the rearing of cattle and swine, bee-keeping, and dairying. The *Hausmutter* was supposed to be able to teach and supervise her corps of female servants as well as her daughters, so that they in turn would know how to spin, weave, dye, prepare vinegar for preservation of meats and vegetables, maintain an herb garden and prepare its products for the household "pharmacy". She was also supposed to know the rudiments of veterinary medicine. All these requirements reflect a view of the family in the original meaning of the word as handed down from antiquity—namely, the entire household that included parents, children, and all those attached to them as servants, farm hands etc.

A little cookbook published in 1844 offers a glimpse into a rural middle-class family that may be somewhat lower on the social scale than the rank of an estate manager.[10] The author "Rosamunda" addresses herself to all "the wives and daughters of the German citizenry", but her curious vocabulary rather suggests that she was writing for Bavarian homemakers. In her introductory remarks she seems to have a fairly comfortable establishment in mind. She does not appear to think that the mistress of the house will do anything other than superintend in the kitchen. She does say that "since so-called ranges or 'household stoves' are not yet among the most common devices, we confine ourselves here to the requirements of that kitchen where cooking is still done on the customary hearth and with the conventional fire."

Industrial products were destined soon to encroach on the rural hearth. In his excellent description of Rhineland manufactures, written in 1848, C. H. Banfield wrote admiringly of the domestic stoves at Sterkerade in Nassau, where the chief operation was the casting of small wares called "pottery". Every house in the lower Rhine had such a stove, he said, calling them "beyond doubt the most practical and economical of all inventions." They were neat, light, and shaped like a square box, opening with a door and showing a receptacle like an oven. "The flame of the fire is drawn between four or six iron pots, imbedded in an oval frame . . . The fire is shut off at will from the pots singly by slides which the cook inserts at her discretion."[11]

Rosamunda offers advice on varieties of firewood, on arrangement of the kitchen, on utensils (prefers copper and tinned pots to iron ones) and on the storage of game, beef, ham, spices, vegetables, flour, lard, butter and so on. She suggests an enormous variety of elaborate 5-course meals. When she comes around to the art of carving, Rosamunda speaks of a side table where the carved meat can be arranged on platters for presentation to the guests. Such a sideboard would have been a ponderous thing in the Biedermeier style. The fortunate people who were to eat the carved roasts of beef, ham, boar's head and capon were alas subject to disease, and for these Rosamunda suggests special diets: for those suffering from apathy and depression, sorrel soup and vegetables; for nerve fever, wine soup and light egg dishes; for hemorrhoids, sheeps' wool tea [sounds disgusting, but it may have been some sort of infusion made from a woolly plant such as a mullen]; for constipation, fruit soups and green vegetables, fine stews with lemon sauce, and lemonade; for diarrhea, egg dishes, cooked without milk; for green sickness (anemia) no vegetables, no fruit, no milk: rather, hearty soups, wine, liver, beer and horse radish. People with worms should avoid fatty dishes, and those who are spitting blood should only take dishes that are cool, advantageously gruel and light almond milk.

All this seems to indicate that the household of the prosperous middle class in the countryside was comfortably housed and well supplied, and that everyone in the household unit had a specific role that not only provided steady useful occupation but must also have afforded a sense of personal worth.

It is to be hoped that the majority of true peasants were fortunate enough to have land that was *spannfähig* [acreage that was sufficient to sustain a team of draft animals], and that it was able to satisfy needs in the matter of household food, feed for some pigs, fodder for a cow or two, and hay for the horses. Some peasants were in fact fairly prosperous because they had enough excess wood to be able to sell it at auction for a good price. Another source of income was land that they rented out to propertyless people who frequently depended on the peasant landlord as the landlord himself had once depended upon the great land-owning lord, and they worked as hired hands (*Heuerlinge*) for a tiny income.

Between the well-to-do farmers and the landless *Heuerlinge* were wretches who barely kept body and soul together on their minuscule holdings and who tried to alleviate their desperate lot by engaging in a form of proto-factory production. The workers in question were usually women, who used materials and tools supplied on credit, returning finished goods (toys, reverse-painted art objects, lengths of woven fabric) to the person who had hired them. Sometimes modern studies call such little outworking operations "factories", but the German word *Fabrik* in the early Nineteenth Century did not by any means describe a large mechanized industrial establishment as it would today. Usually, it meant a dispersed outworking arrangement rather than a centrally located steam-powered shop.[12] In one extreme case, *Fabrik* was the term used to describe Berlin's thirty-one windmills with their thirty-eight workers.[13]

There could be curious variants in outworking, certainly not to be characterized as anything even remotely like a cottage industry, yet on the other hand far from the modern factory . In the Wupper valley, for example, steel blades for knives and razors were ground in tiny shops along the river banks. The grinders owned their wheels, and their source of power was the fast-flowing current. These men were independent contractors for merchant-manufacturers.[14] The use of water-power for mechanized manufacture in the dawn of the age of steam had the effect of retarding the development of centralized enterprises. Again in the Wupper valley, there was an extensive system of spinning mills owned by one family. These mills, along the banks of the Wupper, the Agger, and the Sieg were spread out over distances of some fifty miles.[15]

Another form of independent enterprise was troubling to many small communities. The intrusion of rootless peddlers was regarded as highly disruptive and undesirable, so much so that there were strict ordinances against the practice of *Hausierung* in many localities, and the unfortunate peddlers themselves were personally insulted. People scornfully called them *Böhnhasen*, an epithet that has been freely translated as "groundrabbits".[16]

The sweeping reforms with emancipation of the serfs had unintentionally increased the number of landless people. In Bavaria at least, the state's takeover of secularized church property had theoretically furnished an ample base for settling the former serfs as proprietors. The church had owned 56% of the 29,807 peasant homesteads, and the sovereign had already owned 13.6%, but the supposedly generous arrangement whereby a former serf could become a land owner by payment of a fee actually offered little or no relief because the sum in question could amount to as much as eighteen times the value of the goods and services that the church had previously demanded annually. Many therefore sank to the condition of landless *Heuerlinge*.[17]

King Friedrich Wilhelm's conservative adviser, Joseph Maria von Radowitz, occasionally had a piercingly clear understanding of affairs.

In his opinion, what was known as liberation might in actuality be nothing more than a transition from subjection to persons to subjection to things (specifically, needs and money).

The agrarian reforms of the early years of the century were gradually restructuring usage rights for pasture lands and forests. This was a strained, difficult process because whereas custom had regulated these usage rights primarily by agreement between lord and peasant, market forces were coming into play that distorted the picture. Wood had become a salable commodity, and poor folk who through the centuries had picked up uncut wood, slash, or material that had fallen in storms, and who had peacefully sent their pigs into the forest for acorns, now found that the forests were severely policed by authorities who did not see any virtue in ignoring these little depredations. A complex struggle was developing, not just a classic confrontation of lord and peasants but a wrenching contest between peasants and the landless lowermost classes. Cases are recorded in which disputes were so violent that foresters feared for their lives and there was even a call for protection by the army. An authority on the problem of wood theft comments that the only proposal for resolution of the problem of impoverished classes and those holding private property was "strict justice" in order to protect property. This desire of property-owners for protection, he says, invoked a theme which remained significant throughout the entire Nineteenth Century—the *bourgeoisie*'s fear of revolution.[18]

Forest resources were diminishing not only because of a spurt in population growth that increased the demand for firewood for household heating, but also because of new industrial requirements. Oak bark was needed for leather tanning, charcoal was in demand for forging pig iron, and last but not least, there was the impending heavy demand for railway ties. Wood resources were threatened in all parts of Germany. It is interesting to find that Karl Marx first began to think about the social question when he was a young journalist in the early 1840's and observed wood theft among winegrowers of the Mosel valley near Trier. (Stakes were needed for the vines, wood for casks etc.) [19]

Forest conflict was in fact the most common form of dispute over collective use rights that were being legally questioned, and it was intensified by new forms of productive activity associated with the expansion of the market economy.[20]

There was a vague understanding that some kind of social revolution was taking place. How were all these ignorant unemployables at the bottom of the ladder to be taken care of? Writers fumbled for an appropriate vocabulary. Ever since the middle ages, there had been those who were described as members of the *Pöbel*—a term that through the years has gathered unpleasant overtones, with the result that today it suggests something like rabble. Originally it meant a mass of people who were below the recognized estates but who were useful because they could perform labor that would at least sustain them in a marginal way. But this *Unterschicht* was growing at a threatening rate, a new situation because heretofore the increase had not been rapid. There were so many of them that they could no longer be absorbed as hired hands in rural communities, nor were there openings for them in the towns. It was becoming apparent that they might develop into something like the French *classes dangereuses*. They were starting to make difficult demands, as though they had a right to find support from the community in their desperate need.

The Napoleonic era and the subsequent shakeup had created a social quicksand in German lands. Many aspects of the new dispensation were not covered by the laws. Take the problem of the great landowners, especially the *Standesherren* who had functioned for so long as minor sovereigns, as in the case of the Schönborn family. Some of their rights had been abridged, but there remained areas where everything was uncertain. In the old days, a great lord controlled his serfs by means of corporal punishment: *Peitsche und Knüppel* [cudgel and lash] still prevailed in some parts of Germany, and laws governing their use were ambiguous. The provisions of the general law, of the government, and the pressures exerted by the growing social movement were frequently at odds. In general, reform was moving down from the top, while the lowermost layers of society were the last to feel the effects of any hesitant effort on their behalf.

The landless *Heuerlinge* were a case in point. Theoretically they were free men, but the overlords must have regarded unemployed drifters as somehow subject to control as former serfs would have been if they had rebelled against forced labor [feudal *corvée*; in German, *Robot*] In the good old days, such a rebel would have been beaten. Even after the abolition of serfdom, the state continued to delegate power to punish to the landowners, thinking of it as a means of "education". In Silesia, it was noted as late as 1838 that since there were no police available, it remained to the landowners to maintain order. Many a landowner, need it be said, was not at all unwilling to exercise this authority.—Conditions differed from one region to another, but the problem was enormous. About three hundred thousand peasants had been relieved of *Robot* obligations, but another huge segment of the peasantry still owed some twenty-three million work days to their lords, and obviously there had to be some kind of enforcement if this requirement were not to die out. That the lords were hanging on with grim determination can be seen by the repetition as late as 1832 of regulations against use of the stocks.[21]

The physician C. A. Weinhold had a suggestion, writing in 1827. Permission to marry should be withheld, he said, from beggars and impoverished individuals who were unmarried, from those who were capable of working but who were receiving public support, and from all males (journeymen and apprentices) in the towns or in the country until they were in a position to support not only themselves but also a wife and children.[22] In a similar vein, there was a complaint published in Braunschweig, to the effect that indigent children of hired hands were marrying even before they had earned enough to acquire a bed or necessary clothing, and that "usually their marriages are much more fruitful than the marriages in other classes."[23] The old meaning of the term *Pöbel* was giving way to another term—*Proletariat*—which implied not only need, but also a consciousness of need on the part of the sufferers.

Toward the end of the Eighteenth Century, most of the leading men in Prussia, even the bureaucrats, had been won over by the teachings of Adam Smith, the Scottish economist (1723–1790) and consequently were passionately in favor of his *laissez faire* ideas. In line with this, they had arrived at the conclusion that the guild system as they knew it could not be maintained, but they were reluctant to tamper with anything that enjoyed time-honored recognition. Instead of attacking the system directly therefore, they suggested a certain relaxation of guild entrance requirements. They dared go no further because there was no clear popular movement in the direction of reform. A provincial department head named Strünsee put it this way: "It all depends on ten antique states, twenty record offices, fifty constitutions, a hundred privileges and innumerable personal considerations that I alone can't change or even accommodate . . . What we need is one single reformer who will put through the necessary measures gently or roughly." Prussia found its rough reformer when Napoleon arrived on the scene, followed by two better-intentioned men—the ministers, Karl *Freiherr* vom Stein (1723–1790) and Karl August von Hardenberg (1750–1822). These two did not agree about ways and means. Vom

Stein wanted the overall welfare of the people, but he was inclined to think that Adam Smith was going too far. For this reason he focused attention primarily on unconditional freedom of trade only in the sale of absolute necessities such as bread and meat, and otherwise sought to reform the guild system, not eliminate it. In 1808, for example, he issued a directive to the effect that bakers and butchers were freed from compulsion to belong to a guild, and in that same year he sent out another directive that was effective in eastern Prussia, where guilds had not struck root as firmly as they had elsewhere. This provided that guild membership was no longer a requirement for millers, brewers, and producers of distilled spirits.

Hardenberg on the other hand was wholeheartedly in favor of the *laissez faire* principle. He declared that what he wanted was "a revolution from the top"—democratic principles expressed harmoniously by the monarchy, in other words. When he succeeded vom Stein in 1810 therefore he issued an edict (28 October) that freed millers, brewers and distillers from the requirement of guild membership throughout Prussia, and (edict of 2 November) left as the only people still under restrictions jewelers, manufacturers of surgical instruments, masons, mill builders, carpenters, ship builders and chimney sweeps. Otherwise, if one could furnish a police certification of good conduct, one was free to practice whatever trade one wanted.

The guilds remained, to be sure, but a police law of 1811 made it clear that they had little authority. Only the building trades still required a qualifying examination, but this was to be conducted by a state commission, not by a guild.

It was understood that these reforms were not the result of a powerful impulse from the people. Rather, it was only the educated elite [*die Gebildeten*], especially officials, who were convinced of the necessity of trade reform. The great majority of the middle class did not want to know anything about such extensive reforms and thought rather that there would be harm done to the owner classes. And the lower people and those whose skilled members would especially profit from the new legislation were too little organized and self-aware to raise their voices. For this reason a storm broke loose and petitions flooded into the ministerial offices. It was not only the guilds, but also assemblies of magistrates and city delegates that entered lively protest. Technology would deteriorate and the cities would rot! Decidedly, Germans were not in a revolutionary mood.

Especially in the major cities the first squeeze of industrialization was beginning to be felt by a middle-class group that heretofore had held its head high. With the surge of lackland peasants in search of employment, the master craftsmen felt threatened, if not overwhelmed. Even if they had wanted to do such a thing, they could not accept a great flood of apprentices all at one time, and if the apprentices were eventually to become master craftsmen in their turn, the competition would be highly destructive, they thought, so they were making every effort to freeze them out.

The hostility of the master craftsmen directed against of new potential members of the work force who were drifting in as unemployed landless people was not exclusively based on ideas of economic competition. The social fabric and quality of the community was involved. Traditionally, the guilds were guardians of the collective honor, largely responsible for the moral balance of their towns. In this way, guild masters were insinuated into the fabric of civil activities in addition to their economic functions. They judged applicants for admission to their ranks on the basis not only of proficiency in their chosen work, but also on general steadiness, good moral character, and integrity. A candidate had to present evidence that he was of legitimate birth, even that his parents were legitimate. Who would keep disorderly irresponsible persons from taking up residence in the community and engaging in an honored trade if the guilds were not to do it?[24]

Although the exclusive control of trade that the guilds had exercised for countless generations was no longer legal, there remained in the larger towns individuals who enjoyed a certain status as master craftsmen. It has to be remembered that conditions prevailing in one kingdom or grand duchy did not necessarily obtain in other parts of fractured Germany. At Trier, masters managed to hold together through their mutual benefit associations, one for each of their respective crafts. They had enough confidence to press continuously with a variety of requests addressed to local bureaucrats. They urged the exclusion of peddlers and craftsmen not native to their town who were attempting to establish themselves competitively in their midst.[25]

In Bavaria, guilds had lost much of their power, but even within Bavaria there were different sets of industrial law. The left-bank Palatinate had been controlled by France after 1793, and when it was returned to Bavaria following the Congress of Vienna, it kept the liberal laws that had been introduced in the years of French domination. This meant that guilds had been abolished there. In the main body of Bavaria a law of 1825 had transferred admission to a given trade from the authority of the guilds to that of the state. An applicant had to show proficiency as well as financial soundness, but all the same the field had been opened and was much more competitive than it had been under the guilds' master craftsmen, whose essential aim had always been stability of the community and the craft.

Though they may not have seen it quite in that light, the guildmasters should have been aware that there were cracks in their system, the inevitable product of industry's own revolution. With the advent of steam-powered machinery, a whole new field was opened—namely machine manufacture. This was not an activity that would have ever existed in the old days, and the guild masters had no control over it, though they must have seen that their best workers might move off into this new venture. Textile producers wanted mechanized spindles, mining operators wanted new winches and hauling devices, and of course the locomotives for the railways had to be built. England was the primary source of machinery but could not—or would not—supply it all. Germans would have to make their own tools and machines. The workers ("mechanics") whom the entrepreneurs called in were those from the old guilded crafts who knew how to handle tools and had been accustomed to making their own as required: locksmiths, metal workers and smiths, carpenters, cabinet makers—all of these found ready employment at wages much above anything they had ever earned before. In the beginning there was no specialization because there was as yet no specialized market.

To modern eyes, early machine-building operations look astonishingly primitive. To cite one example, the inventory of a machine-building operation at Moabit lists only simple tools such as vises, turning lathes, drills, punches, grinders, cutting shears, a flywheel, and a machine for cutting screw threads. Most of the pieces are described as having been made "new at the facility", and a sparse few were purchased in England.[26] How would machinists employed in such a plant fit into the revolutionary picture? They may not have regarded themselves as a class that was undergoing severe hardship: machine builders were as a matter of fact held to be the aristocrats of the labor force. The inevitable conclusion is that these workers were too new to their situation to be in a position to frame grievances, in spite of stiff regulation of working conditions and intolerable hours. Moreover, outside agitators who might want to stir them into action would in most cases be defeated by the impossiblity of penetrating the thicket of local dialect that the workers used.

In small communities there were unguilded craftsmen who worked on their own. These would be coopers, locksmiths, glaziers, carpenters, tailors, cobblers and the like. Their shops were usually in their homes, in a room set aside for the purpose. The children of such craftsmen went to the village school for a few years, perhaps, and then learned the father's trade. These individuals were no doubt respected members of the community who knew who they were and where they stood, although they lacked the status that would have been theirs had they been guild masters responsible for the supervision and training of journeymen and apprentices. (Village artisans had never been permitted to take on journeymen or apprentices in their shops.) Even these independent village artisans may have felt the pressure of changing times because the problem of overpopulation and alarming growth of a marginal sub-peasantry was a major concern of small communities, and indeed during the first decades of the Nineteenth Century was not yet drastically affecting life in the larger cities.

Except in thriving free cities like Bremen, a leading urban middle class that had any claim to wealth and distinction was something of a novelty in the early years of the Nineteenth Century in Germany. There were always a few established "old families," to be sure, but newcomers were beginning to appear. Shipbuilders, import/export entrepreneurs, bankers and manufacturers, as well as those who were talking animatedly about railroads. Though their numbers were still small, they were recognizably an emergent factor in society, congregating in major centers such as Krefeld and Leipzig and in almost all the towns of the Prussian Rhineland province.

The level of frustration in this new class of energetic, prosperous businessmen was high. Many a self-confident entrepreneur among them, in command of ample funding, felt a pressing need for some kind of political clout that was consistently denied him. A stockholder with a growing railroad system, a wholesale textile merchant/manufacturer, a steamship company executive, the owners of a large rolling mill—all these people had urgent agenda. They wanted free trade, open markets, free rights of domicile and citizenship, and adequate banking credit. They wanted access to political office and had little patience with the dogged old-style bureaucracy.

In spite of their impatience, the members of this class lived comfortably. Their dignified residences with their huge sloping mansard roofs and innumerable chimneys, their rows and rows of windows and their carriage houses—all bring to mind the image of opulent ease. To tell the truth, it is possible that the majority of this class may have been undemanding, placidly content to accept whatever comforts material success had brought, and complacently waiting for the constitution that the king of Prussia had promised to grant some day.

The inhabitants of the handsome stone-faced residences were bound in time to constitute a distinct upper layer among the townspeople. With development of huge enterprises such as steamship lines or railroads, it was inevitable that the men who controlled them would be far apart from the traditional shopkeeper or small manufacturer, with their own style of social behavior, and forms that were recognizably those of a new elite. Members of the rural wealthy middle class would have recognized the new activities of the city heads of households as productive, if different from their own. They may have looked askance at the women (they were already suspicious of the ladies of the nobility, regarding them as frivolous and self-centered). What did such idle elegant city women know about bee-keeping or spinning? Why, they probably didn't even know how to make vinegar or skin an eel! Imperceptibly, the wealthy city women had acquired a new social role— Veblen's well-known conspicuous consumption was their duty, in order to display their husbands' success.

Thomas Mann's Tony Buddenbrooks, a young wife in a merchant household at Hamburg, is a good example of the new style. Her attire alone showed the difference. Her charming dressing gown with its fine tracery of beadwork, its train, and its delightful row of small scarlet ribbon bows was appropriate for her domestic chores. Her full morning was unmistakably based on the notion of ostentatious ease and leisure. She had presided at the breakfast table with its damask cloth and embroidered runner, its gold-bordered translucent porcelain, its intricately constructed silver bread-basket and glass domes covering butter balls and a splendid selection of cheeses. She had instructed the nurse, who was to take the three-year-old daughter out for half an hour, warmly dressed against the foggy weather. She had had an argument with her husband, not understanding why she could not immediately engage a governess for the small girl. Then she had carried her little lacquered key basket from room to room while she flicked dust from the massive carved furniture, using a "gay little feather duster", and watered the potted palms in her *pensée* room, using a special little brass sprinkler. Tony Buddenbrooks, the quintessential conspicuous consumer. Is it any cause for astonishment that at the time of the revolution, certain rebellious women of this class were to burst out from their frustrating program of dainty household activity, gracious hospitality, piety and good works, becoming active journalists and propagandists for a new more adventurous era?

David Hansemann (1790–1864) was one of the new urban elite.[27] To begin with, he had not enjoyed the elaborate education that was part of the background of many of Germany's liberals. He was not precisely a self-made man in the modern sense, but he had had to struggle up. Born near Hamburg as the youngest child of a clergyman, he was apprenticed at age fourteen to a merchant in Rheda. He was fortunate in that he was intelligent enough to respond to the encouragement and help that was offered him. By the time he reached young manhood, he had read extensively in political theory, history and economics and had acquired some facility in foreign languages. Further, he had made use of the opportunities presented in his job in the town civil service to store up much useful information concerning the intricacies of taxation. His apprenticeship completed, the young man transferred to a textile factory, where his duties sent him traveling all over Europe. By 1817 he was able to set himself up independently in Aachen, where he managed a dyestuffs company that also did a lucrative business in the wool trade. Before long he was able to demonstrate his talents by founding the fire insurance company of Aachen. Since he was keenly aware of the extreme reluctance of government officials to encourage the growth of capital in a venture like his (it might put power into the hands of the middle class), he cannily emphasized the public utility aspect of the insurance company when he presented his documents requesting permission to start such an enterprise.

Hansemann was ahead of his times in his appreciation of the importance of railways. There was much official foot-dragging at first. Both Great Britain and Belgium were ahead of Germany, but in 1836 he started a Prussian-Rhenish railroad company, and for many years thereafter he was active in developing the German railway system as well as he could against official barriers and the objections of petty sovereigns.

He ran into official obstruction continually. The Prussian bureaucrats were past grand masters in the art of holding endless hearings. Initiatives on the part of middle class men were consistently blocked by a state that stubbornly remained feudal in its attitude. There was no organized body through which the candid exercise of *Machtvollkommenheit* [absolute authority] of the bureaucrats could be attacked, let alone broken. There were of course the chambers of commerce—survivals in the Rhineland from Napoleon's times, but they had advisory competence only, and usually the bureaucrats simply ignored them. Hansemann was a member of the Aachen chamber of commerce and constantly struggled to gain public attention for its projects, but in those early days his was more or less a voice crying in the wilderness. His fellow members were apathetic. He therefore sat down to write.

Hansemann's book stated clearly that the essential requirement for a constitutional monarchy should be the abolition of all vestiges of feudal times. He pointed out that power should lie in the hands of those who have the most influence, namely the city dwellers who by virtue of trade and industry were well above rural dwellers in their technical knowledge and political understanding.

The king of Prussia acknowledged Hansemann's book with the dry remark that he had forwarded it to the appropriate ministries for their consideration. He noted that he recognized the author's praiseworthy intentions. The Berlin bureaucrats did not recognize Hansemann's work as at all praiseworthy. Consequently, when he was elected to the provincial *Landtag* in 1831, they hastily brought forward an old regulation, showing that special permission would be required in view of the fact that he had not yet lived ten years in Aachen. Permission to participate in the deliberations of the *Landtag* was denied.

Hansemann promptly wrote another book in which he suggested drastic revision of the tax system. The burden on productive middle class citizens was excessive because noble landowners were exempt from tax. The irritated bureaucrats retaliated by depriving Hansemann of several honorary offices that he held. The members of the Aachen chamber of commerce roused themselves and defiantly made him their president.

David Hansemann was atypical of the new middle class in that he operated almost alone. In most mercantile cities there was a recognizable pattern of concerted family effort. An energetic hard-working merchant would enhance his own savings and property by marrying a well-to-do woman, and together they would produce a young army of offspring who would be guided by their elders and taught that their duty was to contribute to the well-being of the family firm, to marry well, to establish helpful social and business connections, and to produce another young army of offspring. The situation has been examined and described in detail with reference to the family of the well-known liberal political leader of the 1840's, namely Friedrich Daniel Bassermann (1811–1855) of Mannheim.[28]

In 1830, Bassermann's grandfather Friedrich Ludwig, the son and grandson of successful innkeepers, had married well and amassed a respectable fortune in trade and crowned this effort by the purchase of a handsome mansion on Mannheim's bustling *Marktplatz*. He moved into it with his wife and four children. At age fifty, he was prosperous enough to pay 120,000 *Gulden* for his fine house. Friedrich Ludwig was obviously one of a new class of potential civil leaders.

Friedrich Daniel Bassermann the politician was born in his grandfather's house on the *Marktplatz*. Though he was carefully trained for life in the competitive mercantile world (he worked at Trieste with a close business friend of his father's, was helped by his father to purchase a successful drug firm for which enterprise he had prepared himself by the study of chemistry and related subjects at Heidelberg, and also spent time with other firms in France and England), he understood that he ought to play a role in local civic endeavors and therefore founded an arts society at Mannheim and took an active part in the local music society and the natural history society of the city. Like his father, he was elected while still a very young man to the *Bürgerausschuss* [citizens' committee] and quickly gained prominence as a forceful speaker. Soon he was elected to the provincial *Landtag*. From that time on, he devoted himself to politics—a new field for a member of the middle class—to such an extent that he found it advisable to sell his firm to his younger brother Julius. (This, by the way, with the understanding of the family.)

The Bassermann family was equally helpful to Friedrich Daniel's brothers. The second son, Alexander, for example, was sent to London where he worked with one of his father's business associates. He married the daughter of a wine and tobacco merchant, one of his father's partners. Each young man or woman was launched appropriately only after long earnest consultations.

In time, the stately house on the *Marktplatz* was the headquarters of three family firms (a bank, the wine and tobacco enterprise, and the drug firm). There were splendid celebrations there of family anniversaries and birthdays. On those resplendent occasions, each son traditionally received a gift of five hundred *Gulden* from his father, but this should not be construed as sentimental paternal indulgence. The family was functioning as a unit. A family like this unavoidably had a serious interest in business affairs up and down the Rhine. Families like the Bassermann clan understood the advantage that would accrue from more open trade and a dropping of barriers between the multitude of small German monarchies. It is understandable that they would gladly seek ways to support a scion of the family who showed a talent for political life because new pathways had to be opened.

Another Rhenish clan that showed many traits close to those of the Bassermanns was the Gontard family at Frankfurt.[29] Here again there was an impressive succession of energetic men who marshalled their numerous descendants into a bold cohesive force.

The first recorded member of the tribe was one Peter Gontard (1682–1725). His descendants were textile merchants, each of whom married wealth and fathered many children. Jacob Friedrich (1702–1766) had eleven children, and the next two generations averaged five children apiece. The wives of these successful merchants came from the largest and richest families of Frankfurt, with the result that by the time of Clotilde Koch-Gontard's birth in 1815, the Gontards were unmistakably part of the city's merchant aristocracy. By that time, in various ramifications, the Gontards and their in-laws held the reins of many interlocking enterprises, including the wine and tobacco trade (this latter was the specialty of the firm of Gogel, Koch and company, of which Clotilde's husband Robert was a member). The names of the in-laws reveal the proximity of France—d'Orville, de Neufville, de Bary, Passavant etc.

Robert and Clotilde were thus aristocrats in the major commercial city of southwest Germany, and their position was accentuated by the presence there since 1815 of the German confederation diet, with all the attendant glamor of diplomats from the numerous states of the confederation as well as foreign diplomats and observers. Would a young matron like Clotilde Koch-Gontard think of establishing herself as a gracious and witty hostess of a *salon* in the French manner, or would that have been frowned upon as presumptuous? She would be treading dangerous ground, in competition with the haughty *Gräfin* von Bergen, the morganatic widow of Elector Wilhelm II of Hesse-Kassel. Perhaps it would be wiser to confine social activity to the less demanding circle of the city's mercantile princes.

The revolution of 1848 would change the scene drastically. During the sessions of the new Frankfurt national assembly, the *Gräfin* would maintain her exclusive *salon* for the nobility, but they were few in number in Frankfurt of 1848. The Koch-Gontard mansion, on the other hand, was close to the *Paulskirche* where the assembly held its sessions, and it rapidly became a magnet for the new middle class leaders—men of the moderate liberal majority—throwing Clotilde willynilly into a constant round of dinners. She appears to have been original in her approach to the role that was thrust on her, refraining from any foolish attempt to ape *madame* Recamier, but rather offering simple, genuine warm sympathy and hospitality to the weary men who sat at her table night after night. Here they could talk unrestrainedly, like the middle class men they were, about problems that concerned them deeply, without the misery of false social posturing. Many of them wrote in their memoirs of their gratitude to Clotilde Koch-Gontard for her considerate friendliness. Historians have little to say about the *Gräfin* von Bergen's elegant *salon* but they unfailingly pay tribute to the merchant's wife in those extraordinary circumstances.

City life admittedly had its drawbacks, physical as well as political. The town of Elberfeld on the Rhine, for example, was undergoing industrial growing pains. The following comment written by C. H. Banfield in 1848 has an uncannily modern ring. "Here and there spacious and sumptuous houses, often faced with fronts of cut stone and in the best architectural styles, announce the abodes of the wealthy bankers and manufacturers. . . . The river itself is a disgusting object, being an open receptacle for all sewers, disguising the various tinctures contributed from the dyeing establishments in one murky impenetrable hue that makes the stranger shudder on beholding."

Cities were beginning to feel the strain. Landless peasants were drifting in, searching for work, but the cities were reluctant to accept them. It would be an exaggeration to speak of city slums as we know them, but undeniably there must have been many people who lived in comfortless rat-infested quarters where diseases such as tuberculosis could easily spread. Unsanitary urban conditions all over Europe brought on the terrible cholera epidemic of 1832 that killed people by the thousands. (Hegel was one of the victims.) An indication of the uneven spread of education in Europe is the fact that serfs in Hungary blamed the nobility for the cholera scourge. There were two hundred thirty thousand six hundred and forty fatalities that year, and the peasants believed that nobles were poisoning their wells. (They were adding chlorine to the water.) They reacted by indiscriminate murder and the burning of castles.[30]

Within a decade or two, the restless uncertain social mix that was Germany would begin to bubble, showing signs of ferment. Forces only faintly observed in the early decades would come to the surface and the middle-class entrepreneurs and thoughtful theorists would begin to search for ways to solve their many problems.

Among the thoughtful theorists was a new brand of German, potentially creative or disruptive, potentially revolutionary, but difficult to classify. In general these educated individuals (the *Gebildeten*) considered themselves to be members of the middle class, but their position in that group was peculiar because most of these men, well educated and certainly equipped for professional endeavors, were drifting. There was no room for them among the professional ranks and the bureaucrats who dominated civic life. Whatever their success or failure as revolutionists, this educated elite, mingling with the less sophisticated mercantile leaders, would open up the outlook of that essentially conservative group if not actually transform it.

Notes

1 Frank Eyck, *The Frankfurt Parliament, 1848–1849*, p. 63. It must remain a matter of opinion to what extent [the category] should be extended downward.

2 C.A. Macartney, *The Habsburg Empire 1790–1849*, p. 50, note 1.

3 Carl Schurz, *Sturmjahre*, esp. pp. 24–25, 52–53.

4 Priscilla Robertson, *Revolutions of 1848*, p. 146.

5 Walker, *German Home Towns*, p. 135. Even sumptuary rules on clothing for various groups of people "did not actively assert rank and place so much as accept their existence and inhibit the race after status by the display of wealth".

6 Karl Biedermann, *Deutsche Bildungszustände in der zweiten Hälfte des 18. Jahrhunderts,* pp. 100–101.

7 Hans Rainer Giebel, *Strukturanalyse der Gesellschaft des Kgr. Bayern im Vormärz 1818–1848*, pp. 86–87, 108–109.

8 August Bernhardt, *Geschichte des Waldeigentums*, 3:226.

9 Otto Brunner, Das 'ganze Haus' und die alteuropäische 'Ökonomik'," in his *Neue Wege der Verfassungs- und Sozialgeschichte*, pp. 103–127; idem, "Hausväterliteratur" in *Handwörterbuch der Sozialwissenschaften* 5:92–93; Karin Hausert, "Family and Role Division" in Richard I. Evans and W. R. Lee, *The German Family*, pp. 50–83.

10 Rosamunda [pseud.] *Die Köchin ohne Fehl und Tadel, pp. 2–8, 182–201.*

11 C. H. Banfield, *Industry of the Rhine*, ser.2, pp. 39–40.

12 Jonathan Sperber, *The European Revolutions 1848–1851*, pp. 16–17.

13 Kurt Wernicke, *Geschichte der revolutionären berliner Arbeiterbewegung 1830–1849*, p. 27.

14 Sperber, *Rhineland Radicals*, p. 26.

15 Banfield, ser.2, pp. 120–125.

16 So Walker, p. 86. As early as the first decade of the 18th Century, there had been directives forbidding "hunting" members of this class, which seems to have included almost any undesirable individual.

17 Jerome Blum, *The End of the Old Order in Rural Europe*, p. 380.

18 Josef Mooser, "Property and Wood Theft," in *Peasants and Lords in Modern Germany*, pp. 52–80, esp. p. 65; Sperber, *Rhineland Radicals*, pp. 155–156.

19 *Marx-Engels Reader*, p. 3. The *Rheinische Zeitung*, published 1842–1843 in Cologne, carried reports of the proceedings of the Rhineland *Landtag* that related to wood theft.

20 Sperber, *European Revolutions*, pp. 40–41, 117 ff.

21 Koselleck, *Preussen zwischen Reform und Revolution*, pp. 641–659.

22 Werner Conze, *Gesellschaft—Statt—Nation*, p .225.

23 Ibid., p. 226.

24 This aspect of guild responsibility is discussed at length by Mack Walker, *German Home Towns*, passim.

25 Sperber, *Rhineland Radicals*, p. 57.

26 Alfred Schröter and Walter Becker, *Die deutsche Maschinenbau in der industriellen Revolution*, p. 106 ff.

27 Eli Mohrmann, "David Hansemann", in *Männer der Revolution von 1848*, pp. 417–439.

28 Lothar Gall, *Bürgertum in Deutschland,* passim.

29 See Georg Künzel's preface to his edition of Clotilde Koch-Gontard's *Tagebuch über die konstituierende deutsche Nationalversammlung zu Frankfurt am Main.*

30 Macartney, p. 243.

Chapter 3

The Educated Elite: Liberals and Conservatives

Historians who have written about 1848 in Germany have produced a long roster of illustrious names, calling the revolutionists liberals and blandly making common coinage of that slippery word without troubling to define it. In the present case, without constructing an untenable definition or wandering off into a tautological swamp, let us think about the reformers. It may be well to hold it in mind that since they had had little opportunity to confer or to exchange ideas, they may not have even realized at first that they were part of a large heterogeneous group that might be forceful enough to affect the lives of their contemporaries. It might even astound their earnest ghosts if somehow they were to learn that in the Twentieth Century they are thought of as members of a distinct class. They did act as a coherent body, setting off and leading a revolution didn't they? The question must remain unanswered for the present, but in any case there remains another pressing question: What did it mean to be a liberal, a revolutionist?

Revolutionists—successful ones—do not have to have beards and long shaggy hair and flashing deep-set eyes, nor do they have to shout slogans, baring their chests and waving defiant scarlet banners. What they do need is an ability to tap the current of popular discontent, to be articulate and persuasive, and to be clear in their thoughts and motives. It is helpful if they are educated and understand something of the history of the human race, to say nothing of its philosophies. In other words, it helps if the revolutionist is an educated person.

In the nature of things, there was a large group of educated persons in Germany in the opening decades of the Nineteenth Century. Those who were able to do so flocked to the universities because it was only the elite—those with university training—who had access to the ladder on which one might climb to professorships or to most of the bureaucratic positions that offered prestige, privilege, and power. This elite, the *Gebildeten*, constituted the main body of people whose voices were raised in the *Vormärz*[1]. There is a tendency among writers to lump them together, calling them intellectuals. "Intellectuals" ought to be a special term, reserved for those individuals who use whatever ideas they receive during their student years as food for thought. There was plenty of food for thought in Germany in those days. Fortunately, there was a gratifying number of persons who were well equipped by philosophical training who did genuinely think, though their thoughts were not necessarily liberal.

Just what sort of education did the elite *Gebildeten* receive in the first decades of the Nineteenth Century in Germany? Literacy was at a high level there, in contrast to Hungary, for example, where only about 5% could read. In Germany more than 75% of the adult population could read and write. It has to be admitted however that this impressively strong showing did not amount to much. Children in village schools were instructed by teachers who earned little more than the wage of a day-laborer and who additionally had always been firmly under the thumb of the local church. As a consequence, children learned to recite the catechism and sing religious songs but elementary skills such as reading, writing and arithmetic were "thrown in as an afterthought".[2] The religious reformer, Johannes Ronge (1813–1887), remembered that in his school years as a poor peasant boy at Bischofswalde bei Neisse in Silesia, "The names of Schiller, Goethe and Lessing were unknown in our Catholic village." He and his fellow pupils knew hardly anything of German history. All thought was concentrated on religious matters.[3]

Prussian law required school attendance beginning in the sixth year. At Elberfeld there were seventeen schools with forty-three teachers, and an average of one hundred and forty-three pupils per teacher. This inordinate figure was not as alarming as it sounds because the supposed compulsory school attendance until age fifteen was not enforced, in a town where "the temptation to employ children in remunerative occupations is especially great."[4] Secondary schools were attended by about 1% of the eligible age group because most families were unable to pay the necessary fees and allow their adolescent sons to occupy themselves in unremunerative activity. Even though education had been secularized, the curriculum was still strongly reminiscent of the earlier church connection. Such reforms as had occurred can be dated to a Prussian decree of 25 June 1812 that laid out requirements for candidates who presented themselves for a final exam in leaving the *Gymnasium* (the *Arbiturienexamen*). Since the *Gymnasium* stemmed from the monastic and cathedral schools of the Middle Ages, great emphasis was still laid on language study, which originally had been important as preparation for the priesthood. Beginning in the Sixteenth Century, the student was required to learn Latin, Greek and Hebrew. The major change in curriculum, with more emphasis on Greek, reflected the ideas of the neo-humanists of the opening years of the Nineteenth Century. It was not until 1900 that there was a recognized split into *Gymnasium* (Latin and Greek), *Realgymnasium* (Latin and a modern language), and *Oberrealschule* (science and modern languages).[5]

Whereas elementary school teachers were lowly beings subordinate to the church, those who taught at the *Gymnasium* level had been placed under government control (in Prussia at least) by establishment of a special board, under the Finance Ministry. That occurred in 1787. Since most *Gymnasium* teachers were university men, they enjoyed considerable prestige and ranked along with faculty members of the universities. The classics master or the headmaster of a large institution (e.g. Hegel in his early years at Frankfurt) was treated respectfully. There is evidence of this in the bracketing of classical philologists, secondary teachers, and Orientalists in professional conferences that were held, beginning at Nürnberg in 1838. The statutes governing the conferences stated specifically that membership was open to any person who could furnish evidence "to the state to which he belongs that he teaches or has taught at a grammar school or university."[6]

Notebooks preserved by the revolutionary hero Friedrich Hecker from his days at the *Gymnasium* of Mannheim in 1827 offer a view of the exercises that were required of the student in a secondary school. There are compositions written in French, and translations from Julius Caesar, Lucian of Samosata, Cornelius Nepos, Ovid, and Sallust, a summary of Xenophon's *Anabasis*, along with essays on Roman antiquities, Marius on the ruins of Carthage, the *Odyssey*, on "the comfort afforded us by history", and a list of Roman emperors from Augustus to Constantine.[7]

Reformers were raising their voices against the rigid curriculum of the *Gymnasium*. Friedrich Schleiermacher (1768–1834), a Protestant theologian, is quoted to the effect that making ancient languages alone the basis for general education was inappropriate as training for life.[8]

Wilhelm von Humboldt (1767–1835), first rector of the University of Berlin, was calling for a three-fold division, with instruction in languages, mathematics, and science, history and geography. Nevertheless, in this proposed division mathematics was the only one in which a non-linguistic study carried weight because the others all relied heavily on textual materials. The languages of the first division were to be Latin and Greek, one's native language, French and Hebrew. There was resistance in the cities of the Rhineland, where the fathers of future manufacturers and merchants objected to the inclusion of Greek, but they were given to understand that Greek was the crowning glory and flower of civilized education and should so remain.

Friedrich Wilhelm Thiersch (1784–1860) spoke eloquently at a congress of classical philologists to the effect that it is wrong to divide education into separate categories, humanistic and technical. The new industrial class, which he tactfully called "the source of progress" benefits from humanistic training. The industrialist, the owner of large enterprises, the banker, all these people are brought into contact with all the deeper questions of the time and move in circles of world trade. To educate a man for such affairs and raise him to the apex of his profession, to prepare him in his early years is a task for the educator, who must offer the high standard of understanding and culture to the future citizen as well as to the future scholar. In another connection, Thiersch said that "the tree of our culture has its roots stretching through all aspects of past centuries and draws nourishment from everything great, noble and sacred." Innovators, he groaned: "What else do they want but to tear it up with all its roots in order to erect in its place the sapless, branchless and leafless trunk of their theoretical equality?"[9]

The poignant lament notwithstanding, leaders among prosperous entrepreneurs, especially in the Rhineland, were finding ways to educate their sons. The prominent Bassermann family in Mannheim offers an instructive example.[10] The education of Friedrich Daniel Bassermann (1811–1855) served amply to prepare him for his productive life as businessman and later as professional politician. (During the prerevolutionary period he was to become something of a national figure, and subsequently a strong member of the Frankfurt *Parlament* of 1848.) There were no special schools for young aspiring merchants, and he was not interested in a scholarly career. After attendance at a church elementary school, he went through the local lyceum (secondary school, where he elected French instead of Greek), up through the conclusion of the "fourth division", which corresponded roughly to a mid-level of university training that in Prussia would have exempted him from military duty, except for one year. Young Bassermann then entered the firm of his uncle, at age fifteen, and in this connection spent two years in France (one year at Le Havre and one year in Paris). He had become interested in what was generally designated as the drug trade, that included acquisition and sale of botanical, animal and mineral raw products for pharmaceutical and technological uses. With the approval of his family, he went to the university in Heidelberg, for lectures in chemistry, physics and botany in preparation for required qualifying state examinations. Since he was a person of broad-ranging interests, he used the time in Heidelberg for additional study in philosophy and history. Bassermann was then ready for practical training in a drug company in Nürnberg, and this was followed by periods of employment in Trieste and London. He was thus well equipped for his independent, highly successful career. He was twenty-two years old and confident in his knowledge of a couple of foreign languages, extensive business experience, acquaintance with a fair slice of European and English life, and some awareness of the humanities. It is not unlikely that he emerged from his unorthodox training with a better understanding of the world than what he might have attained within the sheltering walls of an old established university.

However distasteful this idea may have been to practical men, the old academic examination as established by the 1812 decree still stood. The candidate would write essays in German, Latin, French and make a two-way translation, from and into Greek. In the oral exam, only Latin would be spoken in discussion of ancient authors. "Deficient knowledge of French and science will not exclude as disqualified those candidates who show satisfactory knowledge of ancient languages, history and mathematics." Entrance exams for the universities were gradually abandoned, and in 1834 it was established by law that the sole entrance requirement was success in the final exam of the *Gymnasium*. In that same year (1834) freedom as to curriculum in the *Gymnasium* that may have existed previously was abandoned. From then on, in a period of reaction to disturbances in the wake of the French revolution of 1830, everything was rigidly set down, including reestablishment of religious instruction. The eternal verities of Christianity must be comprehended and brought into the living awareness of the candidate (circular of 24 October 1837). The Greek flower had withered.

Complaints and theoretical writings continued. The result of all the neo-humanistic reform was a lie, proclaimed K. Mager. "Thousands of young people occupy themselves for seven or even ten years with Latin and Greek and most of them end up with less Latin and Greek than a twelve-year-old would know."[11]

The 1848 firebrand Friedrich Hecker in Baden did not trouble himself much about details but demanded increased state aid for technical education. Such demands had been made before, and answered to some extent. A royal decree of 1833 in Bavaria had provided for establishment of polytechnical schools in Munich, Nürnberg, and Augsburg. In 1840/41 a so-called "4th course" was introduced at Munich especially for the training of civil service candidates in roadway, bridge and hydraulic construction. Later (1856) this training was combined with architecture.[12]

One disagreeable effect of one-sided education was a kind of logjam among educated people, who found no openings in the professional world where their talents might be used. There had been some upward mobility in earlier years, but in the 1840's there was a surplus of educated intellectuals who found no place in the universities or in the bureaucracy. In theory at least, middle-class people had access through the universities to "ennoblement" of a sort, in that the institutions of higher learning were open to them, and completion of their advanced studies would find them on the threshold of prestigious professorships and state offices, but in cold fact the door at that golden threshold was shut. Statistics tell the story. As late as 1910, out of eleven members of the Prussian state ministry, nine were noble. Of twelve *Oberpräsidenten* [provincial governors] twenty-five out of thirty-six were noble. Two hundred and seventy-one of four hundred and sixty-seven county government administrators [*Landräte*] were noble. In 1914, the top echelon of the foreign service included eight princes, twenty-nine counts, twenty barons, fifty-four members of the lesser nobility, and only eleven commoners, and the percentage of nobles was on the rise.[13] "The proletarians of intellectual work are the actual church militant of the fourth estate in Germany. They constitute the large army of the social stratum that has openly and consciously broken with the formerly accepted class structure . . . I include in this group of the fourth estate . . . the civil service proletariat, the schoolmaster proletariat, the perennial candidate for a church pulpit in Saxony, starving academic private docents, literati, journalists . . . In no other

European country is this group so numerous. Germany creates more intellectual products than it is able to use or pay."[14]

Many of those who had thus been closed out had entered the legal profession independently, with the result that there was a disproportionately large number of lawyers. Unemployment was bound to stimulate feelings of discontent and hostility to the existing government. The combination of unemployment and feelings of hostility drove many of the articulate elite into a burgeoning new sub-class—the journalists—who struggled against censorship, writing hotly about various grievances. It has been suggested—and backed up with evidence from successful revolutions, whether French or Russian—that disaffection and alienation among the ranks of the educated ["transfer of allegiance of the intellectuals"] is one of the diagnostic signs of coming revolution.

James J. Sheehan says that liberals regarded themselves as members of the traditional *Mittelstand* (small tradesmen, master craftsmen and farmers), and that they were hostile to the uneducated and unpropertied masses below them.[15] The nobility formed the upper boundary of the middle class, he says. His expression "traditional *Mittelstand*" in conjunction with remarks about liberals brings up bothersome questions. What after all constituted the traditional middle class in the early decades of the Nineteenth Century, and how did the liberals fit into the picture?

Carl Schurz and his family probably were not exactly "traditional" members of the rural middle class. One uncle who was employed in management of a huge peat operation that belonged to the *Graf* was a member of the local guard as a lieutenant, impressive on special occasions in his uniform with shako and sword. Local guardsmen were recruited from the ranks of middle class property owners who could be counted on to sustain law and order in their own interests. The gaudy uniform, shako and sword were paid for by the guardsman himself, not by the state. Carl Schurz's uncle was a great reader, the Voltaire specialist of the family. He was a Freemason, which upset the villagers. He never went to church and when he died he refused extreme unction. Very alarming to yokels who still believed in witches and saw "fire people" near the swamps. Schurz comments that he secretly hoped to see these fearful apparitions (wavering flares of *ignis fatuus*, no doubt).

Whereas the women were all devout, "the men were all more or less touched by the free-thinking spirit of the times," says Schurz. His open-minded father introduced him to Lessing's *Nathan der Weise* after a discussion about old Aaron, a friend of his, who was "wiser than many a Christian". (Aaron was the only Jewish person in the village, and there were no Protestants.)

When Carl Schurz was about four years old, he and his parents and his younger brother moved away from the grandparents' home, to take a modest house in the village. Carl Schurz's *Dorf* had one street, a source of local pride because it was cobbled. The lord of the manor owned the few brick houses along the street, while the rest were timber-framed with tiled roofing The father was a school teacher at first. As his family grew he gave up that work and tried to bring in more funds by setting up a hardware shop in a room of the house that had previously served as a cattle-shed. School teachers were so poorly paid that they sometimes had recourse to work as day laborers in canal construction, just to earn a little extra income. It is difficult to imagine that the Schurz hardware business would ever have been brisk. No matter: the whitewashed walls of the family living room were decorated with framed portraits of Schiller, Goethe, Tasso and Shakespeare, and the modest family library included volumes of Voltaire and Rousseau.[16]

The father had never had much opportunity for schooling and was more or less self-taught, but he was determined to see to it that his sons were well educated. Little Carl went first to the village school but even at a very tender age he took music lessons and ran his scales on a piano at home (this instrument had neither pedals nor dampers). Before long he was walking a long distance through the woods to learn Latin from the parish cleric in a nearby village. In his early teens, young Carl went successfully through the *Gymnasium* and was a university student and enthusiastic *Burschenschaft* member when the 1848 revolution hit. After that his life was one of strange and turbulent adventure, both in Europe and in the United States, where he became a Union General, Senator, and Secretary of the Interior.

If the Schurz family is taken to represent what might be called the rural middle class, it appears that there was a certain degree of upward mobility. Carl went to a nearby city (in the Prussian Rhineland province) in order to receive a higher education than what would be offered in rural communities. He must have seen himself as a future member of the urban middle class. Schurz was a doctoral candidate at Bonn in 1848.

Carl Schurz was a bona fide militant revolutionist. His uncle the admirer of Voltaire no doubt at least sympathized with him, but one can only speculate how it would have been, to be a liberal if one remained in a surly exclusive small village where tradition reigned. In a larger community one could seek out kindred spirits, join together for political action. Or was that a genuine possibility?

Indubitably, every town had its "old familiies"—comfortable merchants, physicians, jurists, university personnel and so on whose status was unquestioned. Sessions at the festive table of Thomas Mann's hospitable Buddenbrooks family have made such people known to modern readers. The Buddenbrooks family was destined to suffer and to fail, but in 1835, the old Consul, head of a prestigious and long-established Lübeck shipping company, and his gentle wife are introduced, awaiting the arrival of guests for their house-warming, seated in their "landscape room" with its idyllic tapestries where pretty shepherds and shepherdesses disport themselves. Before long the pastor, the local gallant and poet, the doctor, the senator and their ladies are ushered into another tapestried room with red damask curtains and massive red damask sofas. "There they all sat, on heavy, high-backed chairs, consuming good heavy food from good heavy silver plate, drinking full-bodied wines . . ." With their massive gold watch chains and beautiful laces, the Buddenbrooks have a serious Biedermeier confidence and awareness of destiny. The men discuss the pros and cons of the new *Zollverein* during their postprandial billiard game and speak tolerantly of Louis-Philippe, but it is clear that theirs is a self-contained, quietly successful world, *die Welt des ganzen Hauses* [the world of the entire household].[17] Tradition and family pride are every bit as palpable as the large gilt-edged copy book in which Buddenbrooks births, marriages and deaths have been recorded for generations. If Thomas Mann had shown a social reformer as an accepted member of this closed household, the reader would have shaken his head at the improbability. (One son had had the temerity to "marry down", and he was an outcast, a black sheep.) Revolutionary ideas were not likely to flourish in such a setting. Nothing much that was new would ever happen there.

Although the major part of the middle class may have been stagnating, something extraordinary had been occurring, especially in the cities and university towns. The new element was the appearance of societies, reading circles, and various organizations made up of people with congenial tastes and interests. Societies had begun to assume a place in the dull uneventful life of the upper middle class as a spinoff of the Enlightenment. The novel activity was in all probability initiated by the restless educated elite, the *Gebildeten*, the articulate people, but the spread brought in many a member of the mercantile middle class as well as a surprizing number of the nobility. Generally speaking, an aristocrat had little need to enter a society because his rank already brought him into close association with members of his own class and he would have little or no motivation for trying to break into the class below him—unless perhaps he had lost some of his influence and power in recent times. On the other hand, what the educated elites were seeking was some means of interaction with other elites who were equally qualified—not necessarily by birth or status, but by education and talent. What they sought was a direct man-to-man "human" relationship. It was a triumph for the advance of democratic ideas that aristocrats were attracted into societies where they would find a genuinely new social sense of "belongingness" based on their personal worth, not on blood and inheritance. The middle class mercantile members no doubt also found a basis for a fresh assessment of themselves, based on talent and accomplishment.

If middle class members of the burgeoning clubs and discussion groups felt uneasy at the prospect of continued suppression or of radical change, they must have welcomed the chance to talk things over with fellow members who were part of the educated elite. These men knew a lot about social problems and philosophy, and it ought to be instructive or at least interesting to listen to them.

The university-trained men had a fairly substantial common knowledge of the various philosophical schools, and whichever set of ideas appealed to them most would find expression in their notions about German society. There might therefore be several different groups within the ranks of the educated middle or upper class, each with specific theories and ideas of how to tackle the problems arising from the peculiar nature of Germany and its confrontation with large-scale industrialization, population growth, pauperism and so on. It is worth while to pause for a moment, considering their options.

Philosophy had received some startling jolts in the wake of spectacular advances in physics and mathematics (Newton, Descartes, Leibniz) in the course of the Seventeenth Century, and it can be said that roughly two schools of thought had emerged—the rationalist and the empiricist.

There had been a joyous leap at first, to the conclusion that philosophy itself could become a genuine science where everything could be mathematically demonstrated, analyzed and quantified, and that before long Truth that all men sought would be revealed, not only revealed but demonstrated just as convincingly as any mathematical theorem. There must be a set of axioms from which Truth and the universal laws of nature could be logically deduced. God said, let Newton be! and all was Light.

The idea was fallacious. Philosophy asks questions and expends most of its energy in search of appropriate tools that can be used in solution of those questions. Before long the jubilant men of the Enlightenment found that their reliance on the Truth of mathematics and physics would not hold.

Giambattista Vico (1668–1744) planted a time bomb when he wrote his *Principi di scienza nuova*, although it was not generally known before the French historian Jules Michelet stumbled on it and translated it into French in 1837. "I have no master other than Vico!" wrote Michelet, overwhelmed. Even a present-day reader experiences a sting of excitement when he opens Vico's little work and labors along through stately antique paragraphs, unexpectedly encountering ideas that tingle with life. The *Scienza nuova* had a powerful delayed effect. Hegel read it, and so did Karl Marx. We understand mathematics, announced Vico, because we made it. Human beings created it, and it cannot be applied to analysis of anything that is not of our own making. Philosophy cannot be a science of cosmic Universals. Metaphysics is a false science. There is no tool for such study anywhere.

In the case of empirical science, if the right tool is found or devised (a telescope, a microscope, a chemical experiment, a set of physical principles, a mathematical model or formula that will test a given hypothesis) concrete problems can be analyzed efficiently and solved, but science can do no more. It can however be expected to continue to break out new disciplines in line with new discoveries. According to Vico, his own "new science" can be successfully utilized in analysis of history which, like mathematics, is knowable because it is a product of human action. In Vico's sedate language,

> In the night of thick darkness enveloping the earliest antiquity . . . there shines the eternal and never failing light of a truth beyond all question: that the world of civil society has certainly been made by men, and that its principles are therefore to be found within the modifications of our own human mind.

It is possible to reconstruct even ancient societies like Homer's Greece by study of the poetry, because poetry is a true expression of the views and experiences of the society that produces it. Many a student in the opening years of the Nineteenth Century must have been startled by Vico's analysis of Homeric society.[18] It is startling even today to the reader who all unprepared comes on it for the first time. How many moderns have been perceptive enough to see that Homer must have lived in a "brutal" pre-philosophical era? Vico was saying that every culture is unique, the product of individual living men, and that there is no timeless natural law. Vico stopped there. He did not go on to say that men's gods and religions are likewise the product of human beings, but he had said enough to put new and daring thoughts into men's minds.

Then along came Locke and Hume, philosophers both. It was David Hume (1711–1776) who contributed to the wrecking of the rationalists' lovely dream palace by stating that science is unequivocally the science of man. We cannot hope to know causal links, ever.

This reexamination of the basic tenets of civilization—especially those deriving from religious beliefs—was a tremendous step. Whether or not the philosophers of the Enlightenment were aware of the magnitude of their deed, they had crossed the threshold that marks the entrance to true secular life where everything is open. To imagine what Europe would have been like if the men of the Enlightenment had not prevailed, one has only to speculate on the nature of European society today if Charles Martel had not won at Poitiers. Gibbon, reflecting on this matter, mused that "Perhaps the interpretation of the Koran would now be taught in the schools of Oxford, and her pulpits might demonstrate to a circumcised people the sanctity and truth of the revelation of Mohammed." It is precisely that static revelation that has been an insurmountable stumbling block to Islam as it struggles to cope with western civilization.

One important outcome of the philosophers' stark finding was scepticism, with a concomitant shift in ideas about ethics and religion. Enter empiricism, a generally tolerant discipline that inevitably fostered a novel intellectual climate. One would imagine that this new climate would have been a relief to Germans, still slowly recovering from the horrors of those inconclusive religion-based conflicts called the Thirty Years' War and still geographically divided between Roman Catholics and Protestants.

Scepticism and tolerance can have serious political consequences. What is one to say about absolute authority and the divine right of kings as claimed by Friedrich Wilhelm IV of Prussia? What about seigneurial rights claimed by the *Standesherren*? What about enormous expensive armies, and wars?

Voltaire was a contemporary of David Hume's. Voltaire the wily unbeliever had one passionate conviction: that man, no matter what the Universals might be, demanded justice. He championed the fight against fanaticism and bigotry and barbarism. How could one ever reach Truth if the way was barred by forces of oppression?

Voltaire was not the only hero of the times. There was Jean-Jacques Rousseau (1712–1778), whose *Contrat social*, whether or not it had actually triggered the great French Revolution as some people proclaimed, had certainly had much to do with establishing and strengthening the revolutionary mood. His egalitarian theories, and his rights of man, as well as his mysterious *volonté générale* [general will] had aroused intense enthusiasm, even though the details of his explanations about the unbreakable link between natural man and his creator remained murky. In Rousseau's view, government was artificial, imposed on mankind by tyrants. Man has been corrupted and must return to Nature. Human beings could recover natural law—the law of equality—and hammer out together a social contract that would satisfy their common needs. Many a heart beat fast at the thought that society's multitudinous ills could be wiped out if only the splendid law of Nature—*a priori* and luminously perfect—were accepted by unhappy humanity.

Most of the German *Gebildeten* must in their youth have received a strong dose of scepticism and at the same time shared a feeling that perhaps society was malleable in some hitherto unforeseen way.

Meanwhile they could consider the difficult thinking of Immanuel Kant (1724–1804). Vico in his obscure professorship in Naples was far from any currents of contemporary thought. Even so, there are strands in his philosophy that might have appealed to the sage of Königsberg. It was Kant who made it plain that the primary role of philosophy had never been to supply answers to questions that properly should only be asked of the empirical scientist. Philosophy should concern itself with analysis of our most general concepts, leaving to physiologists or anthropologists or psychologists the task of devising means that will lead to discovery of the way in which those concepts are utilized by the human mind. Kant offered to the eager men of the Enlightenment some extremely unsettling ideas. Among them was his theory that genuine freedom of the individual lies in his own self-governance, which in turn is piloted by the standards set by the society in which he lives. Kant's conception of *Freiheit* could not be easily equated with the Englishman's notion of freedom, or the French ideal of *Liberté*. To him and his followers, there would always remain the task of balancing societal control and individual liberty.

Here was a place where liberals might split. According to their bent, they might become political theorists or practical sociologists. Some might want to debate, with the intention of extracting some perfect constitutional configuration for an ideal German government. On the other hand, some would think, if we can't fix everything, let's at least do something about censorship and poverty. Among either of these two factions there would be room for those who would say let's overthrow the government, depose the rulers, toss out the nobles and bureaucrats (even the *Mittelstand* if Marx and Engels were to have their way), rely on our own noble aspirations, and make a fresh start.

There was another element that would loom large in the liberals' political and social thinking. A powerful voice had been raised at the university of Berlin by the philosopher Johann Gottlieb Fichte (1762–1814) whose series of *Reden an die deutsche Nation* [addresses to the German nation], calling for resistance to Napoleon, had stirred up a patriotic storm. His students had hurriedly taken up arms, and the romantic spirit of nationalism persisted, buoyed by the university clubs, the *Burschenschaften*. Fichte's philosophical theories that were based on subtle Kantian dialectic remained wellnigh impenetrable, but his political thought was still very much a part of young Germans' intellectual and emotional equipment.

The cult of nationalism led a number of scholarly Germans to a political predilection for reform and constitutionalism on the English model, for an extremely quaint reason. Those who had read their Tacitus managed to persuade themselves that the Anglo-Saxons, revered forbears of the German people, had carried their supposed ancient free institutions across to Britain. They remembered that the distinguished Roman had admired the Germans and spoken respectfully of their Assembly where the people could shout dissent or clash their spears, signifying approval.[19]

Fichte's successor on the faculty of the university of Berlin was a mighty philosopher and political theorist, namely Georg Wilhelm Friedrich Hegel (1770–1831) whose lectures and writings made an indelible impression on a whole generation. "The picture of the intellectual life of the times would be incomplete if one were to disregard the preponderant influence of the man who assumed a position of

absolute dominion in his age and who in the future spread the effect of
German mentality throughout the world in a way not equalled by any
contemporary, including Goethe . . . and who in the immediate future separated out the conservatives' idea of the state as well as that of
national liberalism, and influenced the founders of socialist theory in
the development of their respective positions." Hegelian philosophy
has been called "the hour hand of German life in science and art."[20]
The temptation to bypass Hegel is strong, in part because his elephan-
tine style is so repellent, and in part because of purely subjective dis-
taste. So much of his idealist construction, admittedly with distortions
and modifications, was to be basic to the development of totalitarian
ideology.

Hegelian philosophy is based on a general principle that has been
familiar to philosophers for millenia—at least as far back as Parmenides
and still vigorous in Spinoza—that the whole is the only reality. In
developing his dialectic method and applying it to history, Hegel was
thinking as a metaphysicist, focused on history as the progressive realization of the Absolute. His dialectic bears a shadowy resemblance
to the Socratic technique of reaching truth by reconciliation of opposing statements, but Hegel was striving always for a constant progres-
sion, not only in logic but also in human history, toward an all-encompassing perfection. In his system, one progresses from two opposing
elements to a reconciliation that is an advance over the original two.
The rhythmic beat of the triple dialectic is relentless. Thesis, antithesis, synthesis; synthesis as a new thesis opposed by a new antithesis,
followed by a new synthesis. Over and over and over. As an example:
Thesis, the period of despotism. Antithesis: the classical age. Synthesis: the modern period of universal freedom. In this evolutionary view
of human existence in which the state is a natural organism and repre-
sents a phase in the historical world process, Hegel was denying
Rousseau's theory of the natural freeborn man. No, said Hegel. Early
man was a slave of superstition and passion—an ignorant dangerous
primitive. He could reach freedom to be a valuable person only as a
member of a strong, well-organized state. Hegel seemed to feel that
history had attained the stage of absolute reality in—of all things—the
state of Prussia with its strange medieval-minded monarch who believed in divine right, and his horde of bureaucrats.[21] The mind reels.
What was it that John Stuart Mill said?

. . . where everything is done through the bureaucracy, nothing to which
the bureaucracy is really adverse can be done at all. The constitution of such

countries is an organization . . . into a disciplined body for the purpose of governing the rest . . . the more successful, the more complete is the bondage of all, the members of the bureaucracy included.[22]

Karl Marx in his youth was an enthusiastic member of a group that called itself the Young Hegelians, writing for their *Deutsche Jahrbücher*, but before long he began to detect flaws.

The abolition of the bureaucracy is only possible by the general interest actually—and not, as with Hegel, merely in thought, in abstraction . . . Hegel starts from an unreal antithesis and therefore achieves only an imaginary identity which is in truth again a contradictory identity. The bureaucracy is just such an identity.[23]

In the decade immediately prior to the revolutionary eruption of 1848, the once enthusiastic Young Hegelians began to break away from the master and to promulgate some disturbing ideas. David Friedrich Strauss (1808–1874) picked up an idea of Hegel's, that human institutions are the expression of the particular genius of various peoples. He analyzed the Christian gospels and came to the conclusion that these were not historical documents at all: the whole life of Jesus was a myth, the creation of the popular imagination. Strauss immediately lost his post at Tübingen as the result of this blasphemy, and even the canton of Zurich would have nothing to do with him.

Ludwig Feuerbach (1804–1872) was a man whose thinking shows strands of Vico's courageous exploration of the world, extending Vico's idea to consideration of religion as a manmade product. His *Das Wesen des Christentums* [the essence of Christianity] appeared in 1841 and soon made its way into the hands of various religious protest groups that had begun to gather force in Germany. "Feuerbach uncovered in the most logical way the cradles in the human spirit where all the gods were born, and with them belief's favorite child, the miracle."[24] Feuerbach's way of expressing himself was original and pungent. The course of religion, he said was identical with the course of development of human culture. "As long as mankind represented a simple natural man, his god was a simple nature god. Where men lived in houses, they enclosed their gods in temples. The temple is only evidence of the value that man placed on handsome buildings. Temples in honor of religion are in actuality temples in honor of architecture."

With the rise of mankind from the state of the crude and wild, with the distinction between what is fitting or not fitting for man, there appears simultaneously the distinction between what is suitable for god, and what is unsuitable. God is the concept of majesty, of the highest worth, the religious feeling, the highest feeling of what is fitting. Only the later trained artists of Greece incorporated the concept of worth, of magnitude of soul, of unmoved peace and serenity in their statues of the gods. . . . Bodily strength is a property of the Homeric deities. Zeus is the strongest of the gods. Why? because corporal strength in and for itself is valued as something fine and godly. . . . It was not the property of godliness, but the godliness of the property that was the first true deity.[25]

This anthropological explanation drew much excited attention. It remained for Karl Marx to deliver the final thrust, because in spite of everything, Feuerbach had still somehow remained a Christian. In his much-discussed "Theses on Feuerbach", written in the spring of 1845, Marx argued (Thesis 7) that Feuerbach did not see that "religious sentiment" is itself a social product and that the abstract individual whom he analyses belongs in reality to a particular form of society. He concludes (Thesis 11) The philosophers have only interpreted the world, in various ways; the point, however, is to change it.[26]

This then was the array of philosophical theory that lay open to the Germans. By 1848 all philosophical argument would of necessity have a predominantly political cast.

There remains one more powerful voice that was heard throughout Europe—that of Thomas Paine. His ideas and theories were not presented in an academic setting, but there is little doubt that his words were known and avidly studied by most thinking men. His *Rights of Man* (1791–92) was passed from hand to hand, in English and in translation. Here, in the plainest of presentations, was the clear unadorned expression of the case for democracy and the basic rights of individuals, along with a blistering indictment of hereditary monarchies, titles of nobility, and privilege. To read the work even now, after its two centuries of existence, is to quiver with the excitement of recognition of things thought privately, along with feelings of optimism and even self-congratulation at the refreshing knowledge of one's personal participation in the human experience. *The Rights of Man* is one of those books that one remembers always, recalling the feel of the binding, the thickness of the paper, even the smell of the ink.— Admittedly, Paine had written a polemic. The opening sentences are clear on that point. He had been deeply offended by Edmund Burke's *Reflections on the Revolution in France.*

Paine's argument was that civil rights as they apply to society grow out of natural rights and are "exchanged" for certain rights that are difficult or impossible for an individual to sustain alone (e.g. protection and defense). Among the natural rights that the individual retains are the rights of the mind.

> A man, by natural right, has a right to judge in his own cause; and so far as the right of the mind is concerned, he never surrenders it. But what availeth it him to judge, if he has not power to redress? He therefore deposits this right in the common stock of society . . . Society grants him nothing. Every man is a proprietor in society and draws on the capital as a matter of right.[27]

Paine was impatient when he confronted the theory of social contracts between the governing individual or class and the governed. He thought it was absurd that a hereditary monarch could take it upon himself to "grant" a constitution. Man must have existed before governments, and there necessarily was a time when governments did not exist. Consequently, there could originally exist no governors to form such compacts, he insisted. Each individual, in his own personal and sovereign right, entered into a compact with other individuals to produce a government, "and this is the only mode in which Governments have a right to arise, and the only principle on which they have a right to exist."

In Tom Paine's eyes, the Bastille was the true embodiment of tyranny, and its fall was one of the greatest events of all time. When earnest liberals learned that the key of the Bastille had been given by Lafayette to Paine, and that he in turn had given it to George Washington,[28] they must have felt that in very truth the time was near when all mankind would breathe the air of freedom.

To sum up: liberals were not a class, or even a minority within a class, but rather an inchoate group of educated individuals who were acquainted with the various philosophical schools and who were concerned about the politico-social condition of Germany. Any list of those who wrote, persuaded, and acted during the disturbances that led up to or followed the actual revolution includes many names that have an identifying von, which is incontrovertible evidence that these were persons of status, members of the aristocratic upper class. No cause for astonishment to discover that aristocrats were well educated, but not entirely to be anticipated that some would be ready to imagine possible societal adjustments and reforms. As to the remaining list, it comprises for the most part the names of professors, scholars, journalists and lawyers, along with that of an occasional wealthy entrepreneur. There was a general feeling among them that something was very wrong, and this feeling they shared with the less informed or more timid middle-class members of their various clubs and societies, acting within such groups as a leavening agent. The liberals who were professional people (or who at least had the training to be among the professionals) would have seen themselves as members of the middle class, but though they championed the interests of that segment of society they were in fact not always accepted, especially by businessmen who thought they were too theoretical and did not understand the nuts and bolts of industry or even of society in general. Most individuals of the upper middle class appear to have remained passive, like the fictional Buddenbrooks family, although they had gained a new perception of themselves and their position in society.

Many historians tend to use the terms "liberals" and "intellectuals" interchangeably, but this is a mistake. There were plenty of intellectual conservatives also. "The now almost forgotten opponents of the *philosophes*, even the pessimists who deny the doctrine of progress, are for the most part doctrinaire intellectuals, as unreasonable devotees of *la raison* as the radicals."[29] As Karl Marx once wrote to his colleague Arnold Ruge, "Reason has always existed, only not always in reasonable form." Opponents of the *philosophes* had joined forces at the time of the Enlightenment, when free thought posed an alarming challenge to entrenched monarchs, courtiers, nobility and bureaucrats, along with the ranks of the devout who were led by the clerics, whether Catholic or Protestant. The French Revolution of 1789 had thoroughly frightened them into self-protective unity, and so they remained during the risings of 1830.

An early conservative spokesman, Carl Ludwig von Haller, author of a formidable treatise, *Die Restauration der Staatswissenschaften* (six volumes, written between 1816 and 1822) was determined to beat down Rousseau's pernicious idea of a social contract, which he disdainfully called a self-contradictory aberration. Anybody can see with his own eyes, he said, that there is always inequality among men. The whole idea of the social contract is predicated on a "juridical fiction". Human beings never lived in freedom and equality—it was their nature to form families. This instinctive response to human needs occurred because some, e.g. women and children, are weak and dependent. Haller observed tartly that even the social contract theorists recognized this essential aspect of human life because they excluded women from participation in the social contract simply because of their dependence. The patriarchal system is best. A state is nothing other than the dependent private domain of the independent ruler, and monarchy can be described as the first, most natural, and most durable form, growing naturally from the family. Power should reside with the prince alone, and separation of powers into legislative, executive, and judicial, is the first step toward revolution.

A somewhat later theorist, Friedrich Julius Stahl (1802–1861), a professor of law at Erlangen and later in Würzburg and Berlin, wrote his influential *Das monarchische Prinzip* in 1845. He acknowledged that the nexus of German life was from the patriarchal toward the constitutional state, but his intention seems to have been to reassure conservatives that constitutional development would not necessarily end in something like the English system, where the parliament had rights that clearly spelled out its independence from the crown (right to initiate legislation, right to reject tax bills, responsibility of the ministers to the parliament). In the system proposed by Stahl, it was only the sovereign who could initiate legislation. "Authority, not majority" was his often-repeated phrase. Stahl thought of representative government as a two-way instrument of interaction, in which representatives (neither capitalists nor proletariat, to be sure) who had internalized the law of the state informed the ruler of public opinion, and the monarch in his turn was the instrument of moral education of his people. He should see to it that his power was solidly based on a well integrated administration over which he maintained firm control. "An irreplaceable bureaucracy" could dispose of subversive irreligious tendencies. (Was Stahl, a deeply religious Christian, thinking of Ludwig Feuerbach?) Stahl's program for an ethical realm, a *Rechtsstaat*, presumably offered some room for human creativity. It was in any case the last serious effort to defend traditional monarchy before the 1848 revolution, but it was only in the post-revolutionary period that it was grasped with hope and enthusiasm by conservatives who then had to cope with problems inherent in political parties and elected parliaments. In the dry words of a modern historian, Stahl had proved that it was possible to construct a constitutional monarchy that would not inevitably evolve into a parliamentary democracy.[30]

Less articulate conservatives accepted these views. They were upholding tradition, they announced. Tradition included reverence for institutions that had developed slowly through the centuries and that should not be overturned or altered by constitutions whipped up impulsively on the spur of the moment. Constitutions were untrustworthy constructions, based on abstraction. There was no solidity in them.

Besides, the state was a splendid version of the human family. A position that favored patriarchal principles inevitably made conservatives hostile to any notion of extended suffrage. They did not by any means consider all men to be equal. The king of Prussia was in hearty agreement. No mere sheet of paper called a constitution should ever disturb the trusting, fond, occasionally stern relationship that bound him to his people. He Friedrich Wilhelm IV, the *paterfamilias* ruled alone. Even his close friends among his Kamarilla and the high-ranking bureaucrats would never have a final say.

Through the conservatives may not unanimously have accepted this royal pronouncement, they defended the idea because they were clinging to their old beliefs and values. For this reason they heartily supported the organized church, which graciously supported them in return. Liberals were depriving men of all inward discipline, they asserted. It could only be retrieved by universal recognition of the religious basis of human society. Both von Haller and Stahl were deeply religous men, by the way. The conservative Catholics were ready to back Redemptionists and Jesuits, while the Protestants were quick to come to the side of such men as the Gerlach brothers, who organized supporters of revivalism among the Prussian nobles.

As to the conservatives' agenda in general, they were reluctant to see or encourage industrial development, preferring an economy based on agriculture. They were distressed by the decline of the guilds and looked askance at industrial competition. They thought that railroads might bring more trouble. In Stahl's opinion, "Thus far, industry and machine production are a calamity for the human race." [31] Only the new "capitalist" Junkers were not whole-hearted in their conservatism. On the whole, the conservatives longed for a return to the good old system of Throne and Altar.

The political situation would have to become drastic before men of reflective and scholarly temperament would even think of revolution, and certainly the stolid merchants would think long and hard before they would be capable of entertaining such an appalling notion. Conservatives and reformers alike came from the same social stratum that had inherited a wealth of cultural traditions in which religious beliefs, romanticism—yes, even personal ties—inevitably played a part. During the opening years of the Nineteenth Century there was stagnation and inertia throughout most of Germany, with the exception of the explosive thirties, when excitement spilled over from the 1830 July Revolution in France. Reaction to the disturbances of that time was so severe that up until the volatile fall of 1847 there were no overt divisions into groups of activists, unless we count members of various religious protest groups and certain secret *Burschenschaft* organizations and hot-headed exiles in Paris who seethed with plans to unite German artisans in the overthrow of all existing authority.

Thinking their way along philosophically, discussing seriously, reformers were for the most part envisioning adjustments of the existing system of monarchical government. In essence most people were engaged in theoretical tinkering. They wanted some kind of representative body that could counterbalance the absolutism of the ruler, but tended to have a fuzzy Hegelian notion of respect for political institutions as they were. Some thinkers may have reasoned that whereas Rousseau's basic natural law ought to prevail, full realization of it could only come about if there were overt political action. Few if any of them were clear in their own minds on just what that political action ought to be. The kind of action that had occurred in the disturbances triggered by the French revolution of 1830 had not been encouraging, because it had quickly become evident that Germans were not masters of their own fate. The powerful Austrian minister Metternich had made that abundantly clear when he saw to it that the enthusiastic student *Burschenschaften* were outlawed.

An interesting observation has been made that "intellectuals" and "intelligentsia" are inaccurate terms for those who become alienated and whose transfer of allegiance is symptomatic of coming revolution. A better term would be "publicists", defined as authors, editors, artists, teachers, priests, preachers and "all those whose function is to form and guide public opinion". Johann Jacoby, in discussing the role of the publicist, once wrote to Fanny Lewald that in him there collects as in a burning glass the theoretical knowledge of various doctrines, times, and lands. From the indistinct ambiguous images and concepts he must transmit the core of truth into the transparent understandable speech of the common man.[32] In the everyday course of public life, these people are an intermediate class whose role is the maintenance and transmission of the existing system to future generations. "When the publicists are sure that an institution which they had supposed to be good is really repressive, they attack that institution with a zeal proportionate to their anger at having been deluded as to its nature."[33]

Heine the exiled rebel and quintessential publicist was known for his irony. Whether he spoke ironically or in genuine naive anticipation, here are his words, addressed to the French in 1834.

Beware of kindling the fire . . . You could easily get your fingers burned. . . . German thunder is admittedly German and not well articulated, . . . but if you once hear a crack, it will be a crack such as has never been heard before in the history of the world . . . [at present] there are only small dogs running around in the empty arena barking and snapping at each other, but the hour will come when the gladiators will enter the scene and fight for death or life.[34]

Notes

1   *Vormärz*. Literally prior to March. Used to indicate events, ideas etc that led up to the revolution that occurred in March 1848.

2   Sperber, European Revolutions, p. 33.

3   Sylvia Paletschek, *Frauen und Dissens*, p. 22.

4   Banfield, *Industry of the Rhine*, ser.2, p. 134.

5   Brockhaus *Enzyklopaedie* 7:817–818.

6   Richard Hinton Thomas, *Liberalism, Nationalism, and the German Intellectuals (1822–1847)*, pp. 54–55.

7   University of Missouri. Western Historical Manuscript Collection, Collection 451, box 1, folder 2.

8   Fritz Blattner, *Das Gymnasium*, p. 87.

9   Thomas, p. 73.

10   Gall, *Bürgertum in Deutschland*, pp. 230–233.

11   Written in 1846 and cited by Blättner, pp. 127–128.

12   Hugo Marggraff, *Die Kgl. bayerischen Staatseisenbahnen*, p. 172, note 17.

13   Berdahl, *The Politics of the Prussian Nobility*, pp. 3–4, citing Hans-Ulrich Wehler.

14   Wilhelm Heinrich Riehl, *Die bürgerliche Gesellschaft*, p. 331.

15   James J. Sheehan, *German Liberalism in the Nineteenth Century*, pp. 26, 31.

16   The presence of volumes by Voltaire and Rousseau does not necessarily indicate any high level of erudition. The names of those two were on everyone's lips, in every class, all across Europe, even on the lips of Victor Hugo's dying urchin Gavroche. Wounded, he sings defiantly before he collapses, *Joie est mon caractère, C'est la faute à Voltaire. Misère est mon trousseau, C'est la faute à Rousseau.*

17   The expression is taken from the idea of the self-contained household that found a loyal following among readers of encyclopedic works collectively known as the *Hausväterliteratur* of the late Eighteenth Century.

18   Giambattista Vico, *The New Science*, Book 3, paragraphs 780–902, pp. 245–274; Isaiah Berlin, *Against the Current*, pp. 4–7, 120–129.

19   Tacitus *Germania* 11, 12

20   Bruno Gerhardt, *Handbuch der deutschen Geschichte*, 3:112; Walter Neher, *Arnold Ruge als Politiker und politischer Schriftsteller*, p. 38.

21   In his inaugural address at Berlin (1818), Hegel spoke of the state *der auf Intelligenz gegrundet ist, und Macht und Bildung verbindet* [founded on intellect, and that combines power and education]

22   John Stuart Mill, *On Liberty*, p. 112.

23   Karl Marx, "Contribution to the Critique of Hegel's Philosophy of Right" in *Marx-Engels Reader*, p. 25.

24   H. E. Sachse, *Erinnerungen an die Entstehung und Entwicklung der Magdeburger freie Gemeinde*, p. 27.

25   Ludwig Feuerbach, *Das Wesen des Christentums,* pp. 63–64.

26   *Marx-Engels Reader*, p.145.

27   Thomas Paine, *The Rights of Man*, p. 34.

28   It is preserved today at Mount Vernon.

29   Crane Brinton, *The Anatomy of Revolution*, p. 44.

30   Berdahl, p. 373.

31   Ibid., p. 365.

32   Johann Jacoby, *Briefwechsel 1850–1877*, p. 54.

33   Lyford P. Edwards, *The Natural History of Revolution*, pp. 38–41.

34   Heinrich Heine, *Sämtliche Werke*, 4:72–73.

Chapter 4

Interaction: Societies, Secret and Otherwise

It was inevitable that the first cracks in the solid front that the German states presented against social movement and interaction between classes should come from the outside. The entering wedge was unintentionally driven by English Freemasons. They had become acquainted with certain German merchants, diplomats, and aristocrats who visited England independently, and admitted them into their lodges. The city of Hamburg, with its many overseas shipping contacts and its prosperous Protestant mercantile middle class, was the obvious place for the opening of the first German lodge (on 6 December 1737). From that initial lodge, called Absalom, masonry spread rapidly—to Berlin at the time of the accession of Friedrich *der Grosse* in 1740, to Braunschweig in 1744, to Hannover in 1746, until the network had extended to Oldenburg, Breslau, Königsberg and so on.[1]

Another wave, originating from French lodges, led to the establishment of Freemasonry in Dresden (1738) and Leipzig (1741). In Frankfurt am Main the lodge had an international cast, since it comprised French and Polish diplomats in addition to high-ranking German bureaucrats.

These organizations were legal, in the sense that they were licensed, in spite of a general bureaucratic wariness. Some of the German rulers had been slow to respond to papal denunciations from Clement XII in 1738 and Benedict XIV in 1751, possibly because they were aware that membership included a great number of aristocrats. Even Goethe was a mason. Not unexpectedly, the Catholic Church was vigorous in its opposition, regarding Freemasons as atheists. Certainly churchmen must have resented the notion that men might gather to discuss their ideas privately, in a way that properly ought to have been restricted to the confessional, where appropriate guidance and supervision could be exerted by firmly dependable clerics. The masons were known to be in favor of secularization. A brotherhood that rejected the divinely established human hierarchy must intend to overturn all time-honored social arrangements! Such an organization might even want to overturn the state. A secret society must of necessity be conspiratorial—especially an organization with such a far-flung network that stretched beyond national boundaries to Protestant lands.

The kind of damage that could emanate from secret societies has an excellent example in the German *Tugendbund*, established at Königsberg in April 1808 and presumably a clear offshoot of Freemasonry. This society [literally the League of Virtue: its official title meant something like the Moral and Scientific Union] is said to have originated within the Königsberg lodge, where one of the members observed, "As Freemasons we bear the afflictions of our country and must initiate nothing, but we are also citizens of our state and I think we ought to establish a league that is independent of Freemasonry."[2] Prussia was under the heel of Napoleon at the time, occupied by French armies and obligated to pay enormous sums as indemnity, in return for an unfulfilled promise to evacuate the troops.

The organization technically was not secret because it had been licensed on 30 June 1808 by Friedrich Wilhelm III, who wrote that "The revival of morality, religion, serious taste and public spirit is assuredly most commendable." His Majesty did include a comment to the effect that there must be no "interference in politics or public administration."[3]

The activities of this group somehow came under the control of a conservative *fronde* that was trying to block the work of the great liberal minister, Karl vom Stein, and managed to engage in various foolish enterprises through its "chambers" in Prussia and also in Silesia. An anonymous enemy transmitted to the editor of *Le Moniteur* a confidential message said to have been written by vom Stein and intercepted by a secret agent. The letter was presented in such a way that in the public mind, vom Stein was perceived to be using the *Tugundbund* for his own nefarious purposes. Dated 15 August 1808, it approvingly mentioned the current unrest in Spain and commented that it would be extremely useful to spread the news about it in Prussia. Whether genuine or not, publication set off an uproar, with the result that vom Stein's carefully designed plan to arouse Prussians against the tyranny of Napoleon came into the hands of Napoleon himself. The emperor described himself as "outraged" and quickly placed even more pressure on Prussia than before, in the end unseating vom Stein.

The *Tugendbund* itself, with which vom Stein apparently never had any connection (he is believed to have disapproved wholeheartedly of all secret societies)[4] behaved in "a vulgar and unintelligent way" and was, in the judgment of vom Stein's biographer not a vast union into which all the discontent of Prussia spontaneously threw itself, but was "in reality merely a fantastic attempt of one section of the discontented to give to their movement a peculiar organization." In the words of vom Stein himself (written twenty years later in his autobiography), "An effect and not the cause of this passionate national indignation at the despotism of Napoleon was the *Tugendbund*, of which I was no more the founder than I was a member . . . when later it proposed to exert an indirect influence upon educational and military institutions I rejected the proposal as encroaching on the department of the civil and ecclesiastical governing bodies. As I was driven soon afterwards out of the public service, I know nothing of the further operations of this society." [5] The split between vom Stein's defenders and accusers marks the first beginnings of political parties in Prussia.

The Freemasons were not a genuinely secret society, nor were they conspirators. Their ritual was secret, to be sure, but they were open about their lodges and their membership. The lodges attract attention today because, springing as they did from the liberal ideas of the Late Enlightenment, they were the first organizations in which "brothers" who were members of the aristocracy and those who belonged to the rising middle class met on an equal footing. All recognized organizations in Germany heretofore had been based on birth and social status. In the lodges, moreover, there was close social and business contact between Catholics and Protestants—something that the Catholic hierarchy would surely view with alarm.[6] The Freemasons opened the way for all manner of voluntary associations that one joined at will without consideration of class or religious confession. Even the strange assortment of paramasonic and pseudomasonic lodges spawned in the closing years of the 18th century had this salutary effect.

Masonic ritual has a somewhat infantile look to the outsider—for example, the initiation ceremony undergone by Pierre Bezúkov in *War and Peace*. (Tolstoy wrote to his wife that after he had spent hours examining materials on Freemasonry, he had emerged from the library in a state of deep depression. "What is disturbing is that all those masons were fools."[7]) It is hardly cause for astonishment that the ritual suggested to lively minds various opportunities for ridicule, even farce.

Ritual had its uses, however. In essence, it concealed and facilitated a latent political function, the provision of a stage on which new social interrelationships could be acted out, almost as if in an experimental laboratory. By deliberately cutting themselves off from disturbing issues such as religious profession or politics as they existed in reality, they performed a kind of esoteric balancing-act that allowed the brotherhood to test and examine an atmosphere where mutual consideration and tolerance were possible, at a time when such experimentation was virtually impossible in the rough outside world.[8] The ritualizing of interaction within the lodge had a reassuring and stabilizing effect, much as the disconcerting ceremonies at Diocletian's court (e.g. "adoration of the purple") made things run more smoothly between Roman officials and barbarian courtiers who must have been acutely uncomfortable in their new unaccustomed relationship as colleagues.

The history of Freemasonry is difficult to untangle because its members tend to be less than forthcoming in the matter of access to their archives. Also, there was a bewildering plethora of pseudomasonic societies such as the Asiatic Brothers and the military lodges of the French Clermont-Rosa system, the latter a curious organization deriving from supporters of the exiled royal house of Stuart that claimed to have secret knowledge of alchemy. They could change "sun dust" to gold, it was said.

Masonry seems to have offered a niche for almost everyone, from Benjamin Franklin, who was delighted to escort Voltaire to his honorary induction into the lodge of the *Neuf Soeurs* at Lyons, on down to outright charlatans like Cagliostro (1743–ca.1795), who managed to found a highly successful "Egyptian rite" that could well be taken as a prototype of Amway, since the men and women who made up his lodges (the "Copts") served as an outlet for his lucrative sale of pommades and fortified wines. Cagliostro ended his life in prison, condemned by the Roman Inquisition for activities as a Freemason.

There was a masonic "reform" offshoot called *Strict Observance*, founded by one Karl Gotthelf *Reichsritter* von Hund und Altengrotkau (1722–1776), who strove to prove that his organization was the true successor of the Knights Templar (abolished in 1314). The Templars, maintained von Hund, had lived on in exile in Scotland. Within the ranks of his *Strict Observance*, where one of the chief obligations was absolute obedience, there were ferocious internecine struggles for supremacy before the organization subsided around 1780. For years this rival brotherhood actually outnumbered the original Freemasons.

Rosicrucians asserted that they were the source of Freemasonry which they penetrated to such an extent that "Rosicrucian" became the recognized highest degree in the masonic system. The Rosicrucians were closely associated, apparently, with the *Strict Observance* masons, and they leaned in the direction of esoteric "learning" including alchemy, theosophy, magic and the cabbalistic mysteries.[9] Like the *Strict Observance* rite, Rosicrucianism went into a decline somewhere around 1780, but much damage had been done to Freemasonry, which was banned in Prussia in 1798.

Into the vacuum left by the gradual fadeout of both Rosicrucianism and the *Strict Observance* organization stepped the order called the *Illuminati*, founded in 1776 by Adam Weishaupt, a professor at the university of Ingolstadt. The order spread rapidly through Bavaria as well as to the north and into the Rhineland, but it was fated to be banned because it had the air of a subversive revolutionary conspiracy. In those days, people were looking askance at anything that smacked of conspiracy and irrationality. Weishaupt's *Illuminati* were far from irrational, but they had radicalized the ideas of the Enlightenment. The order was arranged in a three-stage system of degrees like that of classic Freemasonry and its professed goal was to spread pure truth and make virtue victorious—all prosaic enough. However, Weishaupt's program was much subtler and more extensive than that of the masons. Oddly, there are those today who accord to Weishaupt rather than to Karl Marx the title of Father of Communism.[10]

Weishaupt appears to have agreed with Rousseau that mankind and his society had become marred and that there had to be a return to Nature's rule. This could only be effected, he felt, if the *Illuminati* worked in absolute secrecy toward the goal of building an institution of education and training that would be beyond the corrupting reach of state [i.e. Jesuitical] control. He did not hesitate to seek recruits among the nobility and clerics, as well as among bureaucrats, teachers and courtiers whose enlightened talents could be applied to execution of the task within the framework of various learned disciplines—physics, medicine, mathematics, the arts, politics, even arcane knowledge. Although there was perforce a trace of elitism here, in general the *Illuminati* offered an example of an "equalizing" brotherhood. A known membership roster includes aristocrats, school inspectors, physicians, officials, military officers, landowners, teachers and court musicians, even a court baker.[11]

The secrecy of the order would serve strategically as defense against censorship and Jesuitical tampering. Weishaupt was frankly interested in exerting palpable influence on political and educational policy. Unfortunately he was no realist, thinking that he could effect anything so drastic in backward Catholic Bavaria. Beyond Bavaria, in Protestant lands, barriers were already breaking down to the extent that the extreme clandestine nature of the order was no longer perceived as necessary. Nonetheless, the *Illuminati* in particular were the cause of uneasiness and anxiety abroad. Edmund Burke, for example, mentioned the fact that many parts of Europe were in open disorder, and that "in many others there is a hollow murmuring under ground; a confused movement is felt, that threatens a general earthquake in the political world." Referring to two obscure German works but refraining from direct reference to the society, he went on to say that confederacies and correspondences of the most extraordinary nature were forming in several countries.

> In such a state of things we ought to hold ourselves upon our guard. In all mutations . . . the circumstance which will serve most to blunt the edge of their mischief and to promote what good may be in them is that they should find us with our minds tenacious of justice, and tender of property.[12]

Former members, like the Bavarian minister Mongelas, who was dismissed in February 1817 because of suspected illuminist tendencies, later referrred to the order and its rituals as childish.

Sometimes the confusion of interrelated or antagonistic "masonic" lodges is so great that it generates a troubled sensation of wandering in a house of mirrors. Which is genuine? Which is made up of imposters? What is real, and what is the reflection of a reflection? This holds true especially in the case of those lodges that accepted women members. It would be gratifying to believe that those enlightened men of the Eighteenth Century had led the way to a more just attitude toward the opposite sex, but the ground here is treacherous.

There were several lodges that admitted women. The first, established at Hamburg in 1745 by one Christoph Karl Kress von Kressenstein, was known as the order *De la Fidélité*. It was no doubt inspired by a French order with the same name that is known to have existed in 1744, and that was superceded by the *Ordre de l'Ancre*. The authoritative article on Freemasonry in *La grande encyclopédie* comments distantly that "*la pureté morale parait y avoir été médiocre*."[13] The Hamburg order was quickly followed—also in Hamburg—by a so-called "adoption lodge", the Concordia, founded in 1759.

At this point one enters the hall of mirrors, treading cautiously. The order in question was known in Germany as the *Mopsorden*. (In France, the *Mopses*). A *Mops* is a pug dog, here presumably honored as the embodiment of faithfulness. Origins of the order "*im Dunkeln liegen*" [remain in the dark], says Winfried Dotzauer.[14] She then names Clemens August (1700–1761) prince-bishop of Cologne as the supposed sponsor. Another authority named a notorious playboy, *Herzog* Clement of Bavaria as the sponsor.[15] This information, as well as faintly obscene details on ritual, comes from a pamphlet entitled *L'Ordre des Francs-Maçons trahi et le Secret des Mopses révélé* supposedly published in Amsterdam in 1758. Described as anonymous, or alternatively as coming from the pen of one *abbé* Perau, the pamphlet had illustrations showing an initiation ceremony presided over by an elegantly dressed *Grande Mopse*.[16]

The candidate is shown with manacled wrists that are joined by a long catenary chain. One view shows her blindfolded. She stands on a curious "plan" made up of a square and circle, in the center of which stands a *Mops* facing east. There are many symbols of love, sincerity and so on, enclosed in a "cordon of pleasure". Welcoming the candidate, or perhaps threatening her, stand gallants with drawn swords and ladies who hold small dogs. Was this group mocking the Freemasons? Was it being mocked by the author of the pamphlet that described the ritual? Were these people merely bored and enjoying themselves in a silly way? Who, in fact, are the women? Could they be prostitutes?

Here is a judgment that is extremely difficult to make, although it requires quite a stretch of the imagination to accept the idea that any serious-minded woman would ever have allowed anyone to address her as "The Great Pug-Dog".

Though the majority of Freemasons may have been intent on their own personal enlightenment and improvement, they were blamed as forerunners of revolution and disorder. The distrust was accentuated by the fact that later organizations that had distinctly political goals modeled their societal structure and even their arcane rituals along masonic lines. Most groups that patterned themselves after the Freemasons had grades similar to the various degrees that led step by step to the level that supposedly represented the highest understanding of Truth. This pervasive idea was ancient, hardly an invention of the masonic lodges. One need only think of the seven Mithraic orders (raven, *miles*, lion etc.) as they are depicted on a mosaic floor in Roman Ostia. Such a societal structure did of course lend itself well to conspiracy, as in the underground organizations of World War II in France or Norway, for example. (Even under torture, a given individual would have had little to disclose that could endanger the organization as a whole because knowledge was deliberately restricted to the affairs of the member's own cell.) However that may be, before long Freemasonry was denounced as a workshop that actually generated the destructive *Zeitgeist* embodied in such subversive organizations as the French Jacobins and the Italian *Carbonari*.[17]

In 1821, Ludwig Börne wrote a satirical "report" on a conspiratorial group of *Carbonari* that he had uncovered. The *alta vendita*, he said , was in Ludwigsburg, and it had "daughter lodges" in Tübingen, Stuttgart, Frankfurt and Offenbach. Members of this Brotherhood of the Steadfast Hats whose secret goal was to achieve equality, love and courtesy, disguised themselves in public by rough manners. They never removed their hats in greeting but only waved their hands in a military manner. "You will certainly agree with me, *Herr Ober-Tugend-Direktor*, that keeping a hat on heats the head, and we have had enough experience of the disaster spread over the world by heated heads . . . It is clear that the Brothers of the Steadfast Hats constitute a secret militia. It is imperative to suppress these carbonaric excesses. Only by mobility of hats can the stability of heads be maintained in Germany."[18]

The idea of secret conspiratorial bands like the *Carbonari* captured the imagination of the reading public. Honoré de Balzac must have felt confident that his strange brotherhood called "Les Treize" would be accepted. This group of men who were a law to themselves appear in three of his stories, all written in the 1830's—*Ferragus, La duchesse de Langeais*, and *La fille aux yeux d'or*. The reader is given to understand that these men, one of whom is an unscrupulous dandy and womanizer, and another a man who was once a convict, had banded together in their admiration for the audacity and energy of Napoleon Bonaparte. Such was the perhaps unwilling belief in secret societies that Balzac was able to introduce this element into his stories in the knowledge that he was not dragging in anything that would be rejected as implausible.

In the eyes of suspicious rulers and bureaucrats, the Freemasons were suspect because the Craft was international. Events abroad reinforced the suspicion.that this was a dangerous conspiratorial group. Just take the Freemasons of Russia as an alarming example. Freemasonry had struck root there sometime around 1760, and it was believed that there was a deep interest in political reform among members of the lodges. The order had undergone repression during the reign of Catherine, but had flourished under tsar Alexander I, whose successor, Nicholas I, had every reason for clamping down on any secret organization in his realm. In December 1825 there had been a conspiracy directed against him, designed to block his ascent to the throne on the death of Alexander in favor of a more tolerant man, his brother the Grand Duke Constantin. The "Decembrists" were among the first groups in Russian history that had well-formulated plans for political change and even the seizure of power. Among other things, they wanted a constitution. This conspiracy had been put together by members of various secret societies, some of which were derivative from Freemasonry.[19]

One of the earliest organizations was called the *Soyuz spasenija* [union of salvation] which was made up exclusively of members of the Imperial Guard, who were all nobles. In 1817 they had developed a constitution that had different degrees of initiates, like a masonic lodge. When the court moved to Moscow, the meetings continued under a new name and with a new constitution. The organization was then called the *Soyuz blagodenstviya* [union of welfare]. Its constitution closely followed the statutes of the *Tugendbund* that had brought so much difficulty into the life of the Prussian minister vom Stein.

Although one of the leading Russian masonic lodges set down as a principle the idea that a member must be an obedient and loyal subject and must not participate in any secret societies that would be harmful to his country or sovereign, it was clear that the secret rituals and the graded hierarchy of initiates had been congenial to those who found the idea of conspiracy appealing. The Decembrists, as the insurrectionists were called, certainly were involved with other near-masonic conspiracies. Their southern group, for example, had some contact with the Swiss branch of the *Carbonari*.

In any case, they effected a military uprising among the troops stationed at Saint-Petersburg who in their ignorance believed that the popular Grand Duke Constantin had a wife named Constitution, and they shouted for this royal couple with great enthusiasm. Disheartening evidence of the distance that an ignorant populace has to traverse if ever it is to enjoy democracy. Tsar Nicholas had five Decembrist leaders hanged, and one hundred and twenty of them deported to Siberia. Years later, Mikhail Bakunin spoke eloquently of the Decembrists in his first speech that advocated panslavism, addressing a wildly receptive audience of Polish *émigrés* in Paris:

> They are our saints, our heroes, the martyrs of our liberty, the prophets of our future. From the height of their gallows, from the depth of Siberia where they still groan, they have been our light, the source of all our good inspirations, our safeguard against the cursed influences of despotism.[20]

Closer to home, German authorities had observed the Italian *Carbonari*, which was clearly masonic in its origins, as well as the French *Charbonnerie*[21] that had in turn been inspired by the Italian organization. The *Carbonari* first appeared in southern Italy sometime around 1807, when they attempted to defend Ferdinand IV and his queen Caroline, who had taken refuge in Sicily. (The name of the organization was taken from the charcoal-burners, in whose huts the members occasionally hid from the authorities.) With the fall of Napoleon, their effort was directed into revolutionary channels: it was the *Carbonari* who had stirred up both the rising in Naples in 1820 and the Piedmont insurrection of the following year. They were colorful people, meeting conspiratorially in caverns and swearing awe-inspiring oaths in complex rituals where members with such titles as Grand Elected One, Flame, Sword-bearer, Star and so on officiated. It is even asserted that the initiate had to take his oath of absolute obedience on such disgusting objects as the severed hand and head of one who had attempted to betray his brother *Carbonari*.[22] By 1831, the *Carbonari* had been more or less absorbed by Mazzini's Young Italy [*Giovine Italia*].

The French *Charbonnerie*, which first appeared in France in 1820 was distinctly republican in its aims, though at that time the members concentrated on the overthrow of the Bourbons. It had little of the "masonic" degrees and titles that were characteristic of the *Carbonari*, but had a hierarchy that clearly was intended to protect them as conspirators in case any were captured.—The *Charbonnerie* had its system of *ventes* (20 members with a deputy), a *vente centrale* made up of 20 deputies whose elected deputy communicated with the *haute vente*, which in turn sent a delegate to the *vente suprême*. There was never any communication in writing, and each member was required to supply himself with a gun and 25 cartridges. Lafayette was the first elected president at a time when there were fifty *ventes* in Paris alone. There were said to be two thousand *ventes* throughout France, with some forty thousand members. They dedicated themselves to the eternal extinction of all tyranny and the establishment of a *liberté sage et sans fin sur la ruine éternelle des ennemies des peuples*. The organization was ineffective, but was certainly symptomatic of the times, and timorous conservatives were alarmed by it. There were abortive insurrections in 1821, at Belfort and Saumur, but after that as the revolutionist Louis Blanc commented, they could only wallow in the blood of their martyrs. Many rallied around the monarchy of July in 1830, however, and even found places in the government of

Louis-Philippe. (Such a person is the industrialist who appears among the guests of *madame* Dambreuse in Flaubert's *Éducation sentimentale*.)

A known conspiratorial group in Poland was the "National Freemasonry" whose three levels of initiates were devoted to increasingly binding dedication to the goal of Polish freedom. Prince Adam Czartoryski, the best known of all Poles in exile during the troubled years of revolution, had been an active Freemason in his early years, and held the highest masonic degree in his native country. When he went into exile, he was welcomed as a brother by the English Freemasons presided over by the Duke of Sussex, their Grand Master, in 1839. He was also a guest of honor at a lodge in Edinburgh in that year.[23] It is of interest to find that following a meeting of delegates at Dresden in 1820 where the intention was to revive the disbanded students' *Burschenschaften* in a campaign for German unification, contact was made with the Polish masons in order to learn their strategic methods.[24] When the Polish Freemasons were forced to disband following a denunciation, the members reformed as a "Patriotic Society" that abandoned all trace of masonic structure and rituals.

In Austria there was fear and distrust of all secret societies, reminiscent of the Jacobins, with the result that although Mozart's splendid *Zauberflöte* had been presented before the high nobility at Vienna in 1791, the year 1795 witnessed the suppression of Freemasonry. The opera boldly featured masonic themes and symbols, and the tenets of the craft were made clear:

> bald soll der Aberglaube schwinden, bald siegt der weise Mann . . . dann ist die Erd' ein Himmelreich und Sterbliche sind Göttern gleich.[25] [Soon superstition will disappear and the wise man will be victorious . . . then earth will be a heaven, and mortals will be like gods]

One of the opera's crowning moments was the lovely duet of the high-born princess Pamina and the lowly bird-catcher Papagino—a moving hymn to love and the idea of human equality.

What was happening among the German university students during the opening years of the Nineteenth Century? The tradition of student associations was old everywhere.[26] At the Sorbonne or other great universities such as those of Bologna and Padua, there had from the earliest days been a division into nations, and this had been sustained in Germany by the *Landsmannschaften* that mirrored the chopped-up structure of the miniature states in the wake of the Thirty

Years' War. These groups seem to have had no aim other than the acting out of our musical-comedy notion of a life of general youthful disorder, duels, drinking bouts and brawls. There was a shift at the time of the Enlightenment to a sentimental program of lifelong brotherhood and loyalty. Supposedly the new so-called *studentischer Orden* owed its ideas and origin to Freemasonry, but it was still similar to the wayward student corps depicted in Viennese operettas.

A more serious attitude was introduced into student life by Friedrich Ludwig Jahn (1778–1852) who was disturbed by the disarray of Germans under the Napoleonic occupation and thought that young men ought to strengthen both their bodies and their patriotic loyalties by systematic gymnastics. His first *Turnverein* was established at Hasenheide near Berlin in 1811. Jahn fought in the war of liberation in the Lützow *Freikorps* [volunteers], and returned even more convinced that youthful Germans needed to be saved from a vacuous sense of rootlessness that originated in the many political dislocations of the times. He must have understood, judging by his own feelings, that there was deep disappointment among the young veterans of the war. Most of them were members of the middle class, and they must have believed that their patriotism and valor would earn them a place in the government of their country, yet as the Congress of Vienna assembled, the archdukes and kings and princes had resumed their former places and little had changed.

Jahn's original colleague, Friedrich Friesen, was lost during the war, but shortly after the victory over Napoleon the first student organization that embodied Jahn's ideas was founded at Halle—the "Teutonia", established on 1 November 1814, the day of the opening of the Congress of Vienna. The "Teutonia" was an important forerunner of the student movement, acting as a connecting link between the earlier *Landsmannschaften* and the new style of society with its program of German unity and patriotism. It was Jahn who first formally used the term *Burschenschaft* that was soon to be adopted by the student movement. Parenthetically, it should be explained that the name properly implied membership of upperclassmen only, but there were always large numbers of *Renoncen* (lower classmen might be a good translation for the term) associated with the *Burschenschaften*.

Another powerful speaker in favor of student organization was Ernst Moritz Arndt (1769–1860), who had spent some time in St. Petersburg trying to organize a German legion that would participate in an uprising against Napoleon, and who had returned to Germany in 1813.

Professor of history first at Greifswald and then at Bonn, Arndt was influential in the formation of groups at Giessen, Heidelberg and Marburg. Those at Giessen and Heidelberg were known as *Teutsche Lesegesellschaften* [German reading societies]. From these sprang the circle known as the *Giessener Schwarzen* ["black" because they wore old-fashioned German costumes] and the Heidelberg "Teutonen". At Marburg there was a new society called the *Brüderbund*. All these organizations were formed in 1814–1815.

The students who had been taught by Fichte, Arndt and Heinrich Luden of Jena had little use for small-state Germany and spoke of freedom and unity, as well as "purity of the German language". In spite of much fine oratory about unity, there was always a latent—sometimes overt—conflict within the clubs with reference to the traditional idea of the importance of the duel. This unfortunate disagreement had a lot to do with the general weakness of the student movement.

There was activity at Jena, where freedom fighters formed a paramilitary *Wehrschaft* made up of veterans from various *Landsmannschaften*. After a period of stress, a general society was formed, led by the "Vandalia" *Landsmannschaft*, and this new unified organization became the core of a *Burschenschaft* that pledged itself to loyalty to the people and responsibility of individuals for the wellbeing of all. The university of Jena was soon a center for the growing *Burschenschaft* movement. The Jena professor of history, Heinrich Luden (1780–1847), had been calling for the rights of all peoples, even at the time of the Napoleonic occupation. He was not a revolutionist, but admitted that revolution might come. Napoleon is said to have bracketed him sourly with other professors at Jena, who in his opinion were sowing the seeds of revolution among the young. Luden was convinced of the importance of constitutional government.

Through him, the student group at Jena became strong enough to issue an invitation in October 1817 for a festive celebration at the Wartburg near Eisenach,[27] cannily combining recognition of the third centenary of the Reformation with that of the fourth anniversary of the battle of Leipzig, a potent symbol of German unity. Camouflage, no doubt, but in any case five hundred students responded to the call and marched in a stirring procession. It was necessary, they believed, to see to it that all the fruits of the war of liberation were not lost. They intended to work for German unity against the dynastic efforts of princes who sacrificed all rights of the people to their own special interests.

Bearing torches as they ascended to the top of the Österberg, the marchers sang Luther's *Eine feste Burg* [a mighty fortress is our God]. Students were not the only participants. Among the onlookers were officers and soldiers from a nearby garrison, as well as townspeople and local officials.

Not everything that was done that day was entirely admirable. There was some book-burning, though the inspiration for this ill-advised action came from an honorable source. It is thought that the idea came from the venerated *Turnvater* Jahn, who was remembering Luther's burning of the papal bull. The books that were cast into the flames at the Wartburg festival included Carl Ludwig von Haller's conservative work on absolutism, his *Restauration der Staatswissenschaften*, the *Code Napoléon*, and most prominently, the hated *Geschichte des deutschen Reiches*, from the pen of August von Kotzebue (1761–1819), a theatrical director and playwright who was considered to be a spy against the students, in the pay of the Russian tsar.[28]

Kotzebue's activities with reference to the tsar may have been fairly blameless. He seems to have sent extracts and reviews of books currently appearing in Germany, but one of these reports had come into the hands of Luden, who published it. This seems to have been the basis of the popular belief that he was spying for Russia. He had added fuel to the fire by involving himself in a controversy over an anti-*Turnverein* pamphlet that had seemed to him to have valid arguments. In Kotzebue's view, Jahn's nationalism was offensively excessive. When he was asked about the participants in the Wartburg celebration who had burned his book, he answered indifferently that they were merely a handful of malcontents.[29]

About three weeks after the festival, the "Arminia" *Burschenschaft* at Tübingen announced its own dissolution (20 November 1817) in the face of threatened investigation.

The Wartburg festival had been the first opportunity for an exchange of ideas between the leaders of the various budding organizations, who agreed that the time had come for the foundation of an *Allgemeine deutsche Burschenschaft*, a federation with a structure not unlike that of the governing federation of German states that had been established at Frankfurt by the Congress of Vienna. The groundwork for such a general group was laid at a first Jena convocation in March 1818, and on 18 October 1818 fourteen representatives of fourteen different universities met at Jena and signed the document that brought the federated society of students into being. It was at this time that the tricolor black-gold-red was adopted.[30] The leaders, guided by Luden, wrote out their statement of principles but refrained from publishing it for reasons of security. The document called for uniform German law, constitutional monarchy, freedom of speech and press, equality before the law, public trial and trial by jury, and universal military duty. All this anticipated demands and national programs of the future.

There was another, far more radical document that was also the product of the Wartburg era. This draft for a German constitution was written by members of the *Giessener Schwarze* under the leadership of their fiery Karl Follen, who thought that society ought to be self-governing, and that the peasants should lead. Most of Follen's small group of adherents came from families that had suffered in recent times and who no doubt agreed with one of their members. "We poor devils won't ever get our rights unless there is a storm. There has to be a storm that will topple the ones who have robbed us," he said.

Follen was aware that he could expect little support from the student body in general. He organized his followers as a radical group called *Die Unbedingte* ("no holds barred" might do as a translation here, though the accepted one is usually something like "the wholly committed"). Certainly, Follen was not a man to shrink from the idea of violence. He composed a bloodcurdling song, the *Grosses Lied*, that praised regicide as a solemn sacrifice. To give one's life for humanity was as noble as the sacrifice of Jesus on the cross.

Follen and his ardent followers applied themselves vigorously to a campaign of leafleting, propaganda and conspiracy. Follen himself thought that their best hope would be to join forces with known radicals in the Rhineland. They were all sure that a revolution would have to happen in the near future or its chances would fail because a reaction was under way. A revolution could be initiated, they thought, by a terrorist attack on some leading figure of tyranny—the tsar, perhaps. They were impressed by the zeal of Polish revolutionaries at Heidelberg and Marburg, and formed a union of friendship with them.

Among the rank and file of the *Burschenschaft* members, Jahn's influence remained strong. At Tübingen, for example, they called in Karl Völker, a Jahn student and *Freikorps* veteran, who was to introduce the Jahn gymnastics program. With the approval of university *Rektor* Bahnmaier, Völker set up equipment in a hall assigned to him. The city authorities also showed interest and set aside exercise grounds, while the Forestry administration provided young saplings for planting there. Linden trees were set out in the spring and the grounds were dedicated in May 1819. Völker hoped to instill into his enthusiastic young gymnasts an awareness of themselves as Germans. The number of *Turner* increased so dramatically that Völker had to call in no less than seventeen assistants. By summer, the revived Tübingen *Burschenshaft* membership had jumped from a mere forty to one hundred and forty-one, but the organization's days were already numbered because of the action of one of Follen's people.

Karl Ludwig Sand (1795–1820), one of Follen's most convinced disciples, had taken it upon himself to go to Mannheim and stab the hated "traitor" August von Kotzebue to death (23 March 1819). The fanatic young theological student had taken care to resign from the Jena *Burschenschaft* beforehand, thinking to save his fellows from blame, but the damage was done. Unfortunately for the *Burschenschaften*, Sand had a complex background of associations. He had been a member of the Tübingen "Teutonen" before he left briefly during the Napoleonic Hundred Days to join a Bavarian armed unit. He returned to Germany, where he founded the first *Burschenschaft* at Erlangen. He had participated in the Wartburg festival and then continued his studies at Jena, as an active member of the *Burschenschaft*. He seems to have thought that he was making a noble sacrifice for the Christian-German ideals of the students, and that his action was a chivalrous defense of Germany. He was, he said, shielding the honor of the fatherland. Kotzebue was known to have supported the idea of censorship and general repression, criticized Jena's popular Heinrich Luden, and incited mistrust of Germany in the mind of the Russian tsar. For these various reasons, Sand righteously defended his action. In his deposition at his trial, he described in cool analytical terms his penetration into Kotzebue's house, the stabbing and his confused attempt to stab himself before he ran out of the house. On the street, he said, he fell to his knees, thanking God that he had been allowed to do this deed, then stabbed himself again.

He mounted the scaffold quietly, still convinced of the correctness of his actions. He was decapitated on 20 May 1820, in a meadow outside Jena, where an emotional crowd of admirers soaked their handkerchiefs in his blood just as early Christian followers of Saint Cyprian had done at Carthage in the Third Century. They even chopped up the scaffold and carried off fragments of it in devout remembrance, as though these were splinters of the True Cross.

Contemplation of a portrait of Sand is unsettling. A healthy vigorous frame. Manly "arian" face. Clean aristocratic features and a look of firm decisive intelligence. Somewhat distant and aloof, perhaps, but that may be because he had already set himself apart by his bloody assault at the time the sketch was made. His is not the face of a man who has ever experienced the warmth of trusting friendship. But how could anyone with even a deceptive appearance of balance have ever been blind enough and self-deluding enough to accept as his *Führer* a congenital conspirator like Karl Follen?

Popular judgment of Karl Ludwig Sand appears to have been relatively mild throughout Germany, reinforcing the opinion of the German governmental authorities that there must have been a conspiracy. Suspicion lay heavily on Völker, whose gymnastic facility was closed abruptly following an order (17 August 1819) forbidding student assembly. Under strict surveillance, Völker remained in Tübingen until March 1820 when he fled to Switzerland under threat of arrest. *Rektor* Bahnmaier was dismissed from his post at Tübingen because he was charitable in his assessment of the assassin and also uttered words of criticism against Kotzebue. Bahnmaier was not the only one to express himself so. Sand's grave was continuously strewn with flowers, and poems were written about him. Symbolic paintings were made in his honor. Such a portrait, painted by Wedelin Moosbrugger, hung for years in a private room of the handsome home of the prosperous middle class Bassermann family in Mannheim. Young Friedrich Daniel Basserman, then eight years old and a future political leader, was taught that, like Lord Byron in Greece, Sand was a heroic freedom fighter.[31] When Robert Blum—himself destined to be the most famous martyr of the 1848 revolution—received the gift of a flower from Sand's grave, he responded: *Dann greift der Mann zum Schwert mit frohem Muthe, Dass aus der Frevler—aus dem eignen Blute der Freiheit Blume stolz sich neu belebe!*[32] [The man then boldly grasps the sword, that from the sacrilegious one's own blood the flower of freedom may proudly spring up anew]

Speaking at the Waterloo Festival that year, Karl Wächter observed that Sand "was noble and great, but he went beyond his proper sphere. We ought to shed a tear in his memory." Even shedding tears might be risky: the theologian de Wette wrote a note of sympathy to Karl Sand's mother and promptly became the subject of an official investigation.

The term "official investigation" is misleading in its flat tone that suggests some matter-of-fact process. In actuality, such investigation could be disastrous, protracted and maddening as anything described by Kafka. The net of official investigation was cast far and wide. Almost simultaneously with Jahn's arrest in July 1819, police broke into the home of the Bonn professor Ernst Moritz Arndt. His papers were confiscated (and subsequently falsified) . After lengthy hearings, Arndt was released, but forbidden to lecture. This ban held until the accession of Friedrich Wilhelm IV twenty years later, when the new king graciously pardoned him.

Official vigilance was meat and drink to certain bureaucrats like *Geheimrat* Tzschoppe of the Prussian ministry of police, whose target was the Jena professor Heinrich Luden, under suspicion because of his strong influence on the radical wing of the *Burschenschaft* movement. In spite of the fact that Jena was not within the purview of Prussian competence, Tzschoppe eagerly collected documents that incriminated Luden, chief among such documentation being one of "utmost importance", in the form of a set of lecture notes kept by one of Luden's students during a course on political theory given at Jena in 1821.[33] The twenty-two pages of notes were solemnly forwarded to *Fürst* Wittgenstein with a covering letter that urged the elderly minister to refuse admission of any student who had attended Luden's courses into the Prussian civil service. Wittgenstein in turn forwarded the supposedly incriminating material to some learned colleague, who submitted an unsigned comment in which he asserted that this was a repetition of what the demagogues of all Europe were trying to propagate. One has to wonder, wrote this anonymous commentator, if the princes who adhered to the formation of the German confederation at the Congress of Vienna can look on quietly while a professor in one of the states belonging to the confederation teaches German youth that all that was included in the final act of the congress, so faithfully revered in the hearts of thousands, even millions, of German subjects, is nothing but error. Prussian minister of foreign affairs Ancillon found the student's notes disquieting. Luden, he said, was only saying what was being taught in all the German universities, poisoning the youth and the governments as well as the military who, when sent abroad to Italy and Spain, were undermining other governments also. If things go on like this, mused the alarmed minister, in ten years or even earlier there will be no armed force capable of preventing this damage because the army itself will be contaminated by the false doctrine. Only one person (his name not known) wrote a calmly reasoned response. In his view, it was unfair to pull a sentence or two out of context, especially since the document was written by a student who may not have understood the professor's meaning and intent. On the whole, Luden seemed to be advocating a constitution that would assure the happiness of the people by the law of a monarchy. To him, Luden's words were not those of a revolutionary.

Nevertheless, Luden himself saw fit to write (10 September 1823) to Friedrich von Motz, president of the provincial directorate that was competent in matters of Jena university, defending himself and saying that he had no revolutionary intentions and that he had been misunderstood on all essential points. Luden closed with the assurance that he would no longer present any lectures on political theory. He had been giving such lectures regularly ever since 1807. He never spoke again on the subject, right up to the time of his death in 1847. Evidently suspicion, incarnate in the person of *Geheimrat* Tzschoppe and his colleagues, had won a significant victory.

Sand had played into the hand of Metternich, who grasped the opportunity to launch a campaign of repression, though he professed to lament the loss of "my poor Kotzebue". Although he frequently complained of the stupidity of censorship and police surveillance and was irritated when his own movements were spied on, Metternich was second to none in his readiness to apply repressive measures. He once said that Kotzebue's assassination had had an undue influence on the Austrian Emperor Franz, who laid excessive importance on secret societies.[34] He believed that he had found a way to end the evil by keeping the intellectuals under constant surveillance. However that may be, Metternich and the Prussian minister Hardenberg met to discuss the matter, and elaborated a draft document (the "Teplitz *Punktation*").

This agreement was the basis for the notorious "Carlsbad decrees" devised by Hannover, Saxony, Mecklenburg, Nassau, Bavaria, Baden, and Württemberg, in addition to Prussia and Austria, to be submissively ratified by unanimous vote of the *Bundestag* on 20 September 1819. Governmental officials were placed at all German universities in order to supervise discipline and to make determinations as to political attitudes of professors and students. Anyone found to be engaged in "destructive teaching" was to be dismisssed. The *Burschenschaften* were suppressed because of persistent inter-university communication. Members were excluded from all civil posts, and students or professors dismissed from one university were not to be admitted elsewhere. Newspapers, journals, books of more than twenty pages—all were subject to censorship. Not only this. The popular gymnastic societies were forbidden, not to be revived until they were recognized provisionally by an edict of 1842. The *Zentral-*

untersuchungskommission [central investigating commission] at Mainz was charged with responsibility for looking into suspected revolutionary activity, and was instructed to report its findings to the *Bundestag*, which had thus been converted into an instrument for the suppression of any liberal or nationalistic movements.

Evidence of the thoroughness of official repression lies in German passivity throughout the 1820's when a revolutionary wave swept across Europe, from Spain to Greece. Otherwise, what an opportunity for spirited lovers of liberty! There had been wide-spread famine in 1817, as well as a business depression—enough, certainly, to shake the foundations of the post-Napoleonic settlement.

Metternich, who consistently regarded insurrection, nationalism and constitutionalism as inflammatory and dangerous to unsteady Austria, was the only one among the leaders of the major powers who clung stubbornly to the idea that all such movements must be immediately suppressed. In the case of the rebellions in Naples and Sardinia and the Italian Piedmont—all considered to be Austria's special responsibility—he was able unchallenged to send in Austrian troops to control the situation (spring of 1821). However, when trouble erupted in Spain, it was the English, led first by Castlereagh and then by his successor Canning (joined in 1823 by the United States with its Monroe Doctrine) who effectively cut off the proposed police work of France in the Peninsula because they took an unfavorable view of any possible intrusion of French power into their vital economic interests in Latin America.

When the Greeks rose against the *Sublime Porte*—the century's first genuine movement for national independence—there was clear division among the major powers. The English gradually moved into an interventionist position because they wanted to stave off unilateral action on the part of Russia. Metternich resisted, with the result that English and Russian representatives met secretly (April 1826) and then proposed semi-independence for Greece. When war ensued between Russia and Turkey it fell to the lot of Prussia as an outsider to negotiate the peace in 1829. By the terms of the treaty of Adrianople, Greece became independent. German liberals could not claim to have played any part, but they may have been astute enough to perceive that the principle of suppressing all revolutionary unrest had received some serious blows.

From the time of the Carlsbad decrees on, there was little evidence of smooth unity among the students. The *Landsmannschaften* cropped up again, still belligerent in their love of duels, and still clear opponents of the more temperate if moralistic *Burschenschaft* idea. Leadership of what remained of the *Burschenschaften* went into the hands of older, experienced members who tried to control incipient quarrels among the discouraged students. By and large they succeeded. There was a revived *Allgemeine deutsche Burschenschaft* that showed signs of life in its annual meetings (Dresden 1820, Streitberg 1821, and Odenwald 1822). They based their program on the new situation, declaring that they were abandoning political activity and concentrating on more scholarly work, together with gymnastics. There was needless to say an underlying current: there was political discussion in the small groups, the *Kränschen*, but before long there was something more sinister, in the form of conspiratorial groups combined under the name *Jünglingsbund* that was controlled by Karl Follen from his exile in Switzerland. These radicals penetrated the *Burschenschaft* and unrealistically awaited a signal for a general uprising, to be given by Follen. The organization was betrayed in November 1823, with disastrous effects on the innocent members of the *Burschenschaft*. Prison sentences in some cases were for as much as fifteen years.

A typical victim was Arnold Ruge, the publisher.[35] At the university of Halle, he had been impressed by the commitment of the *Burschenschaft* to the idea of national rejuvenation. Ruge was an idealist, and he entered into the activities of the organization with enthusiasm although he first resisted the more intemperate revolutionary ideas that were being clandestinely proposed. Foolish ideas, he thought. Later he joined Karl Follen's secret *Jünglingsbund* in the mistaken belief that senior members of the Prussian army, even including the upright General von Gneisenau, were part of the conspiracy. "Every day we expected the great news of the rising of the army." In actuality, nothing was happening, other than that Ruge himself was running out of money and the organization was deteriorating rapidly. He left Halle for Jena, where he had the good fortune to find a fellow *Burschenschaft* member who was well heeled enough to be able to support him. He became rather too enthusiastic in his activities and was expelled and moved on to Heidelberg. At that point (around Christmas 1823) after the student conspiracy had been betrayed, Ruge was picked up by the police. He was turned over to Prussian authorities and sent to Berlin, where his investigation lasted a year. His sentence of fifteen years' imprisonment in fact lasted six years before he was pardoned. Ruge wrote in his reminiscences that some of his friends broke down both mentally and physically during the ordeal of imprisonment. He himself was more fortunate because he managed to pass the time by reading Greek and making translations of Sophocles and Thucydides.

The *Allgemeine deutsche Burschenschaft* did not recover any strength until 1827, when there was a convocation at Bamberg that was attended by delegates from Erlangen, Heidelberg, Jena, Leipzig, and Würzburg, but once again there were serious disagreements that weakened the whole effort. In brief, all was relatively uneventful until the French July Revolution of 1830 infused new life into the student world.

In the *Vormärz* period, new non-secret societies proliferated at an amazing pace, the trail having been broken for them presumably by the masons and the related pseudomasonic orders. Official surveillance forced everyone to be cautious, so that on the surface these multitudes of societies looked harmless. However, like-minded people were managing to find each other and discuss the problems that confronted them. In time inevitably there actually were secret societies, and many that could have remained open if allowed to express their opinions were driven underground. So many new societies were formed in the late Eighteenth and early Nineteenth centuries that historians and sociologists consider the development to be a phenomenon that requires analysis.[36] Even the German word *Verein*, with no hint of any political connotation, was new. Around 1800 it began to penetrate the language and replace other commonly used words such as association, club, order etc. The new groupings were original in that, unlike corporations with which Germans had been familiar, these were free organizations, their membership not being determined by birth or class. Membership conveyed no special privileges or rights, and one could join a society or leave it at will.

Evidently, societies were filling a definite need. The old corporations were stifling, and many people must have felt claustrophobic. They welcomed the first societies which were likely to emphasize literary or scientific matters and offered them an opportunity to relax in an informal environment and chat over their pipes, but before long they began to break into groups where special talents could be utilized (historical societies, musical societies, choral groups). Through these, the general run of the middle class began to expand its cultural interests into new fields. It became acceptable to attend the theatre and to read serious poetry and novels, even philosophy books. The bourgeoisie began self-consciously to see itself in a new light as an entity that was valuable in the general improvement and refinement of society. Heretofore this role had been reserved for the court and the aristocracy.

Societies had increased in number and variety to such an extent that at the turn of the century there were as many as two hundred and seventy reading societies alone, plus a swarm of salons, "circles", coffee house clubs and so on. Among the most important were the reading clubs or circles, where newspapers and journals were read aloud and discussed. The fact that a newspaper had only a few hundred subscribers did not necessarily mean that it had a proportionately small readership. A club of fifty or more might share a single subscription taken by a coffee house for its patrons. By 1840, the middle-class attitude to formation of clubs and societies had swept them up almost like a craze.

New situations led to new, very specialized bases for organization. The underlying idea of progress and improvement that was inherent in the Enlightenment encouraged establishment of a bewildering variety of societies that were intended to serve economic and social progress. Those that were established in the interests of agriculture and the economy attracted both nobles and middle class landowners as well as estate managers and local officials. Possibly the nobles regarded membership in such organizations as a duty and did not perceive themselves in a new light with reference to their "inferiors", yet something of the principle of democracy may have rubbed off on them. Whatever effect it may have had on the nobles, it had a lasting effect on the bourgeois, who was learning to live with like-minded people without consideration of class. It must be said that the societies by their very nature were also promoting freedom, equality, and solidarity. There were societies for the promotion of schooling for poor children, societies for care of indigent pregnant women, societies for encouragement of potato-growing by the poor, temperance societies, hospital societies, craftsmen's societies, apprentices' societies, worker-education societies. In all these organizations there was the underlying conviction that social action ought to be practical and aimed at the common good. It is understandable that before long people might realize that they could use their clubs and societies in support of this or that political program. The enormously popular gymnastic societies were crypto-political, no doubt,[37] and so were the innumerable choral societies.

Censorship and supervision were restraints, but the new impulses could not be suppressed. The energetically well-run gymnastic society at Stuttgart was subjected to weighty investigation. In that busy club, youngsters exerted themselves prodigiously on parallel bars, on ropes, in races and so on, and took their responsibilities as elected manager, keeper of equipment, or librarian with deep pride and seriousness. With true teutonic orderliness, they issued a modest pamphlet that laid out the various rules and regulations that governed their activities, but as Otto Elben, the journalist, said in his memoirs, "the wise ones" [i.e. the local authorities] could not tolerate the thought that young people could form a society, govern it themselves, carry out elections, and set down their principles. The brochure was suppressed. "There were no more printed statements of principle, but the spirit of it lived in all of us."[38]

The situation differed from region to region, of course, but it is worth noting that in Frankfurt am Main, as early as the 1830's, as many as three thousand individuals (almost half the citizenry in other words) had joined a society or two. Most members were merchants and educators, along with a few artisans. The percentage of workers jumped in the 1840's, through the choral societies, gymnastic societies, and trade organizations. An indication that such involvement could lead to political interest is the fact that in 1832, when two hundred and thirty citizens of Frankfurt signed a petition for freedom of the press, more than one hundred and thirty of the signers were members of societies, and forty-eight of them were society founders. Again, of one hundred and twenty delegates at the Frankfurt constituent assembly of 1848, eighty-three were active in various societies.[39]

Even if a given society were devoid of political concerns, the very fact of membership in an organization offered a training ground for future political action. One learned how to formulate a program, how to reconcile differing views in order to reach a majority decision, how to elect leaders. This informal training must explain the circumstance that when voting actually occurred in the spring of 1848, groups immediately sprang up that were capable of action as political parties.[40] "The way from the special table reserved for *Honoratioren* to the electoral committee, from the reading society, from the 'Harmony club' . . . to the political society was not long and would presumably be rapidly traversed in the period of transition to revolution."[41]

What else? As early as 1731, an "imperial trades edict" was issued with the stated purpose of remedying "abuses among the guilds". This was clearly an expression of distrust of organized political activity among tradespeople. One of the main objectives of the edict was the prevention of the spread of trade organization and communication across state boundaries. That the guilds had in fact engaged in such work is shown by the existence of a guild institution in Württemberg called the *Hauptladen* [high guilds whose prestige was recognized to the extent that they had authority to adjudicate questions that came up in similar guilds in remote localities]. These *Hauptladen* must have generated suspicion among the authorities, because they were abolished in 1764, with evocation of the edict of 1731. Another objective of the 1731 edict was to make the guilds accountable to the civil authorities (i.e. state officials). It was an ineffectual measure at best, in view of the heterogeneous character of the communities involved. In many cases, the civil authorities in question were "in political fact hometown governments in which the guilds themselves participated."[42]

This situation among tradespeople ran counter to that of most Germans, who were struggling through membership in their supposedly apolitical societies to gain some kind of leverage. The guildmasters in that same era felt their power slipping away, confronting as they did the influx of new manufactures not under their control, and legislation that deprived them of exclusive control even of their own trades. It is ironic, that when Germans as a whole had their first opportunity to express their political views few guildmasters were elected as delegates to the revolutionary parliament at Frankfurt in 1848. One would have anticipated a high percentage of guild members among the elected representatives because they probably had more genuine experience in participatory politics than most of their compatriots.[43]

As to the proletariat, a lonely voice on their behalf had been raised at Trier in 1818 [44] (not Karl Marx's: he was born at Trier in that year). A man named Ludwig Gall tried to establish a society with the declared purpose of ensuring work for every German in his homeland, or else assistance in emigration to a more favorable environment. Gall was unable to get official authorization for his society. He left his job with the government service in the spring of 1819 and went to the United States, hoping to arrange some kind of orderly immigration of Germans there, but he came back to Germany in 1820 and took up his government job again. He wrote a two-volume description of his efforts in North America, where he had published a small work of counsel for "my fellow Germans" as to their prospects in the new country. Next he tried to stir up interest at home in the matter of welfare for the poor, establishing a short-lived society in Erfurt that was supposed to deal with the dual problem of industrial underproduction and overproduction. In 1828 he started a paper called *Menschenfreundlichen Blätter* in which he proposed to discuss ways in which the working classes with little property could be helped in the face of the threatening dominance of money in society. This first paper with a socialist program failed, German conditions being what they were at the time.

Next Gall decided that he would have to build up a tremendous fund that would allow him to establish a few "communist" facilities such as community bakeries and laundries, and with this in mind he set about inventing machines that would bring him the necessary fortune, but his steam-distillation apparatus failed to win a patent.

Gall went off to Hungary, to see what he could do there (1835) but nothing came of that either. Following Fourier, Gall clearly saw the opposition of classes, those with possessions and those without. He wanted to paralyze huge capital by associations of small property-owners and workers and spoke unrealistically of communities of two hundred families with five hundred workers who would annually save up the equivalent of forty thousand days' earnings. He came back from Hungary in 1849 and concentrated on steam apparatus after that.

In years prior to a revolution, one would expect to observe activity and organization among the working people. Information on such organizations is oddly sparse. Guildmasters were petitioning local assemblies for a restoration of the control of their respective trades, and well-meaning philanthropists were organizing clubs and societies for journeymen and apprentices that were designed to educate and uplift them. The *Centralverein für das Wohl der arbeitenden Klassen* [central society for the well-being of the working classes] was established in Berlin in October 1844, no doubt as a reaction to the dread experience of the weavers' rising of that year in Silesia. It was an official organization, supported by various entrepreneurs and graciously recognized by Friedrich Wilhelm IV, who offered fifteen thousand *Thaler* as a gift. The society was supposed to encourage workers' self help, and was intended to promote thrift by setting up savings banks. There were also to be elevating lectures, and some kind of assistance for the poor and disabled. There were a few local branches—at Stettin, for example—but the organization itself was more or less dead in the water. Bruno Bauer was disgusted, calling the meetings of the society "a bourgeois parliament" because most of those attending were middle-class intellectuals who welcomed the opportunity to debate. It appears that His Majesty's gift was never accepted because the society could not decide what to do with the money.[45]

The major organizational activity went on abroad, among ardent reformers like Engels and Marx, and the propaganda was brought into Germany by journeymen on completion of their *Wanderjahre*. Paris was a major German city, with a colony that is said to have numbered more than eighty thousand. The German *Bundestag* at Frankfurt passed ineffectual legislation in 1835 that was supposed to block journeymen from travel to "those countries and places in which associations and meetings exist openly aiming at endangering and destroying public order".[46] Men like Stephan Born and Wilhelm Weitling were active in spreading propaganda among the German workers in their numerous clubs (there was an artisans' union in Berlin, an educational society for improvement of the working class in Hamburg, as well as a journeymen's union) which in the long run served to counterbalance the guilds that were dominated by the guild masters. Although they became aware of socialist theory, there does not appear to have been much enthusiasm for radicalism. On the whole, Weitling's Christian morality appealed more than Marx's stern materialism. In the end, Stephan Born's primary concern turned out to be working-class solidarity, a circumstance that offended Marx, who decided that he had been wrong in thinking that "the fellow is ripe for our affairs."

In the Rhineland there was a distinctive institution that offered somewhat unorthodox possibilities for informal interaction that was beyond the purview of official surveillance. This was the *Kermis*, the carnival in honor of a local patron saint. Such jolly, innocent but generally raucous celebrations were marked by a breaking down of social barriers and a freedom of public expression that would be sternly repressed at other times. Like a court jester of the Middle Ages, a determined man might find himself able to make pointed political comments that would be passed on among the cheerful villagers, workmen and townspeople who made up his tolerant audience. Ludwig Bamberger, discussing the political use of the carnivals, remarked that in his boyhood (i.e. in the 1830's) nothing of the sort was known in his home town of Mainz, and that in those days only children and older people from the lowermost strata of society turned up on the streets wearing masks.[47] It was only in the 1840's that the political element entered into these affairs. Two men who made use of the

Kermis just prior to the revolution of 1848 were Franz Raveaux (1810–1851) of Cologne and Franz Heinrich Zitz (1803–1877) of Mainz.[48] Both showed courage and resourcefulness as presidents of their local carnival societies when the suspicious Prussian military moved in to quell disorder with unnecessary brutality. Raveaux and Zitz emerged as popular heroes, and were influential members of the elected Frankfurt *Parlament*.

If carnivals honoring patron saints and the Christian teachings of the labor propagandist Weitling were able to attract the attention of the laboring classes, what about political action through the church?

Notes

1 Agethen, *Geheimbund und Utopie*, pp. 21–64; Winfried Dotzauer, *Quellen zur Geschichte der deutschen Freimauerei im 18. Jahrhundert*, pp. 15–33, 336; Ernst-Guenther Geppert, *Die Herkunft, die Gründer, die Namen der Freimauerlogen in Deutschland seit 1737*, passim.

2 Johannes Rogalla von Bieberstein, "Geheime Gesellschaften als Vorläufer politischer Parteien," in *Geheime Gesellschaften*, 5:1, p. 442.

3 J. R. Seeley, *Life and Times of Stein,*, 2:81.

4 This seems to have been corroborated by the contribution of vom Stein's loyal aide, Ernst Moritz Arndt, to a booklet called *Sechs Stimmen über geheime Gesellschaften und Freimauerei*, in which Arndt wrote strongly against secret societies.

5 Seeley, 2:79.

6 Sperber, *Popular Catholicism in Nineteenth-Century Germany*, p. 14.

7 Cited by Aylmer Maude in his English translation of *War and Peace* (New York: Simon & Schuster, 1942), p. 386, footnote.

8 Norbert Schindler, "Aufklärung und Geheimnis im Illuminatienorden," *Geheime Gesellschaften* 6:1. pp. 208–209.

9 In the words of Mann's character Naphta in *Magic Mountain*, the reappearance of such organizations meant " nothing else than the presence of irrational ferments in a world given over to rational-utilitarian ideas of social improvement". People were weary, he said, of "the rationalistic twaddle of the century".

10 The stated purpose of the *Illuminati* was to destroy all governments, nations, and religions, and "this continuing conspiracy" was behind the revolutions of 1848 and 1871 in Europe, the Mexican revolution, the assassination of Alexander II of Russia, and the Haymarket riots of Chicago. These "facts" are documented by "writers for the John Birch Society". Publisher's introduction to Egon Corti's *Rise of the House of Rothschild*, Belmont, Massachusetts: Western Islands, 1972.

11 Peter Christian Ludz, "Überlegungen zu einer sociologischen Analyse geheimer Gesellschaften des späten 18. und frühen 19. Jahrhunderts," in *Geheime Gesellschaften*, 5:1, p. 94.

12 Edmund Burke, *Reflections on the Revolution in France*, p. 265.

13 *La grande encylopédie* 17:1187

14 Dotzauer, p. 20.—The suspicion that there may be a hoax involved here cannot be avoided. There was another Clemens August, prince-bishop of Cologne at a later time. The name of Clemens August von Droste zu Vischering was on everyone's lips in the 1830's because the archbishop had been placed under house arrest by the Prussian government.

15 Jean-Pierre Bacot, *Les filles du pasteur Anderson*, pp. 6–13.

16 Ibid., p. 8; René Le Forestier, *Maçonnerie féminine et Loges académiques*, p. 22. This book includes the illustrations that have been discussed here.

17 Bieberstein, 5:1, pp. 440–441, citing Friedrich Schlegel.

18 Ludwig Börne, "Monographie der deutschen Postschnecke," in his *Sämtliche Schriften* 1:665.

19 Hugh Seton-Watson, *The Russian Empire 1801–1917*, pp. 183–187.

20 Mikhail Bakunin, *Sozialpolitischer Briefwechsel mit Alexander Iw. Herzen und Ogarjow*, p. 283 [originally appeared in *La réforme* 14 December 1847]

21 A. Crié, s.v. "Charbonnerie" in *La grande encyclopédie*, 9:295–298.

22 Indro Montanelli, *L'Italia carbonara*, p. 383.

23 Marian Kukiel, *Czartoryski and European Unity 1770–1861*, p. 224.

24 Maria Wawrykowa, "Die studentische Bewegung in Deutschland im ersten Jahrzehnt nach dem wiener Kongress," in *Bourgeoisie und bürgerliche Umwalzung in Deutschland 1789–1871*, p. 62.

25 *Zauberflöte* Act 2, scene 7.

26 *Handbuch der deutschen Burschenschaft*, Torsten Locher and Hans-Martin Sass, editors, passim.; Wawrykowa, pp. 49–63; Max Doblinger and Georg Schmidgall, *Geschichte und Mitgliederverzeichnisse burschenschaftlicher Verbindungen in Alt-Österreich und Tübingen 1816 bis 1936*. Burschenschafterlisten, 1. Paul Wencke, editor.

27 It was at the Wartburg that Martin Luther wrote his German translation of the Bible.

28 Gerhardt, *Handbuch der deutschen Geschichte*, 3:109; Tim Klein, *1848: Der Vorkampf deutscher Einheit und Freiheit*, pp. 15–16.

29 Friedrich Otto Hertz, *The German Public Mind in the Nineteenth Century*, pp. 92–93.

30 The arguments relating to the German tricolor are complex, best summarized by Egmont Zechlin, *Schwarz–Rot–Gold und Schwarz–Weiss–Rot in Geschichte und Gegenwart*, esp.pp.11–25. *Turnvater* Jahn appears to have believed that it was he alone who selected the tricolor. Jena students, as members of a volunteer brigade known as the *Lützauer Freikorps* in the war of liberation and subsequently of a club called "Vandalia", and finally of the original *Burschenschaft* (formed in 1815) all used black and gold and some-

times red. During the 1830 revolution in France, the idea of a tricolor cocarde became popular, but it was not until 1848 that black, gold, red were officially adopted as the German national colors.

31 Gall, *Bürgertum in Deutschland,* pp. 221–222.

32 Siegfried Schmidt, *Robert Blum,* p. 26.

33 Hans-Joachim Schoeps, editor, *Neue Quellen zur Geschichte Preussens im 19.Jahrhundert,* pp. 118–125.

34 Desmond Seward, *Metternich, the First European,* p. 241.

35 Harold Mah, *The End of Philosophy, the Origin of "Ideology",* pp. 92–97.

36 Thomas Nipperdey, "Verein als soziale Struktur in Deutschland im späten 18. und frühen 19. Jahrhundert," in Hartmut Boockmann, editor, *Geschichtswissenschaft und Vereinswesen im 19. Jahrhundert,* 1:1 pp. 1–44.

37 Sperber, *Rhineland Radicals,* p. 144: When Krefeld's deputy returned from an unsuccessful meeting of the Prussian united assembly in 1847, he was greeted as a hero by a defiantly supportive parade led by the local gymnastic society.

38 Otto Elben, *Lebenserinnerungen 1823–1899,* pp. 10–14.

39 Ralf Roth, "Liberalismus in Frankfurt am Main 1814" in *Liberalismus und Region; zur Geschichte des deutschen Liberalismus im 19. Jahrhundert.* Lothar Gall and Dieter Langewiesche, editors, pp. 64–65.

40 Wolfram Siemann, *Die deutsche Revolution 1848/49,* pp. 2, 92–93.

41 Manfred Botzenhart, *Deutscher Parlamentarismus in der Revolutionszeit 1846–1850.* p. 320.

42 Walker, *German Home Towns,* pp. 93–95.

43 Eyck, *The Frankfurt Parliament,* p. 95. The social breakdown of the parliamentarians was as follows: civil servants, including local government (19.7% out of a total of 799 members); lawyers (16.3%); university or school teachers (15.4%); judges and public prosecutors (14.9%); businessmen (9.4%); landowners (8.5%); clergy (5.6%); writers and journalists 4.5%; medical practitioners (3.1%); army officers (1.9%); not yet in profession (0.2%); miscellaneous, i.e. unknown (0.5%).

44 Georg Adler, *Die Geschichte der ersten sozialpolitischen Arbeiterbewegung in Deutschland,* pp. 4–7; Dieter Dowe, *Aktion und Organisation,* pp. 43–44.

45 Noyes, *Organization and Revolution,* p. 47.

46 Ibid., p. 50.

47 Ludwig Bamberger, *Erinnerungen,* pp. 28–30.

Chapter 5

Religious Protest and its Ramifications into Politics and the Women's Movement

Although by the mid-forties Germans had become adept at organizing themselves into societies and clubs where they could meet as like-minded individuals and discuss political affairs, there was as yet no organization that could be described as all-German in the sense that it crossed frontiers from one German state to another. There were still the outlawed *Burschenschaft* organizations at various universities, but for all practical purposes the only overarching organization in Germany was that of the Roman Catholic church. Its counterpart, the Protestant church, was broken into a number of sects and did not have the same force that the Catholic church enjoyed by virtue of its ancient hold on the minds and emotions of the peoples of western Europe. Whether Catholic or Protestant, there was always a state church, and this had its political effects. If a citizen did not adhere to the state church, he had few civil rights, and in most cases no vote (like the Jews), no matter how prosperous and competent he might be.

Whether in Prussia or elsewhere, internal migration in the early decades of the century had changed the religious composition of the towns. By the 1840's, even cities that had been predominantly Protestant in the early years had seen their Catholic population increase sharply as peasants, pushed by the sudden jump in population, moved away from the land in search of employment. This development was basic to antagonisms that developed between the growing lower class (Catholic) that made up the force of factory workers and day laborers and the prosperous middle class and leading entrepreneurs, who were almost exclusively Protestant.[1]

Especially in Prussia, the government was struggling to bring the recently acquired Rhineland provinces into harmonious relationship with the rest of the monarchy, and efforts made by Catholic priests to reinforce the piety of their flocks and protect them from the temptations that assailed them in their new surroundings were not acceptable to the bureaucrats. The priests were unpleasantly emphasizing differences that the bureaucrats were hoping to erase.

In one instance, the clash of church and state was vigorous enough to attract public attention all over Germany. This was the famous *Kölner Wirren* [the "Cologne troubles"] in 1834, caused by Clemens August von Droste-Vischering, archbishop of Cologne.[2] Droste-Vischering denounced an agreement made by his predecessor, the more lenient archbishop Spiegel von Desenberg, and proclaimed that he intended to follow the stringent requirements set down by the papacy in the matter of mixed marriages. He would insist, he stated, that offspring of such unions must be brought up in the Catholic faith.

Droste-Vischering was nothing if not a fighter, and under his rule no detail was overlooked. Hermann Körner, who was to become an active participant in the protest movement at a somewhat later date, says that when he was a young instructor at the local *Gymnasium* he ran into difficulties because he had not been accompanying his students in the annual Corpus Christi procession. Much against his will, he marched with bared head in the next procession, uncomfortably feeling that everyone was pointing a finger at him at the various halts before improvised altars set up at important street intersections, where silver bells tinkled and trumpets blared and the monstrance was displayed by priests in gold-encrusted robes. His annoyance boiled over at one of these stops, where he saw Catholic friends and relatives in an upstairs window, watching the procession and obviously making jokes at his expense, in evident enjoyment of his having been trapped in the "carnival". On sudden impulse, Körner clapped his hat on his head and stalked away. The upshot was that he was summoned by the *Gymnasium* directors with demands that he account for his "offense against decorum and his official duty during the procession". Körner's response was to hand in his resignation. He comments that big decisions can sometimes hang on trivial matters: he and his wife soon left the Catholic church.[3]

Droste-Vischering independently ignored governmental efforts to smooth over a controversy involving the writings of Georg Hermes (1775–1831), late professor at Bonn, whom he apparently considered to have been a heretic. A thorough-going rationalist, Hermes had been strongly influenced by Kant. His books had been posthumously placed on the *Index librorum prohibitorum* in 1835 by Pope Gregory XVI. Any candidate for the priesthood, announced the neoorthodox arch-bishop, must shun Hermes' work and affirm that he condemned the professor's theological tenets. There was an active group of "Hermesians" at Cologne as well as at Bonn. These earnest people worked cooperatively in an effort to salvage tenable dogmas of the Catholic church by dialectic analysis, but their efforts had incurred the active disapproval of Rome. The chief objection, supposedly, was the stand against ultramontanist control. The Hermesians wanted a Ger-man primate, or at very least an increased German influence in Rome. Since Hermes had been an appointee of the Protestant Prussian state and was therefore entitled to posthumous respect, rigid Archbishop Droste-Vischering was placed under house arrest in a private dwelling at Minden from November 1837 until April 1839.

The public remained indifferent to the spectacle of a bishop impris-oned by the state, not only in Prussia but throughout Germany. Fur-ther, there were no open moves on the part of the clergy, in part perhaps because the canons of Droste-Vischering's own cathedral chap-ter at Cologne were rationalists for the most part, and hence antago-nistic in their attitude toward him. Some stepped forward boldly, en-dorsing the government's action. This in turn inflamed the orthodox, setting off repercussions among them, but on the whole it remained for the nobility of the Rhineland and Westphalia to send protesting representatives to Berlin (December 1837). The request for an audi-ence with the monarch was sharply rebuffed. Indeed, the *Kölner Wirren* did not die down until the accession of Friedrich Wilhelm IV.

The affair in Cologne would not have attracted much attention in its own right, but it served to focus a light on many below-the-surface tensions (relations of church and state, criticism of papal authority, and resentment of the Rhenish Catholic underclass against the mis-treatment of their bishop by a Prussian monarch). As a rule, liberals would have protested against the abuse of power by the state, but the archbishop was seen by them as a mean-spirited intolerant man, and besides, he represented papal authority which was one of the liberals' targets. It would be difficult to draw a sharp line between Catholic and Protestant, church and state, or even Prussia and its Rhineland prov-inces: in fact, throughout the *Vormärz*, the complex tangle of reli-gious, regional, and social fissures effectively camouflaged the elusive essential fault line where a revolutionary outbreak might be predicted.

Meanwhile, there had been no serious disturbance until the appearance of a provocative piece written by Josef Görres (1776–1848). Agitation then spread like wildfire. Pamphlets and leaflets pro and con poured from the presses by the hundred. Görres' *Athanasius* was no theological treatise. It was a political document, burning with hatred against Prussian tyranny and the tyranny of Protestantism. The *Athanasius* has been called the first great document of political Catholicism in Germany, "epoch-making" in its role in the development of embryonic parties that was taking place in Germany during the *Vormärz*.[4] The significance of the Görres polemic lay in the fact that it made questions relating to national constitutions clear and understandable to those who as laymen had no special competence in legal matters. It opened up to discussion esoteric concerns that had been much too arcane for the general public. There was oversimplification in the discussion of issues of the relationship of church and state, no doubt, but Görres opened the way for an extension and democratizing of the public vocabulary. Görres had written against liberalism and democracy as well as against the Prussian bureaucracy, but his masterful handling of his materials broke open new pathways, making public discussion possible at a highly opportune time.

In August 1844, the Catholic hierarchy undertook a demonstration of its regained strength after the bleak years during which it had been seriously threatened by the Enlightenment. It instituted a pilgrimage to the city of Trier, where the Seamless Robe of Jesus was displayed for veneration. This relic was one of many known unique and authentic Seamless Robes—thirteen as determined by the learned investigations of Professor Siebold of Bonn, or twenty-one, according to J. Gildemeister, in his *Der heilige Rock zu Trier und die 20 anderen heiligen ungenähten Röcke. 3rd ed., 1845.* It first made its appearance in the Twelfth Century, and was displayed to the public in the Sixteenth Century, along with other sacred items in the cathedral treasury. Martin Luther objected strenuously to that new pilgrimage (writing in 1520), saying that it ought to be abolished. The robe was exhibited in 1655 and again in 1810, after Napoleon had assisted in its recovery from Augsburg. The church's objective in sponsoring the pilgrimage of 1844 has been described as an early example of concerted aggression on the part of church and conservative state, with the intention of mobilizing the superstitious lower classes against the *bourgeois* liberal movement, but the argument seems to overestimate the prescience of church and state in the matter of class antagonism.[5]

Pilgrimages had been on the wane for decades. It was common knowledge that they were not entirely an expression of piety, notoriously attracting individuals who were seeking color and excitement in their lives. In many cases, there was a general atmosphere of carnival about them, when local inns eagerly sponsored dances where drinking and revelry overshadowed the mystic ecstasy that was assumed to accompany the contemplation of a holy relic. As early as 1816, the Prussian government had intervened, requiring that all pilgrimages that were to last more than one day be led by a responsible priest, who had to submit a list of participants. By 1827, the government made an additional move, asking bishops to find out if religious processions were being held on days other than the usual holidays, specifically if the processions led to drinking and objectionable conduct, and if they were keeping participants away from work. (Economically, such affairs would be counterproductive.)

The clergy were worried, because this might be an entering wedge for interference in almost any aspect of Catholic practice. However, they were honest enough to concede that since their young people tended to be more interested in dances than in religious ritual, pilgrimages and processions were "highly degrading to the divine celebrations".[6] On the other hand, they were quick to express hostility toward anything that suggested abolition of the public expression of religious belief. They placed blame solidly on the shoulders of the Freemasons and secret societies. These were indubitably conspirators who wanted to destroy Christian faith and to establish an atheistic republic.

Controversial bishop Clemens August von Droste-Vischering had refused to renew a prohibition against pilgrimages that had been in force ever since 1826, but popular interests and attitudes had changed, and participation in pilgrimages had dropped perceptibly. Now in 1844 came the church-sponsored pilgrimage at Trier.

The Trier pilgrimage, carefully managed parish by parish, was of spectacular proportions, successful beyond any cleric's wildest dreams, but it had an unexpected side effect. This huge exercise in mass superstition provoked an equally spectacular protest movement that almost immediately started to spread from city to city.[7]

Figure 1   JOHANNES RONGE (1813–1887)

The man who provided the impetus for the protest among Catholics was the chaplain Johannes Ronge (1813–1887), who was disturbed by the thought that poor peasants were using their tiny savings in order to be part of the devout throng. There are no reliable figures to show the truth or falsity of Ronge's charge. From earlier years, surviving pilgrimage lists show that most participants were artisans and laborers, with a scattering of retail merchants and farmers.[8] More than half a million pilgrims had flocked to Trier in the course of two months in order to offer prayers *Heiliger Rock, bitt' für uns* [holy robe, pray for us] and to buy wonderful little souvenirs such as scarves that had received a priestly blessing, and to witness miraculous cures. Enthusiasm increased when the word spread that the holy robe had been woven by the Virgin Mary herself.

Ronge published an *Offene Sendschreiben an den Bischof Arnoldi* [open letter to Bishop Arnoldi of Trier] in Robert Blum's *Sächsische Vaterlandsblättern*. He charged that the Catholic church had been misleading the people and exploiting them. Thousands of the lower classes, many in extreme want, depressed, ignorant, worn out, and superstitious and to a certain extent degraded, had used their very last penny for the Trier pilgrimage, wrote Ronge heatedly, and the clergy had not been ashamed to accept it. The superstition sanctioned by the church was responsible for Germany's mental and material servility, he went on. He urged Protestants as well as Catholics to join forces against the tyrannical power of the Roman hierarchy. They could impress their opinions on city authorities and community leaders. The inflammatory accusations sank in because the writer was no heretic, no free-thinker or atheist, not even an antagonistic Protestant. This was a Catholic speaking!

Ronge's letter roused Hermann Körner "like a thunderclap". Körner began to write passionately against the practices of the church, against the cult of relics, against pilgrimages. (He secretly participated in one and observed with disgust the harlots who came along as camp-followers.) His articles appeared in the columns of the *Elberfelder Zeitung* and as pamphlets that were distributed far and wide.

Ronge's open letter had traveled across Germany with lightning speed. Almost every major newspaper picked it up. The *Mannheimer Abendzeitung* noted that anyone who said he had not read the letter meant that he had not read it yet, and meanwhile he was thought to be narrow-minded. In Robert Blum's Saxony alone there were at least fifty thousand copies of it in circulation. This was the sort of thing that could rivet the attention of all ranks, from princes to day laborers. Everyone could react to it much more emphatically than to liberal abstractions relating to injustice and reform in general. Such ideas were pallid because many people had no opinion at all about press censorship or constitutions, but in a society still dominated by the church, everyone had had intimate personal experiences that colored his thinking. Church and state were so closely bound together that any discussion of ecclesiastical matters unavoidably had political overtones, and now Ronge had accentuated this by tying church tyranny together with the socio-economic problems. Small wonder that radical activists like Robert Blum fanned the flames.

Starting in October of 1844, a broad popular movement began to spread, inspired by Ronge's letter. The starting point was the criticism of the promiscuous use of relics, but the attack on the Roman hierarchy was unmistakable. Members of the first *Deutschkatholische Gemeinde* [German Catholic congregation] were artisans and their wives, owners of small independent businesses, and also some educated individuals. Usually when a new unit was founded, organization was entrusted to some person who had had experience in a club or society and knew the mechanics of such associations.

The founding members signed a statement that they were abandoning the Roman Catholic church. They subscribed to a program of democratic self-government by individual congregations, with election of the officiating priest. They included in their program abolition of confession and discontinuation of the use of Latin in divine service. They wanted to wipe out celibacy, indulgences, pilgrimages, veneration of the saints, and the marriage sacrament.

By February 1845 there was a *Deutschkatholische Gemeinde* in most of the major cities of Germany. Hermann Körner established a free Christian congregation in Elberfeld at that time.[9] Breslau was an active center, and so was Leipzig, where Robert Blum was the organizer. He was already heavily burdened with various literary and political activities (he was a publisher and a vigorous organizer of clubs and circles where workers might discuss their problems and learn how to express themselves effectively), and this added pressure of responsibility was a load for him. He wrote to a friend, "There are excellent people on our board, but you have to realize that not one of them can write a satisfactory letter, so you can imagine my situation. You would be sorry for me if you saw me getting up at three or four a.m. in this barbaric cold." The energetic Blum could be depended upon in any affair that involved concerted action. In October 1845 he managed the first conference that brought together fifteen representatives from other provinces at Leipzig, where a layman's council was initiated. The council was intended to facilitate close connection among the various congregations.

In its deliberations, the council produced a new version of the general statement of principles. It included a new statement to the effect that the basis of faith should be the Bible but that German Catholics were to regard Christian teachings as historic and not binding with regard to personal actions and decisions. There should be constant revision in view of one's awareness of the times. This association of awareness of current socio-economic and political conditions with the question of accepted teachings was a striking innovation. Section 24 of the revised statement of principles read: "The chief task of Christianity is to promote with all one's might . . . in active Christian love, the spiritual, moral and material wellbeing of one's fellow men, without differentiation." Surely Robert Blum was holding the pen when that paragraph was written. It would be difficult to find its equal in plain democratic tone among other documents of the period.

The congregations were organizing at a time when the law could have been invoked against them. Robert Blum was aware of this. He wrote to his friend Hoffmann von Fallersleben, "Church business takes an inordinate amount of my time, but it is rewarding and I believe it gives us more than people suspect—above all the right of association through which—since we actually took it for ourselves—a great effect [has been achieved] in the shortest possible time."

These were years when it was necessary to move with circumspection in order to avoid police surveillance. Such was the case in Dresden, where coded messages were printed in the local press. "Schneidemühl, Breslau, Leipzig. Dresden, are you asleep?" [4 February 1845 in the *Dresdner Anzeiger*] "Dresden is awake. Friday evening at about 7 o'clock. Conference at Hôtel de Luxembourg, we're ready." [response, same newspaper, a few days later.]—At Konstanz, where Ronge himself had to be cautious because the police at Mannheim had branded him as a criminal, he and his followers managed to thwart police action by locating his speaker's platform just across the border on Swiss soil, while his cheering audience stood within easy hearing distance in Baden.

The movement had attracted the interest of liberals, many of whom had been thinking about the possibility of a German national church that would include Protestants as well as Catholics. These were men like the acknowledged opposition leaders Karl Mathy and Friedrich Daniel Basserman of the lower house in Baden. Bassermann was not a Catholic but he felt that Ronge's movement offered the possibility of an ecumenical union of Christians and Jews. Arnold Ruge thought that the movement was important and supported it by traveling with Ronge. Georg Gottfried Gervinus, one of the famous Göttingen Seven, took the position that the Catholic church was the stronghold of reaction, and that it was necessary to found a new national church for all Germany. Bruno Bauer hailed Ronge as the hero of the lower classes, while radicals like Robert Blum and his co-revolutionist Adam von Itzstein saw in *Deutschkatholizismus* an instrument for attacking the established order in general.[10] This was a miscalculation, because members of the movement were still in the minority among Catholics. They would never be strong enough to tear down the powerful machinery of Rome or win over the masses of pious individuals who treasured their saints and relics and the comfort of confession.

In the pervasive climate of liberal optimism, it was understandable that newspapers that were slanted toward political opposition rapidly assumed a favorable stance. In the turbulent area around Lake Konstanz, for example, the influential *Seeblätter* published by Joseph Fickler abruptly began to look more like a church publication than a political journal. (Fickler, a Freemason, joked that he had never thought to see the day when he would become an apostle.)[11] It was obvious that there was a hand-in-hand relationship between the political opposition press and protest against established religion.

The high point of *Deutschkatholizismus* came in 1845, when Ronge was deluged with invitations. The cities he visited honored him with festive banquets and addresses of thanks that were signed by thousands. The crowds that flocked to hear him speak were spectacular: fifteen thousand at Ulm, another fifteen thousand at Offenbach, even as many as four thousand at little Kreuznach. Thirty thousand greeted him at Königsberg. This was *ein neues Morgenrot* [a new dawn]. Gymnastic societies and choral groups whose political leanings had been strongly in favor of revolutionary change ever since Hambach assembled at city gates in order to welcome and escort him.

Inevitably there was unrest in conjunction with this movement. At Leipzig in August 1845 there were demonstrations where the crowd defiantly sang *Eine feste Burg* [Luther's hymn, a mighty fortress, which in an incongruous twist had become the *Marseillaise* of the German Catholics]. They shouted cheers for Ronge, hurled stones, and were so threatening that the military were called in. There were several deaths. Even Metternich in remote Vienna viewed the affair with consternation—it could herald revolution. Robert Blum was the hero of the Leipzig incident, using his popularity among the lower classes to bring quiet into the situation. There were also disturbances throughout Silesia, this time in popular protest against a Prussian decree that refused joint use of churches by the *Deutschkatholisch* congregations and Protestants.[12]

When Ronge arrived at Mannheim, where police had forbidden a proposed concert by the local *Liedertafel*, he was met by a huge welcoming throng that included a semi-official delegation of *Landtag* members led by Friedrich Daniel Bassermann who, as member of the

"Theatre Committee", had arranged for a public meeting, but police blocked access to the theatre. Bassermann responded to the prohibition by offering public use of the garden of his new residence for Ronge's speech and the welcoming concert, thus asserting the right of assembly. Ronge spent the night at Bassermann's home. In consequence, Bassermann was fined because he had neglected to report to the police that he was offering shelter to an outsider.[13]

The enthusiasm grew to such unhealthy proportions that Ronge became a cult object. His letter to Bishop Arnoldi was printed on kerchiefs that were sold by hawkers who also peddled medallions, tobacco pouches, eyeglass cases and pipe heads that bore his likeness.

Ronge's speeches became increasingly socio-political in tone. The gap between poor and rich must be closed, he insisted. The individual congregations were far from homogeneous, though they all called themselves German Catholic. Heinrich Brüggemann made the astute comment that the movement was "a new form of Protestantism" that had nothing whatsoever to do with the Roman church.[14]

Dissidents supported each other in ways that pointed toward future political action. At Hanau, the order of the government of the Electorate of Hesse forbidding burial of members of the German Catholic movement in consecrated ground caused such a supporting action. A funeral was interrupted by angry members of the local *Turnverein* [gymnastic society], who refused to see a German Catholic placed among suicides and criminals. They carried the coffin to consecrated ground and buried it there, helped by women who supplied scarves and kerchiefs that could serve as improvised ropes for lowering the casket. The *Turnverein* was then officially disbanded on government order because of its "excesses".[15]

Resentment against Ronge and his followers grew in heavily Catholic communities in southern Germany. Armed peasants stood waiting for his coach at post stations. They blamed him for the potato blight. In the Schwarzwald, rotten potatoes were called *Rongekartoffeln*.[16] Rumors were floated to the effect that because of his blasphemies Ronge had lost his fingers or ears—even a leg. Catholic landowners took strong measures, forbidding their people to have anything to do with the movement, thereby causing tradesmen to lose their clientele. The Bavarian authorities issued a pronouncement that equated *Deutschkatholizismus* with radicalism and communism. They understood how the winds were blowing. This religious protest could become a dangerous political movement. In confirmation of that judgment there is the fact that recognized leaders who were encouraging the Catholic protest—among them Blum, Ronge himself, von Itzstein, Bassermann, and Karl Mathy—were all to be members of the revolutionary Frankfurt *Vorparlament* in the spring of 1848.

Meanwhile, what about the Protestant churches? A Protestant reform movement had begun early in the 40's. Originally an assemblage of churchmen (not laymen) had tried to work for the general strengthening of rationalism within the church, in order to counteract the growing effect of pietism that had assumed alarming proportions following Friedrich Wilhelm's ascent to the Prussian throne. Before long, laymen had joined in the effort, attending the meetings. Members of the movement were popularly known as *Lichtfreunde* because they spoke so emphatically in terms of light against the darkness of pietism.

The original thrust of the movement within the church was apolitical. There was implicit opposition to the concept of a state church, but in the initial stages the *Lichtfreunde* were characterized by a broad spectrum of ideologies and interests. However, the impulse toward mass protest and solidarity in a campaign for the right to critical examination of the scriptures, freedom of individual decision, and the idea of a church constitution that would allow independent action within the congregations was indubitably in the very air that people breathed in those days. It was in line with the liberals' political demands for a constitution and electoral reform.[17]

In June 1841 the movement became formally organized under Pastor Leberecht Uhlich of Magdeburg in Saxony, and was known thereafter as the *Protestantische Freunde* [Protestant friends]. Uhlich was a modern man, keeping a close eye on new developments. He suggested that there be meetings *an einem Orte der eine Eisenbahn berührt* [a location on a railway line]. Following his suggestion, there were semi-annual meetings at Köthen, just south of Magdeburg, where there was not only a railway connection but also a large hall in the station. (In anticipation of future developments, it was characteristic of the times that many railway stations had enormous concourses that served as waiting rooms.) Six hundred people attended the Köthen meeting in May 1844, and in the following year three thousand came from many parts of Germany. There were also local assemblies at Halle, Dresden, Königsberg, and Oppenheim. Professionals came in impressive numbers—*Gymnasium* teachers, pastors, lawyers, but also merchants and artisans. There was enough activity to attract the attention of the police. The fact of surveillance inevitably gave a political tone to the work of the movement.

Still in 1844, there was a further development. Uhlich invited free-thinkers in his immediate vicinity to come to what he called *Bürgerversammlungen* [citizens' meetings] for discussion of religious questions. Those who responded to the call wanted more meetings on a monthly basis, for open discussion of current conditions such as local problems relating to poor relief, the development of educational societies for artisans, the improvement of prison conditions and so on.

Bürgerversammlungen were forbidden in Prussia by decree of 6 May 1845, and this was quickly followed by a second prohibition. The *Protestantische Freunde* were disbanded in August 1845 because their meetings had become much too like the *Bürgerversammlungen*. (Friedrich Wilhelm was acting within the bounds of his royal authority because the evangelical church was the Prussian state church.) The two prohibitory decrees had the effect of throwing the *Freunde* and the *Bürgerversammlungen* together as a viable party of citizens' opposition. They soon found a way around the prohibitions against assembly by organizing festivals in honor of historical personages like Schiller. In today's jargon, they coalesced as a counterculture.

Toward the end of 1845, an open letter from Pastor G. A. Wislicenus of Halle started discussion on the direction that development of the protest should take. He welcomed the idea of congregations that would be independent of the state church and at the same time wrote in a most provocative manner about the institution of the church in general. "Away with customary pedantic preaching, bound to Bible texts! . . . away with the cassock in which a priest hides himself! . . . away with forced communion . . . it is against Christian freedom . . . and instead of a church, a hall would be much more appropriate. . . ."[18] Wislicenus underwent disciplinary hearings before the church *Consistorium* and accepted dismissal without protest. He was aware that as a pastor he had been a servant of the Prussian state church, which had legal authority over his words and actions. His obvious assumption that the days of established religion were over was welcomed by enthusiastic Young Hegelians.

By 1846 the former *Protestantische Freunde* reorganized as so-called free congregations [*Freie Gemeinden*], where the respective groups were usually headed by some known pastor who had been suspended from office because of activity among the *Freunde*. Many of these pastors had objected specifically to the requirement that they continue to be bound by the Athanasian or apostolic creed. The first free congregation was organized at Königsberg, followed by Halle.

The publisher Arnold Ruge commented that the Halle group was not so much a church congregation as an association. Indeed, the organizing document of the congregation said as much. "We want no self-contained ecclesiastical confession, but rather a free human society." Further, they applied to the magistrate for recognition as a private society, not as a religious group. Presumably the authorities who were responsible for public law and order accepted this view, because by the end of 1846 meetings for Bible study and discussion were forbidden.

As an organization, the Halle *Freie Gemeinde* was not spectacularly successful. Starting with a membership of sixty, it acquired only another forty in the course of a year. The reluctance of successful middle class people to join such a body was comprehensible. They may have agreed with the principle of independent congregations, and their personal indifference to creeds was a fact, but they were property owners and did not want to surrender any civil rights. At the other end of the scale, the lower classes may have been alarmed by the prospect of social discrimination.

The small group of active members of the Halle congregation produced conspicuous leaders during the 1848 revolution. They were attracted not so much by ideas of reform of the church as by its ideas of social reform. (There were various activities sponsored by the congregation that were aimed at improvement of the lot of workers, of women, and of children.) It is significant that the Baden radical, Gustav Struve, symbolically joined the congregation, showing solidarity with the social program.

Another *Freie Gemeinde* was much more successful than the one at Halle. This was the *Freie Protestantische Gemeinde* in Nordhausen, founded in January of 1847 and led by Pastor Eduard Baltzer. Unlike the Halle organization, the Nordhausen group specifically stated that its separation from the evangelical state church did not imply a break with the Christian religion. This congregation, numbering more than a thousand members, recognized and practiced the traditional rites of baptism, confirmation and marriage. The Nordhausen congregation engaged in numerous activities aside from their central service of worship. They had a choral society, a reading society, and a women's club. Somewhat later (around 1850) they also had a kindergarten.

The true center of the Protestant movement was in Pastor Leberecht Uhlich's Magdeburg. As leading personality of the *Lichtfreunde*, Uhlich had attracted a large following that was embittered by attacks on him.

Awareness of the conflict reached a wide public. The resentment increased when the church *Consistorium* proceeded against him in the summer of 1847, when he was confronted with the alternative of submission or withdrawal from his pastoral office. His loyal followers initiated a protest, circulating it throughout the city for signature. It stated among other things that Christianity was not just a collection of forms—it was a life principle for development. The protesters could not accept the *Consistorium* as a rightful governing body unless there were a true, constitutionally established representation of the members of the congregations. "We are being treated like dependent masses, illiterate in things of belief . . ." This bald rebellion frightened the city authorities and led to police investigation of Pastor Uhlich. (His deviation in matters of belief was that of any rationalist. He objected to the dogmas of Trinity and original sin.) Magdeburg's reaction to the treatment of Pastor Uhlich took the form of mass protest. The people submitted a document to the king, signed by most church leaders and more than a thousand citizens. It named free study of the scriptures and free use of church ritual as basic positions. The monarch was asked to sanction this, in order to avoid a schism.

The city council announced its solidarity with Uhlich, proposing that he be given honorary citizenship, but the city magistrate rejected the idea. He was acting in conformity with the judgment of the police chief, that "the better, more educated part of the citizenry was weakly represented in the city council."

Uhlich and his followers had earned respect and loyalty from the lower classes among the townspeople through their steady support and organization of various societies, such as a trade organization, an educational group, a society for support of artisans, and last but by no means least a savings institution that involved some eight thousand families. It was this savings institution—not the city authorities or the church consistory—that stood by the poor during the dreadful crisis of 1847 when crop failure and its attendant economic failures brought disaster to the region.

It goes without saying that many of Uhlich's most ardent defenders had only a secondary interest in religious protest. They were primarily social reformers. By early January 1848, the number of church dissidents in Magdeburg had risen to about nine thousand, all but a handful classified as working people.[19] The chief of police reported uneasily that there was a novel "deep bitterness" not only against the church and its regulations but also against all forms of authority. Three years before, he noted, there was lethargy as far as public affairs were concerned, but now, even at the "lowermost levels", there was an urgent desire to participate.[20]

State authorities were not indifferent to the phenomenon of protest congregations. There had been secessions in Halle, Nordhausen, Halberstadt, Naumburg and Magdeburg. Combined with the constantly growing number of *Deutschkatholische* dissidents, the organized opposition was becoming formidable. For this reason, a supposedly liberal edict of tolerance was issued (*Religionspatent* 30 March 1847) that opened the way to secession from a church and foundation of new religious associations.

In actuality it was an attempt by the Prussian government to check or at least contain the movement. The document was cannily designed, listing requirements for recognition that were crafty traps. If the state declined to recognize the new groups as true Christian organizations, they became private societies and were then under the law that allowed political surveillance, an instrument that could be applied at any time for abolition of the group in question. There were to be three legally recognized forms of religious societies: a) the publicly recognized "privileged" congregations—Lutheran, Reform and Roman Catholic b) the "tolerated" organizations whose priests were allowed to perform their ecclesiastical functions under the indirect control of the state, and c) private societies not recognized as religious communities, whose members risked loss of their civil rights.

There were additional complications for a congregation that wanted to separate from the state church: these were encompassed in a complex system of required certifications and fees. Furthermore, there were additional fees to be paid for registration of births, marriages, and deaths. These fees ranged from 1 *Thaler* 15 *Grosschen* to 5 *Thalern*—and the daily wage of a manual laborer in Halle in 1848 was 8 *Grosschen*.[21]

Other organizations that had their roots in the religious reform movement were the *Montagskränzchen* [Monday clubs] that sprang up in Frankfurt, Mannheim, Offenbach and Oppenheim in 1845. The Frankfurt meeting was first to accept Jews as members, and gradually became a center for the *Vormärz* liberals. These were the first genuinely public discussion groups of the *Vormärz*. Membership included people from the Protestant free congregations and the *Deutschkatholischer*, along with choral societies that had publicly supported the Catholic protest. There were also members of the gymnastic [*Turner*] movement. Some of these had even turned against the traditional quadruple-F device on their banners because one of the F's stood for the word *fromm* [pious], and this was rejected as "old-fashioned rubbish".

The Monday clubs were clearly overstepping boundaries set by moderates, who found it difficult and dangerous to abolish inequalities that were deeply embedded in European social structures. Progress on all fronts simultaneously would require recognition that Jews with their different culture, laboring people who owned no property, and women whose enforced lack of education had deprived them of useful skills and dignity—all these were groups that if equal before the law would be entitled to vote.[22] Most liberals were incapable of espousing anything so drastic.

At Oppenheim in August 1846, the *Montagskränzchen* organized a meeting of reform advocates from southwest Germany in which leaders from Frankfurt, Marburg, Worms, and Wiesbaden participated. These men were not only members of Catholic and Protestant reform groups but also prominent businessmen. It was disturbing to timid citizens that, as a police report stated, the main objective of the Oppenheim assembly had been to effect the union and merging of all parties that favored progress in religious, political and social life.[23] Meetings like that of the Monday club at Oppenheim tended to harden positions, widening the gap between moderates and radicals. It was indicative of the way the winds were blowing that ultraradical Gustav Struve, who had publicly left the Protestant church in order to join forces with the *Deutschkatholisch* movement, at this point left the Catholics and shifted to the non-denominational *Montagskränzchen*.

In 1847, the Mannheim *Montagsverein* (Gustav Struve was president) invited a speaker from Darmstadt to address them. This speaker, Luise Dittmar (1807–1884), presented a closely argued discussion of *Vier Zeitfragen* [four questions of the day] that was an all-out call for women's emancipation. The speech was warmly received and published at the request of the club, by Gustav André of Offenbach.[24]

Vier Zeitfragen is an extraordinary piece of work, reflecting intelligent broad reading and a courageously cogent analysis of the religious and social background of women's degraded position. Dittmar opened her remarks by stating that if she said that she was not religious, it was because she hated what was usually meant by that word. Her very nature, she said, consisted in resistance to injustice. She refused patient pious acceptance of "the apparently inevitable". She suggested that it was only misunderstanding that interprets spiritual independence as irreligious.[25]

Luise Dittmar was convinced that pressures from church and society in general had brought about in women a destructive lack of self-esteem. It was this that had made them incapable of leading productive, self-reliant and happy lives.

> Without a feeling of self-worth, man has not even reached the lowermost stage of humanity. I therefore demand self-esteem for every individual, for each sex equally.[26]

Dittmar was to go forward with unprecedented daring. In her reading of *Das Wesen des Christentums* by Ludwig Feuerbach (1804–1872), she had arrived at the conclusion that religious faith could only lead to an unhealthy belief in some supernatural power that would solve all problems.[27] She said that if we posit such a higher reason, we scorn our own. She issued a ringing call to women. In a massive, united effort, they should consult, act, believe in themselves and in each other, and claim their rights.

The fact that Dittmar could speak of her respect for Feuerbach's work in a meeting of the *Montagsverein* shows how far the original religious protest had moved from its starting point. The *Montagsverein* was unmistakably a political forum in outlook and interests, and its members were open to ideas inherent in the doctrines of materialism.

For a variety of reasons, Luise Dittmar aroused no enthusiasm among women, not even those who styled themselves as champions of women's causes. If they mentioned Dittmar's work at all in their own writings, there was suspicion, distrust, even jealousy in their comments that sometimes verged on shrillness. Kathinka Zitz-Halein, president of the Humania society in Mainz, obviously irritated by the sight of her estranged husband the celebrated Franz Heinrich Zitz escorting Dittmar into the hall for her lecture, wrote scornfully that Dittmar's remarks were poorly received because women did not want to see themselves transformed into monsters that belonged to neither sex.[28] Others, less emotionally involved than Zitz-Halein may have been, were clearly disturbed by Dittmar's inexorable drive to independence and responsibility for one's actions. Women like Johanna Küster-Fröbel and Luise Otto-Peters were willing enough to contribute to her short-lived newspaper, but they shrank from her forthright ways and demands. They must have been horrified by her piece on Charlotte Corday, in which it was obvious that she thought Corday had acted as she believed an independent woman ought to act.

Although Luise Dittmar repeatedly asserted that she had always felt angered and humiliated by her status as a woman, the impression is unavoidable that she had spent her youth in an atmosphere of eager discussion of the most advanced ideas. Nothing in the home of her father and brothers would have forced her into silence and submission, though she did not hesitate to level accusations against liberals in general. Her network of association with family members, reformers, contemporary publishers and activists shows how, even in the relatively limited confines of Darmstadt, many strands of protest were gradually being bound together, reinforcing each other.[29] Her father, a finance officer of the Hesse-Darmstadt government, was a Freemason, a member of the *Johannes der Evangelist zur Eintracht* lodge .

A welcome house guest in the thirties was a young man from Strassburg, Alexis Muston, who brought messages from Luise's fugitive brother Hermann and her cousin Adolph Heumann, both of whom had been members of the Germania *Burschenschaft* in Giessen and had had to flee because of their involvement in the failed *Frankfurter Wachensturm* of 1833. Muston also brought a report about a young neighbor of the Dittmars, Georg Büchner, the founder of a local *Gesellschaft der Menschenrechte* and publisher of the ill-fated radical *Hessische Landbote*. Luise Dittmar's biographer notes that she probably received copies of the *Landbote* hot from the secret press operated by an in-law of hers, Karl Preller, who had to flee because of accusations against him.

Another in-law, the lawyer Wilhelm Schulz, had been an officer in the Prussian army but lost his commission in 1821, following imprisonment for political activities.[30] (He was the author of a work called *Deutschlands Einheit durch Repräsentation* [the unification of Germany through representation] that earned him a five-year jail sentence, though he managed to escape to Switzerland.) In 1848, Schulz was a member of the Left in the Frankfurt *Parlament*. Schulz was a friend of two of Germany's most radical poets, Freiligrath and Herwegh. One of the local publishers with whom Luise Dittmar was associated was Julius Leske, who published works of Marx, Engels, and Ruge. Three of her brothers emigrated to the United States after the revolution of 1848.

From the Freemasons, through the student movement, the radical underground protests, the liberal movement, and the open religious protest of the 1840's, as well as feminist action, strong forces of resistance were assembling.

Dittmar repeatedly said that throughout her life she had felt humiliated by her status as a woman, yet it is difficult to believe that she would ever have been treated contemptuously like an ignorant little child, in view of the nature of the liberal circle in which she moved. With all due recognition of the feminist cause and its justified expression of grievances, there is evidence in contemporary letters that many intelligent German women enjoyed the absolute respect and confidence of their male associates. Men whose views were as disparate as those of Joseph Maria von Radowitz, Karl Marx, and Robert Blum all wrote to their wives as equal to equal, reporting in careful detail on their political efforts, candidly setting out the record of their triumphs and defeats. They certainly never thought of their wives as toys or child-bearing machines whose proper place was in the kitchen. The same can be said of Johann Jacoby's attitude toward his sisters and close friends like Fanny Lewald.

As time passed, moderate-minded liberals tended to drift away from the religious protest movement, whether Catholic or Protestant, perhaps because they had observed that the most enthusiastic members were those of the far left, like Robert Blum and Gustav Struve.

Though political parties as such had not as yet developed, separation was already occurring. There was considerable freedom of debate in the Baden assembly, for example, because Baden had a constitution that guaranteed certain liberties, unlike Prussia. Although at first glance it might appear that there was a solid division of parties in Baden (Catholic *versus* Protestant) the fact that discussion was possible in the assembly had brought about another cleavage that was more significant insofar as political reform and change were concerned. A motion made by the Baden delegate Karl Zittel, that members of protesting congregations have the same legal standing as those of the established state church, was the precipitating event. The motion set off a storm of petitions in a campaign launched by *Landtag* delegate Franz Joseph von Buss and vigorously supported by Catholic priests in the region, who did not hesitate to instruct their flocks. Hundreds of petitions were therefore brought in, supposedly showing that the majority of the people had no use for the demands of the reformers. The petitions did indeed bring about the closure of the legislative session and a new election, but the voice of the people did not bring down the the reformers. Rather, it confirmed their standing as the majority faction. It was an uneasy majority, however, because a serious split had developed in the course of heated debates in the *Landtag* between radicals and moderates within the ranks of church protesters. In Baden, it had already become possible to speak of "wholes" (radicals) and "halves" (moderates). The break was going to present serious problems in 1848.

Notes

1 Sperber, *Popular Catholicism in Nineteenth-Century Germany*, pp. 42–45.

2 Sheehan, *German History 1770–1886*, pp. 617–619.

3 Hermann Joseph Aloys Körner, *Lebenskämpfe in der alten und neuen Welt*, 1:246–249.

4 Ernst Rudolf Huber, *Der Kampf um Einheit und Freiheit 1830 bis 1850*, pp. 250–255.

5 Wolfgang Schieder, "Kirche und Revolution; sozialgeschichtliche Aspekte der Trier Wallfahrt von 1944." *Archiv für Sozialgeschichte* 14 (1974) 419–454; Rudolf Lill, "Kirche und Revolution; zu den Anfängen der katholischen Bewegung im Jahrzehnt vor 1848," *Archiv für Sozialgeschichte* 18 (1978) 565–575.

6 Sperber, *Popular Catholicism*, p. 25; Körner, 1:307–308. Nine months after any given pilgrimage, there was always a large crop of illegitimate infants.

7 Paletschek, *Frauen und Dissens*, pp. 19–73.

8 Sperber, *Popular Catholicism*, p. 20.

9 Körner, p. 311.

10 Eyck, *The Frankfurt Parliament*, p. 22.

11 Norbert Deuchert, *Vom Hambacher Fest zur badischen Revolution*, p. 200.

12 Paletschek, p. 56.

13 Gall, *Bürgertum in Deutschland*, p. 277.

14 Wilhelm Schulte, *Volk und Staat*, p. 453, note 165.

15 Paletschek, p. 57.

16 Valentin, *Geschichte der deutschen Revolution*, 1:155.

17 Jörn Brederlow. *"Lichtfreunde" und "Freie Gemeinden"*, pp. 49–103.

18 Ibid., p. 50.

19 Sachse, *Erinnerungen an die Entstehung und entwicklung der Magdeburger freien Gemeinde*, passim.

20 Brederlow, p. 60.

21 Ibid., p. 55, note 30.

22   Dagmar Herzog, "Liberalism, Religious Dissent and Women's Rights," in *In Search of a Liberal Germany*, p. 56.

23   Paletschek, p. 53.

24   Gabriele Käfer-Dittmar, *Louise Dittmar (1807–1884)*, pp. 109–128.

25   Ibid., p. 110.

26   Ibid., p. 116.

27   Feuerbach's work found sympathetic readers among liberal communities far distant from Germany. In England, for example, his work was translated into English by none other than George Eliot, whose life unambiguously exemplified the courage of women who expected recognition as worthy members of society.

28   Bamberger, *Erinnerungen*, pp. 28–29. If Bamberger's memory was accurate, *Frau* Zitz-Halein was suffering from raging jealousy. According to his account, she had tricked Zitz into marriage by pretending to have poisoned herself. Zitz struggled for years to obtain a divorce, and meanwhile was exasperated because she always sent wreathes and flowers that were publicly delivered to him whenever he spoke. Bamberger was remotely related to Zitz.

29   Käfer-Dittmar, pp. 9–37.

30   Eyck, p. 137, footnote.

Chapter 6

Railroads and the *Zollverein*: Faltering Steps toward German Unity

The development of new means of transportation and new large-scale manufacture underlay many of the social changes that occurred in Germany, even though railroads were only in their infancy and steam-powered boats were just beginning to appear on the rivers. One thing was understood fairly well: if Germany were ever to solve her many problems, all those boundaries between tiny duchies and principalities ought to be broken down. Wild-eyed radical students and elderly conservatives were united in their comprehension that this was a fundamental problem.

The coming railway systems inevitably trailed with them urgent problems. Barriers between states would create ridiculous situations. Were trains to chug up to a frontier and then stop? Besides, just the laying out of the railroad lines would entail many bureaucratic disputes. In the session of the Bavarian council of ministers of 4 January 1836, for example, there was a lively discussion triggered by a petition from the city of Lindau on Lake Konstanz, which wanted to found a company for the construction of a railroad between Lindau and Augsburg. Lindau wanted its line to Augsburg because in neighboring Württemberg the question of the railway project had been quickly taken up by the state, and a central had been established in Stuttgart. Stuttgart would be connected with the southern area of Württemberg and deflect the stream of north-to-south traffic. In Württemberg they were also contemplating construction of a line from the Rhine to Stuttgart and from Stuttgart to the Danube, which would shunt traffic then passing over the Danube-Main canal. Lindau wanted to prevent the economic ruin of Augsburg, Lindau and Memmingen by thwarting Württemberg's iniquitous planned cutoff of Bavarian trade from Switzerland and Italy.[1]

In the course of the council's discussion, it was pointed out that railroads would be of enormous strategic importance for troop movements. Field Marshal Wrede speaking: "Let there be no mistake. The constantly extending system will bring about a total revision of all military and strategic conditions and relationships."[2] What if there were war with France again? The western flank of Bavaria would require special consideration, obviously. The projected Bamberg-Würzburg-Frankfurt line should be extended, and also the line from Bamberg via Nürnberg toward Nördlingen, where the army could assemble, and thence to Augsburg. (None of these lines existed at the time of the discussion.)

Von Wrede spoke in 1836, fretting about the possibility of war with France and the role of railroads in such a conflict. This military man was not prescient enough to consider the possibility of a German revolution, yet within little more than a decade, the German railway system would be utilized as an excellent means for the dissemination of information and propaganda as well as for movement of insurgents under arms. During the rising in Baden in May 1849, the station at Heidelberg for example was a focal point where connections could be made between Mannheim, Karlsruhe, and Weinheim on the border of Hesse-Darmstadt.

> Pen cannot describe the lively movement in the Heidelberg station at that time. This swarm, this confusion of civil guards, irregulars, troops of the line, and among them the various commanding officers with tricolor scarves, the dress and arming of certain prominent personalities, the constant movement back and forth, running, shouting, the doubled and tripled use of the locomotives, the constant arrival and departure of new troop trains, mixed with the ordinary travelers and ladies, all presented to the eye an animated picture of something that had never happened before.

Franz Raveaux, who wrote these lines, was in the midst of the frenetic effort, and even at times, in the urgency of the moment, did not hesitate to leap from his bed in the middle of the night, ordering for himself in the emergency a special *Extralokomotive* that would convey him speedily to the crisis point.[3]

The matter of rival lines came up again on 6 October 1839, when it was called to king Ludwig's attention that a connection of the Neckar, Rhine and Danube was planned, with interconnection via a Württemberg railroad from Ulm to Heilbronn. The threat to the Main-Danube canal was again mentioned. The *Ludwigskanal* connected the Danube at Kelheim with the Main and therefore with the Rhine.

With its hundred locks, this 176 km waterway was king Ludwig's joy.—
Only a state-owned railroad could reduce the danger posed by the
projected Württemberg railroad.[4]

There was little love lost between the various German states at this
stage, and certainly no spirit of *one for all and all for one* that future
nationalists would dream of. Problems of this kind that involved railroads, trade and military concerns surely contributed to the mix that
underlay the 1848 outbreaks, every bit as much as population pressure, the first stirring of urban industrialization, and the struggles of
land-poor peasants.

Needless to say, nothing was ever simple in a land where religion
played as large a part as it did in Bavaria. By 1843 a strong neo-
Catholic trend had developed, and it found expression even in the
matter of railroad design. The proposed road to Augsburg, for example, would run into trouble because Augsburg was Protestant. It
was suggested that the line that was to connect Nürnberg and Munich
ought to bypass Augsburg in favor of the loyal Catholic cities of
Ingolstadt and Eichstädt.[5]

In Prussia, king and cabinet were locked in a frustrating position.
Even if they recognized the value of a railway system, they felt that
their hands were tied because of a law of 1820 that had set down the
condition that loans for state undertakings had to be approved by an
institution vaguely designated as a united *Landtag* [a united Prussian
assembly]. Such a body had never been summoned, since results of a
meeting of that sort could not be predicted. Would it not lead to demands for a constitution and for a permanent "national" assembly,
reform of the voting franchise, and a dread weakening of the monarch's
power? Best to let sleeping dogs lie, despite rumblings of discontent
from liberals in East Prussia. (Among the East Prussians were grain
exporters and mercantile progressives, and many men in Königsberg
had imbibed their political views from Immanuel Kant.) Not all East
Prussians were in favor of railroad development, however. Many estate owners there were of the opinion that countries like England that
had rapidly expanded their transport systems had laid themselves open
to instability, because the railroad was patent evidence of the dangerous penetration of industry into the heartland.[6]

While bureaucrats wrestled with these tangled issues, worried people
who lived in towns along the projected routes had their own concerns
and doubts. The prospect of enormous crews of railroad construction
workers in their neighborhoods was most unsettling to those who

wanted to keep their communities quiet and unscathed. What if a project were completed near the town and the crews were laid off? What would happen? Where would all those uncouth barbarous people go? Rootless men were always a menace to public tranquility. What if they were to come into town and demand public assistance?

Along the Rhine, railroads were disruptive because they changed traffic patterns drastically, but even before their advent, the people who earned their money in work related to river transport had experienced upsetting innovations. In 1831, free navigation had been established as the outcome of extended diplomatic negotiations. This meant that the cities of Mainz and Cologne were confronted by a new, threatening arrangement. Before that time, all freighted goods had had to be offloaded and put on the market there, but under the new dispensation shippers bypassed both cities and the tonnage going through their harbors dropped to about 60% of its previous levels. Not long after that, the railways began to have their effect. Because layout of the lines had not been too well thought out, feeder lines that were supposed to bring freight to certain cities such as Mainz had the effect of delivering it to rival harbors instead.

Then came steamboats which at first could only be used for passengers because the engines made the craft so heavy, but the problem was solved by putting freight on barges that were towed through shallow waters by the steamboats. Adding insult to injury, the railway companies then put in lines that ran parallel to the river.

All this worked hardship on owners of old-fashioned sailing vessels and reduced haulers and dock workers to desperate near-destitution. Before all these changes, these men had towed boats, or in some cases had made use of mules in the same fashion that those animals were used on the tow-paths of early canals in the United States.

> The long rows of wretched horses that dragged the clumsy but picturesque boats, to which we have so long been accustomed, at a snail's pace up the noble river are gradually diminishing, and powerful tugs are substituted, which smoke away with six or seven barges of 200 or 300 tons behind them, performing the distance that used, with fair wind, to take up to ten days, in twenty-four hours, and often shortening the voyage by at least a month. This is the most important transition to machinery on the Rhine.[7]

The haulers who were hard hit by all the technological changes became "tumultuous", although it appears that in subsequent decades they recovered.[8] As Ludwig Bamberger described them, they were formidable people with whom nobody wanted to tangle. The women seem especially to have alarmed him. Their powerful build was such that they were accustomed to move through the city streets with huge weighty loads on their heads, knitting stockings as they strode along.[9] The haulers indeed became tumultuous during the uprisings of March 1848, when the Rhine river men attacked steamships, firing on them with muskets and cannon.

Efforts had been made to ease problems of merchants with goods to ship, yet there remained a multitude of problems. Consider the plight of a manufacturer who with his wonderful new machinery found himself with an excess of products on his hands that he could not possibly dispose of on the restricted local market. He would want to expand his operations in the new modern world and enjoy the wider market that distant growing cities might offer, but in the words of the impassioned Friedrich List, numerous customs barriers "cripple trade and produce the same effect as ligatures which prevent the free circulation of the blood".[10] If for example the manufacturer wanted to ship his products from Bamberg to Mainz, he would have to pay no less than thirty tolls on the journey, in spite of the fact that Bavaria had dropped internal duties as early as 1807. If that same manufacturer optimistically sent his wares on to Frankfurt am Main, he met further difficulties, because the low import duties imposed by that city on incoming cheap goods that were pouring in from busy mercantile England offered no protection for his own goods. "Germany alone fails to protect her children," lamented seventy Rhenish manufacturers who petitioned Friedrich Wilhelm III of Prussia in April, 1818.[11]

Well, why not at least consider something like uniformity of customs duties all across Germany? Friedrich List had been in the forefront here. As early as 1819, he and certain influential business men founded the *Deutscher Handels- und Gewerbsverein* [commercial and industrial society] which was uncommonly energetic in publicizing its program. Demands included the wiping out of all internal German customs barriers, and the setting up of customs offices at boundaries where protective tariffs would be required. In this way, they hoped to pave the way for free trade throughout Europe but meanwhile to protect vulnerable German enterprizes that were coming along slowly behind the English manufacturers. List wrote incessantly for his organization's own journal and likewise composed voluminous petitions that were submitted to the various state governments. Not all of these writings were consistent because List was trying to appeal to people who had their own special interests and he knew that he had to accommodate himself to that uncomfortable fact.

Merchants and entrepreneurs had long been restive because they had no access to political circles. The effect of this situation becomes clear in this instance. The German people did not have any extensive influence on the events that led to the establishment of the *Zollverein* [customs union]. Rather, the political and administrative problems were solved by the cabinets of the respective states,[12] and what could have been handled briskly under democratic legislative bodies moved with all the whirlwind velocity of a snail's progress.

It is instructive but discouraging to see how much intricate manoeuvering had been involved before 1834 in the process of setting the *Zollverein* on its feet.

In 1818 negotiations had been initiated by Prussia, but though the importance of the principle was clearly recognized by most statesmen, "they took alarm at the power which its adoption threatened to throw into the hands of Prussia".[13]

Even the arrangements of an ostensibly simple customs union arrived at in 1828 between Bavaria and Württemberg showed how warily negotiators had to tread. Each state had its own central customs administration and dispatched a plenipotentiary to the administration of the other. This official had to subscribe to a special oath of allegiance not only to the customs union but also to his own sovereign. Although he was informed of all moves in the state to which he had been sent, he could not veto anything. He could merely object.

As to the similar customs union between Prussia and Hesse-Darmstadt (also 1828), affairs were much more complex because regions along the lower Rhine were more industrialized than Bavaria and Württemberg, and artisans were already restive there. If manufactured goods were to pour in without any customs barriers, it would spell disaster to them. Hesse-Darmstadt had made an abortive effort in the direction of economic cooperation with Baden in 1824, but this venture was abandoned in about a year. It had then seemed for a time that Hesse-Darmstadt might be interested in a customs union with Bavaria and Württemberg, but this also had fallen through after a number of conferences. Darmstadt was aware that her interests were more closely tied to those of Baden, Nassau and Hesse-Kassel, but these states had all refused to consider union with Bavaria and Württemberg. At last, Hesse-Darmstadt approached Prussia (1825), suggesting that there be either a commercial treaty or a customs union. The Prussian response was cool. They would look into the matter, and might be interested if Kurhessen could be included. But Kurhessen (Hesse-Kassel) said no.

Once again Hesse-Darmstadt broached the subject (1827). Problem: Hesse-Darmstadt's relationship with Austria was cordial. What would Austria (i.e. *Fürst* Metternich) think of this? On the whole, it might be advantageous to enjoy Prussian favor. BUT both Baden and Nassau were still close to Austria: Would they see Hesse-Darmstadt as a renegade? Just for the sake of safety, the minister from Hesse-Darmstadt told Prussia that though a Prussian representative authorized to negotiate a commercial agreement would be welcome, it would be helpful if his mission were kept secret.

By January 1828 a shadowy agreement had been developed. Hesse-Darmstadt would conform to Prussian customs law and tariffs and organize customs administration on the Prussian pattern, but otherwise there was at least a semblance of equality. The two states would audit each other's books on revenue collection (but use the Prussian auditing system). All this was ratified by a treaty for "a common customs and commerce system".

All very well, but there had to be special provisions because each state had territories that were geographically split off. The Prussian enclave of Wetzlar therefore was to join the Hesse-Darmstadt customs, and some sections of Hesse-Darmstadt would be incorporated into the customs administration of Prussian Westphalia. There was also a "maze created through secret clauses, supplementary clauses, and an additional secret treaty" which is attributed to lack of experience rather than to lack of confidence.[14] For better or worse, the Prusso-Hessian customs union at last became effective on 1 July 1828.

Meanwhile, other states had not been idle. In that same year of 1828, Saxony and the Saxon states in Thuringia had moved toward a union that was designed to prohibit any adherence on the part of members to any outside customs system. This negative arrangement was bound to fail because its members would not or could not cooperate or bargain collectively. In recognition of this, some northerners tried to set up a union for Hannover, Hesse-Kassel, Oldenburg and Braunschweig, called the *Steuerverein* [tax union] but this body also ran into difficulties through repercussions of the French July Revolution of 1830 that drove out the anti-Prussian Elector of Kurhessen. That state promptly sent a representative to Berlin, asking to join the Prussia-Hesse-Darmstadt union. This provided a geographical link between Prussia and some of her remote territories, but the point was not pressed because of a secret provision for a customs union between Bavaria and Württemberg and the western Prussian provinces.

The *Zollverein* was developed by a series of treaties. First Prussia and Hesse-Darmstadt and Hesse-Kassel signed a treaty with Bavaria and Württemberg. They then negotiated a treaty with Saxony. The Thuringian states came in as a unit, and the *Zollverein* became officially operative on the first day of January 1834. Most provisions seem to have been worked out amicably in spite of various conflicting desires. Mysteriously, all agreed that trade in playing cards and salt should remain under the jurisdiction of the respective members.

A step had been taken in the direction of unity, but the underlying difficulty faced by tradesmen had not been solved. The Mecklenburgs, Holstein, Lübeck, Oldenburg and Hannover remained stubbornly outside the *Zollverein* because they objected to its protectionist tendencies. This refusal deprived members of the customs union of desirable outlets along the Baltic and the North Sea. As far east as Berlin, the commerce of western and central Germany still depended on the Elbe, the Weser and the Rhine, and along those rivers states that had not joined the *Zollverein* continued relentlessly to collect transit duties.[15]

The craftsmen's situation had not been eased either, as the reaction to Hesse-Kassel's entry into the *Zollverein* had clearly shown. In January 1832, mobs attacked the toll houses and threatened customs officers. The disorder spread, and the riots were only ended by the arrival of troops. All through 1832, there were defiant mobs who broke into small shops and skirmished in the streets with the soldiers sent in to quell them.[16]

Among Germans who wanted to see the homeland become a functioning nation, there were those (mostly Protestants), who were not afraid to see Prussia take the lead, but they must have been aware that although there were similarly-minded men within the Prussian establishment, what motivated the dominant conservatives was their desire for something rather disagreeable. They wanted to see Prussia become a major power and had little or no interest in representative parliamentary bodies or constitutions or better education or suffrage. Their king refused even to think of a constitution, on the ground that such an instrument would "come between me and my people". At the outset of his reign, Friedrich Wilhelm IV had raised false hopes by indicating that he would honor the promise of a legislative assembly that had been at least implied by laws passed in 1820 and 1823, but he had managed to convince himself that he ruled absolutely by divine right, and therefore the legislative body had not materialized.

Bavarians must have understood that a Germany weighted toward Catholicism would have to make some kind of adjustment with respect to Catholic Austria, which was already a great power to which Germany could not offer much. Austria was a member of the German *Bund* that had been organized at the time of the Congress of Vienna, and by the provisions of that organization she always saw her delegates presiding over the council meetings at Frankfurt am Main. These presiding officers, to be sure, faithfully followed the directives of that ultraconservative, the chancellor Clemens von Metternich (1773–1859). The council, by the way, was more a meeting of diplomats than a body representative of the people. If Germany were to unify and include Austria, what would be done with all those Slavs who were under Habsburg rule? What, for that matter, would become of the Habsburgs if Austria were included in a new Germany but the Slav portions of the realm were excluded?

Trust in gradual nationalizing through institutions such as the *Zollverein* or the *Bund,* or even through some wonderful as yet undeveloped railroad network was scorned by German radicals. Slow progress was no progress, to their way of thinking. The German monarchies were deliberately thwarting the will of the people! The radicals did not even blink at the notion that because conservatives controlled the armed forces of all the various German states, they might have to call in outsiders to help dislodge them. (The French, maybe?)

The radicals were not being realistic. That assessment can be reinforced by the observation that they were assuming that the German people in general wanted an overthrow of the rulers and experienced some overriding emotional need to see it happen. The radicals were forgetting—or at least overlooking—the fact that Germany was primarily a rural society still, in spite of the beginnings of the Industrial Revolution. A peasant whose most frequent social contact was at the market of his tiny *Dorf* may not even have felt that he had much in common with people who lived in villages twenty or more kilometers from his home. News that circulated in such small communities was probably transmitted by the woman water-carrier as she moved from the well to the various houses along the street. It would have been incongruous indeed if the woman with the water jug had reported on current events in distant capitals. Surely her eye-witness account of a tavern brawl or an altercation between a pair of housewives over the price of a couple of eggs would have been more vivid and commanded close attention.

Fremde (outsider, stranger, foreigner) was the customary term used in reference to someone from another village. There was nothing in Germany to stimulate a feeling of national unity—no common experi-

ences such as the French had had with their huge revolution and all
their amazing farflung military campaigns under Napoleon. Without
stretching the point excessively, it can even be said that the common
experience of the French extended far back across the centuries. In
the time of Emperor Caracalla, the inhabitants of ancient Gaul had
become recognized citizens of the Empire (A.D. 212), and because of
administrative arrangements, they had been subject not only to Roman law but also, in the years of the Later Empire, to the authority of
their own native-born Prefects. Sometimes the region known now as
France had even felt enough unity to entertain the notion of separat-
ism. There was the short-lived "dynasty" of Postumus (A.D. 259–269)
and his successors. Vestiges of Roman life remained, especially in
Provence. The French citizen was familiar with the sight of
amphitheatres, arenas, massive triumphal arches and gateways, ceno-
taphs, even aqueducts like the extraordinary *Pont du Gard*—all powerful reminders of a shared past. The Germans, by contrast, had a
large population of villagers who had never seen anything that could
arouse sentiments of unity other than the stirring pageantry associated with religious processions in Catholic regions. Robed priests,
and incense swirling in shafts of light that streamed through stained
glass windows. Surely, the Church was their nation and their strength.
The emotional appeal of such lifelong experience must have been almost overwhelming. Why transfer devotion to a nebulous concept of
nationhood?

Whatever the setting—whether rural or urban—nationalism in the
Vormärz was not embodied in a recognizable movement. Its goals
were repeatedly mentioned, often with fervor, by liberals and radicals
alike, but on the whole one would have to agree that nationalism was
the experience of marching behind the tricolor flag, of large-scale collective singing, of joining in a large public meeting or a small conspiratorial circle.[17] Even participation of this kind did not develop on a
large scale until the 1830's, when a spasm of revolutionary fervor was
set off by events in France.

What was lacking in Germany was a sense of common experience
that bound generations together. There was little of the unity that
Edmund Burke had in mind.

> The institutions of policy, the goods of fortune, the gifts of Providence, are
> handed down, to us and from us . . . in a condition of unchangeable con-
> stancy . . . we have given to our frame of polity the image of a relation in
> blood . . . keeping inseparable, and cherishing with the warmth of all their

combined and mutually reflected charities, our state, our hearths, our sepul-chres, and our altar.[18]

United activity in the name of the nation suggests the city, certainly not the countryside, where there may even have been some residual affection and admiration for the lords who rode out so grandly to the hunt or who made an occasional conspicuous appearance in the local churches on feast days and high holiday. In this connection, it might be added that even the most radical of the revolutionary activists made little effective effort to engage the rural population in their propa-ganda. There seems to have been no attempt to galvanize the rural people into action, though it must have been evident everywhere that there were desperate issues among them (forest rights, for example) that could have been exploited.

Unfortunately, whatever advances were being made in the develop-ment of customs unions and railroad construction brought little ben-efit to landless peasants or to unskilled workmen drifting toward the towns. The advantages concerned primarily the comfortable middle class entrepreneur. If they had been honest about it, the constitution-alists and the more vociferous radicals would have had to admit that they were not thinking of an open society for all. Property and talent would be the basic requirements for suffrage: few people wanted the proletariat to participate in government.[19] Better to let wiser heads make decisions for those lowly folk, who were to be pitied but not trusted.

It may be that the kind of nationalism that all its champions were advocating (with the exception of those of the extreme left) was in fact a collection of causes that would cut across the boundaries of the petty states of Germany for the benefit of their own middle class. What genuine interest could either aristocrats or lowly peasants or poverty-stricken drifters in the cities have in national suffrage or free-dom of the press, for example?

Fressfreiheit, nicht Pressfreiheit! [freedom to feed our faces, not freedom of the press] yelled an angry man in a crowd at Elberfeld.

Notes

1 Wolf D. Gruener, *Das bayerische Heer 1825 bis 1864*, pp. 92–93.

2 Ibid., p. 94, note 71, citing a *Ministerratsprotokoll* of 4 January 1836.

3 Franz Raveaux, *Mittheilungen über die badische Revolution*, pp. 23, 36, 47.

4 Marggraff, *Die Kgl. bayerischen Staatseisenbahnen*, p. 18.

5 Valentin, *Geschichte der deutschen Revolution*, 1:109.

6 Berdahl, *The Politics of the Prussian Nobility*, p. 340, footnote 89.

7 Banfield, *Industry of the Rhine*. ser. 2, pp. 24–25.

8 Sperber, *Rhineland Radicals*, pp. 30–32.

9 Bamberger, *Erinnerungen*, p. 49

10 W. O. Henderson, *The Zollverein*, p. 22.

11 Ibid., p. 23 note 3.

12 Arnold H. Price, *The Evolution of the Zollverein*, p. 191.

13 Banfield, ser.2, p. 8.

14 Price, pp. 204–243.

15 Hamerow, *Restoration, Revolution, Reaction,* p. 14.

16 Price, pp. 117–119, citing Eisenbart Rothe and A. Ritthaler.

17 Sperber, *European Revolutions*, p. 91

18 Burke, *Reflections on the Revolution in France*, p. 120.

19 Sheehan *German Liberalism*, p. 155. Universal suffrage was generally castigated as "unorganized indiscipline, the recognized hegemony of the irrational".

Chapter 7

Disorder, Alarm and Repression;
The Eighteen Thirties

The news from Paris was stunning. There had been unrest and dissatisfaction for some time under the rule of the unpopular Bourbon monarch, Charles X, but that his regime could be toppled in the course of just three days caught people's imagination everywhere.

In the spring of the fateful year 1830, Victor Hugo had sounded a warning: Addressing kings in general, he urged the sovereigns not to ask the fleeing fisherman about the roar that seemed to come from the horizon. Hasten, O kings! Abandon the old shore! Make way for this sea of men, lest you perish beneath the past century that the flood is about to engulf! [1]

King Charles was an obtuse individual who paid little heed to Cassandras. He had issued four extremely reactionary *ordonnances* on 25 July 1830, among them one designed to change the balance of elections in favor of landowners, and another designed to silence the press, especially the *National* that had been founded by Adolphe Thiers in January of that year. During the spectacular *trois glorieuses* [27–28–29 July] the angry populace rose up in terrifying might, to the tremulous delight of the international community of political exiles in Paris.

Bad harvests and a weak economy had thrown many people out of work, jamming the streets of the capital with unemployed workmen who were only too glad to show their strength by throwing up hundreds of barricades. Students from the polytechnic school joined in, and so did the national guard. Hector Berlioz, the man who wrote the official musical setting of the *Marseillaise*, wrote in his memoirs that he would never forget the wild bravado of the street arabs or the enthusiasm of the men and the frenzy of the public women. There was also, he wrote, "the curious pride which the workmen exhibited in not pillaging Paris though they were masters of the situation".[2] About sixty thousand insurgents took part. They occupied the Hôtel de Ville, the Louvre, the Tuileries, and Notre-Dame, with the result that Charles hurriedly abdicated and a new king came into power. This was Louis-Philippe, of the house of Orléans.

The excitement spread like a prairie fire. Within two weeks, there were disorders all over Germany. Although there had been a change in German society, especially a gradual coalescence here and there of organizations and clubs that were aware of political conditions, the sporadic risings were not revolutionary. There was awareness, in particular among journalists, of the possibility of something remotely ressembling unified reaction within the boundaries of the *Deutscher Bund* in response to action elsewhere. However, it was hardly to be expected that a concerted attack on Germany's various problems would be mounted throughout the thirty-nine states because there was no true recognition of the nature of the political situation in the public mind. Also, there must have been a widespread understanding that on the whole, if there were collective violence—riots, demonstrations, protests, machine breaking etc.—the official response would not be propitiatory. There would be military action, and repression. The only group that might serve as a focal point for some frontal united effort was the student movement, embodied in their fraternities, the *Burschenschaften*, but these were fragmented and still communicating with difficulty as a result of the drastic Carlsbad decrees. The masses were unorganized, the *Mittelstand* for the most part was conservative, grasping, and timid, and there were all too few convincingly articulate liberals.

For decades, all Europe had been haunted by the nightmarish thought of bloody barricades and mobs defiantly flourishing red flags and chanting the *Marseillaise*. When the French rose up and rid themselves of the Bourbons, a reactionary shiver rippled all over the German duchies and kingdoms as well as in Austria, where the ultraconservative *Fürst* Clemens Metternich, who for decades had been almost single-handedly holding the arrangements of the Congress of Vienna together, is said to have predicted that the French *journées de juillet* would cause "the collapse of the dam". The dam he had in mind was much larger than the German-speaking lands that were his bulwark. He no doubt was thinking of all continental Europe as it had been rearranged in protracted debate and agonizing consultation at Vienna in 1815. Metternich had firmly kept Austria clear of any constitutional program that would have undermined the bedrock solidity of his administrative system, and his domestic and foreign policies always interlocked. He was convinced that if constitutionalism were to spread, his whole house of cards might collapse. He had consistently tried to steer the German states—especially Prussia—away from any discussion of a constitution. The situation had become ominous because ideas steaming from the French cauldron might well scald all Europe.

In Metternich's eyes, any political opposition, no matter what form it took, was part of a huge array of conspiracies. In his paranoid state, the Austrian minister was in the unlikely company of the Russian agitator Mikhail Bakunin, whom a friend once told tartly that not even Bakunin himself could believe in the actuality of his imagined infamous league made up of "popes, generals, women, the people, birds and bees".[3] Metternich feared journalists and university professors every bit as much as he feared raving Jacobin demagogues who spewed irrationalities before surging crowds of open-mouthed ignorant rabble. It was inevitable that he would be prepared to apply all available force in his determination to shore up the crumbling structure of post-Napoleonic Europe.

It seemed unlikely that there would be a massive outbreak all over the continent, yet it was obvious that new strains and tensions might soon develop. Liberal West versus conservative East, perhaps? One had only to think of the implications of the spread of revolutionary ideas to Spain or Belgium or Italy or Poland or—heaven forbid—to the heartland of Germany and the streets of Vienna. Altogether, Meternich must have spent those stormy days of July 1830 listening apprehensively to the rumble of distant thunder.

The first lightning flash illuminated the skies on 25 August, barely a month after the Paris revolution. Brussels went into insurrection against the Dutch. A curious revolution. An outsider would have been much puzzled, trying to decide just what the crux of the protest might be. Protestantism? The constitution? The government? The ruling dynasty? How much trouble had been entailed in the settlement of the Belgian problem—all that persuasion and cajoling and threatening that had gone into the construction of that unstable Kingdom of the Netherlands. Catholics and Calvinists together under one king.

It has been wittily said that the Dutch did not hesitate for a moment before stating an opinion—it was an attack by Belgium on Holland, and this brisk definition of the situation gave direction to the course of events. "The rebels overcame their uncertainties; the contradictory nature of their actions was resolved by the nationalist purpose so thoughtlessly placed at their disposal."[4] By the end of September the Dutch held nothing but Antwerp and the new kingdom of Belgium rapidly came into being. Almost immediately there was talk of a constitution modeled on that of the United States of America.

Here was a monstrous event. Other considerations aside, the *Deutscher Bund* would probably lose at least part of Luxemburg to Belgian rule, but the major cause for alarm was the fact that the whole principle of legitimacy as laid down by the Congress of Vienna had been challenged, and this was the very principle that was basic to the entire system of international checks and balances. Suppose France under the new king Louis-Philippe were to invade Belgium. What then? Would Russia allow this to happen, or would the principle of intervention come into play? Would there be a general war?

Another menacing problem: Poland. Always a hotbed of revolution, its universities in constant turmoil, and people all over Europe in sympathy with them. Galicia was under Austrian control, and the region around Posen had become a Prussian grand duchy. With the exception of Cracow, the remaining territory was supposed to be forever united to Russia under Grand Duke Constantin. If revolution caught hold there, liberals everywhere would leap to their feet, shouting wild encouragement.

When the news of events in Belgium reached Poland, the effect was indeed electric. Revolution broke out in November in the Prussian province of Posen.—A nightmare for any conservative statesman who believed that Germany must be held, because this was a clear threat to the integrity of Prussian territory. Prussia was constrained to place a large army on its frontier because otherwise the revolutionary contagion might spread from Posen to the Prussian heartland. This move in itself brought difficulties because there were many Polish conscripts in the Prussian army and they now deserted, rushing to help their fellow countrymen dispose of the tyrants. There was an added internal problem, in that liberals within the Prussian administration were inclined to align themselves with the Poles and express hostility toward actions of their own government.

When the attempted revolution in Poland failed, great tides of refugees flowed across German soil. By 1832, there were an estimated six thousand Polish *émigrés* in Paris.[5] These people probably did as much as any liberal publicist ever did, in popularizing the idea of a fight for freedom. The fact that they gained additional support through public indignation over the papal brief issued by Gregory XVI in 1832 that officially condemned the rebellion in the name of legitimate monarchy must have reinforced Metternich's impression that the pestilence of revolution was spreading.

His only consolation in the aftermath of the Polish rising must have been the split that developed between the two camps of refugees who swarmed into the west. There were moderates who held that in due time France and England would come into conflict with Russia, and that with their victory Poland would emerge free, as an independent state. The leader of this contingent was the indefatigable Adam Jerzey Czartoryski (1770–1861), who settled himself in Paris for three decades of fruitless waiting and complex diplomatic activity.[6] On the other side was a growing radical group. These people busily engaged in conspiracy, planning a violently democratic serf-based revolution.

The July revolution had led to the deposition of Charles X, it is true, but he was replaced on the French throne by Louis-Philippe of the house of Orléans. The new monarch was supported by most French liberals, to the disgust of dreamy romantic German students. The response of the new regime to demands for universal suffrage was feeble. By a law of 1831, French suffrage was extended only to those who were paying a direct property tax of two hundred or more francs. In other words, as a consequence of that high restrictive qualification, only about 250,000 males out of a total of some nine millions were eligible as voters. The dogma of popular sovereignty had been manipulated in justification of the franchise of the property owners.[7] François Guizot cynically advised a questioner that if he wanted a vote, he should exert himself and acquire wealth. The increasingly radicalized set of young Germans who kept alive the flame of liberalism and patriotic ardor that had flashed up at the time of Napoleon's fall was profoundly upset.[8] This was precisely the kind of reaction that Metternich anticipated with so much anguish.

Both Vienna and Berlin kept watchful eyes on the new French government under Louis-Philippe, wondering if it would prove to be stable. A report was filed by the Prussian representative in Karlsruhe that went into detail on the political mood of France in the late fall of 1832. France was still in a provisional condition, in the opinion of the Prussian emissary. There was a prevailing mood of dissatisfaction. The new monarch was not respected, he thought, and for that reason he would always have difficulty in developing a solid ministry that would have the trust of the nation. One candidate for cabinet rank was too doctrinaire, another an excellent military man with no understanding of governmental matters. Another lacked the necessary *trempe d'âme* [firmness: literally, tempering of the soul] that a statesman has to have. Guizot was a man of spirit and wisdom of course, but his was only "school wisdom". French industrialists were mortally afraid of another revolution. The people in general were not calling for war, but they still thought of France as invincible, and if the army were to march into Belgium as national honor seemed to require, fierce patriotism would prevail and party quarrels would be forgotten, but if the war were to end in defeat, there would be disorder and revolution, even terror. The idea of defending the Rhine border still had its advocates. The French would never understand that Alsace would never be French in the true sense. "People in Alsace call Frenchmen foreigners." But the people on the left bank of the Rhine hated Germans and the rabble there would like nothing better than an excuse for raids across the river. "The more I get to know the French, the more I am convinced that they are incapable of enjoying true freedom. What they admire in their rulers is power and force and glitter . . . Louis XIV and Napoleon were the right rulers for the French."[9]

In the immediate aftermath of the July revolution in Paris, Germans were responding to the French excitement by staging spotty uprisings that had little or no revolutionary intent. People were venting their anger against local conditions. In Aachen, so close to Belgium, for example, mobs of excited individuals who had decked themselves with the French tricolor attacked and destroyed a machinery plant as well as the owner's home. There was a minor riot involving tailors in Berlin. In Hamburg there were riots in late August when citizens became incensed over the rise in duties on beef cattle and wheat. At Kassel, bakeries were stormed. In Schwerin a mob burned the contents of the mint and tried to fire the building. In Karlsruhe and Mannheim, there were outbursts as early as mid-September that were directed against Jewish merchants.

The violence of aggrieved artisans and unemployed workmen, and of women rioting because of the high cost of bread, drew little sympathy from most of the liberals. Karl von Rotteck called them "crimes against the community without concern for the fatherland and constitution"—a poignant example of the non-meeting of minds of liberals and the desperate lower classes.

Desperation was acute in Oberhessen. Trouble began on 19 September in the little town of Büdingen[10] and spread from there to Hanau.

Participants in the riots were locals at first, but soon peasants were present in threatening numbers. The shout of Long live freedom and equality echoed. The *Graf* von Isenburg-Büdingen appealed for military assistance, and although prisoners were taken and peace seemed to be restored, it soon became evident that there was a common target—the customs houses. Household industry (linen and woolen goods) had come to a standstill after the Prussian customs law went into effect. So impoverished was the region that an estimated twelve thousand people had emigrated to Brazil in the years 1823–1829.[11] Delegates who had been dispatched to Kassel with instructions that they demand relief from the customs burden returned to Hanau with a document that promised a constitution but failed to mention customs duties. Mobs headed for the customs houses, broke in the doors, destroyed the records and overturned the furniture. All sorts of demands cropped up. The soldiers clamored for a specified term of service, the butchers wanted relief from high taxes, and the guilds wanted their former rights restored.

There was enormous unrest on the countryside toward the end of September, though it did not have the look of a true revolution. It was still only the peasants who were active. Practically all the customs houses were destroyed, and there was serious trouble in areas controlled by members of the high nobility [the *Standesherren*]. The unhappy Isenburg house confronted peasants who demanded relief from manorial duties. Resistance to any idea of relief for the peasants had always been strenuous, and resentment ran high on that account. The peasants regarded themselves as doubly, even trebly taxed [by the state, by the overlords, by the church]. They broke into the home of the *Graf* von Isenburg-Wächtersbach at midnight, forcing him to sign a document in which he released them from all service, direct taxes, payments and punishment. The noble at least saved his castle by these concessions but he fled, only to be captured by peasants at nearby Gelnhausen, where he was again forced to sign a release from obligations.

Excitement continued at Büdingen, where seething crowds called for the release of the rioters who had been incarcerated in the first hours of the disorder. The mob grew until it comprised more than fifteen hundred, who assembled at the town gates with banners. They were going to move on to other towns, and planned ultimately to attack Giessen and Darmstadt. They marched forth exultantly, armed with pitchforks. In each town, they rang the storm bell and the people were ordered to assemble. Each household was required to furnish at least one male for their army. If a family showed reluctance or failed to comply, the house was burned. The new recruits were then marched off to the next town, where the manoeuver was repeated. The marchers were joined voluntarily by people from the various small villages, who stood at the crossroads waiting for them. In every village, papers were burned and mortgage books destroyed. Foresters were forced to throw down all signs that forbade trespass. The mayor, the pastor, the teacher—all were required to join in the march. Later, in defense, the peasants pointed out that they had been accompanied by such authorities, but in fact they had had no leaders.

The major crisis of the Hessian troubles came at Södel on 30 September, when light cavalry blindly attacked the residents of the town rather than the insurgents, who had withdrawn. The innocent people who were killed had come out of their houses simply in curiosity, or to welcome the troops. There was an uproar in the press throughout Germany, and conflicting reports were published, some to the effect that a shot had been fired at the cavalry. Long after the troops had been tried and given negligible sentences and about two hundred of the insurrectionists had been jailed for periods up to fifteen years, the incident was remembered bitterly. Georg Büchner wrote that the aristocrats "drown out your sighs with their drums, and crush your skulls with their clubs if you come around to thinking that you are free men. They are the legal murderers who protect the legal robbers. Remember Södel!"[12]

There was random violence in the cities, and serious trouble in areas where the *Standesherren* still exacted their manorial dues and services. In states where there was a constitution in place, there appears to have been less trouble, and this may even have been the case in parts of Germany where the ruler could be persuaded (or forced) to adopt a constitution. There was a little of both the random action and the more reasoned handling of problems in Saxony. The future radical leader, former tailor and "true socialist" Wilhelm Weitling watched disruptive crowds on the streets of Leipzig. Here is his description of what he saw:

> In one night the people were masters of the city and its environs. Because they did not know what else to do, they set about to destroy a dozen houses. Everyone sought to express his anger in his own way: . . . broke up the furniture of an unpopular lawyer, while some apprentices demolished the house and furniture of an official employed in the passport office who was hated for his harshness.[13]

This is perhaps a suitable place to mention an incident involving Weitling and Heine that shows how difficult it was for intellectual revolutionists like the poet to find common ground with radicals "from the streets" such as Weitling. Heine says that he was vaguely bothered because Weitling did not remove his hat when he addressed him and continued to sit cross-legged, rubbing his leg. At first Heine thought that the posture might be a reflection of previous employment as a tailor who would customarily crouch over his work, but at some point he was moved to ask Weitling why he kept on rubbing his leg. The answer was startlingly simple. While he was in jail the ring of his chains had been too tight below the knee and chafed his leg, which had become chronically irritated. Heine, deeply embarrassed, asked himself how it was that he could not speak and act naturally with this martyr to the cause—"I, who once kissed with burning lips the relics of the tailor John of Leyden . . ." Why did he feel such "insurmountable aversion" to this living martyr?[14]

At Leipzig the rioters were artisans, angry because of the arrest of a blacksmith's apprentice. The uncoordinated Leipzig rising had a positive result, however. Saxony had been badly broken up by the action of the Congress of Vienna, and there it stood as a prime example of the rotten antequated feudal ways of a dying system of statehood. Leipzig, in the center of this, was a lively industrial center where there were intelligent liberal-minded civil servants who understood that the old system could not survive. These civil servants managed by clever manoeuvering to thrust aside the unpopular and rather stupid ruler, adding a co-regent in the person of young *Fürst* Friedrich August. Here the intelligent new regent and the civil servants together framed a constitution for Saxony that came into force in the fall of 1831. [15]

Braunschweig witnessed a personal attack on the detested *Herzog* Karl II. About a decade earlier, his arrogant misrule had been the subject of debate before the *Bundestag* at Frankfurt, where it had snagged on tedious disagreements between Metternich on one side and Prussia and Great Britain on the other. In the meantime, *Herzog* Karl had pleased himself by the grace of God to be utterly irresponsible, but now skilled irenic negotiations led by Wilhelm Bode ended in deposition of the duke and his replacement by his brother, *Herzog* Wilhelm von Braunschweig-Öls. The new ruler promised to set up a constitution for his people, and in this way the violent unrest that was sweeping the country was avoided.

In Hannover there was a violent and exciting three-day student riot that brought positive results. The constitution that had been in place since the first post-Napoleonic years was subjected to close scrutiny and reform, largely the work of Johann Bertram Stüve (1798–1872). Here the lower house gained both middle class and peasant representatives, as well as broadened power for legislation and budget preparation. This constitution unfortunately was destined to be thrown out contemptuously by the next Hannoverian monarch, the Duke of Cumberland who ascended the throne as Ernst August I at the time of the accession of Queen Victoria to the throne of England. Ernst August's arrogant action provoked the famous protest of seven Göttingen professors, some of the most distinguished men of the times.

In Kurhessen (Hesse-Kassel), demonstrations in the capital ended successfully with promulgation of a constitution, but the way that led to this result was a little different in that there was a meeting of minds in Kurhessen. Peasants, university professors, landed people, even the stuffy members of the *Mittelstand* united in their desire to rid themselves of the *Kurfürst* Wilhelm II, who was obnoxious in many ways, including his ill-treatment of his wife. That fine lady had divorced him, but the elector persisted in stubborn infatuation for a mistress on whom he lavished money and attention. He wanted to make her a princess. The coalition of people who opposed him forced him out. He grouchily left the city to join his mistress elsewhere and turned the business of governing over to a nominal co-regent, his son Friedrich Wilhelm. Under the excellent leadership of Sylvester Jordan (1792–1861), a Marburg law professor, a constitution was hammered out, embodying provisions that were a firm protection of citizen's rights. The single house was to have control of taxes and legislation, even the right to initiate laws, which was a novelty in Germany. The co-regent and later *Kurfürst* Friedrich Wilhelm was not much better than his father, accepting the constitution with poorly concealed animosity. It is sad that Jordan himself was fated at a later time to incur the new ruler's dislike and undergo imprisonment.

The various disturbances gradually subsided, but all persons in authority must have been keenly aware of a shift, a something that suggested a sea change. Liberalism was raising its head again, and subversive ideas were afloat. In addition to official concern about possible renewed *Burschenschaft* activity, there was a constant worry that unruly liberals might absorb revolutionary ideas from the French, and that the French might cooperate with them. Besides, the Polish uprising had stirred up great waves of enthusiasm. When Warsaw fell, Polish refugees in large numbers poured through, en route to France and Switzerland. These people of the "Great Emigration" were welcomed as heroic freedom fighters and were much celebrated.

The poet Adam Mickiewicz (1798–1855) was among them. It was understandable that men such as he would exert a tremendous appeal. Aleksandr Herzen met him at a later time in Paris, and observed that his weary eyes suggested unhappiness endured, and that with his obvious acquaintance with spiritual pain he was "the moulded likeness of the fate of Poland".[16]

Political refugees presented a serious problem to the various departments of state who were supposed to maintain good relations with their counterparts among the other European powers. What to do with these immigrants who arrived without passports or diplomatic protection, and who in all likelihood would continue their revolutionary conspiracies? The Poles alone made up about three-quarters of the exiles who had fled to France, and the popularity of their cause complicated affairs everywhere.[17] The French before long were forced reluctantly to institute a system of surveillance, and to arrest one hundred and sixty-eight Polish refugees, and expel forty-seven of them. Others were rounded up and incarcerated at Mont-Saint-Michel and at various designated centers of detention.[18]

The Prussian envoy in Karlsruhe was troubled because Stephanie, the widowed *Grossherzogin* of Hesse-Darmstadt, seemed to be encouraging these undesirable international heroes. At a ball in nearby Mannheim, two guests of hers, Polish officers in full uniform, had collected contributions for their insurrectionary cause, and people had sung the *Marseillaise*. Moreover, it was disturbing that the *Grossherzogin* had already had friendly ties with the new French ambassador Bouillé, even before he arrived in Germany on his present assignment.[19]

Chopin, in Paris, reported to a friend that immense crowds had surged around his neighborhood, enthusiastically wanting to greet the Italian general Girolamo Ramorino of somewhat tarnished reputation, who had taken part in the Polish insurrection, but who was afraid to present himself before the crowd because he thought the government authorities might object. Young men from *la jeune France* with their little beards and special signature manner of tying their ties, numbering about a thousand marched to the *Cité bergère*, shouting *Vive les polonais* and created such a commotion that mounted police rode on the pavements, "shoving aside the excited and muttering crowd, seizing, arresting free citizens," but it all ended around eleven o'clock with singing of *Allons enfants de la patrie*—"You will scarcely realize what an impression these menacing voices produced on me."[20]

Standing up for the Poles was not an activity that Louis-Philippe viewed with dispassionate reserve. Although Lafayette had played an important part in effecting the monarch's rise to power, he lost his position as head of the national guard because of his pro-Poland attitude.[21]

The students' *Burschenschaft* movement in Germany did indeed exist in a somewhat attenuated form which was still enough to cause university officials to watch them suspiciously. The students were following events in France closely. At Munich, for example, the "Germania" *Burschenschaft* brought trouble down on its own head when the July revolution erupted.[22] Radical members hailed the uprising with wild enthusiasm even though they did not go beyond words into action. On Christmas Eve 1830 they clashed with police, and the disorder continued to rage for four nights. Although not many students were involved after the first disturbance, Bavaria's king Ludwig decided that the Revolution had indeed arrived on his doorstep and was threatening him and his throne. The university rector reported that all participants were to be severely punished, the "Germania" dissolved, and its members expelled. This report was followed by a cabinet decision to close the university until the summer term, but the harsh order was appealed and his Majesty graciously allowed the university to continue in session. The students represented a bread-and-butter issue for the local merchants, who did not want to see money-spending customers banished. The Munich *Mittelstand* tended to speak its mind on practical matters, taking to the streets in protest when a new high tax was levied on beer. "Germania" members were excluded at first, but Ludwig intervened on their behalf. Even so, forty-four of them were dismissed. The most important result of the December disturbances was the politicizing of the *Burschenschaften*, whose members thereafter joined in supporting the growing opposition in the Bavarian lower house, the *Landtag*.

The events at Munich were not an isolated phenomenon. A statistical study of popular disorders shows that "In the typical case . . . university authorities suspended and/or facilitated the arrest of local activist students." An incident at Heidelberg where the military were called in is mentioned by way of example.[23] No doubt the authorities were justified in their alarm. Many a student of the 1830's was to become a radical in the revolutionary years. If the revolution had a core, it was the young educated elite.

Disturbances in the year 1832 were especially troublesome in the Bavarian Palatinate. Inhabitants of this region were resentful because they had been annexed to Bavaria, which was a foreign country to them. Ever since the Tenth Century, the Palatinate had been handed around or chopped up and then reassembled in a variety of patterns. The unfortunate region is said to have lost three-quarters of its population during the Thirty Years' War, and after that the devastation continued at the hands of Louis XIV. Following the French Revolution the Palatinate was split between France, Baden and Hesse-Darmstadt, but after the Vienna settlement of 1815 the territory on the right bank of the Rhine had been ceded to Bavaria, which was predominantly Catholic. The Palatinate was a Calvinist stronghold. (Need one wonder that so many immigrants who poured into the United States were Palatinate Germans?)—The new customs arrangements of the *Zollverein* in the 1830's had a disastrous effect on the Palatinate economy, and understandably there was rioting. Matters were not helped when the harvest was unusually poor.

For some reason, press censorship had not been as strict in the Palatinate as in other parts of Bavaria, with the result that journalists with unacceptably liberal views had settled there. One of these was Johann Georg Wirth (1798–1848).

Wirth's was the most fertile brain in the peoples' movement of the thirties.[24] His grandfather was a pastor, and his father before him was "a wild man", an official of the old Empire, benevolent and nature-loving. Wirth himself had known the assassin Karl Ludwig Sand as a fellow student, and Hegel had been his university rector. In his days as a lawyer, one of his earliest productions had been a closely argued proposal for a reform of the Bavarian civil process. As a journalist, he had a high view of the honor of his calling, and campaigned vigorously from the very beginning of his career with sturdy expressions of strong objection to censorship. He saw no value in the idea of joining forces with France.[25] (Here he opposed the views of his colleague Siebenpfeiffer.) In Wirth's view, France stood as an example of the idea of a republic, though perhaps not a permanent one. More important to him was the example of the United States of America. "A spark of freedom glowed in him and was never extinguished."

Philipp Jakob Siebenpfeiffer (1789–1846), who joined forces with Wirth, was a man who was struggling up from the lower classes. His father was a poor tailor in Baden. Siebenpfeiffer had nothing of Wirth's general good humor and charm of manner. He was an embittered man, and a hothead. He was thin and gangly with a shock of black hair and parchment-yellow face, his prominent staring eyes flickering with restless fanaticism. His journal, *Rheinbayern* that he published in Zweibrücken bore a motto: *Licht, Ordnung, Freiheit* [light, order, freedom]. The Bavarian government in whose civil service Siebenpfeiffer was employed, thought to silence him by transferring him to a post somewhere on the upper Danube, but he went to court and managed to be retired with compensation. Authorities in Munich then attacked, revoking the old Napoleonic decree of 1810 that had guaranteed freedom of the press and on that basis forbidding him to continue publication of his paper.

Wirth meanwhile had also run into trouble. The two men's common experience of threats of fines and arrest drew them together, in spite of their differing views.

Wirth wanted to fund his paper. He started the ball rolling by organizing a festival that was attended by three hundred and fifty people, gathered together at Zweibrücken in honor of Friedrich Schüler, a well known opposition leader. Schüler rose to the occasion by praising Wirth and Siebenpfeiffer as champions of the free press. Apparently it was on this occasion—similar to the famous incendiary political banquets of France in 1847 and 1848—that Wirth launched the idea of an all-German press association. (This was in January of 1832.) The *Pressverein* would reunite Germany in spirit. The idea caught on, with membership spreading rapidly to Coburg, Hannover, Leipzig, Halle and Braunschweig. The Prussian government recognized wildfire when it saw it, and immediately suppressed the society as revolutionary. So also Bavaria, Hesse-Darmstadt and Frankfurt. Wirth was imprisoned and his press was sealed. He was accused of having agitated the citizens of Bavaria because his society was calling for the overthrow of the government and the establishment of a conspiracy for attacks that would detonate a revolution.

The appeals court at Zweibrücken freed him in mid-April and the *Pressverein* joyously issued 60,000 flyers announcing the fact. Here, by the way, is evidence of still one more novel element brought into the world by the advent of new technology. It was only with a steam-powered press that such a volume of material could be spewed out so rapidly. Throughout the coming revolution, agitators would be able to flood the streets of great metropolitan centers like Paris, Vienna, and Berlin with massive issues of revolutionary broadsides, pamphlets, and wall posters.

The Bavarian government was angered by Wirth's release, and threatened members of the press society harshly, but the organization flourished. Five thousand joined, most of them from Bavaria proper and the Palatinate. In their zeal, they established more than a hundred branches, not as a political party exactly, yet still the kind of organization that activists tend to join. Branches popped up as far away as Paris (Heine and Ludwig Börne were members there, and so was Lafayette.)

The Paris *Pressverein* soon had about one hundred members. The story of this organization is none too clear, but it is said to have attracted not only political exiles but also artisans who were spending their *Wanderjahr* in France. (So says Georg Adler) This new membership rather altered the character of the society, which changed its name to *Deutscher Volksverein*. The people's organization ran afoul of the French authorities and was disbanded toward the end of 1833, but it reformed in the spring of 1834 as the *Deutscher Bund der Geächteten* [outlaws] and is regarded as an offshoot of the Italian *Carbonari*. They were radicals, declaring that their objective (written in secret documents that were accessible only to initiates) was the liberation of Germany from the yoke of ignominious servitude and . . . establishment and maintenance of social and political equality, freedom, civic virtue and people's unity, first in lands of German speech and custom and subsequently among all the other peoples of the earth.

There were two hundred members of this visionary group, who took a fearsome oath, pledging themselves to secrecy. These people, most of them journeymen, were supposed to return to Germany where they would establish branches in various cities after completion of their *Wanderjahr* abroad.[26]

Another workers' organization split off from the *Geächteten*. This was the *Bund der Gerechten* [league of the just] whose best known member was Wilhelm Weitling (1808–1871). The *Bund der Gerechten* in turn was the immediate ancestor of the Communist League, founded in London in 1847, and it seems to have had a connection of sorts with the *Société des saisons* headed by the French radical Louis-Auguste Blanqui, one of the most famous of the organizers of secret societies.[27] All this is a tangled uncertain story, but the evidence seems to be solid enough to justify a comment on its oddity. Workers' organizations in the land of Karl Marx's birth originated beyond the German frontier.

What was it that Engels once said about Germany? He called it a country where rivers and revolutions run into the sands.

* * * * * * *

To return to Johann Georg Wirth: he rapidly became a recognized hero, honored by torchlight processions, and his paper was definitively suppressed. The not unexpected response was the appearance of a storm of flyers and wall posters. Police began to inspect booksellers' premises and printshops.

A man of Wirth's intelligence and determination was bound to make himself heard. Idealistically, he was saying that "with the help of a democratically organized Poland, a Germany based on a democratic constitution, and an alliance of the French, German and Polish people, the way will be prepared for a European society of nations."

Liberty trees began to show up in various towns, topped with Phrygian-style liberty caps, in defiance of authorities who had the offending trees chopped down during the night, only to confront new plantings on the following morning. At Annweiler where a liberty tree was set up on 6 May, chopped down overnight and replaced in the morning, the local commissioner threatened to call in the military, but the townspeople assembled, armed with axes and pitchforks, and the commissioner hastily called back the soldiers.

Popular assemblies were forbidden in west Germany, but people were becoming bolder. As early as 1827 there had been public celebrations honoring Albrecht Dürer, and the idea of such gatherings caught the public's imagination. *Turnvater* Friedrich Ludwig Jahn was quoted to the effect that the mere act of assembly was an element of patriotism.[28] In 1832, there was a folk festival early in April at Weinheim, another at Badenweiler, still another at Zweibrücken that was attended by delegations from all over the Bavarian Palatinate. Wirth and Siebenpfeiffer had an inspiration and energetically organized a festival that was to be held at the old ruined castle of Hambach near Neustadt, not on 26 May, the day customarily set aside in Bavaria for celebration of the Bavarian Constitution, but rather for the following day. The call for the "German May" festival was addressed not only to German men but also to *Deutsche Frauen und Jungfrauen*— the first time in Germany that women had been invited to join as political activists.

There was alarm in Vienna that spring when it became evident that something extraordinary was brewing in the Rhineland. The Austrian ambassador *Graf* von Spiegel reported to Metternich that both the famed French general Lamarque[29] and Lafayette had been invited to attend. The ambassador was rather put out because the Bavarian minister had not seen fit to inform him that the festival had been officially canceled (he had only learned this from the public press, he said) and he expressed the hope that *Euer Durchlaucht* had been treated more courteously.

The festival had in fact not been canceled after all. Metternich wrote to his friend von Wrede, expressing amazement at the dispatch in the morning paper (21 May 1832) which announced that the proposed festival was to go on as originally scheduled. The magistrate of the little community of Neustadt near the ruined Hambach castle had ruled that the prohibition was counter to the law. "This weakness marks the beginning of the revolution in Rhenish Bavaria," predicted Metternich. "The people of Baden and Württemberg and Hesse, then the people of Nassau, then the people of Frankfurt and so on and so on will not hang back."[30] Much as Metternich and Wrede may have longed to use force, they understood that in Bavaria especially there was an intense desire to avoid anything that might provoke France into interference with affairs of western Germany.

Metternich insisted in his note to von Wrede that he was not just letting his emotions run away with him, but this was hardly the case of the Russian ambassador in Frankfurt, who reported on the festival to chancellor Nesselrode in Moscow.

> It suffices to name the *coryphées de l'orgie* [Wirth and Siebenpfeiffer] to be able to judge the incendiary speeches that were made under these circumstances. Anarchy is complete. Rhenish Bavaria is the model for German insurrection, and the government is doing nothing to put down this perfidious propaganda.[31]

In spite of his excitement, the Russian emissary noticed a few interesting details. Those tricolor cocardes that everybody wore, for example, had been made in wholesale quantities by "the detestable population" of Mainz, where the local government had announced that anyone who wore such an emblem on the city streets would be arrested.

What had happened brings to mind the outpouring of a new generation that occurred at Woodstock. The Hambach gathering (May 1832) attracted about thirty thousand people. The number alone is amazing, in view of the fact that at that time there were still no railroads and everyone must have traveled either by horse-drawn vehicle or on foot. There would have been no overnight accommodations for such a swarm. Many must have slept in the open. Nothing in the records shows that any thought had been taken about sanitary arrangements: if latrines had indeed been dug, reporters were too prudish to mention the fact. There was no shelter, which means that when the rain came pelting down, everyone simply stood there quietly, soaking wet.

The people who attended the festival ranged in age from twenty to about fifty. The older ones would have been members of the early *Burschenschaft* and *Turnverein* movements, and presumably those who belonged to choral societies were also there in force. The impact

Figure 2 HAMBACH (27 May 1832). The speakers' platform was just below the ruined castle (the small flag-topped structure at the top left). This was the first occasion on which women played an active political role: they march prominently just behind the flag bearer in the foreground.

of this enormous assemblage must have been terrific because such meetings were unknown in Germany. Never before had they experienced that strong sensation of affection for one's fellow man that sweeps over a crowd like that. They celebrated their solidarity by waving tri-color flags (black-red-gold) and singing lustily as they marched in orderly procession, arranged in groups led by musicians. Women did not attend in great numbers, but those who did were up near the head of the parade, accompanied by an honor guard, and in turn acting as an informal honor guard for one who carried a Polish flag. Not all could manage to get within hearing-distance of the speakers on the platform up near the ruined castle. Many contented themselves with standing around the foot of the hill, singing.

The speakers, rain or no rain, were cheered in spite of their varying viewpoints. In the words of Heine, "unreasonable things were often said there" (he had his information from Ludwig Börne, who had been present) but he felt that the ultimate authority of reason was recognized. Wirth, the organizer, had a touchingly innocent faith in the power of reason. The best instrument for progress and liberation was an alliance of patriots who intended to teach the people about the reforms that were necessary. "If only twenty such men, bound together by a common cause and led by a man they trusted . . . tirelessly pursued their mission . . . the great work must succeed." Siebenpfeiffer was eloquent. "We devote our lives to science and art," he said.

> We measure the stars, examine moon and sun; we represent God and man, hell and heaven in poetic pictures; we delve into the physical and spiritual world, but . . . study of what the Fatherland needs is high treason. . . . We envy the north Americans for their fortunate fate that they have created for themselves, but we knavishly bend our necks beneath the yoke of oppression.[32]

The festival celebrants were generally well-behaved and orderly, although suspiciously wary officials thought that they were radicals or nihilists or even worse and collected lists of attendees who were regarded as subversives. More than half were academics or booksellers or students.[33] In general they were calling for *Einigkeit und Recht und Freiheit*, as the great anthem *Deutschland über Alles* expresses it.

No matter how earnest and innocent they were, these people were destined to be hounded because Metternich had quickly decided that Bavaria had shown herself unable to shore up the dam and prevent the surge of radical ideas rolling in from France. "*Le libéralisme a cédé la place au radicalisme*," he told his ambassador to Prussia.

The organizers of the Hambach festival were sent to the fortress at Landau for investigation. Wirth made a speech in his own defense that lasted for two days and that gained wide circulation during the 1848 revolution as *Die Rechte des deutschen Volkes* [the rights of the German people]. He and seven others, including Siebenpfeiffer, were cleared of the charge of high treason but most were retried by the annoyed Bavarian authorities. This time Wirth, Siebenpfeiffer and another man—Hochdörfer—were sentenced to two years of imprisonment and the rest of the defendants for lesser terms.

Punishment meant potential economic ruin for the Hambacher men.[34] Siebenpfeiffer managed to escape from prison in November of 1833 and fled to Switzerland, where by the following year he was established as a professor at the university of Bern but in the next year he succumbed to a stroke. Wirth was helped to escape as he was being moved from one prison to another, but refused to run away. After his release in 1836 he was still under police surveillance in his home town of Hof. He moved to Alsace, lived briefly in Nancy, then in Switzerland, where he worked on his history of Germany. At the Frankfurt *Parlament* of 1848 he served first as an alternate, later as a delegate from Reuss-Schleitz-Lobenstein. He died during the parliament sessions, in a shabby little room, on 26 July 1848. His funeral oration was pronounced by Robert Blum, who was destined to become the most celebrated martyr of the revolution.

The one who suffered the most exaggerated persecution was the young student Karl Heinrich Brüggemann [35] (later the well-known editor of the *Kölnische Zeitung*).

He had been one of the leading student speakers at Hambach, A small person whose health was fragile, he was surprizingly tough and daring. He thought of Greek and German civilization with special reverence, and admired English political traits. He had delivered a stirring speech at the ruined cloister of Limburg in celebration of the French revolution of July, and after that he had attracted a heterogeneous circle of idealistic students at Heidelberg who called for a German constitutional monarch, and who were strongly supportive of the Polish revolution and of freedom of the press. Whatever else this mixed group of enthusiasts wanted, they were unified in their belief in a "lawful spiritual revolution". With spiritual power they thought they could do without weapons because spirit is stronger than steel.

After the festival at Hambach Brüggemann was first incarcerated at Heidelberg, then released, then arrested again and sent from Baden to Prussia. He was taken there as a common criminal and forced to walk most of the way under armed guard. Because in the hearings before the Berlin court he refused to name any of his colleagues, he was labeled a "stubborn subject" and placed in solitary confinement in a dark cell. The court sentenced him on grounds of high treason to death "beneath the wheel"—a singularly atrocious idea. The sentence was subsequently commuted to simple death under the blade. This sentence in turn was commuted to life imprisonment and then to fifteen years. In 1836 his sister handed a petition for pardon to the crown prince, and on 14 August 1840 he was released by Friedrich Wilhelm IV in celebration of his accession to the throne of Prussia.

Hambach lives on, still a powerful symbol of the concerted will of the Fatherland, expressed as it had been by people from many walks of life on that extraordinary day. "A whole polyphony", Valentin called it. Here were the first examples of grand style political oratory, where patriotic ideas floodlit the path to 1848. Around the festival "there remains the shimmer of youthful dreams and the melancholy of unavailing effort."

* * * * * * *

Following the Wartburg festival of 1817, the impatient student Karl Ludwig Sand, a disciple of Karl Follen, was moved to take independent action for the honor of his country by his assassination of the playright Kotzebue. The official response to his act took the form of harsh repression from which the whole public suffered. Something similar followed the spectacularly successful Hambach festival.

A small band of *Burschenschaft* hotheads, many of whom were members of the *Schwarze* at Giessen, boiled with impatience because no immediate revolutionary action resulted from the Hambach gathering, and set off on their own independent course.[36] Their adviser was a Protestant minister, the pious Ludwig Weidig, who although he was a convinced revolutionary refused to have any part in the present wild scheme. The *Frankfurter Wachensturm* of 3 April 1833 was so unrealistic in its goal, so miserably conceived, and executed with such a lack of finesse that altogether it has the look of a prank cooked up by bored sophomores on a college campus—certainly not an event that has to be taken seriously as a piece of history. Unfortunately, it had serious results, just as Karl Sand's action did.

For one thing, the puerile *Putsch* at Frankfurt nullified the serious efforts that had been made by an earnest group of men who were trying to sustain the idea that actuated the members of Wirth's

Pressverein. Working with a "central committee" at Frankfurt and using innocuous social activities as camouflage, the membership managed to stage a couple of banquets that were attended by politically-minded individuals, and they had already agreed to engage in quiet political action, under the screen of newspapers that they sponsored. It may be that the simple-minded conspirators who were organizing their *Wachensturm* actually did take the *Pressverein* into their confidence as accusers claimed: however that may be, the investigation that was launched after the failed *Putch* caught the organization in its net. One member, Dr. Friedrich Sigmund Jucho (1805–1884), a lawyer, was sentenced to five years of imprisonment.[37]

It seems to be clear that the *Pressverein* had nothing to do with the planning of the idiotic *Wachensturm* affair. The idea was to capture the guards of the police headquarters at Frankfurt and free any political prisoners they held. Next the building of the *Bundestag* would be stormed, and a republic proclaimed. Why all this commotion in Frankfurt? Didn't they grasp the fact that the true effective power was in Vienna and Berlin?—The plan was to be carried out by a handful of men, about fifty altogether, including students, a few Poles, a workman or two, and some of the Frankfurt street people—decked out in various improvised uniforms and insignia and armed with pistols, daggers and a couple of old French muskets.

The absurd mêlée took about an hour and a half. The prisoners they wanted to release were reluctant to accept freedom at their hands, and when the police reinforcements arrived with firearms and bayonets they made short work of the revolutionary force. About twenty people were wounded, while six soldiers and an innocent bystander were killed.

This cloud-cuckoo extravaganza inevitably stimulated officialdom to exaggerated reactions. A special session of the *Bundesversammlung* was called. The military commission reported on 12 April that the attack had been "powerful, led and undertaken from outside the city". This spurred an order that stationed two battalions of infantry and a squadron of cavalry, all from Austria and Prussia—a total of two thousand men—in and around the free city of Frankfurt. The small area around Rödelheim (Hesse-Darmstadt) received a company of Prussian infantry, an arrangement that set off a protracted and heated argument over this deadly affront to the sovereignty of Hesse. The labored discussion and recrimination about these "foreign" troops continued for years, and there were also long cumbersome negotiations about pay and quartering of the troops and stables and feed for the horses. It was not until October 1842 that the last eight hundred men were withdrawn.[38]

A much more sinister matter than this argument that had kept ambassadors hurrying back and forth so feverishly was the establishment of a new investigating body (like the *Zentralunter-suchungskommission* established at Mainz after the Sand assassination)—the new one known as the *Bundesuntersuchungs-zentralbehörde* [central investigating authority of the *Bund*].

Once again, this was the work of Metternich, who within ten days of the event at Frankfurt had been in communication with courts and ministries in Munich, Stuttgart, Karlsruhe, Darmstadt, Frankfurt, Kassel, Hannover, Dresden, Copenhagen and Oldenburg: it was proposed that separate investigating bodies be established in each of these locations, for collection of data on local episodes of rebellion or unrest, the information then being forwarded to the central office at Frankfurt. An elaborate framework of the new central authority was presented in a series of nine articles . The presiding officer at the time that the new central authority was constituted (8 August 1833) blandly announced that it was neither necessary nor advisable to make public the entire content of any decision that was taken.[39] The delegates agreed that it would be best merely to announce the formation of the office, while results of any specific investigation would only be made known to the authorities in the state concerned. Moreover, the central authority had the right to communicate directly with the court in question. The central authority had thus received the ways and the means for influencing the course of investigations, especially in Prussia and Austria, and they found that judgments by the earlier commission had been too lenient toward the students. On 13 June 1834 it was decided that security was unsatisfactory in Frankfurt, and that the political prisoners should be transferred to the fortress at Mainz. Investigation of the students involved in the *Frankfurter Wachensturm* were not completed until October 1836. One was released at that time, while most of the others received jail sentences that ranged from six months to fifteen years.

In the eyes of patriots and dreamers who had been laboring to develop a united Germany, the establishment of this central authority must have been a supreme irony. The first fruit of their effort for a united Germany was this united all-German action based on principles of suspicion and suppression.

* * * * * * *

Meanwhile life went on. An active agitator and organizer who was busy spreading revolutionary ideas was Georg Büchner, a student at Giessen in 1834, who established a secret society there that was called the *Gesellschaft der Menschenrechte* [society of human rights]. His inspiration came from the French *Sociétés des droits de l'homme et du citoyen*. He seems to have attended some of their meetings as a guest in 1833, while he was a student at Strassburg. He was a fiery young man, calling for a republic. "The relationship between poor and rich is the sole revolutionary element in the world," he declaimed. He did not feel too strongly about the grievances of liberals. It didn't matter, he felt, if "this or that liberal can't get his thoughts published. It's more important that many families aren't able to grease their potatoes." Büchner even preferred monarchical absolutism to liberalism because if the liberals had their way and set up a constitutional monarchy as they did in France, the result would be nothing but a moneyed aristocracy.

Büchner wanted to publish a journal he called the *Hessische Landbote*. (He had already issued his comments on the "bloodbath" at Södel.) The fate of the *Landbote* had its cosmic aspects. The only secret printing press available was under the control of Ludwig Weidig, the reluctant adviser of the *Wachensturm* hotheads. Weidig insisted on checking the contents before printing, and his checking amounted to censorship. The good man earnestly inserted biblical verses and struck out much that Büchner had written. The term "the rich" became "the prominent", for example. Büchner's message was striking enough in spite of the censorship.

> It seems that God created peasants and artisans on the fifth day, and princes and aristocrats on the sixth, and then the Lord said: Rule over all creatures that creep upon the earth, counting peasants and lower class people in with the vermin . . . His [the worker's] sweat is the salt on the table of the aristocrats.

The *Landbote* was circulated in Hesse, but public response was most disheartening. The peasants in whose hands it was placed turned their copies over to the authorities and Büchner had to flee. In July of 1834 Büchner attended an illegal conspiratorial meeting called by Ludwig Weidig,[40] where he reported on his recent visits to Frankfurt, Mainz, Darmstadt, Mannheim and Wiesbaden. In all these cities he had found people who shared his views, he said. The conspirators laid plans for publication of a newspaper in Frankfurt but there was no agreement on Büchner's proposals for radical action. Three of their number engaged in distribution of the *Landbote* and were betrayed by a government spy. Büchner himself fled to France, and Weidig remained free for the moment.

Not long after that the unfortunate Weidig was in chains. Investigations had connected him with the *Frankfurter Wachensturm*. Karl Welcker was to write of him that Weidig had suffered all the fearful consequences of political inquisition. Long secret incarceration while under investigation: a hated and hating judge,—everything that other prisoners endured to a lesser degree or only in part—all was heaped on the head of this unfortunate man. Poor Weidig, who had been rector of the Latin school at Butzbach in Hesse, was a free-thinking man whose ideas did not in any way justify the political torments that he underwent. A pitiful letter to his wife written in prison in March of 1836 spoke lovingly of their children and said that he was trying to keep his sanity by remembering songs "from the time when my mind was clear". He spoke of himself as being one of the *Lebendigbegrabene* [buried alive] and ended by saying that the pain in his head was so "satanic" that he could write no more.[41] By 1837, still languishing in prison, he was suffering from hallucinations and severe pain. He seems to have been beaten on numerous occasions. On 23 February of that year he managed to escape the attention of his jailors long enough to take his own life, slitting his arteries with jagged pieces of a broken bottle.

> *O Vaterland, dein zu getreuer Sohn, er büsste seine Liebe bitter, bitter!* wrote Georg Herwegh.[42] [Oh Fatherland, thy too-faithful son paid for his love bitterly, bitterly]

Members of Büchner's *Gesellschaft der Menschenrechte* were imprisoned in the course of the winter of 1834–35.

* * * * * * *

The damage done to the normal growth of political thought by official repression, surveillance, and censorship affected everyone in Germany. It had promoted what has been described as a large-scale perversion of the public mind.[43]

The contest over freedom of the press, which had the quality of a holy cause among reformers, was bitter.

> I do not believe that the *Bundestag* has the right to forbid me life and breath . . . just as sacred to me as the right to live and breathe is my right to communicate my thoughts and feelings to other men. . . . They have not trusted the moral strength that resides in the people and that grows if freedom of

thought and speech prevail. . . .Censorship is the surest way to destroy the moral strength of the people, as we see throughout history. . . . It is not only the hardest injustice that can happen to writers, publishers and editors, but it is a much broader injustice that is directed against the entire nation, which is being treated like a little child as if one were saying "This and that is not for you to read. You can't understand it. It would lead you into sin."[44]

It is interesting to read, in this same speech, refutation of "an artificial dialectic argument" (Hegel had not been forgotten) that although censorship was directed only to publications within the state of Baden, any criticism in a given article or editorial that could be interpreted as a criticism of the government of other German states would not be publishable.

Yes, Gentlemen: if that is true, writing of newspaper articles and the reading of them would have to be stopped because everything that happens in one state can be referred to other states and the censor would say, "this offends this or that German state and must therefore not be printed."

All this is florid oratory, but there was truth in it. Those who dared to challenge the authorities by publishing items critical of the state risked not just petty interference (fussy checking of travel documents, for example), but it could happen that careers would be destroyed. One could be locked up in prison or exiled.[45] Heine had his troubles as early as 1826, when he published the following ironic piece:

Die deutschen Zensoren - - - - - - - - - - - - - - - - - -
- -
- - - - - - - - - - - - - - - - - - *Dummköpfe* - - - -
- [46]

The juridical council of the German *Bund* issued an official injunction on 10 December 1835 with reference to a school of writers known as the Young Germans. The offending authors are listed by name: Heinrich Heine is one of the five. These men, according to the document, were guilty of attacking the Christian religion in the most insolent way, of speaking disparagingly of existing social conditions, and of attempting to destroy all societal morals. ("If we can weaken people's faith we will make Germany a political force," observed Heine in an optimistic mood.) [47] Governments adhering to the German *Bund* were to apply sanctions against the named writers because of their abuse of the press. This order was intended to affect all editors, publishers, printers, and distributors of the offensive works, who were to suffer the severest penalties for any disobedience. The injunction was extended to include specified publishing houses in Zurich, Herisau, Bern and so on.[48]

An order affecting publishing houses in a foreign country seems inexplicable at first glance but the authorities in Germany knew that the publishers on the far side of the border were not Swiss citizens. They were German refugees and exiles. Revolutionary progaganda flowed into Germany in a steady stream. The creed of these defiant publishers was:

> We believe in freedom. The revolutionary faith is the only religion of our century. Propaganda is its mass or preachment, political association its communion. Its sacrifice is the offering of citizens for the general good, and its baptism is a baptism of blood.[49]

The names of the various offending publishers had come to light shortly after the ill-fated Frankfurt *Putsch*, when the central bureau of investigation had gone to work. They were able to trace German refugees by means of a network of secret agents. Publications had to be smuggled into Germany, where there would be willing readers among former *Burschenschaft* activists who were forbidden to study in foreign universities, especially those of Zürich and Bern.

One of the most famous houses—a target of the German authorities—was *Das literarische Comptoir* in Zürich, headed by Julius Fröbel (1805–1893), a nephew of the famous pedagogue Friedrich Fröbel. It was in this house that the work of the Young Hegelians appeared. Feuerbach, Bauer, Ruge, Marx—all were associated with the *Comptoir*. "Our publishing house is to be the smithy that forges weapons for the party of the future," they proclaimed.

One astonishingly potent weapon forged at the *Comptoir* was a poem written by Georg Herwegh (1817–1875). Carl Schurz recalled that he and his fellow students all chanted this stirring call to arms, not really understanding it but nevertheless deeply moved and excited by it. "It was a frenzy," recalled Robert Prutz. "It caught everybody. Even men of mature years whose political convictions went in an entirely different direction could not resist this poem, the beauty of its rhythms, the glow of its enthusiam. The youth of the country who saw their innermost thought and feelings crystallized in these proud lines were completely carried away."

> *Reisst die Kreuze aus der Erden! Alle sollen Schwerter werden . . . Auch das Schwert hat seine Priester, und wir wollen Priester sein!*[50] [Tear the crosses from the earth. All should be forged into swords . . . The sword also has its priests, and we want to be priests]

"Only one who has known exile understands the love of the Fatherland." wrote Heine from Paris. Exile had strange effects on patriots. Heine was struck by the alteration in his friend and colleague Ludwig Börne when they were reunited there.[51] "There were dangerous sparks flickering in his eyes. He sat or rather lived in a big multicolored dressing gown, as a tortoise lives in its shell, and when he angrily stretched out his little head from time to time, it made an uncomfortable impression. But sympathy took over when he extended his thin hand from the wide sleeve in greeting. There was no trace in his talk of the old harmless humor of the man. Now he was bitter as gall, bloodthirsty and dry. He jumped from subject to subject, no longer out of a madcap mood but rather out of a moody madness. I remember his old comic ways that made me laugh, but now—what treasonous words— what comments—enough to get you twenty years in prison."

When next Heine called on Börne, he found him surrounded by a heterogeneous collection of exiles, among them a couple of German "polar bears" who silently smoked but growled occasionally, and a Polish "wolf" in a red cap whose insipid sentiments were expressed in an unearthly howl. Börne was sarcastic in his remarks and taunts addressed to these followers. He had become bitter about the value of constitutions and seemed to think that the only salvation for the world lay in total destruction. Referring to a newspaper article that announced that Germany was "about to give birth", he snapped that whatever was to be born would have to be torn out with iron instruments.

Aleksandr Herzen wrote some penetrating comments on the condition of exiles. They tend, he observed, to become absorbed in wrangling among themselves, in melancholy self-deception, and they persist in dwelling on the past. Many become "voluntary martyrs, sufferers by vocation, wretches by profession."[52]

Other unhappy exiles who felt strongly about constitutions and who had tried to defend their own were among the heroic "Göttingen Seven", leading faculty members at the famous Hannoverian university whose abrupt dismissal had aroused indignation all over Germany. When he assumed a professorship at Göttingen in 1834, Georg Gervinus had been disturbed by what he described as "a deep silence concerning all affairs and a general flight from scientific discourse itself. Wine and veal roast are more important than the interpretation of Cicero."[53] Such flaccidity probably was a consequence of the oppression that prevailed in Germany at the time. It must have encouraged Ernst August of Cumberland when he ascended the Hannover throne to make the move he did. He abruptly decreed that the constitution that had been established in 1833 was void. He dissolved the *Ständeversammlung* on 1 November 1837 and restored the earlier constitution of 1819 that had been so carefully scrutinized and reformed in 1833. Two weeks later, the arrogant ruler demanded that

Figure 3   THE GÖTTINGEN SEVEN. [From the top] Gervinus—J. Grimm, W. Grimm—Albrecht—Weber, Ewald—Dahlmann.

all officials, who previously had subscribed to an oath supporting the constitution should now take an oath of personal allegiance to him. There was no reaction from the general public to the tyrannical action of their sovereign. The silence that had made Gervinus uneasy continued.

The only reaction was a letter, presented to the *Curatorium* of the university and signed by seven men whose names deserve all honor and respect. They were:

Friedrich Christoph Dahlmann, political theorist and historian
Wilhelm Albrecht, professor of ecclesiastical law
Jakob Grimm, philologist
Wilhelm Grimm, philologist
Georg Gottfried Gervinus, historian
Heinrich Ewald, orientalist
Wilhelm Weber, physicist

The signers explained that they continued to be bound by the oath they had taken to the constitution, and that for that reason they could not participate in the election of delegates to a *Ständeversammlung* that was called on grounds other than those prescribed in that document, nor could they recognize as legal a *Ständeversammlung* that met in contradiction of the provisions of the constitution. The illegal setting aside of the constitution could not be sanctioned by citizens who were mindful of the law. In the eyes of the protesters, the constitution was sacrosanct, a fundamental mechanism that could uphold and promote social justice. Dahlmann, the author of the protest, felt that the state was the basic agent of all human affairs and was especially emphatic about this.

By some route that has never been identified, news of this protest, even its text, was widely distributed even before there had been any official response to it. On the very day that the protest was signed and submitted, a report of it appeared in the *Courrier français*. Two days later, readers of *Gagliani* and *The Times* were informed about it. In their subsequent defense, all the professors asserted that they had no overseas contacts, and even went on to say that "Our tendency is not that of the French revolution. It is not the French liberalism either, that countless people here in this country shudder even to mention."[54]

Apparently it was not the protest in itself that drew a harsh royal reaction on 12 December 1837. It was the speed with which all Europe had received the news that angered the king. Ernst August commanded the immediate departure of Dahlmann, Jakob Grimm and Gervinus from the country. All seven were dismissed from the university.

Gervinus was later to blame the general citizenry for its apathy. It was Gervinus who also understood that although their case had roused intense sympathy that was expressed in torchlight processions and protest meetings, this would all wear off rather quickly. "A few pastors and judges will be moved to look into the matter: a few professors here have expressed themselves honorably, but the whole country is indifferent. The *Mittelstand* that should have gone into action knows nothing of this constitution . . . "[55] Even at that late date, the flint of oppression ignited no revolutionary spark in Germany.

The two Grimm brothers, Gervinus, and Dahlmann were close friends. In subsequent years they maintained contact, writing frequent letters that expressed affectionate concern. Wilhelm Grimm wrote to Gervinus in 1839 from Kassel that he and his brother had decided to undertake an immense project together—a German dictionary that would illustrate the language "as it was from Luther to Goethe, from the historical standpoint". Fifty collaborators were already engaged in this huge work. He said that he was worried about Dahlmann, not having had any word from him for about four months. He had visited him at Jena, where he seemed to be in good spirits and showed improvement in his health, but his last letter had bemoaned "the state of things".

Gervinus wrote back from Heidelberg that he and his wife had spent some time in Italy and had just bought a small vineyard property on the Neckar, planning to build there. (Gervinus and his wife were wealthy, and felt no stress from the harsh turn of events. Some of the others had had to rely on funds collected for them by sympathetic "Göttingen societies.")

If something were to change the situation at Göttingen—the death of the king, for instance—Gervinus felt that he would be in some perplexity what to do. He had had a letter from Dahlmann that reported that his health was poor again. "I think I read between the lines that his spirits are more depressed than his body is burdened." He thought it was ironic, that he and his wife had bought their new home on the anniversary day of the Göttingen protest.[56]

Jakob Grimm wrote a famous piece, entitled "*Über meine Entlassung*" [on my dismissal] that was widely read and had a powerful effect on the public generally.

The lightning that struck my quiet home has moved hearts in wide circles. Is it only human sympathy, or was the stroke propagated electrically, and is there fear that one's own home may be endangered? It was not the arm of the law, the power that required me to vacate a country to which I had been called, where I had performed true honorable service for eight years. "Give the gentleman your hand, he's a refugee," said a grandmother to her grandchild when I had crossed the border on 16 December. And where was I so called? In the land of my birth, that on the evening of the same day had taken me back reluctantly, and even thrust my companion away. . . . I am not such a soft resigned person that I abandon my rights without defending them . . . my good right that, no matter how insignificant it may seem to the world, for me contains all that I have achieved and that I want to preserve unstained and spotless. . . . As long as I draw breath, I shall be happy that I did what I did.[57]

The dismissal of the Göttingen Seven had occurred within weeks of a momentous happening, when intellectuals from all over Germany had gathered in celebration of the centenary of the university. On this rare occasion, 20 September 1837, various scholars took the opportunity to discuss and found a series of annual conferences, the *Versammlungen deutscher Philologen und Schulmänner* [meetings of German philologists and schoolmasters]. Among those who signed the statutes at that time were Jakob and Wilhelm Grimm and Heinrich Ewald, all of whom were dismissed in December.

The meetings began at Nürnberg in the following year and continued up through 1847. The conferences, like those of scientists and phyicians that had been meeting regularly ever since 1822, were daring at a time when even such a thing as a simple meeting of four or more students had to be reported and specially permitted. The men who were engaged in the conferences were all well aware of the risks they were taking. Their nervousness led to extraordinary caution. At the inaugural conference in 1838, one speaker whose subject was the teaching of religion forgot himself enough to remark casually that "we philologists are born rationalists". "Yes yes," interjected the presiding officer in a flurry. "All philologists are born rationalists, but in a good sense, like Melancthon."

Later during the same conference, an informal discussion that touched on politics became somewhat overheated. This so alarmed the chairman that he had the lights extinguished.[58]

Notes

1 Victor Hugo, *Les feuilles d'automne*. Poem no. III. Composed 18 May 1830.

2 Hector Berlioz, *Memoirs of Hector Berlioz from 1803 to 1865*, p. 106.

3 Mikhail Bakunin, *Sozialpolitischer Briefwechsel*, p. 94 Herzen to Bakunin.

4 E. H. Kossman, *The Low Countries 1780–1940*, p. 151.

5 Alain Faure, "À la recherche des réfugiés et prisonniers politiques," in *Répression et prison politiques en France et en Europe au XIXe siècle*, p. 10

6 Czartoryski's adherents as a party named themselves after the magnificent Hôtel Lambert (designed in 1639 by Louis Levau) that was his headquarters.

7 A. J. P. Taylor in *The Opening of an Era: 1848*, François Fejtö editor, p. xix.

8 Thomas Mann's idealistic young medical student, Morten Schwarzkopf, is a touching example of these young people. Tony Buddenbrooks, the Lübeck shipping magnate's daughter whom he loves, and whom he bitterly calls an aristocrat, does not even grasp the significance of his concealed tricolor ribbon.

9 Valentin, *Das hambacher Nationalfest*, pp. 130–136: Document no. 19.

10 Christoph Crossmann, *Die Unruhen in Oberhessen im Herbste 1830*, pp. 1-20.

11 Ilse Spangenberg, *Hessen-Darmstadt und der deutsche Bund 1815–1848*, p. 67.

12 Ibid., p. 69, citing Büchner.

13 Sheehan, *German History 1770–1886*, p. 605.

14 Edmund Wilson, *To the Finland Station*, p. 184.

15 Gerhard Schmidt, *Die Staatsreform in Sachsen in der ersten Hälfte des 19. Jahrhunderts* , passim.

16 Aleksandr Ivanovich Herzen, *My Past and Thoughts*, p. 342.

17 The character Houssonet in Flaubert's *Éducation sentimentale* remarks scornfully that Poland is like the sea-serpent. It doesn't exist. All the Poles, he says, are in Faubourg Saint-Marceau.

18 Faure, pp. 10–11; Slawomir Kalembka, "Les émigrés polonais, victimes de la répression (1848–1870)," in *Répression et prison politiques en France et en Europe au XIXe siècle*, pp. 12–13.

19   Valentin, *Hambacher Nationalfest*, pp. 87–88: Document no. 2.

20   Frédéric Chopin, *Chopin's Letters*, collected by Henryk Opienski, p. 164, to Tytus Wojciecowski, 25 December 1831.

21   Daumier produced a funny picture, called *"Le cauchemar"* that showed Lafayette in bed, staring in horror at an enormous pear [the accepted derisive symbol of Louis-Philippe] perched on his chest.

22   Max Huber, *Ludwig I. von Bayern und die Ludwig-Maximilians-Universität in München (1826–1832)*, pp. 118–139.

23   Richard Tilly, "Popular Disorders in Nineteenth-Century Germany," *Journal of Social History* 4 (1970–1971): 1–40.

24   Valentin, *Hambacher Nationalfest*, pp. 10–11.

25   F. Gunther Eyck, "English and French Influences on German Liberalism before 1848," *Journal of the History of Ideas* 18 (1957):336.

26   Adler, *Die Geschichte der ersten sozialpolitischen Arbeiterbewegung in Deutschland*, pp. 10–11.

27   Samuel Bernstein, *Auguste Blanqui and the art of insurrection* (London, 1971); François Fejtö "Europe on the Eve of Revolution," in *The Opening of an Era*, pp. 36–37.

28   Thomas, *Liberalism, Nationalism, and the German Intellectuals*, p. 13.

29   Maximilien Lamarque (1770–1832) was a hero of the French left. He did not attend the festival, and died of cholera early in June. His funeral cortege served as a rallying point for various radical organizations and thereby set off the ferocious "June days" of Paris. Hugo presented a vivid picture of the extraordinary procession in *Les Misérables*, in the chapter called *Un enterrement*.

30   Valentin, *Hambacher Nationalfest*, pp. 97–98: Document no. 9.

31   Ibid., pp. 98–101: Document no. 10.

32   Peter Longerich, editor, *"Was ist des Deutschen Vaterland?"* p. 63.

33   Sheehan, *German History*, pp. 608–615; Valentin, *Hambacher Nationalfest*, esp.p. 35 ff

34   Valentin, *Hambacher Nationalfest*, p. 78.

35   Ibid., p. 80

36   Spangenberg, pp. 98–102.

37   Friedrich Sigmund Jucho was prominent throughout the revolutionary period. A *Burschenschaft* member, he was an organizer at Heidelberg in March 1848, a member of the *Vorparlament* at Frankfurt, one of the *Vorparlament*'s transitional committee of fifty, and an elected delegate to the Frankfurt

Parlament. When the newly elected chief executive of the German provisional central power, *Erzherzog* Johann, was welcomed at Frankfurt, Jucho was one of three distinguished members of the *Parlament* who rode in the archduke's ceremonial carriage.

38   Spangenberg, pp. 102–103, 109.

39   Ibid., p. 107.

40   Georg Büchner, *Ludwig Weidig, Der hessische Landbote*, annotated by Hans Magnus Enzensberger, pp. 40–63; Adler, p. 7.

41   Klein *1848; Der Vorkampf deutscher Einheit und Freiheit*, pp. 51–52.

42   Wolfgang Büttner, *Georg Herwegh—ein Sänger des Proletariats*, p. 29. The poem was whispered in Nazi concentration camps.

43   Price, *Evolution of the Zollverein*, p. 190.

44   Karl von Rotteck, *Gesammelte und nachgelassene Schriften*, 3:155–157. Speech to the Baden legislative assembly of 18 July 1839.

45   Sheehan, *German Liberalism*, p. 37. More than one-sixth of the liberal elite that was elected to the Frankfurt Parlament in 1848 had been persecuted by the state.

46   Hedwig Walwei-Wiegelmann, *Gesellschaftskritik im Werk Heinrich Heines*, p. 33.

47   A. E. Taylor, in *The Opening of an Era*, p. 22.

48   Klein, p. 54.

49   Hans Gustav Keller, *Die politischen Verlagsanstalten und Druckereien in der Schweiz 1840–1848*, pp. 26–27, citing Johannes Scherr.

50   Klein, p. 57.

51   Heine, *Sämtliche Werke*, 4: 60 ff

52   Herzen, *My Past and Thoughts*, pp. 384–385.

53   Gangolf Hübinger, *Georg Gottfried Gervinus; historisches Urteil und politische Kritik*, p. 111.

54   Ibid., p. 114.

55   Ibid., p. 117 note.38. Extract from a letter of 2 December 1837 to his friend K. Hegel.

56   Edward Ippel, editor, *Briefwechsel zwischen Jacob und Wilhelm Grimm, Dahlmann und Gervinus*, pp. 16–23.

57   Klein, pp. 55–58.

58   Thomas, pp. 51–71.

Chapter 8

The Smouldering German *Vormärz*[1]

Before 1840, there was little true nationalism among the Germans, and there were few people in whose veins there coursed the hot blood of patriotism. Most patriots were veterans of the war for liberation, and that had happened in 1813—a generation past. Ideas of German unity tended to center around such dry topics as the beneficial effects of railway transportation or a customs union, or around political theories relating to the desirability of an English-style constitution (for a small duchy, perhaps). Among liberals there was enthusiasm for freedom of the press or trial by jury, or for representational government. It is true that the banned black-gold-red tricolor symbolized German aspirations, but everyone understood that a tricolor emblem was essentially French, and that liberty, equality and fraternity likewise originated on the other side of the Rhine. The only heirs of the freedom fighters who had known the exhilaration of a joyous bonding love of one's native country were those privileged marchers who had climbed the hill to the old castle of Hambach, carrying their banners and singing in the rain.

There was a sudden change in 1840, when a song took Germany by storm and people everywhere began to sing fervently:

Sie sollen ihn nicht haben, Den freien deutschen Rhein[2]

A simple little song, set to music in at least seventy versions by a host of composers, including Robert Schumann. People sang defiantly about rocky crags and old cathedrals reflected in green water, about boatmen and plashing oars and young lovers, and fish. Sentimental, but the repeated refrain was stern:

You shall not have it, the free German Rhine.

Heretofore, the Rhine had been a simple line of separation between a nation (France) and the German land of non-nationhood. Suddenly a new defensive, uncritical emotion swept over the Germans. The incongruous impetus for the surge of patriotism was a chain of events that were occurring in Egypt, Syria, and Turkey, and in solemn ambassadorial consultations taking place in London.

The Egyptian pasha at that time was a vassal of the sultan of the Ottoman Empire, and he was trying to improve his lot. There had been a previous challenge, in 1830/31, when the pasha managed to capture Syria. Since that victory there had been anxiety in Europe. Would the Egyptian not only strive for independence but try to take over the whole Ottoman Empire? In 1839 he had indeed made mincemeat of a Turkish army, to the acute distress of the major European powers. Russia wanted to have a weak Turkey there on the Bosporus, not only for military reasons (this was her outlet to the Mediterranean and its ports) but also because she wanted to increase her thriving grain export from the Ukraine. England did not care to see any potential block between herself and her growing colonial empire in India. Moreover, she did not intend to see Russia settling the matter unilaterally. Metternich as usual wanted stability on general principles. In the post-Napoleonic settlement, Russia had arrived on the very banks of the Danube, Austria's most important economic link with the world of trade before the coming of the railroads. It would not do, if Russia were to gain absolute control of Constantinople.

In July 1839 a note was sent to the *Porte* on Metternich's initiative, signed by Austria, England, Russia, France and Prussia, to the effect that they were prepared to defend the integrity of the Ottoman Empire and also would be glad to offer their services in negotiation between the sultan and the pasha.

It was after this that the English minister, Lord Palmerston called a conference in London, where he took the position that the pasha ought to be limited to Egypt and forced to relinquish Syria. The French were unhappy because they wanted to see an arrangement that would be favorable to Egypt. Still smarting from their losses at the time of Napoleon's defeat, they proudly recalled their days of triumphant domination on the Nile, and had begun to contemplate development of a new colonial empire in North Africa. For this reason, they felt that it would be in their interest to be on good terms with the pasha, but they were overestimating his military strength. They were also underestimating the determination of England and Russia to settle things in their own way.

On 15 July 1840 the French were suddenly confronted with a disconcerting *fait accompli*,—namely, an agreement that had been made between England, Austria, Russia, Prussia and the sultan. The European powers were promising to give military support to the Turkish sovereign and to force the pasha back into Egypt. Within weeks there was actual military intervention on the part of English, Russian and Austrian forces in Syria, and Beirut was captured. That ended matters as far as the major powers were concerned.

The French were outraged, feeling humiliated because they had been excluded. (The German *Bund* had been excluded too.) The closing months of 1840 were full of alarms and fury. The settlement made by the Congress of Vienna in 1815 was no final settlement, roared the French. There had to be revision. France had to see a territorial revision, a recovery of her natural frontiers, namely the Rhine and the Alps. Lamartine, the velvet statesman, observed coolly that the day would come when the treaties of 1815 *se déchireront d'eux-mêmes devant la force des choses, . . . devant la volonté et la patience de mon pays* [will self-destruct before the force of things . . . before the will and patience of my country]. This then was the connection between the Turkish crisis and the Rhine. This was why the Germans were singing.

The German people had been thrust into a process of self-discovery. French belligerence had injected into them a thrilling sense of unity. Unfortunately, it was not a positive emotion. For the most part it was a feelng of resentment, even hatred, that pulled them together. Two German monarchs were most appreciative, hearing in all those singing voices the sound of loyalty to the *status quo*. Friedrich Wilhelm IV, just having acceded to the throne of Prussia, sent the young author of the *Rheinlied* a gift of one hundred *Thaler*, and a gratified Ludwig I of Bavaria was moved to give him a handsome silver loving-cup. The song would rally loyal subjects everywhere! Speaking half a century later, Bismarck commented that "In those days the song was powerful and had such an effect that it was as though there were a couple of extra army corps standing on the Rhine, more than we actually had."

It was true. The song had inspired a spontaneous burst of popular emotion that found a joyous outlet in a huge celebration of the completion of the Cologne cathedral.[3]

Even the *Herzog* of Baden, in his annual speech from the throne, confidently spoke of the "expression of love and loyalty to the Fatherland" and his faith that the youth of the land would respond to the call to arms.

Negative nationalism like this was depressingly naive, devoid of any political substance. It was the sort of nationalism that demagogues thrive on. Combined sentimentalism and belligerence unfortunately often characterizes mindless situations in which supposed love of country is a mask that crudely covers a disastrous lack of civic understanding and responsibility.

The battle of the newspapers became violent, French radicals implying that any government worth its own salt would be mobilizing. The odd thing is that it apparently had not occurred to the French that Germans might not like to hear the suggestion that Rhenish territory be surrendered to them. They seem to have been astonished and incredulous. How could that happen? There had been so much admiration and cordiality flowing back and forth, beginning with *madame* de Stael's warm words, and besides, the liberals on the other side of the Rhine were pro-French, were they not? And all those exiles in Paris?

Both sides armed and the French rattled their sabres for a while and some new fortifications were built, but in the end the war-scare oozed away. What is of interest is the fact that Germans had taken a new look at themselves, thinking of all their small states as a defiant unit that they passionately loved. The fact that Germany—Prussia in particular—did not act positively in this matter contributed to the general sense of disappointment that had been building up ever since it had become evident that Friedrich Wilhelm IV was not going to live up to the high expectations generated by his initial actions on his accession (June 1840) when he released various political prisoners. "Without the year 1840 and its disappointments . . . there would have been no March 1848."[4]

It is revealing, that the famous *Staatslexikon* published by von Rotteck and Welcker, on which liberals relied, had no article headed either "Nation" or "Nationality". After the war scare, liberals had to think seriously. Was nationality solely a matter of boundaries, or did it encompass complex factors such as language and race? What about culture, and history? Perhaps a nation ought to be defined as a community of citizens dedicated to the same political principles, protecting the rights of the people. In the third edition of the *Staatslexikon*, published in 1864, a sharp line was drawn between nationality as something that marked off what was foreign, and nationality that embraced the inner life and fabric of people living together in the same region.[5]

For better or worse, a new national consciousness had sprung into being, taking the form of an increased interest in German history and

an unsophisticated tendency to center patriotic ideas around stereo-
types. All this was to prove troublesome to the liberals when they
gathered at Frankfurt in 1848 for the purpose of drafting a constitution that would weld Germany into a nation.

* * * * * * *

The chief form of interaction among intellectuals in the early 1840's
was still outwardly nonpolitical. Political organization, especially in an
absolutist state, would have been subversive because it would imply
that the ruler by the grace of God was not invariably right, but future
leaders like Heinrich von Gagern were beginning to understand that if
a man stands alone he is weak. There is political effectiveness only for
the individual who heads a party.[6]

In Germany, there was the known proliferation of social clubs and
professional societies and groups with innocent names like the Thursday Club. Some gathered as professionals at such meetings as the
Versammlung deutscher Naturforscher und Ärzte [conference of
German scientists and physicians], the *Versammlung deutscher
Philologen und Schulmänner* [German philologists and educators],
even the *Versammlung deutscher Land- und Forstwirte* [estate and
forest managers], but to attend such meetings one had to have leisure
and money and privilege in addition to education. Of necessity therefore, most forward-looking individuals with social concerns who were
able to meet and share their ideas were members of the small economically comfortable upper middle class, and though they discussed
the desirability of suffrage and the rights of the laboring classes, they
had very little personal knowledge or experience to guide them. Their
developing concept of nationhood and suffrage had its inevitable
limitations.

In the absence of democratically elected parliaments, and with the
Burschenschaft movement in disarray, a forum of sorts was provided
by the series of scientific and scholarly conferences that had begun in
1822 with the foundation of the annual *Versammlungen deutscher
Naturforscher and Ärzte*. The true founder was Lorenz Oken (1779–
1851) professor of natural science at Jena until 1819, when he ran
into trouble through repercussions from his participation in the
Wartburg festival of 1817. He resigned from a subsequent post at
Munich in 1832, when he moved to Zurich to become a professor in
that city until his death. He is perhaps best known as the founder of
the prestigious journal *Isis*, which appeared regularly from 1816 to
1848.

Oken had been intrigued by the organization of a scientific society in Switzerland, known as a *Wandergesellschaft* [migrant society] that met each year in a different city. Oken attended its conference at Zurich in 1817 and decided that something similar would be successful in Germany. He wrote to various institutions, receiving replies that were hardly to be described as encouraging. Speaking of one such letter, Oken commented that "misgivings are stated about the cost, misgivings about the journey, misgivings about the faces of the people, misgivings about the accommodations, misgivings about the knowledge required, misgivings about the room and finally misgivings about the reaction of the governments."[7]

At the inaugural meeting at Leipzig (1822), many members of the conference refused to allow their names to be recorded. A cabinet order had just been issued from Berlin, forbidding university teachers to discuss political questions. "Political" could mean almost anything. All the same, the conference series throve, and members brought along invited guests who sometimes numbered in the hundreds.

Apparently the reluctant foot-draggers of whom Oken complained had not been perceptive enough to understand the importance of strengthening the cause of empiricism, which was no darling of the rulers. That empirical science could be endangered in the days of men of such caliber as the illustrious chemist Justus von Liebig (1803–1873) of Giessen and Munich, or of Göttingen's distinguished physicists Wilhelm Weber (1804–1889) and Karl Friedrich Gauss (1777–1855) is clear evidence of the narrowmindedness with which the scholars had to cope. Alexander von Humboldt was certainly aware of this aspect of the conferences. His astoundingly popular series of lectures in Berlin (in 1827, with even Friedrich Wilhelm III of Prussia among his auditors) was a clear proclamation of protest against the excesses of speculation that was not based on observation in the laboratory. The lectures were also in a way a protest against surveillance because von Humboldt managed to persuade the authorities that conference members need not undergo the humiliation of registering at police headquarters.

A curious aspect of the early meetings was the inexperience of the university professors in speaking to persons not engaged in their own academic discipline. Just as the early Freemasons had had to learn to address one another as "brother" even though they belonged to different classes, now the learned professors had to be encouraged to speak informally, using "lively and impromptu delivery in place of the painful reading aloud of written texts". It has been suggested that Oken understood that the conferences might serve as training ground for future political work.[8] It was a novel experience for the learned gentlemen to conform to their own statutory rule that "everything must be settled by majority vote"—a departure from general practice in that it brought home to them the fact that as individuals they were required to take heed of their own consciences, not accept dictation from above. The experience of these meetings seems to have reinforced awareness of the common fatherland and responsibility as citizens. In this connection, it is worth noting that Thomas' lists of conference participants, with appropriate markings, indicate that twenty-three conference members were elected to the 1848 *Parlament* at Frankfurt. It is also significant that Jakob and Wilhelm Grimm, Dahlmann, Albrecht and Gervinus, all of the Göttingen Seven, regularly attended the meetings.

* * * * * * *

It was gradually dawning on thoughtful citizens that the wants of the lowest class had to be attended to, unless one were to become reconciled to the notion that pauperism was a fixture in society, and that the lowest classes might coalesce into a violence-prone, virtually criminal proletariat (the term mob occurred to uneasy members of the *Mittelstand*). Afraid as they were of the "huddled masses", the middle class might have been astonished to be told that the royals were afraid of the potential might of their own *Mittelschicht*. General Joseph Maria von Radowitz urged his friend Friedrich Wilhelm IV of Prussia, in the face of the threat of middle class domination, to seek protection and support from the proletariat.[9] He told the pliant monarch that the humble members of the lower ranks of society would be disposed to feel gratitude to their sovereign, whereas the middle classes had been hopelessly demoralized by evil education and the press. Binding the proletariat to the Crown by an eleemosynary program was an essentially Christian process that appealed to the pious monarch. The poor would be grateful for whatever assistance was offered to them but would understand that their role in society as laid out by Jesus himself (The poor ye have always with you) was that of a useful animal that inspires kindly thoughts in the minds of its betters.

A sympathetic analysis of the plight of the artisan was published by Brockhaus in 1848, in the first volume of the encyclopedic work called

Die Gegenwart. What strikes the modern reader is the kindly, didactic tone of the article and the clear evidence that the concepts are assumed to be new to the reader, no matter how self-evident they look to weary Twentieth-Century eyes. Who in all those tiny German kingdoms and duchies would, after all, have given much thought to Capital and Labor or Supply and Demand?

> Up to the conclusion of the last century, all work with but few exceptions was the product of men's hands. Such personal work always makes necessary a shop relationship in which the worker stands with respect to the employer in part as pupil to teacher, partly also as a member of the household. . . . The shop is the family. The situation is quite different where there are machines. . . . The employer does not work himself, and often he has little or no understanding of the work. The bond between worker and master is lost. . . . Machine work is necessarily simple—with development, the work becomes limited to a part of the whole operation and is easier because of repetition.[10]

Notice that it is implied here that in time factory workers will not have special complex skills to offer, only their labor, which will make them more or less like interchangeable parts of a machine, but the language is so stilted that the essential point is obscured.

> The factory worker thus stands in a certain sense related to the machine as the day laborer is related to the farmland. Nothing binds him , other than the need for employment and wages. The employer has lost his feeling of a family relationship between himself and his workers. He undertakes nothing that the master of the shop would have done. He feels no duty to be accountable for the livelihood of his people.

The idea of *bürgerliche Nahrung*—literally civic nourishment, translated here as livelihood—was deeply embedded in the guild mentality. It implied that the guild masters played a combined civic and economic role, as those responsible for the acceptance or rejection of candidates for permanent membership in the guild and hence in the community. The factory owner-employer, in contrast, had no such civic obligations.

> He takes them and he lets them go just as it suits him. The result of this is the important fact that the machine worker for the most part becomes an independent person, who has to look out for himself and because machine-driven industry necessarily requires a large number of such workers, there is a resulting gathering of a mass of independent workers at specific points. . . . The tool can only be built with a significant amount of capital; whereas the artisan had the opportunity to construct his own tools and build his own shop and thus to create capital, the factory worker can never arrive at ownership of a

factory, and never own a machine. . . . There is something else. Because the factory worker cannot work without the machine, he becomes valuable only if the factory owner wants to use him. The labor itself becomes goods, and the price of the goods is determined by the same principles that govern the price of other goods, through supply and demand. . . . The workers and the capitalists are separated into two classes by the law of goods movement, just as sharply as the nobility was separated from the bourgeois in a feudal system. . . . This now is the proletariat. It is, in sum, that class that owns nothing other than its ability to work, and that demands for this ability the same social and governmental rights that thus far only capital can supply.

On the whole, demands of master craftsmen and artisans were not based on this clear explanation. There was a desire to return to the good old days that had been summarily blacked out by the new laws that restricted the power of the guilds. In places like Hesse-Kassel, where they had not been made outright illegal, there had sometimes been official recognition of the problem of the artisan and an effort had been made to encourage handicrafts. As early as 1818, it had been decreed in Hesse-Kassel that henceforth there would be an annual exhibition on the Elector's name day, where prizes and medals would be awarded, and the names of the winners would be published in the newspapers.[11]

Throughout the Brockhaus discussion, it is clear that Germans needed to learn and speak a new language, namely the language of the Industrial Age. A scholarly analysis of the gradual evolution of meaning of the German word *Industrie* as compared to the old term *Gewerbefleiss* shows that the two terms were used interchangeably until well into the mid-Nineteenth Century, when they separated into "machine production and manufacture" versus "hand crafts".[12] In general, those who were concerned about socio-political matters were hampered by their lack of a recognized working vocabulary. It was tiresome to find that even the most elementary argument was bound to end up in a morass of conflicting definitions. Was there any agreement on the meaning of "society", "sovereignty", "constitution", "suffrage", "progress", or "the proletariat" ?

There were attempts at clear definition. The liberal entrepreneur Friedrich Harkort wrote a widely distributed open letter (popularly called his Beehive letter) in which he put his ideas plainly in terms of drones and workers.

"There is a lot of talk about proletarians, but the word isn't defined. I call a man a proletarian whose parents neglected him, who never washed him or combed his hair, and who taught him nothing and didn't send him to church or to school. He hasn't learned any manual skill, has married with no bread in the house, and puts more of his kind into the world." Harkort went on to say that proletarians were heavy drinkers and acted as auxiliary troops of the agitators. He did not count among the proletariat the honest worker to whom "God gave capital in the form of the strength of his hands and his healthy human understanding."

People like that ought to be helped. They ought to get more trade, have credit banks, good instruction for their children, and insurance against sickness and disability.[13] The skilled artisans themselves seem to have been inclined to make similar distinctions, thinking of the proletariat as something apart. This may account for the failure of Karl Marx's campaign to unite all workers in all-out class warfare against the middle class.

One way of dealing with the worrisome problem of unemployment in the cities, social reformers thought, was the formation of organizations that would act rather as the old guilds had done, offering unemployment insurance, accident insurance, burial insurance,—even modest savings banks. It was also proposed that there might be societies that would help unemployed workers to educate themselves. Invoking Rousseau, well-intentioned reformers called for the establishment of educational societies for the impoverished workers. This kind of self-help was popular. Saxony, for example, had about two hundred and fifty branches of its *Bildungsverein* [educational society] that presented lectures and inspirational readings to its seven thousand members. It has to be admitted however that middle class people tended to take over the management of these societies, which therefore probably did not reach the very lowermost levels of the population for which they were originally intended. This of course is a well-known phenomenon in organizations whose goal is the improvement of the masses.

There were two reformers at least who cried for a different approach. They had little use for lectures and inspirational readings. Karl Marx and his colleague Friedrich Engels wanted action. Their *Gespenst* that haunted Europe had flesh—flesh that could be wounded, flesh that could bleed, flesh that could fight for its own cause. To the reader of the *Communist Manifesto* it is revealed that the enemies of the people were not the crowned heads who popularly are the villains of history, but rather the dull unromantic plodding middle class. It was the *bourgeoisie* that had to be demolished so that the workers of the world could unite.

Marx and Engels had nothing but contempt for those members of the *bourgeoisie* who were expressing a smug desire to redress social grievances. These economists, philanthropists, humanitarians, organizers of charity, members of societies for the prevention of cruelty to animals, temperance "fanatics",—according to Marx and Engels, all these wanted the advantages of modern social conditions without the struggle and danger that results from them. "They wish for a *bourgeoisie* without a proletariat," they spat out angrily. The proletariat is simply required to march into the social New Jerusalem but remain within the bounds of existing society. Even those who describe themselves as socialists have no conception of the *bourgeois* relationship to production. They do not understand that there has to be a revolution. The true Communists, however, would never for a single instant cease to instill into the working class the clearest possible recognition of the hostility between *bourgeoisie* and proletariat. "Let the ruling classes tremble at a Communist revolution. The proletarians have nothing to lose but their chains."[14]

These fiery words have been blazing and sending off jets of flame for generations, and it is easy to assume that revolutionists on the German barricades must have shouted about spectres and called for the union of the workers of the world, but although Marx was a known figure of the times, his influence was slight. He had been addressing non-existent legions that were not ready for Armageddon. As Hamerow put it, "They sought to escape from the factory age, not to dominate it. The ideal of traditionalist legitimism was more intelligible to the independent artisan and small farmer than the vision of a classless society." Edmund Wilson pointed out that the *Manifesto* was little read at the time of its publication (February 1848) in London. Copies went to a few hundred members of the Communist League, but it was not put on sale in those days. "It probably had no serious influence on the events of 1848." Sperber's opinion is that the role of the labor movement in 1848 has been grossly exaggerated, and that class struggle and class consciousness were far from the political thought of the times. According to Peter N. Stearns, although Marx played a role in advancing the level of working-class agitation, the revolution did not launch a full-fledged Marxist movement, and "Marx made little headway among the workers."[15]

When the time came for elections to the constituent *Parlament* that was to be held at Frankfurt (May 1848), only one individual from the Marx-Engels circle was able to gain a delegate's seat. This was Wilhelm Wolf of Breslau. Moreover, there was even a split among the communists themselves. The movement at Cologne headed by Andreas Gottschalk boycotted the Frankfurt assembly, but had little or nothing to do with Marx and his followers.

Again to quote Hamerow, "The proletariat, the chosen people of dialectical materialism, preferred to follow other prophets." People talked about the proletariat, but usually the word was taken to mean old-style artisans, not factory workers or railroad construction crews.

There were always little pockets of prosperity where new technologies speeded up production, but it is not unlikely that the mere existence of such prosperity increased the general level of discouragement throughout Germany. New industries could be destabilizing.

A combination of factors had already made life unbearable in Silesia, where heretofore the linen weavers had been fairly well off. They were dependent on middlemen who supplied the raw materials and marketed the finished yarns and fabrics abroad. In actuality, the middlemen were operating illegally, using the mini-state of Cracow as a center for introduction of contraband into Poland and Austria, where protective tariffs were high. Then a general economic depression developed and the demand for linen goods dropped. The effect was devastating. Most Silesian weavers had owned their looms and now found themselves forced to sell them. If any small opportunity for work opened, they would have to rent those same looms from the middleman.

The violent events that occurred in Silesia in 1844 were not evidence of the kind of revolutionary class uprising that Marx and Engels had been calling for. This was an old-fashioned demand for better pay and it took the form of mass machine breaking and attacks on homes of the rich. The rioters were not acting as a class. Quite simply, they were expressing personal outrage against prosperous middlemen who were their perceived enemies. They may not even have been aware of the competition stirred up by technological advances elsewhere in Germany. Did they know, for example, that in the Rhineland there were steam-driven calico printers, or that the growing taste for silk had given rise to a whole new industry where fancy dress goods were produced, with alternate stripes of gauze and satin, with *millefleur* designs printed on the gauze? Did they know that linen was no longer in demand, that customers were calling for silk instead? They wanted proper pay, and certainly were giving no thought to Jacquard looms. They had always woven and sold plain linen. If they received proper pay they would go home quietly. They were not by any means screaming for a new social order.

Whatever it was that the weavers were demanding, the local police lost their heads and the disruptive riots were brutally suppressed. The barrier of official censorship was nearly impenetrable, with the result that even now the story of the Silesian rising is far from clear. In any event, it was viewed in Germany as a harbinger of even greater trouble. From that time, workers' quiescence could not be comfortably relied on. Workers' violence boiled just below the surface, and became more or less a fact of life in the *Vormärz*.

Karl Marx was unwilling to accept the idea that the weavers' riots sprang from blind reaction to need and economic disaster. To him, this was the beginning of class war. Not one of the French or English workers' uprisings had such a theoretical and conscious character as the uprising of the Silesian weavers, he wrote. "The Silesian uprising begins precisely with . . . consciousness of the nature of the proletariat. The action itself bears the stamp of this superior character. . . . Where among the *bourgeoisie* is to be found a book about . . . political emancipation similar to Weitling's work, *Garantien der Harmonie und Freiheit?* . . . It has to be admitted that the German proletariat is the theoretician of the European proletariat. . . . It has to be admitted that Germany is just as much classically destined for a social revolution as it is incapable of a political one."[16]

Heine wrote a terrible poem, *Die schlesischen Weber* [the Silesian weavers] :

There are no tears in the melancholy eyes. They sit at the loom and grind their teeth. Germany, we are weaving your shroud; we weave into it the triple curse—A curse on the god to whom we prayed in cold of winter and famine.— A curse on the king who let us be shot like dogs.—A curse on the false fatherland where only disgrace and outrage flourish.—The shuttle flies, the loom creaks, we weave busily day and night.—Old Germany, we are weaving your shroud, and we weave into it the triple curse.[17]

The *Vormärz* period offered little comfort to those who sought to build a revolution on working-class unrest. The theory that Marx valued so highly was discussed among the Young Hegelians and other intellectuals. "Working-class support was marginal."[18]

This is not to say that social theory was unknown to the workers. They were nearly swamped by the flood of pamphlets that flowed from the socialist presses across the German frontiers, smuggled in and distributed by returning journeymen after their *Wanderjahre* abroad. However, it appears that the most that could be expected of the various workers' clubs in which the communists and socialists placed so much hope was some comprehension of the fact that there was such a thing as class, instead of the old societal divisions that were based on birth. People still used the words *Stand* and *Schicht*, not class.

Emphasis on the difficulties of the urban factory worker was perhaps unwarranted in Germany of the 1840's. Poverty at that time had become more or less endemic everywhere. The Marburg professor, Bruno Hildebrand, made a point of challenging Marx and Engels on that score. He wrote especially about his own province in Oberhessen, where, he said, there were at that time no factories or factory workers, no steam-powered machinery, no unrestricted trade: altogether, the old patriarchal form of society existed there, where masters still accepted apprentices as part of their own households. Only twenty-five percent of the population lived in towns and cities—all the rest were country folk. Even in this situation, the urban artisan was poor. A master shoemaker or tailor was earning about one hundred *Reichstaler* a year, and since a good third of that went for household, fuel, clothing and so on, the family of such a man had to be fed on a few silver coins that—in terms of local tax on bread and meat—turned out to be 3.4 kg ordinary rye bread or 0.8 kg meat for the whole family. In his home town of Marburg, Hildebrand continued, in the winter of 1846/47 when the temperatures dropped to well below freezing, babies were born on the streets, and the estimated proportion of the absolutely destitute was one third of the entire population. In some localities the paupers were organized by the authorities into trains of beggars who daily made the rounds along determined routes through the town.[19]

Incidentally, Bruno Hildebrand's work is evidence that reformers were exemplifying the validity of Vico's arguments. They were developing new "real" manmade sciences and techniques. Hildebrand was more or less a pioneer in his imaginative use of statistics. Statistics in themselves were nothing new. Census-taking for taxation bases was as old as the Pharaohs and the Romans, to say nothing of William the Conqueror's Domesday Book, but this application of Hildebrand's was more subtle. To correlate the known tax on bread with known income levels and thereby to demonstrate the existence of poverty was both creative and useful.

There was near-destitution in the towns not only among artisans but also among clerical workers. An *Aktenhelfer* [rather like a modern clerk-typist, probably] in the Prussian War Department was receiving a princely fifty *Reichstaler* per year. A post office employee received nothing during his first year, then usually free lodging and about five or six dollars a month. After four years, if he passed an exam, he was paid about three hundred dollars per year, and after ten years at that level, he received a raise of about one hundred dollars. A contemporary comment was to the effect that if such an individual wanted to marry then (it would have been impossible before his fortieth year), with a growing family to support, he would inevitably slide into poverty.[20]

In the country, conditions were indeed lamentable among the impoverished and desperate hired hands, but there were factors in play that had little to do with industrialization. There is a telling article by Friedrich List, written in 1842, in which he describes in detail the bad effect of the practice of subdividing one's land holdings among one's heirs. A man with a tiny parcel of land to begin with would split it up among his seven or eight children. Plots were so small that they could not possibly provide subsistence to a family. List may be the one who coined the expression *Zwergwirtschaft* [dwarf economy] to describe this situation. He says that in some Rhenish communities nobody owned a plow because the area under individual cultivation was much too small for such an implement.[21] Aside from the poverty it caused, this fragmentation had another deleterious effect that Karl Marx observed. With small holdings like this, there could be no division of labor, and little intercourse with the rest of society. People in such a situation do not constitute true classes, Marx thought. They were rather like potatoes in a sack that merely form a sackful of potatoes. The identity of their interests generates no unity.[22]

The desperation of the lowest ranks of the rural population (the *Heuerling* or day-laborer class) had been increased by a new practice that excluded landless people from their former use of common pasturelands and forest. Propertied people claimed these areas for themselves, and the lackland peasant who rented a little hut and plot of ground somewhere no longer had any place to feed his cow or his pig. He could not even herd his geese as before, and he was now unable to pick up slash or fallen branches from the forest floor for household fuel. In earlier times, such a man could let his animals roam in good weather and perhaps slaughter them before winter: with the new arrangement, he would have to stall-feed his animals, and that meant purchasing fodder and hay with his non-existent money. It could hardly be a cause for astonishment, that people so pressed would take what was needed, no matter how, by theft if necessary.[23]

Karl Marx had once proved to his own satisfaction at least that if no distinction were made between wood-gathering and theft, there would be a clear invitation to persons so unjustly accused to disregard any distinction between ordinary theft and the offense of accumulating a great deal of property and preventing others from having any.[24]

Even before the terrible famine years (1846–1847), the plight of the rural poor was enough to engender rebellion in its own right. Only in a country long accustomed to absolutism could such deplorable conditions have been tolerated. Here are extracts from an account (Nürnberg 1840) of the situation in an unnamed village, presented case by numbered case:

1. A day-laborer family. The father, a journeyman weaver, has had four weeks of weaving in an entire year. His only other work is wood-chopping in winter. This is all that supports his wife and three small children.

2. A widow without any means, and a daughter who sews and cannot support her illegitimate child and for this reason resorts to stealing from the fields.

3. A single woman with five illegitimate children, one of whom is a grown girl but cannot leave the house because the mother is always sick. The other children survive by begging and robbing the fields.

10. A widower, day laborer and journeyman tailor, unemployed. The field that he carefully tends supplies a minimum of food. There are two grown unemployed sons and a daughter with an illegitimate child.

13. A single prostitute with two illegitimate children (two others have died).

20. A miller, but he and his wife are sick and incapable of working. The oldest son does hand work and has a good job in summer, but nothing in winter.

22. Widow and a grown daughter who herds geese in summer. In winter mother and daughter are not only without bread: they have no potatoes either.

The writer of this account ends by saying that in this whole community there is only one person who receives some kind of public relief.[25]

In passing, it may be noticed that though the illegitimacy rate was high throughout rural Germany, it was excessively so in Bavaria. Community sanctions were directed against the social consequences of "irresponsible" behavior rather than against sexual laxity per se. When the states took control of charitable institutions, something of the cement that had bonded communities together was lost because civil servants who administered them did not have much sense of belonging, and their major concern must have been budget-balancing.

Those who suffered most from the famine conditions of the "hungry Forties" were the marginal people in town and country. In 1846 and 1847 there were poor crops, even outright crop failure as well as an extensive potato blight. Prices on scarce commodities were predictably driven up, and starvation stalked the land. This was especially true in upper Silesia, where it is estimated that some fifty thousand people died either from actual starvation or from famine-related disease. The fact that food costs were so high had the inevitable effect of lowering demands for manufactured goods, so that the poor harvests and the high cost of food reinforced a growing economic depression. In Silesia, the weavers again were in an impossible situation. Austria had annexed little Cracow (1846), thereby cutting off the lucrative outlet for the weavers' goods on a black market.

As usual, the people who suffered most had little comprehension of the social forces at work. Here is an account written by Kraft von Hohenlohe-Ingelfingen that concerns happenings on his father's estate. His words reflect some compassion for the starving people but also not a little impatience with them.

> The people knew nothing of self-help. [Reference to indifference of governmental authorities.] . . . When my father saw disaster coming, he closed all his distilleries and offered to the peasants at half price the potatoes that would have been consumed [in production of brandy]. . . . Not a single peasant bought. Because they imagined that the potatoes must be very bad. . . . When whole families had nothing at all to eat, my father had soup made and fed the people. When they heard that if they stopped working and destroyed their tools they would be fed by the prince, the number rose daily. In the spring of 1848 my father was daily providing food for 1400 persons[26]

In February 1848, the King's adjutant received an indignant report from one of the major landowners, Karl *Freiherr* von Vincke, with reference to affairs in Upper Silesia:

> It is unbelievable that such a condition can go on so long and reach such enormous proportions without notice being taken of it by the government. It is worth noting that when *Graf* Harrach, whom you know and who is truly a

fine noble man first called attention to the situation in the newspapers, the censor blocked him.[27]

The *Allgemeine Zeitung* in Berlin editorialized

Winter has struck with all its strength in recent days. The prices of firewood that have risen so high because of inadequate measures against profiteers press more severely on the poor in such times than even hunger itself. [28]

The crisis increased the general middle-class apprehension and fear of social unrest. Even self-identified liberals had their doubts about industrial progress and thought anxiously that the state ought to take a hand. Much as they despised the censors and the whole apparatus of bureaucracy, they were ambivalent in this because though the state in their estimation was an instrument of repression, they were aware that within the bureaucratic ranks there were reform-minded people.who were potential allies. They were following the lead of Hegel, perhaps. As early as 1821, he had expressed the idea that the state must be prepared to check the disruptive forces that are latent in society. Liberals as a whole were longing for reform, not revolution, but by the mid-winter of 1847, most felt that a new era was about to begin. It was a sign of the changing times that they started to consult each other and to organize professional meetings where they could perhaps formulate some kind of policy. Revolution was in the air. The news from from Switzerland showed that there was about to be some kind of concerted movement in the major European countries.

In spite of everything, German liberals had made progress by their persistent use of newspapers and opposition publications like Karl von Rotteck's *Staatslexikon*, even though they had known all too well what they were risking—dismissal, exile, even imprisonment. Their clubs and societies had at least provided a base of activity, but they had had to communicate in what one might almost call coded abstractions.

The clandestine behind-the-scenes efforts tapered to a close in 1847 when the combination of economic recession and near famine galvanized even the unwilling Friedrich Wilhelm IV of Prussia, who agreed to call a united *Landtag* for the first time. (In Prussia, the legislatures of the various provinces had never been assembled before, and no wonder. Who among European royalty had ever forgotten what happened to Louis XVI when he called the *États généraux*?) If Friedrich Wilhelm thought that he was pouring oil on troubled waters, he was soon to find that this was far from the case. For the first time, liberals had a national platform from which they could speak. Many of them found themselves thus propelled from the world of isolated theorizing into the crowded world of reality. It was helpful to the liberals that at last they were able to meet face to face and speak their minds. The period was even marked by the appearance of the first independent interest group—John Prince Smith's *Freihandelsverein* [free trade association].

The notion of political action fanned out from Berlin, spreading all over Germany, where people began to take to the streets in demonstrations against food shortages and high prices. Political activity at the *Landtag* level was especially impressive in Württemberg and Saxony and Hesse-Darmstadt. To say nothing of Bavaria, where the irritated populace forced out the ultraconservative Abel ministry and effected the summoning of the *Landtag* in special session.

It has to be admitted that a large part of the irritation in Bavaria had little to do with economic conditions. The righteous *Mittelstand* was offended by king Ludwig's mistress, the colorful Lola Montez, who was a law unto herself.[29] Most recent investigation of her life reveals that although she may have been physically charming, she was indubitably arrogant, self-seeking, a liar, promiscuous and reckless. Deaf, aging Ludwig was hopelessly obsessed by her.

When Ludwig conferred the rank and title of *Gräfin* on his adored lady, members of the Schönborn household pointedly closed their palatial residence in Munich and departed, showing unwillingness to accept the lady as a social equal.[30] Crowds assembled outside the inn where Lola was spending the night and treated her to a concert of *Katzenmusik*, a form of public chastisement customarily directed throughout Germany against people who had engaged in sexually irregular behavior. *Katzenmusik* traditionally involved yelling, whistling, jeering, banging of pots and pans—harmless but unnerving to the victim. Occasionally the demonstration could become violent, but police rarely interfered because the noisy affair was supposedly on the side of law and public morals.—Parenthetically, this form of public expression was beginning to assume political coloring. More and more frequently, an official who "voted wrong" in the local assembly might be the target. One interesting aspect of "concerts" of this kind was the participation of women.[31] It was to be expected that they would openly reprove a wayward sister, but it was novel to find them out on the street expressing political opinions. The original use of the *Katzen-*

musik may have made it easier for the women to make the transition to political action.

Ludwig, infuriated by the public disrespect, severely reprimanded his military aides, dismissing them right and left so angrily that at one point he had no personal aide at all. The army officers reacted by demanding that they be protected against overbearing abuse on the part of superiors, basing the demand on their oath to uphold the Bavarian constitution. His Majesty's minister Abel had warned him in a dignified note at the time of his resignation that opinion was against him throughout the realm, and that the army could not be depended upon to defend him. It is possible that the beleaguered king even wondered what kind of support he might find from the Church, which he had so stoutly defended for years. He is said to have stopped a pair of obscure village priests who were wandering along a street in Munich with the glum query, "Are you praying diligently for your knavish king?"

Notes

1   Before March 1848. An elastic term used variously by historians of the period.

2   Hans Blum, *Die deutsche Revolution 1848–49*, p. 63. Song written by Nikolaus Becker, an obscure law clerk in Geilenkirchen near Aachen. Published for the first time 18 September 1840 in the *Trierische Zeitung*.

3   There would be an even more momentous celebration in 1848.

4   Neher, *Arnold Ruge als Politiker und politischer Schriftsteller*, p. 68.

5   Irmline Veit-Brause, *Die deutsch-französiche Krise von 1840*, p. 153, note.

6   Botzenhart, *Deutsche Parlamentarismus in der Revolutionszeit*, p.319. Von Gagern once wrote defensively to his father that he was certainly a party man, defining that as having an opinion and trying to work for its success. On the eve of the revolution, he wrote to his friend Eigenbrodt that there is political influence only if one is head of a party.

7   Thomas, *Liberalism, Nationalism and the German Intellectuals*, p. 30, citing Südhoff.

8   Ibid., pp. 32, 39.

9   Hamerow, *Restoration, Revolution, Reaction*, pp. 72–73.

10 *Die Gegenwart* 1:86–89.

11 C. Brauns, *Kurhessische Gewerbepolitik im 17. und 18. Jahrhundert*, p. 124.

12 Eulen Focko, *Vom Gewerbefleiss zur Industrie*, pp. 58–59, 184; Walker, *German Home Towns*, pp. 121–122.

13 Conze, *Gesellschaft—Staat—Nation*, p. 230. The published letter was headed by a picture of a beehive.

14 Karl Marx and Friedrich Engels, *The Communist Manifesto*, passim.

15 Hamerow, pp. 67, 217–218; Wilson, *To the Finland Station*, p. 160; Sperber, *European Revolutions*, p. 247; Peter N. Stearns, *1848; The Revolutionary Tide in Europe* p. 183.

16 *Marx-Engels Reader*, pp. 128–129. "Critical Marginal Notes on the Article 'The King of Prussia and Social Reform'."

17 Heine, *Sämtliche Werke*, 1:769.

18 Noyes, *Organization and Revolution*, p. 36.

19   Wilhelm Abel, *Massenarmut und Hungerkrisen im vorindustriellen Deutschland*, pp. 7–8; Hildebrand was tried and sentenced to two years' imprisonment for "attempted treason" and fled to Switzerland, where he became a citizen and professor at Bern. Hans Jessen, *Die deutsche Revolution 1848/49 in Augenzeugenberichten*, p. 376.

20   Abel, pp. 11–12.

21   Friedrich List, "Die Ackerverfassung, die Zwergwirtschaft und die Auswanderung," *Deutsche Vierteljahrs Schrift* 1842, in Carl Jantke and Dietrich Hilger, editors, *Die Eigentumslosen*, pp. 114–115.

22   *Marx-Engels Reader*, p. 608. "The Eighteenth Brumaire of Louis Bonaparte".

23   Georg Ludwig Wilhelm Funke, "Zur Lage der Heuerleute," in Janke and Hilger, pp. 101–111.

24   Wilson, p. 124.

25   Johann Karl Porsch, "Aus einer Landgemeinde," in Jantke and Hilger, pp. 149–156 .

26   Jessen, pp. 30–32.

27   Ibid., pp. 32–33.

28   Ibid., p. 33.

29   Unfortunately, the lady's lurid life has inspired a mass of yellow-press publications with titles such as *Queen of Hearts, The Divine Eccentric, The Uncrowned Queen, The Woman in Black, The most Famous Vamp who ever Lived,* and so on. She appears of late to have gained respectful attention from modern psychologists and feminists. For a careful, thorough examination of pertinent documents see Bruce Seymour, *Lola Montez: a Life.* (New Haven: Yale University Press, 1996)

30   Valentin, *Geschichte der deutschen Revolution* 1:127 ff.

31   Carola Lipp et al., "Frauen bei Brotkrawallen, Strassentumulten und Katzenmusiken" in *Transformationen der Arbeiterkultur*, pp. 49–60; Siemann, *Die deutsche Revolution 1848/49*, p. 179. *Katzenmusik* was a special form of so-called "proletarian" action. Called "rough music" in England, *charivari* in France, *scampanate* in Italy. See also Sperber, *Rhineland Radicals*, pp. 86–87.

Chapter 9

Germany's Restive Neighbors

The French rising against Louis-Philippe in 1848 is customarily taken to have been the initial event that led to the European revolutions of that year, but this inaccurate description bypasses much that was happening just prior to the fall of the unpopular French monarch. Germany's neighbors were not by any means waiting for the downfall or death of Louis-Philippe, as events that occurred two years before his hasty abdication clearly showed.

The variety of forms of the insurrections that began in 1846 reflects the differing levels of political development among the European peoples. There was bloody slaughter in Austrian Galicia. In Switzerland there was a brisk little civil war between the two antagonistic groups of cantons, while disorderly and uncoordinated actions marked an Italian nationalist movement that swept up and down the peninsula. Each of these events was watched with keen interest by the Germans, whose thinking was influenced by their perception of them.

There were several factions among the Polish refugees who fled after the debacle at Cracow in the November 1831 uprising.[1] The major group was led by Adam Jerzy Czartoryski, who had been president of the ephemeral national rebel government, and who had had in the past a long diplomatic career as adviser to the czar on Polish affairs. Czartoryski's party in exile took its name from its headquarters, the spectacular Hôtel Lambert in Paris.

The Lambert party that had gathered around Czartoryski was far from revolutionary. Serfdom and the *Robot* system [forced labor] would fit into their scheme of things. At the very most, they would accept a constitutional monarchy. The Lamberts did not shrink from the notion that a major European upheaval—even a major war—might help the cause. The policy pursued by Czartoryski and his followers was astounding in its reach and daring.[2] The elderly Czartoryski had participated in the Congress of Vienna in 1815, and he knew everyone of any consequence in the diplomatic world. In Paris itself, he was welcomed in aristocratic houses, many of which included international figures like the Rothschilds. The Hôtel Lambert became a meeting place for personages from the upper ranks of the Catholic hierarchy, prominent Freemasons, parliament members, and emigrants from many parts of Europe. With adroit management of diplomatic ties, the Polish party could maintain its contacts with the ruling ministries even if there were a shift and an opposing ministry gained control. By personal contact, by letter, or through innumerable agents, their views were presented in all the major capitals. Lambert emissaries were to be found at various times working not only in obvious locations such as London and Paris, but also in Budapest, Croatia, Serbia, Bohemia, Rumania, Rome, northern Italy, the coast of the Black Sea, and Constantinople. Further to establish a "presence", there were Polish legions in farflung regions. (The first French foreign legion in Algeria was Polish.) Unfortunately for the Polish cause, most governments complacently regarded the Polish units simply as mercenaries. They were not at all popular among the bulk of the more democratically minded Polish emigrants, and their reputation sank abysmally when such a unit was sold to Spain.

No stone was left unturned in the Lambert effort to sustain Poland in the international consciousness. It was through the influence of Czartoryski, for example, that the poet Adam Mickiewicz assumed his post as the first professor of Slavic literature at the Collège de France.

A more radical group of Polish exiles wanted outright overthrow of the existing system, drawing strength from the serfs. This faction already had an active membership in Galicia, where many had fled after the failed uprising. These people seem essentially to have been nationalists, but they took up the cause of peasant reform because they needed support.

There was still another faction, the *Mloda Polska* associated with Mazzini's Young Europe that was outright revolutionary, calling for Europe-wide revolt. These passionately left-wing Polish exiles had found sympathetic companions in international communities abroad, and picked up ideas of nationhood that ran counter to the experience of their ruthlessly dismembered fatherland. Throughout the revolutionary period of the late 1840's, the Lambert faction actively opposed the efforts of patriots like Adam Mickiewicz.[3]

There was nothing idealistic about the violent rising of 1846 in Galicia, a land where the majority of the population was made up of Ukrainian serfs. Matters were complicated by Austria's system of administration by which the whole region was fragmented.

In general the so-called political unit known as Austrian Galicia comprised Polish *szlachta* [nobility] and Ukrainian (Ruthenian) serfs. The Poles were Roman Catholic, the Ukrainians Greek Catholic. The Poles thought the Ukrainian language was a Polish dialect that was of no consequence, while the Ukrainians considered Polish to be a Ukrainian dialect. Poles (*Liakh*) were to the oppressed Ukrainian serfs the very embodiment of bondage and humiliation.[4]

It is difficult to accept the innocent notion of the Polish democratic movement that organized the Galician rising of 1846 that all they had to do was assemble the serfs, announce that they were free, and welcome them into their revolutionary ranks.[5] When the naive revolutionists moved toward their assigned meeting places in February 1846, they were met by angry bands of serfs who chopped them down mercilessly. The peasants carted the corpses and wounded (tied hand and foot) to police headquarters, where they were congratulated and rewarded with money.[6] Their blood lust raging, after their massacre of their would-be noble defenders, the serfs went on a rampage throughout Galicia, turning seven hundred and twenty-eight hapless noblemen into so many hideous cadavers, and leaving four hundred and seventy-four manors in smoking ruin before the imperial troops stopped them.[7]

Events of 1846 had nonetheless marked a turning point because Ukrainians had come to see themselves as members of a nation, and from that moment on there were those among them who were prepared to struggle for independence. However, it was not until the abolition of serfdom (September 1848) that there could be anything even remotely like a national movement, and even after that the peasants continued to be distrustful. Not only of the Polish *szlachta*, but of their own would-be leaders.[8] The miserable situation of clashing nationalisms within the Habsburg empire was a handy weapon for those who wanted to beat down emerging freedom and return to absolutism because the nationalists tended to fight each other instead of joining forces.

The spectacle of uncontrolled clashing interests should have served as a salutory lesson to the Germans of the *Vormärz*.

* * * * * * * *

At the other end of the spectrum stood Switzerland, in the center of industrializing Europe. A sophisticated country in startling contrast to Poland with its serfs. Switzerland played a significant role as far as Germany was concerned because it had long been the home of German exiles and revolutionists and innocent targets of royal ire. More than two decades before the crucial revolutionary period, the gymnast Karl Völker took refuge in Switzerland. Karl Follen continued his radical plans (organization of the *Jünglingsbund*) from a haven in that hospitable country. Lorenz Oken the naturalist moved to Zurich, and the Marburg statistician Bruno Hildebrand was able to establish himself at the university of Bern when threatened with imprisonment for "attempted treason". The determined radical Wilhelm Weitling made Geneva his base, finding numerous political exiles there whose views were congenial to him. These are only a few examples, taken at random.[9]

German officials were acutely aware of the kind treatment accorded in Switzerland to persons whom they regarded as dangerous theorists, conspirators and radicals, and kept a sharp eye on these unruly refugees. The refugees themselves had found it possible to establish printing presses and publishing houses close to the German border, and from there they sent floods of propaganda and pamphlets across into the home country. Specific presses in Switzerland had been threatened by the *Deutscher Bund* in the case of Heinrich Heine and the Young Germans. The official attack had included a severe warning to specified houses in Zurich, Herisau and Bern. Another famous publishing organization was the *Comptoir* at Zurich and Winterthur, under the direction of Julius Fröbel. In view of all this activity, it was inevitable that Germans should fight over copies of newspapers that would give them the latest news from Switzerland in November 1847, when the Swiss federal diet declared war on the cantons that had banded together as the Catholic *Sonderbund* two years before.

This was a dangerous situation, involving liberals and radicals on one side and a Catholic party that had the support of Metternich on the other. Trouble had been simmering ever since 1836, when the canton of Glarus limited the rights of the Catholics, who were a minority there, and again in 1841 when Luzern retaliated by curtailing the freedom of the press and denying certain rights to the Protestants. In 1841, Aargau had suppressed monasteries and convents. Gradually, the seven Catholic cantons formed a bloc, and there was considerable excitement when Luzern brought in Jesuits and put them in charge of the leading educational institutions (this occurred in 1844). Anticlerical radicals and Protestants in the country found common ground. In 1845 the seven Catholic cantons formed a military pact, placing their *Sonderbund* under a single command, and in addition to this move they sought assistance from Austria.

Just as in the rest of continental Europe, Switzerland underwent a severe economic crisis that year. The drop in the market could be attributed to the agricultural situation because foodstuff prices went up drastically, and this automatically curtailed private outlay for manufactured goods, and industrial enterprises suffered. The potato blight had struck in Switzerland, and also poor grain harvests. The cantonal governments were forced to buy grain abroad: Switzerland in fact was always in an unsteady position because she could only supply enough grain to care for the population during two hundred and eighty days of the normal year. In the emergency, the *Sonderbund* cantons were in a more favorable position than the others because they had the sympathy of their neighbors and were able to purchase necessities from the nearby Lombardy-Venetian states. In other parts of the confederation, the price of a loaf of bread more than doubled.[10]

The economic situation had its effects on political events. In the cantons of Geneva, Bern and St. Gall there was a swing in the direction of the liberals. In the election campaigns in Bern the radicals were astute enough to play down the matter of Jesuits and the *Sonderbund* and to stress the need for relief from residual feudal dues and taxes. The peasants listened because the poor harvests had made it extremely difficult for them to meet their tax obligations. The conservative *Basler Zeitung* editorialized that this was the first decisive victory that the so-called proletariat had won over all the other classes.[11] Although this may have been an overstatement, it was certainly true that in St. Gall canton the liberals did not hesitate on the eve of election, when it was too late for their opponents to respond, to put out flyers that accused the other side of having profited in the grain trade, to the detriment of the public.

All Switzerland had been in a state of agitation, with the Protestants much inflamed, ever since the defiant introduction of the Jesuits. Half measures were considered everywhere to have become impossible. The conflict reached "the pitch of fanaticism".[12] Matters came to a head in the summer of 1847 when the federal Diet voted the dissolution of the *Sonderbund* on the ground that it was unconstitutional. There was a stormy session of the Diet, where the presiding officer called attention to the fact that the whole conflict was centered around an extremely simple alternative: progress or stagnation. This was not peculiar to Switzerland, he said, speaking of "flames which are leaping up in every state in Europe to rekindle cold embers in the hearths of derelict constitutions."

> The participants themselves in this conflict are fully aware of the fact that the crisis in Switzerland is an integral part of the growing crisis in Europe.[13]

At that point Metternich tried to stir up the major powers. He was successful to the extent that the Austrian, Russian and Prussian diplomats made a dramatic exit. Palmerston and the British diplomats were unmoved.

A curious set of negotiations involving the canton of Neuchâtel (Neuenburg) provides some insight into the general complexity of Metternich's post-Napoleonic world.—This small canton had a dual character, because it was a remnant of territories belonging to the illustrious house of Orange-Nassau as well as a canton of the Swiss Confederation. In the course of many transformations after its original establishment as a *comté* by Charlemagne, Neuenburg had been transferred to Burgundy, confiscated by Louis XIV and so on, but the title and claims of Orange-Nassau had persisted. With the death of the last legitimate ruler, the *Fürstin* of Nemours-Longueville, Neuenburg was recognized as an open feudal estate (no longer in vassalage), and the inhabitants chose the king of Prussia as their rightful lord, he being then head of the house of Orange. Friedrich Wilhelm IV had therefore inherited the little principality, but at the same time he had become a member of the Swiss Confederacy because Neuenburg was a Swiss canton. He had retained his title of *Fürst* of Neuenburg, and once visited there, to the joy of the royalists, but he had relinquished any governmental authority over the canton. When the cantonal war threatened, the citizens of Neuenburg wanted to remain neutral, and called on their Prussian sovereign for help. The emotional Friedrich Wilhelm was stirred. He wrote movingly to Bunsen, his ambassador in London, asserting that he had a duty to the magnificent loyal little country and describing himself as *allein ihren Schutz und Schirm gegen grandiose Unterdrückung* [their sole protector and shield against enormous repression].[14] These communications directed to ambassador Bunsen bristled with multiple exclamation points, and almost every paragraph had its quota of emphatic underlinings, all showing that the Prussian king's mind was not too clear in its judgments.

*Das Blut des Bürgerkrieges ist geflossen und man will in London ???????!
Conferenzen. . . . Dies ist der letzte Augenblick, den Radicalismus der
Gottlosigkeit und Treulosigkeit zu Behandeln, wie Gott und die Ehre es
biethet . . . Das is so gewiss, als ich hier schreibe!!!!*[15] [The blood of civil
war has flowed, and they want to have conferences in London. . . . This is
the last moment for handling the radicalism of atheism and perfidy, as God
and honor command. . . . This is as certain as the fact that I sit here
writing]

He instructed Bunsen to try to arrange an international conference,
preferably to be held at Neuchâtel, where a plan could be devised that
would head off the "terrorist radicals". The agitated monarch was evidently forgetting that his membership in the federation depended upon
the principle of sovereignty of the cantons, and the majority were
clearly among the "terrorist radicals". This fact was borne in upon the
citizens of Neuenburg when the majority of cantons applied pressure,
demanding that they join forces with them. Majority rule was not recognized by Friedrich Wilhelm. Guizot in France was clear in his mind
that the great powers had distinctly guaranteed the Swiss constitution. This was likewise the feeling of Queen Victoria's new minister
Palmerston, but France and England were unfortunately in no mood
at that moment to combine their efforts. (They had recently crossed
swords over the dynastic and political problems involved in the marriages of the young queen of Spain and her sister.) Palmerston was
feeling definitely hostile toward Louis-Philippe. Metternich sympathized
with the *Sonderbund* but had not had much success in generating
enthusiasm for the cause.

The twelve liberal cantons moved cautiously, being unwilling to
engage in war, but the Catholic cantons were in a belligerent mood.
Pope Pius IX sent a letter to his *nuntius* in July 1847, urging peaceful
solutions. The pontiff pointed out that whereas the rest of the world
was watching with bated breath in concern for the stability of the
Confederation, "We from the height of our apostolic office keep religious interests in mind and we recognize above all, with the concern
of a father, in the depth of our heart, the danger for this great nation. . . . Let not the earth of the Confederation be reddened by
brothers' blood." This letter was accompanied by a note, commanding that the papal communication be published. This did not happen
because the Jesuits blocked it. The *nuntius* was later to say that the
Jesuits wanted the war. On the very eve of the outbreak of hostilities,
Nuntius Macioti said, he approached the Jesuit father Roh in order to
discuss a last effort for peace, and Roh answered, "Well, that would be
a great misfortune."[16]

It turned out to be a rather civilized little war, carried out in a brisk businesslike Swiss manner with few casualties and a victory within twenty-six days.[17] Neither side was especially warlike. In fact, in the one hand-to-hand encounter, where bayonets and sabres could have been used, there were only two deaths, both from firearms. From six batteries used in the conflict, a grand total of 378 shots were fired.[18] The Swiss were clearly not eager to kill each other. In the end, there were 74 deaths and 377 wounded on the side of the Confederation, and 24 deaths and 116 wounded on the *Sonderbund* side.

Liberals and radicals all over Europe must have purred: the first armed clash, and the liberals had won! Marx and Engels printed a victory statement in their *Brüsseler Deutsche Zeitung*. This was, they said, "the battle of progress against a feudal past, and of democracy against the baseness of the aristocracy and the Jesuits. . . . Theirs was a victory for the people in every country in Europe."

Switzerland had indeed ordered her affairs well. From then on, the old single vote for each canton was abolished, and the cantons' vote reflected their actual population numbers. The old cantons, with their sparse settlement, could no longer control the actions of the whole. The heavily populated "new" cantons held the majority and were able to swing the confederation into the path of progress, even during the troublesome years following 1848 when all the rest of Europe was once more in the hands of the old guard.

* * * * * * *

The news of the Swiss success was received with enthusiasm in Rome, Florence and Livorno, with noisy demonstrations and torch-light parades outside the Swiss consulates. The demonstrators cheered for the Swiss—and for their own independence.

German liberals usually thought of reform in terms of a united Germany led by Prussia, or a larger unit under the aegis of Austria. Italian liberals confronted much more thorny choices because Italy's major states harbored many an incongruity. In the north there were two provinces that were urbanized and fairly prosperous, with a good proportion of educated people, but these provinces (Lombardy and Venetia) belonged to Austria and were occupied by Austrian troops. Also in the north was Piedmont, whose ruling house of Savoy traditionally rivaled the Habsburgs, but King Carlo Alberto was impossibly conservative. The fact that part of his kingdom was the island of Sardinia was an added difficulty. Tuscany was supposedly independent, but in actuality it was more or less an Austrian protectorate. The largest, most populous state was the Kingdom of the Two Sicilies, down at the bottom of the boot, around Naples and below, ruled by Spanish Bourbons. Very poor and backward, again with the complication of division into two segments, one of them being the unruly island of Sicily. There were smaller states, like the duchy of Parma, ruled first by Pauline Bonaparte, and later by Napoleon's widow, the former empress Marie-Louise. To add to the general difficulty, cutting across the peninsula was Rome and its Papal States.

There had always been a strong undercurrent of anti-Austrian feeling. Ever since the publication of Silvio Pellico's moving little book, in which he vividly described his sufferings during eight years as a captive in the Austrian fortress of the Spielberg near Austerlitz,[19] there had been continuing hostility against the Austrians. Pellico (1789–1854) had been picked up by the Austrian police because his writings in the journal *Il Conciliatore* had led them to suspect that he might be one of the *Carbonari*. On scant evidence, the young man was confined in a cold solitary cell, chained, sleeping on a hard platform without cover, fed on near-starvation rations of bread and watery soup, forbidden to communicate with his fellow prisoners, and deprived of any information from the outside world. He reported that his punishment was rated as *carcere duro*, which was supposedly a comfortable grade above that meted out to common criminals. Only once Pellico had actual physical contact with a fellow prisoner, when that unfortunate had to undergo surgical amputation of a leg and asked that the man next door be brought in to hold him during the ordeal.

For one brief moment, liberals thought that they had found a solution to the problem of national unification. A new pope, Pius IX (Giovanni Maria Mastai Ferretti, 1792–1878) had shown signs of liberal tendencies as archbishop of Spoleto in 1831, when he responded to rebellion there by outlining various administrative reforms. Unfortunately, the popular joy and the liberals' hope did not last long. Pius issued a disheartening encyclical *Qui pluribus* in November of 1846, in which he emphasized his predecessor's condemnation of all the fundamental principles of liberalism. Between the lines there stood an unmistakable message. Pius would never transform the Papal States into a constitutional state, and never would he engage in any war of liberation against Austria.

Though most liberals contented themselves with theorizing, there were the *Carbonari* with their network of pseudo-masonic connections all over Europe in the opening decades of the century. They wanted no monarchs, no papal leadership. They wanted a republic and were willing to risk their lives in a series of unsuccessful insurrections to achieve that end. Among the *Carbonari* was a true revolutionary, in the person of Giuseppe Mazzini (1805–1872), who came from the independent city of Genoa.[20] He was betrayed by a fellow member of the *Carbonari*, arrested, jailed and released after three months because there was no proof of his involvement. Mazzini then fled into exile (this was in 1830), where he remained for most of the next four decades. He had become aware that the *Carbonari* would always be ineffectual because they were so intent on secrecy that they could not possibly have a common program. Perhaps from exile it would be possible to organize the would-be revolutionists and forge them into a real force.

Mazzini's energy and zeal were on the heroic scale. There are said to be more than fifteen thousand of his letters, all written in a beautiful microscopic hand, that he dispatched steadily to all parts of Europe and the New World. Such a voluminous correspondence soon attracted the attention of the censors, who opened and read his letters and passed information about the contents on to Vienna and St. Petersburg and Paris and London, as well as to the various Italian courts and to the pope. For a number of years, in exile at Marseilles or in Switzerland, Mazzini did not dare leave his room because he was in danger of being apprehended and expelled: plenty of time for reflection and letter-writing, in other words. Time too to write to his dear Giuditta Sidoli of whom the world would have known nothing had it not been for the industrious archivists of the foreign governments. Because of the diligence of their secret agents, Metternich and the pope were able to enjoy Mazzini's love letters.

While he was still in Marseilles, in 1831, Mazzini founded his *Giovine Italia* [Young Italy], which was to become a formidable model for secret organizations everywhere. It performed as a genuine political party, its members kept informed about development of the program and formally proving their membership by payment of dues. Within the next year or two, there were similar patriotic groups in Germany, Greece, Spain, Russia, Poland, Turkey, Bohemia, Ukraine, Argentina, Austria and the Tyrol. This was enough to alarm the pope, who organized intense surveillance directed at "the immense designs of this extraordinary man".

Young Italy was decidedly revolutionary, though it was understood that support would be given to any ruler who was daring enough to assume a liberal stance. People joined Young Italy by the thousands and studied Mazzini's detailed instructions for guerrilla warfare. Small insurrections, he felt, would create general alarm yet not do too much damage to private property or cause inordinate loss of life. He knew that violence was inevitable.—Metternich, reading these documents, expressed the opinion that mere membership in Young Italy was high treason and deserved the death penalty. Before long there was a special eighty-man agency in Vienna, charged with the tracking of Italian exiles. Meanwhile, Mazzini's periodical, *Giovine Italia*, most of which he wrote himself, found fascinated readers in all ranks of life throughout Italy.

An attempted military coup in 1833 so frightened Carlo Alberto, the king of Piedmont-Sardinia, that he caused twelve conspirators to be publicly executed. Another hundred were thrown into prison, and hundreds more fled the country. It was in the course of this episode that Mazzini's close friend Jacopo Ruffini killed himself in jail, in order to avoid betraying anyone under torture, an action that was to haunt Mazzini all his life. Mazzini himself was condemned to death, the sentence being read *in absentia* outside his parents' home.

Some of Mazzini's schemes were much too visionary for any hope of realization. There was, for example, his idea that it would be helpful if there were mutiny in the navy of Carlo Alberto's Piedmont. This idea excited Giuseppe Garibaldi (1807–1882), who at the time was a ship's officer in the Black Sea. He signed on with the Piedmontese fleet, thinking to help organize the mutiny, but spies discovered the plot and Garibaldi had to flee, under a sentence of death. In spite of such notably spectacular patriots, it has to be said that on the whole, most people in Italy preferred to stay at home and protect their possessions, not risking their lives. Mazzini was to comment that an Italian nation would hardly come into existence unless the clash of individual rights was transcended by a readiness for self-sacrifice and a greater recognition of collective responsibility. There had to be a revolution in thinking and behavior, in other words.

Mazzini had abused Swiss hospitality by planning the Piedmont mutiny from there, and he was forced to move on, this time to England, where he was to spend most of his life. It is an odd comment on Mazzini as a person that the little Swiss town of Grenchen where he had been living tried to protect him by offering him honorary citizenship. The reaction of the English was equally unexpected. Mazzini found warm friendship there, among such luminaries as John Stuart

Mill , who said that Mazzini was "one of the men I most respect", and
the Carlyles, Thomas and Jane. Carlyle wrote about him that "a more
beautiful person I never beheld. . . . He had fine tastes, [he was an
admirer of Palestrina and was himself a fine musician and singer] but
he gave himself up as a martyr and sacrifice to his aims for Italy. He
lived almost in squalor. . . ."[21] Mazzini was liked for his lively sense
of fun, which masked his depression over what he called the hell of
exile. "That slow, bitter, lingering death which none can know but the
exile himself, that consumption of the soul which has only one hope
to console it"—the wistful hope that some day it may be possible to
return to the homeland.

In 1845, still in London, Mazzini began to cherish the hope that he
might indeed return to Italy. His propaganda campaign had borne fruit,
he thought, to the extent that Europeans generally had become aware
of the fact that there was a problem in Italy, a land still divided into
eight countries, where one might find as many as seven customs stations strung along a thirty-kilometer route, and where despotic rulers
who spoke a foreign language controlled the unwilling lives of their
subjects. In September of that year there was another of those infuri-
atingly incompetent uprisings—this time in Romagna—for which he
was incorrectly blamed. Mazzini was deeply discouraged because some
of his followers had been engaged in the rising, counter to his wishes,
and had joined forces with moderates whose goals were much different—they wanted constitutional reforms, not unification. He found
himself writing twenty or more letters a day, feeling that he was beginning all over again "like a spider whose web has been ruined by some
troublesome flies".

By the end of the difficult year of 1847, the moderates had managed to gain a few reforms here and there that foreshadowed some
kind of Italian unity. There was at least limited freedom of the press,
and it had become possible for scholars to meet freely in a general
scientific congress. Even in Lombardy there was quiet movement toward some kind of recognized responsibility within the Austria-dominated government, though Metternich's response had been harsh. It
was a sign of growing hostility toward him that rich landowners and
wealthy merchants were making conspicuous donations to charity in
that time of near famine. Not so much in the interests of alleviating
suffering as from motives of self-preservation. There was genuine fear
that Metternich's government might repeat its suspected Galician move
of the previous year. It was believed that in 1846 the Galician peasants had been deliberately stirred up against the nobility.[22]

That Austria was prepared to intervene in Italy had been made all too clear by the abrupt occupation of the citadel of Ferrara in July 1847. Much to the irritation of the pope because Ferrera was within the confines of the Papal States, Metternich had made this move on the grounds that he had to protect the garrison there, where there had been a demonstration directed against Austria. Metternich was becoming strangely careless, no longer deeply concerned about the principle of legitimacy that he had championed for so many years. In November of 1846, for example, he had seen fit to annex the free republic of Cracow—a step that was in direct violation of the supposed absolute bar against territorial alterations of boundaries set by the Congress of Vienna and that generated nationalist feelings among the Slavs in the Habsburg empire.—The visibility of foreign occupying forces in the Italian peninsula did much to accelerate and enhance the public restiveness and readiness for revolt, though oddly enough within occupied Lombardy tensions and grievances were not acute, so that any impulse for a rising there would have to come from outside.

In the first months of the actual year of revolution, there had been various risings—at Palermo in mid-January, in Venice a few days later, as well as in Tuscany. But the Venetian leaders were thrown into prison, and Austrian soldiers quelled a student uprising in Padua. These events happened before the serious outbreaks of Paris, Berlin, and Vienna. Authorities everywhere must have understood that it would take little to set off a train of explosions all over the peninsula. As far as the European revolutions of 1848 were concerned, Italy was well in the vanguard.

Notes

1 Benjamin Goriely, "Poland in 1848" in *Opening of an Era*, pp. 355–357.

2 Hans Henning Hahn, "Die Diplomatie des Hôtel Lambert 1831–1847," *Jahrbücher für Geschichte Osteuropas*, n.F.21 (1973): 345–374; idem, *Aussenpolitik in der Emigration. Die Exildiplomatie Adam Jerzy Czartoryskis 1830–1840*, passim.

3 The legion fought bravely in one last-ditch engagement at Lonato in August 1848, following the crushing defeat of the forces of King Carlo-Alberto at Custozza by the Austrian commander Radetsky.

4 Jan Kozik, *The Ukrainian National Movement in Galicia, 1815–1849*, pp. 3–, 161–173.

5 Jerome Blum, *Noble Landowners and Agriculture in Austria, 1815–1848*, pp. 225–226.

6 Goriely, pp. 362–363.

7 John-Paul Himka, *Galician Villagers and the Ukrainian National Movement in the Nineteenth Century*, p. 24 note 157.

8 Kozik, p. 173.

9 Herzen, *Letters from France and Italy 1847–1851*. A fascinating account of the international community of émigrés in Switzerland at a somewhat later date.

10 Erwin Bucher, *Die Geschichte des Sonderbundskrieges*, p. 36.

11 Ibid., p. 37. Bucher thinks that this judgment may have been "tendentious" although he agrees that social causes played a role.

12 Jean Halperin, "The Transformation of Switzerland; Prelude to the Revolution," in *Opening of an Era*, p. 60.

13 Ibid., p. 61.

14 Leopold von Ranke, editor, *Aus dem Briefwechsel Friedrich Wilhelms IV. mit Bunsen*, p. 157.

15 Ibid., p.148.

16 Bucher, p. 40.

17 Ibid., pp. 515–519.

18 Ranke, p. 153.

19 Silvio Pellico, *Le mie prigioni*, passim.

20   Dennis Mack Smith, *Mazzini*, pp. 1–74.

21   Ibid., p. 31

22   Delio Cantimori, "Italy in 1848," in *Opening of an era*, pp. 116–117.

Chapter 10

France en Route to the Barricades

In volatile Paris, everyone with the possible exception of Louis-Philippe (1773–1850) must have been aware that the Orléans monarchy of July was in danger. The king himself was comfortable in his conviction that his dear subjects loved and admired him. The metropolis seethed with unhappy *émigrés* and unemployed workmen, as well as students who viewed themselves as revolutionists whose prime target was the prosperous, self-satisfied middle class. Men had cropped up who, as determined professional revolutionaries, strained their resources and energies in an effort to generate feelings of solidarity among the lower classes, with the intention of overthrowing the existing government.—Men like Auguste Blanqui (1805–1881), that inveterate believer in the effectiveness of secret societies, including the *Société des saisons* and the *Société des droits de l'homme*, whose members, he thought, might act as a trained élite that could lead the proletarian masses to military victory. There was also the flotsam washed up by the tides of human despair (*les misérables*), those wretches whose deplorable condition came to public attention at the time of the 1832 cholera epidemic that swept across Europe. Any small incident could touch off a riot, a situation that people resignedly took almost for granted.

The German revolution has often been described as a movement that started at the top, among the intellectual elite. It may be worth noting that workers' names rarely occur among those of prominent figures of the French revolution of 1848. With the exception of "Albert", a member of the provisional government that was set up at the time of Louis-Philippe's abdication, and a man known simply as "Marche" who had his brief moment in the sun as spokesman for a mob that challenged the new government with its urgent demands when the revolution had come to a conclusion barely twenty-four hours earlier, not one activist appears who was not a politician, an editor, a lawyer, a scientist, a philosopher, or a historian. Even professional agitators like Auguste Blanqui were part of the educated middle class. It seems strange that the revolution is thought of as something organized by the proletariat.

It is true that radical secret societies like the *Charbonnerie* and the *Société des saisons* had a long history among the French working class, but their activities had subsided with the imprisonment of Blanqui and Barbès in 1839. There was an obscure group that called itself the *Nouvelle saisons* ("Albert" was active here), and an even more obscure offshoot known as the *Société dissidente* that has left little or no trace. It is unlikely that either of these would have been effective in promoting worker solidarity.

In the tacit alliance of intellectuals (students, reformers) and manual workers, for example, there was bound to be considerable uneasiness. An editorial in the student newspaper, *La Lanterne* had pointed out, on the occasion of a joint banquet held by students and workers on 14 July 1847 in celebration of the great Revolution that "Our elder brothers of the schools . . . fraternized with the people in combat, but, strange as it may seem, these same men who were truly brothers of the proletariat in battle, in all probability would not have dined in public with one of them three months later: and on their part the proletarian would have refused such an invitation." [1] Although they had closed ranks and fought shoulder to shoulder on the barricades in the July Revolution of 1830, there were inevitable strains of jealousy. The hard-pressed laborers, living as they did on an average daily wage of less than four francs, were aware that university students enjoyed monthly allowances of two hundred francs or more. Animosity was bound to spring up when they reflected that in moments of carefree frivolity some of these young blades might put down as much as ten francs for a meal at Magny's. [2] As sons of judges, lawyers, doctors and so on, most came from mid-level *cadres choyés* [pampered groups]. All were intended for careers in medicine, law, or the civil service. Lowly struggling workmen must have looked speculatively at these allies of theirs. Against such family backgrounds, why would students be inclined to take sides with the rebellious poor, anyhow?—Members of almost any modern generation ought to know the answer to that question. Freed from parental supervision and the strict discipline of the secondary schools, on their own in a huge teeming city—student opposition to governmental authority would almost be automatic. Street demonstrations exerted a powerful pull on such young people, but the workers understood that though times were lean, these cheerful fellow rebels could anticipate a life of relative ease and would readily lapse at a moment's notice into the comfort of *bourgeois* success.

This is not the appropriate place for a description of all the conflicting agenda and misunderstandings that led to the firing of the first fatal shots and the confusion of 22 February 1848, or even of the subsequent misfortunes of the provisional government after the overthrow of Louis-Philippe. What is certain is that Germans, observing the happenings of the next four months in Paris which coincided with their own revolution could have learned valuable lessons about the dynamics of revolt. Even in the case of a unified nation like France, there were innumerable pitfalls. How much more so for thirty-nine small states, clamped between the formidable jaws of the Austro-Prussian vise. How much more difficult in the case of stubborn monarchs like Friedrich Wilhelm IV of Prussia.

It stands to reason that in any nation as troubled as France, serious political differences were to be expected. Since there was no simple two-party system, the factions on left and right were too numerous to be mentioned, but another antagonism that was superimposed on the difference of political opinion must be mentioned: namely, genuine distrust and lack of self-confidence. On the very eve of the outbreak in February 1848, members of the major secret societies which in actuality performed like political parties were conferring anxiously. Trouble the next day was almost a certainty: what part ought they play?

In addition to these factors, there was another social antagonism, no doubt the most pronounced of all—the contempt that Parisians felt for the ignorant unemployable young people on their streets, and the reciprocal contempt of the *gamins* for society in general. These "dregs" threw rocks at lamps and windows as a matter of principle.

Far off in Potsdam, Friedrich Wilhelm IV must have read the news of all this with interest and probably with complacency. Since he was not in favor of the use of armed force against his "dear Berliners", he may have read with peculiar interest any dispatches that recounted the turbulent events of this strange Paris outbreak and its aftermath.

* * * * * * *

For four hectic months, the new republic struggled to maintain a semblance of balance, but beginning on the very day of Louis-Philippe's abdication when the widowed *duchesse* d'Orléans made her gallant though ineffectual attempt to present her nine-year-old son, the *comte de Paris* as the king's designated successor, confusion, mistrust, and violence or the threat of it reigned.

The members of the provisional government were not men who could work as a team. They had been selected in an unorthodox way from lists drawn up by the editorial boards of two leading newspapers, the *National* and the *Réforme* and read off to a tumultuous meeting at the *Chambre des députés* where the mob had broken in during the brief appearance of the *duchesse* d'Orléans and her son. The shouted approval of the mob served as an official vote. These newly named colleagues then walked to the Hôtel de Ville, passing with hesitant difficult steps along the quai de la Mégisserie where there were still barricades at every twenty paces. They picked their way over dry blood and broken pieces of equipment and went around dead horses and discarded bayonets while shouting people crowded the curbs and nearby balconies. At the Hôtel de Ville, their names were again read, and the "vote" was confirmed by the excited multitude. They took refuge in a small room in the Hôtel de Ville, but their deliberations were interrupted by the arrival of the popular socialist Louis Blanc, who had been voted into the administration by the acclamation of the people outside. He was known for his theoretical pamphlet called *Le droit au travail* [the right to work] from which comes the famous phrase "to each according to his need, from each according to his abilities". Blanc was accompanied by three more popularly acclaimed members, Albert Martin, a workman known thereafter to his more sophisticated associates simply as Albert, along with the journalist Armand Marrast and his colleague Ferdinand Flocon. These were the men in whose hands was placed the responsibility of governing France.

Not unexpectedly, there were scenes of wild jubilation as the Republic was proclaimed, culminating when the royal throne was dragged from the Tuileries and carried in triumphant procession to various barricades, where anonymous speakers enjoyed the opportunity to seat themselves on it and utter incoherent inanities. In the end, the throne was deposited at the Place de la Bastille and set afire. Hundreds joined in an ecstatic round dance as it burned.

Harsh reality faced the members of the provisional government all too soon, and their mistakes began to multiply. The insurmountable difficulty that was to plague them was the stubborn fact that the moderates (who were in the majority) wanted reform—a political adjust-ment, in other words—while the street people believed that they had been victorious in a social revolution, although they were not certain just what such a drastic upheaval might imply.

A throng bearing a red flag presented itself the next day before the place where the new government was in session. Their representative, a determined young man named Marche, entered the conference room, banged the floor with the butt of his gun, stared accusingly into the eyes of Lamartine and after an ominous silence announced that he was there to demand that the government recognize and proclaim the universal right to work. "Citizens, the revolution ended twenty-four hours ago. The people are still waiting for results." This was social revolution with a vengeance, but when Marche was asked just what specific plans were involved, he could offer no response and ended by stating that if the government needed more time to work things out, the people would be willing to suffer through another three months of misery. But no more. The government had no plans either.

Within twenty-four hours therefore, the Republic stumbled into the error of making a promise it could not possibly keep. The momentum of revolution was still too strong to be resisted. On that fateful day Louis Blanc composed a decree that pledged the government to pro-vide work for any citizen who needed it. There was a follow-up on 27 February, in the form of a decree that established national workshops [ateliers nationaux] where the unemployed, who at that moment num-bered about eight thousand in Paris, would be assigned to appropriate work. These workshops were set up in the respective arrondissements, where—in the inevitable lack of suitable tasks—the workers were shuttled unhappily from one workshop to another. It did not take long for small knots of potential rioters to collect at these ineffectual offices.

The distracted heads of the new government responded to this prob-lem by assuring the unemployed men that even if there were no work they would be paid 1 franc 50 centimes per day. Provision of food and medical care was also promised. As the word spread, a flood of workers swept in from the departments as well as from abroad. Within two weeks, the administration was forced to declare its inability to handle the problem, turning it over to one Émile Thomas, an optimis-tic volunteer who received the title of commissioner and director of the workshops. There were an estimated seventeen thousand appli-cants at that time, and it was hoped that the number would diminish but on 15 March it had risen to more than forty-nine thousand. The additional applicants had been lured by the prospect of guaranteed pay. By June the number had increased to more than one hundred and ten thousand.[3]

The workshops had some unforeseen effects that were not at all pleasing to the conservative middle class. When all workers were lumped together without consideration of their trades or skills, thousands of them came to see that they had a common interest. This awareness of a shared status was brought home by the workshops more effectively than by the propaganda of the numerous workers' clubs that were proliferating everywhere.

There was another complication that tangled the affairs of the new republic. There were too many rival forces for law and order on the streets of Paris. There was the regular army, the troops *de la ligne*. There was also the *Garde national*, made up of men from each of the twelve respective *arrondissements* of the city who traditionally considered themselves to be a kind of elite organization but that after the proclamation of the republic had been thrown open to all adult males. In addition, there were two new organizations. The first was developed by the self-appointed police chief, colorful Marc Caussidière. These were the *Montagnards*, who presumably replaced the hated *Gardes municipaux* (disbanded by governmental decree). There were more than two thousand members of this organization, all colorfully uniformed and receiving 2 francs 25 centimes a day (more than the army men). This force was recruited from those who had fought on the barricades, or who had belonged to one of the secret societies in days prior to the revolution, or who had been political prisoners.

The second new organization was the *Garde nationale mobile* that was initiated by Lamartine. This guard comprised twenty-four units, recruited from the Parisian proletariat, and perhaps was intended to act as a counterbalance to the Montagnards. Here again the pay was higher than that of the regular army men. Through the democratization of the national guard and the formation of two new units drawn from the proletariat, forces were put into play that would tend to break the solidarity of the working class. In the course of the violent days of June, it became clear that by virtue of military organization, uniforms and regular pay, the *Garde mobile* had forgotten its origins in the Paris slums and felt that it had arrived among the "haves". For this reason it entered the fray as an enemy of the workers, fighting ferociously in defense of the existing government.

Old-time radicals understood that the stakes were high. General elections based on universal suffrage were scheduled for early April and there was precious little time for education of the workers and of the lower classes throughout the country, where conservatives were firmly entrenched. The best way to secure the success won at the barricades would be to engage the minds and enthusiasms of the Parisian working class and then send out well-informed people who could persuade their counterparts in the provinces that their votes must go to the true republicans. After the election of the constituent assembly, it would be a disaster if the provisional government were to be replaced by conservatives. Even in the provisional government the majority was more reformist than revolutionary in its inclinations.

Auguste Blanqui, freed at last from police surveillance, immediately set about organization of a new revolutionary elite. Within a few days, his *Société républicaine centrale* had collected three hundred and twenty-five members. "It goes without saying that there was a core of Freemasons."[4] It is also no cause for astonishment that lists of original members include those who had been tormented, suppressed, or imprisoned under Louis-Philippe. Even in his satellite organizations at the Sorbonne and the Collège de France, Blanqui maintained his preferred arrangement of a small group of elites and the larger rank and file. In spite of initial enthusiasm, there was a drift away from the radical *club Blanqui* as it was popularly known, when it became obvious that the leader wanted to undermine the provisional government, not support it.

Four demonstrations that occurred in Paris clearly showed the gradual disintegration of the united front of the radicals, and with it the failure of the revolution.

Certainly the solidarity of the workers had been broken. In the ensuing days of horror (the *journées de juin*) when the ultimate insurrection broke out, the men and women on the barricades found themselves attacked not only by the regular army forces under General Louis Eugène Cavaignac (1802–1857) but also by contingents of the *Garde nationale* in which members of the workshops were enrolled, as well as by their former allies, the students, and the excitable street kids who had been organized as the *Garde mobile*. To make matters worse, reinforcements came in by railroad, all on the side of the republic. Moreover, though the statistics are admittedly not entirely reliable, it seems that a large percentage of the members of the *ateliers* withheld their support, even though one of the major causes of the outbreak was the knowledge that the newly elected *Assemblée* was feeling its way toward the breakup of the workshops. The explanation of this strange reaction on the part of workshop members may lie in the fact that they were still receiving their pay and were not in the mood to sacrifice it even in defense of workers' rights and solidarity.

The barricade fighters had no true leader. There was a wild unhinged man named Louis Pujol who incited the desperate people to insurrection. He mouthed inflammatory speeches in which he jumbled together Cain and Abel and the kiss of Judas, the wind of the wrath of God, Tarquin, and bayonets in a demagogic shout that brought his uncomprehending hearers to their feet, and even inspired them to fall on their knees to swear an oath that they would fight to the death, but he was no true commander. His enthralled followers marched behind him, shouting *Vive Barbès!* or *Vive Napoléon!*[5] In spite of the lack of any understanding of the issues, and without competent leaders, the workers fought brilliantly and displayed splendid courage in defending their lost cause. Both sides, in fact, performed marvels of useless heroism that one can only deplore.

> The Saint-Antoine barricade was three stories high and seven hundred feet across. Nineteen barricades were lined up in the depth of the streets behind this master barricade. . . . What was it made of? . . . Of the monstrous gathering of all wrath—chairs with the stuffing gone, cabbage stump, tattered cloth . . . and curses. . . . An omnibus presented its shafts to who knows what horses of the air. . . . In this pellmell of despair, fragments of mansards with their painted paper. . . . The few weapons that defended this fortress fired bits of pottery, bones, buttons . . . and one heard shouted commands, song, drum beats, women's sobs, and starvelings' bursts of laughter. It was a pile of rubbish, and it was Sinai.[6]

Estimates on the number of deaths range from one thousand four hundred and sixty to two thousand, not counting the one hundred and fifty prisoners who were shot or bayoneted immediately after the last barricade fighter surrendered. "One would never have supposed that we had so much left in our souls to be destroyed," mourned Herzen.

The level of political sophistication in France far surpasssed that of Germany or any of the other continental countries that were about to be swept along by the tide of revolution, yet evidently the French had not been capable of rising to the challenge of universal suffrage. The middle class had been genuinely frightened by the prospect of proletarian control, and the clumsy improvisations of the provisional government had given them the chance to split the ranks of the workers. Louis Blanc and Albert, the only representatives of the people, had not the strength to insist on aggressive handling of a program that would benefit the workers. Moreover, they were unable to launch any kind of propaganda effort that would have convinced the public at large that drastic measures were required. Perhaps they were themselves so convinced of the rightness of their cause that they could not believe that such propaganda was necessary.

At the height of enthusiasm in the early months of 1848, middle class and proletarians alike cheered *La République*, but banners on the June barricades proclaimed *La République démocratique et sociale*. Here was a cleavage that was to be carried across frontiers to other revolutions.

Meanwhile, in France, Louis Napoléon was going from strength to strength. Before long he would be president, and then by a *coup d'état*, emperor.

Blanqui once stated in a trial that his permanent residence was "prison": this was again the case during the years 1848–1859, 1861–1865, 1871–1879. It is the considered opinion of a modern scholar that at the prison on Belle-Ile-en-Mer (off the coast of Brittany) where Blanqui, Barbès and several hundreds of their followers were confined, it was deliberate policy to demoralize the prisoners, to divide them , and to "assassinate them" physically and mentally because they had committed the unpardonable crime of unseating an established government.[7]

During the hectic months of the Parisian ordeal, Ludwig I of Bavaria had abdicated, Metternich had fled from Vienna, there had been barricade fighting in Berlin, and the newly elected members of a German constitutional parliament had entered the *Paulskirche* of Frankfurt am Main in stately procession, cheered by thousands. Was the chance for successful revolutionary reform any better in these teutonic strongholds than it had been in France?

Notes

1   John G. Gallaher, *The Students of Paris and the Revolution of 1848*, p. 29.

2   Ibid., pp. 5–11.

3   Georges Bourgin, "France and the Revolution of 1848," in *Opening of an Era*, p. 89

4   Maurice Dommanget, *August Blanqui et la révolution de 1848*, pp. 37–38.

5   Daniel Stern, *Histoire de la révolution*, 3:150–154.

6   Hugo, *Les misérables.* *"La guerre entre quatres murs."*

7   Jean-Yves Mollier, "Belle-Ile-en-Mer, prison politique (1848–1858)" in *Maintien de l'ordre et polices en France et en Europe au XIXe siècle*, p. 202.

Chapter 11

The Monarchs at Bay

Brussels was tense in the middle of February 1848. The extreme left-wingers who had congregated there around Karl Marx were in a state of nervous anticipation. The French exile Imbert had managed to make a secret visit to Paris and had returned with the news that this time there was going to be a serious insurrection.

On the evening of 24 February a small group of excited young men waited on the railway station platform. No train had come through from Paris since early morning. Stephan Born, the future labor leader, was among those who stood looking anxiously down the tracks, seeing at last that a train was arriving.[1] Before the locomotive had come to a complete halt, the engineer jumped out, shouting that the red flag was flying in Paris and that *la république est proclamée*. Born and his companions answered with a triumphant yell.

Word of the fall of Louis-Philippe shot all over the city and voices were raised in lively chorus of the *Brabançonne* and the *Marseillaise*. In restaurants and beer halls the older middle class people stared open-mouthed at the shouting youngsters. Born remembered seeing a handsome lawyer named Tedesco who jumped onto a table in one of the restaurants and launched into a flaming harangue. He went then from one café to another, followed by a steadily increasing crowd. Cheers rose in thunderous echo wherever he went.

In spite of all this enthusiasm, Belgium was not to be swept away by the revolutionary wave. King Léopold I was a "clever statesman who piloted his little ship cold-bloodedly and wisely through the stormy sea". He summoned his liberal minister, the *Bürgermeister*, and the Brussels city council and said to them, "The country elected me and as king I have always honored the will of the land. There has been no serious complaint leveled at my administration. For what purpose should blood flow? If the country wishes me to lay aside my crown, I will do it. No citizen shall fight against citizen with weapons. Just say the word and I go." Before long there were shouts on the streets. *Vive le roi!*

Born overestimated King Léopold's power. His success was guaranteed in large measure by England's attitude. The English minister Palmerston was inclined to view the French revolution favorably but he did not want to see an expansion of French power in the direction of Antwerp, and for this reason he extended protection to the Belgian kingdom.[2]

There were a few attempts on the part of members of various radical clubs to stir up trouble but there were no barricades. The clever monarch had made doubly sure that there would be no serious uprising. He called in a regiment of infantry and stationed it on the square in front of the *Rathaus*, and supported it with a squadron of cavalry. The commander announced that there would be three warning drum rolls, and that the square must be cleared. At the third, the infantry moved forward, bayonets fixed. No shots were fired, but the would-be revolutionists fled in disorder.

Born and his companions (Friedrich Engels was one of them) were on the sidewalk outside a café entrance when a cavalryman rode up, seized Wilhelm Wolf—an editor of the *Neue rheinische Zeitung,* in exile because of his activities in the *Burschenschaft* movement—and dragged him away, holding him by the collar. It all happened in a moment. Wolf was in prison for a week, during which time he was repeatedly kicked and beaten. His home meanwhile was ransacked and various papers were taken. On 5 March he was escorted under guard to Valenciennes and ordered to leave immediately for France—without any of his belongings.[3]

The intention of the government was clear. Foreign agitators were to be expelled. This included Karl Marx, who was arrested but then allowed to travel to Paris, where his long-suffering wife Jenny and their three children had already gone a day or two earlier. But not before Jenny had a harrowing night, locked up "by unfortunate mistake" officials said, in the company of a rough band of harlots. Jenny was a heroine in many ways, but she was also rigid in her moral judgments. The fact of having been jailed with prostitutes was a serious shock to her.—Born admired her and made it clear that she was not by any means a "stocking-knitting, kettle-stirring housewife".

The expulsion of Wolf and Marx may have eased king Léopold's life somewhat, but he was unintentionally making trouble for Friedrich

Wilhelm IV of Prussia. Within weeks, Marx, Wolf and others had reassembled in Cologne, where they promptly began to publish their *Neue Rheinische Zeitung,* which called for a single, indivisible, democratic German republic—and war with Russia. To see such inflammatory demands appearing within one of his most important provinces must have been deeply troubling to the uneasy Prussian monarch.

King Léopold ruled with a steady hand, but four days after the stormy events in Brussels he wrote a letter to Friedrich Wilhelm IV in Berlin, intent on enlisting strong united international support. Referring to "the atrocious misfortune in Paris," he stated his firm conviction that it was imperative for Prussia, England, Russia and Austria to set up a conference in London. "Nothing impresses France so much as this holding together of the four powers."[4]

Friedrich Wilhelm meanwhile was writing in agitation to Queen Victoria (27/28 February 1848). His distraught letter declared that "my comparatively insignificant crown will be destroyed" and that the people would confront a fearful century of "disorder, lawlessness and atheism." Above all, it was necessary to impress upon the threatened people that "we know our holy duty."[5]

Throughout Germany, in the days immediately following the Paris revolution, a flood of petitions was directed by earnest subjects to their sovereigns. In most cases, there was an underlying assumption that most problems could be equitably solved within the framework of a constitutional monarchy. The wave of unrest was spreading, however. In small towns, in the larger cities, especially in the countryside, there was a steadily rising chorus of demands all over Germany, for political fairness, for social reform, for justice, for relief from want and desperation.

Because so many diverse sets of individuals with conflicting objectives and so many governments were involved, it is difficult to see all this as a whole and to recognize the chaos as the famous revolution of 1848. It might be more accurate to describe the situation in Germany as a set of revolutions.

To Friedrich Wilhelm the situation must have appeared outrageously complicated. He had to find a solution for Prussia, but he was bombarded by importunate letters from fellow rulers who seemed to believe that he could guarantee their salvation also. To make matters worse, he likewise had to deal with the tsar of Russia and with Metternich in Austria. Within days, his problems would be accentuated by the fall of Metternich.

No doubt the ultimate collapse in 1849 had its seeds in this confusion, this jumble of expectations. Although many strands can be seen distinctly—the almost universal demand for freedom from censorship, for example—there were no recognizable overall organizations to spearhead united action. The liberals hardly even knew each other before they assembled at the Frankfurt *Parlament*. Radicals and moderates were just beginning to recognize and acknowledge their differences. The general thrust of the movement for a constitution was blunted by demands that stemmed from the crisis among the workers.[6] Labor itself was fragmented, broken by the conflicting demands of guildmasters and artisans and factory workers. The peasants, struggling against archaic feudal obligations, monetary inflation, and crop failure, had their own stark problems. At the very most, there were groups with similar ideas that acted simultaneously in various parts of Germany, but they were not necessarily acting in concert or mutual awareness.

As far as Friedrich Wilhelm's Prussia itself was concerned, crosscurrents were symptomatic of the complexity that prevailed everywhere.

* * * * * *

In the Rhineland province, the Cologne community council received a radical document in the form of a petition that might more accurately be described as a manifesto. It called for legislation and government by the people; universal suffrage; unconditional freedom of speech and of the press; substitution of an armed civil guard for the present standing army; free right of association; protection of work; guarantee of social security for the workers; state-funded education for all children. Marx was not the author of this document, which was obviously the work of communists. Rather, it was written by Dr. Andreas Gottschalk, the former army officer August von Willich, and the writer Hocker. Local authorities handled the problem without addressing the king: Gottschalk, Willich and Hocker were arrested. However, their document inspired similar demands that were pushed in other Prussian lands. In Silesia there was serious trouble, especially in Breslau, where a peoples' assembly was forbidden on 6 March and the meeting could only be broken up by the military.

Disturbances of this kind in East Prussia raised the spectre of war with Russia. In Königsberg this was pointed out in a strong address to the king. The liberal debating club there agreed to the wording proposed by the determined revolutionist Dr.Johann Jacoby.

Jacoby was already a hero. In February 1841, with extraordinary daring, he had published a pamphlet, *Vier Fragen, beantwortet von einem Ostpreussen* [Four Questions answered by an East Prussian] that had set out with irrefutable logic the political injustice to the people of the monarch's refusal to honor his own royal father's promises. It also dealt with distortions of a law on community government (the law of 1808) by a new law of 1832 that altered the character of local magistrates, making them officers of the state. In that capacity they exerted harsh control by means of censorship and surveillance. Jacoby quoted Friedrich Wilhelm III, who in so many words had stated that publicity (i.e. through the press) is the most certain safeguard for ruler

Figure 4   JOHANN JACOBY (1805–1877)

and subjects alike against negligence and ill-intentioned measures on the part of bureaucrats.[7] He called for popular suffrage and a constitution. Censorship of the reports of deliberations of the provincial assemblies, observed Jacoby, resulted in *Scheinvertretung* [fictive representation]. The accuracy of Jacoby's comments on control of the press was a matter of common knowledge: he reminded his readers that although newspapers from France were permitted, the government had cynically forbidden use of ordinary newspaper wrappers for them. The "first class postage" rate was about 400 Thaler per year. This amounted to *ein Verbot* [a prohibition]. Jacoby's pamphlet had taken the Prussian public by storm and overnight become the accepted program of the opposition.

Friedrich Wilhelm had responded in his chilliest manner, observing that he did not count "baptized Jews" among his East Prussians.[8] (He had not taken the trouble to check in this matter. Jacoby never abandoned his Jewish faith.) The king demanded that Jacoby be tried for treason, *lèse-majesté*, and provocation against the law of the land, but Jacoby ably conducted his own defense. At first he was sentenced to two and a half years of imprisonment but the case dragged on for almost two years, until the highest Prussian court released him. Jacoby's paper, the *Königsberger Hartungsche Zeitung*, though its circulation was restricted to East Prussia, had nevertheless become one of the most influential of all opposition publications.

In March 1848, Jacoby's debating club agreed with him that after events in Paris, nobody could discuss mere trivialities. Their address to the king demanded popular representation, freedom of the press and a national German parliament. The police stepped in, forbidding discussion of political matters, but on 13 March not only the members of the club were protesting. Outside its building where they held their meeting in Königsberg, there were hundreds of journeymen, workers and students who cheered Jacoby and then headed for police headquarters, which they began to demolish. The military were called in and there was bloodshed and numerous arrests. In reaction to this situation, the local authorities sent their own address to the king, asking for withdrawal of the troops, the establishment of an armed civil guard and the granting of a constitution. Press freedom and freedom of assembly were included as a matter of course.

Jacoby had more extensive demands. On 15 March he wrote that the government of Prussia had too firm a trust in its bayonets and that authorities ought to be mindful of recent events in France, where a government that mocked the rights of the people had been driven out. He warned that Germans generally were "inspired by this example of peoples' justice", and once again brought forward demands for a constitution and universal suffrage He also called for an end to ties with tsarism.[9]

Barometeric indicators of the public mood in Königsberg were on storm. There were rumors that Berlin was in insurrection, and in spite of the fact that Jacoby had forced a granting of the arming of civilians, there was a wild scene when it became known that a dispatch rider was passing through with a message from Berlin to the tsar. The dispatch itself was seized but remained unopened. The provincial viceroy then broke his promise and secretly attempted to forward it, only to find himself surrounded by a howling angry mob that yelled "traitor". The greatest fear in Königsberg at that time was that Russian troops would be called in to quell the revolution.

Tsar Nicholas had issued a threatening proclamation on 14 March, calling up all troops who were on leave, for active duty "for an indeterminate period". When this move became known, it set off violent action in Königsberg, where about four hundred rioters were involved and forty of them were arrested.

In Friedrich Wilhelm's Berlin, crowds milled nightly at the *Tiergarten*, in the popular amusement grounds and pavilions known as *Die Zelten* [the tents]. It would be a mistake to describe these crowds as revolutionary. In the early March days, the police tolerated them as harmless spring celebrants. It was clear, however, that everyone was expecting some sort of decisive action on the part of the monarch. Would he listen to their expressions of discontent and grant a concession or two? Unfortunately, close advisers were stubborn. The ambassador to Württemberg reported that "I hear from all sides that the ultimate moment has arrived in which the king can make concessions that will be gratefully accepted and that would generate great popularity for his Majesty." The remark fell on deaf ears.

Berlin's streets teemed with unemployed men (the great Borsig locomotive plant had found it necessary to release four hundred workers all at a blow). Police files contained reports on the surveillance of seven thousand people, many of them foreign. The situation fostered Friedrich Wilhelm's conviction that there was a revolutionary conspiracy afoot.

The city was heavily armed. In their nervousness the troops launched senseless attacks on innocent civilians, riding down pedestrians and clubbing them viciously. A so-called *Bürgerschutzkommission* [citizens' protection commission] was appointed for the purpose of keeping belligerent troops and citizens apart, but the members were ineffectual and without any power to enforce their commands. By 14 March, the police were so unnerved that they invoked a law of 1798. According to that antiquated document, resistance to orders to disband was punishable by six months in prison.

In the second week of March the inchoate ferment began to take a definite character. Printed posters appeared on the street corners, announcing peoples' assemblies at *Die Zelten*. As soon as the announcements appeared, troops were hurriedly dispatched, ready for action. The young officer Kraft zu Hohenlohe-Ingelfingen reported that the crowd would obediently disperse and the troops would return to barracks, but the whole thing would be repeated on the following day because "invisible hands" would have put up posters again. Defiant individuals taunted the troops, provoking them into vigorous response. The whole affair was satisfactory to the common people, he said, because it dramatically made the soldiers look like brutes.[10] Hohenlohe-Ingelfingen managed conveniently to overlook the fact that on many occasions the troops were atrociously brutal without provocation.

Belatedly, the king announced that he would summon a united assembly of all the provincial representatives, for consideration of a Prussian constitution, but by that time terrifying news was trickling through from Vienna, where insurrection was at its height.

* * * * * *

Grossherzog Leopold of Baden believed that his salvation lay in the hands of Austria The grand duchy of Baden had long been a focal point for political agitation, in part because of its proximity to France. Ideas of the Enlightenment were still a driving force there,[11] and the chamber of deputies was known all over Germany for the quality of its debates. Future leaders in the Frankfurt *Parlament* first came to public attention in that setting (men like the moderates Welcker, Mathy and Bassermann, as well as the radical Friedrich Hecker).

Liberals and radicals had begun to express their desires before the outbreak in Paris and had even clashed, to the extent that they had split into two camps at Offenburg and Heppenheim (fall of 1847).

Against this background, it was hardly a cause for astonishment that the prosperous Mannheim merchant-publisher Friedrich Daniel

Bassermann should speak on 12 February 1848, just days before the Paris outbreak. His measured words, delivered in the lower house of Baden's *Landtag*, were impressively emphatic. The German confederation and its sole political central body, the *Bundestag*, no longer enjoyed the confidence of the people, he observed. This was a national misfortune, and at the same time a serious danger. If the loosely organized federation, held together by foreign diplomats, were not converted shortly into a constitutional federated state, there could be an explosion of unimaginable magnitude. The time had come, concluded Bassermann, for establishment of a federal state patterned after the United States of America.

Within days, there was an enormous popular meeting at Mannheim (it occurred on 27 February, on the heels of Louis-Philippe's abdication). This mass of excited people was so turbulent that its leaders, including Adam von Itzstein and Friedrich Hecker, had to plead for order. Hecker's hearers were saying that they would go to Karlsruhe in a body, bearing a petition that called for the setting up of a national guard with election of officers by members of the guard itself, as well as trial by jury on the English model, and unconditional freedom of the press—in a word, all the classic "March demands". As composed by Gustav Struve, the final address to the government at Karlsruhe was read all over Germany. Its wording had a revolutionary ring.

The German people have the right to demand prosperity, education and freedom for all classes of society without distinction of birth or estate.[12]

Two days after the Mannheim meeting where the address had been formulated, there was an assembly in the university *Aula* at Heidelberg. Here the social makeup of those in attendance cut across all classes. It was "the first major attempt to hold a true people's meeting on the basis of orderly discussion".[13] It was here, under pressure of consternation generated by events in France, that members of the liberal opposition called for immediate recognition of the new provisional government in Paris. (The fear of Franco-German hostility was a governing factor.) They also called for a commission that would prepare for election of a German national assembly. It should be noticed that there was no suggestion that the various monarchies ought to be abolished.

The government at Karlsruhe was troubled because the Austrian ambassador had received an official ruling that the major points of the Mannheim petition were to be categorically denied, whereas there could be some flexibility with respect to the others. The Baden ministry therefore offered some counter-proposals. In its proximity to France, Baden's capital city was a hothouse for rumor. Besides, hordes of workers, peasants, and delegations were arriving by train at the rate of eight hundred people per day, and the alarmed government began a feverish search for military assistance—troops or weapons. The arch-duke meanwhile played a "lamentable" role , and furthermore he drank to excess every evening.[14]

The civil servants and business people who had participated in the Heidelberg meeting were worried too, because it had been their hope that they might be able to steer the government onto a moderate course of reform, with constitutional concessions here and there that would be helpful to their cause. This was the plan of men like Bassermann, but they were aware of the potential damage that might be done by radical leaders. Up to that point the opposition had presented a united front, but from that time on their ranks began to split. This may have been encouraging to Germany's tremulous absolute monarchs but it was troubling to the Baden moderates, who knew that men like Struve and Hecker and the publicist Fickler at Konstanz were all too ready for violence.

Confused by peasant uprisings of extraordinary violence in the Odenwald and Schwarzwald, *Grossherzog* Leopold, appointed a new prime minister—the liberal Karl Mathy—and dispatched the liberal Karl Welcker to the *Bundestag* as his representative at Frankfurt. He had speedily granted the arming of a civil guard and jury trial (29 February) as well as freedom of the press (1 March). These measures were in part expedient, in part of secondary importance, and partly of no further significance, he wrote to Friedrich Wilhelm, in a letter that expressed his devotion and unshakable friendship, in confidence that "you, with Austria, will be able to bind minds throughout Germany in a swift development of the confederation . . ." thus preventing the havoc. It may not have occurred to *Grossherzog* Leopold that Austria was a feeble reed, already on the eve of Metternich's defeat.

Friedrich Daniel Bassermann was prematurely elated. "If we in our small Baden can establish a pattern for Germany . . . that order and law are paired with the freedom that is now dawning, we shall have gained more for freedom for all future times than by any other means."[15]

* * * * * * *

After repeated seesawing and many contradictory ministerial appointments made in an unsuccessful effort to control stubbornly unruly liberals, King Wilhelm of Württemberg unhappily admitted to the Russian ambassador that, stalwart old soldier though he was, *Je ne puis monter à cheval contre des idées.*[16] [I can't go on horseback against ideas.] On 10 March he sent a memo to the ambassador:

> At this time I cannot leave my capital and my country without great danger . . . I try to gain time in order to find out if the German major powers are able or willing to come to my assistance. . . . The tsar will judge things differently from his viewpoint. . . . Explain my position to him. By naming the new ministry I have gained time and avoided bloody scenes. This cannot continue however. It is possible to hold down a city by the power of the bayonet, but not a country. . . .[17]

It was unlikely that the tsar could be induced to intervene in the affairs of a German kingdom at that point. The turbulent French situation must have been uppermost in his mind, and then there were always the Poles. . . . As to his domestic situation, King Wilhelm was speaking with the authority of experience. There had been serious uprisings in both Stuttgart and Ulm in May of 1847, directed especially against bakers because of the high price of bread. When the disturbances had spread to the stage of barricade-building, the king himself had led his counter-attacking troops to quell the rebellion.

Problems in Württemberg were at their most crucial in the countryside, where large estates belonging to the nobility were under attack. Peasant against noble: this was not a Marxian class war. It was a Nineteenth-Century reenactment of the Sixteenth-Century Peasant War. The harsh mobs armed with pitchforks and scythes, calling for the burning of tax and mortgage records were not fighting the ruling class as such, nor were they thinking of attacking the sovereign. They were fighting medieval burdens, seeking relief from the humiliating semi-slavery entailed in seigneurial duties such as transport and road work. They were demanding emancipation from the Middle Ages. The resentful peasants would have recognized a kindred spirit in Berthold Auerbach's Mathes, in his tales from the Black Forest. Hauled up before a magistrate because of a minor infraction of the law (cutting a tree to make a May pole), Mathes addressed the bailiff:

> *Ihr meinet immer, wir sind euretwegen da, damit ihr was zu befehlen habt; wir bezahlen euch, damit Ordnung im Land ist, und nicht, um uns kujonieren zu lassen. Staatsdiener seid ihr, and der Staat das sind wir, die Bürger.*[18] [You always think we're here so you can have somebody to order

around. We pay you to keep order, not to let ourselves be bullied. You're
servants of the state, and the state—that's us.]

Theoretically, the peasants should have formed a natural barrier
against the spread of revolutionary ideas because of their supposed
inborn conservatism,[19] but they were fighting for their own cause.
Occasionally, to be sure, expression of conservative loyalty to the
monarch occurred, as in the case of the Thuringian peasants at Weimar,
who insisted that they loved the *Grossherzog* and the *Grossherzogin*
who had done so much for them, and that they did not want anything
bad—only they wanted their complaints to be heard.[20]

In Württemberg, as in most of the small German states, a new
liberal minister (Paul Pfizer) was appointed. Here again, not excep-
tionally, the liberal replacement was in favor of a constitutional
monarchy.

* * * * * * *

The royals were trying desperately to hold together. In Hesse-
Darmstadt, *Erbgrossherzog* Ludwig, the young co-regent, tears well-
ing in his eyes, spoke with the Prussian ambassador:

> The king must not misunderstand my intentions. Unfortunately, a lot of things
> have to happen that can no longer be prevented, such as the oath of the
> military to the Constitution. It is to be hoped that there will be a time when it
> will be possible to render the work of the present moment partly harmless.[21]

This was characteristic of a number of the beleaguered rulers. They
gave way if it seemed to be expedient, but they did so with mental
reservations. Others, no doubt, were gratefully taking the path of least
resistance in the hope of winning support of the moderates they were
elevating to cabinet rank. In fairness to *Erbgrossherzog* Ludwig, it
must be said that his role at that time was difficult. The old archduke
and his younger brother had many close ties with Russia, and he was
powerless to combat their policies. He once unbosomed himself to
Prussian ambassador Bockelberg, telling him bitterly that "I know their
intrigues and betrayals but I have to keep quiet. The Prussian uniform
is a thorn in the side of many people, but I wear it. Prussia can count
on me."

Ludwig continued, joking. "Tell the King of Prussia that he must
not think of me as a revolutionist." As far as a national guard was

concerned, his cynical judgment was that "All that's needed to satisfy the people is a brightly-colored jacket."—A radical antagonist of his, a *Landtag* delegate, commented sourly that no thanks were due to the archduke for his concessions. Another remark gained ready sympathetic response. "It would be preferable to be free with the French, if the choice is oppression with the Prussians."

The chief importance of events in Hesse-Darmstadt was the replacement of the old minister, *Freiherr* du Thil, by the competent—and moderate—Heinrich von Gagern, who was to become one of the recognized leaders throughout the sessions of the Frankfurt *Parlament*, of which he was the presiding officer. Von Gagern was essentially a law-and-order man. Before the eyes of the assembled chamber of deputies, he deliberately tore up a declaration of renunciation of hunting rights that peasants had forced from *Graf* Erbach in a spillover of disorders in the Odenwald.[22]

Von Gagern was not the only one of the opposition to emerge into the German limelight, and to become a leading member of the Frankfurt *Parlament*. The city of Mannheim had acquired its own hero in what they liked to call the Hessian revolution. This was Franz Heinrich Zitz (1803–1877) of the lower house of the Hessian *Landtag*. Stimulated by the events of February in Paris, the citizens of Mainz twice sent a list of requests in the form of a ten-point petition, addressed to the monarch, but although Zitz accepted the documents and promised to forward them, his colleague Councillor Aull rejected them, and the petition was returned to the indignant people of Mainz. The first public reaction was stone-throwing and window-breaking, but then, apparently encouraged by Zitz, they began to plan a demonstration in the form of a mass march on Darmstadt. It was at that stage (on 8 March) that the *Grossherzog* sent a message, declaring that he was taking into account the desires of the people of his dear city of Mainz, and that he was granting all ten demands listed in the original petition.

In a tumult of joy, the citizens' committee decreed that a marble plate should be set into the wall of the *Rathaus* of Mainz, with bronze letters that would celebrate the victory of Hesse and Germany , achieved for freedom through the moral force of the people, the manly courage of Dr. Franz Zitz, and the magnanimity of the prince. A purse was made up for Zitz, and a Zitz foundation was established for support of needy workers. There was a festival with bell-ringing and a *Te Deum* in the cathedral, followed by illumination of the city, a torchlight procession and many transparencies with the name Zitz in brilliant letters. Ludwig Bamberger, who reports these events in his memoirs, goes on to say that he himself kept a little distance from the festivities because he was not too happpy about so much adulation going to the *Grossherzog*, whose intentions he did not trust. This was hindsight, perhaps. Bamberger was writing fifty years after the celebration.[23]

* * * * * * * *

Herzog Adolf of Nassau attempted to ride out the storm on his own.

If Hesse-Darmstadt had gained a moderate leader and some reluctant concessions from its ruler, the case was different in Nassau. The railroads played a dramatic role here. The peasants had been summoned, and they were given free use of the trains en route to Wiesbaden. Conservative estimates indicate that about thirty thousand answered the call, many armed with hatchets. Their demand was clear enough. They wanted all princely estates to be designated officially as property of the state.

The tumult in Wiesbaden was becoming madder by the moment, in the mysterious absence of *Herzog* Adolf, and the garrison was so small that a complete overthrow of the government seemed to be imminent. But then the ruler presented himself, in full uniform, resolute and calm. He appeared on his balcony and addressed the crowd. Everything is granted. Now disperse, and trust me as I trust you. This man, who had been much disliked, had responded to the challenge with energy, to become for the moment a hero of the revolution.[24]

In the general jubilation, the editors of the Wiesbaden *Freie Zeitung*, emotionally urging unity, ended with an apology for the incompleteness of their current issue. So many typesetters were out celebrating that only a few remained on hand to do the work.

Herzog Adolf had made a specific promise to the milling throng at Wiesbaden. He had declared amnesty for all prisoners who had been charged with violation of laws governing the taking of wood or hunting in the royal preserves. The peasants went home triumphantly to enjoy their newfound privileges. They departed from their farms en masse and invaded the forests, destroying woodlands for miles around. In this wasteland carpenters constructed cheap housing. All this activity should not necessarily be construed as hostile. The ignorant peasants believed that they no longer had to pay taxes. *Herzog* Adolf would take care of it—peasants wouldn't have to pay.[25]

Moreover, since their affairs seemed to them to be in order, they were deaf to pleas of the radicals who begged for their support in revolution. No, said the peasants. They had their spring planting to do. One wonders, in consideration of such innocence, just what the peasants of Nassau thought was at stake. What did they think a constitution was? In their minds, the word might have been synonymous with the comfortable non-payment of taxes. Surely they would have been bewildered, if they had been told that what reformers wanted was a document that would set out the character of political sovereignty and establish a mechanism of some kind for representative government. Would they have understood why there was a demand for the protection of basic rights for all citizens? Would these men who in many cases would have signed their names with an X have understood why censorship of the press was such a threat to their well-being?

These were indeed extraordinary times in Nassau. A new *Landtag* was made up of delegates whose membership was equally divided among peasants and young men from the lower ranks of the civil service.

The Prussian ambassador made no effort to conceal his displeasure from *Herzog* Adolf. Not long before, he had stated in Berlin that nothing could intimidate this brave ruler, that he would never under any circumstances waver. Now this was precisely what had happened. It was literally painful to his ears, said the ambassador, to hear soldiers in the streets shouting *Es lebe die Freiheit!* [long live freedom] It is understandable that—especially in the ambassador's home territory of Prussia—the forces of reaction would set about organizing themselves almost immediately.

* * * * * * *

Kurfurst Friedrich Wilhelm of Hesse-Kassel (Kurhessen) was perhaps the worst, certainly the most detested of all the German monarchs, known for his crudity, obstinacy and capriciousness.[26] Events in Kurhessen showed plainly his dependence upon Prussia.

For fifteen years, there had been a fruitless succession of meetings, appeals, protests, and declarations of principle. This patient reliance on legal process was characteristic of a population that proudly declared itself to be law-abiding. There was a strain of the sturdy Swabian mentality in Kurhessen, where the people have been described as circumspectly stubborn, believers in usage and custom, distrustful of any outsider's slickness, and deeply imbued with a sense of justice. Now, during the March days of 1848, their excitement became so intense that the city of Hanau threatened to secede from Kurhessen and join Hesse-Darmstadt. It is known that a delegation even approached the regent *Erbgrossherzog* Ludwig in Darmstadt, wanting to initiate some sort of separatist arrangement. For all intents and purposes, Hanau was heading toward revolution and a provisional government. There was an armed meeting on 8 March where a "peoples' commission" was elected.

Hanau had become a center of leftist agitation for all southwest Germany. A central correspondence office for the Rhenish states had been established there, and information poured in from active centers such as Offenbach and Friedberg, where there was a strong *Turnverein* movement. (In a police report dated October 1848, on political organizations in Wiesbaden, gymnastic societies were specifically singled out as hotbeds of radicalism, made up of young people who were politically extremely active and oriented toward democracy.)[27] Students at Marburg were enthusiastically supporting Hanau. They themselves had expressed their own grievances in a petition dated 6 March. They complained that they had long been deprived of their excellent professors (e.g. Sylvester Jordan), and that many professorial chairs remained vacant.

The city of Kassel was more circumspect but sent a delegation to the *Kurfurst* that was treated with disgraceful arrogance. Mistaking one of the delegation (a lawyer) for a brewer, Friedrich Wilhelm snapped at him that brewers ought to stick to the business of brewing beer. Government was his business. The ensuing uproar had its effect at last. The *Kurfurst* promised in writing to behave in accordance with the constitution of 1830, and appointed new moderate ministers for his cabinet. *Graf* Galen, the Prussian ambassador, may have had something to do with this change of attitude. It was he who had thought that military assistance from Prussia might be required if matters became any more unmanageable. The Hessian monarch had no armed force of his own available because he had used all appropriated funds on *Paradespielen* [ostentatious military display].

In spite of the reluctant bending of the royal will to the will of his people, there were occasional small riots and episodes of *Katzenmusik* before quiet was restored. "It was fear that turned many greying radicals into semiconservatives," was the judgment of the Prussian ambassador. Even the much-persecuted Marburg professor Sylvester Jordan, released from long imprisonment, spoke against precipitate republican action.[28]

Perhaps something of Kurhessen's traditional good sense and faith in legal processes had prevailed.

* * * * * * *

Ernst August of Hannover (the former Duke of Cumberland) had been viewing events with narrowed eyes from the very beginning. On 13 January 1848, he wrote to Friedrich Wilhelm IV

> I could be mistaken, but in my opinion the political horizon is very black, and I advise everyone to be on guard. I am fully convinced that the radicals in Switzerland are working everywhere to spread their mischief and every government ought to keep its eye on the journeymen, because they are the ones who distribute their propaganda. Thank God, Austria at least seems to be convinced of this, and it is high time for preventive measures.[29]

Ernst August had put his finger on an important aspect of the revolutionary unrest in Germany. It was certainly the journeymen who were the carriers of the virus. Middle class intellectuals, even people like Marx and Engels, had litle or no contact with the workers whose troubles they described so vividly. It was the rootless journeymen who were the truly restless element and who were in a position to be able to communicate with workers who wanted to keep the old guild system as well as with those who wanted to abandon it. They themselves were no longer able to look forward to a satisfactory future as guildmasters, and they saw themselves in danger of sinking into a faceless mass of factory workers. In the course of their *Wanderjahre* they came into contact with more socially conscious workers in Switzerland and France, who initiated them into the arcane doctrines of Fourierism, Babouvism, Saint-Simonism and so on, and who took them into their burgeoning clubs and societies. The journeymen had "fallen between the grindstones of progress"[30] and they were to be articulate organizers, in contrast to lowly peasants and slum dwellers, who had little or nothing to say. Even before the revolutionary years, Catholic clerics had been disturbed by the falling off of church attendance and the lure of the tavern, where Sunday had become a time of drinking bouts instead of worship. Needless to say, the tavern had become the meeting place for the lower classes, where journeymen returning from France would sing revolutionary songs and hand out subversive literature.[31] Inns were to become targets of radical organizers in 1848.

At a later date, the king was to write sturdily to the Prussian monarch to the effect that he would defend himself against republicanism to his last breath. Ernst August was in fact the only German prince who consistently refused to agree to the idea of a parliament at Frankfurt. The old "iron head" as Valentin called him, was firm in his convictions in a way that put many of his fellow monarchs to shame. Moreover, when he granted a concession he had no hidden mental reservations.

In Ernst August's Hannover, the petition movement took hold, led by Dr. Johann Karl Stüve, the *Bürgermeister* of the capital city. In addition to the usual liberal agenda (freedom of the press, etc.), the people of Hannover asked for education for all classes, if necessary funded by the state, improvement of the condition of the working class, and guarantees of employment and pay. Moreover, the artisans managed to compel the rescinding of a law that was to have seriously limited the extent and authority of the guild system. The guilds would be retained, with a few modifications.[32]

Ernst August reacted at first by distancing himself from his people. Petitions were returned signed by a member of the cabinet, and cabinet members were instructed to receive deputations that came requesting an audience with the king. In spite of this determined attitude, in the end a new cabinet led by Stüve was appointed and took over the reins.

The king was unexpectedly calm. He said to his new minister of external affairs, *Graf* von Bennigsen-Banteln, "My people want to be made happy in a way that differs from what I wanted. I will not offer resistance. I am prepared to make concessions that are in line with present circumstances." When von Bennigsen told him that in contrast to previous policy, there would now have to be a policy of openness, the royal response was that he did not want any halfway measures. "What I want, I want wholly."

Counter to all expectation, Ernst August got along well with Dr. Stüve, whom he had heretofore considered to be a demagogue. He found him to be one of the most faithful to the idea of monarchy. As Valentin says, Stüve managed to transform the once malignant despot into an occasionally sulky constitutional monarch.[33] True to form, the sulky ruler wrote to Friedrich Wilhelm that the mess in France was driving the whole world mad.

* * * * * * *

Herzog Wilhelm's tiny Braunschweig may have been the most contented of all the states in the German confederation. The first reaction of the citizens to the revolutionary excitement was a petition for restoration of the civil guard. On the following day (4 March) came a request for popular representation in the *Bundestag.* Wilhelm rejected this as an unclear, impractical idea, but before long he was wearing the revolutionary tricolor and allowing his people to address him as Wilhelm the German.

* * * * * * *

In the dwarf kingdoms such as those of Thuringia, the rulers faced a perplexing situation. Were they to become constitutional monarchs with full-fledged parliaments? What kind of parliament would there be in Schwarzburg-Sondershausen, where there were no more than three thousand potential voters at the most?

Violence threatened, especially at Weimar where peasants assembled in alarming numbers. The crowds sang *Ein freies Leben führen wir* [We lead a free life—(the popular "Robbers' song")] and some people shouted *Erbgrossherzog 'raus!* and demanded relief from the salt tax and access to the forests, but in the end—after a few concessions—all the Thuringian rulers managed to survive. In Schwarzburg-Sondershausen the prince declared in a burst of patriotic fervor that although he was prepared to lay aside his crown, he would not go into exile because he preferred to live out his days among his loyal people.

* * * * ** * *

Ludwig of Bavaria, under a cloud because of his relationship with his unpopular mistress Lola Montez, won high praise and a standing ovation at the theatre in Munich because of his quick action.

On 6 March, he had outdistanced the governments in Karlsruhe, Stuttgart, Wiesbaden and Frankfurt with an extraordinary concession. He agreed to some sort of popular representation in the *Bundestag.* Such representation would open the way for radical opposition to the decisions of the princes and their officers. In the theatre, the wildly cheering audience rose to sing *Heil unserm König, Heil.*[34] Part of the enthusiasm in the theatre audience was inspired by the presence of Ludwig's queen in the royal box, as well as the welcome fact that Lola Montez was not there in her accustomed glory.

Ludwig had been playing with fire much too long, though. He had been earnestly warned by his loyal minister, Ludwig zu Öltingen-Wallenstein, when he handed in his resignation on 9 November 1847. In turning against the Munich students and closing the university in anger set off by the clamor against his beloved Lola, the king had taken action that was *furchtbar ernst* [frightfully serious]. The minister went on to say that he himself could be of no further use to the king, and that the time was approaching when the entire fabric of scandals and lies that had been woven around his Majesty would be exposed to the royal understanding.[35] King Ludwig had disastrously allowed Lola to involve herself in Bavarian political affairs, even to the extent of having her sit in on cabinet meetings. The clerics unexpectedly joined forces with the opposition and Lola was obliged to quit Bavaria. Even this did not mend matters. Ludwig abdicated in favor of his son Maximilian II on 20 March 1848.

* * * * * * *

Meanwhile, much to the annoyance of the Viennese court, the Frankfurt *Bundestag* declared that any state within the federation that wanted to lift censorship and allow freedom of the press might do so. On 9 March there was an even more irritating decree, to the effect that the colors of the federation were now black, red and gold. These were the nationalist colors that originally identified members of the *Burschenschaft* movement. Nothing was said about old Jahn's Lützow affiliation or about the *Burschenschaften*, however. The published decision stated piously that the colors were those of earlier times in Germany, and were taken from the *Reichspanier*[36] [banner of the old Reich].

The poet Ferdinand Freiligrath was moved to pen a warning to the German rulers: His verses, each of which ended with the line *Pulver ist schwarz, Blut is rot, Golden flackert die Flamme!*[37] [Gunpowder is black, blood is red, and the flares of the flame are golden] proclaimed that freedom had not yet come if people still had to break into armories and take weapons into their hands, or if they had to fight by means of petitions. There was still no true freedom if cities took to barricades, and it is not freedom if it is only fear that forces people to do their duty.

Most of the German monarchs were finding that if they granted a few concessions and perhaps agreed to accept a constitution, their thrones would be secure, especially if they could claim protection from

Austria or Prussia. This might not be the case where industry had gained a significant place and radicals were prepared to organize the workers and the members of the unemployed lower classes in the cities. Such a kingdom was Saxony, where Leipzig had developed into a lively industrial center, and such also was the Prussian Rhine province with Cologne as the center of activity.

* * * * * * *

King Friedrich August II of Saxony was acutely aware of his danger. In mid-March, his brother and heir-presumptive, Prince Johann, who shared his views, wrote urgently to Prussian Friedrich Wilhelm:

> Dearest and best of friends . . . I beg and implore you, and Fritz [King Friedrich August] joins his appeal to mine, . . . don't drive affairs to the utmost limit. If forceful suppression fails, the fate of all princes in Germany will be decided, and believe me, public opinion is too strong for you to be able to work against it in the long run with only mechanical means. Fritz has decided to change his ministry and to guarantee a considerable number of present desires. This has gone forward without any disturbance or coercion, and the mood at least in Dresden is now quite good. Imitate our example as far as possible.[38]

Friedrich August's plan of action had evidently not been too successful. On 16 March, Friedrich August sent a note to Friedrich Wilhelm:

> I have to bother you again with a few lines, just to ask you to ignore my earlier proposal that Dresden be the seat of the proposed conference of ministers [by that time Friedrich August's new ministry had been installed] because the mood here is unsettled and unpleasant demonstrations could result.[39]

Affairs in Saxony had indeed been unsettled. As soon as events in Paris were known, the Leipzig professor Karl Biedermann had written an address to the king, proposing various mild measures to which nobody objected. The address was admired as "one of the best" and was read with interest as far away as in England. It was a shade too mild for the worker community of Leipzig, however, and it was with difficulty that serious trouble was prevented. This restraint was largely due to the skillful work of that extraordinary labor leader, the self-taught publisher Robert Blum.

Robert Blum (1807–1848) was one of the few revolutionary leaders in Germany who actually knew the common people, whose love and respectful loyalty he commanded. He himself had experienced all the pressures that life as a manual laborer and factory employee entailed. He was a man of tremendous drive and determination who through contacts at Leipzig had widened his vision by voracious reading and study. He was a born organizer, and his ways of approaching the mass of the people were original in that he managed to draw together middle class people and proletariat. His first effort in organization was an extraordinary Gutenberg festival that gained national attention as early as 1840. In Leipzig, he next established a Schiller society (this was in 1842). He founded a writers' society, and was also an active participant in the first all-Germany opposition group, Adam von Itzstein's *Hallgartenkreis*. This circle, that existed during the years 1839–1847, was basic to the development of political party action during the *Vormärz*.[40] Blum had been one of the mainsprings of the

Figure 5 ROBERT BLUM (1807—1848)

Catholic protest movement, and in cooperation with von Itzstein had worked powerfully to rally liberals to the cause of revolution. It was Blum who almost alone had organized the workers of Leipzig in his *Redeübungsverein* [society for practice in public speaking]. This society, which had branches all over Saxony, was later to be the core of his effective *Vaterlandsverein*. His admirers found something magical in Robert Blum. He looked like a roughly hewn apostle on a medieval altar, people thought. His enemies called him a rabble-rouser but everyone agreed that the man was extraordinarily forceful. Among the fast-growing community of tradespeople, merchants and workers in Leipzig, Robert Blum's word was law.—Because of his firm control, Biedermann's address was duly presented to the king, who rejected it.

There was then enormous commotion in Leipzig. The city reacted by holding a great festival banquet in celebration of the French revolution. A second address was prepared, this time demanding dismissal of the king's ministers. Blum again managed to control the excited populace and the surging crowds of students, to say nothing of his worker following. In the end, a few windows were smashed , but on the whole Leipzig had impressively shown not only self-discipline and ability to reach a consensus but also its animosity toward the old order. Blum's firmness had its origin, no doubt, in his experience at an earlier date in Leipzig, when mob action had ended in bloodshed. The revolutionary poet Ferdinand Freiligrath, referring to that episode, wrote that *niemals hab' ich noch gehört dass man mit Blut zerbrochene Fenster kleibe* [I have never yet heard that shattered windows have been put back together with blood].

The people of Dresden, who had been relatively indifferent at first, were finally aroused and sent a petition signed by some eight hundred citizens to the ministry, asking for better popular representation. Another item of interest was a call printed on 9 March in the *Dresdner Tageblatt* that was addressed to the women of Saxony. They were urged to unite and be strong and sustain law and order, defending the land against internal treachery. The appeal was hardly necessary. The city was essentially loyal to the king . . .

Confronted by the massive movement in Leipzig and its disciplined behavior, Friedrich August gave way gradually. There would be a meeting of the *Landtag* on 20 March. Censorship was lifted.

The chief difficulty came from the Dresden police, who attacked and locked up people who tried to take advantage of the new arrangements. These oppressive actions stiffened the resistance of the king. Leipzig authorities issued a warning, and the guard at Dresden reacted by taking over the railway station. Troops began to gather in the villages, and Prussian forces approached Leipzig. The city authorities of Leipzig went to Dresden and demanded immediate withdrawal of the armed forces, which were endangering the peace.

Friedrich August's government in Dresden was intimidated, and on 13 March the troops were pulled back. The minister of justice had become convinced that the Leipzig movement was serious and advised the king to relent. It was at that point that a new ministry was appointed, which quickly adopted a solid March program of reform. Leipzig rejoiced and Blum was celebrated as a hero. In one of the clubs they even played and sang the *Marseillaise*.

The well known lecturer and literary critic Robert Prutz came to Dresden and calmly told his audience that "Not all the princes now living were made for our significant times". The reaction of King Friedrich August is not recorded.

* * * * * * *

In considering the patchwork of responses to the crisis of early 1848 on the part of the rulers, it would be unfair to stigmatize all their concessions as entirely cynical. It would be much too sweeping a judgment to decide that the solemn royal promises had been made with a hidden determination to withdraw those concessions at the earliest possible moment. The rulers must certainly have understood that their strength would depend to a considerable extent on their firmness in the face of threats to property (riots in the cities, and peasant risings), but that firmness must not be seen as obstinacy. It must have occurred to them that it would be sensible to try to join forces with the opposition, bringing their governments into some kind of alignment with public opinion. To appoint liberal ministers might help to carry their small threatened monarchies through the storm.

Events in Germany since the toppling of Louis-Philippe had provided much food for royal reflection in Germany. It had been borne in on all those diffident, hesitant rulers that they were not at all imperious masters of their fate. Time and again, they had remembered their dependence upon Prussia or Austria. Many a time they had wondered about the tsar. Or about England and France. There was little hope that the action would be played out on the 1848 stage as it had been in 1830, because then neither Vienna nor Berlin had experienced any serious tremors. Now—in the March days of 1848—barricades were to appear on the streets of both those capitals. Whatever happened there would determine the fate of Germany and the disconcerted rulers of all those toy monarchies.

Notes

1   Stephan Born, *Erinnerungen eines Achtundvierzigers*, pp. 75–84.

2   Rudolph Stadelmann, *Social and Political History of the German 1848 Revolution*, p. 104.

3   Walter Schmidt, "Wilhelm Wolf", in *Männer der Revolution von 1848*, p. 44.

4   Jessen, *Die deutsche Revolution 1848/49 in Augenzeugenberichten*, pp. 34–35.

5   Ibid., p. 35.

6   Koselleck, *Preussen zwischen Reform und Revolution*, p. 662.

7   Johann Jacoby, *Vier Fragen, beantwortet von einem Ostpreussen*, p. 8.

8   Berdahl, *The Politics of the Prussian Nobility*, p. 321.

9   Peter Schuppan, "Johann Jacoby", in *Männer der Revolution von 1848*, p. 247.

10   Jessen, p. 74.

11   Stadelmann, p. 34.

12   Valentin, *Geschichte der deutschen Revolution*, 1:340.

13   Ibid., 1:340–341.

14   Ibid., 1:342.

15   Gall, *Bürgertum in Deutschland*, p. 292.

16   Valentin 1:352.

17   Ibid.

18   Berthold Auerbach, *Schwarzwälder Dorfgeschichten*.

19   Hamerow, *Restoration, Revolution, Reaction*, pp. 156–157.

20   Valentin 1:367.

21   Ibid., 1:353

22   Ibid. 1:356.

23   Bamberger, *Erinnerungen*, pp. 28–33.

24   Valentin 1:357.

25   Ibid., 1:358.

26 Ibid. 1:187.

27 Michael Wettengel, *Die Revolution von 1848/49 im Rhein-Main-Raum*, p. 187.

28 Valentin l:359–362.

29 Jessen, p. 18.

30 Stadelmann, p. 16.

31 Sperber, *Popular Catholicism*, p. 18 note 24 cites the case of a journeyman saddler who was distributing such material on Easter Sunday of 1835.

32 Hans Meusch, *Die Handwerkerbewegung von 1848/49*, pp. 40–41.

33 Valentin, 1:362–366.

34 Jessen, pp. 42–43.

35 Ibid., p. 19.

36 Walter Grab, editor. *Die Revolution von 1848/49; eine Dokumentation*, pp. 43–44.

37 *Jessen,* p. 44.

38 Ibid., pp. 69–70.

39 Gerhard Schmidt, *Die Staatsreform in Sachsen in der ersten Hälfte des 19. Jahrhunderts*, p. 109.

40 Siegfried Schmidt, "Robert Blum," in *Männer der Revolution von 1848*, p. 346.

Chapter 12

Vienna Against Metternich— March Days 1848

The empire of inertia known as Austria had been held together for almost four decades by the energy and wiles of *Fürst* Clemens Metternich-Winneburg (1773–1859), the chancellor and apostle of the *status quo*. In theory, the hereditary ruler of this multiracial semi-barbaric entity was Ferdinand I (1793–1875), but he was no more than a figurehead because of his various mental and physical disabilities. His father, Emperor Franz, had left deathbed instructions that he was to be guided in all decisions by Metternich.

Historians have been unkind to Ferdinand, referring to him with contempt or pity. At their most charitable, they patronizingly call him "poor Ferdinand". He has been described as *ein geschwätziger, durchaus nicht immer harmloser Trottel* [a garrulous, not always harmless idiot][1] with the explanation that he was epileptic. Even the term imbecile is used without apology. The Russian tsarina was shocked by his "sickly face" and large head, and most contemporary accounts of him are equally unappealing. However, there are occasional flickers that rouse the suspicion that Ferdinand may not have been altogether a fool. It is said, for example, that he could not sign his name without assistance, yet he kept a perfectly intelligible diary. He may have been garrulous, but he was garrulous in at least three languages. He was "not always harmless" because in his gentlemanly way he tended to grant requests that ran counter to Metternich's rigid principles. There was a refreshing directness in Ferdinand that was rare among all the official obfuscations of the court. In the flurry of consternation on the day of Metternich's fall from power, *Erzherzog* Ludwig had reluctantly told the chancellor that he must resign, describing public hostility and the concessions that would have to be made, but the old fox blandly embarked on an involuted comment that took up an hour and a half.

Various officials were trying ineffectually to bring him to the point, when Ferdinand spoke plainly. "After all, I'm the sovereign and the decision lies with me."[2] In a discussion relating to his forced abdication after reaction had set in (December 1848), Hamerow is unequivocal. He notes that although it would have been feasible to continue with a quiescent, docile sovereign, "Ferdinand had given his sanction to Hungary's [revolutionary] April Laws, and showed an inconvenient disposition to regard himself as bound by his word."[3] After 1848, in his retirement at Prague following his abdication, the former emperor engaged himself in heraldic studies, which is hardly an occupation for the feebleminded.

Metternich's "system" was primarily intended to sustain Austria as a viable European power, in the form attained at the conclusion of the Congress of Vienna, which had been dominated by Metternich himself. His preeminence had been readily recognized, in view of his role as the one who devised and steered the coalition against Napoleon. Metternich's Austria, under Emperor Franz, was a citadel of absolutism that was more impervious than any other outside of Russia. Liberal notions relating to constitutions, equality, the abolition of feudalism, and so on were all classified as disruptive.[4]

Austria had emerged triumphantly from the Congress of Vienna with restoration of all territory lost since 1792, with the exception of the Netherlands and the *Vorlande* [also called *Vorderösterreich*; small fragments of Habsburg territory that were ceded to Baden, Württemberg and Bavaria].[5] She kept most acquisitions made since 1792. She retained the right to co-supervision over the free city of Cracow and dominated Italy, either by outright possession (Lombardy and Venetia), or through family control of such places as Modena and Parma. Germany had been established under Austrian aegis as a federation of sovereign principalities and free cities. Austria, Britain, Russia and Prussia were pledged jointly to maintain the peace settlement.

In spite of these auspicious arrangements, Austria's position remained precarious because of the financial chaos that prevailed in the monarchy. During the final campaign against Napoleon, Austria had undertaken to provision a large part of the allied armies and had wellnigh exhausted her treasury. The difficulty had been compounded by the fact that 1816 was a famine year. (Forty-four thousand individuals died in Hungary alone.)

Metternich was careless or indifferent concerning the financial situation. At the least threat of disorder anywhere, he insisted that the price of order was eternal vigilance. The smallest relaxation might undo all that had been so painfully achieved. It was always possible to borrow, was it not? The Rothschilds stepped into the breach repeatedly, comfortable in their appreciation of the fact that they, with their special status in Vienna as "privileged Jews", were the most powerful family in all Europe. In 1823, for example, they managed to effect a dramatic reduction of Austria's immense debt to England.

Metternich's vaunted system of congresses was already starting to crumble in the years immediately following Napoleon's fall because the great powers, though originally united in fear of France and French ideas, had begun to realize that their own interests had considerable value. England, for example, had no wish to entangle herself in absolutist continental Europe. She had her growing overseas colonial empire to think about.—The disagreements over Greece and the device of making it an independent state had a highly destructive effect on Metternich's "system" because it revealed the flimsiness of the myth that the arrangements of the Congress of Vienna were sacrosanct. The French revolution of 1830 definitely shipwrecked the whole structure. Metternich had understood this at the time, and had performed minor miracles of salvage work (dispatch of Austrian troops to the Papal States, reestablishment of solidarity with Prussia and Russia, agreement on the general principle of mutual support against revolution) but he well knew that an era had ended. However, it may be that the Austrian people had not grasped the fact. The first reaction in Vienna when word came through that Louis-Philippe had fallen was a devastating run on the banks. Holders of Austrian *métalliques* sold frantically, and Viennese banks were forced to close their doors. The fear was palpable that Metternich might launch a ruinous military intervention in defense of his beloved *status quo*. He had in fact actually tried to do something of the sort, sending out a flood of messages to Friedrich Wilhelm in Prussia, to the tsar, and to Palmerston in England.

* * * * * * *

Throughout his reign, Emperor Franz remained convinced that nothing drastic needed to be done for his people in the matter of political power. All they required was material well-being. They could live peacefully without representative institutions under the provisions of the General Civil Code of 1811.

Metternich had been elevated to the prestigious post of chief of the *Haus-Hof-und Staatskanzlei*, but he was soon to discover that Emperor Franz regarded it as his royal prerogative to issue instructions to the various governmental departments without giving any reason for his action, and without informing the heads of other departments. The result was blind, confused execution of misunderstood commands. The administrative machinery lumbered along in so cumbersome a fashion that it was constantly struggling with mountains of trivial cases while truly important matters were disregarded.

A detailed account, written by "an officer of State" [Franz, *Graf von Hartig*] supplies examples of the maddening machinery of Austrian government.

> The conversion of the smallest portions of forest into arable land required the special permission of the throne, because the forest laws enacted, in order to prevent a scarcity of wood, that the extent of the forest should not be diminished. A landlord wishing to purchase a few square yards of ground from his tenant for building, or the formation of a garden, was obliged first to obtain the permission of the emperor himself because the tenant laws forbade the increase of domains by any addition of peasant lands.[6]

A case is cited that involved a cavalryman who would have received a bonus of six florins if he had kept his horse for twelve years. The horse died in battle after eleven years and ten months, and the man asked for the bonus as "an act of grace". The request had to go to the emperor, and passed through the hands of forty-eight officials (twenty-six on the way up, and twenty-two on its way back to the petitioner).[7]

An additional burden was the weight of surveillance and censorship. Metternich was inclined to say that this was the emperor's doing, not his own, though he certainly made use of the massive apparatus of espionage that was available to him. It may be that his statement about Emperor Franz had some truth in it, because indubitably the monarch had a pathological fear of revolutionary ideas, of secret societies, and of the Freemasons. There was a central police office controlled by an excessively timid man who saw threats everywhere, and an additional police system under Metternich's direct control. This one operated both within and outside the lands ruled by the Habsburgs. Both the emperor and his chancellor were inordinately afraid of anything that even faintly ressembled a revolution, and they were in complete agreement that liberalism was to be warded off at all cost—especially the German variety, because they thought that Germans did not just play with ideas as the French did. For this reason, they saw nothing objectionable in their practice of having all incoming and outgoing mail pouches (diplomatic pouches included) opened and all letters copied for their perusal.

As in Germany, detailed information about political currents within the country had to be smuggled in from abroad. Austrians attentively read the *Grenzboten*, published in Leipzig after 1842 by the Czech journalist Ignatz Kuranda, that reported debates in the various provincial diets. Opposition in those provincial assemblies was concentrated on agricultural problems, especially among nobles who were proprietors of large latifundia and who wanted to jettison the *Robot* system in favor of hired labor. The editorial position of the *Grenzboten* was that the nobility was interested primarily in the survival of feudalism. It suggested that Austria was unwilling to undertake the solution of thorny social problems, and in general reflected the viewpoint of the German entrepreneur class. Austria was accused of backwardness in its refusal to adhere to the *Zollverein*. The editor, who had spent his youth in the ghetto at Prague, did not hesitate to call attention to the antisemitism of that city.[8]

Any opposition concerned with general governmental reform and overhaul was centered in Vienna, with its reading clubs and an active *Gewerbeverein* [merchants and trade], but no recognizably constructive program had emerged. Some people looked nostalgically to the "liberal" times of Emperor Joseph, and some thought vaguely of extended representation, but on the whole the emphasis rested on opposition to censorship.

Students who had attended German universities were under surveillance because they might have imbibed dangerous French ideas. At the time of the Wartburg festival (1817), Austrian authorities were appalled to discover that student organizations like the Jena *Burschenschaftt* had cropped up in Vienna, Prague and Innsbruck. This revelation provoked a vigorous campaign against the members of Austria's teaching profession. The professors must have been derelict in their duty if they had allowed this threatening situation to develop.

The Viennese student population differed from that of the French or German universities, where a fair proportion came from prosperous family backgrounds. In Vienna, many were "as poor in purse as they were rich in revolutionary exuberance"[9], whereas the sons of the nobility and upper ranks of the civil or military services usually had their own tutors or attended private institutions. In France and Germany, the students tended to go their separate ways when certain demands were met, but in Vienna there was a closer bond between the university population and the proletariat.

The surveillance that prevailed in Austria was even more rigorous than that in Germany. Professors were watched constantly. Lists of the books that they took out from the university libraries were sent to the police for their consideration. No foreigner could teach in Austria, not even as a private tutor. Emperor Franz is said to have told assembled faculty members at Laibach that he did not need savants. He wanted good, honest citizens. As to anyone with new ideas, "He can go, or I will remove him."

The only major change in the system through the years was that the Catholic church regained some of the political influence it had lost upon the death of Maria Theresa. Emperor Franz's fourth wife, whom he married in 1816, was a Bavarian princess who had been taught by Jesuits. She became the center of a "pious party" at court, with which Metternich promptly associated himself. This move fitted neatly into his policy. He hoped that he could gain sympathy in Catholic southern German states, offsetting the influence of Protestant Prussia. Metternich always kept a wary eye on Prussia. For example, on 11 June 1831, three years before Prussia's projected customs union came into force, he prepared a memo for Emperor Franz that sounded a warning. The Zollverein, he observed, though it originated as a community of commercial interests, would inevitably constitute the nucleus of a community of political interests centering around Prussia that would effectively weaken the Habsburg position.[10]

Vigorous intellectual or artistic life could not be expected to flourish under such conditions.[11] A former United States chargé d'affairs at Vienna observed that "chilled by the restrictions of censorship . . . the literature of Austria possesses no character, and hardly a name."[12] Möring's Sybillinische Bücher aus Oesterreich [Sibylline books from Austria, published in January 1848] contained the dismal comment that in the imperial lands, among thirty-eight million subjects, there was not one man who could say that he was proud to be Austrian.[13]

None of these problems would have seemed strange to anyone who lived in Germany. Such a person would also have recognized the efforts that the intellectuals made, to circumvent censorship and surveillance. After the death of Emperor Franz and the accession of Ferdinand in 1835, surveillance was loosened somewhat. Evidence of this is the fact that various professional men in Vienna had found it feasible in 1842 to establish a juridisch-politischer Leseverein [juridico-political reading society], although they had been cautious enough to organize at a time when Metternich was away on vacation. He grudgingly allowed the club to continue, no doubt because he knew that it would be easy to keep himself informed about the members and their activities. It is known that the police kept lists, not only of the members and their guests, but also of the books in their library.[14] The reading club did not function like the circles in Germany. Rather, it had a tendency to reach out and to attempt to spread its propaganda. The club sponsored a public lecture on prisons, for example. The official reaction was a frowning refusal to allow any more such lectures.

Though Austria and Germany had numerous similarities, there were also significant differences. Whereas there were thirty-nine states in Germany, all were German-speaking, and with the exception of Jewish people and political *émigrés*, there were not many persons of non-German stock living within the boundaries. In contrast, the very title of the emperor of Austria serves as a clear illustration of the staggering conglomeration of peoples that he ruled. By the grace of God, Emperor Franz was *Kaiser von Österreich, König von Jerusalem, Hungarn, Boheim, Dalmatien, Croatien, Slavonien, Galizien und Lodomerien, Erzherzog zu Österreich, Herzog zu Lothringen, zu Salzburg, zu Würzburg und in Franken, zu Steyer, Kärnthen und Krain, Grossherzog zu Krakow; Grossfürst zu Siebenbürgen, Markgraf in Mähren, Herzog zu Sandomir, Massovien, Lublin, Ober und Niederschlesien, zu Ausschwitz und Zator, zu Teschen und zu Friaul, Fürst von Berchtesgaden und Mergentheim, gefürsteter Graf zu Habsburg, Görz und Gradisca; Markgraf zu Ober und Niederlausitz und in Istrien, Herr des Landes Wolhynien, Podlachien und Brzesz, zu Trieste, zu Freudenthal und Eulenburg und auf der Windischen Mark.* Ferdinand as emperor acquired additional titles. His accession diploma showed four more kingdoms. Then in 1840 there were further additions—the Kingdoms of Lombardy, Venetia and Illyria, the Grand Duchy of Tuscany, the Duchies of Modena, Parma, Piacenza and Guastalla, Ragusa and Zara; the Principalities of Trient and Brixen and the Countships of Hohenembs, Feldkirchen, Bregenz, and Sonnenberg. In this list the Kingship of Hungary was designated as "apostolic".[15]

The problem of national unity was difficult enough in *Vormärz* Germany, with its multiplicity of petty sovereigns. The situation was infinitely worse in Austria. The idea of nationalism would inevitably become entangled with the idea of racial identity among Hungarians, Czechs, Poles, Serbs, Croats, Italians, Ukrainians, Ruthenes, or Bulgarians, to name only a few of the more visible groups.

A prime example of the complications that could spring from Austria's heterogeneous ethnic composition appeared immediately after the February eruption in Paris. Lajos Kossuth (1802–1894) delivered a stirring challenge at Pressburg [Pozsony], in a speech delivered to the local provincial assembly. He reminded his hearers that once before, Hungarians had been swirled into a maelstrom of financial disaster through actions on the part of the central administration, over which they had no control. He roared that the "pestilential air from the charnal-house of Vienna" was the cause of Hungary's miseries, and he demanded autonomy for Hungary, especially independent control of finances. But then he went on to say that constitutionalism in any given region could not be expected to survive if absolutism prevailed elsewhere in the realm. There must be "general constitutional institutions, with respect for the different nationalities."[16]

The expression "different nationalities" had ominous overtones. Even Hungary itself was like a set of nesting puzzle boxes, containing a plethora of minority groups. Kossuth himself was a Slovak, not Magyar. He called for a self-governing state under the Habsburgs as kings of Hungary, suggesting that this independent state could include not only the historic kingdom of Saint Stephen but also the southern Slav areas of Croatia, Slavonia, and Transylvania which were predominantly inhabited by Rumanians. As events unfolded, it was to become painfully evident that even Kossuth could not grasp the fact that one nationalist claim begets another. His "revolution by law" provided concessions to the minorities that were to be under Magyar control, but the Croats, Serbs and Rumanians would openly organize against him before long, loudly asserting their loyalty to Ferdinand and his dynasty, and putting forth their own urgent claims.[17]

There was another important difference that may have loomed large in the minds of would-be revolutionists. In Germany, a revolution would mean the overthrow of hereditary monarchs. In Austria, genuinely revolutionary action could take the form of the overthrow of the hereditary monarch's minister, *Fürst* Metternich, who was not of royal blood. In truth, Metternich was not even a native-born Austrian. He was a member of one of the Rhineland families that had fled before the armies of the French. Like other uprooted noblemen, the Metternich family had established itself in Austria, to become landowners there. Even though Emperor Ferdinand was weak, people with any sense of tradition would be reluctant to tamper with the rule of a man whose dynastic credentials extended back through the centuries, at least as far as Rudolph I, who included Austria in his dominion as early as

1278. Metternich on the other hand was fair game. Even conservatives could accept that proposition.

There was still another consideration. In Germany there was no one individual on whom the general public displeasure could focus, whereas in Austria Metternich was an obvious target. His reputation was such that people readily imagined that if only he were to fall all their socio-political problems would automatically vanish.[18] This belief quickly became evident in the wake of the exciting news of the Paris revolution.

There was tension already in Hungary, where Kossuth had spoken so emphatically. On 6 March came the first action in Vienna, where the *Gewerbeverein*, the influential juridico-political reading circle, and the booksellers directed petitions to the emperor. All stated that there ought to be extended political participation as well as trial by jury and abolition of censorship.

In mid-March 1848, Friedrich Wilhelm's special envoy, Joseph Maria von Radowitz, arrived on the scene and reported from Vienna:

> . . . Vienna today is the scene of episodes of unrest . . . they are clear indication that much is wrong in Austria. Beside the love of the royal house, a powerful hate has developed against the "system" and against the officials who represent it. Especially it is against *Fürst* Metternich that this hate is unjustly directed, because one cannot blame him for the despotism of officials and the financial crisis.[19]

Members of the court were divided. A few, including the minister Kolowrat (Metternich's opponent) wanted to make concessions in response to the petitions that had been submitted, but Metternich firmly rejected this proposal.

At about this time, Carl Friedrich Vitzthum von Eckstädt wrote to his mother:

> There are cannon before the court, before the fortress, before the chancellery, and on the Stephansplatz. There are barricades in some of the streets. Several thousand have assembled below the windows of the chancellery, demanding the dismissal of Metternich, whom they call "Austria's curse" . . .[20]

The chief of police surveillance had assured Metternich that the stirrings on the streets of Vienna were insignificant. This may have been a simple error in judgment, but it was a serious one as far as Metternich's survival was concerned. Metternich accepted the assessment because he flattered himself that, as always heretofore, he could divide his adversaries and thus defeat them.[21] In any case, he was indifferent to mob reactions and placed no value on them, having as a young diplomat observed how cynically Napoleon manipulated public acclaim.

On the morning of 12 March, the students assembled in the university *Aula* and drafted a formidable document, petitioning for freedom of the press, for academic freedom, for freedom of religious preference, and a general voting franchise. This meeting could hardly be considered to have been a product of spontaneous combustion, in spite of its close association with the revolution in Paris. The speakers were not rabble-rousers, and it was evident that their demands had been thought out beforehand. The medical men were markedly determined (Adolf Fischhof, for example, who was to become a leader in the succeeding weeks). Two professors—university rector Janull and Anton Hye, the popular archivist who had openly criticized such moves as the annexation of Cracow—persuaded the students that it would be preferable to let them take this petition to the court on their behalf. They had to return empty-handed, reporting that that had received no positive response. The students were profoundly irritated.

Soon the word was spreading: the next day would be the day. The "day" was a Monday, when the workers traditionally took "blue Monday" to recover from their weekend drinking bouts, as everyone knew. Mysteriously, no effort was made to block entrance of workers coming from the outskirts into the streets of the inner city. In consideration of the enormous apparatus of surveillance, it is difficult to believe that there was no awareness of the general currents of sympathy that were running between the students and the workers, or of the desperation of the working people. Many of the students were poor, and they knew that in Vienna at that time, there were often two or three families sharing a single room. Moreover, they must have known of the custom whereby a *Bettgeher* hired the use of a bed for a few hours out of the twenty-four.[22] If agitators were to approach people in such straits, they would find a receptive audience even if the teachings of Marx and Engels had never reached them.

There is some suspicion that the cabinet minister, *Graf* Anton Kolowrat, may have had something to do with the otherwise inexplicable delay in taking measures that would have headed off disorder on the city streets. Kolowrat and Metternich had hated each other for years. They had always done everything in their power to frustrate any plan or action that the other might take.

On that fateful Monday morning (13 March 1848), a huge crowd broke into the courtyard of the *Landhaus* (meeting place of the diet), and while it milled there listening to speeches, copies of a German translation of Kossuth's fiery address at Pressburg were passed from hand to hand, with inflammatory effect. Concerted action was taken at last: a deputation was sent to the court with demands for a constitution, and for the immediate dismissal of Metternich.

Meanwhile the military had been belatedly called in. Inevitably, shots were fired and there were civilian casualties, including four deaths among the unarmed people. The crowd predictably responded by hurling stones and imprecations at the soldiers. The civic guard was summoned, and this action set off still more confusion because the civic guard distrusted the soldiers and the court. As property-owning middle class citizens, they were wary too of the workers. The students, whom the workers trusted, then injected themselves into the volatile mess, demanding that they be armed and organized as an "academic legion".

At the court, Metternich decided that martial law was called for, and summoned *Feldherr Fürst* Alfred Windischgrätz, telling him that he would be given plenipotentiary status and charged with the restoration of order, but before that fierce man even had a chance to go home and change from civilian clothes to his formal dress uniform (even in dire emergency, court etiquette had to be observed, and he could not receive this appointment unless properly attired), a succession of deputations appeared, with demands that unnerved the emperor's ministers.

The first deputation brought a "citizens' petition" for Metternich's dismissal. The second, carried by the rector of the university, called for arming of the students. The third, from the civil guard, set up three conditions, all to be met by nine o'clock that evening: they demanded withdrawal of the troops, arming of the students, and dismissal of Metternich.

The ministry began to give way and troop withdrawal was initiated, with an immediate calming effect on the milling mobs in the streets.

It was at this point that Metternich began his delaying action, talking on and on for an hour and a half, with no sign that he was drawing his wordy remarks to a close. *Graf* Kolowrat drew out his watch in a marked manner and addressed the emperor. "Your Imperial Highness, we have only another half hour. I have been sitting in conference with

Fürst Metternich for twenty-five years, and I have always heard him talk like this without coming to the point."

It was then that "poor Ferdinand" uttered his crisp comment.[23] Metternich resigned and made a speedy getaway, assisted by only one person, Baron Salomon Rothschild, who generously supplied the necessary thousand Thaler for the roundabout escape to England. Frequently in danger, the aged minister traveled humiliatingly under assumed names ("*Herr* von Mayer, landowner from Styria", or "*Herr* von Manteux").

Von Radowitz again wrote to the Prussian monarch, reporting the downfall of Metternich. He was angry because he thought that order should have been restored before any concessions were granted. It would have been possible to do this, he argued, because there were more than fourteen thousand members of the military in the city. They could have expelled the crowds, driving them out and barring the city gates. The Prussian emissary was oversimplifying the situation. There had been too many conflicting interests and purposes in play to allow any clearcut decisions and unequivocal action. In spite of this predictable reaction on the part of a dyed-in-the-wool conservative, von Radowitz was clear in his mind that Metternich had done much damage to Austria with his "purely negative system of domestic and foreign policy."[24]

Jubilant throngs formed long torchlight processions, converging on the palace to cheer the emperor, but the trouble was not over. Windischgrätz had received his plenipotentiary status. News of this sent tremors through the populace in spite of the establishment of a national guard and the issuance of an imperial rescript that abolished censorship. There was a confused effort to pacify the people by means of a strangely worded rescript that appeared somewhat fuzzily to suggest a move toward representative government, but the only thing that quieted the people that day was the emperor's afternoon drive around the inner city. Like everything that Ferdinand did, this move elicited wild cheers and an impressive display of enthusiasm.[25] But disorder still prevailed. At last, on the evening of 15 March, a herald appeared before the palace gates and read a proclamation. It stated that the emperor had taken the necessary steps to convoke representatives of all provincial Estates and of Lombardy-Venetia, with increased citizens' representation, for the purpose of drafting "the Constitution that We [Ferdinand] have decided to grant". When Ferdinand showed himself, he was madly cheered.[26] On the following day there was a

solemn ceremony in honor of the fifty known victims of the disorder—
an unmistakable sign that the revolution had been successful.

The story of the Austrian revolution does not end here. Hungary
was to make herself heard on the following day and before long the
whole new governmental structure started to crack. This had not been
a nationwide revolution. Rather, it was confined to Vienna and fated
to collapse six months later. Even by the end of March, there was a
sharp cleft between the satisfied middle class and the radical student-
worker alliance that had become strongly organized. For the moment
the democrats were confident, with official recognition of their Academic Legion as peace-keepers and the committee steered by the
medical student Hablowsky in collaboration with Dr. Fischhof. They
were still strong enough, at the end of March, to beat back a proposed
restriction on the press, but the days of their power were numbered.
By the end of March it was becoming all too clear that the democratic
movement was isolated. Rural people, the Catholics, and the various
ethnic groups, all had their own conflicting agenda. Proponents of
reaction were beginning to recover their wits, understanding that their
conservative cause had not been lost irretrievably. Metternich may
have given up prematurely, not comprehending the resilience of absolute authority. The secretary of the legation of Saxony in Vienna, Carl
Friedrich von Vitzthum von Eckstädt, may have had a more accurate
view of the situation when he wrote that in a storm the astute captain
casts everything overboard, even the most valuable part of his cargo,
in order to save the ship. Then, when the wind drops, divers can
recover whatever was jettisoned.[27]

Whatever fate might hold in store for Austria, there were already
repercussions in Berlin, where the prospect of a world no longer controlled by Metternich seemed to offer dazzling possibilities.

Notes

1 Valentin, *Geschichte der deutschen Revolution,* I:1.

2 Macartney, *The Habsburg Empire,* p. 330.

3 Ibid., p.408: Hamerow, *Restoration, Revolution, Reaction,* p. 174. It was obvious that the emperor was being retired on account of the pledges he had made to liberalism.

4 Sperber, *European Revolutions,* pp. 102–103.

5 *Oesterreich Lexikon ,* s.v. "Vorderösterreich," 2:575–576.

6 Franz von Hartig, *Genesis, or Details of the Late Austrian Revolution.* Published as an appendix to Walter Keating Kelly, *History of the House of Austria.*

7 Macartney, p. 166, note 1.

8 Josef Polisensky, *Aristocrats and the Crowd in the Revolutionary Year 1848,* p. 69.

9 Arthur J. May, *The Age of Metternich 1814–1848,* p. 87.

10 Hamerow, p. 11.

11 Macartney, p. 213.

12 William H. Stiles, *Austria in 1848–49,* 1:85.

13 Jacques Droz, *Les révolutions allemandes de 1848,* p. 181.

14 Robertson, *Revolutions of 1848,* p. 196.

15 Macartney, p. 834.

16 Ibid., pp. 324–325.

17 Stearns, *1848: The Revolutionary Tide in Europe,* pp. 60, 104–110.

18 Droz, p. 83.

19 Jessen, *Die deutsche Revolution 1848/49 in Augenzeugenberichten,* p. 50.

20 Ibid., 51–52.

21 Droz, p. 184.

22 Macartney, p. 276.

23 Ibid., pp. 328–330.

24 Jessen, p. 60.

25   Macartney, p. 332.

26   Ibid., pp. 332–333.

27   Jessen, p. 67.

Chapter 13

Friedrich Wilhelm IV and His "Dear Berliners"—March 1848

A revolution has to have a geographic focal point as well as a target for popular displeasure. Paris was the focus in February 1848, and Louis-Philippe was the target. In Austria of March 1848, Vienna was the focal point, and Clemens Metternich was the obvious target for the ire of the people. In Germany of March 1848, there were various points where disorder erupted, but Berlin was the recognized center of power. As to a target, rage was not directed against Friedrich Wilhelm IV. There were complaints about his policies, his hesitations, and his ministers, but on the whole the Berliners were loyal to their king. However, they had a clear target—the army. Hostility between the army and the people of Berlin had been a fact of life for decades, and after the violence of the 1847 "potato revolution" there had been a growing cold animosity on both sides.

The situation was understandable. Berlin had become a large industrial city, yet its police force was ridiculously inadequate (a grand total of 110 to 120 men).[1] For that reason even a minor episode that involved nothing more than a few overturned stalls in the market, or a half-dozen shattered windowpanes could be enough to warrant the calling in of the army. The army was hardly the instrument for quiet control of a civilian population because the officers were for the most part arrogant young sons of aristocrats who looked down contemptuously on shop keepers, while the troops themselves were country lads recruited against their will. They knew that city folk looked down on them, and they were resentful because workers in a place like the big Borsig locomotive factory seemed to be lording it over them. The pay earned by those fortunate employees with their valuable mechanical skills must have looked princely to lowly infantrymen. An explosive mixture in March 1848!

In the general nervousness of February and March 1848, Prussia had brought various army corps to full strength and flooded the city of Berlin with cavalry units and infantry battalions. A conservative estimate places the number of uniformed military in the capital at about twenty thousand.[2]

Early in March, while news and rumors trickled in gradually from Paris and Vienna, the potentials for popular unrest were dramatically increased by the agitated reaction of the stock market and the simultaneous dismissal of four hundred workers from the Borsig machine works. The number of unemployed persons then stood at about seven thousand, causing dismay among the police officials, although they seem to have been inclined to think that the local working class was not seriously infected with the virus of communism that was spreading out from Cologne and the Rhenish towns. The surface impression of Berlin's mood must have been deceptive. Karl Gutzkow, the dramatist, recently arrived in the city, remembered at a later date that "I found it so quiet, so peaceful, so patriarchal" that he had been inclined to settle in Berlin for a time in order to write, in spite of the fact that his works, like Heine's, had long been banned in Prussia. He wrote that the coffee houses were full, and that as one passed by on the street one could hear the names of Louis-Philippe, Lamartine, and Ledru-Rollin being read out from the current newspapers. There was as yet no word from Vienna, he noted.[3]

In consideration of the unusual number of idle persons on the city streets, it was to be expected that there would be increasingly large numbers of people gathering near the *Tiergarten*, around the little bandstands and pavilions in the amusement area popularly known as *Die Zelten* (there had originally been tents there, hence the name). The police seem to have thought, with the weather suddenly so fine and sunny, that these crowds were harmless, simply celebrating the springtime after all the cold and rain. However, there was enough purpose and solidarity at *Die Zelten* to generate an official address (on 7 March) to Friedrich Wilhelm IV in which it was firmly stated that it was necessary immediately to establish freedom of the press and to call the united *Landtag*. Even at that late date, the ignorance of the crowds that surged around the speakers' platform could be deplorable. Some believed that freedom of the press meant freedom from taxation (they would no longer be "pressed"), or that henceforth advertizing matter could be placed in the newspapers without charge.[4]

Unemployed laborers in the crowd who were perhaps a little more sophisticated refused to sign the address, saying pessimistically that it

Figure 6 "DIE ZELTEN" [the tents] in the Berlin zoological gardens (early spring 1848).

would not do any good. No doubt they felt justified as days dragged by and his Majesty declined to receive the document.—He did in fact belatedly accept it (on 14 March) and issue a half-hearted order relating to press censorship, and announce that he would call the *Landtag* for a meeting on 27 April, but by that time there had been a clash between armed soldiers and unarmed civilians late in the afternoon of 13 March, when demonstrators returning peacefully from *Die Zelten* were dispersed by a cavalry charge on *Unter den Linden*. Responsibility for this unfortunate skirmish seems to rest on the shoulders of *Freiherr* von Minutoli, the prefect of police of the city, thought to have acted as an *agent provocateur*.[5]

Citizens were cautioned on the following day (14 March) to avoid public assemblies. Friedrich Wilhelm was showing signs of panic. He sent a note to his minister of the interior (Bodelschwingh) insisting that the foreign elements in the crowds must be sent away on "various railway trains" with guards who carried loaded weapons, adding an agitated postscript that "yesterday in whole groups on *Unter den Linden* they were speaking French". This foreign *Literatenpack* must be forcibly removed!!![6] Parenthetically, it is striking to see how quickly the idea of railway transportation had become accepted.

Late that evening an appalling incident occurred in the Brüderstrasse that showed all too clearly that the presence of so many troops was no protection, but rather that it was a provocation or even worse. In this case, cavalry suddenly rushed headlong toward the royal palace, howling, banging on doors, and frightening the residents, who scurried indoors. Then ten people appeared on the empty Brüderstrasse, coming from the direction of the palace, moving quietly in pairs or singly on their way home. The cavalry madly attacked these innocent people with their broadswords, seriously wounding a number of them. This was the most blatant of a series of similar incidents. There was little evidence that the officers were in control of their units.

To put it bluntly, they may not have wanted to control such excesses. A seasoned officer wrote at the time to his mother that these things should not be taken too seriously: there had been an element of "gaiety" in the Brüderstrasse episode. Besides, the people under attack in Berlin at this time were wretches who had come in from southern Germany, probably workers who had been "bought". He was happy to be able to tell her that he and his men had delivered some "good sabre blows".[7]

On the next day (15 March), a civil guard of sorts was established, but it was a body that had little or no organization and no authority. Its members were none too impressive in appearance, being distinguished by a white brassard and armed with a baton. This half measure was annoying: people were asking for a true civil guard and withdrawal of the irresponsible soldiery. That evening popular unrest assumed a more menacing character, when a huge mass of people gathered by the palace. Troops cleared the square, firing into the crowd and causing a large number of casualties as well as several deaths. People had started to erect barricades on the previous day. Now they tore up street pavings and hurled stones at the soldiers in vicious hand-to-hand combat.

The heir to the throne was a trouble-maker. The king's brother Wilhelm had been angered during this encounter because Berlin's governor, *Generalleutnant* Ernst Heinrich Adolf von Pfuel, had been reluctant to fire on the people. The prince had taken it upon himself to order the attack, and his order had then been countermanded by von Pfuel. Two days later there would be a serious altercation when the prince confronted von Pfuel, saying that he was compromising the army. Von Pfuel reacted by going to the king and demanding an apology. The prince indeed apologized, but he was still an angry man. He had complained aloud that he was dissatisfied with the marksmanship of the troops, and he had been overheard saying "rather too loudly" that the people ought to be fired on energetically.[8] He and his supporters must have begun at once to seek ways to effect the removal of von Pfuel and his replacement by *Generalleutnant* von Prittwitz, who tended to look at matters with a hostility that matched their own.

Fürst Wilhelm had shown his true colors on 16 March, when there was again a massive meeting on *Unter den Linden*. The city was in turmoil that day, reacting to the news of Metternich's fall. Infantrymen were everywhere, and cavalry rode through the streets. In spite of this, a crowd of hostile demonstrators collected around the prince's residence (they had begun to understand that he was their enemy), and Friedrich Wilhelm ordered him to come at once to the palace, for his physical safety, no doubt. However, before the prince obeyed that command, a half company of infantry marched out from the arsenal, and then there was a series of confused directives that brought still more troops onto the scene. A couple of innocent bystanders were killed when shots were fired.

An eyewitness of the event of 16 March observed that whereas Austrians had had a detested minister who fully embodied the old system, the Prussian ministers (Bodelschwingh and his colleagues) were indistinct in most people's minds and therefore failed to rouse public anger. On the other hand, there remained before them one object for their rage—the soldiery that ceaselessly injured and infuriated them.

With reference to the event of 16 March, he wrote that in the general turmoil he had been forced over toward the residence of the crown prince.

> When we came to a standstill, an elderly well-dressed man beside me flung down his hat—in a gesture of anger or fear—and wringing his hands heavenward he cried Prussians are shooting Prussians! The tears were coursing down his cheeks. The sight made an indelible impression on me.[9]

Gradually, even citizens whose ignorance of political theory was abysmal were arriving at the conclusion that the military—the mainstay of the king's absolute rule—were at the root of their troubles. Needless to say, the incongruously romantic Friedrich Wilhelm would passionately cling to an opposite opinion because in spite of his dreamy misconceptions he was nonetheless a proud Hohenzollern. He believed himself to be sovereign by the grace of God, overlooking the fact that the divine grace to which he attributed his ineluctable authority was nothing other than arbitrary martial force.

He had also been overlooking the disgraceful conduct of the troops which was surely the result of arrogant mismanagement of the worst sort.

Metternich's fall had thrown Friedrich Wilhelm's ministers into a state of consternation. The royal councillors assembled, anxiously debating a variety of impractical schemes. Indubitably, a turning point had been reached. Cabinet minister Bodelschwingh labored throughout the night, developing a *Patent* that included various concessions that were generally in line with the program laid out by Max von Gagern during his mission from the *Vorparlament* at Frankfurt to sound out the various states on the idea of German unification.

When Bodelschwingh sat down to wrestle with the *Patent* that Friedrich Wilhelm intended to issue, he was facing a difficult task. As a loyal subject of the king, he had always dutifully acted as a rigid conservative, yet now he must prepare a list of concessions that were being forced upon his master. The most influential and "perspicacious" member of the cabinet, [10] Bodelschwingh had become convinced that it was not possible to postpone the granting of a constitution, and he had in fact brought the king around to the same conclusion on 14 March, when it had been first announced that the united *Landtag* would meet at the end of April. Bodelschwingh had in his possession a letter written just days before the fall of Metternich by David Hansemann, the Rhineland business leader. This scorching indictment of Metternich's policy may have helped him to stiffen his resolve in favor of a more liberal approach to government.

Hansemann had written bluntly that the guiding principle of the continental governments under Metternich's leadership had been respect for dynasties, which were considered to be more important than the people. Mercilessly, he listed the "achievements" of the Metternich system: 1) a change in the order of succession to the throne in Spain and Portugal, 2) the deposition of a legitimate ruler in France and the driving out of the rival, supposedly legitimate dynasty, in favor of a provisional republican government, 3) a stronger development of the democratic principle in the Swiss republics, 4) a lively spirit of nationalism in Italy, along with a strong hatred of the Germans, 5) in Germany itself, a total lack of confidence in the officials of the confederation, from whom there had never been any protection of constitutional rights or of German independence, 6) in states that had a constitution only so much was clear, that their uppermost concern was the unlimited power of the monarchs, 7) in the entire German state there was no unitary institution that could represent the nation, 8) Russia was a threat, and so was the unpredictable new regime in France.

Hansemann concluded with the statement that Germans had responded magnificently in 1813, and that they would do so again if Friedrich Wilhelm were to issue a strong call while peace still prevailed in the land where danger threatened. Friedrich Wilhelm should summon a united *Landtag*, guarantee freedom of the press etc etc etc. Hansemann himself was prepared to serve in whatever useful capacity might present itself in those parlous times.[11]

Minister von Bodelschwingh completed his troublesome assignment and respectfully told Friedrich Wilhelm that since, as a loyal servant, he had always played the role of a die-hard conservative, it would not be helpful if he were to attempt to put on a different mask and continue to serve in his Majesty's cabinet under the new dispensation. He would therefore resign immediately, in the best interests of the king and his government. He was to be replaced by *Graf* von Arnim-Boitzenburg, but before his successor actually took his seat, Bodelschwingh pushed through a second *Patent* that abolished censorship.

The two documents went through the hands of his successor and the king. The only change made by Friedrich Wilhelm was substitution of the teutonic word *Verfassung* for Bodelschwingh's original gallic *Constitution*, which his Majesty thought was unpleasantly suggestive of revolutionary tendencies.[12] The main paragraph stood as Bodenschwingh had written it: Germany would cease to be a federation of states, to become a federal state with representation of the members of the various *Stände* of all the German states. There would be a federal army on the Prussian model, a fleet, a national flag, a federal court, freedom of travel from state to state, extension of the *Zollverein*, codification of the law, and standardization of weights and measures. The Prussian *Landtag* would be convened on 2 April. "Prussia has already had her revolution" breathed Bodelschwingh with relief on the morning of 18 March. He was perhaps too weary to realize that the omission of any reference to withdrawal of the troops from the city streets might have a troublesome effect.

That morning the king received a number of delegations, including one that jointly represented the municipal authorities of Cologne, Halle, and Breslau. The demands they presented were drastic and urgent because there was much unrest. Around noon, a delegation of the city council of Berlin was received, and Bodelschwingh sent them into ecstasies of joy when he told them of the impending ministerial changes and read the proclamation to them. They thanked his Majesty "with tears" and assured him that there would be no more disorders in the city. Soon a delirious crowd poured into the palace courtyard. Friedrich Wilhelm appeared on a balcony and was cheered to the echo.

The crowd was enormous because on the quiet previous evening a meeting had been held by the influential editors and agitators of the radical *Zeitungshalle*, where it was decided that there ought to be a powerful demonstration on the following day (18 March), emphasizing the importance of an address that would be presented to the king, calling once again for removal of the troops. Some people attending the meeting had expressed doubts—a huge demonstration like that could turn into a revolution if the military interfered.—It is possible that some of the men who were insisting on a demonstration hoped that something of the sort might happen.[13] As events turned out, this big throng had assembled, and with announcement of the royal proclamation, people felt that at the very least they ought to go to the palace and express loyal thanks.

As the happy mob pressed closer and closer to the palace, cheering their king, they were disconcerted to discover that soldiers were massed in a rear court in a way that looked threatening, although as one observer remarked, they were just standing there patiently. Voices began to call *Militär zurück!* [troops stand back] and the shouting rose to a confused, noisy crescendo. Karl Gutzkow, an eyewitness, recalled that those who first shouted did not number more than twenty "respectably dressed" individuals.[14] The French emissary de Circourt who was present imagined that the shouts were those of foreign agitators. He mentioned Swiss, Italians and Poles but admitted that he had no personal knowledge of such individuals.[15] (It was soon to become the received gospel of conservatives that the revolutionists in Berlin were in fact not Berliners at all, but foreign agitators and riffraff.)

The overall situation had appeared so peaceful that morning that the military commandant, General von Pfuel, had allowed himself the luxury of an hour to check on his family, whom he had not seen for several days. This was just the opportunity that the crown prince and his supporters had been waiting for. In that brief interval they had managed to persuade tired, uneasy Friedrich Wilhelm that an emergency existed and that their candidate, the militant von Prittwitz, ought to command. This unfortunate move was made in a trice. Therefore, when the tumult and shouts for withdrawal of the troops grew louder, it was von Prittwitz who, in response to the king's command to "put an end to this and clear the plaza", led out his cavalry. There was so much noise that the general knew that vocal commands would be inaudible. He therefore unsheathed his sword, raising it above his head. Some of his dragoons imitated the gesture. (The king boldly asserted in his letter which he wrote that night to the people of Berlin that all swords had been sheathed.) To the crowd, the advance of cavalry with naked swords raised had the look of planned aggression.

At that point, two shots were fired into the air. Explanations subsequently offered by the military were disingenuous. (For example, a bystander was said to have caused a gun to discharge by striking the barrel of it with his cane. Obviously, anyone having even the most rudimentary experience with firearms would know that a gun does not discharge unless the firing mechanism has been cocked.) It is worth noting that neither the Russian ambassador nor the Austrian mentioned any accident in their reports.

Eyewitness accounts of the melee that immediately erupted are not in total agreement, but one thing is certain. This was revolution. The newly appointed civil guards promptly ripped off their white brassards, shouting BETRAYAL! ASSASSINS! and hurried to join the fray. Only immediate by-standers would have been aware that there had been no injuries from the shots. To the crowd at large, it was enough to know that the troops were their enemies. A huge white banner was displayed from a palace window, bearing the single word *Missverständniss* [misunderstanding].[16]

In the words of Karl Gutskow, *Wenn hier ein äusseres Missverständniss stattfand, ein inneres gab es nicht.*[17] [If there had been a superficial misunderstanding, there was no internal one]. Gutzkow saw and understood that all those years of repression were bearing their bitter fruit. Why should people care about deposed ministries?—All they thought of was the old familiar brutality and arrogance of officers, the blind raw violence of country kids in uniform. Anything printed was just so much trash to them. A bewildered sixteeen-year-old boy standing near Gutzkow in the crowd, in his blue smock and clutching a bucket of paste against his chest, whined "I'm supposed to paste up the proclamations for the Magistrate but they're shooting at me."[18]

Apprentices, shopkeepers, and women—all were running with eyes furiously raised to heaven. They were shouting "Weapons! Weapons! They've betrayed us!" Everywhere there was frantic activity. The first barricade went up almost as though by magic on the Jägerstrasse. Barrels were being rolled into position, and planks that covered the gutters were being snatched up. Their bodies charged with adrenalin, people were performing prodigies of physical exertion. Circourt observed a scrawny "miserable student" who single-handedly hauled an enormous metal block from one side of the street to the other. Later, three husky soldiers with bulging muscles struggled and strained to put it back.[19]

All in all, this was the catharsis that everyone required. Resentments and foiled expectations had been dammed up too long, and a point had been reached at which citizens everywhere longed for action—almost any kind of action. How good it felt, just to fly into a wild releasing physical explosion, kicking aside the old hates and frustrations and attacking with all one's might whatever lay in the way![20] Bare your teeth, people!

Whatever the infuriated citizens lacked in knowledge of tactics was offset by their determination and energy. A pair of students set off at a gallop in order to summon workmen from the Borsig plant, returning with hundreds, all armed with hammers and iron rods. While women and children panted up stairways, carrying cobblestones and bricks to the rooftops, squads were roaming the city collecting weapons. They invaded the opera house, taking away lances and spears and swords. Others scoured residential neighborhoods, hammering on the doors of private homes. Such a group burst into the quiet, dignified abode of Alexander von Humboldt. The leader at least made an attempt to acknowledge the distinction of the elderly scientist. "Dear and venerable sir," he began. "You are aware that Christians and brothers must help one another. It is impossible that you could have such an impressive collection of stuffed birds in this gallery without being the possessor of an armory of muskets. Give them to us for the well-being of the fatherland." Humboldt's servant gave them an old carbine and tried to usher them out, but the invaders suddenly lost their solemn courtesy and broke the windows, threw the scholar's papers around in disorder, and ended by invading the wine cellar. Humboldt was resigned: at least they had not taken anything.[21]

Even at that late hour, while artillery was being wheeled forward, efforts were being made to quiet the situation. Gutzkow saw the rector of the university and the professors in their long heavy velvet robes hurrying to the palace, where they hoped to persuade his Majesty to arm the students, but already cannon were beginning to speak. The king reportedly said sharply that if the citizens of Berlin were rebels, they had to be treated as such.

The sound of the firing of heavy field pieces was said to have upset Friedrich Wilhelm terribly. Some who had been near him asserted that he had clutched his brow, moaning and even sobbing, and then had flung himself back into a chair in paralyzed apathy. Others, notably the staid von Gerlach, insisted that the king had maintained his calm dignity throughout the ordeal. Modern historians who have critically examined contemporary records have been led to conclude that the descriptions of a distraught, unnerved monarch were derived from nothing more than *Offiziersklatsch* [the disgruntled chatter] of officers who on the whole remained loyal to their king.[22]

The insurgents lacked both weapons and ammunition, but they were prepared to fight with all the instruments of rage and desperation. Circourt reported that people fought with pitchforks, shovels, meatspits and tiles that they tore from the roof tops.[23] They had two small brass cannon that they resourcefully loaded with *Murmeltiere* ["marmots"]—a play on words based on the fact that the actual charge was a load of childrens' marbles [*Murmeln*] crammed into a stocking. One of the heroes of the barricades, the journeyman locksmith Gustav Hesse, managed this extraordinary artillery.

There were no appointed leaders. Gustav Hesse was unusual in that he was able to enforce a certain amount of order and cooperation by taking his stand dramatically at the barricades, iron gunner's rod in hand, and roaring *Citoyens! Liberté!*—Students were everywhere, but they seem to have had no designated leader. It must have been students with a classical background who inspired the coronation of the heroic gunner Hesse. Someone must have remembered that a hero in Roman battles customarily received a crown—a special "mural crown" for being first to scale a city wall, for example—and in a curious throwback to this ancient practice, they contrived to honor Hesse. Throughout the turmoil of the March days, Hesse wore his crown, and there were enough people in the milling throng who understood its significance to cause civil guards to come to attention and salute him whenever he tramped by.

The pandemonium of street fighting began at about three o'clock in the afternoon and continued all through the night. Young apprentices climbed the church towers and rang the bells hour after hour, and flames shot up from fires set at the iron foundry, at the customs offices, and at various factories. It is impossible to know just how many combattants were involved—some think four thousand. As the Russian ambassador reported, "all citizens believed that they had been betrayed" with the result that middle class men readily fought shoulder to shoulder with the workers (nine hundred had come in from the Borsig plant). The revolutionists were indeed genuine Berliners, not outside agitators.

Individuals of all ranks were engaged in this hand-to-hand struggle. Circourt at one point found prince Friedrich-Karl von Hohenlohe, his face black with gunpowder and his garments torn, snatching food in a moment of quiet. He also encountered the spectacular adventurer, Prince Felix Lichnowsky and was "revolted" by the "cruel lightness" of his talk, but made the penetrating comment that Lichnowsky was probably experiencing the *frémissement martial que donne à un homme de coeur l'approche de dangers* [the martial shiver that the approach of danger imparts to a brave man].[24]

The furious struggles at the hundreds of barricades were not executed with much skill, militarily speaking. At first, General von Prittwitz had his men attack frontally, with disastrous results because the men were exposed to fire from the upper floors of houses behind the barricades. *Graf* von Benckendorff, the Russian military attaché, noted that he had seldom heard such massive firing. At one point he counted at least forty wounded and dead among the soldiers.[25] On the other hand, the barricade defenders usually had to retreat rapidly. Sometimes one lone fighter would defend the barricade against a stormy attack. People

Figure 7 BERLIN BARRICADE (March 1848) Friedrich Wilhelm believed that the revolutionists were street rabble, but the men in top hats were clearly men of the middle class. Working classes in the eighteen forties traditionally wore smocks and caps. The iillustration shows how rebellious Berliners were hurling cobblestones if other weapons were not available.

never forgot the 17-year-old apprentice Ernst Zinna who held out valiantly all by himself against an infantry assault until he died.[26]

Prisoners taken at the barricades numbered as many as one thousand. Hundreds of them were herded into the cellars of the palace, where they spent a wretched night jammed into a black hole of Calcutta, subjected to blows and insults and deprived of water or food. One of them reported later that he and his fellow prisoners had been kicked, struck with gun butts and generally mistreated, but he felt that perhaps the soldiers' rage was justified at that point. He himself had been hauled and kicked downstairs from a rooftop from which he presumably had been shooting or hurling stones. The king, seeing these bloody tattered captives, jumped to the conclusion that all of them were scum from the gutters and wondered jokingly if the people would want them back if they saw them—a curious reaction from a man who later that very night was to write so movingly of his concern and love for his dear Berliners.

In his nocturnal wandering, Circourt came upon a new barricade being built in Oranienbaumstrasse. It was made entirely of fire-engine pumps and other materials that could serve to protect a growing city, especially like this in the center of a manufacturing quarter where all kinds of accidents might occur. "I know of nothing more diabolic, more capable of characterizing the face of revolution in a single stroke," he concluded sadly.[27]

The overwrought and emotionally labile Friedrich Wilhelm was being pulled this way and that. Early in the evening of that impossible day, the king received an importunate letter from his trusted emissary and friend, Joseph Maria von Radowitz, written from Vienna on 16 March. Radowitz was clinging to his conviction that whatever reforms were needed ought to be granted by the king after restoration of order. He should under no circumstances act as though under duress. Von Radowitz predicted accurately that there would be a storm of petitions and threatening demonstrations, and that all eyes would be fixed on Berlin. If it turned out that there was a reasonable chance of gaining a genuine victory, his Majesty ought to follow that course to the very end. In other words, if necessary he must leave Berlin and withdraw the troops, because experience had shown time and again that prolonged street fighting only demoralized the men and their officers. Pull back to Spandau, he pleaded. Concentrate the troops there and leave maintenance of order in Berlin to the civilians.[28]

In the opinion of *Graf* Benckendorff, the king had three options.[29] He could continue the battle within the city, reducing the rebels to subjection by persistent massive ruthless attack. He could withdraw along with his troops and cordon off the city. (That would be the most reasonable way to handle the problem militarily, Benckendorff thought.) Or he could hold present positions and wait—a way that did not make much sense and would be excusable only if one needed to gain time.

The militarists around the beleaguered monarch wanted to fight. War is war, they said. Of course, it was also a civil war. If Friedrich Wilhelm were to withdraw, surrounding the city and allowing bombardment, half his capital would go up in flames.

There were other disagreeable possibilities that had to be considered. What if the Rhineland province were to declare itself separate? What would happen if there were risings in Silesia and East Prussia? Would Russia send in troops? What about war with Denmark over Schleswig-Holstein? Austria, of course, was a feeble reed at the moment, but what if the Poles were to rise? What about support of the Prussian army? The crown prince had already been infuriated in discussion of possible withdrawal of the troops, rasping out that he had always known that the king was a garrulous chatterer, but not that he was a coward. "A man can no longer serve you with honor!" With that he slammed his sword down at the sovereign's feet.[30]—If the people of Berlin felt betrayed, so did harassed Friedrich Wilhelm.

Around midnight, Friedrich Wilhelm gave an order to General von Prittwitz. He was to hold whatever parts of the city he controlled, but not to attempt to take any more strategic positions. Prittwitz suggested that it might be necessary to withdraw from the city and bombard it, but the king made no comment. The general understood the unspoken wish that there be no further bloodshed. His Majesty then said goodnight in a kindly way, and von Prittwitz withdrew, seeing that the king had seated himself at his desk, encasing his feet cosily in a fur sack.[31] Friedrich Wilhelm, full of fine resolve, then grasped his pen and firmly composed his fatuous letter *An meine lieben Berliner* [to my dear Berliners].

Friedrich Wilhelm's letter, so full of emotion and pathos, is an interesting example of history rewritten. Within less than twenty-four hours, the king had convinced himself that the voices that called *Militär zurück* had been those of "foreigners" who had infiltrated the crowd of loyal subjects, and that their shouts were "audacious, seditious demands". He also knew somehow that the number of these disturbers of the peace had increased as "well-intentioned" citizens departed. He wrote that the threat to his "brave and loyal soldiers" had necessitated the clearing of the square. This had been done by cavalry who advanced *im Schritt* [at a walk] with *eingestechter Waffe* [weapons sheathed]. These expressions were underlined for emphasis. Indignant citizens were to object that this passage in the royal letter was *grundfalsch* [dead wrong]. Troops had decidedly not advanced at a walk with sheathed weapons. Many witnesses knew better.—His Majesty went on: Two firearms had then discharged *von selbst* [automatically] but there had been no injuries, thank God. However, the foreign miscreants [*Bösewichtern*] who had been infiltrating the good city of

Berlin for more than a week in spite of efforts to detect them, now according to their evil plan incited the people, making them believe the lie that blood had been shed. In that mean dastardly way they had made the loyal people of Berlin themselves responsible for the ensuing bloodshed. The troops,—your brothers and fellow countrymen—discharged their weapons only after many shots had been fired at them from the Königstrasse!

The letter continued: it was now the duty of the people of Berlin to renounce their appalling error, in order to prevent further calamities. He, their king and true friend, urged the people to remove the remaining barricades. He solemnly gave his "kingly word" that as soon as this removal had been completed, the troops would leave the streets, and only places like the arsenal and the palace would continue to be under military guard—and even there, only for a short time.

In a final flourish, Friedrich Wilhelm urged his people to listen to his fatherly voice and to forget the past as he himself intended to forget it. "Your true mother and friend, the Queen" joined her tearful plea to his.

This labored document appears to have met with cynical indifference. Some wit chalked "*An meine lieben Berliner*" next to a cannon ball lodged in the wall near one of the barricades.[32] In any case, on that morning (19 March) a flow of words could not be expected to hold the attention of exhausted barricade fighters and worn-out soldiers. The insurgents had had to give up a few key positions but they were far from defeated, still defiant and prepared to fight on. The troops on the other hand were beginning to waver a little. General von Prittwitz had had to retire the members of the elite *Leibregiment* [the king's own] as unfit for service. (These men were among the units selected to escort prisoners from the barricades to the fortress at Spandau. Their vicious mistreatment of the prisoners may be attributable to their humiliation and anger over this withdrawal from combat.) Fresh troops could be called in, to be sure—there were reserves in the city—but it was doubtful that their morale would hold.

The exhausted Friedrich Wilhelm, who had not slept or eaten throughout the whole ordeal, began receiving deputations at dawn. He told a delegation of city authorities that he was ready to withdraw the troops, but only on condition that the barricades be leveled first, as his letter had stated. The discussion with various officers and cabinet members dragged back and forth confusedly, until at last it became known that a few of the barricades had actually been razed.

(True to their innate sense of orderliness, people went out onto the street and with teutonic domestic tidiness recovered belongings that had formed part of the structure, carrying home their chairs and tables and household goods that had been under fire during the battle.)

In spite of the fierce objections of Prince Wilhelm and his militant backers therefore, gradual withdrawal of the troops—moving from case to case as barricades were leveled—seemed to be the right and successful move. The prince wanted complete withdrawal (and departure of the king with them) in order to continue the fight on a larger scale from outside the city. The king continued to resist that demand but somehow slipped into a new decision, that as soon as work was begun in dismantling a barricade, the troops confronting it should be pulled back. This was clearly counter to his provisions in the "dear Berliner" letter, but Bodelschwingh was told to carry this decision to a delegation that was waiting in a palace anteroom.[33]

General von Prittwitz and Prince Wilhelm objected strenuously, but Bodelschwingh retorted that his Majesty's command was unambiguous and must be obeyed. The command may have been clear, but it handed unambiguous victory over to the barricade fighters, who had not yet won the battle, and handed defeat to the troops, who had not yet lost, and who certainly would have won in the long run.

Around eleven o'clock, the barricade prisoners were removed from the palace cellars and marched off to Spandau. The French emissary de Circourt repeatedly commented on the disciplined behavior of the troops. According to his observations, the men performed their duty with courage, restraint and dignity. Where was de Circourt during the movement of the prisoners? One of them, Ludwig Pietsch, produced a detailed statement. They started off at four in the morning (19 March), escorted by grenadiers and *Ulans* from Pommerania. They went first along *Unter den Linden* to the Brandenburg gate, where they met another group, all of them bound together in pairs. These prisoners had spent the night in the offices of the War Ministry. All the prisoners were then marshalled four abreast in such close ranks that they unavoidably trod on the heels of the men in front of them. They were constantly prodded with gun butts and struck over the head with the weapons. All were regularly struck in the face, their noses bloodied. Special attention went to those who had been wounded. The man next to Pietsch already had a serious wound in the thigh as well gashes on his head. His face and hair were bloody. One of the soldiers dealt him a terrific blow with the barrel of his gun on the fresh wounds, causing them to spurt blood again. The powerfully built young victim shrieked and collapsed. "I pulled him along with some difficulty." A Munich student had such noble bearing and such a fine intelligent face that he attracted the anger of the guards, who struck him on the back of the neck over and over again with their guns and fists, but he somehow haughtily managed to keep silent. The guard next to Pietsch was "on the whole rather merciful". This man did no more than kick him and jab him in the back with the sheath of his bayonet, and pour out a river of insults—traitor—you ought to get a bayonet in your guts etc etc etc. The officers, said Pietsch, sometimes remonstrated mildly, but otherwise did nothing to prevent the torment. There is no reference in this report to pedestrians or by-standers, even though the wretched prisoners were being herded across the whole city. Were people still intimidated and unable to speak up, or did they—like their king—decide that these bloody victims were nothing but human scum? The prisoners were confined in ice-cold cells at Spandau, believing that the people had been defeated and that military dictatorship prevailed in Berlin. They were released late in the day, and a few indignant officials started to take up a collection for them.[34]

General von Prittwitz sent most of his troops back to their barracks, but kept a battalion at the arsenal and seven companies in the palace courtyard. However, the king's commands continued to be contradictory, and the crown prince also was having his say. (Valentin comments that any consistency in the king's behavior existed only in the sense that his instructions were always the opposite of what he did or had previously said, and that if anyone objected he quickly reversed himself or initiated a third command.)[35]

That afternoon, Friedrich Wilhelm learned to his consternation that there were only two battalions left guarding him. "That is not possible!" he exclaimed. It was indeed possible. Karl Gutzkow remembered:

> I saw it myself. Twenty purposeful men would have found the entrance to the stairway completely free. They could have presented a decree of abdication to the king and declared the republic. The palace was only guarded by completely apathetic warriors, most of whom were sleeping. The aristocracy had fled or concealed itself. . . . In the hours between eleven in the morning until two in the afternoon there was neither throne nor government in Prussia.[36]

Someone spoke up, saying that his Majesty ought to go immediately with those two battalions to Potsdam, and he seems to have agreed, but at that moment an unearthly procession entered the courtyard and there was no escape for the unfortunate king. He would have to drink his cup of humiliation.

Slowly, solemnly, an enormous cortege was filing into the palace courtyard. They were carrying the bodies of the slain barricade fighters on stretchers, boards, planks, and improvized biers, all decorated with greens and flowers and accompanied by weeping families. The French emissary Circourt wrote disdainfully that the grim torchlight display of cadavers that had taken place in Paris was more dramatic, but he was mistaken. This sunlit display of open wounds and sorrowing people was certainly effective enough in its own way. One man in the harsh rigidity of death lay with his arm high, the fist clenched. On each body there was an identifying paper, held down against the wind by a stone. As each corpse was set down in the courtyard, someone read the information on the paper: "My only son. Fifteen years old." "The father of five small children." "No quarter was given. Killed after he had surrendered."

A few members of the king's entourage came out on the balcony, including General von Prittwitz, who had the decency to remove his helmet and to order the military who were present to do likewise. Suddenly there was a shout. The king must come. Let him see what he has done! The intrepid Felix Lichnowsky objected, telling the assembled mourners that the king was exhausted and much in need of repose. Various ministers came out and made ineffectual efforts to speak. At last his Majesty appeared, with his deathly pale, half fainting queen beside him. The bodies were brought closer while women wailed and the men growled threateningly. Another shout: Take off your hat! The monarch obeyed, and then attempted to speak to the people, wanting to warn them to keep order, but this time their voices drowned him out. They were singing *Jesu meine Zuversicht* [in whom I trust]. When the hymn ended, the king turned away. His queen was overheard, saying "The only thing missing is the guillotine." As a pious man, Friedrich Wilhelm no doubt understood that one must honor the dead, but at the same time he was a Hohenzollern, a monarch by the grace of God, commander of a huge military machine. He had been forced to do homage publicly to those whom his own army had slain—a bitter pill indeed for a Prussian ruler. "Everything is in question now—even the Crown and the life of the king," said the Bavarian ambassador.

Immediately after this painful scene, Friedrich Wilhelm agreed that the barricade victims should be honored by a state funeral. The public mood changed abruptly. The king had been a traitor: now he was accepted.

Figure 8 LUDWIG MIEROSLAWSKI, THE POLISH HERO, RELEASED FROM PRISON (March 1848) Mieroslawski and his followers had fled from Poland in 1846 and had been imprisoned at the Moabit fortress ever since. The Polish presence had a strong influence on public opinion throughout the revolutionary period. Mieroslawski himself was to command the combined insurrectionary forces in Baden (1849).

On that same evening the troops were definitively withdrawn. They marched away in parade formation, bands playing. There were already Sunday strollers on *Unter den Linden*, but they objected to the jaunty quickstep, demanding something solemn like a chorale.—Perhaps the general release from emotional tension explains what happened next, though it seems odd when one reflects that all those two hundred and thirty barricade fighters were still unburied. The town was illuminated, as for a festival. Professor Fallati of Tübingen, writing to his friend Gustav Mevissen, was to wonder what people in other German countries would think of this *Harlekinade auf blutgetränktem Boden* [buffoonery on blood-soaked ground]. [37] The American embassy glowed: the ambassador reported that Friedrich Wilhelm and his people were now on a firmer footing than before. Feelings of hostility against the king seem to have evaporated. He had paid his debt.

Hatred of the crown prince remained, however. His residence was invaded and on the wall there was chalked derisively, "Property of the entire nation". The prince had become the scapegoat. There was wild alarm that night when rumors flew that he was about to march on the city at the head of the troops in Spandau. Friedrich Wilhelm discovered that his brother was needed in England, and hastily sent him away on an unspecified diplomatic mission.

There were strange festive scenes on the following day (20 March). A political amnesty brought about the release of the Polish revolutionist Mieroslawski and his forty followers from their two years of imprisonment at Moabit. A triumphant procession took them from the prison to the palace, in carriages pulled by enthusiastic Berliners. Mieroslawski waved a black-red-gold banner, proclaiming that Poles and Germans were brothers, and Friedrich Wilhelm stood on his balcony, swinging his hat. Karl Gutzkow had his spy glass trained on his Majesty's face and saw how impatient he was. Evidently he did not enjoy having to salute the flower-crowned *Polenthum*. [38] De Circourt viewed the spectacle with profound displeasure. He had little use for the Poles in the best of circumstances, and the apotheosis of Mieroslawski was rather too much for him. He was much annoyed, watching him as he stood in the carriage in his bizarre "Slavic" clothes. If the poor deluded Berliners had seen those adventurers other than through their tears, they would have found in those round, insignificant faces no traces of the suffering they were supposed to have endured.[39]

On that same morning, Friedrich Wilhelm published a manifesto in which it was announced that there would henceforth be German unity and freedom. The document mentioned general adoption of a true constitutional organization with ministerial responsibility in each of the respective states, and stated with a certain obscurity that *Preussen geht fortan in Deutschland* [Prussia is to be merged into Germany]. Was the king accepting the program being urged on him by Max von Gagern on behalf of the liberals in the south? He did not intend to be a usurper, he wrote, but he saw that at this crucial moment it was necessary for someone to take the helm, piloting a united Germany through dangerous waters. He was prepared to be that man.[40]

With what looks like supreme effontery, Friedrich Wilhelm then proceeded to ride in a stately progress through the streets, wearing a black-red-gold brassard, accompanied by his generals who also wore the revolutionary tricolor, along with his similarly-decorated ministers. Civil guards, a city officer with the German flag and students with the Prussian banner led the way as honor guard. The king saluted the civil guard at the *Brandenburger Tor* and rode on to the university, where he addressed the assembled students in ringing tones. He repeated that he had no intention to be a usurper and that his sole desire was for Germany's unity and freedom.

> I have only done what has so often been done in the past in German history, when powerful princes and dukes have grasped the banner in situations of disorder and placed themselves at the head of the whole people.[41]

The listeners cheered and threw their hats in the air, but in their minds there must have lurked some doubt about this swift *volte-face.* An obscure courtier, Wilhelm von Kügelgen wrote at this time that the various concessions contained something degrading. "To give a promise that I cannot honor makes me despicable." "Oh, what sort of spring this could be if the king took the new path with complete conviction and a really courageous heart!"[42]

Stephan Born, who had arrived in Berlin shortly after 18 March, sensed the uneasiness of the people. "In Paris I had seen a happily excited population that even well into March still had a feeling of the victory that had been so loudly hailed on the evening of 24 February. In Berlin just a few days after 18 March there was hardly any trace of the revolutionary intoxication that had swept all Germany. The intoxication had worn off rapidly. The people looked sober, as if they feared the future."

Born was an honest realist. He observed that people had seen the king on his balcony while the mob threatened, and they knew that he had removed his hat in honor of the fallen because he had been forced to do so. They had seen him ride through the city with his hated chief of secret police Stieber bearing their honored black-red-gold banner. They had heard rumors that during the barricade turmoil the king had been reduced to tears and had been completely unmanned. The people, thought Born, were swinging back and forth between anger and sympathy. They saw him even in those first days surrounded by the old feudal and ecclesiastical councillors there in Potsdam. While it was true that the call for a republic that people in southern Germany were demanding had had no resonance in the north, the Prussians felt discouraged because this successor of Friedrich *der Grosse* "had so little marrow in his bones".[43]

Like people everywhere, the Berliners appreciated bread and circuses, and for this reason they thronged to watch the ceremonial state funeral procession that honored the fallen barricade fighters (22 March). There had been some discussion, in the fervor of unity—possibly the dead officers and soldiers ought to be buried with their victims—but the idea was discarded. Honor was reserved for the heroes of the insurrection.

Local newspapers, including the official *Allgemeine preussische Staatszeitung*, were printed with black borders. Black flags flew from the palace and all public buildings, and heavy mourning wreathes decorated the doors of many private residences. Representatives of the Protestant, Catholic, and Jewish faiths spoke,[44] and then headed the solemn cortege. The civil guard lined up on either side, presenting arms and saluting as Gustav Hesse stalked past, still wearing his crown. The various trades were represented by delegations bearing their colorful distinctive banners. Following custom in the Prussian Mark, these workers provided a medieval touch, each carrying a black gold-tipped rod to which a lemon had been attached. There were young women dressed in black, each with a cushion on which there rested a martyr's crown. There were representatives of all branches of the government, wearing their golden chains of office. The rector of the university and the venerable Alexander von Humboldt led an impressive train of faculty members in their robes, followed by armed students. A huge delegation from the Borsig plant was led by August Borsig himself. There were Poles with their national flag, and some Italians (most of them singers from the opera), gymnasts, members of all kinds of societies, and representatives from many cities. All this mass of humanity streamed in silence past the royal balcony, where Friedrich Wilhelm in full uniform stood with his ministers—all with their heads bared. Twenty thousand marchers accompanied the one hundred and ninety coffins, each of which was borne on the shoulders of six bearers. As the procession moved slowly past, people on the sidelines handed over offerings of wreathes and flowers. It was a devastating sight, "this confirmation of a fact, the kind that is often so easily exaggerated," recounted Karl Gutzkow, who had watched it all from an upstairs window on Königstrasse.[45] When the head of the procession reached the Friedrichshain cemetery, where a mass grave had been dug, people were still being marshalled at the starting point. Altogether, the streets were filled with marchers for more than three hours. Circourt was impressed. This people that had so recently undergone terrifying stress was so quiet—not a single cry for vengeance or any expression of bitter recrimination. "One would have believed, witnessing this, that the Berliners were ripe for the exercise of the most extensive political liberty."[46]

What about the military? There was something furtive about their funeral ceremony. At five o'clock in the morning on 24 March a modest cortege set out from the garrison hospital near the *Brandenburger Tor.* There were eighteen bodies in individual coffins, carried on horse-drawn vehicles. Because there was apprehension, various precautions had been taken. (Guards posted along the streets and at the cemetery.) The procession with its appropriate escort moved along streets where the windows were full of watchers, most of whom appeared to be sympathetic. There was even a crowd at the churchyard, but these people were not hostile demonstrators. They remained quiet but *teilnahmslos* [not participating].[47]

Friedrich Wilhelm had attempted to hold out his hand to the German people, but the offer was coolly received. "The hand was bloody, and it trembled."[48] He had not understood that he was too much a Prussian, too much a Hohenzollern, to become ruler of a united Germany simply by virtue of a manifesto. When Ambassador von Bockelberg suggested that as a first step the royal residence might be shifted from the north to Cologne, the king scratched a short notation in the margin of von Bockelberg's memo. "Is Bockelberg deranged?"

Soon he turned away from Germany, back to Prussia. There he addressed his officers in Potsdam (25 March), only to have them snarl and rattle their swords, smarting with indignation. He had blandly told them that upon the withdrawal of the troops from Berlin, he had never been more secure.[49] If he had hoped to initiate some kind of counterrevolution, the king must have understood that such an attempt was premature, even though he had at least made contact with those dissatisfied warriors, who were calling him the king who fell, though not in battle.

Meanwhile, his new liberal ministry, led by Ludolf Camphausen and David Hansemann, (appointed by the king on 29 March) was more or less left to its own devices in Berlin, while the monarch in Potsdam was comfortable in the company of his old friends, especially the ultraconservative Gerlach brothers. A counterrevolution might not be too far off. As early as 26 March, Ernst Ludwig von Gerlach had written a passionate call to his fellow conservatives.

> Not only our well-being, our possessions, but all bases of German rights, German freedom—everything on earth that is precious and holy to us—is

threatened. . . . The loyal troops of his Majesty the king, as true sons of the Fatherland, fought victoriously against the unrest that had broken out in Berlin until a superior command put a halt to their efforts. What followed has been experienced as shame and pain by many thousands of loyal Prussian and German hearts. It is of the utmost urgency to come to the aid of the Throne and the Fatherland . . . defending them against revolutionary tyranny.[50]

On that same day, the communist Andreas Gottschalk in Cologne wrote to his friend Moses Hess in Brussels, warning him not to become involved in a proposed invasion of Germany under the leadership of the radical poet Georg Herwegh. "You have no idea of the fear that our *bourgeois* have of the very name of the republic. To them, it is identical with theft, murder, Russian attack, and your legion would be seen as a troop of murderous arsonists."[51]

Still on that same 26 March, there was an enormous rally at Göppingen (Württemberg) where a speaker described recent events in Berlin, asking if Friedrich Wilhelm could ever be accepted as ruler of Germany. Thousands of voices roared NEIN![52] There was in fact deep anger and disillusionment among the German people. Friedrich Wilhelm's portrait was publicly burned on the streets of Munich. Whatever confidence Germans in general had placed in Friedrich Wilhelm had been destroyed on the fatal night of 18 March.

Germany was destined not to experience much more armed violence. The revolution had moved into a political phase in which there was unfortunately plenty of room for conflict and misunderstanding. There were liberals who believed, even after 18 March, that Friedrich Wilhelm was genuinely a friend of German unity. It was so, in a way. He wanted German unity but what he understood by the term would have astonished the liberals. He thought it was obvious that Austria should lead, and that the princes ought to decide the basic questions, not representatives of the people. It never occurred to him that the revolution could be utilized as a firm basis for Prussian power.

With the king in Potsdam and his liberal ministers in Berlin, there was little actual communication, much to the advantage of the Gerlach party of conservatives. Before long there would be two additional centers of activity—the newly elected Prussian national constituent assembly (successor to the second united *Landtag* that had met in early April), in which there was a fairly large number of radicals whose prime interest was in social reform and freedom), and the *Parlament* at Frankfort where most delegates represented a middle-of-the-road electorate that was interested in national unity.

At this critical juncture, all Germany was in desperate need of a calm, intelligent, steadfast ruler, but the man of the hour was Friedrich Wilhelm. He had never been a steady man, but in the spring of 1848 he was more and more under the influence of the Prussian nobility and the military. He had been brooding over the events of recent months, and with mental processes not unlike those of Alice's White Queen who could believe as many as six impossible things before breakfast, he had arrived at certain convictions that he hastened to communicate to his friend, Christian von Bunsen, his ambassador in London. Bunsen must have read this letter warily because even the introductory sentence was ominous: "I have something on my heart against you, my valued, loyal Bunsen, and it has to be discussed because I am your true friend." His Majesty was troubled because Bunsen had written that it was his considered opinion that there had been no conspiracy involved in the March unrest. Friedrich Wilhelm set out to correct the ambassador's error.

> Stones for the stoning of my loyal soldiers were collected in all the houses of Berlin, Cologne, etc. People had observed them being brought in from long distances, like the grass sods that were to serve as barricade breastworks, and nobody had been able to explain this unusual requirement for stone and sod. Moreover, in the main thoroughfares all buildings were put into communication [by passageways] so that it would be possible to torment the troops as they moved back and forth by shooting and hurling stones from the top-floor windows. It has been proved that more than ten thousand—probably twice that number that were not traced—of the most disreputable scoundrels had streamed into the city over the course of weeks . . . This included French riff-raff (convicts from the bagne), Poles and South Germans, especially people from Mannheim, but also others,—Milanese counts, merchants etc etc. . . . They came from Paris, Karlsruhe, Mannheim, Bern . . .

> Liberalism is a disease, just like tuberculosis of the spine. [Here follows a remarkable set of "clinical" details.] Liberalism works like that on the soul. Appearances become deceptive and the consequences of clearly present causes are dismissed as superstition. There are people even now who don't believe that Napoleon was in Moscow. . . . The most shameful products of godlessness destroy human feelings of nobility . . . Black becomes white, darkness is called light . . . . I have, as in the case of physical disease, mentioned the mental symptoms of the final stages. God forbid that you, my friend, should be seriously ill. But you seem to me to be sick, because disbelief in conspiracy is the first unmistakable symptom of the liberalism that dessicates the soul.[53]

The author of this wild document was the man on whom the moderates pinned their hopes. This was the man to whom the delegates of the Frankfurt *Parlament* would offer the crown of united Germany.

Notes

1 Droz, *Les révolutions allemandes de 1848*, p. 195.

2 Valentin, *Geschichte der deutschen Revolution*, 1:427.

3 Karl Gutzkow, *Rückblicke auf mein Leben*, pp. 332–333.

4 Stadelmann, *Social and Political History*, p. 56.

5 Droz, p. 195.

6 Schoeps, editor, *Neue Quellen zur Geschichte Preussens im 19. Jahrhundert*, p. 413.

7 Droz , p. 196, citing a report by city councilman Nobiling.

8 Valentin, 1:425.

9 Karl Frenzel, *Die berliner Märztage und andere Erinnerungen.*, passim.

10 Droz, p. 197.

11 *Vormärz und Revolution 1840–1849*, Hans Fenske, editor, pp. 266–270.

12 Adolphe de Circourt, *Souvenirs d'une mission à Berlin en 1848*, 1:198. The emissary from France's provisional government recalled somewhat contemptuously that all the "sacramental" expressions used by the German revolutionists were taken from the French: *Militär* for *Kriegsvolk, Revolution* for *Umwälzung* and so on.

13 Droz, p. 199; Valentin, 1:425–426.

14 Gutzkow, p. 336.

15 Circourt. 1:159.

16 Valentin, 1:430.

17 Gutzkow, p. 337.

18 Ibid., p. 338.

19 Circourt, 1:162.

20 Stadelmann, p. 76.

21 Circourt, 1:168.

22 Gunther Richter, "Friedrich Wilhelm IV. und die Revolution von 1848," in *Friedrich Wilhelm IV. in seiner Seit*, pp. 117–120.

23 Circourt, 1:163.

24   Ibid., 1:165.

25   Valentin, 1:435.

26   Ibid., 1:434.

27   Circourt, 1:167.

28   Klein, *1848; der Vorkampf deutscher Einheit und Freiheit*, pp. 149–150.

29   Valentin, 1:438.

30   Richter, p. 116, footnote 30, citing Varnhagen.

31   Karl Ludwig von Prittwitz, *Berlin 1848*, p. 230.

32   *1818: Augenzeugen der Revolution*, p. 187.

33   Valentin, 1:440.

34   Ibid., 1:443–444; Ludwig Pietsch, "Gefangeneaussage," in *1848; Augenzeugen der Revolution*, pp. 142–145.

35   Valentin, 1:436.

36   Gutzkow, p. 339.

37   Ludwig Bergsträsser, "Die parteipolitische Lage beim Zusammentritt des Vorparlaments", *Zeitschrift für Politik* 6 (1913): 619.

38   Gutzkow, p. 343.

39   Circourt, 1:175.

40   Ibid., 1:224. His Majesty appeared to be assuming the scepter of Otto the great (Saxon emperor, crowned in 936), and asserting the claims of Charles Quint, (King of Castille 1516, emperor of Germany 1519 until his death in 1558).

41   Valentin 1:450–451.

42   Stadelmann, p. 75.

43   Born, *Erinnerungen eines Achtundvierzigers*, pp. 116–118.

44   There were 16,000 Catholics, more than 10,000 Jews, and about 380,000 Protestants of various denominations in Berlin.

45   Valentin, 1:455; Gutzkow, pp. 343–344; Klein, pp 214–216, citing A. Wolff, *Berliner Revolutionschronik*.

46   Circourt, 1:225.

47   Klein, p. 217 — Letter from Adjutant General von Natzmer to his wife.

48   Valentin, 1:458.

49   Richter, pp. 127–128.

50   Ernst Ludwig von Gerlach, "Anruf an seine Standesgenossen," in *Vormärz und Revolution 1840–1849*, pp. 274–275.

51   *Vormärz und Revolution*, pp. 275–276.

52   Bergsträsser, p. 620.

53   Ranke, editor, *Aus dem Briefwechsel Friedrich Wilhelms IV. mit Bunsen*, pp. 184–187.

Chapter 14

Radicals *versus* Moderates; Tests of Strength

Prior to the year 1847, there had been no distinct division between those who pressed for reform and those who wanted a more drastic overhaul of the German states. Those who at a later date took sides as moderate constitutionalists *versus* radicals were in the habit of meeting amicably. Furthermore, the constitutionalists presented a united front in the meetings of the provincial assemblies, although in the future there would be various splinter groups among them. It would be safe to say that thus far there had not been any formal party organization at all.

Stages of political development differed from one state to another. There was a perceptible difference between the attitudes and capabilities of provincial assembly opposition members as found in absolutist states like Prussia under Friedrich Wilhelm IV and in constitutional states such as Baden. Further, it must be held in mind that Baden was not only a constitutional state but also that it bordered on France and Switzerland. Political thought consequently had a revolutionary tinge there that can be traced as far back as the Hambach festival of 1832. The Hambach liberals and their defiant orators had been severely repressed in Bavaria but their ideas had survived in the nearby Baden *Wetterecke* [storm quarter].

Throughout Germany by the fall of 1847, those who wanted to break the governmental stalement that rose like a barrier against all change or progress had arrived at a general agreement that censorship was evil, that the system of criminal justice needed an overhaul, and that there ought to be freedom of assembly, speech and conscience, as well as academic freedom, but there was no consensus on the means of arriving at this desirable state of affairs. The members of the opposition in the various provincial and state assemblies had thought at first that they could make common cause, but even before the events in France, the general parting of the ways in the religious protest movement—as in Baden—had shown them that this was not necessarily the case.

In Prussia meanwhile, the subjects of Friedrich Wilhelm IV were nursing expectations for a representative government and a constitution, but their hopes were repeatedly dashed. On five separate occasions, Friedrich Wilhelm's predecessor had given them what appeared to be legal grounds for hopeful anticipation of reform. As early as 27 October 1810, there had been a financial edict that referred to a future constitution, and this had been specifically repeated in a second financial edict issued on 7 September 1811. Even before that, on 23 February 1811, there had been promising signs of royal intent, with the opening of an assembly of provincial deputies. Beginning in April 1812 and continuing through July 1815, there had been periodic meetings of elected representatives of the estates [upper social classes] for regulation of war debts of the provinces and towns. There was a cabinet regulation issued on 5 June 1814 that again referred to an intended general constitution and representation of the estates. There was a fourth promise in the royal edict of 22 May 1815 after the battle of Waterloo. The fifth and last such promise was to be found in the ordinance of 17 January 1820 in which a summoning of the estates of the kingdom was solemnly mentioned. In spite of the best efforts of ministers like Hardenberg, the promises had never been kept—a fact that can be attributed to the diligence of the Austrian chancellor Metternich. Keeping Prussia permanently opposed to the ideas of freedom and true to the concepts of a feudal nobility and rule of the bureaucrats was his "masterpiece".[1]

Friedrich Wilhelm IV occasionally wrestled feebly with the problem of popular representation, but his ideas were hardly practical, and besides, he placed great confidence not only in the judgment of Metternich, but also in the opinions of his brother-in-law, the Russian tsar and of his own brother and heir presumptive, the prince of Prussia. These three were firmly united in opposition to democratic reform.

Members of the various provincial assemblies called attention to the true character of the promises made by Friedrich Wilhelm's predecessor, but in vain. At the formal opening of the meeting of the assembly of East Prussia in the fall of 1840, for example, there was a vote of 89 to 5 in favor of "general representation" as promised by the law of 22 May 1815. The response of the king was that his father had kept himself withdrawn from "prevailing concepts of so-called general representation" for the sake of the well-being of his loyal people.

In reaction, Dr. Johann Jacoby of Königsberg published his widely read *Vier Fragen, beantwortet von einem Ostpreussen* [four questions answered by an East Prussian] that quickly transformed the question of a Prussian constitution into an all-German, even a European concern.[2]

The *Landtag* [provincial assembly] of the Prussian Rhineland involved itself energetically in the matter of general political objectives, working through petitions that related to specific items, e.g. naming of the speaker in the published minutes of the assembly, extension of the franchise, openness of assembly meetings, abolition of censorship, etc. It was the Rhineland assembly that especially incurred Friedrich Wilhelm's displeasure. He was much upset when a respectfully worded petition reached him that reminded him once again of the promises implicit in the law of 22 May 1815 and that called for a constitution that would allow representation of the wishes of all classes of the population in a correct proportion. It was distasteful to him to see that the names of the leaders were not respected members of the nobility, and that he would have to adjust himself to the idea that businessmen like Ludolf Camphausen, Hermann von Beckerath, and Gustav Mevissen could have the temerity to address him.

Friedrich Wilhelm had no inclination to listen to those among his loyal subjects who might have given him excellent advice. General Gustav von Below, for example, wrote to his son-in-law (in 1846) that "if people could see that we have a constitution under which they live better than elsewhere, they would rapidly become good Prussians, just as the Alsatians politically joined the French, not wanting to belong to Germany even though they did not adopt the French language and customs."[3] If members of the nobility ventured to express opinions like that, Friedrich Wilhelm was quick to call them traitors. He was immensely angered when Ernst von Saucken-Julienfelde told him that the party of the old nobility was the true disturber of the peace, and should not be permitted to build a barrier of rusty weapons from the ancient times of tournaments against the powerful flood of the new life of the people. The people had been waiting for thirty-one years, he said, for the fulfillment of the law that was an absolute necessity not alone for the well-being of the state but also for its continuation. The power of Prussia was no longer what it had been. "Prussia can only survive if people and sovereign are one in mutual trust and love. The former has been shaken, and the latter decreases from day to day."[4]

On 3 February 1847, Friedrich Wilhelm reluctantly issued a summons for a meeting that would bring together the members of the eight provincial assemblies of Prussia. Had the Prussian king actually taken a meaningful step and met the demand that had been building in the minds of his people? Public opinion was divided on this point. The royal *Patent* seemed to be based on the financial edict of 1820, but not on the four other pronouncements of his predecessor that had constantly been invoked with respect to a promised constitution.

Many guesses and possible interpretations of the monarch's words were offered, and people waited in suspense for Friedrich Wilhelm's *Thronrede* [speech from the throne] which would be delivered on 11 April 1847, ceremonially opening the first meeting of the united Prussian assemblies. In view of the king's long history of reluctance and refusal, it must have been with a sense of profound misgiving that the members of this historic united *Landtag* settled down in order to hear Friedrich Wilhelm's opening remarks. After pious reference to his father of glorious memory, the ruler plunged into the body of his message.

> I declare that I shall never allow a written page to intrude between our Lord God in Heaven and this land, to rule us with its paragraphs and thereby to supplant the ancient holy trust. You have not been called here to represent opinions. . . . I give you my kingly word that I would not have summoned you if I had had the slightest suspicion that you had some inclination toward so-called popular representation.[5]

A foolish joke made the rounds. All Germany grieved over the *Thronrede* with the exception of two villages [the German word for village is *Dorf*]. The "villages" in question were Trauttmannsdorff (*Graf* Trauttmansdorff was the Austrian ambassador) and Meyendorff (the Russian ambassador). Friedrich Wilhelm is said to have laughed heartily when he heard this witticism. As a matter of fact, the Austrian ambassador failed to express much approval, and the Russian ambassador declared that the speech was good, but sharp. He said it was fortunate that censorship still existed.

Among the assembly members, the reaction was mixed. The Prussians were angry but the more sophisticated Rhineland people hinted that all was not lost. It was just possible that their work might be easier.

In Vienna, Metternich expressed amazement that the whole speech had been permeated by ideas so distinctly counter to general opinion, and one Austrian liberal was heard to grunt, "When I read that speech, once again I was glad to be an Austrian."[6]

There was a fierce wrangle over the official response to the monarch's speech. Hermann von Beckerath wrote a draft that was much too pointed for the majority of the delegates. He wanted to say that according to the laws of 1820 and 1823, the united assembly should have much more power than the king's *Patent* allowed. There should be periodic meetings, unlimited right to approve all new loans, and collaboration in disposition of state domains, etc. In the end these details were discarded, but the demand for periodic assembly remained. Friedrich Wilhelm answered that he would think over what had been said, and would accommodate himself to proposals that did not touch his absolute authority. He would summon the united *Landtag* again within four years.

The delegates then settled down to work, or rather to acrimonious debate over a long roster of topics (military duels, the public debt, the condition of the treasury, notes put into circulation that the Bank of Prussia was reluctant to accept, the urgent need for a loan of thirty million *Talern* to cover construction of the important *Ostbahn* [eastern railway line], the civil status of Jews, and so on).

Aristocratic members who conservatively favored the authoritarian military state and liberals who wanted a consitutional *Rechtsstaat* were deeply divided. Hermann von Beckerath made this contrast clear during the debate on the duel. "If the duel is declared to be the keystone of the officer class, I ask—can this promote a common ground for the military and the *Bürgerstand* [middle class citizenry]? Can we regard the duel as the keystone for the private citizen? The keystone for the *Bürgerstand* is observance of the law, but the law says Thou shalt not kill."

At first glance, duel as a topic for debate by the united assembly might seem to have been inapposite, but in fact it was highy relevant to the struggle on the part of the liberals who wanted to establish a true parliament. Duelling had not been dragged in just for the sake of chest-thumping argument. The larger issue was that of eligibility for membership in the hoped-for parliament. The conservatives, backed by the king's government, wanted to retain the principle of exclusion of *bescholtenen Personen* [disreptable individuals] that prevailed in the provincial assemblies. The government reserved the right to declare that a man was unworthy—and liberals suspected that political

motivation could be the triggering mechanism.[7] In a new law proposed by the Prussian government, one cause for exclusion would be
expulsion or dismissal by a military honor court. An officer could be
dismissed because he had refused to fight a duel that military honor
required. In other words, the proposed law would impose the military
code on society as a whole. Noble honor and civil rights were being
unacceptably mixed, in the view of the liberals. Gustav Mevissen, agreeing with Beckerath, said hotly that in the military *Stand* the duel was
honorable, whereas in civil society it was a punishable crime. The
argument became extravagant. One conservative member quoted
Guizot, saying that the duel was "the culmination of civilization". No
doubt the majority of liberals agreed with Mevissen, who felt that only
a criminal conviction should annul the right to serve in an assembly.[8]

The question of a loan for the essential *Ostbahn* was brilliantly
handled by the opposition. They pointed out that funds like that had
to be approved by a united *Landtag* and that they could not claim that
status, given the fact that their continued existence had not been guaranteed. The young Bismarck fumed that this was blackmail. The vote
against the *Ostbahn* loan was 360 to 179. It was smugly suggested to
the angry monarch that he could allow work on the railroad to continue, and submit another request for a loan at the next regular session of the assembly. Friedrich Wilhelm petulantly stopped following
the deliberations of the assembly and also stopped inviting opposition
members to balls and dinners at his palace.

The proponents of the existing absolutist system were not being
stubbornly irrational. Many of them were honestly convinced that their
duty as aristocrats was to "represent" the people by protecting them.
There were few among the lower classes, they thought, who were
sufficiently aware of the complexities of political issues. Some of these
conservatives—notably Georg von Vinke—espoused a theory of historical law and aristocracy even though they knew that ideally self-
government ought to be in the hands of the communities and their
elected officials.

The Rhineland members of the assembly perceived themselves as
Staatsbürger who were fully equal to the task of self-government. The
most insistent speakers at the united *Landtag* were men like David
Hansemann and Gustav Mevissen, who were accustomed to responsibility and authority within their own spheres of mercantile activity
and understood the potential value of a constitutional system. They
had observed how effectively the shipowners and merchants of the

great free Hanseatic cities managed their affairs through their elected consuls, senators and so on, and they were also aware of the developments in southwest Germany.

They became increasingly urgent when, during the assembly sessions, unrest broke out in many cities—Stuttgart and Ulm among them, and especially in Berlin—in the so-called *Kartoffelrevolution* [potato revolution] that had been brought on by high food prices in a period of inflation and poor harvests. Riots were the order of the day, quelled by application of the bayonet. Barricades had been erected, but as revolutions go the disturbances hardly qualified for the name. However, the half-measures and general incompetence of the Prussian ruler and his ministers were clear evidence that authority was in the wrong hands. In spite of pleas for a civil guard in Berlin, for example, the military had been mobilized for guarantees of protection for the haves against the have-nots.

When the sessions finally dragged to a conclusion, everyone was surly and dissatisfied, even though there had been certain advantages for the liberals. They had had the opportunity to meet face to face and to become aware of their various strengths. Besides, they had been able to stand up publicly and express their views, which had actually been laid open by publication of stenographic reports—a novel step that had never been taken during the sessions of any provincial assembly. During the course of the meetings, various groups had begun to gather for informal discussion, as embryonic political parties. David Hansemann had started this by renting a large apartment where he received liberal delegates from different parts of Prussia. The Hôtel de Saxe became a meeting place for liberals, and so did the Russischer Hof.

Meanwhile, events were moving at a swift pace in southwest Germany. In Baden, the incipient split among the ranks of reformers had come to the surface. The radicals who assembled at Offenburg on 12 September 1847 laid out such a drastic program that the moderates who met on 10 October at Heppenheim were filled with dismay. In spite of the fact that a few Offenburg men, including the Baden opposition leader Adam von Itzstein attended the Heppenheim meeting, a line was being drawn in the sand.

At Offenburg near the Schwarzwald, the meeting led by Gustav Struve and Friedrich Hecker, called "The Whole" to indicate scorn for half-way measures,[9] demanded a set of sweeping reforms, both political and social. The Carlsbad decrees along with the Frankfurt decrees of 1831 and 1832 were condemned as instruments of oppression. Most demands were so characteristic of those generally put forward all across Germany in the course of the spring uprisings of 1848 that they are sometimes collectively called the "March program"—namely, a call for freedom of speech, freedom of the press, freedom of assembly, and freedom of conscience. In addition to these more usual goals, there were others that were unmistakably revolutionary. The Frankfurt *Bundestag* should be transformed into a parliament duly elected by all German citizens. A civil militia should replace the standing armed forces. Tax reform was a necessity. All aristocratic titles and privileges as well as all obligations laid on the rural population should be immediately abolished.

In spite of these demands, the Offenburg program was not radical enough to include a call for establishment of a German republic. It is significant that when similar meetings were banned, there was vigorous protest from the constitutional monarchists, especially Karl Mathy.[10] Members of the embryonic party groups were still fighting shoulder to shoulder for many a common cause.

There were indignant rumblings from the sidelines even before the Heppenheim gathering. Moderate Karl Mathy received a letter from Karl Huetlin, the *Bürgermeister* of Konstanz,[11] who raged against the "brainless squabble", denouncing it as an impudent declaration of war on the part of the journalists, and ending in severe denunciation of the banditry of the communists, whose "standing army" was made up of apprentices and booty-hungry followers of Babeuf.

The moderates who gathered at Heppenheim near Darmstadt included many parliamentary opposition leaders, men like Mathy and Friedrich Bassermann (Baden), Gustav Mevissen and David Hansemann (Rhineland), and Heinrich von Gagern (Hesse-Darmstadt). This group, in the opinion of the minister of the interior for Württemberg, was not extremely democratic, but represented wealth and intelligence.[12] These were the men who in the coming months were to step into positions of power, replacing cabinet ministers of the conservative old guard under their respective frightened monarchs.

The program document that they presented (it appeared in the *Deutsche Zeitung*, Heidelberg 15 October) pointed out that as constituted by the provisions of the post-Napoleonic settlement, the *Bundestag* had not met its obligations. Problems of adequate representation, free trade and commerce, freedom of the press, etc., had not been properly addressed. The only body that genuinely represented Germany's common interests, the *Zollverein*, had not been created by the confederation, but rather was the outcome of negotiations and treaties among the several states. In contrast to the fire-breathing radicals at Offenburg, the Heppenheim moderates were cool and cautious. They suggested that the *Zollverein*, which had already demonstrated its usefulness, might be accorded extended authority over matters of commerce, trade, taxation, etc., and that the existing customs conferences might have an expanded, more representative membership. They thought that the budget for the army could be cut, and were emphatic in stressing the urgent need for consideration of problems that originated in inadequate public education and in pauperism. They urged appointment of a special commission for study of conditions among the lower classes, but refrained from inflammatory Marxian terms.[13]

Oddly enough, it was the Heppenheim gathering, not the one at Offenburg, that set off alarm bells in the minds of anxious officials, who considered themselves and their administrations to be threatened.

Graf von Beroldingen, the minister of foreign affairs for Württemberg, was deeply worried, and wrote to the Württemberg delegate at Frankfurt, *Freiherr* von Wächter, saying that the Heppenheim meeting was a deliberation on the part of a faction that was obviously against the monarchical principle. It was clear that the purpose was to bring about elected representation of the German people. It was true that this was not exactly a "society for illegitimate purposes" but it was a meeting of a large number of individuals who had come together as private persons. They had had the audacity to discuss the idea of subjecting the decisions of the *Bundestag* as well as measures taken by individual state governments to the control of delegates of *all* the German states, and they were setting themselves up as an influence on the political life of Germany. This had to be stopped! No German government could be in doubt of that. Maybe the *Bundestag* ought to take steps to forbid a repetition of such meetings. Von Beroldingen intended to instruct the Württemberg ambassador at Vienna to consult Metternich on this matter, because one could anticipate only the worst possible outcome from such irresponsible activities.

The minister of foreign affairs for Baden, *Freiherr* von Dusch, attempted to allay von Beroldingen's fears, explaining to delegate von Wächter that the German *Bund* had indeed made serious blunders. It had done nothing for justice, for trade or navigation, for the postal service, etc. The confederation needed some kind of new element to help it perform its duties, but the state governments should not let the radical "party of movement" win out. There were plenty of people to help—there were meetings and discussions everywhere. Everyone was meeting, with the exception of the princes.

This explanation upset von Beroldingen, who wrote back in agitation, "When he says representation, does von Dusch mean representation by *elected representatives of the people?* This would surely be greeted with joy by the radical party, and it would be the beginning of a change in German law, the end of which could be nothing other than the dissolution of the German monarchies."[14]

When an article appeared in the *Deutsche Zeitung,* reporting on the Heppenheim meeting, there was objection from Württemberg because the paper was giving undue political importance to the event. Meetings like that, held at an inn, should not take action as if the participants were officials. Such gatherings were far from innocuous! The ruler of Württemberg called assemblages of this kind "illegal, even unconstitutional", but his minister, von Maucler, wrote a memo on 3 January 1848 to the effect that the *Bundestag* had presented a deplorable record for more than thirty years. Inadequate measures, petty special interests, regrettable absence of an elevated political viewpoint, and a complete lack of understanding of human conditions. Maucler went on to say that a response to the irregular "usurping congress" of Heppenheim would be a legitimate conference, held in some place such as Munich, where there could be a meeting of authorities from neighboring states in order to constitute and organize a large national opposition.[15]

The Frankfurt *Bundestag* received a suggestion from Württemberg that it take measures against the "recently increased activities of the radical party". To be designated as a party must have been a source of satisfaction to men like Hecker and Struve. The upshot was that Baden and Württemberg named police officials who would exchange information for purposes of political surveillance, but the relationship of Württemberg and Baden was badly strained when Struve wrote an insulting article about the Württemberg government in his *Deutscher Zuschauer* (28 January 1848). Indignant officials in Württemberg demanded that the lax censor in Baden who had passed the offensive article be severely punished.[16]

Struve's paper, *Der deutsche Zuschauer,* was banned in Hesse, but the publisher managed to send out thousands of copies in which he included the program of the Offenburg meeting under the title, "The people's demands". The Prussian ambassador observed gloomily that it was just an illusion that prohibitions could have any effect, in view of the new ease and multiplicity of means of communication.

The same was becoming true of meetings, discussions and protests. These could be strictly forbidden, yet in Mainz, for example, women were defiantly wearing black in protest against a revocation of the liberal law on marriage that had been on the books in Hesse-Darmstadt for more than two decades. A new law empowered town councils to prevent the marriage of anyone who was considered to be

Figure 9 HEINRICH VON GAGERN (1799–1880)

unable to support a family. This was a continuation of the struggle of small towns to retain control over the quality of their communities that had formerly been exercised by the guilds.[17]

That particular debate developed in a bizarre way, with the result that Heinrich von Gagern gained spectacular attention and acclaim. He wrote a pamphlet in which he passionately attacked what he called the erosion of the people's rights with respect to their established laws. The laws should not be tampered with so lightly. Everyone had a right to enter civil society. Gagern went on to say heatedly that Hesse-Darmstadt appeared to be on the threshold of becoming a police state. Ever since 1833, a period of decline of popular representation had been under way, and it was high time for correction. These remarks deeply offended the cabinet and officials of the Hesse-Darmstadt administration.

At this point von Gagern received an improbable challenge to a duel from the detested *Landtag* delegate Georgi, who seems to have thought that he could recover from his ignominious condition as an object of scorn by rising dramatically in defense of the *status quo*. Georgi was generally believed to have driven Weidig to suicide during his dreadful imprisonment following the misguided Frankfurt *Wachensturm* of the thirties.

The absurd challenge placed von Gagern in a delicate position, in the crossfire of blunt statements by aristocrats, who thought that unquestionably he ought to go through with the duel, and anguished pleas of those who wanted to save him as a political figure. If he fought a duel and survived (Georgi's seconds were calling for revolvers at six paces from the barrier), he would be tried because duelling was outlawed—among civilians at least. In the end the storm blew over, and von Gagern suddenly found himself surrounded by cheering crowds, waving banners, garlands, and triumphant marching companies of gymnasts. Valentin comments that all this was an odd defense of civil marriage, but the people had found a hero and a champion.[18] The people collectively were thought to be radicals, and Gagern was decidedly a moderate.

There was not as yet open hostility between moderates and radicals. They were spinning different yarns from the same wool, as it were. The moderates were gradualists, ready to accept the historical situation as a given. They were great believers in working things out in detail, careful step by careful step. However, the groundwork had been laid. Revolutionary events in Paris, with the fall of Metternich almost immediately thereafter, would precipitate a rapid separation of German moderates and radicals, with the subsequent birth of political parties.

After the events in Paris, the radical Offenburg contingent in Baden wanted to plunge ahead, full steam. It would soon become evident that whereas the moderates were unwilling to accept anything more than a cautious opening up of the franchise, the democrats would refuse to temporize and would clamor for immediate universal suffrage. In March 1848, Heinrich von Gagern, leader of the moderates, was to say:

> I too would be a republican if the German people were to decide on the republican form of state. I can be a republican because I quite simply have learned to live, but I don't want any government by the mob, no flirting with the mob.[19]

Friedrich Hecker, a member of the Baden *Landtag*, an out-and-out radical, countered:

> I want freedom, total freedom for all, no matter what the form of the state may be, to achieve this. But no freedom must be soely for the privileged or for the rich. In a word, I am a social democrat.[20]

In the Baden *Landtag* by this time there was a distinct separation between liberals and radicals. Moreover, the moderates worked as a party in collaboration with the delegates of the right. Even men as clearly in the opposition as Karl Mathy and Friedrich Bassermann took this route, causing the radicals to jeer. The break had become apparent to all.

Members of the new "parties" at the Frankfurt *Vorparlament* were destined to be disconcerted to find themselves required to fight on two fronts simultaneously, not only against recognized antagonists who had no sympathy with their goals but also against men who shared many of their objectives but advocated different methods of attack. As lines were drawn with increasing clarity, the opposing groups would inevitably move respectively farther and farther to extreme left or right.

There was already one small coherent group of extremists among the fifty-one *Vaterlandsfreunde* to whom Gagern and Friedrich Hecker spoke at Heidelberg on 5 March 1848. Ostensibly the liberals and democrats were still united, although it was becoming difficult to sustain the fiction. With the astounding developments in France uppermost in their minds, those who wanted change to occur in Germany were suddenly aware that their tight solidarity might no longer offer them the chance to effect the reforms that were dearest to their hearts. They would have to decide not only just what changes might be brought about, but also select the way that would best lead to their objectives. Although they hastened to declare that it was imperative to recognize the new French government in order not to become entangled in a war by following the Metternich formula of intervention whenever revolution occurred or threatened, and were in full agreement also that Germany must not ally herself with Russia, they were casting anxious glances at each other.[21]

The members of this Heidelberg meeting came from many parts of Germany. Loosely organized gatherings like this were typical of the period, harking back to the conferences and clubs of the early *Vormärz*. Baden was heavily represented, and it was in Baden that reformers held the most radical views. David Hansemann had come to the meeting with the direct intention of impressing on all those in attendance the understanding that moderation and prudence were highly important. He and his colleague Gustav Mevissen were determined to hold the line against the growing pressure of a faction that might not steadily adhere to the principle of monarchy.[22] Another who firmly supported the monarchical principle was Heinrich von Gagern. Parenthetically, there was once a controversy among scholars because Gagern was thought to have spoken favorably of the republic at times. The explanation is to be found in the fact that the word "republic" had a special meaning for him, as it did for all those who had enjoyed a classical education.[23] No doubt, he assumed that his hearers would automatically think of *Res publica sive societas civilis sive societas rationalis*. This minor latterday misunderstanding points up a major problem. As Herzen observed, the liberals never knew the people. They had to translate the moan of humanity into Latin and arrive at their ideas through the Gracchi and the Roman proletariat.[24]

The political center of gravity in Prussian lands was shifting to the Rhine region, where there was double danger. The radical forces were strong and vociferous in places like Cologne, and the financial underpinnings had become so fragile that they were on the verge of collapse. When the great Schaffhausen bank in Cologne failed late in March, the worst fears of the *Bürgerstand* seemed to be realized because so many workers were thrown out onto the streets (the banks could no longer advance credit to employers) and in places such as Solingen there was violent destruction of foundries and manufacturing plants. Uprisings of this kind, paralleled by peasant insurrections, led to an extremely grave situation. The industrialist König had written to his brother-in-law Mevissen on 29 February that "the most liberal among us have now become conservatives."[25] In this paradoxical confusion, it was the Rhenish industrialists who became the mainstay of the constitutional monarchies, even sustaining the throne of Friedrich Wilhelm IV.

The Heidelberg participants took upon themselves the responsibility of deciding that an all-German parliament ought to be created, and also of deciding how such a parliament should be organized. The initial action was formation of a *Siebenausschuss* [committee of seven] that was charged with issuance of invitations to a preliminary gathering (a *Vorparlament*) where preparations for a constituent assembly could be hammered out. Invitations were sent to all past and present delegates of the various provincial assemblies, plus a wide selection of individuals who had never been members of those bodies—people like Robert Blum, for example. In an effort to reach as many participants as possible, those who received invitations were given blanks that they could send to persons whom they considered to be potentially helpful.

This preparatory *Vorparlament* was packed, the annoyed moderates suspected, by what they regarded as the unscrupulous work of radicals in the committee of seven. Suspicion lay heavily on Adam von Itzstein, who for years had been an indefatigable organizer of the adherents of the left. It is certainly true that the doctrinaire leftists had more experience in organizing themselves than the others did. A letter from Robert Blum to Karl Theodor Welcker of 16 February 1843 uses a code name, "our old uncle in Mannheim" in reference to Adam von Itzstein and one of the meetings he customarily sponsored among a group known as the *Hallgartenkreis*.[26]

This circle of reformers with democratic leanings had shown much resourcefulness in establishing what today would be called a network. They had been successful in evading official surveillance by meeting casually at the vineyards in Baden owned by the popular von Itzstein, a wealthy judge who exerted strong and persistent efforts to coordinate all important activities of the opposition, beginning as early as 1832. Von Itzstein's vigorous work had not been limited to Baden. For example, when Dr. Johann Jacoby of Königsberg published his *Vier Fragen,* Robert Blum quickly established contact with him, and suggested that Jacoby be invited to one of the Hallgarten meetings.[27] Inevitably, in the spring of 1848 when the committee of seven issued its invitations to the *Vorparlament*, von Itzstein, Blum and Jacoby had ready to hand a list of activists who were thinking along lines congenial to them.

The suspicion that the *Vorparlament* was deliberately packed seems to have been unfounded, in view of the wide spectrum covered by the opinions of the invited participants. In the event, it turned out that packing would have been unnecessary if the principal objective was to outweigh conservative opinions held by members of the *Bundestag*. During the ten days that intervened between the establishment of the *Siebenausschuss* and the first meeting of the *Vorparlament*, there had been a gigantic upheaval—the fall of Metternich—with the result that many agitated sovereigns had seen fit to supplant their conservative ministers, appointing new men like Heinrich von Gagern, who in turn sent new representatives to the Frankfurt *Bundestag*. These new representatives, in the spirit of the times, authorized formation of a committee of seventeen *Männer der öffentlichen Vertrauens* [men who enjoyed the public's confidence], who would be given the responsibility of drafting a new constituton for the *Bund*. This committee, appointed by the new "March ministers", included famous liberal warriors like Dahlmann and Gervinus, who had won popular esteem as members of the Göttingen Seven. The confederation had thus become pliant, submissive, even cooperative. Constitutionally, it was the *Bundestag* that would arrange elections for a general constituent assembly. In hindsight, the moderates might have acknowledged that there had been little need for a *Vorparlament*.

The revolutionary events in Europe had jolted German reformers into an extraordinary feeling of new life, as if they had miraculously floundered into the Fountain of Youth. France was leading the way. Before long all Europe would be a paradise of liberty, equality and fraternity. An illusion and a potential betrayal, of course, as all dreams of the Fountain of Youth are bound to be.

Frankfurt, the great free city where emperors had been crowned, was a fitting place for new beginnings, an ideal location for loud, heartfelt singing of Hoffmann von Fallersleben's revolutionary "Lied der Deutschen". *Einigkeit und Recht und Freiheit für das deutsche Vaterland* [unity, justice and freedom for the German fatherland].[28] On the eve of the opening of the *Vorparlament*, crowds surged along the festively decorated streets. Ludwig Bamberger described the scene in a dispatch to the *Mainzer Zeitung*. The sensation of hope and triumph was so pervasive that it seemed that victory would be an anticlimax, he wrote. Flags and banners everywhere, and throngs of elegantly dressed people. Dishearteningly few ordinary folk, though.

Republicans with long beards and hair combed back. Courtier types with bristling upturned waxed moustaches, their hair elaborately teased and combed forward. There seemed to be a fair number of republicans, Bamberger thought. "At least, they talk loudly and the others are silent." Hearts of the townspeople were full of fear. "Are you a republican too?" they asked the newcomer, looking anxious.[29] There were in fact a few unpleasant incidents—the rough encounter of monarchists from Darmstadt and *Türner* [gymnasts] from Hanau, but there were few who genuinely feared that men like Hecker would turn the *Vorparlament* into a *Sturmparlament*.[30]

Johann Jacoby was caught up by the contagion of hope. He wrote to his friend Ludwig Moser early in April:

> You in the north can hardly imagine the excitement that prevailed here in recent days. Thousands of people pushed through the streets with noise and song. . . . The houses are at their most festive, decorated with carpets and wreathes of flowers. Here there is celebration and rejoicing, there arguments and reckless party strife. In all the public spaces there are orators who demand attack on Russia, deposition of princes, and proclamation of the German republic.[31]

The ardent believers in drastic measures were optimistic in their conviction that they would carry the day at the *Vorparlament*, but in actuality their numbers were insignificant in that assemblage of more than five hundred, and besides, they were unable to hold together as a unit.

As matters stood, the moderates in the *Vorparlament* quickly adopted tactics of obstruction that effectively blocked all proposals coming from the radical left. They had suspected that their gathering had been packed, but in fact there were only eighteen genuine radicals, and they themselves were not uniformly in Gustav Struve's camp. Robert Blum associated himself with a group that was calling for a unitary republican German state that could encompass both constitutional monarchies and republics. Moreover, in contrast to the radical republicans, he thought at that time that the coming revolution could move along the orderly line of parliamentary majority rule. In Blum's opinion, the old ruling class would be so weakened before long that it would then be possible for a revolutionary parliament to create a republic if the people exerted sufficient pressure.[32]

The radicals of the Baden opposition had been receiving encouragement from the "German Legion" that had been organized in both France and Switzerland. They made no secret of this support, intending to use the threat of armed invasion in order to gain their point. Definite lines separating moderates from radicals had not yet been distinctly drawn, and sometimes they did not know precisely who their allies or opponents were. Johann Philipp Becker, president of the Swiss committtee of the German Legion, wrote urgently to Karl Mathy, offering "a well armed force with many cannons" because in his view, if a republic proclaimed by a German parliament were to run into difficulties, the danger and storm that would follow such rejection would be tremendous all over Germany. "We Germans in Switzerland are preparing ourselves."[33] Bloody revolution, thought Becker, might be the only way to attain a German republic. Moderate, irenic Karl Mathy was hardly the man to respond cordially to such a message.

Even at that early stage there were divisions among the radicals. Blum refused to support the program that Gustav Struve was proposing, and he was not alone in taking that stand. Struve's platform called for an immediate declaration that it was the will of the people that a German republic be created. The *Vorparlament* as a whole refused even to discuss Struve's proposal.

Struve was a theorist who rarely troubled himself over distinctions between his goals and what was practically attainable. Besides, he had difficulty in grasping the notion that his arguments would not sweep the moderates into whole-hearted cooperation. Only a dreamer could ever have believed that a majority of those in that large assembly would join him in a united call for elimination of the standing armies, for abolition of all privilege, for dissolution of all cloisters and monasteries, for absolute separation of church and state, for abolition of hereditary monarchies, for universal suffrage, for balancing out the economic differences between capital and labor, for a united Germany, etc., etc., etc. Struve did not even seem to realize or care that his all-encompassing, emotional demands might offend the sensibilities of cautious, deliberate northern liberals whose ideas had been hammered out in lengthy philosophical disquisition.

On the second day of the *Vorparlament* sessions, Friedrich Hecker rose to deliver a powerful speech in favor of an undivided German republic, again challenging the moderates. In his strong baritone voice, he carried his hearers along so forcefully that the presiding officer obviously did not dare interrupt to tell him that his allotted ten minutes had expired. The Bremen senator, Arnold Duckwitz, described the scene.

> Hecker, an engaging person . . . made a terrific impression, and when he finished there was a roar that seemed endless. Up to that point, people had been climbing over each other to reach the speakers' platform, but after Hecker it stood empty. Then a knightly figure moved onto the stage with measured step, laid his hands on the railing and allowed his steady gaze to sweep over the noisy assembly until it became mouse-quiet. It was Heinrich von Gagern. With raised voice, he proclaimed himself to be for constitutional monarchy and developed his thought brilliantly. The impression he made, following the other [Hecker's] speech was overwhelming. The mob in the gallery that had just screamed for the republic now—carried away by von Gagern's words— screamed bravo for the monarchy.[34]

The fickle response from the galleries (there were about two thousand spectators up there)[35] reinforced the moderates' conviction that universal suffrage would not bring a satisfactory solution to Germany's problems. People like Gagern should not ever be thought of as revolutionists, as men who intended to overthrow existing governments. Extremism was never in their blood. They valued continuity. What they dreamed of was thorough reform—not so much limitation of the power of the sovereigns as an expansion of the capabilities of an increasingly able, creative working class.[36] They failed to see any contradiction between the notion of an egalitarian society and the concept of restricted voting rights because they believed in progress and the glorious results of education of the masses.[37] In due time, all adult Germans would be well-informed, intelligent, qualified voters.

When Hecker brought up the question of permanent status for the *Vorparlament*, Gagern moved quickly because he wanted at all cost to prevent the conversion of the *Vorparlament* into a provisional revolutionary government. Here was a head-on collision. The radicals knew that it was essential for their cause to win and maintain control of the *Vorparlament* which, after all, was revolutionary in its origins. If moderates could be made to see that there was no hope of progress through cooperation with existing governments, especially with the *Bundestag*, they could be brought around to acceptance of drastic measures.

Von Gagern managed to derail the radicals' plan by proposing that they elect a *Fünfzigerausschuss* [committee of fifty] that would replace the *Vorparlament* and serve as a liaison with the general constituent parliament that was to be elected. The motion in favor of the committee of fifty was carried by a vote of 368 to 148. Hecker stamped out angrily, but only a handful of left-wingers followed him. In his subsequent book that included his version of events in the *Vorparlament,* he wrote contemptuously that instead of the permanence of the *Vorparlament,* there would be the boredom and narcotic effect of a permanent committee of fifty, which would amount to "permanent impermanence".[38]

Hecker had definitely split the ranks of the left. In retrospect, Blum was to observe that Struve and Hecker had been lurching around like slaughtered oxen, and that they had made victory "frightfully difficult for us."[39] Karl Theodor Welcker was heard at one point to mutter that the radicals of the left seemed to think that they had a greater claim on the grace of God than any living ruler. The irrepressible Mikhail Bakunin, that perennial nihilist, left Frankfurt in a sour mood, commenting that one could not find "even a germ of unity in this new tower of Babel."[40]

It is true that Hecker returned briefly, but there was now a sharp division between him and Blum, von Itzstein, and Raveaux. "Nothing can be done in Frankfurt," Hecker announced. "We have to strike in Baden."[41]

Gagern showed considerable acumen when he proposed that his brother Max von Gagern be dispatched on a tour of inquiry, in order to sound out the governments of the German states on their reaction to the idea of a constitutional Germany united under Prussia. He no doubt would have been able to move with equal address in developing a true, well organized party of moderates, but like a number of his colleagues in the *Vorparlament* he was desperately pressed for time. As a new minister in Hesse-Darmstadt, he knew that he had to return quickly in order to solidify his position in a wary, resentful court. Five days was the absolute maximum that he could afford to spend with the *Vorparlament.*

Altogether, may who were attending that meeting must have been under stress. Just weeks before, they had been outsiders, objects of scorn and resigned to the fact that the controlling petty aristocracy in the conservative courts dismissed them contemptuously as silly dreamers who had been led astray by alien ways of thinking. They had been shrugged off as nothing more than "birds of plumage that roost in the upper branches of the tree of knowledge," as Thorstein Veblen wittily expressed it.[42] Now they were undergoing a sobering experience. The reins of power had abruptly been thrust into their hands. They were learning that whereas it is one thing to be an outsider, demanding reform, it is another thing entirely to be charged with the responsibility for effecting the salutory change. They were also becoming uncomfortably aware that the united opposition had started to crack. Karl Mathy was certainly aware of this situation because in Baden he had observed at close range the drastic actions of Hecker and Struve and the influential publisher, Josef Fickler. He must have understood that the path ahead was a thorny one.

The *Vorparlament* was not an official body, and its membership reflected the rather helter-skelter way in which the *Siebenausschuss* had handled the summoning of members. Austria was entitled to almost a third of the seats in the *Bundestag*, for example, yet there were only two men representing Austria in the *Vorparlament*, and there seems to be no record anywhere of who sent them. Prussia's large delegation (one hundred and forty-one individuals) was closer to the percentage that might have been expected, but its members were not the people who would have appeared if it had not been for the circumstance that the long-postponed united Prussian assembly was simultaneously in session, and many deputies were absent for that reason. They had been invited to send alternates in their stead. Hesse-Darmstadt's delegation of eight-four men was out of proportion, almost matching the ninety-four from Bavaria.[43]

The moderates were in the majority, but in spite of this, the left managed to force through their demand for universal suffrage. According to the final decision, every subject of every state of the confederation, if he qualified in terms of age and economic independence, could vote for the coming Frankfurt *Parlament*. If the moderates had not been so pressed for time, and probably also so weary, and so anxious not to allow the *Vorparlament* to become a permanent body, like a provisional government *à la française,* they might have stiffened their resolve and toned down the suffrage decision. They may have thought that there could be a little leeway here because it was left up to the state governments to interpret the provision in their own way.

It was certainly poor judgment that allowed an unofficial group like the *Vorparlament* even to attempt to handle the nightmarishly complex problem of the two duchies of Schleswig and Holstein in the course of a crowded five-day meeting, but they may have been relieved to find here an issue on which there was comforting unanimity of moderates and radicals. Therefore they pressed forward recklessly and voted to demand admission of Schleswig into the German confederation of states.

Is there anyone among the readers of this book who can recall high school history classes without wincing at the mere thought of Schleswig-Holstein? In its complexity, it snarled almost all aspects of the difficult European age of transition from dynastic to democratic rule into an inextricable tangle.

In brief, the king of Denmark was a member of the German *Bund* by virtue of his rank as *Herzog* of Holstein, a territory that was originally a fief of the Holy Roman Empire. Schleswig had been a fief of Denmark in times past. In 1460, Christian I declared that the two duchies would never be separated, but this promise had not been kept. They were divided among the three sons of Frederick I in 1544, and reunited about two centuries later under a Danish king.

The kings of Denmark were Oldenburgs, most of them German speakers. The two duchies were subject to the salic law of succession (only males in the male line could inherit the throne), and the Danish male line was about to be extinguished. In a complicated argument, it was claimed that Schleswig-Holstein ought to go to Germany, to be ruled by the agnate male collateral line, the Augustenburg dukes.

On the eve of the revolutionary disorders of 1848, the Danish king Christian VIII died and was succeeded by Friedrich VII, who had no male heirs. He immediately summoned a fifty-two-member commission—half Danes, half delegates from the two duchies—that was charged with completion of the constitution drafted by Christian VIII. This document had provided for the union of Denmark and Schleswig-Holstein.

A strong ultranationalist political party known as the Eider Danes was rapidly gaining strength at this time. (The Eider is a river that marks the southern boundary of the duchy of Schleswig. The Eider Danes regarded the river as the southern frontier of Denmark as a whole.) They wanted a declaration that Schleswig was integral with Denmark, while Holstein was to have its own constitution.

Both duchies promptly erupted, angered by this plan of separation. Their resistance was strengthened when news of the February revolution in Paris and the following German disturbances of early March was received. In Rendsburg consequently, on 18 March an assembly of leaders from both duchies decided to send a petition to the Copenhagen government, demanding common representation for Schleswig and Holstein, as well as entry of Schleswig into the German

Bund in view of the fact that the major part of the population of southern Schleswig was German. The petition included the usual March demands for freedom of the press, freedom of assembly, arming of the people, etc. Meanwhile, before the petition reached Copenhagen, the Eider Danes came into control and their leader Orla Lehmann entered the Danish government administration.

Influenced by the new political power in the Danish kingdom, the royal response to the Schleswig-Holstein petition was cold. "We have neither the right nor the power nor the desire to incorporate Schleswig into the German confederation. On the contrary, we want to affirm the inseparable connection of Schleswig and Denmark by means of a common free constitution."

This response implied forced annexation of Schleswig. The Schleswig duchy regarded it as an act of legal resistance when it asserted that the citizens would defend themselves against incorporation into the Danish kingdom, and Holstein also rejected the royal decision. They issued a declaration from Kiel that justified their action. They said that when the king submitted to the Eider Dane party, he had lost his competence to rule over them. They seem to have thought of their own revolt as a revolution against revolutionists (the Eider Danes). They established a provisional government in the accepted style of 1848, the leaders being Wilhelm Beseler, *Fürst* Friedrich von Augustenbug, and *Graf* Friedrich zu Reventlou-Preetz. In all of the German revolution of 1848, it was in Schleswig-Holstein alone that there was such a direct attack on the ruling dynasty and its representatives.[44]

The presumed heir to the duchies, *Herzog* Christian August von Augustenberg, appealed to Friedrich Wilhelm IV for support. The Prussian monarch had no love of rebels of any kind, but in spite of this he answered that as protector of the existing provisions for legitimate male succession in the duchies, he would aid them by intervention and appropriate measures. He fruitlessly sent an emisssary to Copenhagen in early April with this intent, and after that failure decided to engage in military action. Since the Frankfurt *Bundestag* had asked Friedrich Wilhelm to attempt to mediate the quarrel between Denmark and the duchies, Prussia was presumably acting on behalf of the German confederation.

Prussian troops moved into Holstein but were reluctant at first to cross the Eider. Friedrich Wilhelm was all too aware that sympathy for Denmark prevailed in London, Paris, and St. Petersburg, and that any abrupt action on his part might precipitate a European war. The Prussian monarch knew also that he had no navy, and that Denmark had a fleet powerful enough to make serious trouble for export/import merchants of the German ports on the North Sea and the Baltic.

The provisional government of Schleswig-Holstein appealed not only to Friedrich Wilhelm and the *Bundestag* in Frankfurt but also to the *Vorparlament*. In the latter case, their emissary asked that Schleswig be allowed to send delegates to the coming Frankfurt *Parlament*, a request that was readily granted on 31 March 1848.

In the *Vorparlament* there was solidarity between moderates and radicals on this point, and in their excitement they eagerly voted in support of the provisional government. The fever had swept all Germany, in fact. In hotheaded enthusiasm, the members of the *Vorparlament* brushed aside objections that Britain and Russia were seriously displeased by the notion of a German advance into the tight Baltic-North Sea region. By espousing the Schleswig-Holstein cause, the impetuous *Vorparlament* was proving that there are times when two-party strife has its advantages. Certainly, a split vote might have saved them from future disaster. But who among those weary men had the prescience to look ahead from March 1848 to September of that fateful year?

There was too much thunder in the air in early 1848–not an atmosphere conducive to the formation of lasting party alliances. However, the men of the *Vorparlament* were learning the rudiments of political action. They were finding that it was advantageous to consult and develop strategy in the quiet of small groups. When the time came for deciding on the makeup of the slate of candidates for the committee of fifty that would be the stand-in until the general *Parlament* had been duly elected, the moderates considered Robert Blum's rather strange motion that every member of the *Vorparlament* should vote for fifty candidates of his own selection (potentially damaging to the left), and came to the conclusion that it would be fair to include some radicals on their own slate. For this reason, Robert Blum, von Itzstein, Jacoby, and Raveaux all became members of the *Fünfzigerausschuss,* but not Gustav Struve or Friedrich Hecker.

The subsequent moves of Hecker and Struve were unfortunate for the radicals because they revealed with depressing clarity just how unrealistically radical they were, and had the net effet of depriving them of power in the elected *Parlament*, arousing distrust among the moderate middle class that yearned for peace, and driving them irrevocably into the arms of the propertyless proletariat. Whether they intended to engage in civil war, class war or revolution is not clear. In any case, their base of operations was Baden, where they found more sympathy than they would have found elsewhere.

Notes

1 Valentin, *Geschichte der deutschen Revolution,* 1:27.

2 Robert Prutz, *Zehn Jahre,* 2:lxxxix–xcvi. Jacoby underwent serious persecution because of his boldness and was charged with treason. The text of his impressive self-defence is here included as an appendix.

3 Valentin, 1:42.

4 Ibid.

5 Eduard Bleich, *Der erste vereinigte Landtag in Berlin 1847,* 1:20-27.

6 Valentin, 1:66–67,

7 The governor of Silesia had in fact ruled that *Graf* Reichenbach should be excluded because he was being investigated on charges that he had distributed probibited politcal pamphlets.

8 Berdahl, *The Politics of the Prussian Nobility,* pp. 342–343.

9 Deuchert, *Vom hambacher Fest zur badischen Revolution,* p. 151. Reference to conflict between *"Halben"* and *"Ganzen"* [half-way liberals and whole radicals].

10 Bergsträsser, "Die parteipolitische Lage beim Zusammentritt des Vorparlaments," p. 596.

11 Karl Mathy, *Aus dem Nachlass von Karl Mathy,* pp. 64–65.

12 Valentin: 1:161–162.

13 Grab, *Die Revolution von 1848–49,* pp. 30–32. "Das heppenheimer Programm der südwestdeutscher Liberalen".

14 Valentin, 1:162–163.

15 Ibid., 1:164.

16 Ibid.,1:165.

17 Walker, *German Home Towns,* pp. 360–361.

18 Valentin, 1:177–179.

19 Jessen, *Die deutsche Revolution 1848/49 in Augenzeugenberichten,* p. 111.

20 Ibid.

21 Grab, pp. 40–41. "Erklärung der heidelberger Versammlung".

22 Bergsträsser, p. 603.

23 Ibid., p. 604, footnote 2, citing a dissertation by G. Hebeisen.

24 Wilson, *To the Finland Station*, p. 163.

25 Droz, *Les révolutions allemandes de 1848*, pp. 212–213.

26 Robert Blum, *Briefe und Dokumente*, p. 23; Siegfried Schmidt, "Der Hallgartenkreis 1839–47," in *Wissenschaftliche Zeitschrift der Friedrich-Schiller-Universität Jena* 13 (1964): 221–228.

27 Rolf Weber, *Johann Jacoby*, pp. 91, 131–133.

28 The last stanza of the anthem popularly called *Deutschland über Alles* (written in 1841).

29 Jessen, p. 112.

30 Droz, p. 230.

31 Weber, p. 146.

32 Schmidt, "Robert Blum," in *Männer der Revolution von 1848*, p. 353.

33 Mathy, pp. 151–152; Bergsträsser, p. 616.

34 Jessen, pp. 114–115.

35 Eyck, *The Frankfurt Parliament*, p. 156.

36 Stadelmann, *Social and Politial History*, p. 36.

37 Dieter Langewiesche, "The Nature of German Liberalism," in *Modern Germany Reconsidered, 1870–1945*, p. 102.

38 Friedrich Hecker, *Die Erhebung des Volkes in Baden für die deutsche Republik im Frühjahr 1848*, p. 24.

39 Schmidt, *Robert Blum*, pp. 155–156.

40 Edward Hallet Carr, *Michael Bakunin*, p. 153.

41 Willy Real, *Die Revolution in Baden 1848/49*. p. 61.

42 Thorstein Veblen, *Imperial Germany and the Industrial Revolution*, p. 76, note 1.

43 Eyck, pp. 40–41.

44 Ernst Rudolf Huber, *Der Kampf um Einheit und Freiheit 1830 bis 1850*, pp. 666–667.

Chapter 15

Insurrection in Baden.
The *Heckerzug* of April 1848

A cynic might characterize the episode of the April rising in Baden under Hecker's leadership as farce, but it must be borne in mind that Hecker and his fellow insurrectionists were in deadly earnest and had not so much as a shred of power-hungry egotism in their hearts. In spite of its foolish aspects, their quixotic effort had a serious effect on the thinking of reform-minded Germans. The event is occasionally described as one that undermined the influence of the *Vorparlament* moderates by demonstrating that liberals who said they represented the wishes of the people were sailing under false colors. This, at least, was the interpretation that the radicals chose to publicize. A moderate might have retorted that the rebellion had regrettable consequences for everyone because it frightened off many citizens, driving them into the ranks of the reactionaries.

In Baden, lower middle class people and peasants alike wanted some kind of direct action for alleviation of their financial and social difficulties, but their leaders had been in the opposition for so long that they had little comprehension of delicate political balances. Although they had had much experience in participatory politics, they failed to see that they first ought to be staunch defenders of the fragile liberty that was emerging in many German states, where only a small minority was equipped to handle the novel situation.

As far back as 1842, Metternich had been keeping an observant eye on Baden, aware of what he chose to call a journalistic conspiracy and the radicalism of German exiles in Switzerland, with specific reference to the poet Georg Herwegh among others.[1] Konstanz even then was a hot spot because of the active propaganda that Josef Fickler (1808–1865) was spreading in the pages of his influential *Seeblätter*.

Fickler was born in the Tyrol whence his family fled in Napoleonic times to Konstanz. Orphaned in early childhood, he had no formal education but his mind was lively. Because his penetrating editorial comments related ostensibly to Switzerland, he was impervious to attacks by the censor, though what he wrote had definite implications for his German readership.[2]

Fickler was always in financial difficulty, and in his early youth had made his way as best he could as salesman, warehouse manager and so on. His *Seeblätter*, which first appeared in 1836, was supported by a group of unidentified wealthy men who paid fees (and fines) for him. He was married to a sickly young woman who had an illegitimate daughter (his, perhaps: he adopted her when she was not quite three years old). He entered the radical camp around 1840 when he came under the influence of Johann Georg Wirth (one of the organizers of the Hambach festival) and Georg Herwegh. Those two were at that time publishing their *Deutsche Volkshalle* in Switzerland in order to circumvent German censorship, confident that their radical paper would be smuggled across the border into Konstanz. Always a defender of the poor and the oppressed, Fickler acquired enemies among the local merchants because of his active work on behalf of hawkers at the weekly market in Konstanz, and in 1846 he initiated a successful campaign for justice toward Jewish people. Because Baden had had a constitution as early as 1818, the political effectiveness of his small newspaper was greater by far than it would have been in absolutist Prussia, where radicalism was more or less confined to the intellectual ranks of the Hegelians.

In Baden's *Landtag*, representation was not divided by classes, but rather all the population in the large urban and rural districts was represented in a process of indirect voting. On the whole, elections in Baden reflected a broad range of opinions, much more so than in the rest of the German states. Within the lower house, there were no distinct party divisions, however. One member was quoted to the effect that "We have no right and no left. Today the man who speaks against the government may tomorrow be the government's best friend, depending upon his point of view."[3] Even in those early days, Fickler was doubtful about the liberals in the Baden *Landtag*. He himself had never been able to gain a seat in that supposedly representative body, perhaps because of some obscure personal animosities. In any case, it is a matter of record that Adam von Itzstein was among those who deliberately blocked his candidacy.[4]

The moderates won a majority in the Baden *Landtag* in a stormy election campaign in 1842, but the result of this shift was deeply disappointing to Fickler, who thought that as citizens of a constitutional state, the new majority ought to have been boldly pushing through reforms that he viewed as desperately needed by the lower classes. "Indignation in this matter fills many a breast, and many—even the strongest—are inclined to cast a stone against the constitutional system, because the tree has produced no ripe fruit." [5]

As the years passed, Fickler had arrived at the conclusion that the middle class liberals were politically self-centered and retarded, and that truth resided in the untarnished minds of the lower classes. The middle class was no longer on the cutting edge of progress, he decided. He began to use the word *Volk* [people] in the classic revolutionary sense.

Within the *Landtag* were signs of incipient confrontation. About half a dozen delegates in the lower house of the *Landtag* sided with Fickler, among them Karl Mathy and Friedrich Hecker, but even Fickler himself had not reached a hardened mind-set. During the Constitution festival in 1843, for instance, he stood with von Itzstein, who was saying that there must be the most peaceful behavior possible, in order not to scare off the timid.

By 1848 Fickler had become convinced that insurrection was the only route to justice for the people, and he was impatiently prodding Hecker. Fickler himself was already engaged in a storm of pre-revolutionary activity. As early as 16 March, Karl Mathy wrote to his wife that Fickler was rushing from one mass meeting to another, working for the republic. When Mathy went on a mission to Baden for the purpose of sounding out the situation there, he thought that on the whole the people were not in a belligerent mood. He met with Fickler in the course of this trip and tried to persuade him that declaration of a republic at that stage would cause irreparable damage.[6]

On 1 April at Achern, Fickler met in consultation with emissaries from the motley army of German insurrectionists that Herwegh had led from Paris to the banks of the Rhine, and spoke to a peoples' assembly there. Apparently it was at Achern that he met the Russian nihilist, Mikhail Bakunin, because a few days later they were together in Frankfurt. Bakunin enjoyed nothing so much as an opportunity to roil already troubled waters. He was just the man to inflame Fickler, who reacted to his presence by allowing himself to go into a paroxysm of rebellion. His overwrought editorial blast was published in the issue of 2 April 1848 of his *Seeblätter*.

Gather up all your strength, shake off the heavy yoke of servitude, of tyranny that has pressed for so long on your wounded neck. Burst the fetters and chains that your strangler has forged with hard iron . . . Strike down the thrones of the traitors of the people . . . who have robbed you of all rights to which you are entitled and have torn from you your goods and property for their own use—to maintain and feed their mistresses, spies and lackeys . . . Take the scepters from the bloody hands, abolish and destroy their satanic power.[7]

On the day that this wild summons was published (2 April), there was commotion in Baden when a huge meeting occurred at Offenburg. The demand there was for creation of a ministry of labor. At almost the same time, an independent corps was organizing at Mannheim under the leadership of Franz Sigel. This group was calling for a merging of the regular army of Baden with the civil militia.

Hecker himself enjoyed the confidence of rebellious citizens in Baden, where the rumor had spread that he was a brother of the mysterious Kaspar Hauser, whose growing legend had caught the popular imagination. Glory rubbed off on Hecker, as the supposed true hereditary ruler of the region. In his enthusiasm for revolution he showed more talent for eloquent inspirational speech than for hard-headed organization and leadership.

Here is immediacy, when he enters and shakes his long brown hair away from his face. This is a full-blooded healthy man. You see at once that he is not coming from the writing desk, not from the study of the *contrat social*, but rather from the vigorous people who want a drastic change in the life of the state. His grasp of affairs is poetic, not just socialistic. It comes from the whole human condition, not from the imperatives of theory. . . . He's like a student . . . and it is this quality that explains his rousing effect on the young men of western Germany, who are very different from the young revolutionaries of the north, especially the Berliners. The young men of south and west Germany have no use for theorists and their abstractions.[8]

Volksfreund Hecker could rely in Baden on a fairly cohesive network of political clubs. As chairman of the central committee of the *Vaterlandsvereine* he was adept at impressing his ideas on his audiences. When he asserted in ringing tones that only an armed uprising could solve the question of German unity, he was met with resounding cheers. Even before he left Frankfurt for Baden, the Prussian emissary at Karlsruhe, Siegmund von Arnim, observed that Hecker's power was so great that "with a word—that may have already been spoken—an army of more than twenty thousand desperate and fanatic proletarians could unite under his command, coming from southern Germany and Alsace, where according to most recent information numerous German factory hands have been released."[9]

It was believed that Hecker could draw strong support from abroad. He was in touch with Becker in Switzerland with his twenty thousand member German committee and his "German Legion", but Swiss authorities were firmly blocking the way of this potential army that wanted to move across the frontier into Germany. Hecker received some arms but no troops from that quarter.

Other possible assistance from abroad took the form of the dubious military force assembled in Paris by the poet Georg Herwegh. He and his wife had been in Paris at the time of the February revolution and had been swept into a fever of optimistic excitement. It was Herwegh who penned the exalted address of thanks to the French people. "Greetings and thanks to you, O people of France! In three magnificent days you have broken with the past and raised the banner for all the people of the earth."[10]

Herwegh believed that just a few determined men would suffice to sweep away all the peoples' wrongs and abolish the German monarchies. The fact that in Paris alone there swarmed thousands of eager democratic-minded Germans was so overwhelming that he readily accepted the notion that an armed band crossing the Rhine from France would have a decisive effect on the history of the world. (More than four thousand had crowded into the Valentino Hall in Paris to cheer his rousing address of thanks to the French people.) He sent a letter to Hecker, stating that it would be possible to organize and arm a corps of about five thousand, trained and headed by competent officers.

A *Deutsch-demokratische Gesellschaft* had been organized in mid-March, chiefly under the aegis of Adalbert von Bornstedt, the editor of the *Brüsseler deutsche Zeitung*. Herwegh took over its vaunted Legion, which boasted a membership of some eight hundred German workers and journeymen. The Legion immediately began its military training under members like Otto von Corvin, who had been an officer in the Prussian army and who had some sense of reality. Corvin found that although most of his men had been barricade fighters in Paris, when they were closely questioned about serious intention to fight in Germany, all but sixteen of his company chose to withdraw.[11]

Herwegh was convinced that there was unity in planning the overthrow of German monarchs. He would have done well to observe that confirmed revolutionists like Marx and Engels were looking at him scornfully, rejecting his *Revolutionsspielerei*. A band like Herwegh's, coming in as invaders, would fall into the hands of German troops and all would be lost. (Lamartine, as minister of the French provisional government, is supposed to have agreed with this assessment.)

Much of the blame for Hecker's failure may therefore be laid on the shoulders of the excited Germans in Paris. At the same time, much of Herwegh's own failure may be attributed to the swift reaction of Marx and Engels, who wanted a strong workers' movement within Germany, not a bourgeois revolution from the outside.

In the Baden *Landtag* meanwhile, the split between moderates and radicals had become painful. On 4 April, alarm at the possibility of some kind of invasion by sympathetic radicals coming from France had led the Baden government to call for protection from troops of the German federation, and the prospect of such a response gave the radicals an excuse for vigorous protest. Von Itzstein had immediately set out from Frankfurt, intending to use his influence to cool tempers. He felt that the outcome of the *Landtag* debate was uncertain, and was appalled by the thought that the majority might declare in favor of the insurrectionists, thereby destroying any hope of a peaceful solution of Germany's problems. He was joined by the moderate delegate Karl Mathy, who like him was a member of the new *Fünfzigerausschuss* [committee of fifty] that had been selected by the *Vorparlament* at Frankfurt.

The fact that Mathy was proposing to head off Hecker, Fickler, and Struve offered an interesting contrast in personalities. Karl Mathy (1807–1868) was an unusually calm, rational person. His father, Arnold Mathy, was himself an original man, the product of a Jesuit college who had come into serious conflict with the Jesuits and their followers and had been denounced as "refractory" and dismissed from the priesthood. He had been a private teacher for a number of years, and had gone over to the reformed church in 1805, and married his housekeeper, who was to become the mother of his eight children. Known as a Kantian and a freethinker, he had nonetheless been invited by the government of Baden to teach in a new nondenominational school at Mannheim. Karl was the eldest son of this independent man. He had been active in the Heidelberg *Burschenschaft* but his youthful idealism had gradually hardened into political realism. As early as Hambach, he had been annoyed by the irresponsible talk of the extremists. He probably had come to the conclusion that a government controlled by hotheads like Struve, Hecker and Fickler would not show much more tolerance than one controlled by an absolute monarch.

The radicals were infuriated because they thought that Karl Mathy was a disgusting turncoat. They knew that he had interrupted his studies at Heidelberg, just before his final examinations, because he wanted to join a philhellenic corps that was being organized in France, to fight for Greek freedom. He went to Paris and tried to enlist himself in the group of volunteers, but when his hopes failed to materialize he returned to Heidelberg and finished his exams so satisfactorily that he was immediately accepted as a member of the *Praktikantendienst* of the Baden finance ministry.

Mathy's interest in politics had always been serious, and during the 1830's he began to write for various journals, where his article on a proposed tax reform caught the attention of Karl von Rotteck, one of the leaders of the opposition. Rotteck arranged to have Mathy become a correspondent for the influential *Augsburger allgemeine Zeitung*, where he reported on debates in the Baden *Landtag*. Mathy had helped some of the participants of the unfortunate Frankfurt *Wachensturm* to escape, and for that reason had himself been briefly imprisoned. Still threatened with investigation, and severely dealt with by the press censors, he fled to Switzerland in 1835, where he associated himself at first with Mazzini, although he was careful to function only as a translator, not involving himself in political conspiracies. In spite of his caution, he was again arrested—by the Swiss this time—and was badly treated in his second incarceration. He learned in the course of this experience that even democratic governments are not automatically just. After his release, he spent several years in a small town in Switzerland, where he taught school and established a family. He had returned to Baden in 1841.

Elected to the *Landtag,* he soon became an acknowledged leader. An article in the *Deutsche Zeitung*, describing Mathy's manner as a speaker, noted in admiration that "Behind an iron calm, one recognizes the steadiest character and the most energetic force."[12] Mathy and Friedrich Daniel Bassermann, who by that time had become one of Germany's leading political figures, joined forces as partners. They were active as publishers and book sellers in Mannheim. Respected, cool-headed, and definitely a moderate, Karl Mathy was the one who now intended to stop Hecker and the man who was encouraging Hecker's reckless plans, the brains of the insurrection, namely Josef Fickler.[13]

On 7 April, at a mass meeting in Mannheim, Fickler declared that the time had come to throw out the tyrannical *Grossherzog,* and that he himself was about to leave for Konstanz to start the uprising.

On that same 7 April, at a meeting of the lower house of the Baden *Landtag*, the radicals opened fire. There was no danger of an invasion from France, they asserted impatiently. This call-up of federation troops was an insult. Hecker levelled charges especially at Mathy, angrily calling him a hypocrite who was using the monarchy for his own purposes. Mathy's response was chill.

> Delegate Hecker is right . . . to warn against hypocrisy. . . . The true friend of the Fatherland goes with the nation and abandons his personal wishes when they are not in accord with the will of the majority. . . . He has called German brothers under arms 'foreign troops'. Is this the union in brotherhood of all Germans? . . . A man ought to be ashamed to have so poor an understanding of the great idea of German unity. . . . Do you believe that disorder is a republican virtue? . . . He who is against defense of the land and works for civil war is no friend of the people. [14]

Hecker stormed out of the hall, scowling and resentful because he was unable to frame a crushing rebuttal. After the general session of the *Landtag* there was a closed meeting of a committee in which the presiding officer revealed that he had in hand evidence of high treason, and presented letters and documents that showed the insurrectionists' plans. Fickler, who was still in Mannheim, was to proclaim the republic at Konstanz, Hecker at Offenburg. Mathy wanted to know why, with this evidence, the government was not acting. Was the government afraid of these people? No decision was reached, and Mathy departed in anger. That evening he learned about the Mannheim meeting that had occurred on that very day, where Fickler called so belligerently for the immediate overthrow of the "tyrant". Mathy wrote immediately to the *Bürgermeister* of Mannheim, requesting an emergency meeting of the local council for the following day. He would be there, he said. (Mathy was a member of the council.)

The situation had become at once tense, confusing, and menacing. Mathy was aware that his former friend and colleague, Josef Fickler, who was an impressive organizer, had immense influence in the area around Konstanz. It would be almost impossible to attack Fickler on his home ground but at the moment he was passing through Karlsruhe, en route back to Konstanz from Mannheim. If action were to be taken against him, this was the moment. A swift, decisive move would have the effect of dislocating whatever purposeful military thrust Fickler, Hecker and and their colleague Gustav Struve might have in mind.

Historians are not in agreement about the actual events of 8 April on the railway station platform at Karlsruhe. Some believe that Mathy went there for the sole purpose of stopping Fickler. Gustav Freytag's account sounds accurate.[15] In his version, the dramatic encounter was unplanned.

The trains for Konstanz and Mannheim arrived simultaneously at Karlruhe. Mathy was there, heading for Mannheim, when he saw Fickler in a compartment on the Konstanz train. The two men had a brief, hostile discussion, after which Mathy called a policeman who was standing nearby and told him that Fickler should be arrested, but the policeman was frightened. Fickler meanwhile shouted to the engineer that the train should start immediately, but Mathy went to the stationmaster and said crisply, "You are not to allow this train to depart before *Herr* Fickler has been arrested." "My god, I don't have any order from the government!" "On my responsibility," said Mathy coolly, charging Fickler with high treason.[16] In the end Fickler was arrested after some hesitation.

Mathy's train went on to Mannheim. The passengers were in an uproar, and after arrival word of the Karlsruhe event was spread throughout the city. Mathy's house was surrounded by a furious, shouting mob. Police protection was effective, but from that time on, there was a vast gap between radicals and moderates. Mathy was a hero, receiving letters of thanks signed by thousands from many parts of Germany, but he was also constantly in danger of having stones hurled at him. Fickler, meanwhile, was effectively behind bars, locked out of action throughout the insurrection.

One idea that had been floating in the *Vormärz* was definitely buried—that the *Volk* and the middle class were striving for common goals in brotherhood and unity. From that day on, it had to be acknowledged that the moderates and radicals would go their separate ways.[17]

Hecker was badlly shaken by Fickler's arrest and made his way furtively to Konstanz via Bavaria, France and Switzerland. He arrived in Konstanz on 11 April. There he found Gustav Struve and Franz Sigel, who had reached the city ahead of him. Their mood was cool, sceptical, almost detached. The imprisonment of Fickler had deprived the movement of its most dependable propagandist. Hecker himself admitted that he was bombarded from all sides with appeals to abandon any thought of insurrection, but he had already been pushed too far. At Frankfurt, petitions from German partisans in Switzerland and France were pouring in, urging armed revolution.

Konstanz itself was in a state of deep consternation. The city council had sent a protest to the Baden ministry of the interior on 9 April.

The council stated that it had been forced to the conclusion that thousands of men from the mass of the people regarded the arrest of Josef Fickler as an attack directed against themselves personally. Josef Fickler had done no more and no less than thousands of his fellow citizens would have done. "We must express our conviction that the holding of Fickler in prison can provoke a popular uprising, the extent and outcome of which cannot be predicted, but it could certainly have the most serious consequences."[18]

It is impossible at this late date to decide why everyone seems to have been convinced that an uprising of thousands upon thousands was imminent. Fickler had told Hecker that he could count on some forty thousand from the Konstanz area alone, but when Hecker bravely proclaimed his provisional government and issued an order that all able-bodied men should present themselves, armed, with money and rations for a week, he had to march off to war with a troop of about sixty men. His call to the authorities in various neighboring communities met with resistance, doubt and confusion. Gustav Struve, serving as advance man, had announced to a large audience at Überlingen that Hecker was coming with thousands at his back, and he asked the men of Überlingen to march with this army to Karlsruhe, but only two dozen indicated any willingness to participate, and even they wanted to be paid first.

Since Josef Fickler's influence was powerful throughout the Konstanz region, where he was a recognized champion of the lowly, it would seem reasonable to think that Hecker's revolutionary force must have included a high percentage of peasants and manual laborers. It has been possible to look for verification of this hypothesis by examining records from the ministry of justice that include detailed indictments and citations against participants in the spring uprising. Even though they do not include Hecker's original sixty followers, the records of one hundred and thirty cases allow a fairly dependable assessment of the situation at Konstanz, where the police lists can be checked against parish records and other pertinent data.[19]

The general assumption that the revolutionists were almost exclusively peasants and manual laborers proves to be incorrect. On the contrary, of the artisans in the study, 22.5% were on the master level and another 21.7% were journeymen. Independent workers accounted for 15% of the whole, while 10% were students. Day laborers and hired hands were present in small numbers, making up only 5.8% of the total. The major occupational group was made up of shoemakers, but there was an interesting variety—carpenters, tailors, painters, butchers, masons, brass founders, book binders, haberdashers, and surgeon's assistants. Moreover, there was an array of occupations represented by single individuals: physician, innkeeper, postal clerk, lithographer, cigar manufacturer, calico printer, drawing teacher, saddler, hatmaker, plasterer, nail smith, watch maker, typesetter, rope maker, etc.

The same records from the ministry of justice provide information on age cohorts. Most participants were in their thirties and mid-twenties, with only a minuscule number over forty or under twenty.

Still, most of these people may have been at the lower end of the social scale. What about the more affluent members of the middle class, those who presumably were the steady readers of Fickler's *Seeblätter*? There are traces of them in the membership lists of a *Bürgerversammlung* [citizens' assembly] and its *Ausschuss* [committee] that was organized after word of the French February revolution reached Konstanz. The parent organization had its own library and reading rooms, and it customarily sponsored concerts and festivals that were intended to further the interests of the middle class. The special committee was established on 5 March 1848 for the purpose of consultation and discussion of matters that related to the Fatherland. Originally the committee had only eight members, but an editorial in the *Seeblätter* encouraged admission of artisans and farm workers, with the result that membership was expanded to a total of twenty-six. The committee then included merchants, lawyers, and other professional individuals, while the artisans were without exception prosperous masters whose personal property and cash incomes were far above the average for their respective occupations. It seems likely that affluent middle class persons in Konstanz were more strongly represented in the committee discussion group than they were among the people who actually took up arms for the revolution.

Hecker's own comments about recruitment are revealing. "The women and girls were much more enthusiastic than the men. Many who marched with us were driven by the women and girls who told them it would be cowardly to leave us in the lurch and stay home while we were striving for freedom. We found signs of bravery, enthusiasm and resignation in the women . . . In front of fathers who wanted to protect their sons, the sisters stepped forward and called out, 'Go! Go! Don't be misled! Go with God and fight for the freedom of your people!'"[20]

Friedrich Hecker.

Figure 10 FRIEDRICH HECKER (1811–1881)

Hecker unfortunately had no conception of the international forces in play, and he had not even the most rudimentary understanding of military strategy and tactics. He does not appear to have given any thought to logistics, or to the problem of arming and feeding his troops.

He believed that the army of Baden would join him (he had led a meeting of soldiers not long before, in which there was talk of a pay raise and introduction of formal address—"Sie" instead of the patronizing "Du"). He rejected Herwegh's offer of help not out of strategic considerations but solely because he believed that the German Legion from Paris consisted mainly of French and Polish insurgents.

Maps of Hecker's movements reveal the woefully erratic nature of the campaign.[21] Less than forty kilometers northeast of Konstanz, at Stockach, there was supposed to be a three thousand man reinforcement, but the total number marching with Hecker was increased there to about two hundred at the most. The only munitions that his army received at Stockach were two old *Feldschlangen* (a curious long cannon with serpent handles, technically known as a culverin) that Hecker thought might have come from the Thirty Years' War, but he accepted them because they were still capable of firing, and made "an impression" on the people.[22] In spite of his determination to be noble, Hecker did not object to the opening of mail at Stockach, over the protest of the postmaster. He had hoped to find communications from Struve and others there, but was disappointed. He also allowed his people to raid a shipment of munitions intended for the civil militia, and confiscated four thousand cartridges.[23] The campaign map has a large black arrow pointing toward Stockach, marked *Bavarian government troops*.

"Indubitably, a mass rising was taking place," wrote Hecker cheerfully. "We lost our way and moved toward Allersbach, where we were invited to stop. We were received with joy, and I spoke to the citizenry assembled at the *Rathaus*, and my words were received with enthusiasm. . . . The blue sky smiled down from the torn rain clouds beside the bright magnificent lake. In the distance were the free Alps, and before us lay . . . a world full of ancient sagas. . . . Martial songs sounded, and white gulls swirled over our heads . . . We moved to the drum beat through a small village where people shook our hands and called out wishes for good luck. . . . Men, women and children came toward us with loud cries of joy, swinging a German banner."[24] Much joy, song, enthusiasm and waving of flags, but few volunteers.

About thirty kilometers to the east lay Donaueschingen, where Struve had been supposed to prepare an uprising in the southern Schwarzwald. According to him, their combined forces could overpower the fortress there and take possession of the area. However, the armed forces of Württemberg had arrived ahead of him, two thousand strong, so that Struve was forced to retreat. He led his men to Bonndorf, sixteen kilometers to the south of Donaueschingen, and met Hecker there.

The original plan for a two-pronged assault against Freiburg and Offenburg, as shown on the campaign maps, had had to be abandoned, and the republic proclaimed at Offenburg lasted only one day.

It was during a halt near Engen, not far from Donaueschingen, that Hecker received a visit from Emma Herwegh, the poet's wife, who had reached this place by a devious route from Strassburg. Her husband was anxious to be given concrete instructions as to time and place of a rendez-vous. Herwegh's situation at Strassburg was fraught with tensions.

The French administration was eager to rid itself of unemployed foreign workers, and coldly viewed Herwegh's troop of Germans, Swiss, Poles, Italians, Hungarians, Russians—even one lone American and a single Turk—who made up the German Legion. French displeasure had increased when this revolutionary band arrived in Strassburg and was joined by fifteen hundred Poles, all of whom had been living there on funds supplied by the French government, which customarily provided at least minimal support to political exiles. At that very time (mid-April 1848) the French provisional government was struggling for its own existence. This was no season for hospitable relationships with a troublesome foreign legion, no matter how splendid its appearance. The Legion looked as if it had come straight out of the Middle Ages. The revolutionists wore blue blouses with daggers or pistols thrust into their belts, slouch hats with feathers, high boots, and big scarlet neck scarves.

Emma Herwegh, the emissary of this wonderful army, was every bit as picturesque as the rest of the troop. She dressed like a man, wore a big slouch hat, and had a pair of pistols in the belt of her dark blouse. Brave, observant, and with a delightful sense of humor, she would have been an excellent addition to any army, though it must be admitted that her generous enthusiasm covered an almost total ignorance of military matters. In the present case, at Engen, she noted that in addition to his troop of about six hundred fighting men, Hecker had cavalry—one horse, in fact. (There are occasional references to horses in Hecker's account. At Schönau, for example, Hecker gratefully accepted a mount "that was most welcome because of my weary legs".)[25]

The village of Engen was festive as if there were some big celebration going on, and the street was full of peasants with wide eyes and open mouths, who had come to stare at *Volksfreund* Hecker. He had spoken so movingly to the crowd that women were weeping and older men were wiping sweat from their brows and the young boys were clamoring for permission to go to war.

Frau Emma delivered her husband's importunate message: his Legion was difficult to control. His men were ready to fight like lions for the cause. He needed a definite rendez-vous date. Hecker responded with vague instructions that she contact this person and that. He wanted her to look up Becker in Switzerland and tell him that he ought to come so that Herwegh could cross the Rhine. Just where this crossing ought to be, Hecker left to the judgment of the people on the spot. He himself was going to move on 17 April, he said . He would send a message to Herwegh. Goodbye, goodbye.[26] Hecker's evasiveness may be explained in part by the fact that he believed that the regular army of Baden would come over to his side. He would not want to compromise himself by accepting help from what might be regarded as a foreign army.

Herwegh envisioned himself as in command of a column of about five thousand, including the Poles. He accordingly issued a grandiose proclamation addressed to the German people, announcing that the Legion assembled on the left bank of the Rhine had come for the sole purpose of fighting for German freedom. "We are a well-equipped auxiliary in the service of the German People," he wrote, unabashed by his patent lie. Equipment was not the strong point of this remarkable army, many of the troops being armed with pitchforks and scythes. *Die Zukunft kämpft mit der Vergangenheit* as a current revolutionary poem expressed it.[27] [The future is fighting with the past] Repeatedly, he reassured the Germans that they were not greedy freebooters, and that "we have no intention of touching your property."[28]

Herwegh had reckoned without the authorities in Strassburg, who promptly initiated energetic negotiations with the ministry at Karlsruhe, announcing that they intended to drive Herwegh and his army out by force of arms if necessary. They suggested that the Poles could be sent down the Rhine to Cologne and transshipped there to Poland via Danzig, and that the Germans could swiftly be sent home. The Baden commissioners offered free railway transport to the birthplace indicated on the Germans' baptismal certificates but the proposal was haughtily rejected. (Here again is evidence that Germans had rapidly accepted the idea of railway transport as a part of their lives.)

Herwegh then had a brilliant inspiration. He and his legion could be transported across Germany to Schleswig-Holstein, where they would show their republican enthusiasm by fighting for Germany. The provisional government in Schleswig expressed serious doubts and the Prussian ambassador to the confederation at Frankfurt received a sharp message from Berlin: such additional forces were not wanted. Switzerland refused admission when Herwegh attempted to enter negotiations there. Herwegh was not dismayed. When a delegation arrived at Strassburg from the *Vorparlament*'s committee of fifty, they found that he had already left, moving in the direction of Basel.

The planned capture and occupation of Donaueschingen had failed, and both Struve and Hecker had moved south, to Bonndorf. From Bonndorf, the combined force moved north again, with the intention of heading toward Freiburg. The Württemberg army had blocked the route, however, so that the insurgents had to move south again as far as St. Blasien, where Hecker moved west to Bernau and Struve marched toward the Swiss border in order to join a group commanded by his colleague Joseph Weisshaar. The intention was to take the Konstanz area and the southern Schwarzwald and then march on Karlsruhe.

Franz Sigel (1824–1902) meanwhile was having more success as far as organization was concerned. He had once been an officer in the army of Baden and therefore was somewhat more brisk in his military movements. His report is direct (no torn rain clouds or swirling gulls here). He states frankly that even as early as 13 April he had been in doubt about the prospects of the undertaking. After Hecker's march toward Stockach, Sigel returned to Konstanz, where he found a tumultuous mass meeting under way. Most people seemed to be against the idea of an armed uprising, but after Sigel addressed the crowd, admitting that there was much danger while insisting on the necessity for a massive uprising if the monarch were to be convinced that the revolution was serious, he managed to recruit about one hundred volunteers, whom he led two days later toward Stockach. It was ominous that a messenger arrived with the news that Hecker had changed his plans because troops from Württemberg were already in Donaueschingen, where they had agreed to meet. Altogether, in spite of much confusion and many reverses, Sigel managed to collect some three thousand men and lead them to Todtnau, which was a favorable site. Once again, there was no contact between him and Hecker, and the enterprise that had started so well ended in disorder. Sigel's route on the campaign map has the look of a hairpin—first due south, then on the following day, due north.

His report of events in the spring campaign is appended to Hecker's.[29] It is a depressing narrative, full of missed rendez-vous, commands not obeyed, misunderstandings, bone-wearying marches in impossible weather, without rations. Sigel's small army had a more martial look than Hecker's. He refers repeatedly to his baggage train of twenty carts, for instance. At one point, where the forces of Württemberg were assembled in large numbers, he found a strong force of defenders, but he had to send them away because most of them were middle-aged men, many in their sixties. (Could these willing stalwarts have been veterans of the war of liberation of 1813?)

Although Sigel and his men were kindly and helpfully received in a number of places along their march, they were not always able to count on a hearty welcome. People were beginning to be afraid, and sometimes there were unpleasant rumors being circulated. At Todtnau, where they were sheltered and fed, a rumor was spreading that twenty thousand Württemberg troops as well as peasants were in the region, ready to attack. The source of this rumor turned out to be the local priest, a Jesuit. This man then came to Sigel, full of smiling flattery, to say that the people were mistakenly suspicious of him. This, says Sigel in a matter of fact tone, was his first experience with the Jesuits, whose ways were unfamiliar to him.

The reader gains the impression that if the revolutionary forces had not been so aimless and out of contact, they might have been able to present a united front of some six thousand insurrectionists, but as matters stood, Sigel was receiving snatchy reports: Becker had crossed the frontier from Switzerland with German workers. Herwegh had arrived at Neu-Breisach, on the far side of the Rhine, and was ready to cross over. There was unrest in Freiburg, where the *Turnverein* was ready to defend the town. The railroad above Freiburg had been torn up, in order to delay the royalist armies' advance. Hecker was somewhere . . .

Two delegates sent by the committtee of fifty of the Frankfurt *Vorparlament* traveled to Bernau for an interview with Hecker. They found him and his fellow insurrectionists wearing borrowed garments and mismatched footgear, happily singing and drinking wine at an inn while their sodden clothing dried after several days of floundering (without rations) through knee-deep snow, bending against stinging rain and hail in difficult mountain passes.

On behalf of the national assembly, delegates Jakob Venedey and Carl Alexander Spatz offered Hecker an amnesty if he would disband his forces, "in order not to destroy, by the spilling of German citizens' blood, the peaceful development of our Fatherland toward unity and freedom that has been started so magnificently." Hecker responded caustically that he in turn would offer amnesty to all German princes if they would abdicate within two weeks. There was some ironic joking. Maybe Venedey and Spatz ought to be retained as hostages. Somewhat uneasy, the delegates perceived that this was a jest, but they departed in some haste.[30]

Hecker's account is full of comments to the effect that the people were truly with him in his effort, but it is just possible that this was not the case. The *Parlament* was about to convene at Frankfurt, and many must have seen in this fact their true hope for Germany's future. Venedey and Spatz had issued a general proclamation in the name of the committee of fifty, from Lenzkirch on 18 April in which they wrote:

> Our mission of peace to the leader [Hecker] was a failure. For this reason we turn to you, brave citizens of Baden, and beg you by all that is holy to you not in any way to participate in an undertaking that destroys the inner development of Germany, that puts in jeopardy the free action of the National Assembly that has been called together for 1 May, and that could expose our great Fatherland to endless civil war and the intervention of foreign powers.[31]

The Baden government was unsure of itself and of its army, where two general officers in turn had resigned from the overall command. The new commander was an outsider, the highly respected Friedrich von Gagern, elder brother of Heinrich and Max. General von Gagern was an exceptional man, splendidly fitted for this duty. He had held numerous responsible commands in the Netherlands and Luxembourg, and he had served on diplomatic missions in England and Russia and even in the Netherlands Indies. He was currently on leave from his regular duties in the Netherlands. The *Bundestag*, in line with provisions of the Congress of Vienna, mobilized parts of the Eighth *Bundescorps* (troops from Hesse and Nassau), and placed the federation troops together with the army of Baden under von Gagern, who received this new temporary command on 16 April. Friedrich Daniel Bassermann was the man who engineered this arrangement, according to the note he sent to his colleague Mathy, who was on a mission in Berlin (the letter was dated 14 April). He expressed trepidation, reporting that Hecker and Struve were accompanied by "Polish officers". He planned to go immediately to Mannheim, intending to move his wife and *Frau* Mathy to a safe distance from any potential scenes of armed conflict.[32] Bassermann's alarm seems excessive. A formidable force totalling thirty thousand men then stood ready to crush the *Heckerzug*.

Georg Herwegh is usually counted among the dreamers, but in fact he had a clearer view of his situation than Hecker did. His wife reported that while he was still at Strassburg he had assembled his army and addressed them because he was aware that before long the Legion might find that it had only one possible action before it—namely, to disband. He told them that if any of them wanted to go to Schleswig-Holstein or to Poland, or to return home peacefully. they were free to do so. They had come voluntarily, and were just as free to leave the Legion if they wanted to. When they left Paris, the situation in Germany was such that they all believed it would take only a little push to bring the revolution to full outbreak.

> We could not know that the red flame that shown toward us from the Fatherland was nothing more than the reflection of the great world conflagration that France had kindled.

Our only hope now, continued Herwegh, lies at this moment in the insurrection in the Lake area. If it fails, then we have no choice because our material means are dwindling to an end. Someone ought to go there, to determine just what is happening.—Emma Herwegh was sent once again to Hecker's headquarters.

When she reached Kandern and stepped out of her carriage, Hecker greeted her with the somber announcement that "We are in a mousetrap." He led her into the building where he and his companions were resting. Some were lying on the floor, some were in lively argument around a table, and others stood thoughtfully leaning against the door frame. "There was complete anarchy in clothing and weapons. . . . What struck me most favorably was the untroubled good humor."

Frau Emma had only about five minutes with Hecker, because as he explained in his own account, he had to go to the war council, but she did manage to corner him for a few moments. She told him that she had to have a definite answer of some kind because supplies were almost exhausted. Either they would have to starve, separate, or hurry to Hecker immediately. She had to have a decisive answer, she said.

"Well, tell Herwegh that I cannot call him, but if he wants to come, quickly, and in large numbers, I would like it."[33]

The observation that there was untroubled good humor was accurate. Here is an extract from the diary of Theodor Mögling, one of Hecker's companions. (There were no officers in the corps because they felt that rank was undemocratic. The lack of a chain of command may in part account for the ragged behavior of Hecker's army.)

Communism has indeed caught up with us [wrote Mögling]. Feyerlen von Donaueschingen is wearing Doll's coat because someone else is wearing his, and in the same way many are going around in other's boots. . . . On Thursday 20 April I buy a blue blouse, pay nothing at the inn but leave a tip, take a kiss from the innkeeper's very pretty daughter, and travel on.[34]

The day on which Theodor Mögling started off so jauntily with the kiss of the innkeeper's daughter on his lips was the day of the disastrous encounter of the insurrectionists with the combined command of General von Gagern. Near Kandern, the opposing forces drew up, facing each other, and waited while their leaders held a parley on a small bridge. The discussion lasted only a few minutes. Von Gagern, the "citizen general" with a sabre belted over his brown civilian coat, told Hecker that "You are a brave man, but a fanatic", and required him and his men to lay down their arms. Hecker seems to have thought that in the few minutes available to him, he could convince the general of the rightness of his cause. "If devotion to the freedom of a great people is fanaticism, you are free to use the term, but there is fanaticism on the other side, the one you serve." Two men with powerful names and powerful ideas, as Valentin put it.[35] Both behaved with rigid military correctness and courtesy, parting to ready themselves for battle.

The revolutionary force stationed itself on the nearby Scheidegg, where there would be the advantage of defending a high pass. The Hessians, shouting and laughing, followed closely. Von Gagern had expressly forbidden them to shoot.

Hecker's men returned the Hessian shouts, calling "Come over, brothers! Join us! Come to freedom!" Some of the Hessians hesitated. The insurrectionists were encouraged and renewed their shouting, this time "Let the general come forward!"

General von Gagern rode to the front.

One of the rebel leaders, Dr. Kaiser, shouted again, "Don't shoot your German brothers!"

Von Gagern, angered, raised his voice. "Lay down your weapons and go home!"

Again, some of von Gagern's men wavered. He must have understood that the situation was critical. He brandished his sabre, shouting "Forward!" and the Hessians automatically responded.

It appears that the insurrectionists were the ones who opened fire, though there is argument about this point. (Hecker denied it, but he was not on the front line at the time and therefore could not qualify as an accurate observer.) In any case, there was von Gagern, who had exposed himself so that all the rebels knew him by sight, in his brown coat and green cap. A clearly recognizable target, easily distinguishable from the mass of uniformed men who followed him. Von Gagern was among the first to fall.

The infuriated Hessians hesitated no longer, seeing this as deliberate murder. They attacked, dispersing the rebels. There was only one brief pause, when von Gagern's body was exchanged for a captured rebel battle flag. After that the exhausted revolutionists retreated in disorder. Hecker himself, disguised as a peasant, fled to Switzerland.

Sigel's column had been moving along successfully in the direction of Todtnau, where Hecker was supposed to arrive at any moment. Sigel had already ordered his men to quarter overnight near various small towns, when the information reached him that there had been a battle at Kandern. "I was astounded," wrote Sigel. "I had had no word from Hecker during the previous days and believed for this reason that he was already in the vicinity of Freiburg." News also reached Sigel that part of the Hecker troops had pulled back toward Zell, where they were trying to help the town's inhabitants to defend themselves against attacking forces. They were calling for assistance. Sigel thought that it was of the utmost importance to get to Freiburg as soon as possible, but he responded to this urgent appeal by dispatching about six hundred men. The royalists had already turned away toward Steinen, and Sigel therefore doubled back toward Schopfheim, in order to meet some of the fugitives from Kandern. All were exhausted, including Sigel's men who had performed a ten-hour forced march in drenching rain.

Hecker's men then went off on their own, hunting for Hecker, of whom they had had no report since the battle. Sigel waited for their return, but learned at last that both Hecker and Struve had crossed over the Rhine. Struve's band, as well as that of Weisshaar, had been dispersed.

Sigel was much alarmed because in the course of all this confusion he had lost two days in his proposed march to Freiburg. The royalists had taken advantage of the delay and had formed themselves before Freiburg (troops from Baden and Hesse), while the Württembergers threatened to cut off Sigel's northward route. The Bavarians had arrived in Stockach. The only path that appeared to lie open was through the mountains of the Schwarzwald. He made careful plans for disposition of his available forces, including the Swiss Legion under Becker, and he thought that he had developed a workable plan for a successful cautious advance against Freiberg, only to find that his first column had somehow decided to move along on its own and had already engaged troops from a royalist outpost. When he arrived at the edge of the forest and was able to look down into the Güntersthal, he saw his first column already shattered and in retreat. He started an orderly march, hoping to reassemble the insurrectionists, but soon heard the desperate cry, "Run! Run! All is lost!" Down in the valley, he realized that his whole second column had vanished. "So there I stood at the edge of the forest with my third column. This was all that was left of three thousand men whose victory would have been assured if they had not acted against my commands and against all military measures of precaution." Sigel did manage to slip into Freiburg and ultimately to make his escape, but as far as he was concerned, the battle was lost.[36]

Herwegh meanwhile had crossed the Rhine, only to learn that on the previous day Hecker's men had lost the battle at Kandern. On the actual day of their crossing, Sigel had lost his battle at Freiburg and in the Güntersthal. In their ignorance of the true situation, the Herwegh force marched to Todtnau, believing that they would meet Sigel and Struve there. They cautiously entered a village (Mutten) where all houses were locked and the shutters closed. Once in a while a pale face would peer out. The women and girls had fled to the forest. They learned that the villagers had been frightened because they thought that this was a French army attacking. When the mistake was rectified, the villagers were friendly, but all the same Herwegh cautioned his men to avoid use of the French language.[37]

Emma Herwegh wrote sadly that "Because of all kinds of misunderstandings and delays" Sigel had suffered a serious defeat. All weapons were in enemy hands, and the three thousand man column under Sigel had been reduced to thirty. All the others were either captured or scattered to the four winds, to come together in Switzerland if they had luck for it. Herwegh and his followers decided that they had no choice: they would have to find the quickest and most honorable withdrawal route into Switzerland, there to join the others on neutral ground and at some favorable moment cross the border again together.

They set out in pitch-black night but made the mistake of borrowing a couple of lanterns which quickly disclosed their whereabouts to the enemy. Above Dossenbach they entered a forest, where a sense of threat silenced the marchers. One whispered, "*Frau* Herwegh, I believe we ought to sing a requiem for the German republic today." They were ambushed and a furious skirmish ensued in which the insurgents lost eight men, the Württembergers forty. The angry Württemberg force then began to scour the woods, intent on capturing Herwegh, who had a price on his head.

The number of fallen given by Emma Herwegh was not correct. Von Corwin reported that about thirty died, either in the battle itself, or drowned in the Rhine, trying to swim across to Switzerland. Some who were caught in the woods were shot (one was hanged), and those who had been wounded were treated with cruelty.

The two Herweghs meanwhile were taken in by a farmer, who disguised them in peasant clothing and put them to work in his field, where they could hear and observe the bloodthirsty talk and action of troops that were hunting for them. The couple reached Switzerland, still clinging to their pitchforks.

On 3 May Robert Blum wrote to his wife, "Hecker and Struve have betrayed the country in the eyes of the law—that's trivial—but they betrayed the people by their insane insurrection and checked us on the way to victory. That is a hideous crime."[38]

* * * * * * *

The monarchy tried with all its means to crush the first republican rising. It did not succeed in achieving its goal. Our repressed but undefeated cause is at home in the peasant's hut and the townsman's household. Like a glorious saga it lives in the mouth of the people. It decorates the graves of our fallen brothers, and if the flowers wither in the evening, there are fresh ones in the morning, placed by unknown hands. In the lonely huts on the mountain heights, in the valley dwellings, there hang thousands of pictures of "the rebel leaders", and the people praise their names in songs. Yes, they live and sound in the games and little songs of the children. Hecker[39]

Hecker's modest use of the plural with reference to pictures that had been hung with respect in hovels and cottages does not mask the fact that it was his picture that was so honored. A *Heckerkultus* had developed. In addition to the pictures, there were also statuettes, showing him in his picturesque blouse, boots and feathered slouch hat, with sword and pistols belted, and grasping a long musket. (He protests in his account of the rising that he never used any of his weapons.) Pilgrims flocked by the hundreds to see him in Muttenz in Switzerland, coming not only from Baden but from all Germany. He was twice elected to the Frankfurt *Parlament*, which after strenuous debate refused to seat him. Pamphlets written by him flooded Baden.

Thousands of copies of his *Plan zur Revolutionierung und Republikanisierung Deutschlands* fell into the hands of admirers in Germany, and his paper, *Volksfreund* was read in Baden, Hesse-Darmstadt, and the Palatinate. For a short time it appeared that he might be preparing some kind of armed assault, but the cold reception in Strassburg deterred him. (He was told to quit the city within twenty-four hours.) In mid-September he sailed for America from Southampton.[40]

Hecker's role in the death of General Friedrich von Gagern was harshly judged by his brother Heinrich and by most German moderates, who agreed with the assessment of the matter in Heinrich von Gagern's biography of his fallen brother. After a careful review of all available evidence of the events at Kandern, he concluded that *Sie war ein als Kriegsmittel völkerrechtlich unerlaubter feiger Mord.*[41] [As a means of warfare, in terms of international law, it was impermissible cowardly murder]

Throughout the summer of 1848, Switzerland swarmed with refugees—Poles and Sardinians and Italians in addition to the Germans. Various combinations were formed, and strange plans elaborated. Struve published *Die Grundrechte des deutschen Volkes* [basic rights of the German people] in which he called for the arrest of police, bureaucrats, landowners and princes. All Germans were to stand ready to begin a life-and-death struggle. Struve wanted all royal families to be banished from German soil, their property to be turned over to the people. He even went so far as to issue a map of Germany, divided into twenty-three republics (Upper Rhine, Middle Rhine, Lower Rhine, Tyrol, Upper Saxony, Brandenburg, Silesia etc etc.) On the basis of some obscure reasoning, Struve asserted that this arrangement would effect an annual saving of seven hundred million *Gulden.*[42]

The patient Swiss bore with all the turbulence of refugees in their midst, but officials in Germany were disturbed. In mid-summer, the confederation sent a special envoy to Switzerland, demanding that the refugees be disarmed and their belligerent groups disbanded, with removal of their leaders from the border cantons. If this were not done, troops would have to be stationed along the border, and that would of necessity be harmful to trade. The Swiss rejected the note, saying that its requirements did not correspond to the facts—that the refugees were not gathering in a warlike manner and that the Swiss police were responsible and capable of controlling them.

This then was the situation at the time of the opening deliberations at Frankfurt, where the duly elected *Parlament* had assembled.

Notes

1 Deuchert, *Vom hambacher Fest zur badischen Revolution*, p. 147.

2 Elmar B. Fetscher, *Die Konstanzer Seeblätter und die Pressezensur der Vormärz 1840/41*, pp. 41–58.

3 Helmut Kramer, *Fraktionsbindungen in den deutschen Volksvertretungen 1819–1949*. pp. 40–42.

4 Deuchert, p. 148. In Metternich's opinion, von Itzstein was the first genuinely practical radical; Ibid, p. 65.

5 Ibid. p. 149.

6 Mathy. *Aus dem Nachlass*, p. 133.

7 Deuchert, p. 266.

8 Heinrich Laube, *Das erste deutsche Parlament*, pp. 22–23.

9 Real, *Die Revolution in Baden 1848–49*, p. 63.

10 Büttner, *Georg Herwegh– Sänger des Proletariats*, p. 82.

11 Wolfgang Dressen, *1848–1848. Bürgerkrieg in Baden*, p. 31.

12 Mathy, p. 316.

13 Eyck, *The Frankfurt Parliament*, pp. 185–187; Gall, *Bürgertum in Deutschland*, pp. 261–264.

14 Gustav Freytag, *Karl Mathy*, pp. 265–267.

15 Ibid., pp. 268–269.

16 Mathy regularly used the term treason with reference to Fickler and Hecker. See for example Mathy, p. 73, his letter of 14 December 1847 to Franz Peter Buhl, discussing the Offenburg meeting of September 1847.

17 Gall, pp. 306–307.

18 Dressen, pp. 37–38.

19 Reinhold Reith, *Der Aprilaufstand 1848 in Konstanz*, pp. 17–29.

20 Hecker, *Die Erhebung des Volkes in Baden*, p. 34.

21 Franz X. Vollmer, *Vormärz und Revolution 1848/49 in Baden*, passim.

22 Hecker, pp. 39–40.

23 Ibid., pp. 37, 41.

24 Dressen, pp. 42–43.

25 Hecker, pp. 51–53. It was at Schönau that a local shoemaker repaired the footgear of Hecker's men.

26 Dressen, pp. 47–48.

27 Valentin, *Geschichte der deutschen Revolution,* 1:389.

28 Dressen, pp. 44–45.

29 Hecker, pp. 105–119. "Erlebnisse während des ersten Schilderhebung der deutschen Republikaner im April 1848".

30 Dressen, pp. 49–50.

31 Friedrich Lautenschlager, *Volksstaat und Einherrschaft,* p. 126.

32 Mathy, pp. 194–195. With reference to the appointment of von Gagern, Bassermann wrote, "I arranged this myself last evening".

33 Dressen, pp. 51–52.

34 Ibid., p. 53.

35 Valentin, 1:497.

36 Sigel [with Hecker] pp. 108–119.

37 Dressen, pp. 61–62, quoting von Corvin.

38 Schmidt, *Robert Blum,* p. 161; Bergsträsser, *Frankfurter Parlament,* p. 361.

39 Dressen, p. 75.

40 Karl Schurz visited him in his little log house, where he and his wife were struggling as Latin farmers. Hecker was morose, bitter, and wretched with malaria. Before the interview ended, Schurz cheered him a little by suggesting that if ever war were to break out in the United States over the slavery question, they would offer their services.

41 Heinrich von Gagern, *Das Leben des Generals Friedrich von Gagern* , 2:835-910.

42 Valentin, 2:173–174.

Chapter 16

The Frankfurt *Parlament*

Faust: Wohin der Weg?
Mephistopheles: Kein Weg! Ins Unbetretene

Even the most prescient of the delegates who moved in solemn procession with such pride and determination through the cheering crowd into the huge echoing chamber of the *Paulskirche* at Frankfurt probably had only a faint idea of the innumerable pitfalls that lay ahead. They could hardly be blamed if they trembled a little as they crossed the threshold of that noble building, aware that like Goethe's Faust they were setting forth into the new, untrodden unknown. Some of the delegates had been sent from states that already boasted possession of a constitution, but those constitutions had all been granted by hereditary sovereigns who could rescind them at any time according to their royal whim. Many of those attending the constituent assembly treasured in their hearts Thomas Paine's lucid words:

> A Constitution is not a thing in name only, but in fact. . . . A Constitution is a thing antecedent to a Government, and a Government is only the creature of a Constitution. The Constitution of a country is not the act of its Government, but of the people constituting a Government.[1]

All Frankfurt was redolent of history and German destiny. It was along its splendid medieval streets with their timbered houses, their imposing vistas of fountains and grand public buildings that newly crowned rulers of the Holy Roman Empire moved toward the famed *Römersaal*. (Ten emperors were crowned in the *Dom* at Frankfurt, the first in 1562, the last in 1702.) The *Paulskirche* itself was not ancient, yet it had its own aura of classic grandeur. Its drumlike central room with its ring of simple Ionic columns that supported the encircling overhead gallery, the grave arched windows and severely plain doors, the clerestory and shallow dome all reflected the architects' impressively sober sense of spatial integrity.[2]

Noble though the structure certainly was, the *Paulskirche* was far from ideal for the purposes of a large body of delegates because there was no provision of suitable rooms for conferences or committee meetings. In some extreme situations, members even conferred outside, in pouring rain. Another problem was presented by the huge

Figure 11   The *PAULSKIRCHE* at Frankfurt am Main.

galleries overhead that could accommodate as many as two thousand members of the general public. They were often full of shouting agitated men and women (to the clear advantage of the radicals, who did not shrink from appeals to popular emotion), because all meetings were open. Members of the press and distinguished visitors were crowded in an outer circle, right on edge of the floor where the delegates were assembled. Small wonder that as parties began to be formed, their meetings were held in Frankfurt's inns, where there was at least a semblance of privacy and quiet for discussion.

In the course of the brief interim between the meetings of the *Vorparlament* and the opening of the sessions of the elected *Parlament*, the members of the *Vorparlament*'s committee of fifty (the *Fünfzigerausschuss*) had precariously survived the turmoil of Hecker's insurrection in Baden. They had also been uneasily aware of the seething unrest in Berlin, typified by the threatening activity of the "Rehberger" gangs of quasi-employable workmen on the one hand and a printers' strike purposefully led by Stephan Born on the other.

Crisis after crisis had brought in a deluge of petitions, demands and complaints The use of troops in coping with the Baden insurrection was viewed with great displeasure and alarm. A so-called people's council at Hanau addressed the *Fünfzigerausschuss* on 21 April, expressing anger and dismay at the presence of forty thousand troops from the Electorate of Hesse in the Hanau area. In the view of the council, this was an unwarranted interference in the internal affairs of a German state and an attack on the sovereignty of the German people as a whole. It was thought to be a symptom of the beginnings of reaction, and the *Fünfzigerausschuss* was blamed for this situation.

Rhineland unrest had pointed up the weakness of the parliamentary committee. Sections of the Taunus railway line at Kassel had been destroyed, and the steamship company of Cologne had found itself "anarchically" attacked by barge men and others whose living depended upon the river traffic. They may have been in essence expressing outrage against modern technological developments, but their mood played into the hands of radical agitators. The *Fünfzigerausschuss* dutifully sent a three-man committttee of investigation (Blum and Raveaux were members). They were courteously received, even celebrated, but they had to report back that along the Rhine opposition was not monolithic. Rather, there was a combination of many heterogeneous elements. They could do no more than admonish because the committee and its appointed delegates had no true authority.

Another delegation from the *Fünfzigerausschuss* was dispatched to Kassel, where trouble stemming from long-lasting hostility between the townspeople and the cavalry stationed there erupted into violence. An officer had been subjected to a round of *Katzenmusik* that angered his troops. When the men encountered a peaceful, unarmed procession of citizens who were celebrating the new arrangements brought on by the March revolution, they accordingly attacked with broadswords. The people responded by rushing to the local armory and taking weapons. In the end, the offending cavalry unit was transferred to another station and peace was restored, just at about the time that the delegation from the *Fünfzigerausschuss* arrived on the scene.

The delegation had set out prepared to deal with the trouble in a dictatorial manner if circumstances required firm action against the old government. As the affair developed, they had had no reason to try to assume command. Nevertheless, they were satisfied, apparently believing that their presence had restored order. One member of the delegation was reckless enough to boast that "We have the whole people behind us." The head of the Hessian finance ministry scorned this bold claim. "And if Prussia beats its drum, that's the end of it," he snapped. At Kassel, the minister of Saxony told the delegation that if intervention of this sort had been attempted in his home region, "I would call for the immediate arrest of the members of the Frankfurt committee." These remarks ought to have warned the members of the *Fünfzigerausschuss* that they were in fact weak and without any recognizable mandate.

Perhaps, since all this was now behind them, the elected members of the new *Parlament* enjoyed the refreshing thought as they entered the *Paulskirche* for their inaugural session that the path ahead lay broad and open. They would write a splendid constitution for united Germany.

The Frankfurt *Parlament* was an assemblage of educated men.[3] Seven hundred and sixty-four of them had attended a secondary school, and at least six hundred and fifty-three of them (81.6% of the total) had a university education. Not only that. Most had studied law. Two hundred and forty-nine members had practiced law as judges, public prosecutors or lawyers, and then there were also university law professors. Anyone who served in the upper ranks of the civil service would have presented knowledge of the law as a normal requirement for his office.[4]

Altogether, the hasty elections for the *Parlament*, without any recognized parties that could establish a slate of candidates and campaign for them, and without any uniformity of qualifications, had brought into being a gathering that consisted for the most part of people known for their scholarship, or for their ability as professionals (judges, members of the provincial *Landtag*, leading businessmen and civil servants, etc.), or simply for their prominence as local *Honoratioren*, who might be major landowners, teachers at the *Gymnasium* level, physicians, wealthy innkeepers, or members of the clergy. In Frankfurt, many were meeting for the first time, and it was only gradually that they were able to sort themselves out into rudimentary parties.

When they first filed into the *Paulskirche* there was no formal seating on right or left. People just sat down wherever they found a place, facing the rostrum. Apparently, there was never even any thought of orderly seating by state delegation. On the whole, the irregular seating was a reflection of common experience in provincial *Landtag* arrangements. In those assemblies, there had never been any physical disposition that might have promoted formation of parties. In Saxony, for example, two delegates wanted to exchange seats because the light bothered one of them and the other wanted to be nearer the speakers' podium, but this was not allowed since it was believed that this rearrangement could be an entering wedge for some sort of partisan organization.[5]

Members of this new historic assembly had no experience in legislation. A *Landtag* had competence to prepare a budget or to offer petitions, but no authority to initiate laws. (The sole exception was the upper house in the Electorate of Hesse.) Usually, there was no cooperation between the *Landtag* and the ministry. Ministers could not be called to account. Moreover, the government had the right to close the *Landtag* at any time—in itself a powerful weapon against party formation.

Liberals were in the majority at Frankfurt. Their goal could be quickly attained, they thought—namely, reform in the name of justice, under a monarchical system. They would have done well to reflect on the general complexity of German affairs, both domestic and foreign, and to remind themselves that although the troublesome Hecker and Struve were absent, the radicals still had some formidable big guns—Robert Blum, Franz Raveaux, and Franz Heinrich Zitz, to name only a few. These men would make themselves heard, and their primary goals did not necessarily coincide with those of the moderates. They were certainly in conflict with the idea of sustaining the monarchies. They would surely have rejected the notion that "Slow progress is a characteristic of freedom," as Paul Pfizer said.[6] Many would have listened to Robert Blum's warning about excessive reliance on law. The historic legal foundation, in his opinion, was like a treacherous sheet of thin ice over running water. The running water was the stream of revolution.[7] They would also have disagreed with the moderates who, like Pfizer, acknowledged the importance of the state in shaping fundamental institutions that hold society together, in spite of their hostility to a state that abused its power. The moderates had their own big guns—among them, Heinrich von Gagern, Karl Mathy and Friedrich Daniel Bassermann.

The out-and-out radicals were few in number, but even before the actual opening of the sessions, Robert Blum had worked to gather them together into what he hoped would be an effective voting bloc. Less than one hundred elected members could be identified as belonging to the left, but they presented a wide spectrum of opinion and could not all be classified as radicals. Most were from the Rhineland. About fifty clustered around Blum. In connection with the left-leaning members, it should be noted that there were ninety-two known former members of the old university *Burschenschaft* movement at the *Paulskirche*.

Agitation over regional problems in areas under Habsburg control was a factor that generated many vacancies. The Czechs, for example, flatly refused to participate. The Slav boycott accounted for nearly all unfilled slots (sixty constituencies were not represented).[8]

If it had not been for the Austrian situation, Catholics would have outnumbered Protestants at Frankfurt. There was an additonal weakening of the Catholic position because denominational considerations led people like Archbishop Geissel of Cologne, a strong activist, to seek election in a state assembly (Berlin, in Geissel's case) rather than at Frankfurt. The leading Roman Catholic prelate among the Frankfurt delegates was no activist. Prince-Bishop von Diepenbrock of Breslau had even declined to involve himself in the turmoil around the imprisonment of archbishop Droste-Vischering at Cologne in the thirties. At Frankfurt, Diepenbrock called a meeting of leading Catholics, including General Joseph Maria von Radowitz and the judge August Reichensperger. This meeting marked the founding of a *Katholische Vereinigung* of which Radowitz was president.

Von Radowitz had a complicated, sophisticated mind, and he saw no benefit in making his new society into a political party. He had already stated his views on possible reform of the German confederation, and although he was a devout Catholic, he would not ever be the man to try to force Catholic views on the rest of Germany. He had considerable prestige at Frankfurt because of his writings and also because it was common knowledge that he was a close friend of Friedrich Wilhelm IV of Prussia. The monarch, who had little faith in parliaments, wrote to him that he feared his "precious Radowitz" would be wasted at Frankfurt. *Satan und Adrammelech haben dort ihr Hauptquartier.*[9] [Satan and Adrammelech (Babylonian deity) have their headquarters there]

The Roman Catholics by and large tended to join forces with the party of the right, which had its quarters in the same building (the *Steinernes Haus*) where the Catholic society held its meetings. Von Radowitz was president of both the Catholic society and of the organized Right. He had been elected to the *Parlament* by a constituency in Westphalia, where the electors included a few conservative Protestants. Since von Radowitz was the son of a mixed marriage, this interdenominational support was comfortable as far as he was concerned. As the sessions of the *Parlament* progressed, the Catholics found that they could function most effectively in conjunction with non-Catholic conservatives. Among non-Catholics, there were not only the *Deutschkatholiken* but also a scattering of Jewish members.

The leading Jewish delegate was Gabriel Riesser, a vice-president of the *Parlament*. In addition to Riesser, there was the well-known editor of the *Grenzboten*, Ignaz Kuranda, and the publisher Moritz Veit. Johann Jacoby of Königsberg joined the *Parlament* only toward the end. There were eleven other delegates who were converts to Christianity (Eduard Simson and Heinrich Simon among them). All these men appear to have been able to function without embarrassment or restraint of any kind. Anti-semitism does not seem to have been a serious or troublesome factor at Frankfurt.

In theory, there were five hundred and ninety constituencies represented in the unwieldy assemblage at the *Paulskirche*, but in actuality the number of members present at any one time fluctuated because some who lived at a distance were trying to handle their regular commitments at home, to say nothing of people like Heinrich von Gagern, who had recently become a minister in the government of Hesse-Darmstadt. He was not the only one with this difficult problem of split responsibilities. State ministers from Württemberg, Nassau, Prussia, Bavaria, and Saxe-Weimar participated at Frankfurt, and as time passed some of them became entangled in questions that related to their own states, to the detriment of their supposed concern for overall German well-being. For many reasons, there was always a lot of coming and going. This circumstance had a complicating effect. It was extremely difficult to make any precise estimate of the strengths of the various groups within the *Parlament*. [10] At one stage or another, nearly eight hundred delegates were elected and took part in the sessions.

Individual states had served as organizing instruments for election of the *Parlament*. There were a few general directives but on the whole each state fitted its requirements to its own situation. It was the states that had the responsibility of breaking up their respective quotas of delegates into constituencies. In the Rhine province there was a fairly successful attempt to work out population statistics, with the result that the various constituencies were not unreasonably different in size, but there was no uniformity in the sub-districts in which the *Urwähler* [original voters] chose one single *Wahlmann* [elector]. In the subsequent election, such a man might represent anywhere from three hundred to nine hundred and ninety-nine voters.

A serious drawback in conducting the elections was the fact that there was no national citizenship. Hence there was no uniformity in the matter of age requirements. (In the Rhine province, minimum voting age might be twenty-one, or twenty-four, or even twenty-five.) A voter was supposed to be economically independent [*selbstständig*]. In certain states, independence meant that the individual in question was not on the public dole. Elsewhere it might mean that he paid direct taxes to the state. Again, it might mean that he was not a hired hand, or a domestic servant. In some states journeymen were not allowed to cast a vote.

Voting procedures themselves had many peculiarities. There is the report, for example, of voting in a village of Westphalia. The election took place in the church, where the congregation listened quietly to the explanations of the priest. They were going to affect the future of the Christian religion, of the Holy Church, and therefore were in duty bound to select thoughtful men. When the written ballots were collected, it was found that there had been an almost unanimous vote for two men who were to serve as deputies in the indirect choice of electors for the simultaneously occurring Prussian united provincial assembly and Frankfurt *Parlament*. The first was the priest, and the other was the former feudal lord of the village.[11]

Such monolithic voting was counterbalanced to a certain extent by the vigorous efforts of the radicals, who as early as 4 April had organized a central committee for the elections for the constituent assembly. This group published an appeal for support of representatives who would favor Gustav Struve's revolutionary program that had been so firmly rejected by the *Vorparlament*. Publication provoked an indignant response from Georg Gervinus of the Göttingen Seven, who wrote in the *Deutsche Zeitung* of 11 April that the time had come when the prestige of government had to be reestablished. The base of government must not be undermined, he insisted. Otherwise, "we hand ourselves over helplessly to anarchy."[12]

The example of the Westphalian parish and the pro-Struve propaganda cannot be taken as evidence of an out-and-out clash between Catholics and radicals. On the contrary, since Catholics were in the minority under Protestant rule in the Rhineland, radical agitators were to find that they could play on their discontents, gaining sympathetic hearing among them.

The first formal meeting of the elected assembly (18 May) was marked by unadulterated chaos. The pro-tem chairman was an elderly gentleman who proved to be incapable of establishing order. Nevertheless, the occasion was memorable. In the general confusion, someone noticed that the "martyr" Ernst Moritz Arndt wanted to speak, and cleared the way for him. What happened next was extraordinary.

As they saw that venerable man, emotion swept over the assembled delegates with the force of a shock-wave. He was the epitome of everything that had gone before, as well as the one person whose name through his writings had become synonymous with the idea of a German nation, and who therefore symbolized not only the past but also the future. They hailed him in a storm of applause, shouting, cheering, in a moment of intense unanimity.

Arndt's earliest published work had been a protest against serfdom as it still prevailed along the Baltic and on his native island of Rügen in his youth.[13] Speculators there were buying and selling whole estates and villages in ruthless indifference to the havoc wrought in the lives of the powerless serfs, who were nothing more than chattels. He was so old that he could remember the French occupation of Prussia and the conspiracy to dislodge Bonaparte. (Arndt was born in 1769.) He had been closely associated with the military leaders, August von Gneisenau (1760–1831) who was to be a commander at Waterloo, and his colleague Gerhard von Scharnhorst. Those two were the men who reorganized and restored strength to the crushed Prussian army.

Figure 12   ERNST MORITZ ARNDT (1769–1860)

Arndt been a propaganda specialist for the reformer, Karl vom und zu Stein during the final years of the Napoleonic occupation. He had been active at St. Petersburg, organizing a German legion, and it was he whose powerful words most effectively galvanized the German people into armed resistance in the war of liberation (1813). Arndt remembered that war. He remembered rigid corpses of soldiers, stacked on sledges like so much cordwood, and slinking wolves.[14] Arndt's work as professor of history during the thirties at Greifswald and later at Bonn has already been described in an earlier chapter. In those days he was influential among student groups that anticipated the *Burschenschaft* movement which was to spread through the universities. In the turbulence following Sand's assassination of Kotzebue,

Arndt underwent years of humiliating investigation, was deprived of his academic post, and forbidden to speak. This silencing of a patriot continued until the accession of Friedrich Wilhelm IV to the throne of Prussia.

Now Arndt stood before that emotion-charged multitude, symbolizing all that lay in ruins in the past and all that lay ahead in dreams for Germany's future. Certainly none who took part in the spontaneous act of homage to the man and to Germany would forget that stirring moment. All their lives, they would stand a-tiptoe when this day was named. Alas, it was the only occasion when unanimity flowed like a river through the *Paulskirche*. From that day on, there was discord.

The first order of business—election of a presiding officer—moved along smoothly because a number of centrists, including Friedrich Christoph Dahlmann (famous as a member of the Göttingen Seven) and his friend and colleague Georg Beseler had quietly decided that Heinrich von Gagern would be ideal for the post. Like Arndt, he was an avatar of an earlier day: he had been one of the youngest who fought at Waterloo. Beseler and Dahlmann traveled hastily to Darmstadt on 19 May in order to sound out the absent von Gagern, who had pressing duties as a new minister there. On their return they were confident enough to have voting slips printed with Gagern's name on them. In Beseler's admiring words, a personality of such rich natural endowments is a rarity. Gagern, he said, combined an imposing chivalrous appearance with mannerly civility. He possessed genuine love of the fatherland, nobleness of mind, a courageous temperament, and a rare power of speech, so that even in the *Vorparlament* he had been recognized as the leader of the moderate reform contingent.[15] Unfortunately, the noble von Gagern was unable to live up to all these high expectations. Beseler admits that his way of conducting the business of the *Parlament* left much to be desired. During the final days of the *Parlament*, when hatred among the delegates was palpable, an observer noted that Gagern as presiding officer swung his bell [calling for order] with such passion that it seemed that he might fire it into the raging assembly like a projectile, so great was his anger and frustration.[16] At the moment, however, he was elected by the assembled delegates, who no doubt were moved to a certain extent by their sympathy for him in the recent grievous loss of his brilliant brother on the battlefield of Kandern at the hands of Hecker's forces.

The radical delegates had hoped to elect Robert Blum, who despite his revolutionary ideas was to show himself to be more the statesman and more the conciliator than many of his colleagues. He may have understood the implication of von Gagern's words in his inaugural speech, in which he made a distinction between *National-* and *Volkssouveränität* [sovereignty of the nation as opposed to sovereignty of the people].

Franz Raveaux probably also understood. He was a man of sharp political instincts. On the very first day of business, he rose to pose a question that encompassed one of the major problems that confronted the assembly. Prussia had simultaneously elected delegates for the Frankfurt assembly and for its own united provinces assembly. Raveaux proposed the adjournment of all provincial assemblies while the *Parlament* was in session. His clear intention was to make the assembly competent to overrule provincial legislative decisions. Implicit in his proposal was a total bypassing of the *Bundestag,* and an assumption that states and rulers would have to conform to decisions of the *Parlament*. This would in effect be popular sovereignty [*Volkssouveränität*] masked as national sovereignty.

The heated debate that took place on 27 May ended in a rare compromise action. Raveaux, who was one of the more astute members of the assembly, withdrew his motion and supported another that was proposed by J. P. Werner of Coblenz, which specified that the German national assembly, as the instrument developed by the will of the people and the votes of the German nation for establishing unity and political freedom, declared that all determinations of individual German constitutions not in agreement with those of the *Parlament*'s constitution were to be regarded as valid only after decision by the latter assembly, quite apart from any previous validity. The motion was acceptable by both right and left, whose members were beginning to see each other as antagonists, because it was ambiguous enough to allow a variety of interpretations.

The resolution's smooth references to national unity, political freedom, and a constitution temporarily glossed over deep underlying problems. Past unsuccessful efforts to attain constitutional guarantees of fundamental individual rights in the several states had led many delegates to the belief that such guarantees could only be arrived at through a national constitution. This pervasive yearning for security of individual rights was the glue that held the *Parlament* together in its early days. Aside from the obvious difficulty inherent in gaining assent among the rulers, as well as drastic structural reorganization within the states that a new national constitution would require, there remained an unsolved question. Just what was the German nation? Did it include

German-speakers everywhere, even in Belgium, and embrace those in Austria where there was a huge Slavic population? Did it extend to German-speakers in such places as Schleswig-Holstein (under Denmark), Alsace (part of France), and Posen, where Prussians ruled a Polish-speaking native population? Prussia, Austria and Bavaria were all powers that could not be expected to yield easily to changes in the Metternich system. All this would inevitably come to the surface in the sessions of the Frankfurt *Parlament*.

Antagonists there may have been in the early stages, but it would have been unrealistic to describe the various developing factions as political parties. Many who came to Frankfurt as delegates were profoundly averse to the very idea of parties. They were convinced that the concepts of justice, right and liberty were inherent in the human mind. Basing their argument on Rousseau's *volonté générale*, they felt that somehow the entire assembly would arrive at correct decisions, and viewed party alignments with distinct antipathy. Georg von Vincke wondered if there were not something unsuitable, if factions met in the evening in order to consider a common course of action on an issue that would be discussed on the following day.

At the far left, on the other hand, the general will was thought of as the will of the people, and this conviction tended at least temporarily to impart firmness and unity of purpose to those who wanted to destroy monarchical governments. In any case, the left held a temporary advantage, in that experience in efforts to raise the level of political awareness among the workers had taught them that of necessity they would have to bend occasionally, for the sake of building a consensus. Such accommodation was foreign to the moderates, who looked on it with suspicion. As members of a fairly homogeneous sophisticated group, they relished argument and made a point of sharpening distinctions. This attitude was obviously detrimental to the formation of solid party alliances.[17]

Gradually it became apparent to everyone that party structure and discipline were inevitable and necessary, and like-minded delegates sought each other out in Frankfurt's various inns. As time went on, they spoke of the Milani, meaning the extreme right, the Kasino, meaning the center, or of the Landsberg as right center, the Württemberger Hof as the left center, the Augsburger Hof as the offshoot of the left center, the Deutscher Hof as the left, and Donnersberg as the extreme left. However, people drifted from one group to another as various issues came to their attention, and it was not until the fall of 1848 that formal statements of party programs were published.[18]

Georg Beseler described his curious problems in struggling to gain a winning majority for the Kasino party to which he belonged.[19] The center was in the majority, he said, and in most cases had a clear advantage over the left, but they had to have help from the conservative right. The difficulty lay in the circumstance that there were many factions within the conservative right, and at times even the Kasino itself had a certain amount of division. In fact, about forty members, most of them from Hannover, separated out to form a new group, the Landsberg, although on many questions they were still in harmony with the Kasino party. The exodus of the Landsberg group inspired some members of the conservative right to move over to the Kasino. It still was necessary to coax part of the left center away from the Württemberger Hof, where a more leftwing contingent had broken off to form a faction that met at the Westendhalle. There remained about one hundred members in the Württemberger Hof. Beseler had some secret conferences with three of the Württemberger Hof people, who thought that perhaps about forty of them might split off and commit themselves to a sort of cartel with the Kasino and Landsberg, but only on the condition that the conservatives who had recently joined the Kasino be excluded.

Since it had soon become evident that the tasks confronting the *Parlament* were of staggering complexity, standing committees were formed (fifteen in all), each charged with one specific aspect of the assembly's work. The most prominent among them were the committee on priorities and petitions, the committee on economic matters, and the committee on the constitution. The first, headed by Gabriel Riesser, was so nearly overwhelmed that it soon had to double its membership, from the original fifteen to thirty. Petitions and suggestions and demands were flooding in by the thousand, from every conceivable special interest group in Germany. The economics committee, led by Friedrich von Rönne, boasted experts like the industrialist Gustav Mevissen, Professor Bruno Hildebrand, and Karl Mathy, publisher and politician. The committee on the constitution included such luminaries as Friedrich Dahlmann, the venerable academician Theodor Welcker, Max von Gagern, and Robert Blum. Inevitably, discussion would be long, ardent, learned, and passionate. *Im Parla-Parla-Parlament das Reden nimmt kein End'*, mocked the poet Georg Herwegh. [In the *parla-parla-parlament* there's no end to the speech-making.]

The first major debate, on the nature and establishment of some sort of provisional central power, quickly revealed the threat of interminable discourse. Two hundred and twenty-three delegates had indicated their intention to speak, even before the debate started.[20] The attempt to find means for curtailing speeches in support of various motions evolved into a hot discussion of parliamentary order of business. This offered a way for the left to mitigate its disadvantage as a minority. The left wing factions in the early stages were much more tightly organized than those of the moderates or the far right. (They owed this to their experience in working more or less as an underground during the *Vormärz*.)

Arnold Ruge rose to offer a suggestion that appeared to be guileless enough. It might be practical, he said blandly, to cut down debate by causing the *Parlament* membership to divide into four parties. The proposal meant in practice that three well-organized groups on the left would confront one party on the right, namely the Kasino. Clearly, Ruge's idea was full of guile. It was countered by a suggestion from Gabriel Riesser, who was reluctant to recognize parties as such. He thought that the presiding officer might be given the option of arbitrary limitation of the number of speakers. This was followed by a proposal from Felix von Lichnowsky (extreme right), whose idea was that a speaker ought to be required to show that at least twenty members supported him, not necessarily as a formal party but as a group that held similar opinions on a given issue. Gagern responded that this seemed to him to be workable. "If you insist that republican views are to be doubly represented [by the Blum and Zitz factions], more speakers will have to be heard from the right."[21]

When the debate on the provisional central power finally got under way, disturbing news was arriving from Paris, then in the midst of the horrifying turmoil of the *journées de juin* in which workers on their hopeless barricades were being mercilessly crushed by the general Eugène Cavaignac. On 24 June, the executive commission (Arago, Garnier-Pagès, Marie, Lamartine and Ledru-Rollin) was required to surrender its power to Cavaignac as dictator. The four days of bloody conflict had cost some one thousand four hundred and sixty lives. Cavaignac declared martial law in Paris, setting an example for Berlin and Vienna in travails that lay ahead. Wholesale executions and arrests and deportations were to follow.

Even four months prior to the present debate, the liberal-minded industrialist Hermann von Beckerath had understood that German constitutional development could be seriously undermined by events in Paris that might cast an unfavorable light on the reform movement.[22] Writing to his intimate friend Fanny Adelson, the extreme leftwing

Figure 13 THE FRANKFURT *PARLAMENT* IN SESSION (1848–1849) Beneath a gigantic image of Germania as well as the imperial double eagle sat Heinrich von Gagern as president of the assembly, flanked by two vice-presidents and their secretaries. Below them was the speakers' podium, and in front of that were tables for stenographers and secretaries. Members of the press were accommodated behind the row of Ionic columns, nearest to the podium. There were reserved seats for guests—ladies on the right and gentlemen to the left, with the diplomatic corps crowded in behind them. The galleries above were open to the general public.

leader Johann Jacoby of Königsberg, made it clear that the bloody defeat of the workers had marked the turn of the European revolution. For the *bourgeoisie,* the June days were the signal that they must join the counterrevolution of the nobles against any forces that stood for a continuation of the revolution and for a democratic republic. "There is cowardice and prostration, and the hucksters and philistines are happily on top once more. In Germany as in France the old barefaced regime of self-interest and servitude [prevails]. Only the masters have been changed. Instead of the absolute monarchs there is an absolute *bourgeoisie*."[23] Any speaker who rose at Frankfurt, intending to address the subject of a provisional central power for Germany at that deplorable point in European history, must have been either blind or else a man of dauntless stoicism.

Onlookers like the Prussian ambassador to the still existent *Bundestag* viewed the prospects of the *Parlament*'s assembly with scepticism. The revolutionary body indubitably had the strength to knock down Prussia and united Germany, thought *Graf* August von Dönhoff, but its belief that it could create a living organism from the resulting wreckage was ill-founded. *Diese Macht glaubt sie vielleicht zu besitzen, besitz sie aber nicht.*[24] [It believes it has this strength, but does not possess it.]

Various proposals were advanced, and candidates considered, for a three-man directorate. People like Karl Mathy were named. Some of the proposals for membership in the executive triumvirate were extraordinary, almost to the point of being ridiculous. For example, there was the idea of what was jokingly referred to as the "three uncles" central power. The royal uncles in question were 1) *Erzherzog* Johann of Austria, the youngest brother of the late Emperor Franz and hence uncle of the reigning emperor, 2) Wilhelm the elder of Prussia, brother of the late Friedrich Wilhelm III and uncle of the regnant Friedrich Wilhelm IV, and 3) Carl of Bavaria, brother of Ludwig I, who had just abdicated, and uncle of the new king. The uncles, if chosen, would have formed an unsteady unit that would have been characterized by little initiative—obviously nothing more than a stop-gap. In her diary, Clotilde Koch-Gontard reported a dinner-table discussion in which Gagern reiterated his notion that there ought to be three princes heading the government. When Mathy commented that it would be preferable to have three members of the assembly instead, Gagern responded with some heat that this would be an insult to the princes.[25] Various involuted schemes were developed that were supposed to base a three-man directorate on the old *Bundestag*. This would have been extremely unpalatable to the left, whose members were calling for a single executive responsible to the *Parlament*.

The concept of a single chief executive brought suggestions that there might be a provisional *Reichsverweser* [vicar], an idea that had a certain attractiveness because it seemed to be simple and clear. The delegates on the left thought hopefully that such an office might serve as a bridge to subordination of the princes and transition to a republic under an elected chief executive in the American style.

Originally, Heinrich von Gagern had felt that Prussia ought to lead the new Germany, but as he witnessed the general weakness of Prussia in the ongoing Schleswig-Holstein affair, he began to have doubts. As presiding officer of the Frankfurt assembly, he was perforce sensitive to the mood of the delegates. The right wanted a multiple directorate of princes, nominated by the several governments, whereas the left wanted determination to be made by the *Parlament,* and furthermore they wanted one man to function as chief executive.

It is said that Karl Mathy was the man who coined the expression *kühner Griff* [bold stroke] that von Gagern used in proposing his solution to the impasse. The assembly could take matters into its own hands, he said, and create the new central power—an idea that delighted the left. They could choose one man as *Reichsverweser*—again delight on the left. AND, they could elect a prince—certainly a source of vast satisfaction to the right, where it was felt that the new arrangement must be headed by someone strong enough to compel recognition from the royal governments. The man proposed by von Gagern was none other than *Erzherzog* Johann of Austria (1782–1859), a person whose quiet dignity commanded respect, and whose marriage to a commoner (a postmaster's daughter) was a comfort to the left. "A familiar figure from an old-time legend."[26] Gagern's noble earnest demeanor carried the day, his speech provoking a storm of applause.

The sovereignty of the people had been sustained and the assembly voted enthusiastically for this Austrian candidate. "Not because he is a prince, but in spite of it," as Gagern said. In cold figures, there were 436 votes for *Erzherzog* Johann. For Heinrich von Gagern, 52 (from the left). Twenty-seven of the extreme left abstained. They might have cast votes for Robert Blum, but Blum had refused to allow his name to be used.

The event marked a tremendous victory for Gagern, who was cheered every bit as loudly as *Erzherzog* Johann, but in the quiet of his heart he should have known that he had destroyed all hope that Germany could be led by a Prussian Hohenzollern when he brought an Austrian Habsburg into the fabric of the new Germany.

The jubilation in the *Paulskirche* hid the fact that this was a hollow victory, the product of desperate improvization because the *Reichsverweser* was not to be responsible to the national assembly, and his ministers would have no clearly defined competence. The Frankfurt *Parlament* had "created a lance tip without a shaft."[27]

On 13 June 1848 the first *Demokratenkongress* was opened, meeting in Frankfurt under the presidency of Julius Fröbel, a far-left member of the *Parlament*. This congress gathered in full awareness that the radicals' cause was endangered, since they were in the minority at the assembly. It was hoped that the members from the left at Frankfurt could be joined by extra-parliamentary radicals, applying pressure on the *Parlament*. Indeed, sixty-six cities had sent two hundred and thirty-four delegates, representatives of eighty-nine democratic and workers' societies, who were calling for a *Gegenparlament* [counter parliament], thus fostering the threat of secession at Frankfurt. Blum's faction did not participate, but men like Zitz and Feuerbach of the Donnersberg party were there.[28] In the end not much was accomplished, although committees were established for the purpose of spreading and reinforcing the idea of true revolution.

There was deep discouragement in some quarters. Hecker wrote to Emma Herwegh on 11 July, "Greet Herwegh and tell him that if the people remain at the end of the year as they are today, the best he can do would be to go hunting buffalo with the Choctaws and Comanches. . . . If he wants to be happy and cut loose from civilization, I'll go with him."[29]

At almost the same time (12 July), Robert Blum wrote to his wife Jenny. He had met the celebrated *Erzherzog* Johann, and "I must tell you that he has such a worn out, dead, impassive face that he makes the most miserable impression, and any spark of hope attached to him is obliterated. . . . It is maddening . . . that Germany puts its trust in this man."[30]

Germany was not only putting its trust in *Erzherzog* Johann. Without clear awareness, trust was also being placed in the good faith of the old German *Bund*. A sign that this confidence was misplaced took the form of a statement by the still-existent *Bundestag* in its declaration of transfer of power to the Frankfurt national assembly on 12 July, a deceptive document that did not correspond to the spirit of the law establishing the provisional central power. It had not been the intention of the *Parlament* merely to suspend the *Bundestag*. It wanted to liquidate it, immediately and finally.

In theory, the competence of the Frankfurt assembly would rest on the fact of revolution, and any suggestion that it rested on agreement on the part of former governing bodies would have been rejected. But implicit in the declaration of 12 July was the idea of continuity. The *Bundestag* was asserting that although it was delegating certain authorities and powers, it remained competent to claim for itself the right to decide its own fate, in that its activity would end only after the act of transfer. It did not elect to dissolve itself, but only suspended its activity. The *Bundestag*, in an underhanded way, was putting itself into a state of suspended animation but holding onto its right to resume activity at a future time, if the provisional central power were to disintegrate for some reason. In other words, the declaration of 12 July 1848 was an assertion of the principle of agreement (*Vereinbarungsprinzip*) that was to be a potent weapon in the hands of Friedrich Wilhelm IV and even in the hands of the elected provisional central power.[31]

Ludwig Feuerbach sent a letter to his wife from Frankfurt on 14 July, saying that the torchlight procession honoring members of the extreme left in which multitudes of working people participated was much more imposing than all the "theatrical, ostentatious celebrations" that had welcomed *Erzherzog* Johann, in which no workers' association had taken part. He wondered if the *Reichsverweser* might not turn out to be something of a sham.[32]

Not long after the *Parlament* had organized itself into its committees and elected its chief executive, the unfortunate assembly began to betray itself. Inevitably, in the early decades of the century, the Polish question loomed large, and dragged with it the strands of incipient nationalism that had never quite subsided after the crisis along the Rhine in 1840 had first stirred the people. In April of 1848, the Frankfurt *Bundestag* had received a request from the Prussian government, in response to which it had declared that a part of the theoretically independent Grand Duchy of Posen was incorporated into Prussia. About six hundred thousand inhabitants of the territory were involved. Then on 2 May, there was a second annexation that brought another two hundred and eighty thousand individuals under the rule of Friedrich Wilhelm. General von Pfuel was charged by the Prussian government with the task of establishing a new line of demarcation between the Polish and German portions of Posen, with the understanding that German territory would take in some two-thirds of the Grand Duchy. Decision concerning this new frontier was published on 4 June, and the Poles objected fiercely, especially the super-patriots who had fled to France in earlier times. They regarded Posen as the core of a future Polish state and were outraged at what they called a fourth partition of their country.

In May delegations from a number of Polish organizations had presented themselves in Frankfurt, demanding that the new *Parlament* declare itself in favor of a reconstitution of Poland. They stated that the future independent nation would be democratic and would respect the rights of other nationals living within its borders.

In recently annexed Posen, twelve delegates had already been elected to the Frankfurt *Parlament*. The Prussian government was highly displeased to see Frankfurt entering into the picture. France meanwhile had officially protested against the incorporation of part of Posen into Prussia, somewhat cynically invoking the Congress of Vienna settlement. Russia began to fish in the troubled waters by associating herself with the Polish refugees in Paris, which had the effect of heightening Polish antagonism against Germany. The end result at Frankfurt was a burgeoning of chauvinist feelings. National pride became important—more so than unity or freedom.

On 24 July the actual debate on Posen began in the *Parlament*, where somehow the idea began to circulate that Poland's rebirth ought properly to originate in Warsaw, not in Posen. There were, after all, so many Germans living in Posen—about four hundred and nine thousand of them, plus almost seventy-seven thousand Jewish people, as opposed to about eight hundred and forty-eight thousand Poles.[33]

Robert Blum tried to inject an element of restraint into a discussion that was rapidly becoming febrile. He asked the assembly to be consistent, not to swing back and forth on territorial and ethnic considerations from case to case, as it seemed to be doing. He repeated an argument that he had already offered on an earlier occasion. If ethnic issues were to be decisive in the Posen question, "we would logically have to advance the same requirement for Alsace and logically also for the very large German population in Italy, and the same for the large German population in Belgium—in other words, we would have to declare war on the entire world." Blum thought that any changes in boundaries ought to be made in consultation with other powers. A statesmanlike contribution, in other words.[34]

Blum's reasonable remarks were countered by Wilhelm Jordan of Prussia (also speaking for the left). This speech has frequently been singled out by latterday historians for bitter attack, with dark hints that the ultranationalism of Bismarck and Hitler might have its source here. A more sympathetic assessment would be that Jordan was speaking in 1848, and at that time impulses of nationalism were stirring all over Europe, and it is only fair to remember that he was speaking as a man of his day. Misguided, perhaps, but hardly excessive or evil.[35] However, his actual words were chilling and it is difficult, with late Twentieth-Century hindsight, not to think of their dread implications.

Jordan's argument was based on the fact that at least parts of Posen had originally been German, and that it was to Germans that Posen owed its prosperous cities. True, much had been taken by German conquest, but on the other hand, Germans had conquered in Posen just as much by the plough as by the sword. They had doubled, even tripled the productivity of the region. There were other considerations: realistically, little could be done to restore Poland to her original status because the eastern territories could only be recovered by bloody conflict with Russia, which of course was not at all in Germany's interest. Besides, an independent Poland would probably claim Baltic regions that Germany would certainly defend in a struggle to the death if need be. The well-being of the Fatherland had to come first.

> Our right is nothing other than the right of the stronger, the right of conquest—The German conquests in Poland were a natural necessity. . . . The right of history knows only the laws of nature . . . that a people through its mere existence has not yet any right to political independence but can only assert itself through force, to be a state among others. . . . The much deplored partition of Poland was not the murder of a nation but nothing more than the proclamation of a death that had already occurred, nothing more than confirmation of the dissolution of a corpse that could no longer be tolerated among the living. . . . The enthusiasm of Polish agitators is . . . unadulterated religious fanaticism. . . . Prussia has planted the seed of a Polish people . . . prepared a cradle for it in which, under German protection . . . it can develop without hindrance.[36]

Blum indignantly tried to persuade his fellow leftists to expel Jordan from his Deutscher Hof party as an undesirable apostate, but the effort failed. (Jordan ultimately left Blum's party and moved over to the Landsberg group.)

Jordan's speech found resonance throughout the assembly, with the result that the majority voted to recognize the Prussian annexation of Posen and to seat the delegates who had been elected, rejecting Blum's attempt to push through a motion that the question of Posen be carefully examined in more detail, and Arnold Ruge's call for a European congress. Carried along by its wave of patriotic fervor, the *Parlament* surged against the Poland decisions of its own *Vorparlament* and even went so far as to vote down a resolution that it was the sacred duty of the German people to work together toward the reestablishment of an independent Poland. The erstwhile liberals had lost sight of their original dream for Germany, and had placed their reliance on Prussia instead. All this had an ominous look as far as the overall success of the national assembly was concerned.

All this aside, there remains the evidence of an astonishing collective oblivion as far as the past was concerned. Were the men of the

Frankfurt *Parlament* truly so ignorant, so obtuse—or so innocent—
that they were able blandly to overlook all the excruciating negotiations of the Congress of Vienna that had taken place just barely a
generation before? Had they forgotten the pulling and hauling that
went on between peace-loving Castlereagh, the impressively intelligent Tallyrand, wily Metternich, and unpredictable Alexander I of
Russia?

Storm clouds continued to gather throughout the summer. There
were distinct signs of discord in the wake of a decree issued by
Erzherzog Johann's newly appointed war minister to the effect that
all troops in the states that made up the German confederation were
to express "fealty" to the *Reichsverweser* on 6 August.[37] On that
auspicious day, there would be parades, the statement that the
Reichsverweser would from that time on be the commander-in-chief
of Germany's armed forces would be read, and the troops, led by their
officers, would greet this announcement with a resounding triple cheer.
The order was ambiguous, not requiring an oath of loyalty to *Erzherzog*
Johann or to the provisional central power, or even to the Frankfurt
assembly, but the intention was clear enough. If there were any revolutionary moves made against the Frankfurt assembly, federal troops,
united under their new commander-in-chief, would be ready to quell
them.

Commanding officers responded in various ways, none of which
offered much encouragement to those who were intent on establishing German unity. In some places—at Aachen, for example—there was
an out-and-out boycott, with a military parade on 5 August instead of
on the appointed day. During that celebration, one set of troops cheered
Friedrich Wilhelm IV while another remained silent. This episode ended
in street brawls. At Krefeld, the festivities were boycotted by Protestants, but celebrated by Catholics. Some towns draped their main streets
with Prussian flags. Protestant towns like Elberfeld were in a hostile
mood. Their citizens seem to have felt that the Catholics were gloat-
ing over them. On the other hand, a flamboyant editorial appeared in
the *Rhein- und Moselzeitung* that urged election of *Erzherzog* Johann
as emperor of a Catholic Rhineland. The civil guard at Worms avoided
the officially appointed day, but on 5 August proclaimed loyalty to the
new central power rather than to the new commander-in-chief. At
Düsseldorf, the democrats split into two groups, one of which celebrated under the aegis of the moderate local association for democratic monarchy, while the radicals in their *Volksverein* held a rally of

their own. At the end of the day there was a torchlight procession that culminated at the foot of a new statue of Germania, where flags of the states of the *Bund* were laid down by students from the Düsseldorf academy of art, all theatrically garbed in medieval costumes. A herald then arrived bearing the black-red-gold colors and the crowd raised its deep voice in Arndt's anthem *Das ganze Deutschland soll es sein.*[38] [All Germany it shall be.]

Clearest evidence of undercurrents of popular feeling appeared in the textile manufacturing town of Mönchengladbach, where there had been clashes between Catholics and a Protestant minority even before the festival. In June, youths from neighboring Rheydt (Protestant) had marched into the city behind a Prussian flag. This had precipitated a riot. The Prussian flag again figured in pre-festival arguments, where Protestants called for display of their black-and-white Prussian banner beside the new tricolor. The dispute remained unresolved, with the result that the Protestants of Mönchengladbach declined to have anything to do with the festival. On the eve of the celebration, a mob attacked the homes of two defiant Protestant manufacturers, who displayed the Prussian flag. The Mönchengladbach festival ran smoothly the next day, with a grand procession that included young boys carrying the tricolor flag, girls in white, wreathed with oak leaf crowns and wearing tricolor sashes, followed by members of the local gymnasts, the *Bürgerwehr* [civil guard], and the choral societies. That night, when houses were festively illuminated, stones smashed the windows of Protestant pastor Zilleisen's house. This clergyman had been a conspicuous leader in the pre-festival discussions. Protestant-Catholic and Hohenzollern-Habsburg rivalry had become interwoven, and the event had become "a festival of disunity".[39]

In Potsdam there was a parade and a huge folk festival, but the king refused to participate, and not far off, in Berlin, handbills appeared that were conspicuously headed "Hurrah for Prussia!—Is the Prussian army to offer its allegiance to an Austrian prince? No!" [40]

Most ominous of all was the deluge of addresses that swirled around Friedrich Wilhelm. The drive had been organized by four new conservative societies under the leadership of a publication called the *Neue preussische Zeitung* (popularly known as the *Kreuzzeitung* because of the Iron Cross on its masthead). Forty-six thousand signatures had been collected for this massive protest against the Prussian army's homage to *Erzherzog* Johann as commander-in-chief.[41] This was clear evidence that a conservative counterrevolutionary force was beginning to gather strength.

The Frankfurt parliamentarians were destined to spend an uncomfortable summer. The debate over basic rights dragged along to such an extent that caricatures began to appear in shop windows, depicting the speakers as self-important wind-bags.

To compound the difficulties, a new problem had arisen. The cathedral construction society at Cologne was planning a spectacular celebration of the sixth centennial of their *Kölner Dom*. The cathedral had stood unfinished for centuries, and work had only been resumed upon discovery of the original plans. The decision to complete the structure according to those plans had inspired a successful *Dombaufest* in 1842, when Friedrich Wilhelm had laid a new foundation stone.[42] At that time, the cathedral had become romantically associated in the public mind with ideas of German unity and Germany's future. Now the builders, anticipating their second celebration, had issued invitations to Friedrich Wilhelm, to *Erzherzog* Johann, to an impressive number of bishops, and also to the newly appointed ministers of Johann's cabinet, as well as to leading members of the Frankfurt and Prussian national assemblies. Possibly because of the moderates' general uneasiness and distrust of the radicals within the *Parlament* at Frankfurt, reaction to the invitation had originally been reluctant, but had gradually changed into a resounding consensus on their part in favor of it.[43] The radical left reacted by boycotting the festivities and going off defiantly to a meeting in the Rheinpfalz.

The moderates took ship on two steamboats (the *Schiller* and the *König*) and sailed downstream in beautiful sunny weather, cheered all along the route by flag-waving crowds. The boom of military salutes from the fortresses of Koblentz and Ehrenbreitstein unnerved them somewhat because it was an all too vivid reminder of Prussian military might, but *Erzherzog* Johann aboard the *Schiller* accepted the salutes of Prussian troops smartly lined up along the shore as a satisfactory acknowledgment of his status as commander-in-chief.

Friedrich Wilhelm meanwhile was the victim of a dreadful reception at Catholic Düsseldorf as he passed through en route to Cologne. No military display there. On the contrary, his Majesty had to face an angry crowd that pelted him with horse manure.[44] When an indignant delegation of Protestants loyal to their Prussian monarch arrived from Elberfeld, the Düsseldorf mob attacked. There were brawls in the taverns and crowds in the streets wore red ribbons and sang Arndt's *Was ist des Deutschen Vaterland?* [What is the German's Fatherland?] at the top of their lungs. The loyal delegation was jeeringly serenaded by leftist fellow citizens with *Katzenmusik* when it returned home to

Elberfeld, but the town itself rallied and offered a wild welcome to Friedrich Wilhelm on 16 August. Elberfeld was Protestant, to be sure, in sharp contrast to Düsseldorf, which was not.

Erzherzog Johann had had his own difficulties en route to Cologne. At Mainz there were enormous hostile crowds who watched him in silence. Flags fluttered everywhere, but they were red.

At Cologne itself, the Prussian king arrived amid such a thunder of heavy ordnance that there could be little doubt about the identity of the true commander-in-chief of the assembled forces.[45] As the festivities progressed, religious and political differences did not seem to carry much weight. Everybody was eager to watch all the pageantry, though many were taken aback when they saw the *Reichsverweser* decked out in a Prussian uniform.

The men from the Frankfurt *Parlament* went almost unnoticed in the general crush. In the initial meeting, they stood packed so tightly that when Heinrich von Gagern attempted to present them to the king, he could do no more than introduce a few who happened to be in the front row. Friedrich Wilhelm was not too interested, and even interrupted Gagern's courteous words in order to speak to *Erzherzog* Johann, who was passing by in the hall, and in his response to Gagern's remarks, he said in a clear voice that his hearers should not forget that there were still princes in Germany, and that he was one of them. Georg Beseler adds a discreet footnote to his account, to the effect that "That is the wording of the official version. I believe I heard *and I am one of the most powerful.*"[46]

The processions that marked the celebration had certain disturbing aspects. In the first one, though the artisans who were engaged in the actual work on the cathedral marched, carrying their tools, the masters and foremen marched separately from the journeymen. In the second parade, following the reconsecration of the cathedral, there was a gaudy assemblage of municipal authorities, mercantile leaders, local notables, military units, and clerics from a wonderful variety of religious orders, but workers were totally missing.

Altogether, as a symbol of national unity, it was curious to see how much emphasis was laid on the presence of the nobility (not only Friedrich Wilhelm and *Erzherzog* Johann, but also other princes of the Prussian royal family), and so little on the people. As Jonathan Sperber observed, the symbolism relating to unity was constantly represented by the unity of Germany's princes.—Moreover, it was significant that the unity of the secular princes was "quite literally blessed by the princes of the church".[47]

Figure 14 FRIEDRICH WILHELM IV, KING OF PRUSSIA (1795–1861)

On the following day a festive gathering was held at the small abbey of Saint Alban's at nearby Gürzenich, where Friedrich Wilhelm was purposefully gracious. His Majesty was an unpredictable man, everyone knew,[48] and they braced themselves when he stepped forward, wine glass in hand. His first toast was in honor of *Erzherzog* Johann, who returned the compliment. The king then raised his glass again, this time in honor of the Frankfurt assembly — a gesture that generated wild, somewhat stunned enthusiasm. *Und Fürstenwein ist teuer Wein* [and princes' wine is expensive wine: Georg Herwegh] Gagern followed with a toast to German unity, drawing even lustier cheers from the *Parlament* members. In spite of all this general good humor and sense of a crisis successfully weathered, the Prussian ruler had dominated the Cologne affair, and it was well understood that accommodation would have to be made to princes.[49]

The delegates returned to Frankfurt and reopened their exhausting debate on basic rights and the constitution. These unfortunate men have been jeered at as self-important windbags, but the problem did not lie in their supposed arrogance. What critics have failed to understand is that the men of the *Parlament* were wrestling with their disastrous lack of a shared working vocabulary. *Liberty* and *equality*, for example, were conflated and confused in their minds. Reformers and radicals alike were using these concepts recklessly, talking past each other in a heedless manner, each speaker applying his own meaning to the potentially explosive terms. It has even been asserted that this product of their inexperience held within it the seeds of ultimate defeat for the whole revolutionary reform effort.[50]

Before long they were to confront another formidable problem.[51] Friedrich Wilhelm's defense of the provisional government of Schleswig-Holstein had developed into a troublesome war from which the Prussian monarch was anxious to extricate himself. He had never been happy in the thought that he was defending revolutionists, and although his ground forces had been successful, not only occupying the disputed duchies but also crossing the frontier into true Danish territory, the military operation had proved to be a serious threat to the prosperous free ports along the Baltic and the North Sea because Denmark had a strong naval fleet, which Germany did not. Moreover, England, Sweden and Russia had expressed deep displeasure. To continue military aggression against Denmark would mean not only difficulty for the ports but also the risk of a general European war. The extreme demands of the superpatriots in Frankfurt and in the political clubs were alienating England more and more, in the opinion of Prussia's ambassador Bunsen.

England had offered to mediate the dispute, even going so far as to outline a proposed partition of the disputed duchies, and Sweden had supported the idea of an armistice. In Germany itself meanwhile, hot feelings of patriotism had spread, and the Frankfurt *Parlament* felt committed to the liberation of Schleswig and its incorporation into the new German *Reich*. Wilhelm Raabe was to write of young volunteers who had left school or the parental home with Arndt's *Vaterlandslied* on their lips, feathers waving on their hats, their weapons gleaming in the sun, and who were streaming north in order to join the fray. One of the most ardent speakers in the *Parlament* was Friedrich Dahlmann, who proclaimed that the cause of the German nation would be decapitated if justice were not done to Schleswig and Schleswig's cause. He was so convinced of its importance that he was indifferent to the general equilibrium of Europe as a whole.[52]

With an increasingly chauvinist mood prevailing, it was therefore a shaken, pale-faced Johann Gustav Heckscher, *Erzherzog* Johann's new minister for foreign affairs, who took the floor, announcing the painful news that an armistice had indeed been signed between Prussia and Denmark at Malmö, under the aegis of Sweden, on 26 August 1848. "A terrible thunderclap," wrote Heinrich Laube, recalling the stressful scene.

One major difficulty lay in the uncertain status of the Frankfurt assembly vis-à-vis the old *Bundestag*. In April, the *Bundestag* had decided that the Danish attack not only against Holstein but also against Schleswig fell under the provisions of original Vienna decisions at the conclusion of the Napoleonic war and had therefore placed its tenth confederation army corps, comprising forces from Hannover, Mecklenburg, Oldenburg, Braunschweig and the free cities under the command of the Prussian field marshal, General von Wrangel. Denmark's naval blockade had been the response to this move.

As early as June, the Frankfurt assembly had declared that the Schleswig-Holstein affair concerned the German nation as a whole and was hence within the competence of the national *Parlament*. With the election of *Erzherzog* Johann as head of the new central power came his designation as commander-in-chief of the armed forces of the new German *Reich*, with assent on the part of the *Bundestag*. From that time on, presumably the Prussian forces in Schleswig-Holstein were acting on behalf of the new governmental head in Frankfurt.

In reaction to the announcement of the *fait accompli* of the Malmö armistice, the Frankfurt assembly was aghast. Prussia had entered into the agreement unilaterally, without consulting the new authorities in Frankfurt. It was true that in the beginning, Prussia had been charged by the *Bundestag* to act on its behalf, using its troops, but with the election of *Erzherzog* Johann, all military forces had come under his jurisdiction. Furthermore, in preliminary negotiations, General von Wrangel had insisted upon ratification of any ensuing treaty by the *Reichsverweser*, but the Danes had pointed out (correctly) that the new German *Reich* had not yet received international recognition. This preliminary discussion therefore had broken down on 24 July.

The Prussian government then asked for—and received—agreement from *Erzherzog* Johann's cabinet, under the leadership of Karl Leiningen, the distinguished half-brother of Queen Victoria, that it might act in the name of the *Reich*, but only on condition that a number of stipulations were honored. The new Prussian negotiator, General Gustav von Below, found that the Danish government was reluctant to accept these restrictions and had therefore concluded the armistice agreement of 26 August in total disregard of the ministry's requirements. Overlooked therefore were the Leiningen cabinet's stipulation that all laws and regulations of the Schleswig-Holstein provisional government should stand, that part of the German federal troops should remain in the duchies, and that ratification should depend upon the decision of the *Reichsverweser* and the *Parlament*. Furthermore, the negotiations with Denmark had been conducted in what might almost be called a furtive manner, with the unmistakable intention of excluding Max von Gagern, the emissary from the Leiningen cabinet.

Von Radowitz sent a detailed report of the situation to his constituents, outlining the difficulties that confronted the Prussian government, the *Bundestag*, and the Frankfurt *Parlament*.[53] Schleswig, he reminded his readers, had never belonged either to the old German *Reich* or to the German confederation, and could not legally be incorporated into the German *Bund* without the consent of the princes. Moreover, part of northern Schleswig had a preponderance of Danish inhabitants. The governments of Russia, Sweden, England and France were inclined to side with Denmark, regarding the use of force on the part of Prussia as reprehensible aggression.

Because of the burden placed on Prussia and the possible consequences (even a full-scale European war), it was Prussia's duty to seek a peaceful solution. The new central power had given authority to Prussian negotiators under certain formal conditions, but to reject the resulting treaty would be highly inadvisable. Denmark had been driven from the duchies, but in no way in such fashion that arbitrary conditions could be imposed, as if Denmark had been totally defeated. Denmark was still master of the seas, and the northern powers could be expected to enter into the hostilities if Jutland were occupied by the Prussians.

Figure 15 JOSEPH MARIA VON RADOWITZ (1797–1853)

Admittedly, continued Radowitz, there were certain disadvantageous arrangements made in the armistice document. A man hated by the duchies had been made head of the government there, for example, yet there was nothing to preclude a future settlement that would be satisfactory to Schleswig-Holstein. The members of the radical left at Frankfurt were of course in favor of rejection of the treaty because it fitted well into their overall plan. In Radowitz's eyes, the extreme left was deliberately destructive, working toward further revolution. It should be understood, he repeated, that the whole burden of the Schleswig-Holstein operation would fall on Prussia and the northern cities, not on the southern provinces that were so clamorous for continuation of the war.

Public opinion throughout Germany was placing the new *Parlament* and the *Reichsverweser* in an extremely awkward position. Recognition of the treaty would imply the *Parlament*'s approval of the independent action of Prussia. On the other hand, a demand that the treaty be rejected would throw the weight of responsibility onto the shoulders of *Erzherzog* Johann and his cabinet, who knew full well that they had not the means for conducting a war against Denmark and the Danish fleet. Besides, the *Erzherzog* and his ministers felt the ground shifting under their feet. They were, after all, creatures of the *Parlament,* even though Johann himself bore no responsibility to it.

Everything was threatening to break loose. All the dammed-up animosities and frustrations were rising to the surface—the antagonistic attitude of the extreme left toward Prussia, the straining of the center not to have a rupture with Friedrich Wilhelm, the ill-concealed satisfaction on the part of the rightist advocates of the small states and the leftist radicals who were pushing for a renewal of the revolution and abolition of all monarchies. The unfortunate duchies of Schleswig and Holstein were almost forgotten because what was at stake was the future of the Frankfurt assembly and of Germany as a whole.

There was a furious debate within the assembly (4 September). The most impassioned man at the *Paulskirche* was Dahlmann, raging that Germany's truth, honor and justice were hanging by a thread. Reasonable arguments were presented by various members of the moderate center, but to no avail. Speakers included Bassermann and Radowitz and Blum and Lichnowsky. Objections to the treaty began to coalesce around the disappointing conditions set by that document. Even in London, there was dissatisfaction. At the end of a stormy session, the treaty was rejected by a vote of 238 to 221—much too close for anyone's comfort.

This unprecedented victory for the left was managed by an uneasy combination of the true left, the Westendhall, and the left center along with the delegation from Schleswig-Holstein, but it was too precarious to be sustained. When the Leiningen cabinet submitted its resignation and the responsibility for forming a new cabinet was handed over to Dahlmann, it soon became obvious that the task was beyond him. Dahlmann, in the opinion of the historian Valentin, had preached and issued prophetic pronouncements but he had never had any instinct for the actual state of affairs, and was unable to perform like a practiced politician who knows that he has his own cabinet already in his pocket when he is called on.[54] By the eighth of September, he realized that he was incapable of forming a cabinet and handed his appointment back to *Erzherzog* Johann, who promptly requested that Friedrich von Hermann, a delegate from Bavaria and a vice-president of the assembly, take over the task. Hermann also failed.

Meanwhile, diplomatic notes were flying and pressure was being brought to bear on the Frankfurt men. The hapless *Reichsverweser* consulted representatives of various factions, trying at least to gain a sense of public opinion. When he was told of a rumor that he himself might resign if the treaty were not recognized, he responded wrathfully that this was a downright lie. However, he went on to say that "You can do what you want about Schleswig-Holstein, but there must be no halfway measures. Either or! The situation is such that a decisive step has to be taken."[55] Evidently *Herzog* Christian August of Augustenburg was of the same mind. He arrived in Frankfurt, where he urged the delegates from Schleswig-Holstein to learn patience. All Europe must not become inflamed over this problem.

The united committees of the *Parlament* had been in steady consultation and appeared on 12 September with their report. A majority of twelve sustained the original vote against the armistice, while a minority of ten spoke in favor of accepting the treaty. The respected Ernst Moritz Arndt originally sided with the majority but during the discussion he shifted his position, so that the committee vote was broken evenly, eleven to eleven. The debate lasted three days. Two speakers who had firmly insisted on rejection of the treaty spoke now in its favor, but Robert Blum stood fast; he warned that the revolution had halted before the throne, but this time there could well be a mighty uprising that would overthrow the monarchs. Four delegates from Schleswig-Hostein suggested surprizingly that the armistice ought to be ratified because the Danes would no doubt modify their position. The words of *Herzog* Christian August must have carried weight with them. It was this action on the part of the Schleswig-Holstein delegates that brought about a reversal of the original vote. Now there were 257 in favor of the armistice, with 236 opposed. Even fiery Dahlmann voted affirmatively. Many of the delegates on the left sprang to their feet and departed from the hall.

For various reasons, everyone in the *Paulskirche* was astounded and full of dismay. Even the action of individuals seemed strange and contradictory. If Dahlmann had stormed out, it would have been understandable, but he reversed his vote. The superpatriots, those who had been most vociferous in their expressions of love and loyalty for the Fatherland, had supported Prussia, to the humiliation of the assembly. The leftwing extremists, those suspected internationalists, were the ones who had stood firm, calling for recognition of the assembly's authority and the honor of the Fatherland. Schleswig-Holstein—well, what could one say? And what were the prospects of a constitution and a unified Germany now? What about the people in the streets?

Ever since Frankfurt had become the designated center of official activity, the city had attracted agitators and organizers of every leftist stripe, and numerous democratic societies and workers' congresses had met there. Once again, the new railway system played its part. Rapid transit for large numbers of people had become the accepted norm.

On 17 September therefore, it was inevitable that a huge crowd of irritated members of the working classes should assemble at the popular meeting ground called the *Pfingstweide*. Here, in the thousands, they were harangued by fiery speakers, some of them leftist delegates of the *Parlament*. One of the most inflammatory was Franz Zitz. There was all manner of irrational talk—the *Parlament* should be disbanded and a new election called. The left should leave the assembly and proclaim a republic. Various leaders like von Gagern and Heckscher (a member of the new cabinet), and Mathy should be hunted down. In the end, it was decided that the *Parlament* should be confronted with the statement that those who voted in favor of the armistice were traitors to the German nation.

Erzherzog Johann, aware of the general desperation of his predicament, appointed a new cabinet head, in the person of Anton von Schmerling of Austria, who had already been a member of the Leiningen cabinet. Schmerling was a man of incisive intellect, capable of quick coldblooded decisions. He immediately called for troops whose assignment would be the protection of the *Parlament*. Those who were moved into place were Prussians and Austrians (two thousand of them) from nearby Mainz.

Early in the morning of 18 September, Reinhard Carl Theodor Eigenbrodt, the deputy of the Hesse-Darmstadt government, sitting in his study, became aware that excited people were running back and forth as if something were about to happen. Eigenbrodt was a close friend of Heinrich von Gagern, and knew that Gagern's physical danger was great in those overheated days. He worried about the safety of Gagern's children because the house where the family lived was remote and unprotected. In his anxiety, he went to the Gagern residence, and found Clotilde Koch-Gontard there. She too was concerned and suggested that Eigenbrodt might take the children to Darmstadt, where they would be safe. (Gagern's wife meanwhile would remain with Clotilde Koch-Gontard.)[56] A note was sent to Gagern at the *Paulskirche*, asking for his permission to send the children away. This assent was quickly given. With some difficulty, a driver was found, though he was reluctant to move through the city—his vehicle might be taken for building a barricade. After a roundabout trip and a crossing of the Main by ferry, Eigenbrodt and the children safely boarded a train, hearing gunfire in the city. By that time, it was about two in the afternoon, Eigenbrodt thought.[57]

What Eigenbrodt had heard during his departure was the firing on the square in front of the *Paulskirche*. In spite of the fact that troops had been deployed near the church, one of the rear doors had been breached and members of the mob started to break in. They were halted by von Gagern's roar that entry into this "holy place" was treason. Behind barred doors, the assembly tried to go on with its business, in spite of the rattle of muskets and sporadic gunfire outside. An artillery attack on the barricades by incoming Hessian troops started just at about the time of Eigenbrodt's departure with the Gagern children.

The square had been quickly cleared, but menace was in the air. During the previous night, Heckscher, the one who had had to announce that Prussia and Denmark had agreed to an armistice, had been stoned and escaped being hanged only by fleeing to Höchst, where he was taken into protective custody by the police. The Westendhalle inn was stormed and devastated. In fact, disorder prevailed in many of Germany's major cities, especially in Cologne and at Worringen am Rhein, where thousands gathered and the red flag of revolution was defiantly unfurled.

Revolutions have to have their martyrs. Two *Parlament* delegates, both men with considerable military experience, namely General Hans von Auerswald and Felix Lichnowsky, rode out in order to reconnoiter and were trapped by wandering members of the Frankfurt mob. They were dragged from the place where they had concealed themselves, and Auerswald was killed on the spot. Lichnowsky suffered a much grimmer fate. His name had been conspicuously on the list of those to be hunted down, and therefore he could expect no mercy. From the very beginning of the Frankfurt sessions, he had been the most talked-about man in the *Parlament*. His arrogant manner, his careless use of

Figure 16 THE MOB ATTACKS LICHNOWSKY AT FRANKFURT (18 September 1848)

the German language, his wealth, his much publicized amatory exploits—all had brought down on his head a combination of public wrath, envy and hatred, as well as the witless adulation that today surrounds a Hollywood figure. A drumhead court pronounced the death sentence on him and the protracted, sadistic murder began. According to Clotilde Koch-Gontard, he was hacked at, his bones broken,[58] and after that he was tied to a tree as a target, with a placard attached to him. *Vogelfrei* [outlaw] it read. Although the victim had been the object of public hatred, this could hardly justify the viciousness of the lynch mob.

Ludwig Bamberger, a man of the far left, met with colleagues late that night at the inn called Zum hahner Hof—a remote place on the edge of town that offered easy access to incoming peasants. As they sat around a table discussing the appalling events of the day and trying to estimate the damage to their cause, two unknown persons arrived, much excited, with eyewitness reports of the death of Lichnowsky. One of them had a souvenir—a piece of cloth ripped from Lichnowsky's coat as a trophy. He was a private tutor from Bockenheim, and "he did not say that he himself had participated in the killing, and I thought it unlikely because of his personality, but he slowly related details of the death of innocent Auerswald with precision, and with a foul coldbloodedness that made a sinister impression on me."[59] In 1849, after he had fled to the United States, Julius Fröbel experienced a chilling throw-back to this event when a round-faced, "well-nourished" young man affably greeted him by name on the streets of New York. Finding that Fröbel did not know him, the young man was astounded. "Why, I'm the one who murdered Lichnowsky!" [60]

The two martyrs were buried with all the pomp that Frankfurt could muster, but dreadful hurt had been suffered by the *Parlament*. Any semblance of trust and cooperation between moderates and radicals had been wiped out. There were calls for the arrest and investigation of members who had addressed the public gathering at the *Pfingstweide* meeting on the eve of the killings. Von Radowitz wrote gravely:

> I am far from giving biased hearing to current rumor, but it is impossible to close one's eyes to the truth that the intellectual instigators of the incident were not those who stood behind the barricades. In word and writing, there has been an incessant effort everywhere in the course of the past three months to represent the democratic republic as the form desired by the people, the only form that will satisfy it, and to present the National Assembly as the sole hindrance.[61]

Discontent and rebellion had not subsided in Baden after the defeat of Hecker's spring insurrection, though leadership had fallen into the hands of Gustav Struve, who had taken refuge in Switzerland. In Basel, he occupied himself as editor of the newspaper, the *Deutscher Zuschauer*. Word of the Frankfurt uprising generated tremendous excitement among the veterans of the *Heckerzug*. They were eager to make a second attempt, this time with the intention of proclaiming a provisional republican government, in the hope that a revolutionary movement would spread across Germany.

Accompanied by a handful of unarmed insurgents, Struve crossed over to Lörrach in Baden on the afternoon of 22 September. There they were met by volunteers, all armed and ready for action. Briskly, the revolutionists issued a printed proclamation of the new German republic, using a local press that they had commandeered. All "medieval" burdens and obligations were declared void, and all lands belonging to the state, church or to royalists were confiscated for public use. There was a general call-up of all males between the ages of eighteen and fifty who were capable of bearing arms. Further, funds from *sämmtliche in Lörrach befindliche Kassen* [all money chests located in Lörrach] were taken over in the name of the republic.

Eduard Kaiser, who lived in Lörrach, was making his peaceful way along a country road near the Swiss border when he was picked up by Struve's men and taken to an inn where Struve himself told him that he was a prisoner. Under guard, he was hustled to the main square of Lörrach, where the appropriated press was busily turning out proclamations. Even a "Great Seal of the German Republic" was hastily devised by a local manufacturer. Before he was released, the prisoner heard Struve's harangue to the populace. In that speech, Struve assured his hearers that at that very moment the republic had been acclaimed with enthusiasm in Karlsruhe, Stuttgart, Mainz, Frankfurt, Berlin and Saxony. "This was a deliberate big lie. A lesser lie would not have been so quickly and joyously believed. That's the way people are."[62]

By 24 September, Struve estimated that his army comprised about ten thousand well armed men, though "well armed" has to be taken with a grain of salt, in view of Struve's further remark that hardly suggests adequate ordnance for an army. "Two casks of powder were quickly supplied. One contained cannon powder, however, and could not be utilized. The second cask was used at once for flintlock cartridges, which were prepared on the upper floor of the town hall."[63] Struve's formidable force was dispersed in a two-hour battle with a couple of battalions of regular troops, a squadron of dragoons, and a few pieces of artillery. Struve himself was captured.

Like the Frankfurt rising, which brought about an irreparable split in the Parlament, this fruitless little revolution of Struve's caused serious damage, in that public opinion began to shift toward indignation and disgust. Private property had been taken by the revolutionists! Property-owners everywhere were grim. When it was realized that there had been minor outbreaks elsewhere—at Kassel, Berlin, and Cologne—the anger level rose perceptibly. Struve, passing among the previously enthusiastic inhabitants of the Wiesenthal as a prisoner, narrowly escaped being torn apart by enraged citizens. The cause of

Figure 17 GUSTAV STRUVE PROCLAIMS A GERMAN REPUBLIC (22 September 1848)

the radicals suffered even more than that of the *Parlament*, and the forces of reaction started to gather. Frankfurt was under martial law, civil guards were disbanded in many municipalities, and newspapers were suspended. Even Switzerland moved in the direction of hostility. Finding that more than half the participants in the *Struvezug* had been refugees from the Hecker insurrection, the government at Bern decreed that all individuals who had enjoyed the right of asylum and had taken part in the recent uprising were not to be allowed to return.

A nasty little saying gained popularity. *Gegen Demokraten helfen nur Soldaten* [only soldiers can handle democrats]. This was the title of a pamphlet published anonymously by the conservative Prussian officer, von Griesheim. It was repeated and relished by conservatives everywhere, including *Erzherzog* Georg von Mecklenburg-Strelitz, who wrote to his nephew Friedrich Wilhelm IV that Goethe never wrote anything that pleased him so much.[64] The term "democrats" was extended to include many social reformers who had not been revolutionists at all.

A disheartened Robert Blum wrote a disconsolate letter to his beloved Jenny on 4 October. "If it would not be disgraceful to separate from one's fellow combattants in misfortune, I'd be inclined to scrape together everything I have and either emigrate or buy myself a mill or something of the sort in some peaceful valley of southern Germany, and never go back into the world again. Just watch it all from a distance, without taking part."[65]

The story of the 1848 revolution was far from played out, and it had not been confined to south Germany and the Rhineland. While the men of Frankfurt debated and the men of Baden fought, another drama was unfolding in Berlin. Following the September disaster in Frankfurt, Arnold Ruge wrote to his wife that "The Berlin assembly is the true national assembly. Its victory is a victory of the revolution, whereas the victory of the present [Frankfurt] assembly is a victory for the Right."[66]

While the liberals of Frankfurt were casting anxious eyes in the direction of Berlin, conservatives in Potsdam in their turn were watching the course of events in Austria with keen attention.

Notes

1 Paine, *The Rights of Man*, p. 36.

2 The *Paulskirche* was built between the years 1789 and 1833 as a Protestant church. Johann Georg Christian Hess and his son Johann Friedrich Christian Hess worked with plans developed by the city architect Liebhardt. The completed building seems to suggest acquaintance with the drawings of Friedrich Gilly (1772–1800). The edifice was destroyed by the bombings of World War II, but was restored in time for the centenary celebration of the first meeting of the *Parlament*.

3 Eyck, *The Frankfurt Parliament*, p. 95.

4 Valentin, *Geschichte der deutschen Revolution*, 2:2. A detailed breakdown: 49 university professors and docents, 57 professors from higher educational institutions, 157 judges and legal authorities, 66 lawyers, 118 upper echelon civil servants, 20 mayors, 3 diplomats, 5 librarians and archivists, 18 physicians, 43 writers, editors and publishers, and 33 clerics (evangelical and Catholic, in virtually equal division).

5 Kramer, *Fraktionsbindungen in den deutschen Volksvertretungen 1819–1949*, p. 19.

6 Sheehan, *German History*, p. 602; idem, *German Liberalism*, p. 9.

7 Valentin, *Die erste Nationalversammlung*, pp. 54–55.

8 Eyck, p. 74.

9 Jessen, *Die deutsche Revolution 1848/49 in Augenzeugenberichten*, p. 130.

10 Eyck, p. 296.

11 Sperber, *Popular Catholicism* , pp. 48–49.

12 Droz, *Les révolutions allemandes de 1848*, p. 234.

13 Arndt, *Versuch einer Geschichte des Leibeigenschaft in Pommern und Rügen*.

14 Arndt, *Erinnerungen aus dem äusseren Leben*, pp. 107–114.

15 Georg Beseler, *Erlebtes und Erstrebtes 1809-1859*, p. 60.

16 Fanny Lewald-Stahr, *Erinnerungen aus dem Jahre 1848*, p. 112.

17 Grab, *Die Revolution von 1848/49*, p. 23.

18 Ibid., pp. 130–156.

19 Beseler, pp. 74–76.

20 Valentin, 2:35.

21 Werner Boldt, *Die Anfänge des deutschen Parteiwesens*, pp. 26–27.

22 Joseph Hansen, *Gustav von Mevissen*, 2:332.

23 Weber, *Johann Jacoby* , pp. 170–171.

24 Valentin, 2:29.

25 Koch-Gontard, *Tagebuch*, p. 12.

26 Wilhelm Döhl, *Die deutsche Nationalversammlung von 1848 im Spiegel der "Neuen Rheinischen Zeitung"*, p. 109.

27 Valentin, 2:41.

28 Ernst Rudolf Huber, *Der Kampf um Einheit und Freiheit,* p. 687; Rolf Weber, *Die Revolution in Sachsen 1848/49,* p. 116. It may have been the non-participation of the Blum faction that was mistakenly interpreted by Weber as a total boycott by the *Paulskirche* left.

29 *Revolutionsbriefe 1848/49*, p. 202.

30 Ibid., p. 203.

31 Huber, pp. 631–633.

32 *Revolutionsbriefe*, p. 205.

33 Valentin, *Geschichte* 2:124.

34 Friedrich Sigmund Jucho, *Verhandlungen des deutschen Parlaments*, p. 156; Eyck, p. 276.

35 Hertz, *The German Public Mind,* pp. 251–252.

36 Ruddolf Haym, *Die deutsche Nationalversammlung bis zu den Septemberereignissen,* pp. 85–87.

37 Sperber, *Rhineland Radicals*, pp. 306–310; Valentin, *Geschichte* 2:91.

38 Sperber, "Festivals of National Unity in the German Revolution of 1848–1849," *Past and Present* 136 (1992): 131–132.

39 Ibid., pp. 120-121.

40 Valentin, 2:228.

41 *Neue preussische Zeitung* no.60 (9 August 1848), cited by Wilhelm Füssl, *Professor in der Politik,* p. 148.

42 Nikolaus Pevsner, *An Outline of European Architecture,* p. 384.

43 Laube, *Das erste deutsche Parlament,* p. 113.

44 Sperber, *Rhineland Radicals*, p. 310, citing contemporary newspapers.

45   Laube, pp. 114–115.

46   Ibid., p. 116; Beseler, p. 66.

47   Sperber, "Festivals", p. 128.

48   Valentin, 1:29. This was a king who could not govern himself . . . He could insult and abuse those close and loyal to him in words and gestures up to the point of rawness . . . but then he would again be charming and bubbling with quips. David E. Barclay, "Ein deutscher 'Tory democrat'?" in Hans-Christof Kraus, editor, *Konservative Politiker in Deutschland,* pp. 37–67 applies the following adjectives to Friedrich Wilhelm: ambiguous, mentally gifted, confused, contradictory.

49   Laube, pp. 117–120.

50   Jozsef Eotvos advanced this thesis in his *Der Einfluss der herrschenden Ideen des 19. Jahrhunderts auf der Staat,* recently translated into English by D. Mervyn Jones. The work has not been available to me. See however Elizabeth A. Drummond, "Review of Jozsef Eotvos, *The Dominant Ideas of the Nineteenth Century and their Impact on the State.* Vol.1. *Diagnosis* [Michigan State University] HABSBURG, H-Net Reviews, May 1997.

51   Döhl, pp. 112–118; Huber, pp. 679–681; Beseler, pp.66–76; Johann Gustav Droysen and Karl Samwer, *La révolution danoise de 1848,* 2:107–123; Valentin, 2:138–157.

52   Valentin, *Geschichte,* 2:144.

53   Radowitz, *Gesammelte Schriften,* 3:414–432. "Bericht aus der Nationalversammlung zu Frankfurt am Main, 5. 17 September 1848."

54   Valentin *Geschichte,* 2:154.

55   Ibid., 2:156.

56   Koch-Gontard, pp. 36–37.

57   Reinhard Carl Theodor Eigenbrodt, *Meine Erinnerungen aus den Jahren 1848, 1849 und 1850,* pp. 154–155.

58   *Revolutionsbriefe,* pp. 222–223. Friedrich Theodor Vischer wrote on 19 September that he had just viewed Lichnowsky's body, which had "frightful head wounds" and his arm was riddled with bullets, hacked, and shattered. "A terrible victory for the Right".

59   Bamberger, *Erinnerungen,* pp. 131–132.

60   Julius Fröbel, *Ein Lebenslauf. Aufzeichnungen, Erinnerungen und Bekenntnisse,* 1:280.

61   Radowitz, 3:424–425.

62   Dressen, *1848–1849. Bürgerkrieg in Baden.* pp. 81–83. Excerpt from Kaiser's *Aus alten Tagen.*

63   Dressen, p. 83. Excerpt from Gustav Struve's *Geschichte der drei Volkserhebungen in Baden.*

64   *Revolutionsbriefe,* p. 338.

65   Ibid., p. 231.

66   Ibid., p. 228.

Chapter 17

The Background for Counterrevolutionary Action

The great German revolution of March 1848 was not proceeding according to the hopes of the moderates, the fears of the conservatives, or the plans of the leftwing radicals. Uneasiness had settled in all quarters even before the events of September, and determined leaders of extreme right and left had already begun to prepare for action, grasping the opportunity presented by the freedom of assembly and association that had become possible in the course of the hectic March days.

Those who saw no good in revolution or reform were finding evidence that in all probability the revolutionary movement would be unable to sustain itself. They had already observed the chaos of the Parisian *journées de juin*, which had pointed up the lack of solidarity among the workers. The class war that Karl Marx so ardently preached had not materialized there because the new government's clumsy handling of the national workshop problem had ended with fierce bloody confrontations that cannot with any degree of accuracy be described as a clash between property owners and the propertyless workers. True, there were thousands of artisans on the barricades, but it was the mobile guard, recruited from the ranks of the proletariat, who fought the defenders of the workshops. In addition, French radicals and members of the labor organizations had split apart.

Encouraging news came from Austria also. The turn of events there was startling and abrupt. When Metternich fled in March, the Habsburg regime seemed to be moribund, yet in August it was the revolutionists and the nationalists who were in disarray. At Frankfurt, even in the first flush of enthusiasm, it had been disconcerting to discover that the Czechs were boycotting the *Parlament* because, they said, they were not German but Czech nationalists. (Germans and Czechs had seemed to present a united front at Prague in the beginning, but gradually German radicals and liberals alike had resigned from the newly organized Prague national committee.) Voices were raised in Prague, singing a defiant new song: *Forward against the German, forward against the murderer, against Frankfurt.*[1] Mikhail Bakunin, the Russian anarchist, defending his fellow Slavs against the charge that they did not even have a common language, responded that all Slavs from the Elbe to the Urals, from the Adriatic to the Balkans, understood the phrase *Zahrabte niemce!* [down with the Germans].[2]

It was easy for paranoid outsiders to misinterpret the aims and motives of the nationalists when they called their Slavic congress that met at Prague in June, presumably with the intention of demonstrating their anti-Frankfurt unity. The members of the congress thought that they were making everything clear by decorating their assembly hall with the black and gold of the Habsburgs. Their proclamation that announced the congress had been carefully worded, with invitation to "all Slavs of the Austrian Empire", with a qualifying statement that "If the Slavs living outside our monarchy desire to honor us with their presence, they will be welcome guests". With the Czech liberal, Frantisek Palacky (1798–1870) as their leading spirit, the members of the congress were in fact hoping for a constituent assembly that would write a constitution for all Austria, providing a voice for Slavic national groups. Delegates from three nationalities—Czechs, Moravians, and Slovenes—even went so far as to issue a joint statement that declared them to be opposed to any policy [emanating from Frankfurt] that would result in their incorporation into a unified Germany.[3] But outsiders saw the meeting as an ominous foreshadowing of disintegration because of the presence of so many Polish guests, and even decided that the congress must be made up of nihilists—probably because of the incendiary presence of Mikhail Bakunin, but that disorganized man was never a representative of anything. He had the destructive personality of an arsonist, dashing from one trouble spot to another all over Europe with pathological if passionate enthusiasm. In a way reminiscent of T. S. Eliot's laughing Mr. Apollinax, Bakunin was as irresponsible as a fetus.

Admittedly, the principal action of the congress—issuance of a manifesto—was the work of the Polish contingent, with Bakunin's collaboration, although the final version adopted on 12 June by the congress had little of Bakunin's fireworks. It must also be conceded that on the whole, the manifesto was constructive in its attempt to find some way to handle the conflicting requirements of antagonistic Slavic blocs. To speak of the peoples involved as "nationalists" can be misleading, because nationalism among the Slavs had an artificial tinge, being the outcome of struggles toward self-determination that in the early 1840's had found an outlet in the promotion of distinct languages which were in fact not at all familiar to the political leaders of the various groups who called themselves Croatians or Serbs or Ruthenians or whatever. The chief difficulty resided in the relentless fact that different nationalist movements were trying to claim like groups that were also being claimed as part of different nations.[4]

The congress was held just at a time when daily street demonstrations in which workers and students participated were alarming the authorities. Prague's cotton mills had felt the strain not only of the introduction of machinery but also of the fact that expected shipments of American cotton had been blocked at Trieste by the military events in Italy.

Whatever hopes the nationalists may have had were rudely crushed by the deliberately provocative moves of Prague's local garrison commander, the harsh German-speaking aristocrat, *Fürst* Alfred Windischgrätz, who had arrived in Prague on 20 May, and who promptly placed troops threateningly around the city outskirts as if in preparation for quelling an uprising of anarchists. His conviction had been sharpened, that a revolutionary conspiracy was back of the workers' agitation and the general excitement of the Slavs at their congress. New street demonstrations erupted immediately because the students especially were inflamed. There were huge rallies at which the removal of Windischgrätz was openly called for, and this defiant attitude only served to deepen the suspicions of the commander. The presence of the Slavic congress added to the general tension, in spite of the lack of interaction between congress participants and the demonstrators. Rumors spread that hostile Germans were about to attack.

On 12 June (Whitmonday) a mass was held that was attended in large numbers by people of various social classes. Following the mass, there were shouts of "Let's march past Windischgrätz", and it was in front of the unpopular marshal's headquarters that the first clash occurred. Barricades went up almost instantaneously, starting six bloody Czech *journées de juin*. Among the victims was Windischgrätz's wife, killed by a stray bullet.

All this public disorder offered an excellent pretext for bombardment. Windischgrätz followed the surrender of the poorly armed, heavily outnumbered insurgents by arresting the leaders, dismissing the Slav congress, and proclaiming martial law. In the widespread confusion, the fact that most of the troops involved were Slavs was overlooked, and so was the loyalty of the Czech nationalists to the Habsburgs.

By the final day of the rising, the movement had perceptibly weakened, and middle class citizens obviously wanted the hostilities to end. The students were worn out. Among the workers, there were those who took money for dismantling the barricades. The Czech movement was still led by those of the extreme left, but they were so intent on their demands as nationalists that there was little chance that they would ever join the left in Vienna. They were in fact rather inclined to support the Austrian dynasty, with the thought that in that way they might win some kind of approval and reward at some future time.

Windischgrätz meanwhile had enjoyed a triumphant moment, proving that the military was valuable for drawing the teeth of a national movement. "Amid the multitude of setbacks—in Hungary, in Italy, and in Vienna itself—the forces of reaction could point to the crushing of the June uprisings as their first major victory, a milestone in leading the people back into the darkness of absolutism."[5] It was a strange victory in which distorted perception played a significant part. Constitutionalists throughout the German-speaking world were adding their enthusiastic voices to the praise of Windischgrätz. Because of the complexities of nationalism, there were people in Bohemia, Vienna, Saxony, even in the Frankfurt *Parlament*, who felt that a fine blow had been struck against Slavic aggression.[6]

The nationalists in Austria's Italian territories had a different perspective. Theirs was not so much a movement for social change and liberal reform as it was a struggle for liberation from foreign (Austrian) intruders. Inevitably, armed force was again the useful tool of the oppressor. If Austria had been unable to withstand the pressure of the nationalists, much essential territory would have been lost. A military victory in Italy was hence a *sine qua non* if the Habsburgs were to survive.

The initial spectacular clash during the "five days" of March in Milan had routed the inadequate forces of the Austrian commander, Joseph Radetzky (1766–1858)[7] in furious combat before the insurgents' unusually stylish fortifications that included stacked-up pianos and gilded silk-upholstered sofas supplied by wealthy middle class liberals. The revolutionists' victory had its drawbacks, however, because in subsequent developments it proved to be more favorable to the moderate constitutionalists than to the determined radicals. The Piedmontese government chose not to pursue Radetzky but rather to court its neighboring provinces in northern Italy (Venetia and Lombardy), with the result that the majority favored constitutional monarchy, limited suffrage heavily weighted for property owners, and evinced an almost total disregard of the lower classes.

Because of the general confusion, Radetzky was able to perpetrate a dreadful compaign of terror in the northern countryside—for example, everyone in the village of Montebello (Venetia) was slain and the community itself was burned to the ground—thereby annihilating any potential support on the part of the peasantry. The battle at Custozza on 23 July was a decisive victory for Radetzky, who returned to Milan in triumph. The cease fire of mid-August left all northern Italy in Austria's possession, except for Venice itself, which remained under siege.

Carlo Alberto of Piedmont-Savoy had declared proudly that *Italia farà da se* [would handle matters on her own], but there were always lurking hopes in his government that support would come from England and France, and that the mere hint of armed intervention by these major powers would bring Austria around to the cession of her Italian provinces. In both France and England, however, there was no appetite for risking a general European war. This reluctance was useful to Austria because all her struggles—in Bohemia, in Italy, and in Hungary—thus retained their local character, and the adversaries could be picked off one at a time.

Once again, conservatives at the court of Friedrich Wilhelm in Potsdam could plainly see that military force was still an excellent tool for reaction, and that in this case also the revolutionists had been too much split among radicals and moderates to make any serious headway. Besides, as in the case of the Czechs, the Italians were allowing nationalism to outweigh their social concerns. They had forgotten Mazzini's insistent demand that Italy's peasantry be involved.

A hero-worshiping biography of *Feldherr* Radetsky states categorically that it was only after his victories that conservatives elsewhere raised their heads and attempted to fight the revolution in their own states.[8] His recovery of Austria's Italian lands had another portentous aspect. Austria would be able to recall forces that had been heavily engaged in Italy, for use against Hungary if need be. These troops included Croatian units.

Hostility among the nationalists that sprang up almost immediately after the March explosion complicated the Hungarian problem, where there quickly developed "a wild political free-for-all into which violent antagonisms between lord and serf were mixed".[9]

In a series of national assemblies [Croats in Zagreb as early as March, followed by those of Slovaks, Serbs, and Romanians in May] enormous crowds were involved, most of them calling for the establishment of independent states under the Habsburg crown. The bewildering plurality of dialects and even of distinctly different languages—on their own a potential cause of bitter dissension—erected an almost insurmountable barrier to any true comprehension of basic issues. Moreover, there were so many cross-purposes that it was not always clear just who was fighting whom for what.

In Transylvania, Hungarian nationalism was championed by distinctly non-liberal Magyar nobles. Passionately clamoring for independence, they were serf-owners who had not a shred of interest in social reform. To their chagrin, liberal-minded Romanians of Transylvania found that the Magyars of the new government at Budapest were determined to suppress any political action on their part. The Romanians therefore not only agitated for resistance among the serfs but also sent a delegation to the emperor, who in the new arrangement remained emperor of Austria and had additionally become king of Hungary.

In Croatia, which was under the control of a *Ban* [provincial governor] appointed by Vienna, that official selected Josip Jelacic (1801–1859), a colonel who was totally loyal to the Habsburgs, to assume command of the border forces. Jelacic refused with patriotic fervor to have anything to do with the new Budapest government. (Emperor Ferdinand had signed the so-called April Laws that granted Hungary at least a semblance of independence, with her own national assembly, treasury, and army.) This government (constitutional monarchist with allegiance to Ferdinand as king of Hungary) claimed control of all its putative national territory and attempted unsuccessfully to remove Jelacic, who insisted that he only served Ferdinand in his capacity as emperor, not as king of Hungary. Fantastic collisions of authority ensued because two supposedly lawful governments—at Vienna and in Budapest—were struggling for control of the regular armed forces stationed in Hungary.

Vienna focused attention on Jelacic, who was made *Ban* (end of August). He was given to understand that if he were to attack the Budapest government, the move would be viewed with favor by certain unnamed influential persons. The Budapest government, facing Jelacic's invasion, quickly set up a national defense committee headed by Lajos Kossuth, who had been prominent for years in the struggle against Habsburg rule. During the summer, Kossuth had been demanding appropriations for an armed force so large that it could only be thought of as an army of aggression.

Vienna retaliated by appointing *Feldherr* Franz Lamberg commander-in-chief of the Hungarian armies, meaning Jelacic's troops plus the regulars of the Budapest army that was setting out to attack Jelacic. The ill-fated Lamberg was viciously lynched by a Budapest mob two weeks later, and Jelacic was appointed to replace him. The monarchist ministers at Budapest understood that this was war. They resigned, and Kossuth and his defense committee assumed leadership.

Jelacic was an ineffectual military commander. He was severely trounced by the Hungarians, whereupon the Richter battalion of the Vienna garrison was ordered to march out to support him. This precipitated a terrifying crisis in Vienna. The soldiers mutinied, refusing to march, and about half of the national guard stood by them while the rest took their stations, ready to fight the rebels.

Vienna was in such a chaotic state that the city was ripe for the bloodiest of armed confrontations. The incongruous constituent assembly (the *Reichstag*) already had "a Hippocratic face".[10] What kind of reasonable unified action could be expected from a group that presented such marked contrasts in ethnic background, class, and conviction? They had no common ground on which to stand, and tended to speak past each other rather than to engage in dialog. Party affiliations entailed insoluble contradictions, and showed many improbable combinations: German conservatives and Czechs and Ruthenes on the right, for example: centrist-minded Germans driven farther and farther to the left. The only accomplishment of this confused, disconsolate body was an important one: they voted passage of a bill introduced by Hans Kudlich of Silesia, himself the son of a serf, that abolished serfdom within the Habsburg realm.

Meanwhile, outsiders came to fish in troubled waters. Ronge, the German-Catholic firebrand arrived. So did Karl Marx. Hecker visited Austria briefly before departing for the United States. All had axes to grind.

Through most of the summer of 1848 there continued to be a loose alliance of students and workers. The students at least were enjoying themselves, swashbuckling through the streets in outlandish costumes, their scabbards rattling on the pavement as they strutted along. The middle class was understandably becoming uneasy and was moving toward some policy of law and order, like the wealthy property owners. The workers began to tire of the theatrical behavior of the students. The typesetters and book publishers were the first to make independent moves. They formed the first workers' education society, and this was quickly followed by a general workers' society (the *Wiener Arbeiterklub*). These organizations pressed demands for higher wages, shorter work hours, limitation of women's work, etc.

There were hordes of unemployed people whom the government tried ineffectually to help with depressing make-work assignments, but the financial strain was too great. In August pay was lowered for women and, though the measure was necessary, it set off troubling disorders in the streets. The committee of safety and the national guard clashed, the end result being eighteen deaths and two hundred and eighty-two wounded. The ministry saw this as an opportunity to dissolve the committee of safety. Accusations and violent recriminations were flying on all sides, so that leadership went more or less by default to the democratic society. As unrest increased in the city, grenadiers were called in to support the national guard. It was not long before barricades began to go up as a result of the growing suspicion, internal weakness and general lack of recognizable goals.

In reaction to this gloomy situation, 15 September witnessed the foundation of a new organization, the *Monarchisch-Konstitutioneller Verein*. Within the first forty-eight hours of its existence, this conservative society was able to boast a membership of six thousand, and the number was multiplied by four within the next few days. They were turning their backs on anarchy, they announced.

It was on 6 October that Viennese troops had been ordered to march out to reinforce the embattled Jelacic and his Czech army that had been beaten off by the Hungarians. In one of the most degrading episodes of all 1848, a lynch mob attacked Theodor von Latour, the elderly war minister whose known intellectual dishonesty had made him a public target. They hanged him twice, first from the crosspiece of a window frame and then (already half dead) from a lamppost.[11] Apparently no intervention was even thought of when street ruffians and women savagely trampled the victim's naked body. The incident, like the lynching of Auerswald and Lichnowsky at Frankfurt, left a permanent stain on the reputation of the radical left, and enraged the troops of Latour's own regiment in Prague. It was unfortunate that the discouraged Robert Blum lost his customary detached perspective and was heard to remark that a lot of people would have to be "Latourized" before the story ended.

With Vienna in chaos, the doughty *Feldherr* Windischgrätz moved from Prague, heading toward the capital. The alarmed *Erzherzog* Johann now dispatched emissaries to Austria. These two men (Karl Welcker and Ludwig Mosle) arrived at Passau on 19 October, where posters were put up, explaining that they were on a mission of peace and reconciliation [*des Friedens und der Versöhnung*]. They believed that all German Austria would stand as a unit with the Viennese, but when they discovered that this was far from the case, they attempted to go to Vienna. Warned away, they decided instead to accost Windischgrätz who, in a surly mood, brushed them off with the gruff statement that Austria was strong enough to take care of herself and had no need of soldiers from Baden and Oldenburg, as if he had not troubled himself to find out who Welcker and Mosle were or why they had sought him out. The two determined emissaries went next to Olmütz, where the court had fled. Anyone coming from *Erzherzog* Johann could hardly expect to find a welcome there. What was going on in Vienna was merely a rising of the proletariat, they were told. Frankfurt was not recognized as competent to intervene.[12] Welcker and his colleague returned to Frankfurt, where they faced harsh criticism.

Meanwhile, four opposition delegates from the Frankfurt *Parlament* (Robert Blum, Julius Fröbel and two others) had arrived in Vienna, bearing an address signed by sixty-five members of the left at Frankfurt, who extended warm and sympathetic greetings to the heroic people of Vienna. They were received by the constituent assembly, the city council and the students' committee. Blum and his colleagues were given sabres and made honorary members of the famous Academic Legion.

Blum especially, who had long harbored a dreadful sense of defeat at Frankfurt, threw himself into the revolutionary turmoil without reserve. The historian Valentin wrote sympathetically that "politically he was exhausted in the fall of 1848 and had no hope other than that a new popular movement might develop". Here in Vienna he saw all at once a rump *Reichstag*, students' fervor, military gone over to the revolution, arming of the people, German patriotism, international "democracy"—all the dream wishes of his political fantasy. "Blum, the tactician, the calculator and moderator, was overwhelmed by his political emotions."[13] When Windischgrätz arrived before the gates, and surrounded the city with his largely Slavic army sixty thousand strong, Blum unhesitatingly went to the barricades. He would have seen himself a coward if he had done otherwise. As the poet Freiligrath expressed it, *Wenn wir noch beten könnten, wir beteten für Wien* [If we were still able to pray, we prayed for Vienna].

Windischgrätz proceeded to bombard the city, quickly reducing it to submission in spite of desperate defense by the barricade fighters, whom the visitor Richard Wagner admired, calling them "beautiful people". It was ironic that two potential sources of help did not respond to the desperate calls of the Viennese. The peasants, so recently freed from serfdom, might have been expected to hurry to Vienna, but in their ignorance, many thought that because ultimately Emperor Ferdinand had signed the order for emancipation, it was to him alone that they owed allegiance. In another variety of indifference, the Hungarians were slow to try to rescue the Vienna barricade fighters. Here the reasoning was that since ties had been cut and Hungary was now independent of Austria, problems in Vienna were not a matter of vital concern to them.

Commanders like Windischgrätz were staunch loyal defenders of the Habsburg dynasty, but officers who rode with them carried sabres marked with the initials W-J-R [Windischgrätz, Jelacic, Radetzky], signifying personal loyalty to the army and its leaders rather than to the ruling house.

Windischgrätz, who had been hated by the Czechs in Prague and cheered by enemies of what they perceived as Slavic aggression, now found himself being wildly hailed by the Czechs because this time they saw him as their champion against German nationalists. He certainly allowed his Slavs to express their wrath in the most brutal way. The actual count of the dead on Vienna's streets has never been determined, but they numbered in the thousands, and the physical destruction of buildings was appalling. In actual fact, the victory of the imperial forces was a victory over all nationalist movements and over the hopes for a constitutional monarchy.[14]

Though it is not clear that he ever signed any order, it was on Windischgrätz's watch that Robert Blum of the Frankfurt *Parlament* was captured, heard briefly by a court martial, and shot. With the city under martial law imposed by Windischgrätz and a new government being set in place under Windischgrätz's brother-in-law, Felix zu Schwarzenberg (1800–1852), Blum was caught in the trammels of the cruel unreason of war.

Figure 18 ROBERT BLUM BEFORE THE FIRING SQUAD

The revolution had been betrayed, wrote Blum to his wife Jenny on 30 October. He would leave for Leipzig as soon as possible, and report there on the events in Vienna. On 2 November he and his fellow delegates applied for exit visas. Blum and Fröbel had understood that the Viennese revolution was hopeless, and although Blum especially had performed well in a thirty-six-hour defense of one of Vienna's bridges, they had withdrawn to their hotel during the worst of the fighting, awaiting a response to their request for permission to leave the city. Under Schwarzenberg, any foreigner without a passport was to be expelled, but through the diligence of an officious underling, Blum and Fröbel were arrested, even though they presumably had diplomatic immunity as members of the Frankfurt *Parlament*. The other two members of their delegation hastily took flight, but Blum and Fröbel entered a vigorous appeal at Frankfurt and confidently waited for their release.

When Windischgrätz first became aware of the arrest (6 November), he wrote to Schwarzenberg that he intended to release the Frankfurt delegates simply in order to avoid diplomatic complications, but in the meantime a bitter enemy of Blum's, *Graf* Alexander von Hübner, former Austrian consul general at Leipzig, went to Schwarzenberg to say that Blum ought to be executed because he was one of Germany's most dangerous anarchists, and his death would have a salutory effect.

Schwarzenberg, as the historian Valentin expressed it, suddenly saw himself in possession of a great prize—the very embodiment of revolution![15] He therefore told Windischgrätz that he would take upon himself the responsibility for the execution because "Blum deserves it all".

At dawn on 9 November therefore, Blum was placed before a firing squad. The sentence had been for hanging, but there was no hangman available. At the very time of the execution, Windischgrätz received a letter from Schwarzenberg, who had changed his mind. Blum ought to be freed, on condition that all material against him be presented to a court. Blum had already become a martyr, but Fröbel's death sentence was revoked, and he was unconditionally pardoned.

Fröbel went immediately to Frankfurt, where on 18 November he presented his account of the events to a *Parlament* that listened in glacial, suspicious silence. How had Fröbel managed to extricate himself? The execution of Blum marked a turning-point that none could fail to recognize.

Old Arndt wrote (19 November) in disgust that everything appeared to be favorable for the reds. "This includes the Windischgrätz stupidity . . . If [Blum] had been sentenced by court martial to rope or bullet and then (just because he was a member of the *Parlament*) held in prison and an inquiry put to Frankfurt about his fate, he would ultimately have been released. There would have been some sort of onus [*Klack*] clinging to him and to his party along with him. Now he's a saint and martyr, and a flame of anger and revenge flares from him that can be utilized by his followers to ignite more fires."[16]

The multitudes who flocked to memorial demonstrations were evidence of the accuracy of Arndt's comments, but the acts of the Austrian government had greater significance for the course of the 1848 German revolution. No matter how arguments were twisted, it was obvious that there had been the utmost—one might almost say deliberate—disregard for international law. It was fruitless to quibble that Frankfurt's law concerning immunity of delegates had not been published in Austria. The action against a Frankfurt delegate was against the underlying principles of representative government. In the constitutional system, immunity is inherent in the status of every delegate of a representative body in which the independent and free will of the nation is manifest. No sentencing is allowable without the concurrence of the representative body in question. Taken in conjunction with the contemptuous treatment of the official emissaries Welcker and Mosle, Blum's execution was perceived by the Frankfurt *Parlament* as the first signal of Austria's rejection of the overall goals of the movement that the *Parlament* and its provisional government represented. Austria was disclosing by this intransigeance her program for causing Germany to revert to the status of a member in a federation in which Austria, as before, would hold a strong hand.[17]

Notes

1   Stanley Z. Pech, *The Czech Revolution of 1848*, p. 89.

2   Carr, *Michael Bakunin*, p. 158.

3   Pech, p. 135.

4   Sperber, *European Revolutions*, pp. 96–101.

5   Pech, p. 155; Macartney *The Habsburg Empire*, p. 366.

6   Sperber, p. 205.

7   The old hero survives in popular memory through the enthusiastic playing of Strauss' *Radetzky March* as part of Vienna's traditional New Year celebration.

8   Hugo Kerchnawe, *Radetzky*, p. 7.

9   Sperber, p. 135.

10   Valentin, *Geschichte der deutschen Revolution*, 2:188.

11   *Revolutionsbriefe*, p. 234. Carl Friedrich Vitzthum von Eckstädt (apparently not an eye witness) wrote to his mother that Latour was first bayonetted, then thrown from a window, then hanged from a lamp post.

12   Ernst Rudolf Huber, *Der Kampf um Einheit und Freiheit*, p. 71.

13   Valentin, 2:205.

14   Sperber, p.217.

15   Valentin, 2:212.

16   *Revolutionsbriefe*, p. 269.

17   Huber, pp. 717–720.

Chapter 18

Friedrich Wilhelm and the Prussian National Constituent Assembly

The turmoil in Austria was grist for the mills of those Germans who hoped that the revolution would ultimately collapse. Even as early as March 1848, conservatives in Prussia had begun to search for ways to undo the work that was going on in the Rhineland and at Frankfurt. The spectacle of the gradual fracturing of revolutionary and nationalist forces in Austria was encouraging to them.

In the immediate aftermath of the March events on the streets of Berlin, the courtiers of Friedrich Wilhelm's entourage as well as the feudally-minded landowners of East Prussia had been reduced to stunned silence. The king's former ministers withdrew, urging the shaken sovereign to rely on his new cabinet, led by Prussia's first constitutional minister, Adolf Heinrich von Arnim-Boitzenburg, but this officer quickly decided that he was not the man for the task. He ought to be replaced, he thought, by someone from the liberal contingent. Therefore, only ten days after the bloody scenes in the capital, a new cabinet was formed under Ludolf Camphausen (1803–1890), an entrepreneur from the Rhineland, with the financier David Hansemann (1790–1864) as his treasurer. It was the Camphausen-Hansemann ministry, as king Friedrich Wilhelm's executives, who would confront the second united Prussian *Landtag* that assembled in Berlin on 2 April. The original date for that meeting that Friedrich Wilhelm had reluctantly called was 27 April, but when the revolution boiled over in the streets of Berlin the date had hurriedly been advanced.

On the morning following the appointment of the new ministry, Friedrich Wilhelm's longtime friend and adviser, Leopold von Gerlach (1790–1861), arrived in the king's chambers with the intention of beginning the desperate and painful process of salvaging the authority of the Crown. Immediately after the March days, there had been glum despair among the king's close associates. Gerlach placed an entry in his journal on 10 April 1848—"Evening with the king. 'You must call on me in the morning. I have so much to discuss with you.' What should we discuss? We have already spoken too much to each other, I thought. What should one say to the king? The most shameful experiment with the elected constituent assembly must be gone through, and only then will we be able to see ahead. . . . How fine it was *in politicus* when people were fighting each other way off in Turkey. Now it's here."[1]

It was the second united *Landtag* that determined the conditions governing the vote for *Die für die zur Vereinbarung der preussischen Staatsverfassung zu berufende Versammlung* [the assembly to be summoned for agreement on the Prussian state constitution]. The term that suggested reconciliation or agreement was important because, in the opinion of his Majesty's ministers, the Crown was the responsible executive unit. Democratic opponents on the left saw no virtue in the principle of reconciliation. They saw themselves as a constituent body, free of any ties with dynastic tradition. Although it does not seem to have been recognized as such at the time, the fact that the principle of conciliation and agreement was pushed through was a victory for the conservatives. On the other hand, the *Landtag* decision on the franchise was fairly democratic, with few restrictions based on income or class.

At close range, Leopold von Gerlach had observed the volatile Friedrich Wilhelm's strange mixture of apathy and desperation, and he now urged him to insist that his new ministers must invariably come to him in Potsdam. He should hold firmly to his royal dignity and never any under circumstances demean himself by going to Berlin to meet with them. Furthermore, Gerlach suggested changes in the cabinet appointments. He noted in his journal that "I was thinking of the possibility of restoring monarchical authority by proceeding from the army and from foreign policy."[2] This move marked the initial effort on the part of an underground *ministère occulte* that began quietly to take shape among Friedrich Wilhelm's close associates, the men whom historians call his Kamarilla. They felt constrained to move with extreme caution, knowing that in a way they would have to "reinvent government" as Washington's modern parlance would have it.

The newly elected Prussian national constituent assembly had little to offer the conservatives in the way of consolation, although it must have been evident that the assembly itself would find many a stumbling-block in its path. In any case, the actual makeup of the assembly presented a curious contrast to that of the Frankfurt *Parlament*. This in itself was odd, given the fact that the elections had been simultaneous. In contrast to the professorial cohorts at Frankfurt, the Berlin assembly had sixty-eight peasants (half from Silesia), including day laborers and illiterate cottagers. When they received their compensation for daily expenses, many of these rural innocents kissed the hand of the man who paid them. There were about forty merchants and manufacturers, and twenty-eight craftsmen. Twenty-seven teachers were among the delegates, but a larger group was made up of clergymen (fifty), divided among Rhineland Catholics and leaders of various evangelistic splinter sects. Representatives of the legal profession were present in great numbers, most of them junior bureaucrats.

Fanny Lewald, one of the more perceptive observers who reported on the revolutionary scene, was a guest at a soirée given by David Hansemann in the first week of June. This was to initiate a series of twice-weekly social evenings throughout the sessions of the Prussian national assembly, at his elegant official residence, in rooms so enormous that the two hundred delegates who had received invitations looked almost lost in the impressive vistas of chandeliers and elaborate furniture. Lewald noticed Hansemann himself listening courteously to a rough individual, obviously a day laborer, in hobnailed boots and coarse blue jacket, who shared a red velvet-upholstered sofa with his host.

Lewald spoke at some length with *an alter Beamter* [old bureaucrat] who asked her querulously what contribution she thought people like the day laborer or the Polish-speaking Kiul Bassan could contribute to the new government. She responded stoutly that their presence in the chamber and here in the salon would remind the other delegates of their duty to see that the needs of such people were recognized. "And do you know why this Kiul Bassan was elected?" "Yes, I do," she replied, not in the least embarrassed. He had been drunk in the electors' meeting and the provincial governor was rough with him because he hadn't removed his hat. Kiul Bassan was furious, attacking the governor, and the peasants promptly decided that a man who defied their governor was the very man who ought to go to the assembly because he would be just as self-confident and bold in talking to the king.[3]

As at Frankfurt, the members sorted themselves out into parties—right, center, and left, with the difference that most at Berlin gravitated toward the left, which was in favor of a unicameral system that would be an expression of the sovereignty of the people. The jurist Franz Benedikt Waldeck was the leader of this party. Another powerful speaker for the left was Johann Jacoby from Königsberg, who shone as a party organizer and opinion-builder, though he has been judged "too brittle" ever to be a leader.[4]

The Frankfurt *Parlament* had inaugurated its sessions in a mood of hope and euphoria. A brave new world was about to be conceived! At Berlin, even the most sanguine understood that there were serious problems inherent in the fact that somehow a new constitutional state had to be grafted onto an existent despotic monarchical system that was resilient in many subtle ways.

When she first arrived in Berlin (end of March), Fanny Lewald had been disconcerted to observe the general listlessness of the Berliners. Fresh from the exhilaration of revolutionary Paris, she had been expecting enthusiasm, song, patriotic shouts and general confidence, but she found instead that people were "acting like children who have been kept too long in their go-carts and suddenly set down on the ground. They don't trust their own feet, they're afraid . . . they want to know if the king or the members of the previous ministry are also pleased with what has occurred." They'd like to avoid extremes and make the hard soft, the rough smooth, and in order not to offend anybody they weren't speaking of the revolution and its results, but rather of the "agitation" of the March days and of the need for an "agreement". Lewald returned to this topic in another connection, when the prime minister Camphausen used the term *Begebenheit* [event] with reference to the revolution. She called this an *unselige Halbheit* [unfortunate half-way expression].[5]

Reflecting that there were large numbers of Berliners who felt genuine affection for the royal family, and that many in Berlin had derived personal satisfaction from their flimsy connections with the royals (e.g., the weeping nursemaid who had once cared for the children of the crown prince's cook and had "belonged to the court for years"), Lewald observed that Germans returning from exile in France would soon discover that they had been mistaken in their assumption that subjects accustomed all their lives to the absolutist monarchy would show unqualified enthusiasm for the idea of a republic.[6]

The first official task therefore was to inject confidence into the new government and assert the authority of the Prussian assembly. Friedrich Wilhelm had not been at all helpful in this matter on the opening day, when he prevailed upon the delegates to come to him at his palace for his inaugural *Thronrede* on 22 May. Not only this: his government promptly laid before the assembled delegates its own draft of a constitution, modeled on the Belgian but lacking many essentials that a genuinely democratic constitution would have. In addition, an order of business was imposed on the inexperienced assembly—the draft constitution should go first to committee, then to a special board for markup, then back to the committee, and only after all that tedious process, to the full assembly, where debate would be concluded within one day, with a definitive vote immediately thereafter. This left the assembly delegates with practically nothing to do during the opening weeks. The conservatives must have been quietly pleased.

At the beginning of June, the Prussian assembly had its first open debate. The mood of the delegates was not conducive to amicable discussion. The heir to the throne had made a sudden appearance as a delegate from an obscure locality in the province of Posen, to which office he had been elected during his enforced exile in England. Since he was considered to be the focal point of any counterrevolutionary endeavor, his arrival was most unwelcome. Members on the right rose when he entered the chamber but those on the left hissed. His Highness made a brief speech that was poorly received, and departed hurriedly, not returning to the assembly for any of its subsequent sessions.

Against this unfortunate background, the book publisher Dr. Julius Berends (1810–1853) immediately rose to propose a motion that was heartily supported by the left. The intent of the Berends resolution, that the assembly, in recognition of the revolution, declare that the fighters of 18 and 19 March had well served the Fatherland—was to place the assembly and its acts on a foundation of legality. As Berends explained, the people were taking back their inalienable right to self government and to the promulgation of their own laws.[7] It implied recognition of popular sovereignty and at the same time obliterated the legal foundation of past royal acts.

Minister Camphausen struggled to convince the assembly that its competence was not based solely on the revolution, but that at the same time it derived from decisions of the united *Landtag* that had been legally summoned by the king. The hot debate only ended when a more moderate resolution was introduced by delegate Zachariä and sustained by the combined votes of the right and right center parties. The question of the legality of the revolution was ignored, and the principle of collaboration between assembly and the king was affirmed.

The harsh reaction on the streets of Berlin to the rejection of the Berends resolution could have been anticipated, in consideration of the restive state of the population. The danger—or even the threat—of disorder had had a depressive effect on Berlin's economy. People had moved away if they could, and many residences stood empty. With the departure of the court, merchants and tradesmen had lost valued customers, and unemployment had reached alarming levels. Because of this, the remaining property-owners in the city were in a constant state of apprehension, anticipating wild outbreaks among half-starved idle people.

So it was that after the vote on the Berends resolution, delegates emerging from the assembly were roughly handled. One of them, the clergyman Sydow, who had warmly lauded the March victims at the state funeral, was the object of bitter anger. It was only the intervention of some civilians that prevented his being hurled half-conscious into a canal as punishment for having voted in favor of the Zachariä resolution. There was a huge demonstration that night, where the angry crowd sang the *Marseillaise*. This was followed by what has been called the high point of the Berlin peoples' movement—the storming of the arsenal. In a city where there was a steady undercurrent of disillusionment and distrust, it was only a step to a demonstration of mass unreason that even the assembly members on the left were to deplore.

The outbreak known as the *Zeughaus Sturm* [arsenal attack] came on the evening of 15 June when a crowd approached the arsenal, demanding weapons. There followed a scene of violence, confusion and stupidity. The weapons that were taken included valuable ancient pieces that had been preserved in memory of glorious battles in the past, as well as a number of guns that had a newly-invented firing pin mechanism that was among the most secret of the military's top-secret devices. These ultra-modern weapons were useless in the hands of the marauders, since they were unfamiliar with them and also had no appropriate ammunition. In the melee were law-abiding civil guards, a group of excited students, and members of the proletariat with Polish flags and the flaming red flags of revolution, whereas in a nearby public park vendors were busily engaged in the preparation and sale of sausages, cakes, brandy, etc. to a milling crowd of curiosity-seekers. Rumors flew. The defenders of the arsenal, grossly outnumbered, believed the story that a republic had been proclaimed, that Berlin was in the hands of the revolutionists, that the royal family had fled, etc.

Figure 19 A MOB ATTACKS THE ARSENAL IN BERLIN (JUNE 1848)

By the end of the messy affair, almost everyone was anxious to disavow any connection with it. Stephan Born (1824–1898), who had participated as a member of the civil guard, was convinced that the arsenal break-in had been engineered by forces of the reaction who, he said, were using every means to start a counterrevolution. "I published in my paper, *Das Volk*, my suspicion that here we had an organized, paid-for political move."[8]

The display of lack of control brought about the downfall of the Camphausen ministry, which was quickly replaced by another headed by Rudolf von Auerswald, a boyhood friend of Friedrich Wilhelm's, and the able Hansemann.

The party of the left may have been heartened by the notion that Berlin remained a revolutionary city, with its workers' organizations and democratic clubs, but they would have done well to reflect that the general atmosphere of sullen rebellion would in the long run cause many an anxious citizen to shift his allegiance in the direction of law and order. Labor organization was in its infancy and there was not at that stage a movement that could bind Berlin's working population together for concerted, responsible political action. Admittedly, a *Centralverein für das Wohl der arbeitenden Klassen* [central society for the well-being of the working classes] had been organized, but this had been developed from above, not by the workers themselves. Bruno Bauer scornfully referred to it as a true *Burgher* parliament.

In the spring of 1848, the workers of Berlin still tended to group themselves by trades (they marched behind banners that so identified them in the funeral procession for the fallen, for example, though on that occasion there was for the first time at least one organized band of workers who bore arms).[9] There had never been any opportunity for united labor action, because the Prussian trades ordinance of 17 January 1845 had included provisions for imprisonment and heavy fines in the event of strikes,[10] and the first informal gatherings for self-improvement and political study had been preceded by liberal middle-class groups such as the *Politischer Klub* that was founded on 21 March, even before freedom of association had actually been approved for Prussia (6 April).[11]

A workers' colony on the outskirts of Berlin, made up of unemployed individuals who had been assigned to a public-works project for leveling land for future cultivation beyond the Oranienburg gate was popularly regarded as a revolutionary cell. The "Rehberger" as they were called because of the site where they worked were an unruly band of about fifteen hundred men who were relatively well paid. They made themselves conspicuous not only by their defiant ways, their indolence and heavy drinking but also by their appearance. (They wore big yellow straw hats decorated with scarlet cock feathers.)

Though the Rehbergers were anything but organized, they occasionally put in a public appearance that alarmed the law-abiding Berliners. On 1 April, for example, three hundred of them massed for attack on the middle class *Politischer Klub*, and repeated the action toward the end of the month. They apparently had been paid eight *Silbergroschen* each by an agent of the conservatives who wanted to cause a rift among the workers as a first step toward counterrevolution.[12] The rabble-rouser Friedrich Wilhelm Held had briefly played some ill-defined role in the club and seems to have been present on the occasion of the attack.[13] On another occasion (19 April), the Rehbergers appeared on Berlin's streets in threatening numbers, successfully demanding the release of three of their fellows who had been arrested. Finally, in something most closely resembling concerted labor action, they marched on the builders of the Moabit-Charlottenburg canal, forcing them to give up acceptance of their piece-work rate in favor of a fixed wage. Their method of "persuasion" had been assault.[14]

The most cohesive effort in the post-March period was that of the typesetter Stephan Born, who had been associated with Marx in Brussels. Born, a thoughtful young man, understood the complexities of an age of rapid technological innovation, and though he was ready to adapt to the use of machinery, he was convinced that the key to the solution of the workers' problems was organization plus state attention to their interests. Because of his steady effort during the month of April, he was able to start his campaign to persuade the workers that they must learn what their rights were in order to be able to defend whatever gains the revolution had brought. He preached against riots and machine breaking, and even expressed a hope that in Germany there might be a reservoir of good feeling and cooperation between workers and manufacturers. Under his leadership, his ideas were put to the test when six hundred Berlin journeymen printers went out on strike (28 April). The demand for higher wages was met—by promises that were not kept—but the strike action had been effective enough to give the workers confidence. They decided to defer further action until a general congress of workers could meet.

Although the arsenal affair lent comfort to the conservatives, and little to the forces of organized labor, there were few among the royalists who believed that the monarchy might indeed be salvaged, and those few had various ways of looking at their problem. The unhappy king's close associates were by no means in agreement among themselves. Against their own personal backgrounds of experience in Napoleonic times, they tended to see all developments since 1789 as chaotic and destructive. They detested the growing secularization of the European world, and clung to the idea of a monarch who ruled by the grace of God. Even if they were not unanimous in wanting a reversion to the *status quo ante*, they were highly sceptical of the supposed advantages of constitutionalism and national assemblies that claimed legislative powers and expanded suffrage.

Leopold von Gerlach was one of the more intransigeant. In his mind, revolution was nothing short of satanic. His was the rigid incomprehension of the aristocrat: he quivered with outrage when he learned that the workers had the audacity to say that they wanted to be addressed formally as *Sie*, instead of with the patronizing, slightly contemptuous *Du*.[15] He abhored constitutions and the absolutism of bureaucracy with equal intensity. In spite of his clear perception of the flawed character of Friedrich Wilhelm, Leopold von Gerlach was intensely loyal to his king. "If authority comes from above, so too does Friedrich Wilhelm IV," he wrote to his brother.[16]

He was arguing with Ernst Ludwig von Gerlach (1795–1877), the Magdeburg jurist, who, though he subscribed to the idea of the divine right of kings and was convinced that the institution of monarchy as such had to be sustained, yet had calmly asserted on several occasions that he was not entirely averse to the idea of Friedrich Wilhelm's abdication.[17] In the spirit of Edmund Burke, he was able to contemplate change in the system of government as continuous development. The effects of the revolution's sudden interruption of the normal course of history could be repaired.[18] He went so far as to compare Friedrich Wilhelm with Austria's weak Emperor Ferdinand.[19] Besides, he thought that Friedrich Wilhelm was arrogant, and he was fiercely critical of his Majesty's performance during the March days in Berlin. The king was in crying need of "self-reliant men," he insisted.

That astute observer, Fanny Lewald, wrote a sharp comment while she was in Frankfurt.

> Above all, one sees how well articulated the faction of the right is. You have to respect them, as one respects the Jesuits—not for their system but for their cleverness and endurance. [They] work with such harmonious unity that not the tiniest occurrence goes unutilized by them, so that all happenings . . . are lined up as useful links of the chain that they once again fling around that part of humanity that has tried to free itself.[20]

Ernst Ludwig von Gerlach was himself a man of prodigious energy. He had already expended it to some extent in journalistic work as a contributor to the *Evangelische Kirchen-Zeitung* [evangelical church newspaper] which, as the months passed, had gradually changed from its original character as the organ of Lutheran orthodoxy to become one of political conservatism. It tended to condemn Christians who participated in the revolution, and to work toward establishing Biblical justification for the concept of political authority.[21] (Von Gerlach had always been convinced of the rightness of Haller's paternalistic theories.)—By early summer, he was vigorously launching a new publishing venture, the *Neue preussische Zeitung* which was to become the voice of the conservatives. The first issue appeared on 16 June (by happy coincidence immediately on the heels of the storming of the arsenal that had already upset anxious Berliners), after a struggle to find enough stock-holders to support the enterprise. The original stockholders were almost without exception members of the high aristocracy (the *Fürst* von Hessen, the *Grossherzogin* von Mecklenburg-Strelitz, the *Prinz* von Preussen, the *Herzog* von Braunschweig, the *Graf* von Brandenburg and so on).[22] Even in its earliest days, the revolutionists regarded the new paper as an ominous challenge. The editor, Hermann Wagener, received death threats, and stated that persons delivering the paper had copies torn from their hands and tossed into the gutter.

Known popularly as the *Kreuzzeitung* because of the Iron Cross [a decoration first awarded for valor in the war of liberation] on its masthead, this influential paper soon was publishing controversial contributions by Friedrich Julius Stahl (1802–1861), the political theorist. Joseph Maria von Radowitz was also a contributor, but his ideas diverged so much from those of the main body of conservatives that he came to be known as "our opponent in the *Paulskirche*".[23]

Friedrich Julius Stahl's writings were based on his well known book, *Das monarchische Prinzip* (1845). He did not want to see a rigid monarchy like that of the *Vormärz* revived. Rather, he chose to regard Friedrich Wilhelm's concessions as a praiseworthy expression of his royal power. Consultation with the parliament and its ministers, responsibility of the parliament on budgetary matters and taxes—all these were reasonable and necessary *Anforderungen der Zeit* [requirements of the times], and his Majesty had correctly recognized the fact. On the other hand, Stahl was firmly against the French notion of sovereignty of the people.[24] On no account would he advocate any modifications that would have the effect—as in England—of making the monarch subject to the parliament. Leopold von Gerlach, much disturbed, could see nothing good in Stahl's flexibility. He snapped that "I reject constitutionalism of this kind. It is impermissible and impossible."[25]

In Stahl's view, being a conservative meant retention of the Christian character of the state. He was in profound opposition to the actions of the Frankfurt *Parlament* as well as to those of the more radical assembly in Berlin. Both were urging separation of church and state, and the mere notion of such separation was anathema to him.

He staunchly defended his opinion that public law and order were of major importance. With this in mind, he contributed an article to the *Kreuzzeitung* in which he discussed the vexed question of hunting rights. It was important to preserve them, Stahl argued, because it was essential to maintain order among the working classes. There would be danger if they were to carry arms, and also they might become so enamored of hunting that they would be lax in performance of their duties as farmers or laborers.

In line with the assembly's official order of business that had been imposed during the introductory session, discussion of the constitution on which king and assembly were to reach agreement had been effectively buried in committee for months, but at last, on 26 July, the constitution committee emerged, boldly presenting its own draft that came to be known as the Waldeck charter because it had been developed under the leadership of its determined chairman, Franz Benedikt Waldeck. The government's original draft, based on the 1830 Belgian constitution, had been drastically modified. The Waldeck charter emphasized most of the standard "March demands" and guaranteed personal freedom, respect for a writ of habeas corpus, trial by jury and prohibition of retroactive punitive laws. House search could only be conducted on the basis of a search warrant. Freedom of speech and press were assured, as well as freedom of religious confession. Civil marriage would become legal. Citizens would enjoy the universal right to bear arms, while the military would be split into a *Landwehr* [national army] and a *Volkswehr* [militia]. The monarch would no longer exercise an absolute veto on laws passed by his bicameral legislature.

The whole of these provisions was grasped by the conservatives as a distinct target that could be utilized in order to concentrate agitation among all levels of Prussian society against supposed Jacobins and anarchists whose program would indubitably lead to ruin. This was the propaganda line that was vigorously pursued throughout the succeeding months. They were also able to make use of Prussian displeasure over the election of *Erzherzog* Johann at Frankfurt.

Following closely on the launching of the *Kreuzzeitung,* a conservative society was founded (July 1848) that was destined to become the core of a political entity, the *Kreuzzeitungspartei*. This was the *Verein für König und Vaterland* [for king and fatherland]. Its original goal appears to have been to work discretely in the background. The leadership—*angesehenen Männern in Berlin . . . deren Name nicht genannt werden dürfe* [distinguished men in Berlin whose name should not be mentioned]—was hampered in the first months of its activity by the veil of secrecy. The press carried warnings against the society as a "wolf in sheep's clothing", even as a "gang of worthless conspirators."[26]

Leopold von Gerlach was the connecting link between the *Verein für König und Vaterland* and the growing *Kreuzzeitungspartei*, although by the end of 1848 Stahl seemed to be the controlling force, as member of the so-called central elections committee. A more moderate course would then be followed, in contrast to Leopold von Gerlach's rigid policies.

Cautiously, deputations from other conservative organizations attended early meetings of the *Verein für König und Vaterland*. Among these were the *Preussenverein für konstitutioneller Königtum* [Prussian society for constitutional monarchy], most of whose members were middle class Berliners, the *Patriotischer Verein,* made up primarily of high-ranking clerics, officers, academics, and civil servants, and the *Bauernverein,* whose name was misleading because there were no farmers or peasants among its members. They were in fact members of the lesser nobility, professors, and middle-rank bureaucrats. The objective of all these societies was to stir up anxiety with reference to the revolution, and to attack decisions made by the Frankfurt *Parlament* or the Prussian assembly at Berlin.[27]

Step by step, a conservative party came into being, with recognition of the *Kreuzzeitung* as the official organ of the society for king and fatherland. The hesitation and unwillingness to present themselves as a target even resulted in some talk of forming a secret society that would closely resemble the structure of the lodge system of Freemasonry, but this idea was abandoned. Instead, by the end of August a new decision had been reached. The three societies that had sent deputations to meetings of the *Verein für König und Vaterland* joined together as a permanent committee whose assigned task was to bring together like-minded organizations on a local basis, and to organize new societies by profession or occupation, and to arrange demonstrations in order to encourage participation in political action. (The conservatives were learning from the radicals.)

Shortly after the organization of the central committee, an article appeared in the *Kreuzzeitung* that emphasized the need for a conservative party. Differences of opinion were admissible, to be sure, but it was important to hold together on the basic goal—preparation for coming elections, in the interest of giving voice to conservative views. An early result of this call for united action was the massive campaign of letters to Friedrich Wilhelm against recognition of *Erzherzog* Johann as commander-in-chief of Prussia's armed forces.[28]

The *Kreuzzeitungspartei* was not alone in its fight for the conservative cause. As early as July, a society with an imposing name had been founded—the *Verein zum Schutze des Eigentums und zur Förderung des Wohlstandes aller Klassen des Volkes* [for the protection of property and for promotion of the wellbeing of all classes of the people]. This conservative body met for the first time in August. Its so-called *Junkerparlament*[29] included former members of the Prussian *Landtag* (Otto von Bismarck among others) who appeared in substantial numbers. It was not exclusively a group intent on preservation of feudal aristocratic interests. On the contrary, it also embraced the modern neo-feudalism of agrarian economy. Because of this, the first general meeting of the society was marked by a change in nomenclature. The organization significantly became the *Verein zur Wahrung der Interessen des Grundbesitzes* [for the safeguard of the interests of land ownership]. The wellbeing of all classes had been dropped as irrelevant. Moreover, the clear-sighted members of the new society went on to elect a committee of fifty that was intended to sustain the new organization (i.e., political party) as a permanent representative of Prussia's conservatives. In a word, the conservatives were going to fight fire with fire: they would face the middle class progressives sternly, holding together and mobilizing as best they could the old dominant orders (monarchy, military, civil service, landowners and the church). With connections to the royal court, the conservatives had created for themselves not only a political organization but at the same time a special-interest lobby for their growing agribusiness, in a way that foreshadowed developments characteristic of capitalist enterprise of the present day.

Other special interest organizations rapidly came into being. In north Germany, for example, Hansa city exporters joined in a German *Verein für Handelsfreiheit* [unrestricted commercial activity, as opposed to free trade in the classic sense] while importers in the Rhineland, Baden, Württemberg and Saxony formed a protectionist German *Verein zum Schutze der vaterländischen Arbeit* [protection of domestic industry].

Religious orthodoxy and conservatism went hand in hand all over Germany, while people who were temperamentally daring enough to join splinter sects or to become free-thinkers were more in sympathy with the left. In Bavaria, the Gerlach organization was matched by a society for constitutional monarchy and religious freedom. There were sixteen hundred members in Munich alone, with sixty local branches, most of them headed by priests.[30] No doubt, subjects who were accustomed to the rigidity of an established hierarchy and a catechism had no objection to a sovereign who ruled by the grace of God, no matter what his faith. The king of Bavaria was a Roman Catholic, and the king of Prussia was Protestant.

In the welter of conservative undertakings in 1848, the number and variety of Catholic societies that sprang up was startling. The Catholics in the Frankfurt *Parlament* failed to constitute a political party, but tended rather to gather from all parties as members of the Catholic club headed by Joseph Maria von Radowitz. Outside the parliament, however, there was enormous activity. Aside the *Vinzenzius Verein* and the *Bonifatius Verein*, both of which focused on problems relating to pauperism and charity, the most spectacular in its spread all across Germany was the *Piusverein für religiöser Freiheit* [Pius society for religious freedom].[31] The organization took its name from Pius IX who, it is true, had symbolized the struggle for freedom in the early years of his pontificate, but who in the revolutionary period had evolved into an opponent of liberalism.

An indication of the zeal of the Pius societies is the fact that by August 1848, one thousand one hundred and forty-two petitions, with a total of two hundred and seventy-three thousand signatures, had been submitted by them to the Frankfurt *Parlament*—more than 90% of all petitions received at that point by the assembly.[32] These petitions came from Aachen, Berlin, Freiburg, Hannover, Hildesheim, Koblenz, Cologne, Mainz and Münster. Most demanded complete freedom of the church from the state in its teachings and cult, its constitution, the appointment of its clergy, its discipline and control of its property. There was also a wellnigh universal demand for foundation of "private schools", as well as a Catholic university.

In the late autumn of 1848, there were as many as four hundred local Pius societies, with one hundred thousand members in Baden alone. On 6 October there was a general conclave at Mainz that included not only bishops but also delegates from various provincial assemblies as well as from the Frankfurt *Parlament*. The unambiguous statement of views at this meeting had the effect that suppression of the Jesuits disappeared from the provisions of the Frankfurt basic statement of rights, and the call for church supervision of education was restored.

In spite of these gains, the Pius societies were not as effective as they might have been, had they not—like the Catholic members of the

Frankfurt *Parlament*—tended to adopt a multiplicity of political positions. They performed as a unit only when specifically religious issues were involved.[33]

Not only the courtiers and the churchmen were aroused. It was inevitable that the members of the proud Prussian army would prepare for action. They had accumulated a number of grievances, not the least of which had been Friedrich Wilhelm's behavior during the March days in Berlin. They were disturbed by the posture of the Prussian army in Schleswig-Holstein, and deeply offended by the idea of allegiance to *Erzherzog* Johann of Austria.

Military defiance was expressed repeatedly in a series of anonymous pamphlets that came from the very heart of the Prussian war office, written by *Oberstleutnant* Karl Gustav von Griesheim, the acknowledged spokesman for the general staff coterie. His writings set out the matter plainly enough. In the first one, *Die deutsche Zentralgewalt und die preussische Armee* [German central power and the Prussian army], were the following sentiments: German unity is an abstract idea. A unitary north Germany is to be sought for, with Prussia as its core. The attack of the Frankfurt *Parlament* is directed against Prussia. Austria is weak. The fame of the Prussian officer corps is two centuries old. The Prussian army must not be abolished by the Frankfurt *Parlament* and dispersed into a *Reichsarmee*.[34]

The Prussian military quickly grasped the potentials of the new freedom of the press. As early as July, they were publishing their *Deutsche Wehrzeitung* [defense journal], which later more honestly was named the *Preussische Wehrzeitung*. They also cleverly camouflaged their interests in the conservative *Neue Volkszeitung* which sounded democratic but put forth warnings to the effect that the people must hold together for the sake of law and order.[35]

Since they were by no means sealed off from the everyday world, traditional antagonisms persisted, as for example in the clash between the commandant of the regular troops of the line and the new civil guard at Schweidnitz in Silesia (31 July 1848).

In the steamy post-revolutionary climate, what might have been a minor scuffle over use of drums to call out the civil guard for its daily drill exercises ended in a hot altercation that left fourteen civilians dead. The immediate reaction to the Schweidnitz affair had been the customary explanations and accusations—someone had hurled stones, a soldier had been injured, a gun had gone off by accident, the civilians had fired first and so on and so on—all in the time-honored pattern of unconvincing army-civilian post-mortems[36]—but these were no ordinary times. This was the first clash of regulars and civic guards after the guards had been accorded official status (in mid-April).

Because the Prussian constituent assembly was in session, the scope of the quarrel was disproportionately enlarged, the passionate arguments between cabinet and assembly delegates ending in the resignation of Friedrich Wilhelm's new Auerswald-Hansemann ministry that had been in office since June. This was no idle display of legal pyrotechnics. The very nature of the assembly and its competence had been called into question.

The general public had interpreted the episode at Schweidnitz as a sign of the overall attitude of the army—a kind of test run for a counterrevolution.[37] This accounts for the sharp reaction of the Berlin assembly. The original decision by the petitions committee, which had received expressions of public resentment about the incident, was that the offending troops ought to be removed from Schweidnitz. Though this move might have been reasonable enough in anyone's view, it was perceived at the Potsdam court as an assault on the power of the king as commander of the army. It was he alone who traditionally had authority to shift military units from one place to another.

Members of the left on the other hand thought that the petition committee's decision did not go far enough. They supported a resolution by Dr. Julius Stein (1813–1883), a delegate from Breslau, who thought that army officers should be ordered by the war minister to distance themselves from all reactionary efforts, demonstrating their intention to cooperate with the citizens in establishing a new regime. Attempts along this line had already been made in various provincial *Landtag* meetings, where it was suggested that officials known to have opposed the ideas of the revolution ought to be removed. (This had entailed specific votes in Kurhessen and in Hannover, for example.)

In the Berlin assembly itself, the Stein resolution was not an isolated phenomenon. The delegates on the left had repeatedly expressed the opinion that not much in the way of freedom would be achieved by a constitution alone. If the old guard remained in place, they remained the true agents of power. Even Waldeck himself had asserted that the constitution he sponsored would be nothing other than a framework, and that all depended on the "organic" laws on such aspects of public life as the military and educational systems. Also, the left had even been attempting to control various executive offices of the government through the medium of investigative committees.[38]

To the moderates, the Stein resolution had the look of Jacobin-style cleansing of the public service, and consequently they were uneasy, but the Schweidnitz happening had stirred up so much popular emotion that the Auerswald-Hansemann ministry hesitated to oppose it. The resolution was passed by a strong majority.

This vote set off serious repercussions at the court, among the nobles and officer corps, as well as in the various conservative societies. The ministry was under heavy fire from the right. Friedrich Wilhelm was incensed, feeling that his honor and his status as army commander had been violated. There was outrage on the left also, because of the slowness of the ministry in taking action against suspect army officers.

Because of their preoccupation with the problem of the Stein resolution, Prussian assembly members may not have paid much attention to the *Arbeiterkongress* [workers' congress] that assembled in Berlin on 23 August and continued in session through 3 September. The workers had been invited by the central committee organized by Stephan Born among Berlin's workers. This congress, representing thirty-one organizations, arrived at a new form of association that they called the *Arbeiterverbrüderung* [workers' brotherhood] led by a central committtee that established its headquarters in Leipzig. No communist groups had participated in the congress, which in fact issued a manifesto that was in direct opposition to known Marxist goals: "We, the workers, are by nature the supports of peace and order".[39] By the spring of 1849, the brotherhood was publishing its own paper, *Die Verbrüderung,* and was able to claim fifteen thousand members, based in one hundred and seventy locals. Though labor organization during the early months of the revolution had been loose it had become obvious to leaders like Stephan Born that the potential was there, in view of the wave of strikes (by textile workers, metal workers, and construction workers, all demanding higher wages) that followed in the wake of Born's typesetters' strike in April at Berlin.

On 2 September the Auerswald-Hansemann ministry announced that an executive order in the sense of the Stein resolution was incompatible with the spirit and being of the army. Choice of means for execution of the goal of the resolution had best be left to the discretion of the war minister as a member of the executive branch, and not touched by the assembly. This non-execution of the provisions of the Stein resolution quickly precipitated the constitutional crisis that brought down the ministry, although the Prussian constituent assembly, in its transitional character before the actual adoption of a constitution had in fact no competence to interfere in executive matters, which remained under the lawful control of the monarch.[40]

Delegates on the left bitterly contested the right of the government to decide whether or not to comply with the provisions of the Stein resolution. Stein himself insisted that the honor and dignity of the assembly required that the government execute all terms of the resolution, and this position was applauded by members of the right center, whose spokesman, Hans Viktor von Unruh (1806–1886), warned that they had come to a critical divide between counterrevolution and a second revolution. He suggested that the assembly ought to express its lack of confidence in the ministry if it persisted in its delay with respect to the resolution of 9 August. In this way, the right center was declaring itself open to a parliamentary system of government.

With certain factions on the left threatening to withdraw from the assembly, a number of mediating suggestions failed, along with the Unruh resolution of no confidence. On the contrary, the assembly voted on 7 September (219 against 143) that it was the most urgent duty of the ministry to comply unreservedly with the resolution of 9 August. There was an implicit threat here of renewed revolution. Leopold von Gerlach saw it in those terms. This was not a cabinet question, he thought. It was revolt [Aufruhr] because it was a barefaced demand that the ministry obey the orders of the assembly majority.[41]

The ministry objected firmly that it was not within the competence of the assembly to interfere in executive affairs. Then, unable to find any prospect of solution, the Auerswald-Hansemann ministry resigned (8 September).

This downfall of the ministry entailed broad implications. Since the parliamentary majority had forced the issue, the government for its part had bowed to the rules of a parliamentary system. Now Prussia appeared to be headed fully toward parliamentary government, but resistance hardened among the court conservatives and the military party, as well as in the heart of the ruler himself. Forces already in play were joined by those of liberal citizens' groups that had begun to send petitions to the king, asking him to parry the dangerous thrust of radicalism.

One anonymous appeal was worded in terms that would surely inflame the king. "Loyalty to Prussia remains as it was of old—yes, the old formula With God for King and Fatherland has not lost its magic power. There is still time, but perhaps it is high time, to draw the long dormant spark from the steel. It needs only the firm sure stroke to make it spray forth. May it please the wise judgment of Your Majesty to secure in this way the welfare of the land." In another address to the king, published on 10 September, the Rhineland constitutional society of Elberfeld [described as "liberal"] pleaded that he immediately dissolve the assembly and call a new election "in order to eliminate the threatening power of absolute parliamentary control, and to protect the freedom of the people from despotism".[42]

The king and his courtiers were encouraged by this evidence of opposition, and started to consider formation of a cabinet that would frontally attack the assembly and enter into deliberate open conflict with it. Leopold von Gerlach had already presented a *Regierungsplan* [plan of government] to Friedrich Wilhelm in a memorandum of 3 September.

For years, it was accepted as fact that on 11 September Friedrich Wilhelm set down his own detailed plan for a *Streik*, with clear reference to dissolution of the assembly and the royal grant of a constitution.[43] He would reject the Stein resolution as illegal, shift the assembly from Berlin to Brandenburg, refuse to accept the draft constitution, and forbid public meetings, societies, and uncensored press as incompatible with public law and order. Recent scholarly investigation has proved that the king's ambitious program was by no means adhered to, and that by no stretch of fact or imagination can it be said that he provided a blueprint for counterrevolutionary moves that occurred in November and December.[44] Nevertheless, a memorandum written by the king in response to a petition of 14 September that was signed by many of his *Standesherren* definitely shows that Friedrich Wilhelm had given serious thought to the idea of overthrowing the troublesome assembly. He observed that he wanted "responsible ministers" who would be willing to act according to "my convictions", and he wrote of an encircling military force that could be utilized in case of rebellion.[45]

In view of the upset conditions in southern Germany during the month of September, anyone could appreciate the fact that this was an extremely inopportune moment for installation of a defiant ministry in Prussia. Provocative moves on the part of the sovereign would surely have caused the Berlin radicals to dash to the barricades once again, erupting into vigorous protest and revolutionary violence.

Friedrich Wilhelm decided that some kind of transitional figure was needed, if he were to gain the upper hand, and unexpectedly appointed the elderly general, Ernst von Pfuel (1779–1866), as his new prime minister, supplying him with a ministry of bureaucrats, instead of the members of the assembly who had previously held cabinet posts. Von Pfuel was a man of independent mind, the "last representative of the great Prussian reform era, and as such not willing to strike down radicalism solely by reaction."[46] Rather, he would seek a middle way for state reform. It was Pfuel who in March had refused to order his troops to fire on the crowd in Berlin, thus enraging the crown prince, and again it was he who had promptly gone to the king, demanding that his royal brother be ordered to apologize.

Although Friedrich Wilhelm had surrounded the city of Berlin with an army of some fifty thousand men under the command of Friedrich von Wrangel and was obviously in the mood for a showdown, he had been mistaken in his selection of a transitional minister. Old von Pfuel quickly set about what he considered to be the essential task of conciliation, saying that he wanted to "reach the majority of the national assembly" and above all obtain agreement on the constitution "in order to limit the legislative actions that they would undertake." Peace and order must be restored in Berlin by legal means, he commented. As a precaution, and with the intention of controlling the belligerent von Wrangel, Pfuel reserved for himself the cabinet post of war minister.

To the deep chagrin of his sovereign and at the same time delighting the radicals, Pfuel issued an *Anti-Reaktions Erlass* [decree][47] directed to army commanders. He pointed out that the draft constitution stipulated that members of the army and the civil service would be required to take an oath to the constitution. Pfuel's decree continued, to the effect that all anti-constitutional endeavors would therefore be incompatible with the position of army officers. The interests of the fatherland demanded cooperation with the "statutory powers" and avoidance of any appearance of dissent. The concept must be spread that the free development of the constitutional state was not threatened by the fatherland's armies, but rather it was protected by them. The hearts of the radical members of the assembly were won because they themselves were part of the "statutory powers", but the military party was infuriated. Pfuel was a traitor to the tradition and honor of the corps! Further to fuel the conservatives' ire, the new minister accepted an act of habeas corpus and another that abolished the noble landlords' hunting rights.

Backed by the assembly's confidence in him, Pfuel also allowed debate on the draft constitution to open early in October, no doubt in the belief that his *Erlass* to the military would have had a mollifying effect and that the delegates on the left would not make excessive demands. He could not have foreseen that ranks and titles (even decorations) would be eliminated, the death penalty abolished, and that Friedrich Wilhelm would have to face the terrible prospect of ruling without the grace of God. The conservatives began to raise the cry that this was pure Jacobinism, straight from the French *Assemblée nationale.*

All this, by prior agreement, would have to be thrashed out with the government, but the sovereign was so angered that his god-given royal backbone stiffened. It should be remembered that the current news arriving from Vienna was most invigorating. If the Habsburgs could resume their absolute rule, why not the Hohenzollerns?

On 7 October, General von Pfuel handed in his resignation, accompanied by a dignified justification of his action. His Majesty had told him that never, under any circumstances, would he ever regard the draft constitution that had been presented to him as acceptable. In Pfuel's opinion, his Majesty would have to accept the constitution just as it came from the plenum of the national assembly, because otherwise there would be *eine masslose Verwirrung* [immeasurable confusion]. In their last meeting, von Pfuel reminded the king, his Majesty had stated unequivocally that if the ministry did not wish to keep to the path he proposed, he would act alone "in full consciousness of his right and power."[48]

A critical conflict arose in Berlin before Pfuel's resignation could become effective. For months, friction between the proletariat and Berlin's property-owning middle class had been generating heat, the problem being exacerbated by the inability of the civil guard to maintain order. Trouble broke out in earnest in consequence of an ill-advised move on the part of the constituent assembly, which ruled on 13 October that the minimum age for admission to the ranks of the civil guard would be twenty-four. This automatically excluded the ephemeral groups of young apprentices, students, artists, etc., who had until that time legally borne arms,[49] although they were not officially recognized as part of the established *Bürgerwehr.* This was a sly blow at the radicals because the main body of the civil guard was made up of middle class citizens, while the youngsters of the semi-official corps were unmistakably in sympathy with the left. However, there was fission among the members of the civil guard itself. As the disorder expanded, some were in open agreement with the demonstrators, and about one third actually withdrew from the service.

The new regulation was never put into effect, but the actual vote had been preceded by angry street demonstrations and riots. The canal workers contributed to the trouble by engaging in machine-breaking (they viewed the new steam pumps as a menace to their own livelihood in any case), and this violence spread to such an extent that it was inevitable that the civil guard would begin to fire into the milling throngs. Before order was restored, hundreds of workers had joined the fray, carrying red flags and shouting "Long live the Republic!"

A delegation of workers appeared before the constituent assembly, demanding that the civil guard be punished, but the assembly was firm, refusing to be terrorized. The dreadful affair ended on 20 October with the public display of corpses and an enormous procession in which there marched representatives of some twenty-six manufacturing establishments as well as assembly members from the left. Within the assembly, there were those on the right who accused the left of having instigated the trouble. On the left, there was bleak discouragement. There were too many factions—social revolutionists, workers' clubs, Marxists—and the orderly middle class was deserting them.

There was enough turmoil to warrant Friedrich Wilhelm's demand that Pfuel put the city under martial law, but once again there were constitutional snags. It was questionable, whether the executive branch at that time had the competence to issue such an order. Pfuel's refusal to proclaim martial law was no doubt based more on his conviction that some kind of peaceful solution had to be reached.[50] Pfuel again offered his resignation (16 October). The king accepted it but ordered him not to publicize the fact. Meanwhile, conflict within the assembly had led to shifts that brought Hans Viktor von Unruh to the chair as presiding officer.

Friedrich Wilhelm IV wrote from Potsdam to his sister Charlotte [the tsarina Alexandra Feodorovna] on 25 October 1848.

I thought of my holy duties as the authority established by God for protection of the right . . . I acted. More than 30,000 men were united around Berlin, and I demanded from the ministry those things that you know about from my letter to the tsar. It [the Auerswald-Hansemann ministry] refused to obey. Thereupon I dismissed it and named the present one [Pfuel's ministry] in its place. Pfuel has come three times to resign. I have provided [*Graf* Friedrich Wilhelm von] Brandenburg as his successor[51] . . . I wrote a proclamation to the people on the fifteenth. However, because I set up the building of our freedoms on the sole basis of authority "by the grace of God", in rejection of the striking down of that title (by the assembly on the previous Thursday), the ministers refused to countersign my proclamation. . . . *Aidez-moi de Vos prières*. . .[52]

In desperate last-ditch moves, the radicals opened their second *Demokratenkongress* on 26 October, and on the next day their *Gegenparlament* assembled. At first glance, one might wonder why two separate gatherings were necessary. They embodied different aspects of the far-left movement in that the *Demokratenkongress* was made up of representatives from workers' societies all over Germany, whereas the *Gegenparlament* [53] was intended to rally elected delegates of the extreme left from the Prussian national assembly, the Frankfurt *Parlament*, as well as provincial *Landtag* representatives.

The *Demokratenkongress* was the successor of the congress that had been held in Frankfurt in June under the chairmanship of Julius Fröbel. The central committtee had issued a manifesto on 3 October, calling "in the name of the peoples' sovereignty" for the abolition of the Frankfurt *Parlament*. Only by such a measure, the manifesto asserted, could the necessity of a new, bloody revolution be avoided. Since recall of the *Parlament* delegates was out of the question, this was a thinly-disguised call for a second revolution. [54]

The two hundred and thirty-four delegates who attended the second congress that opened in Berlin on 26 October indeed represented Germany's extreme left. Though there was a superficial unity in their drive toward a republic, beneath the surface there were so many conflicting views and goals that the unity was in actuality not much more than a staunch opposition to monarchy. Stephan Born had hoped to persuade the congress to express solidarity with his workers' congress and the principles of *Verbrüderung* but the cross-currents were too strong. Attempts by the delegates from Cologne met similar obstacles. They tried to push through a resolution that outlined the communist program, but many participants in the congress had already left in protest before the motion came to the floor. The pervasive essential disunity flowed from a shift of viewpoints on revolutionary tactics. Originally the thrust had been toward a democratizing of all Germany—united—but convictions concerning the effectiveness of such an approach had drifted.

There were those who were beginning to feel that a unification of all the German states might be unattainable, and that it might be better to aim at constitutional government in the individual states, leaving the matter of an overall national union until some later day. In their minds, Berlin rather than Frankfurt had become a focal point, as indicated by the choice of the Prussian capital as the appropriate meeting place for their congress. An article signed by H. B. Oppenheim, editor of the *Reform* (no. 167 of 5 October) makes the point (cited by Gustav Lüders) that

> the Frankfurt central state is floating in the air, and the basis of our reality, the place of choice for our battles lies elsewhere. As certain as it is that German unity is to be founded only on and by freedom, just as certain is it that the victory or failure of democracy will be decided in the individual states and—as most recent events have shown clearly enough, in the German states of the first rank, in their capitals, in Vienna or Berlin. Dynasties do not fall before paper storms that have been flung at Frankfurt—but they waver before the hammer blows of social democracy in Berlin and Vienna. If Prussia goes backward, German freedom is lost, but if democracy is victorious in Berlin, it is victorious for all Germany.[55]

Members of the *Demokratenkongress* were united in their acute awareness of the plight of the Austrian revolutionists in Vienna, where their former presiding officer Julius Fröbel together with Robert Blum and three other delegates from the Frankfurt *Parlament* left arrived on the very day that the congress opened, their mission being to carry affirmations of sympathy and encouragement. News soon arrived that Windischgrätz had begun his bombardment, and not long after that came reports of the capitulation of Vienna's barricade fighters. (Robert Blum would face a firing squad on 9 November.)

The other last-ditch effort which was under way in Berlin at the same time, the *Gegenparlament*, was also transfixed by the evil fate that hung over Vienna. The opening meeting of the *Gegenparlament* [opposition parliament] had taken place on 27 October, one day after the opening of the *Demokratenkongress*. Called by Johann Jacoby and five other delegates of the Prussian assembly, this counterparliament had been thought of as a meeting of the extreme left from all the German provincial assemblies. The intention had been to develop a revolutionary body that would counterbalance the Frankfurt *Parlament*. The difficulty lay in the fact that participants other than the radicals of the Prussian constituent assembly were so few. Five came from Frankfurt, including Ludwig Simon of Trier and Franz Zitz of Mainz, but the discouraging total of delegates who were not members of the Prussian assembly was only eight.

The most urgent issue as they saw it was the need to support the Viennese. A proposal that an uprising in Berlin be promoted was rejected. Waldeck especially was convinced that parliamentary action alone should be attempted. Jacoby and the communist Karl Ludwig d'Ester failed to garner enough votes for a motion that the German people ought to rescue Vienna by the armed intervention of volunteers. In the end, there was agreement that the left ought to press for a vote in the Prussian assembly, calling for intervention by the Prussian armed forces.

In the *Demokratenkongress*, in spite of concern over the Viennese situation, there was little unanimity among the delegates. They were reluctant with respect to Arnold Ruge's effort in urging support of a resolution that Waldeck intended to present to the Prussian assembly, calling for military aid by the standing army of Prussia. The only result was a call for a general mass meeting in Berlin on 29 October. At this meeting, it was agreed that the people of Berlin regarded the Vienna revolution as their own. Ruge then engineered a "storm petition" to the Prussian assembly that would support the Waldeck resolution.

On the following day, about one thousand marchers headed for the assembly, but from the very start it was obvious that they were heading into trouble. With their red flags, they were led by Ruge, who unfortunately was escorted by two of Berlin's well-known *Kannegiessern* [compulsive spouters of political nonsense]. The presence of a disheveled street orator like the well known "Karbe" did nothing to build public respect and confidence.[56] The document that Ruge and his marchers bore was duly presented and handed over to the assembly's presiding officer. Ruge was informed that there would be no vote until late afternoon, and he told his followers that they could meet again on the following day at the *Zelten,* at which time they would learn the result of the assembly's deliberations. Ruge then discovered that he had lost control of the force he had brought together. The marchers refused to leave, and they were rapidly joined by hordes of unpleasant riffraff (popularly called "Bassermann types").[57] Newspaper reports on the following day described the mob as made up primarily of boys and unemployed older men.

When delegate Waldeck offered his motion to the effect that all means available to the state should be applied for the defense of freedom ("Civilized Europe urgently expects from the major German people [Prussia] that it will place its money and arms in the scales, making them available to the government in Vienna . . ."), he was voted down 229 to 113.[58] Liberals and moderates of the assembly had joined the right in defeating the proposal for Prussian military intervention in Austria[59] which would have been an opening wedge for a revival of the particularist individual-state system in lieu of the originally sought-for German unity. Instead, a cynical vote was carried in favor of a motion by Karl Rodbertus (left center), that the Frankfurt central power should be asked to intervene. This was an obviously empty gesture because it was common knowledge that *Erzherzog* Johann and his administration had no means at their disposal for execution of any action in Austria, but even von Pfuel voted in favor of the Rodbertus resolution.

Meanwhile the roar of the multitude outside was reaching a crescendo. At one point, Julius Berends, one of the most popular members of the assembly, tried to go outside and reason with the crowd, but before he could even open his mouth he was flung rudely back into the building entrance, where pale Waldeck and Jacoby stood in consultation. Berends fell to the floor, screaming. Someone had thrust a flaming torch into his face.

The doors were now hammered shut. Inside, along with the delegates, was a detachment of the *Bürgerwehr* and its commanding officer, Rimpler. This meant that the major part of the guard out on the street was without a commander. The outside group managed to beat its way to a side door, opening it. The delegates then made a precarious trip through store rooms, up and down ladders and so on, on their way to this exit. As they emerged from the building, a shot was fired, and a pitched battle began, the guard using their clubs, the crowd using its torches. An unarmed band of machinists appeared and made a valiant attempt to break up the fight. They were successful, but then the guard turned on them, with the result that more shots were fired and bayonets were used. The machinists then retired, saying that they were going for weapons. The heroic Rimpler rushed to their meeting hall and promised them that there would be no further attacks.

When von Pfuel attempted to leave, he was told that this was impossible. In the end, the old gentleman was able to depart, escorted and protected by Jacoby and two other delegates of the left, who hurried him to safety. On the following day, his resignation was announced.

In its effort to engage in the struggle against counterrevolution, the *Demokratenkongress* had achieved nothing more than an ineffectual demonstration that pointed up the growing split between the proletariat and the Prussian constituent assembly. At the same time, the moderate middle class had been forced toward the right.

Whether or not there had been active *agents provocateurs* in the crowd outside the assembly chamber has not been determined. There is however a damning statement by Hermann Wagener, who had been the editor of the arch-conservative *Kreuzzeitung*, in his *Die Politik Friedrich Wilhelms IV,* written in 1883.

> In the interval between the resignation of the Auerswald-Hansemann ministry and the opening of the Pfuel ministry, the peoples' representatives moved from the Singakademie to the theatre, chiefly because the large plaza of the Gendarmenmarkt was especially suitable for putting crowds on the scene and thus acting on the assembly from the outside. This was, as we were convinced at the time, a cheap diversion and cost exactly a hundred *Taler* and three kegs of brandy, one *Taler* each to a hundred trusted individuals stationed at various points on the plaza, who were to shout the appropriate words and supply the brandy for firing up enthusiasm.[60]

In any case, it would be an obvious advantage to the conservatives if they could spread the impression among middle-class citizens that the vaunted revolutionary assembly was nothing but a tool of the radical, mindless proletariat. It would therefore be useful to them if the street rabble could be stirred up in such a way that they would appear to be dictating to a servile assembly. The public support of the Waldeck pro-Austria resolution by unsavory characters like old Karbe and Ruge's thousand marchers, followed by rough reaction on the streets to rejection of the resolution, had precisely the desired effect.

> Recipe, from an anonymous broadside: Take 20 earth workers, 4 quarts Kümmel, some Karbe, 2 or 3 pitch torches, 6 lengths of heavy rope, 1 1/2 kids from the Berlin streets, 2 sticks with blood-red linen, 1 obligatory pistol shot. Stir together vigorously until three to four thousand curiosity-seekers collect, then throw in a few shouts of "reaction—treachery—citizens' blood", let the alarm sound and—*probatum est*—unless it rains.[61]

The only "evidence" of conservative activity centers around one *Graf* Bressler who was a contributor to the *Kreuzzeitung* and had been a member of the *Preussenverein* as well as of the *Junkerparlament*, though he seems to have parted from that group because he thought it was not energetic enough. Apparently acting on his own, he was twice arrested—once for urging workers to go to the barricades, and on a second occasion for inciting to riot. Bressler was jailed for three months on the latter charge—but that was in September, before the disastrous October episode around the assembly chambers.[62]

With announcement that the Pfuel ministry would be replaced by that of *Graf* Brandenburg, there was great indignation among the members of the Prussian assembly. They had seen themselves as law-abiding and loyal. The mob that surged around them on 31 October had been against them, attacking them! The majority decided to submit an address to Friedrich Wilhelm, protesting the appointment of Brandenburg. They wanted a ministry of commoners, preferably taken from their own ranks.

With some difficulty, a royal audience was arranged for twenty-five delegates from all parties. They presented their respectful address and then stood in silence, awaiting a response. The king took the proferred document, folded it up, and stalked toward the exit. This was too much for Johann Jacoby, who ignored all courtly protocol, asking the monarch if he was refusing to listen to the deputation. They had come not only to submit their address, but also to report on the

Figure 20   DR. JOHANN JOCOBY CHALLENGES THE PRUSSIAN MONARCH (November 1848)

state of the country. The king continued his walkout, tossing a disdainful "No!" over his shoulder.

It was then that Jacoby uttered his memorable observation. *Das ist das Unglück der Könige, dass sie die Wahrheit nicht hören wollen!* [That's the trouble with kings. They don't want to hear the truth!] Jacoby's fellow delegates were upset by this shocking outburst, but his words rang through Berlin. He had struck a sensitive nerve in the city's proletariat, who poured out onto the streets, honoring him with a torchlight procession. They began to set up a cry for "a last fight for the fatherland and right and freedom". On 5 November, some fifteen hundred men gathered with the intention of organizing a new volunteer corps. The time for action had come.

The new ministry was bombarded with conservatives' demands that the "excesses" and "complete lawlessness" be stopped. The *Preussenverein* wrote on 3 November that there must be protection from terrorism in this state of utmost anarchy. The Prussian constituent assembly was pacified by soothing messages from Friedrich Wilhelm and kindly assurances from *Graf* Brandenburg, though members on the left remained wary and suspicious. The right was quietly engaged in negotiations with Brandenburg, discussing the possibility of removing the assembly from the capital. General Wrangel meanwhile was calling attention to the difficult situation of his troops. Cold weather was coming, and there they were in the city outskirts, quartered in sheds and barns. Morale, health, and discipline were threatened.

Fanny Lewald had been absent from Berlin for four months. She returned to the city on 8 November and reported that everyone was waiting for a *coup d'état* that would be marked by martial occupation and dissolution of the assembly. She recalled that in the hot summer of 1846, which she had spent at Castellammare, Vesuvius was quiet but everyone was shuddering in anticipation because all the wells were drying up. It was like that in Berlin. The hatred between the parties had assumed a bitter character, and among the stable friends of order there was tooth-grinding and longing for a blood bath that would destroy the Bassermann *Schreckengestalten*. The watchful waiting, she thought, could be explained by the fact that the government was hoping for some kind of riot that would justify intervention. She talked at length with her friend Johann Jacoby who seemed to her to be unaccountably optimistic. He explained that the feeling of subjection and submission was still rock-solid in many Germans, and that nothing would so effectively combat that as absolutism. "The princes are wearing out the trust and faith of the people. They are teaching them. . . . They're undermining the only foundation on which they can stand."[63]

On 9 November (the day of Robert Blum's execution), *Graf* Brandenburg appeared before the Prussian assembly and read a royal message. In consideration of earlier ill-treatment of the delegates and the events of 31 October, the assembly lacked freedom and the delegates were without adequate protection, with the result that their debate was hampered. The king was therefore moving the assembly to the city of Brandenburg, and adjourning it until it could resume its work there on 27 November.

Accepting the ministerial dismissal, seventy-seven members of the right promptly filed out. Called to order by Hans Viktor von Unruh, the remaining members voted 252 to 30 that the act of the minister in closing the session had been illegal. Another nineteen delegates departed. The rest voted almost unanimously to continue in session. They would meet wherever president von Unruh summoned them. They then went on to debate the question that was before the house, and also passed a warm vote of thanks to von Unruh for his courage.

Even a peaceful, bloodless winding down of a revolution is depressing to contemplate. Von Unruh was determined that he and his fellow assembly members would remain strictly within the law. He was obdurate when he received a peremptory message from *Graf* Brandenburg, to the effect that he and the assembly delegates had arrogated to themselves unwarranted rights and had acted against the constitution, passing the legal barriers and disobeying his Majesty's commands. When he consulted commandant Rimpler of the *Bürgerwehr*, Unruh was told that if regular troops were to appear, only half of the guard could confront them, and that if there were actual conflict, only one quarter of them would have sufficient ammunition. Besides, most of the officers were reactionary, Rimpler said. Unruh then canvassed the delegates of the left: what about the various democratic clubs? They responded that defensive action from that quarter would be hopeless. Unruh decided that passive resistance was the only practical course.

In the night of 9 November, commandant Rimpler received an order from the chief of police. He was to block all entrances to the assembly chamber. He refused, saying that he and his men were supposed to protect the freedom that would be endangered by ruthless treatment of the assembly members. The delegates met early on the tenth, and after listening to von Unruh's arguments, they agreed with him that as long as freedom of the press and of assembly remained, the despotic regime could be overturned by the people.

At two o'clock in the afternoon (10 November), Wrangel and his thirteen thousand troops marched into the city. The people and the civil guard watched them coldly. Fanny Lewald saw women weeping at the spectacle of pipe-smoking soldiers sticking their heads out of public buildings, where they were quartered in detachments of two hundred or more. From these *Alarmhäuser*, as such housing was called, fully armed troops could appear almost instantaneously on the streets, in solid ranks. In the museum, which was being used as barracks, the huge rotunda echoed "like the noise of a thundering waterfall" from the voices of men settling in there, putting their caps rakishly on the heads of the Capitoline faun and the Minerva Medica.[64]

The assembly voted to issue a proclamation to the people. "Hold fast to the freedoms that have been won, but never for one moment forsake the foundation of the law. The peaceful and resolute behavior of a people ripe for freedom will secure the victory of freedom, with God's help."[65]

There followed a public interchange between Rimpler and General von Wrangel.

> Wrangel: he would remain until the delegates had been removed.
> Rimpler: the *Bürgerwehr* would not leave the area before the delegates of the National assembly.
> Wrangel: he did not know of any national assembly or any president of such an assembly.
> Rimpler: The troops would not withdraw until the gentlemen in the chamber had left the building.

At five o'clock, Unruh sent word that the assembly delegates and the *Bürgerwehr* would depart together. He added a formal protest against military intervention, and then led the delegates out. They moved solemnly in formal procession, escorted by the civil guard.

Von Unruh had already been in search of another meeting place. The university rector had refused use of the *Aula*. The sharpshooters' association found space for them at the Hôtel de Russie, where two hundred and forty-seven delegates assembled on 11 November. On that same day the civil guard was disbanded on Friedrich Wilhelm's order, an act that the assembly promptly branded as illegal. Members of the left next offered a proposal that taxes be withheld from the Brandenburg ministry (presumably at the suggestion of Johann Jacoby), but the moderates still had the upper hand in the assembly, and the motion was side-tracked.

Then came the lightning stroke. Quiet, passive, unresisting Berlin was declared to be "under siege" (12 November), threatened by Wrangel's encircling heavy artillery.

In this appalling situation, the assembly began to look shabby in the eyes of the citizens, hounded as it was by the police and driven out of each of its successive meeting places. In the death throes of its last meeting in Berlin, the radicals managed to put through their tax-with-holding measure, with its assertion that the Brandenburg ministry had no right to use state funds or to collect taxes so long as the assembly could not continue its deliberations undisturbed.[66]

The conservatives eagerly welcomed this misstep, which admittedly was not within the competence of a constituent assembly. Now they could claim that wild-eyed radicals were in control!

Before the members had mastered their problem of persuading enough delegates to attend the scheduled session at Brandenburg to constitute a quorum, the king formally dissolved the Prussian national assembly (5 December 1848), not even troubling himself to call for new elections, and enabling himself single-handed to solve the problem of a constitution. He "granted" (imposed) a constitution of his own devising. Friedrich Wilhelm had resisted, announcing dramatically that he would never grant anything so shameful as a constitution but would kill himself instead, but in the end he had bowed to the inevitable. Though ultraconservatives objected strongly, the moderates—*Graf* Brandenburg and Otto von Manteuffel, his minister of the interior among them—were in favor of this realistic concession.

The assembly had attempted to base its authority on the fact of revolution. Friedrich Wilhelm based his authority to dictate a constitution on the fact of his right to engage in a *coup d'état*.[67] It was an act of illegality and at the same time the beginning of a new stable system under which Prussians were to live for seven decades.

Though ostensibly based on the Waldeck charter, the imposed constitution had significant modifications. Reintroduction of the death penalty. Restoration of the monarch's absolute veto. A new emergency power that allowed the king to suspend the civil rights he had so graciously granted (freedom of person, freedom of religious confession, freedom of assembly and association etc.). His Majesty remained as before ruler by the grace of God, and it had dawned upon him that constitutions are subject to revision.

Provisions for voting had an unexpectedly liberal aspect, yet May 1849 found a new election law already in place that classified the voters in three categories based on the amount of direct tax they paid. The resulting three classes in a given locality would end in proportionate voting for one single representative. Such a *Destillierapparat* [distillation apparatus], as Ludwig Simon was to describe it in writing to his friend Johann Jacoby from his Paris exile in 1861[68] was hardly an adequate instrument for democratic government.

The drama had ended.

The view of Prussian affairs from Frankfurt was somewhat distorted. Karl Theodor Welcker, growling about the left's "sovereignty swindle", had commented with sour displeasure that the radicals believed that through the grace of God they were superior to everyone else.[69] Friedrich Daniel Bassermann had his own ideas about sovereignty. He thought that in the new state it resided in the parliament. He was also convinced that the will of the majority that he represented had become invincible. He was destined to suffer rude disappointment early in November, when the Frankfurt *Parlament* sent him on a mission to Berlin, where the forces of reaction were steadily advancing. He viewed *Graf* Brandenburg's actions and Wrangel's entry into the city as healthy measures against the street rabble and the radical left. Just before his departure from Frankfurt on 7 November, he told a friend that Berlin was the last place of retreat of "our modern tyrants", and that he anticipated open discussion with the king in the interest of unity.

It is true that Bassermann had his discussions with Friedrich Wilhelm, but there was hardly a meeting of minds. Bassermann confidently believed that the middle class liberal majority and the monarch were fighting shoulder to shoulder against the radical left. He did not grasp the idea that the king and the extreme right had already decided to lump all revolutionaries and reform-minded liberals together with the radicals and toss them all into the trash bin. Worse still, Bassermann did not see that more and more of the middle class—not just in Prussia but also in the south, even in his own home town of Mannheim—approved of such a course.

In his memoirs, Bassermann mentioned that after their interviews, Friedrich Wilhelm had wanted to know if he would accept the Order of the Red Eagle in recognition of his service to the Prussian crown. "This was saddening evidence of the king's lack of understanding of the situation."[70] He himself still failed to understand that Friedrich Wilhelm had seen how matters stood: the hour of Bassermann and his political allies had passed.

Wealthy Berliners, calmed by the presence of the troops, quickly resumed the even tenor of their ways. Though the poor were still poor and the unemployed remained idle and hungry, elegant ladies accompanied by their liveried footmen once again visited the luxury shops, in anticipation of balls and routs that had long been abandoned. A disgruntled Fanny Lewald commented resentfully that the purchasers of stylish black-and-white striped goods must have envied zebras, whose hides were modishly striped by the grace of God. Her friend Johann Jacoby was more relaxed. He shrugged off scurilous reports in the *Kreuzzeitung* that named him as a spy in the pay of the Russians, remarking that he could quote Ireland's O'Connell, who once boasted that he was the most calumniated man in the kingdom.[71]

When word reached Frankfurt that Friedrich Wilhelm had moved against the press (on 15 November), the forces of the left saw that the "feudal" reaction of Vienna and Berlin was threatening even the concept of democracy. They viewed their own Frankfurt *Parlament* as futile and incompetent because of its "upper class" majority. Also, they considered that their own left wing membership was becoming dangerously remote from the proletariat. There had been a move toward withdrawal from the *Paulskirche,* but now at a joint session of the delegates from the Donnersberg, Deutscher Hof, and Westendhall it was decided to form a great umbrella association that would work throughout Germany with the Frankfurt *Parlament* in an effort to preserve gains made in March 1848.

Because the counterrevolution might annihilate the campaign for German unity, the new *Zentralmärzverein* [Central March Association] would accept the fact that there were serious divisions among its own ranks and would consciously search for common ground.[72] This was a novel phenomenon. Germans, struggling toward unity and reform, had had so little experience with the kind of bridge-building and conciliation that is the very essence and bulwark of viable democracy that usually, at the slightest provocation, they had tended to break apart.

The statement of principles published by the Central March Association was the result of a number of significant compromises on the part of the extreme left. The question of monarchy *versus* republic was left open, for example. However, there was an unambiguous demand for self-determination

by the people as a whole, as for the people of any particular state, [who] determine and establish for themselves their own form of government, and improve and transform it as it appears to be advantageous to them, because every government exists solely by and through the will of the people.[73]

Moreover, the manifesto specifically stated that only parliamentary means—not armed force—were to be applied in building a peaceful, just and united Germany. The intention to achieve reconciliation with the moderate liberals was unmistakably spelled out.

Karl Marx's *Neue Rheinische Zeitung* jeered that legal resistance was the favorite expression of "all those who believe they can circumvent revolution" by pretty speeches. These people were in fact a *bewusstloses Werkzeug der Konterrevolution* [an unwitting tool of the counterrevolution].[74]

The Central March was well structured, with a system of branch societies and associated societies that all received directives from the Frankfurt headquarters. "March societies" sprang up all over southern Germany. At the peak of its activity, toward the end of March 1849, there were nine hundred and fifty affiliates with a total overall membership of half a million or more. Most action of these organizations centered around leafleting and publication of articles relating to current political problems, as well as public demonstrations, e.g. in celebration of the introduction of the constitution's fundamental rights. In this last instance, Central March members split. Those on the far left thought that the fundamental rights were meaningless unless those states that were resisting them were forced into acceptance. Such disagreements were ominous. The knell of revolution was tolling not only in Vienna and Berlin, but all over Germany, especially at Frankfurt.

Notes

1 Leopold von Gerlach, *Denkwürdigkeiten* , 1:150.

2 David E. Barclay, "The Court Camarilla and the Politics of Monarchical Restoration in Prussia, 1848–58," in *Between Reform, Reaction, and Resistance, p. 127.

3 Lewald-Stahr, *Erinnerungen aus dem Jahre 1848*, pp. 79–81.

4 Valentin, *Geschichte der deutschen Revolution*, 2:45.

5 Lewald-Stahr, pp. 75–76, 90. The comment on the evasive vocabulary is interesting in conjunction with the caustic remark of de Circourt, who observed at the height of the March days that German revolutionists used French words in referring to their most sacred objectives—constitution for *Verfassung*, *révolution* for *Umwälzung* etc.

6 Ibid., pp. 77–78.

7 Ernst Rudolf Huber, *Der Kampf um Einigkeit und Freiheit*, p. 725.

8 Born, *Erinnerungen*, pp. 138–141; P. H. Noyes, *Organization and Revolution, p. 85, citing Bernstein's *Geschichte der berliner Arbeiterbewegung*, 1:38; There is no direct evidence of any plan to use Rehbergers and canal workers as a nucleus for a counterrevolutionary army.

9 Wernicke, *Geschichte der revolutionären berliner Arbeiterbewegung 1830–1849*, p. 105.

10 Ibid., p. 45.

11 Noyes, p. 124.

12 Wernicke, p. 133.

13 Valentin, 2:58.

14 Noyes, p. 130.

15 Gerlach, 1:154.

16 *Von der Revolution zum Norddeutschen Bund*, 2:529.

17 Ibid., 2:530, footnote. Ludwig von Gerlach countered his brother's argument by saying that voluntary abdication would in itself be an act of sovereign authority, but at a somewhat later date he said that on the whole he was not in favor of it.

18 Hans-Christian Klaus, "Das preussische Königtum und Friedrich Wilhelm IV. aus der Sicht Ernst Ludwig von Gerlachs," in *Friedrich Wilhelm IV. in seiner Zeit*, p. 50.

19   Barclay, p. 139.

20   Lewald-Stahr, pp. 118–119.

21   Füssl, *Professor in der Politik*, p. 140.

22   Ibid., p. 128.

23   Barclay, p. 136.

24   Füssl, p. 145.

25   *Von der Revolution zum norddeutscher Bund*, 2:551.

26   Füssl, p. 145.

27   Ibid., pp. 146–149.

28   As previously noted, forty-six thousand signatures were collected in that campaign.

29   Berdahl, *The Politics of the Prussian Nobility*, p. 16. The term *Junker* as generally applied to the Prussian landowners derives from an old term that originally referred to the younger sons of the nobility (the *junk-herre*), whose dominance can be traced as far back as the mid-Fifteenth Century.

30   Siemann, *Die deutsche Revolution von 1848/49*, p. 112.

31   Ibid, pp. 108–109.

32   Huber, p. 687, footnote 15.

33   Sperber, *European Revolutions*, p. 162.

34   Valentin, 2:229.

35   Ibid., 2:232.

36   Ibid., 2:238–239.

37   Huber, p. 735.

38   Botzenhart, *Deutsche Parlamentarismus in der Revolutionszeit 1848–1850*, p. 525.

39   Huber, p. 693. Though communists were not officially represented, forty-eight leading members of the *Arbeiterverbrüderung* were communists.

40   Ibid., pp. 737–738.

41   Gerlach, 1:190.

42   Friedrich Frahm, "Entstehungs- und Entwicklungsgeschichte der preussischen Verfassung," *Forschungen zur brandenburgischen und preussischen Geschichte* 41/2 (1928): 265–266.

43   So, for example, Huber, p. 739.

44 Barclay, p. 144, agreeing with Gunther Günthal, "Zwischen König, Kabinet und Kamarilla," *Jahrbuch für die Geschichte Mittel- und Ostdeutschlands* 32 (1983): 135–137: Botzenhart, p. 533 also cites Günthal with approval.

45 Frahm, pp. 267–268.

46 Huber, p. 740.

47 Ibid., p. 742.

48 Frahm, p. 270; Botzenhart, pp. 34–535.

49 *Korps der jungen Kaufmannschaft, Künstler-Korps, Studenten-Korps, Korps der bewaffneten Handwerker* (Stephan Born was a member of this last group).

50 Huber, p. 745.

51 Brandenburg (1792–1850) was the son of Friedrich Wilhelm II and his morganatic wife, *Gräfin* Sophie Dönhoff. He was therefore a half brother of Friedrich Wilhelm III and uncle of Friedrich Wilhelm IV.

52 *Revolutionsbriefe*, pp. 248–250.

53 Lüders, *Die democratische Bewegung in Berlin im Oktober 1848*, p. 36, footnote 3. This was not a term used by the democratic leaders themselves, but was first applied in an article that appeared in the *Augsburger Allgemeine Zeitung* no. 288 (14 October 1848).

54 Huber, p. 706.

55 Lüders, p. 39, footnote 2.

56 The first was "Karbe," a grey-bearded former confectioner, and the other was "Lindenmüller," who customarily held forth every evening at the intersection of Friedrichstrasse and *Unter den Linden*.

57 Friedrich Bassermann, on a mission of conciliation in Berlin, had commented that the streets there were full of *Gestalten* he had never seen before.

58 Valentin, 2:263 calls the motion "an absurdity".

59 Huber, p. 708; Lüders, p. 117, footnote 1 cites an article in *Deutsche Zeitung* no. 295 of 4 November which observes that the resolution of the extreme left with reference to Vienna was essentially directed against Frankfurt. Its intention was opposition to the central power and the Frankfurt *Parlament*, and it originated in the failed *Gegenparlament* and *Demokratenkongress*. Lüders himself comments that the struggle of the republican forces had reached not only its peak but also its turning point.

60 Lüders, p. 124.

61 Ibid., p. 133.

62 Ibid., pp. 127, 128, footnote 3; Valentin, 2:247, citing Lüders.

63 Lewald-Stahr, pp. 130–131.

64 Ibid., pp. 130–131

65 Valentin, 2:270.

66 Ibid., 2:272.

67 Huber, p. 765.

68 Jacoby, *Briefwechsel 1850–1877*, p. 151.

69 Valentin, *Die erste deutsche Nationalversammlung*, p. 113.

70 Gall, *Bürgertum in Deutschland*, pp. 318–321.

71 Lewald-Stahr, pp. 140–144.

72 Weber, "Centralmärzverein (CMV) 1848–1849," in *Die bürgerliche Parteien in Deutschland*, pp. 227–235. Weber's statements have to be taken with a large grain of salt because he ignores documentary evidence when it conflicts with his chosen thesis. For example, he says that the Central March manifesto had no reference to popular sovereignty. See however the quotation from that document presented by Michael Wettengel. [footnote 73 below]

73 Wettengel, *Die Revolution von 1848/49 im Rhein-Main-Raum*, p. 345.

74 *Neue Rheinische Zeitung* no. 181 (29 December 1848).

Chapter 19

Collapse of the Frankfurt *Parlament*

The *Parlament* had survived a number of serious crises—notably the debates over Posen and Schleswig-Holstein and the selection of officers for the provisional central power. The September crisis on the other hand was much more life-threatening to the revolutionary effort, with its violence and bloodshed that followed the reversal of the vote on the Schleswig-Holstein armistice. The city of Frankfurt itself bore its scars, remaining under martial law as an official precaution against barricade fighting and further disruptive action on the part of the proletariat. The murder of Lichnowsky and Auerswald had not been forgotten. Jakob Venedey (1805–1871), one of the staunchest democratic believers in the cause of the moderate left, observed sorrowfully that during his long sixteen years of exile he had never had to endure the unwarranted suspicion that had been thrown at him since that fateful night. A depressed Fanny Lewald found that fast-living arrogant Lichnowsky had acquired something not unlike sainthood in the conservatives' memory. Lichnowsky's reputation during his lifetime had never been high. Johann Jacoby's friend Max Hobrecht had written in the spring of 1848 that the dashing prince was a *treuloser Mantelträger* [faithless opportunist].[1] This had in fact been the general opinion of the man.

In the course of the weeks immediately after the murders, party alignments at Frankfurt shifted in such a drastic way that it constituted a setback for the left. The split between moderates and radicals revealed the intense hatreds all too clearly. Specifically, forty or more members of the left center Württemberger Hof had already founded an independent faction at the Augsburger Hof, where it was hoped that it might join forces with the Westendhall with some reliance on the true left, but after the September crisis, the Augsburger Hof re-

Figure 21   PRINCE FELIX LICHNOWSKY

fused to have anything to do with the left and moved toward the moderate Landsberg and Kasino parties. The effect was a secure majority of some sixty to eighty votes for the center. The left was further weakened by an internal breakup. In October, twelve departed from the Deutscher Hof because of a disagreement over sending the fated Fröbel-Blum delegation to Vienna (the new small faction moved to the Nürnberger Hof).

Meanwhile, after the overthrow of the September uprising, new revolutionary cells began to spring up, to the acute alarm of the ruling princes of the minor states, who sought to interest larger neighboring states in their plight. It was these smaller states that tended to cling to the central power in Frankfurt, where a rudimentary party that favored a hereditary German monarchy was coalescing. Prussia herself was showing no interest in any proposed incorporation (mediatizing) of smaller states.

In spite of these disturbing developments, the committee that had been charged with drawing up a statement of citizens' fundamental rights [*Grundrechte*] which was to serve as a theoretical introduction to the new constitution had doggedly continued its work and had reached a point at which it was ready to submit the results to the assembled deputies who were attending the *Parlament* in the capacity of designated plenipotentiaries for their respective governments. The opinion of these representatives had gained weight after the shifts at Vienna and Berlin toward reaction because it had become imperative for the Frankfurt *Parlament* to gather support from the individual states in its effort to establish a true viable German state.

The *Grundrechte* "did not smell of the lamp, but of German blood and German need", binding together the results of the bitter experiences of the age.[2] This enumeration of basic rights had been hammered out by men who remembered a time of sudden house searches, of imprisonment on hearsay without trial, of interminable humiliating investigations. They remembered honored professors who had been dismissed and sent into exile. They remembered a time when it was difficult even to arrive at an opinion, and dangerous if not impossible to express it. They remembered a grasping nobility that was completely indifferent to the welfare of its peasants. They knew poor men who had remained uneducated because of their poverty. In anger, they remembered episodes like the Trier pilgrimage, when churchmen had traded on the ignorance and superstition of the people for the glory of God. They knew of the difficult lives of Jewish people and freethinkers. They were declaring that henceforth in Germany there would be no arbitrary arrests or imprisonments or investigations, no death penalty, and no state church. There would be freedom to travel, no limitation on instruction, and no more patrimonial rights for the nobles. Furthermore, governmental officials would be responsible to the people.

To the acute dismay of the committee, the official deputies of Germany's numerous states were by no means sympathetic to the reformers' ideas. Though Württemberg, Hesse-Darmstadt, Baden and the city of Frankfurt expressed immediate concurrence, other governments set up a variety of stumbling blocks. The representative from Bavaria, for example, stated blandly that he had no instructions in this matter, but in his personal opinion the estates would have to be consulted, and if not, the principle of *Vereinbarung* [agreement] would be endangered. Hannover objected strongly to publication of the *Grundrechte*. A disconcerting throwback to the past was embodied in the objections of Oldenburg, Lübeck, Bremen and Hamburg. Section 3 of the *Grundrechte* was troubling to them because they viewed *Freizügigkeit* [freedom to travel] as an entering wedge for communism and socialism. What alarmed these old gentlemen, no doubt, was the thought that it was journeymen returning from France who were spreading pernicious radical ideas among the workers' clubs. There was also a tinge of the old custom whereby entrance into guilds had been controlled by guildmasters for the good not only of the guild but also for the maintenance of the smooth cadence and virtuous tenor of community life. "If a community is required to accept any proletarian who has not been legally declared to be a vagabond, for operation of any branch of occupation, then all the efforts of every state and every community will be fruitlessly expended in providing work and necessary support in cases of want."[3]

In the first flush of excitement after the March revolutions, Austrian delegates had been elected to the Frankfurt *Parlament* and there had been grandiose talk about the German mission in the world, where a greater Germany (including Austria) would extend across Europe with lands that separated Russia and France in a fine assertion of teutonic might. There would be a strong German influence all along the Danube, and there would even be German colonies at the mouth of the great river. Austria would serve as a bridge for lands "into which German influence must penetrate". The new European *Riesenstaat* [mega-state] would be "an outer bastion" and "corner pillar" that would be a vivid symbol of the German mission in the world.[4] Those delegates who professed a strong interest in such a role for Austria were the conservatives. They were attacked in debate by the majority, who saw a threat to Germany's interests at the very time when the new united Germany was trying to establish its constitution.

The shape of the German constitution had largely been decided on and the document was therefore presumably ready for presentation, but when the actual four-day debate on it opened on 19 October, there was gloomy awareness that one question that had been postponed could no longer be swept under the carpet. What states would the new Germany include? In a word, what about Austria? In their days of early optimism, the radicals especially had thought that Austria could easily be disregarded, cast aside, ignored. The resurrected forces of reactionary conservatism in both Vienna and Berlin loomed threateningly now, when the Frankfurt *Parlament* was most in need of strength and unity. It was obvious that the Germans could no longer act independently. Austria once again had to be considered, accommodated—perhaps even obeyed.

With no little nervousness, the introductory statements of the constitution were accepted.

Paragraph l: The German Empire consists of the region of the former German Federation [*Bund*]. The relationship of the Duchy of Schleswig and the determinations of the boundaries of the Grand Duchy of Posen are reserved until the definitive arrangement.

Paragraph 2: No part of the German empire may be united to form a state with non-German lands.

Paragraph 3: If a German land shares the same head of state with a non-German land, the relationship between the two must be arranged according to the principles of purely personal union.[5]

In other words, if German Austria were to join Germany, it would give up its union with the rest of the Habsburg lands and limit its connection with the non-German regions to a dynastic relationship. Discussion of this problem highlighted the contrast between so-called *Kleindeutschen* and *Grossdeutschen* [those who favored construction of a narrow Germany comprising the lands of the original states, or those who wanted to expand to include German-speaking parts of Austria]. Friedrich Dahlmann delineated the alternatives clearly. Either dissolution of Austria and the joining of German-Austrian lands to Germany, or retention of great Austria and separation of all its parts from the German *Bund*.

The question before the house had been set down in splendidly unambiguous terms. What, indeed, about Austria? In the past, there had been much confident talk about arrangements that could no longer be contemplated. The romantic notion of a *Grossdeutschland* that would embrace not only all the minor and major states of Germany itself but also the ethnic German parts of Austria had to be discarded. The political situation in Austria was in flux at the moment. In mid-October, Hungary was marshalling forces for attack, and Windischgrätz was about to bombard Vienna, and Robert Blum was still alive. But then came Blum's execution, and the total disregard of Frankfurt as a diplomatic entity. An antagonistic Austria stood there nakedly. The changed situation had become so charged with danger that in November 1848 even the radicals understood that Austria under the new Schwarzenberg ministry might be strong enough to dictate Germany's fate.

Reporting to Paris from Dresden on 14 November, French ambassador Reinhard wrote that the cruel event served as an indicator of Austrian policy. What was most upsetting, he thought, was the fact that choice had fallen on Blum to be judged before the Austrian leaders, and the speed that accompanied the execution of the sentence. There seemed to be an intention to strike the Frankfurt *Parlament* in the person of Blum, and thus to respond to decisions of the assembly concerning the Austrian question.[6]

Frankfurt's initial reaction to Blum's execution took the form of a mild note signed by Prime Minister Schmerling, in which it was obliquely observed that the closing down of Viennese newspapers and the shift of the Austrian *Reichstag* away from Vienna to Kremsier were unwarranted. Rights gained in the spring revolution had to be retained. The true opinion of the Austrian people with respect to relationship with Germany must be ascertained. "We want to know the whole truth."

By 18 November Frankfurt was ready to turn openly against the Austrian government. Schmerling wrote, "Frankfurt was the first place in Germany where disorder was handled with justice." There followed complaint against Austrian terrorism and the execution of Robert Blum, with the comment that this act had the character of "a declaration against Germany." (In the judgment of Friedrich Engels, this protest was offensively insipid. In 1851, he was to write with withering scorn that the "softness and diplomatic decency of its language was more an insult to the grave of the murdered martyr than a damning stain upon Austria.")[7] There was also objection in the Schmerling message to the open break with the constitutional system. The note concluded with the statement that the overwhelming majority of the German people stood for constitutional monarchy.[8]

Schwarzenberg's response was sharp. "Austria's continuation as a unit is a German as well as a European necessity." Only after the reorganized Austria and reorganized Germany had reached new solid form would it be possible to determine their mutual relationships. Until that time, Austria would continue faithfully to execute her duties within the German federation.

Did this imply that there was no German *Parlament* at Frankfurt in which duly elected representatives of lands belonging to the Austrian empire had been seated for months? Schwarzenberg was deliberately ignoring the *Parlament* in his reference to the German federation that was supposed to have gone out of existence when the central power was chosen at Frankfurt.

On 1 December the *Wiener Zeitung* editorialized: Frankfurt wants to destroy Austria. The Frankfurt assembly has such enmity against Austria that Napoleon never thought of expressing. The Frankfurt assembly is thus at present the greatest enemy of the Austrian monarchy as well as the greatest enemy of Vienna.[9] Ruffled feathers in Vienna had to be taken seriously. It was on the day following publication of the truculent editorial that Emperor Ferdinand had been forced to abdicate in favor of his eighteen-year-old nephew, Franz Joseph.

Frankfurt's delegates of the left raised their voices: If Austria had no intention of joining Germany, why were Austrian delegates seated in the *Parlament*? What was the basis of the authority of Austrian *Erzherzog* Johann and his minister von Schmerling? Schwarzenberg, the new master at Vienna, was setting up a Greater Austria, for all practical purposes jeering at the proponents of a greater Germany. *Erzherzog* Johann held onto his office precariously, helped by the attention that was focused suddenly on Prussia, where Friedrich Wilhelm and his conservatives were showing their strength. Emissaries dispatched to Berlin by the *Parlament* received the same kind of contemptuous dismissive treatment that had been the fortune of the delegates to the Austrian court. Deeply offended by both Austria and Prussia, the *Parlament* members pulled themselves together in a semblance of unity, supporting *Erzherzog* Johann, but his prime minister lost his post and Heinrich von Gagern became the new head of the ministry, while his place as president of the *Parlament* was taken by the able Eduard Simson (1811–1899).

Schmerling had always been in favor of a hereditary emperor and had regarded the election of Johann as a step in that direction because what he had in mind was a Habsburg emperor. He now supported von Gagern, considering him to be the liberals' only hope. What Schmerling wanted at this moment of disappointment and chagrin was nebulous, but he put considerable effort into convincing the right and center that they ought to seek some kind of negotiation with Austria over a future connection with Germany. Heretofore, he had been able to function smoothly in his ministerial office because he was supported by opponents of the scheme to elect the Prussian monarch as hereditary emperor and by all those who wanted to retain Austria in the federation. (They had joined forces to form a new party, the Pariser

Hof.) The heterogeneous group included people like Welcker and representatives of small states of the south and northwest, as well as Catholics and Austrians. Moderate Austrians shifted from the Kasino party, actively supporting Schmerling. But now he realized that he had become head of a party whose primary goal was to break the Gagern program that leaned toward Prussia. He had never been popular in the *Parlament*. At this critical point he confronted active opposition from various parties (Landsberg, Augsburger Hof, Kasino), and consequently he was constrained to hand in his resignation on 15 December.

With Schmerling's resignation from the cabinet, it was therefore the decision of von Gagern as new head of the ministry (he assumed the office on 18 December) that led to the premature publication of the disputed *Grundrechte* in the *Reichsgesetzblatt* on 28 December. This move was short-sighted because it made all too obvious the opposition of the major states, especially Prussia, which refused to publish the document. Resistance to the concept of the *Parlament*'s sovereignty was a fact that all could see.

In spite of discouraging reports that Friedrich Wilhelm would not be inclined to accept an imperial crown without the assent of the German princes, Gagern remained hopeful that the program he presented to the *Parlament* would once again set an independent course for Frankfurt, and help to push matters toward a favorable conclusion. Austria's future relationships with Germany would have to be determined through diplomatic channels, he asserted. He was proposing an "empowerment" of the provisional central government, with Austrian leadership over the future ties with Germany, while at the same time the Frankfurt *Parlament* would press on in its work on the constitution. He was wary of any injury to the concept of a national state, declaring that the governing idea of the times was the development of freedom on a foundation of nationalism. "The requirements of nationhood are not compatible with the proposition that we allow ourselves to meet here with a dozen foreign nations."[10] Gagern spoke of the *Vaterland* in terms that unmistakably referred to a restricted *Kleindeutschland*.

Gagern had regarded the opening paragraphs of the constitution as queries presented to Austria, not as irrevocable decisions. In line with this thought, he said that the "world power" Austria, should as a whole stand closely at the side of Germany, while those peoples along the Danube that had neither the vocation nor the claim for independence should be included "like satellites in our planetary system." He suggested that Austria might be threatened by the opening provisions of the German constitution, and he added that a partition of Austria was not anything to be wished, and certainly not in Germany's interest. A way out, Gagern thought, might be a double indissoluble *Bund* that could be developed by means of a new act of federation. The constitution of the German states could not be the subject of discussion or negotiation with Austria. Gagern therefore asked the *Parlament* for its consent to such arrangements.

To Gagern's consternation, the *Parlament* responded to his veiled challenge to Schwarzenberg by appointing a special committee that included among its fifteen members not only delegates from the extreme left but also Austrians. Gagern had thought that since articles 2 and 3 of the constitution still stood, the Austrians could be ejected. The Gagern project of a *Kleindeutschland* under Prussian guidance did not appeal to those who had so sincerely engaged their strengths, even in the *Vormärz*. The committee reached a formulation of goals. The central power must arrive at a constitution of such nature that German Austria could be fully accommodated. Furthermore, in view of Germany's interest in its colonization, industry, trade and influence on lands of the Danube region, it must declare that Germany found an intimate political and commercial relationship of non-German lands, hence with Austria as a whole, to be most desirable. The leader of the committee's majority was none other than Jakob Venedey.

Schmerling had wanted to remain in the ministry, as head of the department of domestic affairs perhaps. The Catholic press grumbled that his defeat was the work of the pro-Schleswig faction, who "moved heaven and earth if a few square miles of Schleswig had to be given up, but who tossed off Austria as if it were a village."[11] Even after his downfall, Schmerling's star appeared to rise when he was dispatched to Vienna for talks with Felix Schwarzenberg. In those discussions, he thought that he had managed to convince Schwarzenberg that Austria ought not surrender her position vis à vis Germany needlessly, and he was delighted when, in the course of his return journey to Frankfurt, he found that he had been appointed Austrian plenipotentiary (on 5 January 1849). Schmerling's satisfaction was short-lived.

What Schwarzenberg had actually decided was something that Frankfurt could not accept. Because both Prussia and the central power had more or less tabled the problem of the minor states, he had seen his opportunity. He had already spoken to the Prussian ambassador about his idea of a division of Germany into six (seven at the most) complexes in which the ranking prince would govern through a common assembly. Baden, "the most dangerous point" would have to join some stronger state, he thought. He also suggested that Prussia could assimilate Nassau, Kurhessen, Mecklenburg, Anhalt, etc., into its own military and legislative system. He resisted the thought of Prussian control in south Germany. (This conversation with the ambassador took place on 27 December.)

Then, on 28 December, Schwarzenberg had dispatched a note to Frankfurt. Austria remained a power in the German federation and intended so to remain. Austria would henceforth participate in work on the constitution. The idea of work through diplomatic channels was rejected. Only by clear understanding between the governments could a solution be found. "We will not allow ourselves to be ejected from Germany."

With the Schwarzenberg note of 28 December, the independence of Germany in establishing its ultimate political form had been thrown into question. Everything might depend on Austria. Suspicion of Schmerling deepened at Frankfurt, and increased when on 9 January 1849 he informed von Gagern that the Austrian government had empowered him to enter again into direct intercourse with *Erzherzog* Johann and his ministry. But on 3 February there came an abrupt decision from Schwarzenberg. The Frankfurt model of the German state was rejected as unworkable.

Discussion in the *Parlament* had dragged on for so many months that the weary delegates were approaching exhaustion. Radicals elsewhere in Germany and abroad meanwhile had become impatient, thinking of renewed armed revolution in order to focus attention on their demands. There was so much agitation among them that Swiss authorities had been stirred to action. On 30 November, a circular had been dispatched to members of the federation's cantons that bordered on Germany. Lists of German refugees were to be filed with a special commission. Participants in the two earlier risings in Baden were to be expelled from the bordering cantons. All suspicious individuals were to be interned. On the German side, troops from Württemberg and Baden had moved into territories along the Swiss border, and the public mood in Switzerland had consequently become distinctly hostile.

Because of the Swiss regulations, many German refugees crossed over into Alsace, where French authorities shunted them away within forty-eight hours, sending them to Besançon, under police escort if necessary. The would-be revolutionists were undeterred. In mid-November, for example, a shipment of ammunition moved through Meerburg to Karlsruhe. Military units began to train near Haltingen. About seven hundred individuals were involved. The execution of Blum and events in Berlin had had a stimulating effect. The refugees at Besançon gathered in barracks, under the leadership of the militant former Prussian officer, August von Willich.

Some projects had a tinge of swashbuckling insanity. A letter was intercepted, dated 22 November, written in Berlin, from an excitable man named Georg Fein. He referred to a proletariat that was demanding social justice and religious freedom. There were dark threatening remarks concerning Windischgrätz and Wrangel ("the two German Albas") and to Friedrich Daniel Basserman as one who betrayed Lichnowsky and Auerswald. The whole *Gesindel* [rabble] of kings should be wiped out.

In February 1849, Karl Vogt and Julius Fröbel arrived in Switzerland and set about agitation among journeymen and apprentices. They should prepare to cross over into Germany. The military mobile units in Frankfurt and Thuringia were put on alert because it was thought that a mass uprising could be anticipated at any time. The railroads especially would be under attack. The whole work of the Frankfurt *Parlament* was threatened.[12]

The debate over the constitution was still in progress at Frankfurt when Schwarzenberg delivered his crushing blow. On 4 March 1849 a constitution for the whole of Austria was imposed, and on 7 March the revolutionary Austrian *Reichstag* was dissolved. On 9 March a demand was presented at Frankfurt, that a draft constitution for a German empire be accepted. This document was intended for an Austria-dominated empire of seventy million subjects.

Meanwhile, starting on 12 December, debate had begun in the *Parlament* on the question of the future head of the newly constituted Germany. The radicals' idea of a president was tacitly ignored, and the question was: Elected sovereign or hereditary sovereign? It was becoming clearer and clearer that the ruler would be Prussian. It was agreed that the King of the Germans, the sole executive, would be elected (Article 1, section 68) and would be "a reigning German prince". His successors would constitute a hereditary dynasty (Article 1, section 69). The federative aspect appeared only in the legislative arrangements. At the price of accepting universal franchise and a suspensive veto for the executive, the *Kleindeutsch* liberals led by Gagern won over part of the left for a hereditary emperor.

As the stunned delegates tried to digest the implications of the Schwarzenberg move, one of their own members, the veteran Theodor Welcker, rose to deliver an astonishing counter-blow. He moved that the whole of the constitution be adopted as it stood, and that a head of the government be elected immediately. The measure was voted down, but it had stirred the *Parlament* into raging debate, in the course of which Gagern announced his intention to resign (22 March).

Arguments swung this way and that between those who were demanding that no change be made in the constitution and those who wanted to admit future amendments. The issue was complicated by the circumstance that there had already been changes, between the first and second readings. During this stressful period, the delegates learned severe lessons about the fundamentals of parliamentary life. To their shock and dismay, idealists among them were forced to realize that parties play a decisive role in development of workable compromises, that there has to be a readiness for shifts of position, and that there are times when one strong person, single-handed, can bring about necessary changes of opinion within a given group.

The constitution was adopted on 27 March 1849, incorporating changes that had been effected after the first reading of the document. The elected hereditary ruler would have a suspensive veto, and there would be a general franchise. The *Parlament* then went on to assume a competence to elect a ruler that theoretically it did not legally have.

Ever since the war of liberation, Prussia had been the chief German state and for this reason—for better or worse—Prussia remained the fulcrum for the lever of political action.[13] On the following day therefore, Friedrich Wilhelm IV of Prussia was elected King of the Germans by the vote of two hundred and ninety, with two hundred and forty-eight abstentions. (One of the delegates, a prince, stated coldly that he was not a *Kurfürst*.) On the same day the constitution was proclaimed. The bells of Frankfurt, even the cathedral's great Emperor bell, rang in triumph.

While the bells clanged their brazen message over Frankfurt's rooftops, the new government was making a lamentable mistake. It was refusing to accept *Erzherzog* Johann's resignation, urging him to stay on until Friedrich Wilhelm had reached a decision about the crown. Johann appears to have been encouraged to follow this course by members of the *grossdeutsch* contingent, led by Schmerling. It was not to be anticipated that the Austrian *Erzherzog* would exert himself prodigiously to attain quick recognition of a constitution that excluded his native land and placed power in the hands of a Hohenzollern. Certainly, he would take no action that could be interpreted as stemming from the provisions of that constitution. It would have been preferable to accept the resignation and install a regency that would enforce constitutional provisions until the crown had been accepted. Such a regency would have been able to go forward at once with the election of the two legislative houses. There would have been numerous difficulties, to be sure, but on the whole the possibilities for ultimate success would have been substantially enhanced by the presence of an interim authority that was backed by the constitution. As matters stood, with *Erzherzog* Johann at the head of the government, there would be little or no progress. The constitution would hang in mid-air while the world awaited Friedrich Wilhelm's decision, and that monarch himself would feel little pressure or threat to his own powers.[14]

Friedrich Wilhelm IV, the man of the hour, was not blessed with a personality and temperament that suited the role. Schwarzenberg at least had been an open antagonist, but the Prussian monarch habitually engaged in trickery and deceit,[15] like a Shakespearean king traversing all classic by-paths and indirect crook'd ways. To make matters worse, he was now in the eye of the storm, urged and cajoled and tugged hither and yon by contending factions. Gerlach and the *Kreuzzeitung* party approached the question of an imperial crown with all the hostility born of anachronistic Old Prussian—one might even say obsolete Borussian—attitudes. In their view, Prussia should always remain genuinely Prussian. They wanted nothing to do with middle-class movements, and they thought that the new constitution that had been developed with such care and stress at Frankfurt was a crass manifestation of the revolutionary principle. To accept a crown from such a source, with the golden symbol of power presented atop a copy of that constitution by a delegation of uncouth lawyers instead of on a velvet cushion offered by kneeling princes would be appalling. It was probably from this group that Friedrich Wilhelm gathered that it was accurate to refer to "a pig crown" and to sneer that it was nothing more than a pretzel concocted by butchers and bakers.

Not all conservatives in Prussia were as ultraconservative as the *Kreuzzeitung* courtiers. There were many, in fact, who were definitely in favor of acceptance of the Frankfurt constitution. In the newly elected second chamber, where moderates were in the majority, and

even in the new first chamber which was preponderantly conservative, there was an inclination to urge acceptance of Frankfurt's offer.

Still another group, the one that favored the concept of a Greater
Germany, fell into line because its members were attracted by the idea
of increased Prussian power, seeing an advance to outright Prussian
hegemony in Germany as an acceptable goal. With von Vinke as their
spokeman (he was no longer a delegate at Frankfurt but had gained a
seat in the new Prussian second chamber) these bureaucrats and army
officers were ready to move into a new era. There were other powerful
figures who joined their ranks—men like Friedrich Wilhelm's close friend,
his London ambassador Bunsen, and Prince Wilhelm, heir to the throne
of Prussia, and his wife the Princess Augusta. These people all wanted
a conditional acceptance of the crown, and enumerated reservations
that the monarch ought to make. They were proposing that the king
demand assent on the part of the individual German governments,
and insist that the new constitution be subject to revision and amend-
ment. They were calling for restoration of the absolute veto for the
ruler, and abolition of universal suffrage. It was also suggested that
the king might accept the role of chief executive without accepting the
title of emperor, on condition that the princes subsequently declare
their agreement with the election.

Everyone was reckoning without any thought of what might be in
the royal mind. Friedrich Wilhelm was medieval, and *grossdeutsch* in
that he still dreamed of the old Holy Roman Empire headed by the
Habsburgs. He wrote to his friend Bunsen in December that the claim
of the Habsburgs to the old crown had not been extinguished in 1806.
Any election by a national assembly would be a revolutionary measure, and any acceptance of the results of such an election would be
theft of the true crown.[16] "The king and his time spoke two different
languages, yet the king's proclamations and words frequently were
expressed in terms so nearly modern that they always aroused hopes
and concealed the unbridgable contradictions."[17]

A deputation of thirty-two delegates, led by Eduard Simson as presiding officer of the assembly, departed from Frankfurt on 30 March,
and after hard traveling arrived in Berlin on 2 April. Berlin was under
martial law still, and for that reason the reception of the men from the
Parlament was subdued—no general illumination of private homes
and public buildings, for example. At a cabinet meeting held on the
day of the deputation's arrival in Berlin, Friedrich Wilhelm told his
ministers that the *Parlament* had no crown to offer.

What his Majesty chose to say to the Frankfurt delegation was not quite that brutal, but the tone of his remarks was indubitably negative. With reference to the election, he remarked that he could make no decision without the free assent of the crowned heads, the princes and the free cities. He did not even say that acceptance of the crown was contingent on such a unanimous agreement. He would think about it after the princely judgment had given. As to the constitution, this would have to be the subject of discussion among the governments of the individual states. Would they find that the constitution assured him the prerogatives that would be necessary if he were to rule with a strong hand? Friedrich Wilhelm's most daunting comment came at the end of his speech. "Proclaim this throughout all the regions, gentlemen. If the Prussian shield and sword are needed against external or internal enemies, I shall not fail. I will then faithfully go the way of my house and people, the way of German honor . . ." Internal enemies. This was surely a threat to use force in counterrevolutionary measures.[18] A few of the deeply disappointed Frankfurt men (Dahlmann, Riesser, and Biedermann) wanted to believe that all had not been definitively shattered, but the majority understood the monarch's meaning. He was throwing the crown back into the gutter whence he said it came.

Not only between Berlin and Frankfurt were there cross-purposes. In Friedrich Wilhelm's own cabinet there was movement that ran counter to what the monarch was saying. On the very day of his response to the Frankfurt delegation [3 April], his ministers issued a circular dispatch that was addressed to all the other German governments. This document carried the suggestion that they provisionally accept the leadership of the Prussian ruler in overall German affairs. The tone and content of Friedrich Wilhelm's response to the Frankfurt men was glossed over. Hannover was the only state that answered in a cautious affirmative. The twenty-eight states that had already recognized the constitution joined in sending a collective note [14 April] to the effect that Prussia ought to accept the new constitution, as they had.

The disheartened delegation returned to Frankfurt, where they confronted a message from Vienna. All Austrian delegates to the Frankfurt *Parlament* were recalled. Schwarzenberg found no merit in an assembly that had accepted the idea of a hereditary German empire under a Hohenzollern. This move caused a shift of power among the parties at Frankfurt because the moderate Austrians had helped to ensure a majority for the center. The radical left now held the advantage.

Friedrich Wilhelm meanwhile had become increasingly agitated, not least because his newly elected Prussian assembly was not cooperating with him. The lower house on 21 April expressly urged his Majesty to recognize the constitution and was rewarded by prompt dismissal. The upper house, where the majority also wanted recognition, was abruptly adjourned. Prussia's official plenipotentiary at Frankfurt, Ludolf Camphausen, seeing the writing on the wall, resigned his post on 22 April. In his view, the prospect of some kind of positive interaction with Frankfurt had become mere fantasy. Frankfurt however made a last-minute effort to bridge the widening gap by sending Friedrich Daniel Bassermann once again to Berlin on a mission of reconciliation. He was supposed to endeavor to persuade the stubborn monarch that he ought to recognize the constitution, the election and the general franchise. He was also authorized to attempt certain adjustments such as Friedrich Wilhelm's agreement to be a provisional head in the place of *Erzherzog* Johann. On a strictly confidential level, without actual authorization, Bassermann was also to suggest that Friedrich Wilhelm could summon a German *Reichstag* that might be given power to amend the constitution. All this was to no avail, as Bassermann found to his chagrin.

On 28 April 1849 the king through his ministry not only definitely rejected the imperial crown but also declared his definitive refusal to accept the constitution. The chief objections related to the so-called interference in internal affairs of the respective states, to the suspensive veto, and to the unlimited franchise. Taken together, the constitution was a means for gradual and to all outward appearances legal abolition of the supreme governing power and transition to a republic.

The Frankfurt *Parlament* reacted on 4 May 1849 by addressing the governments, parliaments and free cities, asking for immediate recognition of the constitution and election on 15 July of a "peoples' house" that would meet at Frankfurt on 22 August. If Prussia declined to respond to this summons, the ruler of the next-largest state represented at the new *Reichstag* would head the government. Prussian ultraconservatives immediately grasped this move on the part of Frankfurt as potent ammunition, denouncing it as a summons to revolution.

By his rejection of the imperial crown and the constitution and the dissolution of his own Prussian assembly, Friedrich Wilhelm had opened Pandora's box. All the tensions and cross-purposes and elements of discord that seethed below the surface ever since the beginning of the century escaped into the light of day. The instability of the foundation of so-called German unity was cruelly exposed, making obvious the fact that the whole elaborate structure was nothing more than a house of cards.

The *Zentralmärzverein* [Central March Association] swung into action on 6 May, sending out two calls from its congress at Frankfurt, signed by Julius Fröbel as president and Franz Raveaux as vice-president. The first was addressed to the German army. German warriors should place honor and love of the Fatherland above the arbitrary rule of princes. They should obey the will of the sovereign National assembly, which now summoned the entire people to support the constitution. The second call was addressed to the German people. It stated that the Prussian government had declared its intention to meet risings of the people in support of the constitution with force. Let there be unity of plans, and unity of action! Parenthetically, it should be noticed that the Central March was the major politically-minded organization that worked through campaigns for elections to provincial assemblies in the spring of 1849, in order to strengthen the pro-constitution forces. The largest labor organization, Stephan Born's *Verbrüderung*, had only fifteen thousand members, in contrast to Central March's half million.

The Frankfurt government attempted on 8 May to persuade *Erzherzog* Johann to make a pronouncement that although there was recognition of the fact that the duty of the *Parlament* was to act as moderator, and the central power should only exert moral pressure, it would nevertheless oppose any intervention of one or more individual states for suppression of movements in other states that were directed toward recognition of the constitution. This was an open rebuke to Prussia, which had in that week dispatched troops to Saxony.[19] *Erzherzog* Johann responded in a handwritten note that the legal means for action were lacking, and that he was reluctant to begin anything that he could not carry through to a conclusion.

The days of Frankfurt's power had passed. The dispute between *Erzherzog* Johann and Heinrich von Gagern over the course to be followed with respect to Prussian intervention in Saxony had led to Gagern's final resignation [10 May]. His resignation marked the breakup of the party that had favored hereditary monarchy, which in truth had always been more of a loose coalition than a strongly motivated group. The left-tending Westendhall and Nürnberger Hof returned to the democratic left.

Some time after the dissolution of the Prussian assembly, Dr. Johann Jacoby had gone to Frankfurt, not intending to remain there long, but when he discovered that *Parlament* members were being recalled or were drifting away without such summons, or were holding onto their posts with considerable uncertainty, he took over the place of von Raumer, the Berlin delegate who had decided to leave, rather to Jacoby's disgust. He sought out Heinrich von Gagern in order to discuss the current situation with him. "How old and worn this man has become in a single year! In spite of all the calumny, I have the firm conviction that Gagern's intentions are honorable and that he is prepared to make any sacrifice for freedom. What he lacks is strength and above all self-confidence. He is a brave man but not the type that the times require. Gagern is the *Paulskirche* personified. He is Germany personified!" wrote Jacoby to his friend Simon Meyerowitz on 19 May 1849 after his conference with the weary von Gagern.[20]

On the day after the Jacoby interview [i.e., 20 May 1849], Gagern and sixty of his colleagues withdrew from the *Parlament*. In a signed joint statement, they declared that the National assembly now faced two alternatives. It could enter the path of civil war, or it could abandon any further effort to establish the constitution. Gagern and his fellow delegates felt that the latter was the lesser of two evils as far as the German Fatherland was concerned.

All semblance of parliamentary government had vanished with the resignation of von Gagern. In theory, *Erzherzog* Johann should have called on some member of the radical left to form a new cabinet since they were in the majority. Instead, he had called on a peevish, dry old anachronism from the extreme right, the fusty jurist, M. C. F. W. Grävell, to be his "sacrificial lamb". Here was an opening for the embittered left with Karl Vogt as spokesman. Vogt pointed out that this deplorable situation had been created by the moderates who, in their "learned enthusiasm" for the constitutional system, had enacted the law of 28 June 1848 that allowed the chief executive (the *Reichsverweser*) to function without responsibility to the National assembly. They had dug their own grave by that naive oversight.[21]

The appointment drew fire from Karl Theodor Welcker, who entered the following acid motion: "The National assembly declares that after it has considered the appointment of the [Grävell] ministry and its program, it cannot have the slightest confidence in this ministry but rather must regard this nomination . . . as a grave injury to national representation." The motion was adopted by a vote of 191 to 12, with 44 members abstaining. Alas, this occurred almost one year to the day after the grandiose, hopeful opening of the assembly in May 1848.

Grävell was unmoved. He responded that he had only accepted the unpopular assignment because he did not want to see *Erzherzog* Johann confronting a void, without a cabinet. He would not resign. In a strange convoluted argument, he made a distinction between the office and the power of the *Reichsverweser*. Whereas the actual office derived from the National assembly, its power had been conferred by the governments united in the old *Bundestag*. For this reason, Grävell asserted, the *Reichsverweser's* tenure did not depend wholly upon the will of the *Parlament*. In other words, the old *Bundestag* which had always operated under the shadow of the Habsburg imperial house, was not extinct. Its authority had thus far remained in abeyance, but now it was beginning to stir and exhibit signs of life. The *Bundestag* was far from extinct, and it could be restored to vigorous life at any moment.

Grävell's disconcerting argument had a certain legality, harking back to the statement issued by the *Bundestag* on 12 July 1848, at the time of transfer of certain portions of its authority to the provisional central power. Although Prussia had taken back the powers it had vested in the *Bundestag, Erzherzog* Johann still retained powers delegated to him, e.g. by Bavaria and Austria. The concept of continuity had never been effectively handled, and the members of the Frankfurt left were justified in their caustic reminder of the blunder that the *Parlament* moderates had made in the early days.

The Central March members meanwhile were aware that the very existence of the association had been severely threatened by Friedrich Wilhelm's rejection of the imperial crown. The Heidelberg *Volksbund*, for example, had severed its ties with the association, saying that there remained only one weapon for the people, and that weapon was revolution. The *Märzverein* had blocked the old revolution by its hesitations and indecisions, and thus made the new revolution necessary. The separation was quickly followed by the departure of the Donnersberg delegation of the Frankfurt *Parlament*, led by Wilhelm Adolph von Trützschler of Dresden. The extreme left at Frankfurt, shifting to a revolutionary posture, sent out a message to the March associations throughout Germany asserting that the organization was endangering the solidarity of the democratic party.

This was the beginning of the end. On 15 May 1849 the society burned its records in anticipation of a counterrevolutionary attack.

The *Parlament* membership had been so much reduced by recalls (Austrians on 19 April; Prussian delegation, 14 May; Saxony, 19 May;

Hannover, 23 May) as well as by individual or group withdrawals that there was no longer a recognizable quorum, even though the remaining stubborn delegates lowered the required number to one hundred.[22]

The individual withdrawals had been based on principle, not on frustrated irritation. The last to depart, among them those stalwarts Riesser and Welcker, did so because they reasoned that even the loyal minority of a parliament bears moral responsibility for the decisions that are made and that only withdrawal can effect a release from such an obligation. With the affirmative vote on a motion by Ludwig Uhland that in essence called for general armed resistance, these men found it to be their duty to lay down their mandate as delegates.—It would have been a gross exaggeration to refer to the few leftwing delegates who still held on in Frankfurt as a body representative of all Germany. Aware of their anomalous situation, they stoutly called themselves a "core" around which a new *Parlament* could be built up by future elections.

On 27 May, Jacoby wrote to Simon Meyerowitz, "I am passive in the assembly. Under prevailing conditions, I expect little from it and only wish that it may have an honorable conclusion."[23]

There were sharp disagreements among the one hundred and thirty men still meeting at the *Paulskirche*. These became clear when the question of a shift away from Frankfurt was brought up (30 May). Those who wanted simply to act as stand-ins for a future assembly objected that to break away from the *Paulskirche* would alter the character of the assembly, exposing it to the danger of more fissions and party re-alignments. If they were to become too closely associated with the uprisings that were breaking out in southwest Germany, they would lose all claim to identity as a German national assembly. This was the argument of the moderate Venedey, for example. Others felt that the time had come for bold action and that they ought assuredly to break away from the central power and distance themselves from the sphere of influence of Prussian military might.

There was an invitation that they might consider, from the *Gemeinderat* [city council] of Heidelberg, sent on 22 May. If the *Parlament* members wanted to come to Heidelberg, the city would be honored to have them hold their sessions in the university *Aula*, they wrote.[24] At Frankfurt, they rather thought that Württemberg was the place of choice. From Stuttgart, where they would surely find a sympathetic hearing, they could extend their activities in support of the constitution to the Rhine-Main area, for example. When a vote was taken and carried, it was obvious that many were agreeing to the shift simply out of loyalty to their comrades, not out of conviction.[25]

For a few brief days during the transfer to Stuttgart, the harassed delegates had a sunny respite that filled them with hope and good cheer. Jacoby , who back in the days of the Frankfurt *Vorparlament* enjoyed the festive aspect of the city, writing to friends about the fluttering banners, the surging crowds, the singing, and the general atmosphere of enthusiasm, once again was writing words that reflected the glow of his renewed hope. He reported that "In Heilbronn, where we met several delegates, we had to halt for an entire day. The house in which we lived was richly decorated with black-gold-red banners and an honor guard was placed before it. When we left, the excellently organized civil guard formed a cordon along the street, and half the city accompanied us with cheers to the railway station. If the people in Württemberg over all are as keyed up and energetic as those in this area through which we passed, the National assembly has found the place from which it can combat the absolutism that is breaking in."[26]

The rump parliament at Stuttgart had itself been keyed up and energetic. Jacoby went on to note that in the first three sessions, Friedrich Wilhelm's imposed Prussian electoral law had been declared null and void, the members of the central power had been removed from office, and in their stead a *Regentschaft* [government] had been chosen, comprising five individuals. The hopeful glow had begun to fade by the time Jacoby reached this part of his letter. "We cannot conceal from ourselves the fact that, with the apathy into which a large part of Germany has fallen, the prospect of success of our initiatives is only slight, but we believe we are obliged for the honor of the nation and above all for the honor of peoples' representation, to make this last effort."[27]

Conditions in Stuttgart were far from harmonious. Karl Vogt remarked that "If we had foreseen this, we would have brought cannons along."[28]

Two of the chief actors in Württemberg were redoubtable Wilhelm I (1781–1864) and his minister, Friedrich Römer, who had double responsibility as a delegate to the Frankfurt *Parlament*. Römer had written to the king, urging acceptance of the constitution on the grounds that states refusing to recognize it might face annexation, and that "Your Majesty stands among the German princes as the sole genuine representative of the idea of the new era. . . . If, counter to expectation, the Prussian king declines, then in the National assembly your

Majesty's name will lead in the discussion." Wilhelm, he argued, should therefore proclaim adherence to the constitution in order to forestall any misapprehensions on that score. Römer may have entertained certain personal ambitions. In any case, it was he who suggested that the Frankfurt *Parlament* ought to be invited to shift its headquarters to Stuttgart.[29]

His Majesty had been cool to the proposal, wanting to pursue a wait-and-see policy with respect to Vienna, Berlin, and Munich. Watchful waiting was none too easy because the people of Württemberg were stirring. There was an enormous rally on the Stuttgart market place, where representatives of a multifarious assortment of parties united in a resounding call for support of the constitution. (The king kept his troops in their barracks, thus preventing their entry into the demonstration.)

As early as 16 April King Wilhelm had spoken at a meeting of his council of ministers against the proposal for a hereditary emperor. Römer, his minister, although he was inclined to agree with the king on that point, continued to urge immediate acceptance of the constitution. King Wilhelm refused to budge, and Römer offered his resignation. The council of ministers, unshaken, wrote to his Majesty that the constitution must be recognized at once, because otherwise it would look as though they were being forced to accept it. If Prussia rejected the imperial crown, Württemberg would be in a painfully delicate position. It was pointed out that all prior orders and decrees issued by the king had implied, if not indeed specifically asserted, that the decisions of the Frankfurt *Parlament* were to be unconditionally binding.

Wilhelm meanwhile searched aimlessly for a new head for his cabinet, but everything was against him. Even military help was not available, because the treasury was almost empty and most of his troops were on the Baden frontier as a barrier against the revolutionary explosions in that area. On 21 April the distracted ruler received a delegation from his chamber of deputies and delivered himself of an excited, rambling speech that created nothing but confusion. Prussia itself had not yet accepted the constitution, he remonstrated. "What am I supposed to recognize? something that doesn't exist yet? Give me time! . . . I shall never subject myself to the house of Hohenzollern, I'm responsible to my country, my family, and myself. If all the other German princes did it, I would also make this sacrifice for Germany but my heart would be broken. . . . If you set yourselves on the basis of revolution and force me to give my word . . . you know yourselves . . . word forced from me wouldn't be binding and I could call it back because my will would be free. I will execute the German constitution in my land, just as I have already introduced the fundamental rights. I give you my word, I will not subject myself to the house of Hohenzollern" etc. etc. etc.[30]

The king departed for Ludwigsburg on 23 April, warning against "premature decisions" in the matter of the constitution. He grumbled to the Russian *chargé d'affaires* that attempts had been made to wheedle him in many ways. "They've shown me the imperial crown, offered me command of the armies in Schleswig-Holstein in a war that I consider to be criminal. . . . Even last summer, I told Gagern he would push Germany into a civil war." He was sending his family to safety at The Hague, he said, adding that he hoped the Russian tsar shared his views and apprehensions.[31]

When the Württemberg chamber voted to accept the constitution (25 April), thousands of singing, cheering people thronged the streets of Stuttgart, but the jubilation was short-lived. News from Baden was too alarming, and solid citizens set up a cry for law and order.

By the time the Frankfurt group arrived, minister Römer's position had become unstable and tormented. He appears to have been power-hungry, wanting to retain his ministry, yet fiercely patriotic as far as Württemberg was concerned. Wilhelm Löwe, president of the rebel Frankfurt parliament, suggested to him that the king might be willing to accept the new post of *Reischsstatthalter* [governor]—or that possibly even Römer himself might assume that office. The king meanwhile, in a quiet move, summoned Adolf Schoder, a member of his chamber of deputies, telling him he understood that the Frankfurt party was short of funds. He would supply a little, on condition that they leave Württemberg for the sake of public order. Schoder told his Majesty that he had been misinformed.[32]

Heavy pressure was being exerted against Württemberg from all sides. From Frankfurt came a severe note from *Erzherzog* Johann's new minister, *Fürst* August Wittgenstein-Berleburg, stating that the move to Stuttgart and the naming of the governing committee was illegal, and that it was open anarchy. If the Württemberg authorities were unable to handle this matter, the central power was prepared to do whatever was required. The Prussian ambassador in Stuttgart received instructions to protest that the Prussian government was "astounded" to see that Württemberg had not reacted in due time. Was Württemberg going to tolerate this situation, or was it ready to accept assistance? If this deplorable situation continued, Prussia was prepared to recall its ambassador. Prussian combat troops could be furnished if requested. If no satisfactory response was received, Prussia would consult other states as to appropriate measures. An angry Römer rose in the chamber of deputies to say that apparently "we have now a central power in Frankfurt, another in Stuttgart, and perhaps soon still another in Berlin."

The king was adamantly refusing to return to Stuttgart while the Frankfurt group was there. The new *Reichsregentschaft* was calling for five thousand troops to defend the fortresses of Rastatt and Landau against possible Prussian invasion. Römer rejected the request, countering with a demand that the *Reichsregentschaft* retire to some other country.

At Heilbronn, where Jacoby and his colleagues had been received with such warmth and enthusiasm, the civil guard assembled, announcing that they were ready to protect the constitution from attacks by "princes and treacherous governments". The Württemberg government responded by recalling troops from the border of Baden and deploying them throughout the country. Armed units were dispatched to Heilbronn, with orders to disband the civil guard and confiscate its weapons. The guard marched smartly up into the height above the city, their number increased to some four thousand by the volunteers who swarmed in. A mob surged into the arsenal, carrying off weapons, but the next day marked the beginning of defeat when cavalry patrols arrived on the scene. Heilbronn was soon declared to be under siege.

All highways around Stuttgart were occupied by the military, and artillery was stationed on the surrounding hllls. The provisional *Reichsregentschaft* issued a general call to arms (17 June), fighting to the last ditch. The Württemberg ministry sent word that there must be no further meetings of the rump parliament. These gallant men must depart.

Fanny Lewald wrote to Jacoby in deep anxiety. "I worry about you, as if I were watching you build a temple on quicksand. . . . For the first time, belief is leaving me. . . . I need to talk to you, to know what you're thinking, in order to be able to believe and hope with you."[33]

On the morning of 18 June Stuttgart's streets were packed with milling soldiers. Infantry occupied the riding hall where the Frankfurt men had been meeting. Under the command of their general, sappers entered the hall and quickly demolished everything—tables, speakers' platform, chairs, benches. They even tore banners to shreds, leaving nothing in the building other than splintered wood and tattered rags.

Adolf Schoder, as a member of the Württemberg chamber, spoke the last word. "The National assembly will go down today. The cause of Germany will perhaps be trodden in the dust for a time, but the spirit, gentlemen, you shall not tread in the dust. In spite of all bayonets, it will soon again lead the way. The German people have at least learned to know the men who have not forsaken the cause of freedom in the moment of peril."[34]

The poet Ludwig Uhland (1787–1862) suggested to his beleagured colleagues that they could assemble at the Hotel Marquardt, where they had been meeting informally. From there they set out in silent procession, their president Löwe leading, flanked by Uhland and another member of the group (the elderly father-in-law of minister Römer). Four abreast they advanced, slowly, with all the dignified solemnity that had marked their inaugural procession to the Frankfurt *Paulskirche* in May 1848. Unhesitatingly they moved toward the line of soldiers who blocked the way. *Wenn alle untreu werden, so bleiben wir doch treu* [If all others become faithless, yet we remain true].

A strange, unreal confrontation. Sober, mature, determined men, marching against youthful soldiers who hesitated at the command "Fix bayonets!" The commanding general, viewing the scene from a distance, ordered the cavalry to move in. As they came from the side streets, at a walk, reluctant to obey the command to unsheath their sabres, the delegates closed ranks, standing back-to-back. In the scuffle there were a few injuries (some were kicked by the horses, or struck by scabbards, and all were rudely jostled and bruised). Threatened and shouted at, the parliament members retreated to the Hotel Marquardt, where the indignant innkeeper took them in even though he did not agree with them. He was irritated, he said, by the way these men were being treated.

On 19 June they were officially expelled from Württemberg. They departed, most of them heading for Switzerland, agreeing to meet again at Karlsruhe, but that meeting never took place.

A Schwabian newspaper, the *Beobachter* published the following on 21 June: "Everything is quiet here, as though nothing had happened. The city looks as if there had been a funeral, where everyone goes his usual way afterward, and only those few who were related by blood or by close ties of mutual understanding bear their deep grief inwardly as they move about in the everyday world."[35]

Criminal charges and trials for high treason soon began. The net pulled in not only the leaders but also many teachers and innkeepers, a few physicians, some soldiers, peasants and manual laborers. Sentences were as high as twenty-five years' imprisonment. (The editor of the *Beobachter* was sentenced to eighteen years.) Though many escaped to foreign lands, their life prospects had been seriously damaged. Ludwig Pfau, editor of the famous satirical journal, *Eulenspiegel*, avoiding his sentence of 21 years, wrote to his friend Carl Mayer, a refugee in Switzerland, in 1850 that "You'll understand that I am a total shipwreck on the sands. Often in the morning I don't know if I'll have enough to eat all day. I am literally in a state of siege." In the immediate aftermath of the forced dissolution of the parliament at Stuttgart, Prussia sent out warrants for the arrest of Löwe and others—especially Johann Jacoby.

During the summer of 1849, Jacoby rested in Switzerland along with his friends, the Austrian poet Moritz Hartmann (1821–1872) and Heinrich Simon of Breslau. In that peaceful refuge, he gradually recuperated from the experience which had "deeply disturbed" him. Reflecting on recent events, he was able to say that with the conclusion of the first phase of the revolution, the only advantage thus far was the fact that the people had gained *Selbsterkenntniss* [had learned to know themselves] and that in general it was to be understood that any future revolution would be lost if it allowed old well organized powers to coexist with it.[36] He had already written to the chief public prosecutor in Berlin (from Frankfurt on 25 May and again from Vernex near Vevey on 10 August) that he understood that the Prussian police were searching for him, and that it was his intention to return home shortly.[37]

At that time Jacoby was being deluged by floods of apprehensive, anguished letters from friends and family, and even from anonymous well-wishers, all warning him that by no means ought he consider setting foot on Prussian soil. Simon Meyerowitz wrote on 27 July that he must see clearly that governmental vindictiveness was focused on him because they felt that they had old accounts to settle, regarding him as the prime instigator of the whole revolution.

They could take this position with a certain degree of justification, because Jacoby had indeed been in the thick of things from the very beginning. Who else among the revolutionists could point to a consistent record such as his? In 1841, his famous pamphlet, *Vier Fragen*, had stimulated serious thought in many unexpected quarters. Twice he had had to face trial during the *Vormärz* because of his courageous political actions. He had worked closely with Adam von Itzstein and Robert Blum in the early days of the *Hallgartenkreis*. He was at Frankfurt as a member of the *Vorparlament* and of its *Fünfzigerausschuss*. He served throughout the life of the Prussian national assembly, challenged Friedrich Wilhelm directly, and was among the last who were expelled by Prussian troops. On that occasion, it was Jacoby who was the spokesman, addressing the military commander. After the dismissal of the Prussian assembly, Jacoby undertook the hapless task of membership in the waning Frankfurt *Parlament*, and he was among the stoic marchers at Stuttgart who confronted the soldiers there.

Jacoby understood the import of the warnings. The punishment for high treason (this was the charge against him) was death by decapitation. A letter of his, written to his sisters Betty and Karoline from Vevey on 18 August 1849, came to light after the death of Betty Jacoby in 1890 and was then published as a "classic" by the *Königsberger Hartungsche Zeitung*. This letter deserves to be quoted and respectfully remembered.

> I know the power and ill will of the government, before which the most innocent is not secure, and I know the political apathy of the people, who will quietly accept any injustice. I know what lies ahead of me at home, and know that a favorable shift in affairs is not to be expected so soon. Nevertheless I cannot act otherwise. . . . So long as my fellow citizens—persuaded to take political action by my word and example—are suffering in prison, I would also have no happy moment in a freer foreign land. The foreign land would only be a larger prison for me, in which—dissatisfied with myself—I would go to ruin physically and mentally. You write that in Prussia force can now do anything that is to its advantage because all are silent from fear. I believe it. . . . A long absence under the present circumstances would be equivalent to flight, and would properly be regarded as a confession of fear and guilt.[38]

The *Arbeiterverein* [workers' society] at Königsberg composed an address to Johann Jacoby on 29 October 1849. "To the Man of the People: A sorrowful time has broken in over our poor German Fatherland. The betrayed people seek their representatives and friends in the light of day, and find them only in the darkness of the dungeon."[39] True to his word, Jacoby had returned to Königsberg and was imprisoned from 21 October until 8 December, the day of his trial for high treason.

When the actual trial date arrived, all Königsberg quivered at the thought of the fate hanging over the city's famous son. Little reason to hope that the members of the picked *Schwurgericht* [jury] would assess the case fairly. The event was reported in the *Kölnische Zeitung* on 13 December, reprinting a dispatch received from Königsberg that was dated 8 December 1849:

> After one hour's deliberation, the jury released Jacoby. . . . It was a magnificent, exhilarating moment when the assembled masses raised their voices, singing "Was ist des Deutschen Vaterland?" There were thousands who joined in this song, which at the end of each stanza was followed by uninterrupted thunderous cheers for Jacoby, for freedom, and for democracy.[40]

Jacoby was once more the recipient of a flood of letters—all of them congratulatory and joyful. Fanny Lewald concealed her emotion by writing lightly that *es ist etwas, die Freundin oder der Freund Jacobys zu sein* [it's something to be the friend of Jacoby]. There are always people, she commented, who glory in being *les neveux de leurs oncles* [the nephews of their uncles] and she was trying to avoid this. She was happy to think of the public demonstrations, because "no address inscribed on parchment can take the place of men's shouting voices." Her forthcoming book (her recollections of the year of revolution) she would not dedicate to him, much as she would like to do so, being reluctant to be *le neveu de son oncle* at this happy time when Jacoby was "the god of the day". If the judgment had gone against him, then the book would certainly have been dedicated to him.[41]

Many a historian has been moved to observe that the revolution of 1848 produced no great men. The judgment must be challenged.— Johann Jacoby was noble, fearless, honest, and a true patriot. In short, he was a great man by any standard, a superb human being. Let it always be remembered that this person who strove throughout his life with selflessness and unflinching integrity to bring his fellow Germans to a promised land of freedom, dignity, and justice—let it always be remembered, I say, that this German hero who loved his Fatherland was a Jew.

Notes

1   Lewald-Stahr, *Erinnerungen*, 114; Johann Jacoby, *Briefwechsel 1816–1849*, p. 453.

2   Valentin, *Geschichte der deutschen Revolution*, 2:313–314.

3   Ibid., 2:312: Indignant argument of Bremen's mayor, Johann Smidt.

4   Günter Wollstein, *Das "Grossdeutschland" der Paulskirche; Nationale Ziele in der bürgerliche Revolution 1848/49*, pp. 284–285.

5   Valentin, 2:303.

6   Kretzschmar and Schlechte, editors, *Französische und sächsische Gesandtschaftsberichte*, p. 213.

7   Friedrich Engels, *Revolution and Counter-Revolution in Germany*, p. 99.

8   Valentin, 2:216.

9   Ibid., 2:220.

10   Wollstein, p. 295.

11   Valentin, 2:306.

12   Ibid., 2:333–337.

13   Hellmut Diwald, *Ernst Moritz Arndt*, p. 17.

14   Ernst Rudolf Huber, *Der Kampf um Einheit und Freiheit*, pp. 842–843.

15   Valentin, 2:351 refers to the king's *Unklarheit, Falschheit, Bauernfängerei* and *Klopffechterei* [lack of clarity, falsehood, con artistry, bullying]. In Valentin's opinion, Friedrich Wilhelm betrayed Heinrich von Gagern.

16   Huber, p. 847.

17   Wilhelm Mommsen, *Grösse und Versagen des deutchen Bürgertums*, p. 69.

18   Dieter Grimm, *Deutsche Verfassungsgeschichte 1776–1866*, p. 205. Friedrich Wilhelm's thought was expressed in a forthright way in a letter to his friend Bunsen, written on that same day. His letter described his meeting with the Frankfurt delegation and ended with the popular saying, *Gegen Demokraten helfen nur Soldaten*.

19   Valentin, 2:463.

20   Jacoby, *Briefwechsel 1816–1849*, p. 570.

21   Botzenhart, *Deutscher Parlamentarismus in der Revolutionszeit*, p. 702.

22   Ibid., pp. 704–705.

23   Jacoby, p. 579.

24   Valentin, 2:671, note 39.

25   Botzenhart, p. 706.

26   Jacoby, p. 582. Letter to Simon Meyerowitz, written at Bad Canstatt 9/10 June.

27   Ibid., p. 583

28   Valentin, 2:502.

29   Ibid., 2:496.

30   Ibid., 2:498.

31   Ibid., 2:500.

32   *Die Gegenwart*, 6:152.

33   Jacoby, p. 584. Written in Berlin, 16 June 1849.

34   Valentin, 2:506.

35   Ibid., 2:508.

36   Jacoby, p. 586. Written 19 June to Simon Meyerowitz from Bad Cannstatt.

37   Ibid., pp. 574 and 588.

38   Ibid., pp. 589–590.

39   Ibid., p. 592. "Dungeon" may have been poetic license, but at that very moment Franz Benedikt Waldeck, the former head of the Prussian assembly, was known to be confined in an evil-smelling dark cell that was infested with bedbugs.

40   Ibid., p. 594, footnote.

41   Ibid., pp. 600–602.

Chapter 20

Saxony, the Prussian Rhineland, and the Bavarian Palatinate in 1849

This chapter deals with chaos. In May 1849 the Prussian counter-revolutionary steam-roller was on the move and would soon flatten all opposition. In the 1848 round, the impetus had arrived from abroad and the people of Germany had not by any means been organized for revolution. In a general way, liberals and moderates had known quite well what reforms they wanted, and radical agitators had known that the old system had to be destroyed root and branch, but in spite of these essential differences in outlook there had been a concerted push toward something different that had had the deceptive look of unity.

In the course of a difficult year, the members of the Frankfurt *Parlament* had learned to their chagrin that unity was not the characteristic feature of their beloved land. Disagreements had evolved into antagonism—even hatred—and as opposing views hardened, not only in the assembly but also throughout Germany, an astounding multiplicity of political organizations had sprung up. If anything, the Germans were now too organized. The resulting fragmentation made opposition to the much more unified counterrevolutionists almost impossible from the very start. This time, the attempts at revolution were bound to fail simply because the people who supported movement toward reform and change had coalesced into groups that could not present anything other than a fractured, shifting front.

Although theoretically this was a struggle to sustain the Frankfurt constitution, the term *Verfassungskampagne* [campaign for the constitution] is a misnomer that hardly applies to the *Bürgerkrieg* [civil war] that was going on in various parts of Germany. The people of Dresden rushed to action when they learned that Prussian troops were poised for invasion of their beloved Saxony. In Prussia's Rhine region, what stirred the people into action was anger over the mobilization of the Prussian militia [the *Landwehr*] for the purpose of beating back efforts in support of the constitution. Among those who took up arms in the Palatinate were Franconian or Swabian separatists whose homelands had been annexed by Bavaria in the post-Napoleonic settlement, and who in the very nature of things resented being part of Maximilian's realm, whereas in Baden, there was traditionally a strong strain of radicalism and hostility toward the whole principle of monarchy. Mixed into this were conflicting sentiments about Prussian hegemony *versus* Austrian dominance, along with old-Bavarian pride in the ancient royal dynasty. There were also incipient class antagonisms (an increasingly self-aware working class *versus* prosperous manufacturers) and so on. Red banners as well as the black-red-gold of Germany flourished at mass meetings or on the barricades.

* * * * * * * *

King Friedrich August of Saxony had been in communication with Friedrich Wilhelm, sharing his views. He immediately followed the Prussian monarch's example, dismissing his own troublesome *Landtag* on that same 28 April on which the imperial crown was rejected. The Saxon cabinet resigned on 30 April when the king declined to publish the Frankfurt constitution.

At first glance, Saxony would appear to have been ideal revolutionary territory. For centuries, this country of about two million inhabitants, with the densest population in Germany, had been concerned with industrial production. Unlike the industrialized Rhineland, however, Saxony had no centralized large-scale factory operations or heavy industry. Decentralized textile production and outworking was dominant (about 74% of all Saxon workers were so engaged).

Up to that point, the extreme left in Saxony had been apathetic as far as the constitution was concerned, considering it to be far too undemocratic for their taste, but now they responded vigorously to the call of the local *Vaterlandsverein* for a rally in Leipzig. The summons to that meeting declared that the constitution must be supported, not so much for its own sake, but for the sake of a future constitution that would conform to the will of the people. Various extreme motions were voted down at the meeting, but the question of republic *versus* monarchy had been effectively raised, especially by Samuel Erdmann Tzschirner, who opposed the ideas of the Saxon republican club that had been attempting for almost a year to infiltrate the moderate *Vaterlandsverein*. Within the republican organization there was a majority (*Burschenschaft* members and journalists for the most part) that deliberately took the position that intellectuals ought to lead. This elite blandly asserted that it would avoid working through the masses, who would easily be misled by rabble-rousers. Tzschirner himself belonged to a democratic organization that relied on the proletariat and the lower middle class.[1]

The guiding hand in Saxony at that moment was the Dresden *Vaterlandsverein* and its moderate democrats. With the thought that they might force the king to make concessions, they had already set up (on 2 May) a committee of three that would make decisions for the society throughout the duration of the crisis. This committee sought to lower the level of popular excitement.

The government meanwhile, for its own reasons, was also trying to lower the pitch by keeping its military men in barracks, away from the people on the streets. The ministry was at the same time appealing to Prussia for military assistance. When news of this move trickled through to the populace, the Dresden uprising erupted spontaneously.

With the appalling realization that in this unplanned insurrection they might be facing Prussian troops, the *Vaterlandsverein* sent out a call for help from all members of the democratic movement. *Eilt schleunigst mit Waffen und Munition herbei.* [Come at top speed with weapons and ammunition]. The *Dresdner Zeitung* reported that there was a complete lack of organization, and that the proletariat had only farm implements as weapons, and that food was being collected for the weak units manning the barricades.

For some forgotten reasons, the monarch and his ministers fled, departing by river boat for the fortress of Königstein. It was unfortunate that the steering committee of the *Vaterlandsverein*, informally assuming the function of a provisional government, made the error of agreeing to a short armistice, to last until noon of 5 May.

During the brief pause in hostilities, Tzschirner grasped the initiative. In view of the flight of the ruler, he argued, it was time to conduct a formal election of a provisional government. Fifteen of the delegates of the recently dismissed Saxon provincial assembly [*Landtag*] responded to his call and voted unanimously for Tzschirner, Otto Heubner, and Karl Gotthelf Todt. The trio were in effect a coalition government because Tzschirner was a leader of the extreme left, Heubner a member of the left, and Todt a liberal constitutionalist. Tzschirner regarded the campaign for the constitution as merely a takeoff point since his interest was in total German democratic revolution. Heubner on the other hand genuinely wanted to further the work of the *Paulskirche*. Todt, finally, thought that the provisional government had a double obligation—to effect recognition of the constitution and to stop the insurrection.

The middle class property owners as a whole viewed the election of the provisional government with suspicion because they knew that Tzschirner had consistently been an explicit opponent of the Frankfurt constitution although now he was its most vigorous advocate. As Engels once remarked, those who were in earnest about the movement were not in earnest about the constitution, and those who were in earnest about the constitution were not earnest about the movement.[2]

The forces of counterrevolution had utilized the short interruption in hostilities to collect a formidable army. At the expiration of the truce, the Saxon military had five thousand men in Dresden, plus another eight hundred who were moved in from western garrisons. The first Prussian unit had arrived, with artillery and the new hand guns with their vaunted firing-pin mechanism.

Bitter house-to-house combat began. Richard Wagner was busy here, climbing church towers in order to ring storm bells at some risk of his life, and two of the commanders formed an unlikely pair—Mikhail Bakunin the anarchist, and Stephan Born, the sturdy, methodical labor leader.

Born at least understood that the cause was lost. In his memoirs, he depicted Bakunin as a constant nuisance, always interrupting discussions at headquarters with a host of impractical proposals. (Nihilist that he was, Bakunin saw no reason to honor the established truce. He thought it would be advantageous to storm the arsenal on 4 May).[3] Though Born managed through his organized worker followers to effect a few imaginative operations (e.g., breaking through walls of adjacent houses in order to afford quick safe movement and communication without exposure to gunfire, and having some of his miners drive a tunnel toward a nearby mirror factory that they hoped to destroy by detonation), he was painfully aware that the best one could hope for was preservation of the honor of the uprising and an orderly withdrawal. On the barricades on 5 May, he saw that the two little four-pounders that the Freiberg miners had brought along served more as noise-makers than anything else. They could not compete with the Saxon artillery.[4]

Figure 22 INSURRECTION IN DRESDEN (May 1849). Fires had destroyed the opera house and the famed *Zwinger* pavilion.

It was not only lack of adequate preparation or the scant supply of arms that was the undoing of the defenders of the constitution. Their own ranks had shattered. The moderates who had thought of themselves as brothers-in-arms with the left discovered that their hearts were in fact with the reaction. As apprehensive property owners, they had no inclination to join in the bloody struggle. Within the forces on the left, there were contentious arguments, conflicting moves, and disagreements that reached disastrous proportions.

Apprehensions concerning Prussian troops had not been unjustified. French ambassador Reinhard, who had been on the scene in Dresden throughout the uprising, reported to Paris on 12 May:

It is only to be deplored that after the arrival of the Prussians the combat received a character of cruelty that it had not had before. The first unit that appeared in Dresden had already fought in the streets of Posen and Berlin, and in those two cities the soldiers had seen men who had threatened their lives and whom they had captured walking around free several weeks later. They had promised themselves not to give quarter this time. This example was followed by the Saxons.[5]

The brave determined barricade fighters in this desperate affair were mostly from the working class (miners, machine and textile workers), plus a students' contingent. Among the eight hundred and sixty-nine insurgents who had been subjected to investigation by mid-summer, five hundred and sixty-nine were of the working class. Because distinctions between various groups of workers (manual workers, apprentices, journeymen, masters, and "proletariat") are uncertain, the many attempts at statistical analysis of data on participants are rarely enlightening.[6]

Stephan Born managed to effect an orderly withdrawal by two thousand of his followers. He dismissed them at Freiberg, urging them to return peacefully to their homes. They had done their best.

At Freiberg, Born was greeted with theatrical effusion by a stranger who embraced and kissed him, exclaiming that "All is not lost. Youth, ah yes, youth, youth will restore everything." The excited speaker was Richard Wagner, whom Born had never met before. He was also urged by an effervescent Bakunin to take his two thousand battle-exhausted men to Prague, where they could fight for the Slavs. Born detached himself from the two woolly-minded enthusiasts and went on his solitary way by a roundabout route to Switzerland. During that journey he found sympathetic help from people who were tactful enough to refrain from questioning him, though they clearly observed his physical condition and accepted his coins that were grey from the gunpowder in his pocket.

There had been sporadic armed resistance throughout Saxony, though the whole affair is generally thought of as the Dresden uprising. About twenty towns had recognized the authority of the provisional government and attempted with varying degrees of unanimity to support it.[7]

* * * * * * * *

In Saxony the violent events had erupted more or less spontaneously, but this was not the case in other parts of Germany, especially in the Prussian Rhine provinces. On the surface this industrialized theatre of activity with its workers' associations, communist agitators, and the Central March organization would appear to have been fertile and promising ground for purposeful united action against the forces of counterrevolution, and indeed many a leader there had thought in those terms, but general disorder prevailed among the shifting, often bitterly antagonistic organizations during the early months of 1849.

Though it was more and more probable that violent revolutionary action might soon break out, this was not by any means a smooth continuation of the revolution that had swept across Germany in the spring of 1848. At that time there had been a deceptive appearance of a people united in a common angry crusade. At that time, people surged out onto the barricades in direct response to the revolutionary stimulus of the day. By the spring of 1849 Germans were organized, not only in the metropolitan centers like Berlin but also in the countryside. The counterrevolutionists were coalescing around their Prussian king, the middle class moderates were anxiously trying to hold the fort against the terrifying "masses", and the left wing radicals were busy marshalling their forces for Armageddon.

Rhinelanders—even those not actively engaged in the politico-social struggle and who had not felt concerned enough to join any of the supposedly national organizations like the *Zentralmärz* or even the Catholic *Piusverein*—were finding their loyalties divided. As monarchists, many were profoundly disturbed by the attitude of Friedrich Wilhelm. The Catholic majority was none too pleased to contemplate a future under a Protestant dynasty. Besides, in spite of the advantages they saw in the new Prussian constitution, they objected to having it imposed arbitrarily. Protestants on the other hand, though they rather liked the idea of a Protestant monarch, were unhappy with Friedrich Wilhelm's dictatorial ways and objected strenuously to his policies with respect to education.

Rhenish citizens who served in the regular Prussian army were known to be resentful of the dominant "Old Prussians", yet though their commanders were dubious about their loyalty in case of civil insurrection, they themselves were not at all sure that they would mutiny. In their anxious minds there lurked awareness of the death penalty. Civil guardsmen, most of whom were property owners, felt impelled to defend property, even though on the whole they were inclined to sympathize with the rebellious *Landwehr*. Within the *Landwehr* itself, there were those who objected to the proposition that they ought to take the oath of allegiance to the Frankfurt constitution.

The ranks of labor were seriously divided over problems of priorities. Those who assigned prime importance to the program of widespread class action (e.g. the Marxists) as opposed to those who favored the type of trade organization advocated by Stephan Born were often at loggerheads.

Constitutional monarchists and republicans, radicals and capitalists, Catholics and Protestants, all showed signs of wanting to reach some kind of non-violent center. There were few who openly sought to stir up a second revolution. When that ardent agitator Friedrich Engels attempted to pull the Elberfeld committee of safety toward revolution, he was promptly expelled. The committee, first organized by radicals, had deliberately included former moderate council members in its group of town executives.

Effective civil war or revolution does not spring from such moderation and uncertainty. Besides, the people lacked arms. Even the local *Bürgerwehr* had turned in most of its weapons in December of the previous year. Though in some cases (in Düsseldorf, for example) the few armed soldiers confronted milling thousands on the streets, their ordnance soon carried the day.

If anything, the trouble lay in the fact that although there was a spectacular increase in organizational activity, there was no unity of purpose. Even within individual organizations, there were so many cross purposes that there was a constant splitting into factions, a bewildering chain of secessions, followed by shaky tentative alliances that were in turn followed by further division, with the result that initial goals were hopelessly buried and forgotten. The membership and even the purpose of certain organizations changed drastically almost from day to day. Bakunin, the arch revolutionist, was moved to observe that anarchy was fundamental to the German character, in odd contrast to today's popular notion that the revolution failed because of German "obedience" and "passivity". Bakunin may have put his finger on the trouble. In Germany of 1849, every man had his own opinion and felt that he could only function in the company of true believers like himself. *Einigkeit* indeed.

So far, little attention has been paid to local politics because emphasis rather has been on alignments at Frankfurt. Consideration of the strengths and weaknesses of the multifarious political groups and parties that existed regionally—in this instance, specifically in the city of Cologne—offers an opportunity to take stock of the situation in post-Frankfurt Germany, and even to gain some understanding of the easy victory of the counterrevolution. In the heady springtime of the people following Friedrich Wilhelm's unwilling capitulation, the people of Cologne, like Germans almost everywhere, joyfully hailed their illusory unity as fact, but within a few short weeks they began to understand that they were not unified at all. They discovered this disagreeable fact as soon as their representatives at the Frankfurt *Vorparlament* returned to Cologne (on 5 April) in order to prepare for the vote that would elect delegates not only for the weighty sessions of the Frankfurt *Parlament* where a German constitution would be hammered out, but also for the united Prussian assembly so reluctantly summoned by Friedrich Wilhelm that would be meeting simultaneously in Berlin.

Cologne was one of the Rhineland's great growing industrial centers, the city where conspiracy and struggle to engage the heart and soul of the working people had gone on long before the March days of 1848. Conservatives and order-loving Germans in general looked at Cologne with misgivings.

The vicissitudes undergone by the local *Arbeiterverein* [workers' association] first organized by the popular physician Andreas Gottschalk in April of 1848, are almost too involved for brief exposition. Starting with a membership of about three hundred journeymen and laborers, the society grew by leaps and bounds, claiming as many as five thousand members by early May. Even in that short period there had been an abrupt shift of focus. When Gottschalk issued his original call, he was still a member of the *Bund der Kommunisten*. In that capacity, he had helped spearhead a mighty petition movement on 3 March 1848, when the city council had had to consider a document that demanded legislation and government by the people, general franchise, unlimited freedom of speech and press, dismissal of the standing army and introduction of general arming of the people under elected leaders, freedom of assembly, protection of work and social security for all, as well as education of all children at public expense.[8] From this radical position, Gottschalk had moved by the time he established his *Arbeiterverein* to one of willingness to support a monarchy based on democratic principles. His followers must have been confused when he urged them to boycott the coming elections for the Frankfurt *Parlament* and the united Prussian assembly. Besides, after he had attended the first enormous *Demokratenkongress* at Frankfurt (14–17 June 1848), he was full of enthusiasm for a workers' republic.

Next came a phase in which a merger of sorts was considered, of the *Arbeiterverein*, the Cologne *Demokratische Gesellschaft* of which

Karl Marx was a leading member, and the local *Verein für Arbeiter und Arbeitgeber* [for workers and employers]. This ended in formation of a joint directorate comprising two representatives from each of the three organizations in question. It was intended to serve as a regional board for democratic societies throughout the Rhineland and Westphalia.

Gottschalk was arrested in July 1848 and imprisoned through December of that year. During that six-months period, Marx became the interim head of Gottschalk's *Arbeiterverein*, managing to transform it so drastically that it lost most of its members (down from its thousands to about two hundred and sixty). Whereas it had started as a socialist league that relied primarily on the effect of petitions and demonstrations, it had become an educational society, more or less an arm of Marx's *Demokratische Gesellschaft*. After many a twist and turn, during which the regional directorate came to be fully in the hands of Marx's supporters, those in control were faced with the realities of the successful counterrevolution as it was soon to be played out on the streets of Dresden in the spring of 1849.[9]

The response was tactical. They promoted a series of political banquets as a means for propaganda. The most successful marked a celebration of the Paris February revolution. More than two thousand attended, responding with enthusiasm to toasts proposed by Cologne's leading democrats. Troops patrolled the streets meanwhile, because of a rumor that a synchronized rising in Cologne, Düsseldorf and Elberfeld impended. On 19 March there was still one more spectacular banquet in memory of the March days of 1848. Here there were toasts to the proletarian revolution, to the red republic, to the sovereign people and so on. Affairs appeared to be in full swing, but suddenly on 14 April 1849 Marx and his colleagues withdrew from the regional directorate, with the crisp announcement that "the present organization of democratic societies has too many heterogeneous elements within it."

The sprawling remnants of the combined organizations were left in the lurch. They attempted to pull themselves together by announcing that a congress would be held at Cologne on 6 May 1849, to include all workers' groups of the Prussian Rhineland and Westphalia that adhered "with decisiveness" to the principles of social democracy.

The supposedly promising attempt of a "united" opposition to energize and in a sense reawaken passive middle class citizens by means of elections and propaganda had meandered off into inconsequential political byways. Parliamentary and revolutionary programs that had coexisted more or less harmlessly, with odd compromises such as at least verbal acceptance of the idea of a red democracy by the moderates and half-hearted participation in petition campaigns by the extreme left had produced meager, inconclusive results. The brusque announcement by the Marxists that they could no longer function in the midst of a plethora of heterogeneous elements was in fact a disclosure that the democratic opposition had split. Thereafter there was a party of action and a distinct labor party.[10]

The day appointed for the congress (6 May 1849) turned out to be an eventful one known thereafter as "Congress Sunday", at the very time of the explosive impromptu insurrection in Dresden. Delegates of twenty-five clubs from various parts of the Rhineland responded to the call, but on the same day Marx and his colleagues also assembled a congress at Cologne, this one made up of representatives from twenty-one Rhineland organizations plus five from Westphalia. Adding to the excitement, there was still a third congress at Cologne on that day, made up of left-leaning groups that had seceded from the constitutional monarchist federation. In spite of the simultaneous occurrence of a trio of congresses, as many as half the democratic organizations known to have existed during the 1848 revolution seem to have disappeared.[11]

For simplicity's sake, it may be said that four major organizational efforts can be distinguished at Cologne in 1849, all of them jockeying for advantageous positions in view of the disarray at Frankfurt and the violence in Saxony. The *Demokratische Gesellschaft* promptly showed its colors in violent objection to the Frankfurt *Parlament*'s election of Friedrich Wilhelm as King of the Germans. When the Frankfurt delegation passed through Cologne on its way to Berlin, where it would offer the imperial crown to the Prussian monarch, the *Demokratische Gesellschaft* organized a demonstration—noisy *Katzenmusik*—setting up a din that was in embarrassing contrast to the festive welcome prepared for the delegation by the local citizens' association, the *Bürgerverein*. The latter organization, favoring constitutional monarchy, had been founded on 20 May 1848 as a direct opponent of the *Demokratische Gesellschaft*.[12]

The history of the *Demokratische Gesellschaft* of Cologne is a tangled one, going back in a way to Adam von Itzstein's annual *Hallgartenkreis* meetings, and through them to the Heidelberg meeting of 5 March 1848 that called for an immediate assembling of representatives for "the whole German Fatherland". Among those invited to the *Vorparlament* at Frankfurt were a number of far-left radicals, including Franz Raveaux, the dealer in tobacco and real estate who had used his office as president of the local carnival association to attain prominence and popularity among his fellow citizens. After the *Vorparlament* disbanded, turning over its work to an interim body (the *Fünzigerausschuss* [committee of fifty]) that would function until delegates to the coming Frankfurt *Parlament* were seated, Cologne's *Vorparlament* delegation returned, ready to prepare for the coming election. Raveaux, as a member of the committee of fifty, and charged by it to try to settle the problem of angry longshoremen and tow-path workers who were up in arms against the steamboat companies, had not too much time to engage in the election campaign—or so he craftily said. Raveaux, parenthetically, seems to have been a consummate politician, quick to understand the potentialities of any given situation, and also capable of making the kinds of concessions that true democracy requires. (E.g., his famous motion at Frankfurt that was intended to establish the priority of Frankfurt's decisions over those of provincial assemblies, and his willingness to withdraw it in favor of another that left more elbow-room for parliament members of the right and center.)

Political outlines were blurry. The *Zentralwahlkomitee* [central election i.e. nominating committee] that had formed was made up for the most part of Cologne's upper class *Honoratioren,* half of whom were members of the city council. To bind this group together with returned *Vorparlament* radicals like Raveaux and the radical Karl d'Ester into a smoothly functioning unit was going to be a formidable task. The first split, into a group of liberals and a radical group occurred almost at once, even though both Raveaux and d'Ester seemed willing to abandon part of their revolutionary fervor in a willingness to support the idea of a constitutional monarchy. The original break, which came on 16 April, was based, to put it baldly, on elitism on the part of the liberals.[13] Nettled merchants who were championing Raveaux's candidacy were moved to publish a statement:

> We make use of this occasion to print the speeches of our deputies because we are proud of being so worthily and honorably represented, doubly proud because Raveaux is a man of the people, and triply proud because we are able to certify that our delegate has proved that he has enough scientific training to be able properly to represent the people, his city and the Fatherland.[14]

Raveaux soon had his own so-called party, which met the desire of many of his fellow citizens to have their own group that opposed the forces of reaction. Democrats were uneasy, not wanting to inject a third element into the political picture, but by the end of April many were becoming sharply aware of the decided differences between themselves and the liberals of the central election committee. They began to speak bitterly of "moneybags" and "arrogance". A breakaway group that included former members of the election committee had been meeting at Cologne's Stollwerk café. It founded its own association, the *Demokratische Gesellschaft*, at a public assembly on 25 April 1848.

The hopes of the new *Demokratische Gesellschaft* for a sweeping victory in the spring elections were dashed. They had underestimated the effect of Gottschalk's boycott of the election, and also underestimated the strength of the Catholics. The only outstanding victor in the whole proceeding was Franz Raveaux, who had managed to stand above the fray and was rewarded by an impressive landslide vote for a seat at the *Paulskirche*.

Another organization at Cologne was the group that favored constitutional monarchy—the *Bürgerverein* [citizens' association] that had been founded on 20 May 1848, with the purpose of direct confrontation with the *Demokratische Gesellschaft*.[15] It was this association that made such a point of hailing the Frankfurt delegation that passed through Cologne on its way to Berlin with its offer of the imperial crown.

Here again, shifting undercurrents brought about strange affiliations. Even though the *Bürgerverein* was unmistakably on the side of law and order and sharply opposed to the radical faction, their proposal that there be a general consultation by representatives of Rhineland communities, with subsequent presentation of their findings to his Majesty Friedrich Wilhelm, was sharply rebuffed. The Prussian ministry of the interior prohibited such a "quasiparliament" because even the newly imposed Prussian constitution would not permit such gatherings for consideration of matters outside their immediate field of competence. The members were defiant enough to act as private persons and not as members of the city council, organizing a conference. In January 1849, a congress of constitutionalists was attended by members of forty-six clubs in the Rhineland, including some that were about to secede and affiliate with the democrats.[16]

The gymnastic societies—the *Turnvereine*—had had a political character ever since the early days under *Turnvater* Jahn. It has been said that the mere fact that they separated into two national organizations because of divergent views is proof of the political nature of the movement. The respective groups were called the *Allgemeiner deutscher Turnerbund* and the *Demokratischer Turnerbund*. The latter wanted a republic, while the former were more moderate, favoring a constitutional monarchy.[17]

There remains the organized group that represented political Catholicism, namely the *Piusverein* that had originally been started by neo-orthodox Catholics at Mainz in March 1848. During the whole course of the revolution, only twelve such societies were created in the Rhineland province, where three-quarters of the population were Catholic.[18] In their early days, the Cologne Catholic clergy and also the lay activists had supported the radical resistance of the democrats, but by the spring of 1849 their position had reversed. They were then in favor of the monarchy and its ministers and strongly opposed to the left and to Frankfurt as well. Their admiration stemmed from Friedrich Wilhelm's refusal to become emperor of a Germany from which Austria was excluded. Catholics would have perpetually been in the minority in such a case. In the eyes of the *Piusverein,* the question had become, should Germany be Catholic or Protestant?

Such then was the general confused situation among recognized political organizations. Throughout Germany, under varying circumstances, the same kind of confusion seems to have prevailed, presenting a welcome opening to the determined, much more unified counterrevolutionists.

In one exceptional case, that of the national *Zentralmärzverein* [Central March Association], there was a conscious attempt to go against the tide of dissent and fission. It is of interest here because one of the founders was that skilled political personality, Franz Raveaux of Cologne. Although he and his fellow founders, all members of the Frankfurt *Parlament*, were definitely on the left in their beliefs and actions, these men were willing to make a last effort in the face of the counterrevolutionary tidal wave.

They had in mind a closing of the ranks for the sake of German unity, freedom and sovereignty of the people. Their rival factions had in fact come together as the *Vereinigte Linke* [united left] in the fall of 1848. Now they were aiming at a universal organization that would be an umbrella for all varieties of individual societies that could work toward the common goal of German unity without surrendering any of their own methods of action, or of their specific views. They would all be tied, through the Central March organization, to the Frankfurt *Parlament*. Though the headquarters of the Central March would be at Frankfurt, this did not imply that the main office would act as a directorate. Rather, since unanimity was not required, communications from the head office would be in the form of suggestions and recommendations. Raveaux himself made the explicit point that in congresses of the society, it was the delegates, not the officers of the organization, who would be responsible for resolutions that were adopted.[19] Marx and his followers thought this was highly amusing, not to say offensive, but in all fairness it must be admitted that Raveaux had the more accurate view of the way a democracy has to function.

The fact that the *Zentralmärzverein* had such close ties with members of the *Parlament* was at once its strength and its undoing. On the plus side was the fact that the members of the executive office, as members of the parliament, were financially secure and were by the very nature of their duties assembled in one place. Furthermore, again as parliament members they had close ties with their constituents, and what they said was heard with attention. On the negative side was the circumstance that the collapse of the *Parlament* entailed the collapse of the society.[20]

In the long run, it must be said that the Germans had not mastered the political process that leads to consensus. They persisted in the view that disagreement entailed separation. For this reason, the *Zentralmärzverein* remains the lone prototype of modern political parties. If further evidence of the essential non-functional situation of Germany in 1849 is required, there is the depressing analysis presented by Michael Wettengel as a preamble to his detailed list of political organizations.[21] He arranged them by categories, as follows: conservative, Catholic-conservative, Catholic-constitutional, constitutional-conservative, liberal-constitutional, liberal-democratic, moderate democratic, democratic, republican, socialist-republican, and communist. *E pluribus unum* would have been a highly inapposite motto here.

* * * * * * *

The rival congresses that were struggling for the allegiance of the industrial population that took place on Congress Sunday (6 May 1849) have already been mentioned. In his analysis of the situation, Jonathan Sperber offers the interesting comment that "affiliation with one of the two congresses seems to have been based more on personal connections than on political principles or social structure." He further observes that "strangely, the democrats seemed to lag far behind the city councilmen, and even the constitutional monarchists in both the militancy of their views [toward the Frankfurt *Parlament*] and their willingness to make them known to a mass public."[22] He attributes this to behind-the-scenes activity that was intended to lead to armed insurrection. It is certain that Marx's *Neue Rheinische Zeitung* was refusing to endorse the movement that supported the Frankfurt constitution, and that the *Arbeiterverein* was calling for a tax boycott and stating that the Frankfurt assembly had consistently betrayed the people. On the surface at least, there seems to have been little firmness of purpose among the democrats. Insurrection was in fact already brewing at Elberfeld, where the members of the *Landwehr* were showing distinct signs of mutiny, but that was not the work of the *Demokratische Gesellschaft*.

Matters had been taken out of the hands of political organizers by the Dresden uprising and the subsequent call-up of Prussian militia for use in combat against insurrectionists. The *Landwehr* [national guard] was in no mood to cooperate with the projected mobilization for work against pro-Frankfurt sentiment. Under the threat of immediate call-up, those at Elberfeld, for example, had been organized in early spring into a unit that marched belligerently under the German tricolor. As early as 3 May 1849, they met and published the following firm resolution:

> The undersigned members of the Elberfeld *Landwehr* recognize and declare that the ministry surrounding the Crown is to be regarded as hostile to the people, and consider themselves to be released from duty to the absolute Crown. On the contrary, the said members declare themselves to be in accord with the constitution established by the Frankfurt Assembly and to be determined to bring about the introduction of this constitution for Germany with their persons and their honor.[23]

Similar declarations were sent out from such places as Gerresheim, Mönchengladbach, Krefeld, and Neuss. Of these, the group at Giesenkirchen was bold enough to display a red flag and take an oath to the Frankfurt constitution.[24] Though all this was certainly a major challenge to Friedrich Wilhelm and his government, as the month of May progressed, there was considerable disunity below the surface.

The bloodiest encounter was at Iserlohn, where *Landwehr* insurgents were concentrated, and the lower classes were to a certain extent in real economic distress. The democratic societies had about eight hundred members there, and made use of the employment situation for their propaganda. The arsenal was stormed and plundered, and local authorities fled, to be replaced by a radical committee of safety. *In toto* there were about three thousand rebels in the town, although some eight hundred withdrew before the affair became serious. Apparently the townspeople in general had become terrified by the actions of the revolutionists and actually welcomed the arrival of regular troops. There was a fierce confrontation at the barricades, where one hundred Iserlohn workers died at the hands of Prussian soldiers, many of whom were veterans of the Dresden uprising and inclined to be ruthless on that account.[25]

Of the forty known dead among the locals, there were twenty factory workers, ten craftsmen or apprentices, a policeman, two merchants, a night watchman and a road worker. Those who fled to exile were academics.[26] On the whole, middle class observers had a low opinion of those who fought at barricades. "The workers have no understanding of the constitution and fundamental rights, but where they can strike a blow with their sledge hammers and punch a hole in the existing state structure, they won't fail to do so."[27]

It is useful at this point to consider the account of one of the participants in the disturbance at Iserlohn, not for its drama but for the evidence it offers of the general confusion among the revolutionists of 1849. This was written by the industrialist Karl Wilhelm Sudhaus (1827–1915), who looked back with a certain amount of amusement at his activities as a student at Hagen, a few kilometers from Iserlohn.[28] Labor relations in his town were relatively smooth-running, he observes, because many of the employers had been workers themselves in their day. In August 1848 a handful of brash youngsters had made themselves obnoxious at the time of Friedrich Wilhelm's passage through the town, returning to the north after the festivities at the Cologne cathedral, but otherwise the students seem to have confined their revolutionary activities to beer drinking and singing songs written by people like Herwegh and Freiligrath.

When Friedrich Wilhelm rejected the imperial crown, there was general indignation. He refused it because it was offered by the people, and the people would have to force him to receive it from their hands! At Hagen, mass meetings began, and there was excitement when word arrived from Iserlohn that the people had stormed the arsenal there. The Iserlohn *Landwehr* battalion was stationed at Hagen and was thrown into turmoil by the arrival of agitators. When an officer tried to control the assembled *Landwehr*, he could not even make himself heard. The narrator, on his way to school the next day, learned that the town was in an uproar and that there was a plan to march to Iserlohn to join the fighting there.

The agitators were telling the *Landwehr* men, "You could all be sentenced to death for your disorder here. Since things have gone this far, it would be better to join the brothers who are fighting in Iserlohn. You can't have anything worse happen than be shot to death, but if the revolution wins, you'll not only go unpunished but you'll be heroes who saved the Fatherland, and you'll be praised and honored." The crowd took up the cry "On to Iserlohn!"

"So before I quite knew what was happening, I handed my books over to a fellow student and went on my way to get a gun." The young man was put up at the front of the marchers, along with two others who like him wore green smocks, because they would look like sharpshooters. The narrator thought that there were about eight hundred marchers: other eye-witness reports estimate the number at about four hundred. They were all without ammunition, and without rations. Country people along the way gave them food, and on they marched with loaves of bread or sausages on their bayonets, "like Hussites before Naumburg."

The revolutionists from Hagen were hailed at Iserlohn, given quarters, and assigned picket duty, to be on the watch for Prussian soldiers. For some days they saw none, but when the Prussian troops actually arrived, the townspeople of Iserlohn were anxious to rid themselves of the revolutionists, in order to allow the regulars to march in peacefully. The Hagen troop slipped through the gates and went home, where they were hailed as heroes—all before the fighting began in earnest at Iserlohn.

Revolutionary activity and insurrection were brought under control almost as soon as it began. This was, after all, an internal affair in Prussia, and armed force was readily available. Some of the rapidity can be explained by the availability of railway transport for the troops. There was another factor—new in this second year of revolution— namely the telegraph system that the military was able to use. Telegraphy was still in its infancy. Samuel Morse (1791–1872) had become aware of the potentialities of the work of Gauss and Weber on electromagnetism and had received a patent for his apparatus in 1840, but practical application of the device had been slow. Both Alexander von Humboldt and David Hansemann had attempted to promote the use of the telegraph as early as 1842, but it was not until 1848 that Prussia became interested enough to initiate experiments. In February 1849 a line was opened between Berlin and Frankfurt, and thereafter the work advanced rapidly. The new lines followed the new railroads, for reasons of economy. Therefore, Prussian military authorities had both railways and telegraph at their disposal in the crucial spring of 1849.[29]

* * * * * * *

Bavaria had the usual divisions characteristic of the times. It had an eighty-thousand-member conservative society for constitutional monarchy and religious freedom, a *Märzverein* at Munich, an *Arbeiterverein* and an *Arbeiterbildungsverein* [education of the workers]. a *Piusverein*, plus assorted *Vereine demokratisch gesinnter Bürger* [societies of democratically-minded citizens] and *Bürgervereine für Freiheit und Ordnung* [citizens' societies for freedom and order], in addition to regional groups such as the *Pfälzische Volksverein* [Palatinate people's society] at Kaiserslautern. It also had a new elected lower house that had sixty-nine delegates representing the left, all from the recently annexed regions of Franconia and Swabia.

The struggle for the constitution in Bavaria had its own special features.[30] The problem was intertwined with dismay over the supposed settlement of the *kleindeutsch-grossdeutsch* question by the Frankfurt *Parlament*. Geographically, Bavaria's position was exposed, and reliance on Austria was not to be denied. A ministerial questionnaire directed to authorities in Bavaria's various districts had evoked responses indicating that on the whole there was a sense that Austria should never be excluded. There was also a well-defined dislike of Prussia's Hohenzollern monarch, Friedrich Wilhelm. The government moreover had a fairly strong position in that it could call attention to the fact that Bavaria already had a constitution that guaranteed most of the Frankfurt *Grundrechte*. There would have to be discussions and adjustments, not immediate unconditional acceptance. The ministry's assertion that in Bavaria the *Grundrechte* had not been acknowledged inflamed the pro-constitution radicals. Oh no, they were told. The *Grundrechte* had merely been *veröffentlicht* [published], not *verkündet* [proclaimed]. The implications were obvious: the Bavarian ministry was saying that there had to be *Vereinbarung*—agreement—concerning the constitution, and that this agreement would in fact have to be double-barreled: between the Frankfurt *Parlament* and the several states, and also within the states, between the respective rulers and their assemblies.

This provocative assertion caused leftwing publications to snarl that Frankfurt was sovereign and that the states would have to conform. They also started to issue threats of secession by the Palatinate and even by Franconia. These portions of Bavaria had only come under the sovereignty of the Wittelsbach rulers after the Congress of Vienna, and they traditionally were much more receptive to democratic ideas than were the citizens of Munich.

A ministerial declaration denying the validity of the constitution was officially issued on 23 April, causing Karl Mathy as undersecretary of state for the Frankfurt central power to rush to Munich in the hope of persuading Maximilian II to change his mind. His Majesty refused to treat with Mathy as a duly accredited emissary and let it be known that nobody was more eager than he to see a strong united Germany, and that his negative reaction had nothing to do with his own dynastic position. Rather, he was responsible for the welfare of all his people. He saw no reason to shift his attitude, this view having been strengthened by the decision of the Prussian government of 28 April (Friedrich Wilhelm's rejection of both crown and constitution).

Mathy was not the only one whose eyes were directed toward Munich in those days. The congress of the *Zentralmärzverein* at Frankfurt, meeting on 27 April, had decided that it would be useful to establish a provisional central office for Bavaria. Although the staff there reported to Frankfurt that there was substantial doubt about the ability of a new united Germany to control the old *Bundestag*, they were able to organize an enormous meeting from which an address bearing twelve thousand signatures emanated, this document calling for immediate unconditional recognition of the Frankfurt constitution.

Not to be outdone, the *Verein für konstitutionelle Monarchie und religiöse Freiheit* had swung into action. When Mathy called to bid farewell to the king, therefore, he encountered a deputation that had in hand an address to his Majesty, signed by some nine thousand citizens of Munich. The document expressed heartfelt thanks for the firm conduct of the Bavarian government in the face of a constitution that would fragment Austria and convert Bavaria into an endangered borderland state—a situation that would cause economic havoc and was fraught with the danger that Bavaria might come into thralldom to the north. The address went into detail, delineating the woes that would visit the beloved native land if the new constitution were recognized. Bavaria would be inundated by a flood of unemployed drifters from the north. There would be burdensome taxes—for a Baltic navy. This constitution, it was suggested, would mediatize *nicht nur unsere Fürsten, sondern auch unsere Landtage*.[31] [not only our princes but also our provincial assemblies] All true Bavarians were prepared to close ranks in defense of "the holy rights of the Throne."

The executive committee of the Palatinate *Volksvereine* had also been active on 27 April. It summoned the Frankfurt delegates and those of the Bavarian chamber, as well as members of the Palatinate *Landrat* [council], along with electors, mayors, and representatives of various political organizations to a preparatory meeting to be held at Neustadt on 1 May. They also summoned all Palatinate citizens to a peoples' assembly on 2 May, for the purpose of taking a position against his Majesty's government in Munich. "Bavaria's king, through a 'constitutional' ministry, has declared to our parliament that he wants to know nothing about a *Reichsverfassung*, does not want to know anything about a single powerful German Fatherland. For him there is only a hereditary Bavaria, always the tax-paying domain of the house of Wittelsbach. If the government has become a body of rebels, the free citizens of the Palatinate will execute the law." The preparatory meeting at Neustadt decided that the constitution, with its fundamental rights and law on the voting franchise was binding for Bavaria. The Bavarian government's actions against this constitution were branded as high treason. Until the government complied with the law, a ten-member provisional *Landesverteidigungsausschuss* [national defense committee] should be elected.

The peoples' meeting on the following day confirmed these inflammatory statements and decisions, and elected the proposed defense committee. This body immediately ordered recognition and publication of the constitution, and required all officials in the Bavarian Palatinate to subscribe to an oath to the constitution on pain of removal from office. Private citizens were told to call their sons home from military duty. Having taken this step, the committee went on to make contact with radicals in the Rhineland, in Hesse, in Baden—even in Paris. They called for volunteers from Switzerland , and went so far in their exuberance as to invite staid General Dufour, the Swiss military hero, to head their armed force. Dufour declined, needless to say, and the command was turned over to Fenner von Fenneberg, whose military exploits had been none too brilliant.

Moderates and extremists alike were well aware of the depleted condition of the Bavarian state treasury after the abdication of King Ludwig, and they had also observed the extreme weakness of the Bavarian army. For reasons of economy, a large portion of the armed force was always on furlough. Furthermore, the army had been drained by the stationing of two full-strength companies at Frankfurt ever since the September crisis there. The danger of mutiny was imminent. About three-quarters of the soldiers in the Bavarian army were Palatinate Germans, who soon felt pressure from their home towns and villages. Some communities physically prevented their men on furlough from returning to active duty. Others were held back by the local civic guards, who removed the Bavarian insignia from their caps and decked them out with tricolor ribbons—even with red ones. The two companies at Frankfurt were deluged with letters from home and surrounded by shouting crowds in railway stations. "Don't shoot your brothers! Stand by the people!"

The major fortresses were experiencing serious defections, especially at Landau, where almost half of the provincial troops were stationed. The commanders at Landau and Germersheim on the Rhine both appealed to Munich for reinforcements, which Munich simply did not have. There was too much danger of insurrection in Franconia and Swabia. The Bavarian government responded weakly that officials must act resolutely, arresting the members of the provincial defense committee.

In desperation, moderates directed their plea for help to Frankfurt. Mayor Kolb of Speyer argued that the men of the defense committee, while unquestionably honorable people were blind to the fact that revolution could not succeed and would play into the hands of the counter-revolution. If at all possible, he urged, steps must be taken to legalize what had already happened. Delegates approached von Gagern, imploring him to send a *Reichskommissar* who could contain the revolutionary actions and restore order. Gagern appointed Bernhard Eisenstuck, a deputy to the Frankfurt assembly and dispatched him to Speyer on 6 May.

In this surreal situation, the Bavarian provincial governor and the military commanders at Speyer and Landau also turned to the central power. They were asking for "troops of the *Reich*". Gagern responded to this appeal by sending some of the forces that were protecting the

Frankfurt assembly, including Prussian infantry. He did this without apprizing Eisenstuck—and Eisenstuck had specifically said that such forces should under no circumstances be sent to Bavaria.[32]

Eisenstuck, whose actions and motives have been subject to heated argument among historians,[33] was doing his utmost to pour oil on troubled waters and above all to keep control out of the hands of the extreme radicals of Neustadt. To that end, one of his first official acts was the issuing of a proclamation that legalized the provincial defense committee, by authority of the central power. The intention was clear enough if the conditions attached to the proclamation are considered. The committee was empowered to take any action necessary in defense of the Frankfurt constitution, insofar as it did not interfere with the authority of legally existing provincial officers. (In a word, the committee would not be allowed to threaten officials with loss of office if they refused to take an oath to the constitution, nor would it be permissible for it to take over public moneys or demand the payment of taxes.) Eisenstuck was effectively drawing the teeth of violent revolution.[34]

He was able to demonstrate the wisdom of his policy when the first Prussian troops arrived at Landau (on 8 May). He dashed to Landau and met with the commandant of the fortress, urging him to order the Prussian troops to withdraw from the Palatinate. He said nothing about the Badenese troops who had also arrived from Frankfurt, because these men came from a state that recognized the Frankfurt constitution. The uncomfortable, much alarmed commanding general managed by indirect means to accede to Eisenstuck's request. The Prussians departed peacefully, but the government at Munich was outraged and demanded the dismissal of Eisenstuck, seeing him as a revolutionist instead of as the peacemaker that he indubitably was. He was recalled by the central power, but not by Heinrich von Gagern, who had resigned from the ministry of *Erzherzog* Johann on 10 May, to be replaced by the reactionary Grävell.

Although in a cantonal election the moderates were in the majority, the extremists managed to insinuate themselves into a position of power as a provisional government (no longer a defense committee), helped by vociferous enthusiasts who, like so many Jacobins at a French Convention, shouted down the moderates. This new provisional government, which by the way insisted that it would remain in office only until the Frankfurt constitution came into force and never ventured to proclaim a republic, was elected on 17 May. During the month of its precarious existence, it attempted to impose taxes and to raise an adequate army by conscription, but was constantly hampered by its tacit compromise with the moderates. Since the effort to collect taxes failed (resistance to taxation had always been a strong point among Palatinate Germans), voluntary contributions had to fill the gap, and these were so meager that the government was constantly in debt. Without money or qualified officers and practically devoid of efficient weapons and ammunition, the government faced a formidable problem in recruitment. Difficult enough to bring in young conscripts during the hay-making season. They were sorely needed in the fields at home.

The Palatinate had friends who had hurried to their side, especially radicals in nearby Hesse-Darmstadt, whose own ruler was one of the twenty-eight princes who had acknowledged the Frankfurt constitution. A provincial congress of democratic clubs, held like those at Cologne on Congress Sunday (6 May 1849), had seethed with plans for insurrection. Incendiary speeches were colorful, like that of Philipp Wittmann, who shouted that although the princely caterpillars had been shaken from the Liberty Tree in the past year, they had not been trampled, and the time for action had arrived.[35]

Workers from Mainz moved ahead to Wörrstadt, where they set up an arms co-op on 9 May, to be followed by hundreds of gymnasts and members of the *Arbeiterverein* who were ready to march off to Bavaria. In fact, on 10–11 May two columns of insurgents departed in response to an invitation of the Palatinate defense committee. About fifteen hundred men moved toward Kirchheimbolanden under the joint command of Franz Zitz and Ludwig Bamberger.[36] Another column of some thousand men (mostly civil guards from Worms) moved out smartly toward Ludwigshafen under the command of Ludwig Blenker, the local wine merchant and colonel of the guard. These eager insurgents arrived in Bavaria at an inauspicious moment of confusion and general disarray, just at the time of Eisenstuck's recall, and immediately before the provincial government came into being.

In later life, Ludwig Bamberger (1823–1899) wrote an account of the military action in the Palatinate in 1849.[37] There is more than a tinge of self-justification in his narrative, but it has to be remembered that he was writing toward the end of a long career of disheartenment and disappointment.[38] In spite of its flaws, Bamberger's work on 1849 offers a distinct picture of the flounderings of inept inexperienced leaders and their demoralized rank-and-file followers in a region where genuine interest in their cause underwent disconcerting fluctuations. The Palatinate has always been considered to have had its separatists. When Bamberger speaks of his on-the-spot observations, it is perhaps worth reflecting that his field of activity was regionally quite small, centering around Kirchheimbolanden, Neustadt, Kaiserslautern and Ludwigshafen (all in the southern part).

Bamberger thought that the terrorism and brutality of the Prussians at Dresden had had its effect on the people of the Palatinate.[39] In his travels back and forth across the region, he found only two individuals who were recognizably convinced democrats, but they had no talent as propagandists. He found no traces of excitement . "Once in a while there would be a mild liberal, but just as often there would be a decided reactionary. On the whole, . . . people were going about their business in their usual way."

The description of the members of the provisional government (originally the defense committee) sounds like something designed for a farce. The five men, now designated Minister President, Minister of Finance, Minister of the Interior, Minister for Foreign Affairs, and Minister of Justice, shared a space where they worked together on any problem that arose. Since they had no staff, and not even any office supplies, they handled even the most minute details in person. The Minister of Finance, for example, had to find time to arrange for the purchase of three yards of black-red-gold bunting. Once, during an important "plenary" session, the Minister President ran downstairs in order to break up a noisy argument between two people on the street. The Minister of Finance (a physician) had at times a total treasury of sixty florins. "What they absolutely did not comprehend was governing."

They had established their headquarters at Kaiserslautern, which, in Bamberger's disillusioned eyes, was nothing more than an overgrown village, where half the population went barefoot and cows and swine were herded on the street, and where there was no workable communication with the outside world (no notion of what was happening at Munich, for example). They had only one miserable small printing press. Nothing had been prepared or organized ahead of time. Bamberger noted gloomily that this was the situation in Württemberg and Baden also. At one point the headquarters was shifted to Speyer, where facilities would have been better, but the government returned almost immediately to Kaiserslautern because of a false rumor that an enemy army was approaching.

The most dismal part of the Bamberger story relates to the various military commanders, who succeeded each other with dizzying rapidity. When Bamberger and Franz Zitz arrived at Kirchheimbolanden on 11 May with their "Rhine Hesse Legion", Ferdinand Fenner von Fenneberg (1820–1863) was the provisional commander-in-chief. An Austrian officer, he had fought at Vienna in October. Bamberger never found it in his heart to blame Fenner for the general disorder, because it would have been almost impossible to conjure up anything from *Nichts*, as he expressed it, but he did feel that Fenner was no administrator.

Fenner was briefly replaced by a five-member board. There was vague discussion of a possible arrangement whereby Franz Sigel, whom the Badenese had summoned from his exile in Switzerland to serve as their commander, might act as head of a joint Badenese-Palatinate force, but in the event the five-member board appointed Polish general Sznaide as commander. This stumpy, short-legged little man with a paunch and grey whiskers, was a superannuated soul who had fought in the revolution of 1830 and had been living ever since in much reduced circumstances in Paris. Militarily, Sznaide had only one idea. He would organize the Palatinate forces in three camps. He seemed to have an inordinate faith in those camps, although at one point he confided honestly to Bamberger that if he had realized what he was getting into, "*Il ne restera qu'à me faire tuer*" [the only thing left for me to do would be to get myself killed].

The recruiting effort was pitiful. All males between the ages of eighteen and thirty were supposed to report, but "most had to be dragged in by the hair." They obviously had no confidence in the revolutionary army, which had no officers, no money, no equipment, no ammunition, and only eight thousand muskets. Even after a modest amount of money was collected and paid for the purchase of weapons at Liège, there was no way to effect delivery. France would not allow shipments, and Belgium was equally adamant. Passage through Switzerland was forbidden. Once half a dozen cannon were miraculously acquired, but there were no horses to pull them.

There was a pathetic attempt to storm the formidable fortress of Landau because in wonderful self-delusion, it was believed that the men stationed there would desert in a body to the revolution. The attacking force here assembled on 19 May under the popular Ludwig Blenker (1812–1863), who had acquired some military experience as a cavalry officer in Greece. The attacking force was made up of three hundred regulars (deserters from the Bavarian army), and fifteen hundred members of the local *Bürgerwehr* and volunteers, plus peasants carrying pitchforks and scythes. They boldly approached the main gate, Blenker shouting, "Brothers, don't shoot!" but the guard responded by immediately opening fire. Blenker, slightly wounded, found himself standing there with only two armed men beside him. The others had hastily retreated.

There was no overall plan. As Bamberger put it, there were only episodes. *Es marschirte nichts als die Zeit* [the only thing that moved forward was Time].

Among the gymnasts whom he and Zitz had brought to Kirchheimbolanden as the Rhenish Hessian Legion, most were men who had left their shops, their desks, their small businesses, or their farms, thinking that they were about to participate in a three-day operation *à la française*. When they found how dreary the actual situation was, about a quarter of them departed within the first week. The rest, demoralized, complained bitterly in spite of determined efforts on the part of the leaders to impose some organization and discipline. They put shoemakers and tailors to work, supplying shoes and shirts for the troop. But food was lacking, and shelter. It did no good to apply to the authorities of the provisional government. They were helpless and disorganized, and General Sznaide only pulled out his trusty map and described the three camps he intended to establish. In response to desperate pleas, Sznaide at last appointed a commander for the troop, but the man he sent—one Major Ruppert—was singleminded like his general, and thought that everything could be solved by rearrangement of the men in *pelotons* [platoons], and he spent all his energies shuffling the exhausted men around according to the plan he sketched with pencil on a scrap of paper. The men meanwhile were being shuttled hither and yon in response to conflicting orders from headquarters, often marching in one direction for five hours, only to be told to return to the original position. Many were barefoot. All were hungry. In view of their hardships, Zitz and Bamberger reached the conclusion that they would be wise to dismiss the troop. (This was on 2 June, twelve days before the actual Prussian attack.) They would attempt to lead their men to Alsace, and Zitz was saying that he wanted to pay for the operation.

In spite of everything, they stayed on, being marched up and down the Alzens valley several times, as reports and counter-reports as to the location of the Prussians came to headquarters. Bamberger himself meanwhile was constantly being shuttled around for consultations and negotiations with the Badenese, whose statements were hopelessly contradictory. *Wirrwarr* [confused situation] is the word that comes from Bamberger's pen over and over.

On 11 June some of the more clear-headed officers, including Blenker, met with members of the provisional government at Grünstadt to hold council. Franz Zitz was with them. They issued a memorandum that set out the situation in all its bleakness.

The whole northern border was occupied by Prussians with their artillery and cavalry—at least twenty-eight thousand strong. On the Palatinate side, the Hessian legion of Bamberger and Zitz had nine hundred men. Blenker had a corps of four hundred and eighty. At Göllheim there was a two-thousand-man body of armed *Volkswehr*. (Some had scythes. The other units lacked adequate arms.) There were about six hundred men at Neustadt. The memo included the proposal that all forces retire to Neustadt, where possibly they might reorganize in a siege of the fortress of Landau. This group had had to take matters into its own hands because there had been no orders from the Kaiserslautern headquarters for weeks. Their own immediate commander, Ruppert, was intently reshuffling his *pelotons*. And the Prussians were on Bavarian territory, already skirmishing with the revolutionary forces.

Bamberger and Zitz were acutely aware that as members of a force that all Germany was watching and that was in fact Frankfurt's last hope, they would be blamed as the ones who precipitated the defeat if they decided to withdraw. As one reads Bamberger's sad pages, it is easy to see that he still felt responsible.

On 18 June the remnants of the Palatinate force (about six hundred infantrymen including the volunteers and the members of the provisional government) crossed the Rhine on a pontoon bridge near Knielingen. "For me, this was the clearest preview of the fate of Baden." No provision had been made for the retreating army by their supposed allies, the Badenese. In desperation, seeing his men sleeping on the bare ground, cold and hungry, Bamberger decided to go to Heidelberg in order to appeal to Mieroslawski, the young Polish commander of the Baden army, but at the railway station in Karlsruhe he encountered a friend who told him that such a mission was impossible. The Prussians had already advanced as far as Bruchsal, cutting off communication between Karlsruhe and Heidelberg.

The Prince of Prussia and his armies had the firm intention to crush the rebellion. On the left bank of the Rhine there were twenty-five thousand men under von Hirschfeld. On the right bank were another twenty-five thousand under von der Gröben. Württemberg had supplied some eight thousand. They had not waited for the Bavarians, who were infuriated to have their land treated so summarily. Under their commander, *Fürst* Theodor von Thurn und Taxis, they finally fielded fifteen to sixteen thousand troops of the line.[40]

Part of Bamberger's legion joined the Badenese revolutionaries, and part went their own way home. "I myself left Baden without even the shadow of a shadow of hope for the resistance of the Badenese."[41]

Notes

1 Weber, *Die Revolution in Sachsen 1848/49,* p. 330.

2 Ibid., p. 340.

3 Ibid., p. 341; Born, *Erinnerungen,* p. 226.

4 Ibid., p. 222.

5 Kretschmar and Schlechte, editors, *Französische und sächsische Gesandschaftsberichte,* p. 397.

6 Christopher Klessmann, "Zur Sozialgeschichte der Reichsverfassungskampagne von 1849," *Historishe Zeitschrift* 218/2 (April 1974): 294–297.

7 Weber, pp. 327–355.

8 Valentin, *Geschichte der deutschen Revolution,* 1:416.

9 Marcel Seyppel, *Die demokratische Gesellschaft in Köln,* pp. 157–158. 218; Dowe, *Aktion und Organisation,* pp. 172–173; Sperber, *Rhineland Radicals,* pp. 223–231: Sperber suggests that the importance of the *Arbeiterverein* may have been "exaggerated in retrospect".

10 Seyppel, pp. 271–272.

11 Sperber, pp. 360–361.

12 Seyppel, p. 273.

13 Ibid., p. 74. The political separating lines were not according to substantive differences between democrats and liberalism. Candidates for the Frankfurt *Parlament* were assessed in terms of character, intellectual probity and closeness to the people.

14 Ibid.

15 Ibid., p. 159.

16 Sperber, p. 188.

17 Wettengel, *Die Revolution von 1848/49 im Rhein-Main-Raum,* p. 522; Richard Noack, "Die Revolutionsbewegung von 1848/49 in der Saargegend," *Mitteilungen des Historischen Vereins für die Saargegend* 18/2 (1930): 246.

18 Sperber, p. 205.

19 Wettengel, pp. 345–346.

20 Ibid., p. 349.

21 Ibid., pp. 522–524.

22 Sperber, pp. 361–362.

23 Valentin, 2:471.

24 Sperber, p. 365.

25 Klessmann, p. 302, citing W. Schulte, *Volk und Staat.*

26 Ibid.

27 Ibid., citing Johann Philipp Becker and C. Enselen, *Geschichte der süddeutschen Mai-Revolution des Jahres 1849.*

28 Wilhelm Schulte, "Zustände und Vorgänge in Iserlohn und Hagen 1848/49," in *Fritz Kuhn zum Gedächtnis*, pp.106–122.

29 Josef Reindl, *Der Deutsch-Österreichische Telegraphenverein und die Entwicklung des deutschen Telegraphenwessens 1850–1871*, pp. 64–70.

30 Michael Doeberl, *Bayern und die deutsche Frage in der Epoche des frankfurter Parlaments*, pp. 153–199.

31 Ibid., p. 153; Valentin, 2:674, note 76.

32 Georg Friedrich Kolb, *Lebenserinnerungen einer liberalen Demokraten*, pp. 197–201.

33 Sperber, pp. 400–403.

34 Ibid., p. 402.

35 Ibid., p. 394.

36 Like Raveaux at Cologne, Zitz had come onto the political stage via carnival presidency, and like him he was an influential member of the left at the *Paulskirche*. Bamberger was a young journalist.

37 Bamberger, *Politische Schriften von 1848 bis 1868.*

38 Sheehan, *German Liberalism in the Nineteenth Century*, pp. 194–195. Bamberger's pamphlet, *Die Sezession*, written in 1880, expressed little faith in the proposed separation of the liberals in protest against their treatment by Bismarck's government, and has been called a "bleak assessment of German liberalism" that "deserves a place as an important milestone in the movment's long downhill journey through the imperial era".

39 Bamberger, p. 85.

40 Valentin, 2:526.

41 Bamberger, p. 158.

Chapter 21

On to Rastatt

Like the final act of a theatrical performance, the 1849 uprising in Baden offered one last look at the heroes and villains, one more round of show-stopping arias and a reprise of familiar choruses before the curtain was rung down. Veterans of the *Hallgartenkreis*, of the *Vorparlament* and the Frankfurt *Parlament*, and of the 1848 risings of the people all took a farewell bow. Engels made a brief appearance. Franz Raveaux was frenetic as a current actor and also as member of the rump parliament at Stuttgart. *Erzherzog* Johann and Friedrich Willhelm IV remained offstage in the wings, pulling strings. The perennial revolutionary Becker arrived from Switzerland. Struve was released from prison, and Fickler was locked up again. The Polish man for all revolutions, Ludwig Mieroslawski, assumed the role of commander-in-chief. Friedrich Hecker returned from America. All alas were destined to swirl away in the dust when *Fürst* Wilhelm of Prussia swooped down onto the scene, for all the world like an antique *deus ex machina*.

The danger signals had indeed been serious enough to rouse the forces of counterrevolution. Baden was a land that had long been regarded as the dangerous hot spot from which the flames of revolution might sweep across all Europe. Only in Baden did the troops mutiny and go over practically *en masse* to insurrection. Frankfurt had upset traditional arrangements with its new provisions governing the armed forces, and had brought in large contingents of Badenese soldiers who in civilian life had been exposed to agitation on the part of the *Volksverein* and who were much more politically aware than the men of Baden's old-fashioned pre-Frankfurt army. In the good old days, about one third of Baden's fourteen-thousand-man standing army had been *Einsteher* (mostly sons of impoverished peasants who were

"stand-ins" for more affluent citizens. These substitutes served as sub-
alterns, fife-and-drum corps members and so on.) According to the
new dispensation as established by law at Frankfurt, two percent of all
eligible males would be expected to perform military duty. Therefore,
replacing the indifferent *Einsteher* there were newcomers, ripe for
insurrection.

After publication of the Frankfurt basic rights, freedom of assembly
had resulted in Baden in a vigorous campaign for the establishment of
a chain of radical *Volksvereine*. These organizations actively engaged
the army men, spreading ideas that were readily accepted by men in
new surroundings, away from home, and discontented with the low
pay. Agitation was especially successful in the vicinity of the great
fortress of Rastatt, where political prisoners were held. Before long,
the soldiers began to ask each other why, if Fickler had been released,
was Struve still behind bars? (He had received a six-year sentence
after the September rising, this "mildness" being largely attributable
to the brilliant defense conducted by the rising political figure, Lorenz
Brentano. In less skilled hands, Struve might have been condemned to
death.) This, after all, was Hecker country. Not too astonishing therefore that the soldiers should clamor for Struve's release.

The citizens of Baden, despite the noisy enthusiasm of the insurrectionists, were far from unanimous. In Rastatt itself there were resentful people who at the most assumed a mask of acquiescence. There
is evidence of this in a memoir written by Albert Förderer, an unpleasantly self-serving individual who described at first hand all the events
of the 1849 disturbance in his home town and at the fortress.[1] A
student and future cleric, he had easy entrée everywhere and cannot
have been alone in his readiness to denounce the revolutionists as
cannibals. He was a law-and-order man, and reported beatings of prisoners by their Prussian captors in a most matter of fact way. He saved
his own skin by changing sides as required by the dangers of the
moment. At the conclusion of his work, Förderer listed those who
were executed by the Prussian military, noting the innocence of a
number of the victims but without so much as a hint that he or his
fellow citizens ought to have engaged in any action of protest.

Announcement that a great people's assembly sponsored by the
Volksverein would take place at nearby Offenburg on 13 May 1849
set the stage for the military rising at Rastatt. Struve's wife was in
town, calling for the release of her husband, and the restless soldiers
wanted to participate in the meeting. Excitement was growing be-

cause nearly forty thousand people were bearing down on Offenburg, representing some four hundred local clubs.

Franz Raveaux, as a *Reichskommissar* appointed by *Erzherzog* Johann and his new minister, Heinrich von Gagern, on his way to Offenburg, where the united *Volksvereine* intended to demand a constituent assembly for Baden, arrived at Mannheim on 13 May. He found the place in turmoil. When he showed his credentials to the station master, asking for a special train to take him to Offenburg, Raveaux was told by an excited official that the Rastatt garrison had mutinied, that the soldiers had massacred all their officers and were drunkenly plundering the town. "If I provide a train for you," he ended, "you must send it back at once because people here in Mannheim will

Figure 23 FRANZ RAVEAUX (1810–1851

be wanting to flee ahead of the soldiers."[2] In truth, there had been a mutiny and the rebels were in control of both fortress and town of Rastatt, but the rest of the man's tale was the product of his over-heated imagination.

Raveaux traveled on a train crammed with eager people heading for the Offenburg meeting. The train itself was festooned with the German tricolor, and at every station there were cheering gymnasts, civil guards and *Volksvereine* in a body, all scrambling to climb aboard.

The victorious garrison men at Rastatt addressed the Badenese minister of defense, General Hoffmann, in resounding tones:

> *Herr General*, we want nothing that is unjust . . . We want only the basic rights and the German constitution. You have promised so much and have kept your word in nothing. We are tired at last of this shameful behavior.[3]

The preliminary meeting of the national committee [*Landes-ausschuss*] of the people's organization was already in progress when Raveaux arrived. These men, operating under pressure and aware of the seething impatient crowd outside their cramped conference room, were having difficulty in keeping their tempers. There were internal stresses that would become increasingly apparent as the weeks wore on because there were two divergent factions within the *Landesausschuss*. These were headed respectively by popular Lorenz Brentano, who wanted to push through reforms without general pandemonium and mayhem, and Armand Goegg, a true-blue socialist whose heart throbbed violently in his desire for the ultimate republican victory of the revolution.

It was indeed a colorful crowd out there—people from the Schwarzwald in their characteristic fur caps and scarlet vests, gymnasts, soldiers, private citizens, women and girls—but, according to Raveaux, who had great familiarity with mass meetings and was an observant person—*vom Proletariat, wie man es in Norden Deutschlands in Volksversammlungen angetreffen pflegt, nirgends ein Spur*[4] [of the proletariat, as you usually find them in people's meetings in northern Germany, not a trace]. There were shouts of Hecker *hoch*! from the youngsters, but this was no call for revolution. "I took away the impression that the Badenese had no faith in their government, and had no inclination to believe the assurances that the ministers were making that they would respect the constitution." On the other hand, wrote Raveaux, it was clear to him that the members of the *Landesausschuss* were decided republicans who were willing to go along with the rest of Germany in establishing the basic rights and the constitution—but only for the time being.

Raveaux, intent on returning quickly to Frankfurt with the report of his mission, was constrained before departure to call on Minister Bekk, in response to an urgent message from him. He found the distraught gentleman at his residence, pale and wan, his head wrapped in a towel. His plea to Raveaux was twofold. First: Return to Rastatt and restore military order and discipline there if you can. Raveaux, quoting his document of commission signed by *Erzherzog* Johann and von Gagern, responded that he would be overstepping his authority if he were to attempt anything of the sort. Then came the second woebegone appeal. "Have you then no *Reichstruppen* that you could put at our immediate disposal?" Raveaux answered that the Frankfurt garrison could not be weakened at that point. The minister then *schien allen Muth verloren zu haben*[5] [seemed to become completely dispirited].

The rebels at Rastatt may not have been as invincible as they appeared to frightened Minister Bekk. When the members of the *Landesausschuss* appeared before the gate of the Rastatt fortress on 14 May, leading a huge crowd of enthusiasts who wanted to burst into the place, they found to their dismay that the gate was barred to them.[6] During the night, the few remaining officers had worked feverishly and had reestablished a measure of authority. They had placed selected reaction-minded soldiers at the gate. The very sight of this guard was enough to intimidate certain members of the *Landesausschuss*, who departed in a hurry for the railway station. Undaunted, Armand Goegg demanded that he and his colleagues be admitted to the fortress for discussion with the commanding officer. After an inconclusive conference, there was a pause, followed by a meeting before the *Rathaus* late in the evening. Here Goegg read to the assembled soldiers the socialistic program adopted at the Offenburg meeting, and addressed them in such stirring words that they agreed to meet again on the following morning.

The first item of the Offenburg agenda was this: The government of Baden must unconditionally recognize the Frankfurt constitution and support "with all its armed might" the execution of it in other German states, first in the Bavarian Palatinate.[7]

The drastic demands of the republican faction had been successfully pushed through in the absence of Lorenz Brentano and his colleagues.

Meanwhile the cavalry had been called out and cannon were put in place, while the infantry advanced from the fortress. It was a night of storm and stress, but the tables were turned when the leader of the artillery—with Goegg's permission—arrested all the reactionary officers and locked them up. The volatile soldiers and the people of Rastatt became revolutionists once again, enormously cheered by unexpected news from Karlsruhe.

The soldiery at Karlsruhe had followed the Rastatt example. Raveaux traveled on to Heidelberg, where he settled in for what he sorely needed—a night of uninterrupted sleep—but within an hour there was alarm among his companions. There was a big crowd outside, muttering, and mentioning Raveaux by name. This ominous crowd turned out to be made up of enthusiastic students who had come to hail Raveaux, cheering him as a hero.

This was only the first of a series of interruptions. First came a comically pompous new *Civilkommissar* appointed by the *Landesausschuss* who wanted to assure the weary Raveaux that he could sleep in peace because he had personally checked the situation at the railway station etc. etc., and there were no Prussians in the vicinity. Next came a city director who wanted to know what he ought to do in the present danger. Go home and go to bed, suggested Raveaux. Then the commandant of the *Bürgerwehr* entered Raveaux's chamber, reporting on his activities. All night long, deputations came and went.[8] The weight of authority was heavy on the shoulders of the anxious revolutionists.

On the morning of 14 May, when the citizens discovered that under cover of night their ruler, *Grossherzog* Leopold had fled to Alsace, there was no hesitation in inviting the people's *Landesausschuss* to assume control of the government. There was an effort on both sides to conduct this power shift in an orderly manner. After the disorders at Karlsruhe ended, the *Bürgerwehr* had placed itself at the disposition of the state and the city council had sent word to the government's ministers that they were not to leave the official residence, and further sent an invitation to the *Landesausschuss* in Rastatt, asking them to come to Karlsruhe in the absence of the *Grossherzog*. Raveaux observed in his account that representatives of the Frankfurt government had found throughout Baden that the city councils were unanimous in expressing appreciation of the action of the *Landesausschuss* in protection of persons and property at that difficult time.[9]

This was a period of anguished hand-wringing for Armand Goegg, the new minister of finance, and his party. They could not unseat the popular Brentano, who was determined to conduct an orderly government. To the extreme disgust of Goegg, Brentano stepped onto a balcony at Karlsruhe and addressed the crowd in "honey-sweet" words. He insisted that his was a strictly provisional government, and expressed regret at the "unnecessary" flight of the *Grossherzog*. The leading theme of his speech was the maintenance of order and the support of the Frankfurt constitution. To Goegg's acute displeasure, even the oath to uphold the constitution was watered down. The old bureaucrats were charmed by Brentano, he said, because they would be required to subscribe to the Frankfurt constitution only to the extent that they would obey the orders of the *Landesausschuss* if those orders were not in conflict with regulations that had prevailed heretofore. Indubitably, even at that early date, this was *der Todesstoss der Revolution*[10] [the death stroke for the revolution]. From that time on, according to Goegg, there were splits and disobedience in the army, in the government, and among the citizens. From that time on there was negotiation but no action.

Disorganization was severe in the important war ministry. If only Fickler and Sigel had been here, lamented Goegg. Fickler had gone to a people's congress at Reutlingen in the mistaken belief that the Württemberg army could be drawn into the insurrection, and had been arrested there. Sigel was recovering from illness in Switzerland. In Goegg's opinion, Sigel would not have hesitated to cross the border into Württemberg with an armed force.[11] In the absence of those two stalwarts, the offensive—such as it was—was in the hands of Gustav Struve, who was a *Niederreisser, kein Aufbauer* [a destructive man, not a builder]. His was an *Oppositionsmanie* [a mania for opposition], and he suffered from an unwholesome need to get himself talked about and always to be first.

Incidentally, most of the people involved in the last throes of revolution in Baden had a poor opinion of each other. Their sole agreement involved Heinrich von Gagern. Raveaux bitterly denounced him as "one of our former friends, bastards between absolutism and freedom who know no god other than their own ego."[12]

The revolutionary force that Struve assembled was a motley disjointed creation. There was a German legion made up of fugitives, a Swiss legion, a German-Polish legion, a German-Hungarian legion under an Italian commander, a free corps from Karlsruhe, a workers' battalion from Mannheim, a band of gymnasts from Hanau, and a Swabian legion.[13] This conglomerate was under the overall command of Johann Becker, the man who had served in the Swiss *Sonder-*

bundskrieg and who ever since had been an incessant, determined organizer of refugees in Switzerland, holding them in presumed combat-readiness for an assault in Germany.

Brentano meanwhile was struggling during the last weeks of May to hold the military in a strictly defensive posture, in his wariness of intervention on the part of troops under the command of *Erzherzog* Johann that inevitably included some Prussians.

The arrest of Fickler and his detention in Württemberg was a serious blow to the radical cause. Raveaux admired him, seeing in him a practical man who was capable of suppressing the immature enthusiasm of the radicals. He felt more than anyone else that a movement that was not based on support of the Frankfurt constitution would be bound to fail. Besides, he was capable of instilling firmness and determination in the sometimes vacillating Brentano, yet keeping the overblown demands of Struve and his party in check. Fickler, in Raveaux's words, had a conception of the rising in Baden that was *ein grossartige, rein deutsche*[14] [magnificent and truly German].

The assembled ministry of Brentano's group, reorganized as a provisional government, issued a prompt protest to Württemberg on Fickler's arrest, declaring war. They were doubly disturbed because a six-thousand-man force was massed on the border under the command of the Württemberg general von Miller, who had been requested by *Erzherzog* Johann to occupy the Rastatt fortress on behalf ot the Frankfurt government.

In the fast-moving kaleidoscope of the Baden insurrection, Franz Sigel had arrived and assumed military command (on 25 May). He wanted to lead a troop of some five thousand across the border into Württemberg, where ranks would be increased, he thought, by sympathizers in the Württemberg army. The *Reichsarmee* [Frankfurt troops] was not yet in a position to interfere, he believed. It was encouraging that a deputation had arrived from Tauberbischofsheim that urged the Baden insurgents to come over. Sigel received a strong order from Brentano to remain in a defensive posture along the Neckar river.

It was at this point, encouraged by the Baden-Palatinate defense pact, that Sigel arranged his feint against the Hessians that was intended if possible to push through Hesse-Darmstadt to Frankfurt, where it would save the *Parlament* from being ejected by Prussian troops. Its actual result was the temporary triumph of the Palatinates under Ludwig Blenker at Worms. Overall, the whole operation was a failure, though. The Hessians drew back for a day or two and then returned, bombarding Worms (29 May). Blenker had to retreat to the Palatinate,and Sigel was removed from his command and appointed to the office of Minister of War instead. It has been suggested that the unsuccessful invasion had demonstrated that there were radical sympathies in Hesse, and that perhaps the insurrectionists might have done better to organize an offensive to the west rather than on the right bank of the Rhine.[15]

Backstage activity during the closing weeks of May and early June had brought many conflicting desires and impulses to the surface. From Frankfurt, for example, the *Erzherzog* had sent a pair of *Parlament* delegates to Baden for the purpose of sounding out public opinion. They had reported (on 30 May and 3 June) that the desire in Baden was for regulation of affairs by the central power, not by Prussian troops. Both the military and the people in general were loyal to the dynasty. Prussian troops were both hated and feared. Troops of the Frankfurt government must come in, bearing white flags, requiring the people of Baden to submit to the central power.[16]

Military operations were soon to begin in earnest because the effort to head off Prussia had failed. This was largely the result of the duplicity of Baden's fugitive ruler, *Grossherzog* Leopold. On 9 June, the *Grossherzog*, through his minister von Dusch, appealed to the ministry of the central power for assistance, but on that very day, he allowed von Dusch to appeal to the Prussian government for military support. The Austrian government at the same time was in agreement with the southern German states and the central power that engagement on the part of Prussia must be prevented at all cost. Baden's *Prinz* Friedrich, who was popular with his people, was given to understand that if he could persuade his father the *Grossherzog* to abdicate, he would find willing support as regent from both the central power and Austria.[17]

In spite of all this, Prussia was ready to march not only against the Palatinate and Baden but against the revolution in general, with the intention of making an example of the insurrectionists. Prussia had the further intention of preventing any victory on the part of the Frankfurt troops under General von Peucker, whose command included Hessians and Prussians, plus troops from Nassau and Frankfurt. Peucker's first indication of Prussian antagonism came from the Hessian *Grossherzog*, who abruptly refused to permit him to march across his territory. The *Herzog* of Nassau swung into line, putting his own troops directly under the command of *Fürst* Wilhelm of Prussia. The enormous force assembled by the Prussians has already been mentioned, with reference to its threat to the Palatinate. It was only on 16 June that the Bavarians officially joined the action, under *Fürst* Theodor von Thurn und Taxis.

The new commandant of the revolutionary army was the uncommonly effective Polish general Ludwig Mieroslawski (1814–1878). His dispatches issued during his ill-fated efforts constitute one of the few documents of the period that suggest that here was a man who knew what he wanted to do.[18] As veteran of many a campaign (he had first fought in Poland as a fifteen-year-old stripling), Mieroslawski was an individual who harbored few illusions. He knew at the start that defeat was practially inevitable.

Mieroslawski cast a cool appraising eye over his new command, of which the left wing was roughly disposed around Weinheim, the center at Heidelberg, and the right in the Baden Odenwald.[19] There were about twenty thousand men all told, but only two thirds could be utilized, and only half would be capable of participating in battle action. He found ten line battalions, twenty-four cannon with gun-carriages, ten squadrons of dragoons of extremely dubious loyalty, and two or three *Volkswehr* units that had been well enough trained and equipped so that they might not present any problems if subjected to enemy fire. The remaining civil guards were full of burning patriotism but could only serve to guard positions already occupied. The line infantry were adequately trained but had no officers, with the effect that they had lost all organizational and tactical capabilities. As they stood, these men were merely random collections of soldiers with no sense of group identity, purpose or discipline. Besides, added Mieroslawski disapprovingly, they had been softened by frequent *Spazierfahrten* [jaunts] on railway trains and by the comforts of cantonment life. They had forgotten how to march or bivouac in the field as a proper army should.

As to the volunteer units, supposedly organized by the revolutionary Palatinate government at Kaiserslautern, in Mieroslawski's judgment this army existed *immer zum grossten Theil auf dem Papier* [it existed largely on paper]. Taken together, there were units commanded by Schimmelpfennig,[20] Blenker, and Willich that totalled about three thousand recruits, plus another twenty-four hundred under Sznaide. Miersoslawski decided that it would be impossible to think of these troops confronting the advancing Prussians and Bavarians who were pouring in simultaneously from the north and west. He therefore ordered Sznaide to put up only so much resistance as would prevent the insurgents from being cut off from each other, or pushed away from

Figure 24 WOMEN OF THE REVOLUTION. Women participated in a variety of ways throughout the German revolution. Some, like Fanny Lewald, were observers and reporters or historians. Others actually went into battle. These included Robert Blum's daughter, who rode carrying a banner that read "Vengeance for Robert Blum", and *Frau* Emma Herwegh, wife of the poet. The present illustration shows the wife of Ludwig Blenker in revolutionary costume.

the Rhine. They would have to be brought over into Baden, using the Knielinger bridge. (It was there that Bamberger crossed. In the light of Mieroslawski's statements, Bamberger's scornful comments may have been unjustified.)

"I have come too late to be able to change this dangerous situation," explained Mieroslawski in his second dispatch, dated 13 June. "We may have to accept decisive battle as early as tomorrow."[21] He had nonetheless effected rapid redeployment so that "we are now able, in half a day, to concentrate ten thousand men and twenty cannon at any point on the Rhine or Neckar without excessive weakening of our defensive position."[22]

In the ensuing month-long chess game, Mieroslawski executed some masterful evasive moves and even felt justified in claiming a victory or two over the Prussians. At the very end, on the glacis at Rastatt, he still had his army, all his artillery, and all his flags intact. Raveaux, who despised him, wrote that Mieroslawski's so-called successful retreat was to be attributed to the clumsiness of the enemy.[23] He also was moved to repeat the rumor that Mieroslawski was not even in Baden, but was writing his glorious dispatches in Switzerland.[24] But the ubiquitous Förderer saw him at Rastatt on 25 June, and heard him mightily shouting French curses at his bewildered men, who did not understand a word that their infuriated general was yelling at them. Hostile assessments are not at all in line with the general appreciation of his performance. "Mieroslawski extricated himself from the noose with wonderful, most excellent skill," wrote a reluctantly admiring Prussian general staff officer, as reported at Karlsruhe on 27 June.[25]

There was plenty of blame for everyone. Mieroslawski himself found it shameful that Baden's provisional government had not had the acumen to rush assistance to the Palatinate at the very beginning. They should never have allowed the fortresses of Germersheim and Landau to fall into enemy hands. Germans never seem to get it into their heads that there has to be unity in revolution![26] He also felt that he had been betrayed by defecting officers and troops, and laid specially harsh blame on the citizens of Mannheim, which he was inclined to see as the seat of a conspiracy against the insurgents. Karlsruhe, he wrote wrathfully, is a city *das nichts von Freiheit wissen will* [that does not want to have anything to do with freedom].[27]

On 26 June, Mieroslawski held a general review, thinking that he would deploy his army along the Murg, but to his disgust he found that a third of his cavalry had gone over to the enemy, a third of the infantry had taken its slinking way home, and so had two-thirds of the *Volkswehr*. There remained about thirteen thousand men.

After a few more days of ineffectual manoeuvering, Mieroslawski realized that he could do no more. On his resignation, it was Franz Sigel's lot to be commander-in-chief for the remaining period during which the insurrectionists' army evaporated. Many crossed over into Switzerland. The poet Gottfried Keller wrote to his mother from Heidelberg:

> If only people will be decent to the Badenese soldiers, because they are great kids and have defended themselves bravely. The Prussians paid dearly for

their victory although theirs was the superior force. Especially the Baden gun-
ners have been heroic. They worked in their shirtsleeves like bakers at their
ovens because it was very hot, yet they were energetic and cheerful by their
cannons. They shot their own wounded dead so that they would not fall into
the hands of the Prussians.[28]

Sigel is generally dismissed coolly by modern historians as an incompetent. His contemporaries had a different opinion. "As long as I
have the cold-blooded young hero Sigel at my side, I can have no
doubts."[29] "There was an intimate friendly relationship between us,
and I must say that of all the military leaders, none made such a pleas-
ant impression on me as Sigel, in his character and behavior."[30] "The
indispensable Sigel."[31]

Nothing remained in early July, other than the force penned up
under siege in the fortress at Rastatt. Not exactly what could be called
a homogeneous assemblage. There were about six thousand there,
including one whole infantry regiment and the standing artillery of the
fortress. Otherwise, there were scraps and patches from the Polish
and Hungarian legions, some people from Freiburg and the Swabians,
as well as the Robert Blum legion. In other words, about two-thirds of
the men under siege were soldiers, the rest volunteers and members
of the *Volkswehr*. The so-called governor was a bombastic useless
individual named Gustav Nikolaus Tiedemann, who had fought in
Greece. The person who won the trust and affection of everyone was
Ernst von Biedenfeld, a retired infantry major from Baden who had
fought against Napoleon and who had no special political feelings.
With the rank of colonel, he kept good discipline among his infantrymen even when, unnerved by the siege, deplorable disorder broke out.
(Förderer witnessed a dreadful manhunt against a supposed spy but
was not noticeably upset by the victim's wretched bloody death.) Along
with the two commanding officers there were people like the adventurer von Corvin, Mniewski, the Polish officer, the leader of the workers' association at Cologne, the writer Ernst Elsenhans, and the brave-
hearted young student Carl Schurz. All must have at least suspected
that their situation was hopeless.

The Prussians were not even bothering themselves to attack ag-
gressively. Why bombard a fortress that, when it was all over, would
have to be expensively repaired by the victors? Meanwhile, the fortress was tightly sealed off by von der Gröben, who on 2 July sent a
demand for capitulation that was promply and emphatically refused.
There were still adequate supplies within the fortress. Mieroslawski
and his army might yet come to the rescue.

Gröben was willing to be patient—even courteous. At Tiedemann's request, he sent a thousand leeches for treatment of the wounded among the insurrectionists.

The men at Rastatt had no information from the outside. They did not know that Mieroslawski's entire army had disintegrated. About two thousand of them had already taken refuge in Switzerland, and the rest were making their way home by devious routes. (Raveaux saw how crowded the trains were, carrying the fugitives away from the scene of their defeat.) As the siege wore on, people in the fortress began to have second thoughts. At last, Otto von Corvin as chief of staff and another officer agreed to go out , escorted by Prussians, to view the situation in Baden. They returned to deliver their report on 21 July. The whole revolutionary army had been destroyed, they said— there was not a trace of it to be seen anywhere. They, alone and surrounded, were the only remnants of the brave enterprise.

On the following day (22 July), governor Tiedemann penned a message to von Gröben:

> The soldiers and members of the *Volkswehr* conformed to the government that existed and was recognized in the country and fought for the constitution, which they had sworn to support while still under the *Grossherzog*, and that had been accepted by most of the German princes. The *Grossherzog* had left the country with his ministers, and thus the soldiers were obliged to obey the government that had replaced him. The proclamations of the *Grossherzog* have been withheld from them and they have even less been aware of the proffer of pardon for all that was to obtain until 5 July, because the fortress has been so closely surrounded since the end of last month that no paper could have come in.[32]

Tiedemann's message concluded with a request for a clear statement on their position. Gröben himself seems to have been inclined toward clemency, but over him was the implacable *Fürst* Wilhelm, who wanted revenge for the Berlin episode of March 1848. Gröben's response was an uneasy one, referring to the fact that Prussia was not fighting for itself but for the unity of Germany, for its true freedom. If the surrender is made to the Prussian troops before Rastatt, it is being made only *auf Gnade und Ungnade* [unconditionally]. The general concluded by saying that he could not discuss special conditions but that he would do what he could so far as the situation permitted. Corwin and von Biedenfeld signed the capitulation on 23 July. They were surrendering unconditionally to the *Grossherzog* of Baden and were putting themselves into the hands of the Prussian troops standing before the fortress.

Five thousand men then marched out to lay down their weapons, and then were hustled back into the casemates of the fortress as prisoners. Altogether, this was an anomalous arrangement. The Prussian commander had been dealing with the commanders in the fortress as though they were officers of a recognized enemy, but now they immediately began to treat the captured force as rebels. The court martial that was established also had an ambiguous character. The court itself, which held its first session on 7 August, was made up entirely of members of the Prussian army, yet it pronounced its decisions in the name of Baden's *Grossherzog*. Furthermore, there was no appeal from the court's decisions.

The writer Ernst Elsenhans was condemned to death and shot. Unassuming old Biedenfeld was condemned and executed. Tiedemann was shot. So was Konrad Heilig, the heroic artilleryman. Simple men in the ranks, like Philipp Zenthöfer, a gunner, and Ludwig Peter Schade of the infantry were arbitarily condemned. Others received sentences of life imprisonment, ten years—whatever these military men with little or no knowledge of the law elected to impose. Otto von Corvin was released. Why?

There were similar hearings at Freiburg and Mannheim. There were fewer death sentences there, but one execution was bitterly lamented throughout Germany—the victim was Wilhelm Adolf von Trützschler, who was shot. He had been civil commissioner in Mannheim and had been highly respected. There are many drawings from popular publications and broadsides that show Trützschler quietly kneeling before the firing squad.

Warning! Johann Ludwig Maximilian Dortu of Potsdam, former royal Prussian junior barrister and subaltern in the 24th *Landwehr* regiment, on the occasion of the uprising that occurred in May of the present year in this country went over, upon the entrance of the royal Prussian army against the troops of his own lawful sovereign, taking weapons in his hand against his own brother soldiers and fellow countrymen. On 11 July the said Dortu was placed before a court martial on the grounds of treason. The finding of the court released yesterday is confirmed by me, that the accused is to be degraded to the rank of common soldier, placed in the second class of the soldiery and deprived of the national cocard, and to be punished for treachery by death by shooting. This legal judgment was carried out this morning at 4 o'clock in the vicinity of the Wiehre cemetery, and is herewith brought to public knowledge. The commanding general of the first army corps of the royal Prussian Army of operation on the Rhine, von Hirschfeldt. Headquarters, Freiburg, 31 July 1849.[33]

This is a sample of the announcements that issued from the courts martial. Dortu's body was at least buried in a cemetery, in a marked grave that was visited by loyal mourners. Those executed at Rastatt were flung into a pit that served as their common grave.

One death sentence that was much resented was that of Gottfried Kinkel, the Bonn professor who had been a determined revolutionist. The sentence was commuted to life imprisonment, again to great popular disgust that he should be treated so cruelly. It was to be Kinkel's good fortune that his young student Carl Schurz would come to his rescue in a daring foray at Prussia's prison at Spandau, at the risk of his own life.

Carl Schurz was a darling. There is no other way to describe that open-hearted nineteen-year-old. For genuine reading pleasure, his reminiscences are in a class by themselves. As Valentin says, Schurz was not typical of his times, but rather a lucky exception—this wholesome youngster knew nothing of poses, of self-importance, of sentimental twaddle.[34] At the time of the Rastatt surrender, young Carl wrote a farewell letter to his parents, saying that he was sorry to have caused them so much grief and anxiety but that he had done what he had to do for the fatherland, and that he knew that, as a Prussian subject, he would probably face a firing squad.

But then he noticed an opening into a storm sewer. With two hardy companions, he dropped out of sight as the surrender was taking place. Then follows a splendidly unheroic yet gripping escape story.[35] Bent over uncomfortably in the four-foot-high sewer, sloshing along in ankle-deep water, pausing gratefully to straighten up whenever they reached an overhead grating in the Rastatt streets, where they breathed a little cleaner air and listened to the Prussians, dodging into the water to pass below bars, escaping for four tense days into a loft above a stable that housed boistrous *Ulans* and their horses, subsisting on a little bottle of brandy, palmsful of rainwater coming through the overhead gratings, a little green apple and some bits of bread, they emerged at last into a field, made a run to the river bank and were ferried to an uninhabited island in midstream from which they were able to call for the help of some Alsatians on the farther shore of the Rhine. Filthy dirty, wet and cold, hungry as a bear, but still in lively good spirits, young Carl was free, and he would go to America. Carl Schurz *hoch*!

Notes

1 Albert Förderer, *Erinnerungen aus Rastatt 1849,* passim.

2 Franz Raveaux, *Mittheilungen über die badische Revolution,* pp. 4–5.

3 Ibid., p. 6.

4 Ibid., pp. 10–11.

5 Ibid., p. 14.

6 [Armand Goegg] *Nachträgliche authentische Aufschlüsse über die badische Revolution von 1849,* pp. 107–109.

7 Ibid., p. 100.

8 Raveaux, pp. 17–18.

9 Ibid., p. 20.

10 Goegg, pp. 110–111.

11 Ibid., p. 112, footnote.

12 Raveaux, p. 129.

13 Goegg, pp. 114–115.

14 Raveaux, p. 67.

15 Sperber, *Rhineland Radicals,* pp. 408–409.

16 Valentin, *Geschichte der deutschen Revolution,* 2:522–523.

17 Ibid., 2:523.

18 Ludwig Mieroslawski, *Berichte des Generals Mieroslaski über den Feldzug in Baden,* passim.

19 Ibid., pp. 2–4.

20 Schimmelpfennig appears to have simplified the spelling of his name after he fled to the United States. Mark Mayo Boatner, *The Civil War Dictionary,* p. 725: Schimmelfennig.

21 Mieroslawski, p. 5.

22 Ibid., p. 6.

23 Raveaux, p. 104.

24 Ibid., pp. 93–94.

25 Valentin, 2:528 and 2:679, note 168.

26 Mieroslawski, pp. 44–45.

27 *Ibid.*, p. 24.

28 Karl Obermann, *Einheit und Freiheit,* p. 859.

29 Mieroslawski, p. 19.

30 Raveaux, p. 38.

31 Goegg, pp. 143.—Even in the Union Army, where he was regarded as anything but brilliant, German soldiers proudly announced that "I fights mit Sigel".

32 Valentin, 2:532.

33 Obermann, p. 861.

34 Valentin, 2:531.

35 Schurz, *Sturmjahre*, pp. 194–254.

Chapter 22

A Climate of Vindictiveness and Distrust

"A living man craves for air that has not yet been breathed a thousand times over, which does not smell of the picked bones of life," wrote Aleksandr Herzen in deep weariness.[1] Among the refugees in Switzerland, he was profoundly depressed by the tendency of his companions to wallow in their memories and to persist in contemplation of their disillusionment.

Any assessment of the overall damage among the Europeans as the reaction set in victoriously is far beyond the scope of this book. There are whole libraries devoted to this disturbing subject. However, within limits, the question remains. Why did so many people feel that they could no longer live in Germany? Some fled with a price on their heads, and others were forced into exile, but this was not universally the case. There was economic pressure, of course, but again this was not universal. Why did so many Germans feel suffocated and in desperate need of the fresher air of an untried country overseas? Some who had been active revolutionists managed to stay on, pursuing successful careers. Johann Jacoby, for example.—Secure in the esteem of his fellow citizens at Königsberg, he was able to resume his medical practice there, although he did undergo the annoyance of a police search of his home.[2] Men like Friedrich Daniel Bassermann and Karl Mathy distinguished themselves, but these were people who had already made a mark in the world prior to the revolution and enjoyed a degree of financial independence as well. There were unnumbered individuals who returned to their quiet private lives, sometimes even with a little sigh of relief. But still, what pushed those thousands overseas?

Baden as a whole suffered most from the consequences of the revolution. The people were under the heel of the Prussians, whose military occupation continued relentlessly. The public mood was expressed by the well known cradle song.

> *Schlaf, mein Kind, schlaf leis! Dort draussen geht der Preuss. Deinen Vater hat er umgebracht, Deine Mutter hat er armgemacht, Und wer nicht schläft in stiller Ruh, Dem drückt der Preuss die Augen zu. Wir alle müssen stille sein Als wie dein Vater unterem Stein . . . Gott aber weiss wie lang es geht Bis dass die Freiheit aufersteht. Und wo dein Vater liegt, mein Schatz, Da hat noch mancher Preusse Platz.*[3] [Sleep softly, my child. Out there goes the Prussian. He destroyed your father and made your mother poor, and he presses closed the eyes of anyone who doesn't sleep quietly. We must all be quiet like your father under his gravestone. God knows how long this will go on until Freedom rises. And where your father lies, my treasure, there is room for many a Prussian.]

Grossherzog Leopold had returned, it is true, but he had been forced to disband his entire army, and he was totally controlled by the ministers of Friedrich Wilhelm. His government, even in late 1851, was still struggling with the unwieldy problem of political prisoners, who had become a heavy financial burden on the state. There had been tentative efforts to find a place for these expensive unfortunates, basing the plan on an edict of 1803 that called for transfer of convicts against their will to remote foreign service—but the Netherlands Indies had refused to take them, and so had France when it was suggested that they might be accepted as a foreign legion in North Africa.[4]

There were a few experiments with deportation, but it was cumbersome and costly and could not by any means be adopted as a general solution. A classic example was the complicated departure of Gottlieb Rau, a glass manufacturer of Garlsdorf in Württtemberg.[5] This prisoner, who was to travel with his wife and daughter to New York via Le Havre, had to be accompanied to the port by a guard, and there had to be special security arrangements with police authorities along the route (at Heidelberg and Mannheim, for example). Since there would have to be extraordinary precautions against demonstrations in favor of the popular Rau at Heilbronn, a circuitous route had to be devised in order to bypass the town. Finally, the Württemberg consul at Le Havre had to certify arrival there, and embarcation at last on the transoceanic vessel *Advance*.

Reluctance was strong among officials to discharge insurrectionists after a brief term in prison. A minister in Baden expressed his alarm, fearing that those who were freed would spread out all over the country and *vergiften fortwährend die besseren Säfte des Staats-organismus*[6] [continuously poison the better juices of the state organism]. In this dread situation, it would be preferable to encourage large-scale emigration to the United States.

In general, few obstacles were deliberately placed in the way of anyone who was willing to leave Europe for good. At one stage, selected prisoners were even approached with queries as to their feelings about permanent exile. Results from the questionnaire (this was in Baden toward the end of 1849) were not encouraging. About two hundred prisoners indicated that they would accept transfer to the United States, but they were bold enough to set numerous conditions— the state or the home community would have to pay travel expenses for them and their families, and some also demanded financial support to establish them overseas.[7]

Especially in southern Germany, officials were desperate as they wrestled with the overwhelming task of investigating and sorting out prisoners and suspects. In Baden alone, there were an estimated twenty thousand persons involved (six thousand imprisoned insurgents and some nine thousand fugitives in Switzerland, to say nothing of a large number of people held for investigation in scattered local prisons). Von Corwin is said to have remarked cynically that you couldn't very well shoot two-fifths of the population and lock up another two-fifths.

The reaction handled its problem of former insurrectionists who were not in prison in the most clumsy manner imaginable. "Densely stupid, cowardly, in its dotage," growled Herzen.[8] An appalling survey of the fate of German parliamentarians (at Frankfurt, Berlin, or at the rump parliament at Stuttgart) first published in 1857, shows this all too painfully.[9] Death sentences and lengthy imprisonment were no doubt to be expected for people like Ludwig Bamberger and Franz Zitz. After all, Friedrich Wilhelm had written that "in my opinion, what is . . . necessary is a comprehensive, serious and rapid action against all those Prussian subjects who involved themselves in the revolutionary movements of the Palatinate and Baden and who in part took up weapons against my army."[10] What is distressing in this list is the evidence of the inordinate number of broken careers. Here are a few examples, taken at random.

> *Pastor* Baltzer of Nordhausen. After various monetary punishments, forbidden in January 1852 to engage in private teaching, or even to instruct his own children in religion.

Fehrenback, attorney at Säckingen. Arrested in January 1852 for activities as president of the Freiburg reading club.

Hoffbauer, physician at Nordhausen. November 1851 condemned by the court at Heiligenstadt for attempted treason (i.e., participation in the Stuttgart parliament) to five years imprisonment, five years of police surveillance. Prohibited from engaging in medical practice.

Graf Reichenbach, Silesian landowner. His case tried seven times by various courts for participation in the Stuttgart parliament. September 1851, sentenced to ten years in prison and ten years under surveillance. When he fled to Belgium, the Prussian government demanded that he be expelled.

Schoder, government council at Stuttgart, died 12 November 1852. The military was forbidden to take part in his funeral. Members of the Tübingen *Burschenschaft* were arrested and investigated because of their participation.

Pastor Töbe of Namslau was freed after lengthy imprisonment but was removed from his office. When he started a private school it was closed by the police (September 1851), and parents of the pupils were threatened.

Members of the Stuttgart rump parliament, journalists and clergymen seem to have been more harshly treated and persistently harassed than others, but on the whole, the picture is one of unpredictable, petty vindictiveness. Those included in this list had at least been openly active during the revolution. Would it have been possible for an insignificant relatively inconspicuous person to live undisturbed during the period of reaction? Maybe not, in the prevalent climate of mean-spirited retaliation and suspicion.

There is another list, even more troubling than the first. This comes from the secret archives of the ministry of external and domestic affairs at Munich. It was submitted to the ministry of Swabia on 10 September 1852.[11] Beside each name there are entered remarks that are designed to explain why the individual in question is suspect and not to be trusted.

Dr. Johann Emanuel Nusser, physician was "an enthusiastic member of the *Märzverein* at Augsburg", and was "in a confidential relationship with Dr. Kronacher of Bamberg, who has been deported".

Kaufmann, typesetter, "agitated for the introduction of the German basic rights".

Neuss, engraver "produced forbidden commemorative medals for Blum and Hecker"

Schwarz, Aloys, teacher "joined democratically-minded people, and for this reason is not politically reliable".

Fichel, Franz "expressed himself against the government in a suspicious way".

Wacker, district forester at Fischen "in uniform, took up a collection for Blum's widow".

Butcher, Franz, hat maker's apprentice "carried a sign in a demonstration for the republic".

[9 individuals] "took part in a raft trip to Ulm, had decorated the raft with the German colors and picture of Hecker".

And so on. All obviously dangerous to society, but society seems to have been dangerous to them. The people who took part in that jolly raft trip may have paid dearly for their imprudence. Transpose such notations to modern times. What innocuous member of our society has not at one time or another slapped a newspaper angrily, expressing disapproval "in a suspicious way"? Who has not worn a campaign button on his jacket, or placed a bumper sticker on his car, or called in to a talk show? Who has not "carried a sign in a demonstration"? Or collected money for some unfortunate victim of a perceived miscarriage of justice? In a climate of suspicion, the interpretation of trivial, unverified information can be dark indeed.

As one final piece of evidence of the kind of damage that was done by the arbitrary actions of vindictive officials in the wake of the revolution, there is the case of Friedrich Fröbel, the educator who is recognized today as the man who first developed the concept of the kindergarten. In his long life he had been a loyal citizen who, it is true, had been viewed with a certain amount of suspicion because of his original methods. A student of Fichte's, Fröbel fought in the war of liberation as a member of *Turnvater* Jahn's legendary volunteer corps, where he found friends who were to be his loyal colleagues for decades. In a followup of the Carlsbad decrees, his infant establishment had been subjected to official investigation, supposedly because of the presence of former *Burschenschaft* members on his teaching staff. Although the school had been declared to be free of objectionable taint, the local Thuringian newspapers published a statement to the effect that no pupil coming from the Fröbel school could ever expect to be admitted to a reputable German university. As a result of this, the more affluent parents promptly withdrew their children, and the student body was reduced to a mere handful.

In spite of various setbacks, by the 1840's Fröbel was receiving recognition, and even during the disturbances of the revolutionary period he managed not only to maintain his school but also to establish a kind of normal school for training young women as kindergarten teachers—a new career opening that was appreciated by feminists. Fröbel was also receiving public attention as the uncle of radical Julius Fröbel, who had been one of his very first pupils.

In August 1851, the blow suddenly fell. By decree of Friedrich Wilhelm's Prussian government, all Fröbel's kindergartens and training centers for teachers were closed. This move can only have been based on the stupid notion that if the institution could produce a subversive person like Julius Fröbel, it must indeed be a dangerous hotbed of sedition and labor unrest and atheism and revolution.

Though the blow was too much for Friedrich Fröbel, who died a few months after the closing of his schools, the idea of the kindergarten was spread around the world by his followers, many of whom as revolutionists had fled for their very lives. Two of Fröbel's young trainees—the Meyer sisters—married such fugitives (Johannes Ronge, the leader of the religious protest movement, and Carl Schurz, the future US senator and Secretary of the Interior). These two women, with the full support of their husbands, promptly established kindergartens—Bertha Ronge's in Britain, and Margarethe Schurz's at Watertown, Wisconsin. (This was the first kindergarten in the United States.) The idea was taken up enthusiastically by Elizabeth Palmer Peabody after her meeting with Margarethe Schurz. In this way, official Prussian vindictiveness became instrumental in the spread of the Fröbel initiative far beyond the borders of Germany.

In spite of the overloaded condition of the prisons and the impossible backlog of cases before the courts, there continued to be a determined roundup of suspected individuals. Once more there was heavy censorship of the press, and prohibition of assembly. In Valentin's opinion, the revolution and its aftermath did not appreciably increase the number of emigrants from Germany, although he does mention the fact that there were about ten thousand fugitives in Switzerland alone.[12] More than one million left Germany in the period 1849-1854. How many of these left for political reasons cannot be determined, but it is certainly a fact that Forty-Eighters flocked to the United States in those years.[13] They made their contribution there, especially in the Middle West, and most particularly during the Civil War. They are still remembered with pride and affection.

Notes

1   Herzen, *My Past and Thoughts*, p. 383.

2   Jessen, *Die deutsche Revolution 1848/49 in Augenzeugenberichten*, p. 377: The Königsberg *Arbeiterverein* was dissolved on 15 April 1850. In the early morning of 6 June, a dozen police house searches were conducted in the homes of known democrats, including Jacoby's. Reported in *Die Verbrüderung*, 22 June 1850.

3   Valentin, *Geschichte der deutschen Revolution*, 2:541–542.

4   Ulrich Klemke, *"Eine Anzahl überflüssiger Menschen,"* pp. 114–118.

5   Ibid., pp. 77–86.

6   Ibid., p. 119.

7   Ibid., p. 124.

8   Herzen, p. 384.

9   Jessen, pp. 369–396.

10   Obermann, "Karl d'Ester, Arzt und Revolutionär," in *Aus der Frühgeschichte der deutschen Arbeiterbewegung*, 2:199.

11   Dietmar Nickel, *Die Revolution 1848/49 in Augsburg und Bayerisch-Schwaben*, pp. 230–254.

12   Valentin, 2:552.

13   Readers will find valuable material in a work published in recognition of the 150th anniversary of the revolution—Don Heinrich Tolzmann, editor, *The German-American Forty-Eighters, 1848–1998*.

Chapter 23

A Few Words on
Emigration to the U.S.

Though investigations relating to the personal history of my ancestor, Captain Anton Joseph Kilp, were not crowned with spectacular success, a few questions that occurred to me during my search were answered in a way that ought to be of interest to any descendant of a Forty-Eighter who came to the United States. Specifically, I wondered just how such a journey was accomplished.

The outward-bound traffic from Germany was of such proportions that catering to the needs of emigrants developed into a flourishing business along the North Sea. The city of Bremen was a major point of departure, and so were ports in England, but the preferred one was Le Havre. Developing steamship lines along the Rhine and railroads in Belgium and France made this route attractive, with the result that enterprising agencies sprang up, ready and willing to help uneasy, hurried travelers.

A popular guidebook, written by one Traugott Bromme (his *Hand- und Reisebuch für Auswanderer nach den Vereinigten Staaten von Nord-Amerika*) was issued in an up-to-date fifth edition in 1848, published by Büchner at Bayreuth. This comprehensive guide listed the names of the agents in various German cities—Louis Marckle at Speyer, for example, who would undertake arrangements by Rhine steamer to Lille, and by rail from there to Paris, and then on to Le Havre.

According to Bromme's authoritative little book, which must have been in the hands of many Germans who were already feeling the threat of anticipated post-revolutionary conditions, there were regular sailings four times a month all year around from Le Havre. These were the Finlay company's postal vessels, the *Burgundy, Admiral, Baltimore, Argo, Zurich, New York, Utica, Splendid, Silvia de*

Grasse, Louis-Philippe, Saint Nicolas, Duchesse d'Orléans, Iowa, Havre, Oneida, and *Bavaria*, a fleet that comprised a few steam-powered craft as well as more conventional three-masted sailing ships.

Transatlantic crossings under these auspices cost one hundred and twelve florins, this price including free conveyance of two hundred pounds of goods and payment of the landing fee in New York.

Unfortunately the two hundred pounds of goods had to include the voyager's food for the three-week transit. The shipowners furnished wood for cookstoves on board, as well as potable water. Recommended supplies such as potatoes, vinegar, smoked ham and zwieback could be purchased (at a price) at Le Havre, right on the dock.

There are drawings that show those crowded docks, where many a departing family appeared to be camping out in a small tent, in the very shadow of the ship's hull. There may not have been much more comfort on board the ship during the twenty-two day crossing. Each passenger was furnished with a clean straw-filled mattress. A small area was assigned to him for his exclusive use, and he was responsible for its cleanliness. He stowed personal gear and food supplies in the hold, and did his own cooking. There was access to the upper deck in fair weather, and the passengers sometimes danced.

Many warnings were issued about the danger of unscrupulous sharpers in New York. It was to be hoped that the wary immigrant would go to the headquarters of the travelers' aid society that had been established especially for Germans. New York offered a variety of accommodations—the famous Shakespeare Hotel among them—or inns and boarding houses.

Bromme's handbook offered a wealth of information about the new country. Here is a sample:

> The state of Illinois is a huge plain, cut through by two chains of hills, one near the eastern bank of the Mississippi, the other along the western bank of the Illinois. The land itself is very rich, and yields incredible crops, and the trees that cover the part that has not been built up are of colossal size. The agriculture of Illinois is a veritable gold mine. Few states have such rich prof-itable soil as this one. Indian corn is currently the staple article, the yield on the average being 50 to 80 bushels to the acre—if well tended, even 100 to 120 bushels. Cattle raising is just in its infancy but is well supported by the extensive natural pastures. Of wild life, foxes, bears, wolves, panthers and wildcats are plentiful. In the woods there are cottonwood trees, sycamores, elms, oak. Wild vines with sweet grapes grow in quantity along the banks of the Mississippi and Illinois. Thus far Illinois has no large factories, yet even now half of all requirements are met locally. Household industry provides

coarse cloth and calico. Tanneries, breweries, mills, works for production of acorn sugar and potash already yield enough for export, and what the state otherwise produces in grain, tobacco, cattle, horses, skins, furs and salt more than covers domestic needs. There are at present 716,284 inhabitants, including 3,598 free colored. Originally there were French Canadians, but the main stock now is made up of Anglo-Americans, Scots, Irish, English, and about one-tenth are German, most of whom arrived after 1824. The Indians include Chippewas, Delawares, Pottawattamies, and Kickapoos. There are about fifteen thousand of them. Schooling is well supported. 1,241 elementary schools, 300 Sunday schools, 42 academies and five institutes of higher learning as well as a seminary.

The state has undertaken extensive works of internal improvement. The Illinois and Michigan canal extends 106 miles below Chicago to Peru, connecting with shipping on the Illinois. The canal was begun in 1836 but has not yet been completed.

Admittedly, this is pure conjecture, but as a descendant of a Forty-Eighter, in my mind's eye, I see my great grandfather closing Bromme's little book with an air of quiet decision. Peru Illinois sounded to him like a place for new beginnings, far far from Bamberg's archepiscopal palace and clustered steeples.

If the newcomer decided to seek his fortune in the Middle West, Bromme's guide gave the necessary details about northbound shipping on the Hudson, transportation along the Great Lakes, railway lines, canals etc.

Certain it is that whatever his background, and whatever his destination, with the Rhine journey and the confused hurly-burly of Le Havre behind him, the departing Forty-Eighter stood on the deck of the sailing ship as moorings were slipped off, waving a brave farewell to Europe. He was a German, and where there are Germans there is always song. Across the years, we hear his voice, raised in the full-throated chant of the well known emigrants' chorus—*Wir reisen nach Amerika.*

Bibliography

Abel, Wilhelm. *Massenarmut und Hungerkrisen im vorindustriellen Deutschland.* Göttingen: Vanderhoeck & Ruprecht, 1972.

1848: Augenzeugen der Revolution. Briefe, Tagebücher, Reden, Berichte. Berlin: Rütten & Loening, 1973.

Adam, Reinhard. "Johann Jacobys politischer Werdegang, 1805–1840." *Historische Zeitschrift* 143 (1930): 48–76.

Adler, Georg. *Die Geschichte der ersten sozialpolitischen Arbeiterbewegung in Deutschland, mit besonderer Rücksicht auf die einwirkenden Theorieen.* [1885] Frankfurt am Main: Verlag Sauer & Auvermann, 1966.

———. *Ueber die Epochen der deutschen Handwerker-politik.* Jena: Gustav Fischer, 1903.

Agethen, Manfred. *Geheimbund und Utopie; Illuminatien, Freimaurer und deutsche Späterklärung.* Ancien regime, Aufklärung und Revolution, 11. Munich: Oldenbourg, 1984.

Agoult, Marie de Flavigny, *comtesse* d' see Daniel Stern.

Albart, Rudolf. *Rundwanderungen Steigerwald.* Stuttgart: Fink, 1973.

Alton-Shée, Edmond d'. *Mes Mémoires (1826–1848).* 2 vols. Paris: Librairie internationale, 1869.

Arndt, Ernst Moritz. *Erinnerungen aus dem äusseren Leben.* Breslau: Korn Verlag, 1944.

———. Meine Wanderungen und Wandelungen mit . . . vom Stein. Breslau: Hirt, 1941.

————. Versuch einer Geschichte der Leibeigenschaft in Pommern und *Rügen*. Berlin: Verlag der Realschulbuchhandlung, 1803.

Artz, Frederick B. *Reaction and Revolution, 1814–1832*. The Rise of Modern Europe. New York: Harper & Row, 1963.

Auerbach, Berthold. *Schwarzwälder Dorfgeschichte*. Mannheim, 1843.

B., Victorine. *Souvenirs d'une morte vivante;* préface de Lucien Descaves. Paris: François Maspero, 1976.

Bachmann, Siegfried. *Die Landstände des Hochstifts Bamberg*. Sonder-Ausg. aus dem 98. Bericht des Historischen Vereins Bamberg. Bamberg, 1962.

Bacot, Jean-Pierre. *Les filles du pasteur Anderson; deux siècles de franc-maçonnerie mixte et féminine en France*. Paris: E.D.I.M.A.F., 1988.

Bakunin, Michael. *Sozialpolitischer Briefwechsel mit Alexander Iw. Herzen und Ogarjow*. Berlin: Kramer Verlag, 1977.

Balzac, Honoré de. *La cousine Bette*. Collection folio. [n.p.] Gallimard, 1972.

————. *La duchesse de Langeais; La fille aux yeux d'or*. Saint-Amand: Gallimard, 1976.

Bamberger, Ludwig. *Erinnerungen*. Berlin: Georg Reimer, 1899.

————. *Politische Schriften von 1848 bis 1868*. Gesammelte Schriften, 3. Berlin, Rosenbaum & Hart, 1895.

Banfield, C.H. *Industry of the Rhine*. London: Cox, 1846–48.

Barclay, David E. "The Court Camarilla and the Politics of Monarchical Restoration in Prussia, 1848–58." In *Between Reform, Reaction, and Resistance. Studies in the History of German Conservatism from 1789 to 1945*, pp. 123–156. Providence: Berg, 1993.

Bauer, Bruno. *Der Untergang des frankfurter Parlaments. Geschichte der deutschen constituierenden Nationalversammlung*. [Berlin 1849] Aalen: Scientia Verlag, 1970.

Baughman, John J. "The French Banquet Campaign of 1847–1848." *Journal of Modern History* 31 (March 1959):1–15.

Bekk, Johann Baptist. *Die Bewegung in Baden von Ende des Februar 1848 bis zur Mitte des Mai 1849.* Mannheim: Bassermann, 1850.

Berdahl, Robert M. *The Politics of the Prussian Nobility. The Development of a Conservative Ideology, 1770–1848.* Princeton: Princeton University Press, 1988.

Bergsträsser, Ludwig, "Die parteipolitische Lage beim Zusammentritt des Vorparlaments." *Zeitschrift für Politik* 6 (1913): 594–620.

Berkeley, G. F.-H. *Italy in the Making, 1815 to 1846.* Cambridge: Cambridge University Press, 1932.

Berlin, Isaiah. *Against the Current; Essays in the History of Ideas.* New York: Viking Press, 1980.

Berlioz, Hector. *Memoirs of Hector Berlioz from 1803 to 1865.* New York: Dover Publ. 1960.

Berlitz Travellers' Guide to Germany. 4th ed. New York, 1991.

Bernhardt, August. *Geschichte des Waldeigenthums, der Waldwirtschaft und Forstwissenschaft in Deutschland.* 3 vols. [1872–75] Berlin: Springer, 1966.

Bernstein, Samuel. *Auguste Blanqui and the Art of Insurrection.* London, 1971.

Beseler, Georg. *Erlebtes und Erstrebtes 1809–1859.* Berlin: Wilhelm Hertz, 1884.

Bezzel. Oskar. *Geschichte des Kgl. bayerischen Heeres von 1825 mit 1866.* Geschichte des Kgl. bayerischen Heeres, 7. Munich: Verlag Max Schick, 1931.

Bieberstein, Johannes Rogalla von. "Geheime Gesellschaften als Vorläufer politischer Parteien," in *Geheime Gesellschaften,* 5/1, pp. 429–449.

Biedermann, Karl. *Deutsche Bildungszustände in der zweiten Hälfte des achtzehnten Jahrhunderts.* New York: Holt, 1905.

Blättner, Fritz. *Das Gymnasium, Aufgabe der höheren Schule in Geschichte und Gegenwart.* Heidelberg: Quelle & Meyer, 1960.

Blackbourn, David and Eley, Geoff. *The Peculiarities of German History; Bourgeois Society and Politics in Nineteenth-Century Germany.* Oxford: Oxford University Press, 1984.

Blanc, Louis. *Histoire de dix ans, 1830–1840.* 6th ed.. Paris: Pagnerre, 1846.

Blanqui, Louis-Auguste. *Oeuvres complètes.* Paris: Galilée, 1977.

Bleich, Eduard. *Der erste Vereinigte Landtag in Berlin 1847.* [Reprint.] Vaduz: Topos Verlag, 1977.

Blum, Hans. *Die deutsche Revolution 1848–49.* Florence: Eugen Diederich, 1897.

Blum, Jerome. *The End of the Old Order in Rural Europe.* Princeton, 1978.

———. *Noble Landowners and Agriculture in Austria, 1815–1848. A Study in the Origins of the Peasant Emancipation of 1848.* Johns Hopkins University Studies in Historical and Political Science, series 65, no. 2. Baltimore: Johns Hopkins Press, 1948.

Blum, Robert. *Briefe und Dokumente.* Leipzig: Verlag Philipp Reclam jun., 1981.

Boatner, Mark Mayo. *The Civil War Dictionary.* New York: David McKay, 1959.

Börne, Ludwig. *Sämtliche Schriften,* 1. Dreieich: Melzer Verlag, 1977.

Boldt, Werner. *Die Anfänge des deutschen Parteiwesens; Fraktionen, politische Vereine und Parteien in der Revolution 1848. Darstellung und Dokumentation.* Sammlung Schöningh zur Geschichte und Gegenwart. Paderborn: Ferdinand Schöningh, 1971.

Born, Stephan. *Erinnerungen eines Achtundvierzigers.* 3d ed. Leipzig: Georg Heinrich Meyer, 1898.

Bosl, Karl. *Bayerische Geschichte.* Munich: List, 1971.

———. *Handbuch der historischen Stätten Deutschlands,* 7. *Bayern.* Reihe Kröner 277. Stuttgart 1961.

Botzenhart, M. *Deutscher Parlamentarismus in der Revolutionszeit 1846–1850*. Handbuch der Geschichte des deutschen Parlamentarismus. Düsseldorf: Droste Verlag, 1977.

Braun, Harald. *Das politische und turnerische Wirken von Friedrich Ludwig Weidig. Ein Beitrag zur Geschichte der revolutionären Bestrebungen im deutschen Vormärz*. Schriften der Deutschen Sporthochschule Köln, 11. 2d ed. Sankt Augustin: Verlag Hans Richarz, 1983.

Brauns, C. *Kurhessische Gewerbepolitik im 17. und 18. Jahrhundert*. Staats- und sozialwissenschaftliche Forschungen 156. Leipzig: Duncker & Humblot, 1911.

Brederlow, Jörn. *"Lichtfreunde" und "Freie Gemeinden". Religiöser Protest und Freiheitsbewegung im Vormärz und in der Revolution von 1848/49*. Studien zur modernen Geschichte 20. Munich: R. Oldenbourg Verlag, 1976.

Brinton, Crane. *The Anatomy of Revolution*. Rev. ed. New York: Vintage Books,1965.

Bromme, Traugott. *Hand- und Reisebuch für Auswanderer nach dem Vereinigten Statten von Nord-Amerika*. 5th ed. Bayreuth: Büchner, 1848.

Brunner, Otto. s.v. "Hausväterliteratur" in *Handwörterbuch der Sozialwissenschaften*. Stuttgart: Fischer, 1956.

———. *Neue Wege der Verfassungs- und Sozialgeschichte*. 2d ed. Göttingen: Vandenhoeck & Ruprecht, 1968.

Bucher, Erwin. *Die Geschichte des Sonderbundskrieges*. Zurich: Verlag Berichtshaus, 1966.

Büttner, Wolfgang. *Georg Herwegh—ein Sänger des Proletariats. Der Weg eines bürgerlich-demokratischen Poeten zum Streit für die Arbeiterbewegung*. Berlin: Akademie-Verlag, 1970.

Burke, Edmund. *Reflections on the Revolution in France and on the Proceedings in Certain Societies in London Relative to that Event*. Harmondsworth: Penguin Books, 1969.

Calman, Alvin R. *Ledru-Rollin and the Second French Republic*. Columbia University Studies in History, Economics, and Public Law, 234. [Reprint] New York: Octagon Books, 1980.

540 Bibliography

Cantor, Norman F. and Samuel Berner, eds. *The Modern Era 1815 to the Present*, Problems in European History, 3. New York: Thomas Y. Crowell Co., 1971.

Carr, Edward Hallet. *Michael Bakunin* [1937] New York: Octagon Books, 1975.

Caussidière, Marc. *Mémoires de Caussidière, ex-préfet de police et représentant du peuple*. Paris: Michel Lévy, 1849.

Chevalier, Louis. *Le choléra; la première épidémie du XIXe siècle*. Bibliothèque de la révolution de 1848, 20. La Roche-sur-Yon: Imprimerie centrale de l'Ouest, 1958.

———. *Classes laborieuses et dangereuses à Paris pendant la première moitié du XIXe siècle*. Civilisations d'hier et d'aujourd'hui. Paris: Plon, 1958.

Chopin, Frédéric. *Chopin's Letters, collected by Henryk Opienski*. New York: Dover Publ., 1988.

Circourt, Adolphe de. *Souvenirs d'une mission à Berlin en 1848*. vol.l. Paris: Picard & fils, 1908.

Clapp, Edwin J. *The Navigable Rhine; the Development of its Shipping, the Basis of the Prosperity of its Commerce and its Traffic in 1907*. Hart, Schaffner & Marx Prize Essays, 9. Boston: Houghton Mifflin, 1911.

Clark, Kenneth. *Civilisation*. New York: Harper & Row, 1969.

Conze, Werner. *Gesellschaft—Staat—Nation*. Industrielle Welt 52. Stuttgart: Klein-Cotta, 1992.

Corvin, Otto von. *Pfaffenspiegel* [4th ed. of a work originally published as *Historische Denkmale des christlichen Fanatismus*, 1844] Schwerte: Verlag Hubert Freistühler, 1974.

Crémieux, Albert. *La révolution de février; étude critique sur les journées des 21, 22, 23 et 24 février 1848*. [1912] Geneva: Mégariotis reprints, 1977.

Crié, A. s.v. "Charbonnerie" in *La grande encyclopédie*. Paris: Limarault et Cie [1898?]

Crössmann, Christoph. *Das Unruhen in Oberhessen im Herbste 1830*. Quellen und Forschungen zur hessischen Geschichte, 8. Darmstadt: Hessischer Staatsverlag, 1929.

Dauzet, Pierre. *Le siècle des chemins de fer en France (1821–1938)*. Fontenay-aux-Roses: Bellenand, 1948.

Demandt, Karl E. *Geschichte des Landes Hessen*. 2nd ed.. Kassel: Bärenreiter-Verlag, 1972.

Deuchert, Norbert. *Vom hambacher Fest zur badischen Revolution; politische Presse und Anfänge deutscher Demokratie 1832–1848/49*. Stuttgart: Konrad Theiss Verlag, 1983.

Deuerlein, Ernst. *Bayern in der Paulskirche*. Altötting, 1948.

Diesbach, Alfred. *Die deutschkatholische Gemeinde Konstanz 1845–1849*. Mannheim: Freireligiöse Verlagsbuchhandlung, 1971.

Diwald, Hellmut. *Ernst Moritz Arndt—Das Entstehen des deutschen Nationalbewusstseins*. Vertrag gehalten an dem Mentorabend der Carl Friedrich von Siemens-Stiftung am 27. Januar 1970. Munich, 1970.

Doblinger, Max and Georg Schmidgall. *Geschichte und Mitgliederverzeichnisse burchenschaftlicher Verbindungen in Alt-Österreich und Tübingen 1816 bis 1936*. Burchenschaftlisten, 1. Görlitz: Verlag für Sippenforschung und Wappenkunde Starke, 1940.

Döberl, Michael. *Bayern und die deutsche Frage in der Epoche des Frankfurter Parlaments*. Bayern und Deutschland, I. Munich: Oldenbourg, 1922.

Döhl, Wilhelm. *Die deutsche Nationalversammlung von 1848 im Spiegel der "Neuen Rheinischen Zeitung"*. Inaug.-Diss. Bonn. Dillingen a. Donau: Schwäbische Verlagsdruckerei, 1931.

Dommanget, Maurice. *Auguste Blanqui et la révolution de 1848*. Paris: Mouton, 1972.

Dotzauer, Winfried. *Quellen zur Geschichte der deutschen Freimauerei im 18. Jahrhundert*. Schriftenreihe der Internationalen Forschungsstelle. Demokratische Bewegungen in Mitteleuropa 1770–1850, 3. Frankfurt am Main: Lang, 1991.

Dowe, Dieter. *Aktion und Organisation. Arbeiterbewegung, sozialistische und kommunistische Bewegung in der preussischen Rheinprovinz 1820–1852*. Schriftenreihe des Forschungsinstituts der Friedrich-Ebert-Stiftung, 78. Hannover: Verlag für Literatur und Zeitgeschehen, 1970.

Dressen, Wolfgang. *1848–1849. Bürgerkrieg in Baden. Chronik einer verlorenen Revolution.* Berlin: Klaus Wagenbach, 1975.

Droysen Johann Gustav and Samwer. *La révolution danoise en 1848.* Paris: Firmin Didot frères, 1850.

Droz, Jacques. *Les révolutions allemandes de 1848.* Publications de la Faculté des lettres de l'Université de Clermont sér 2, fasc 6 Paris: Presses universitaires de France, 1957.

Drummond, Elizabeth A. "Review of Jozsef Eotvos, *The Dominant Ideas of the Nineteenth Century and Their Impact on the State.* Vol. 1. *Diagnosis.*" [Michigan State University] HABSBURG, H-Net Reviews, May 1997.

Eckermann, Johann Peter. *Gespräche mit Goethe in den letzten Jahren seines Lebens.* Berlin: Aufbau Verlag, 1982.

Edwards, Lyford P. *The Natural History of Revolution.* The Heritage of Society. Chicago: University of Chicago Press [1927] 1970.

Eigenbrodt, Reinhard Carl Theodor. *Meine Erinnerungen aus den Jahren 1848, 1849 und 1850.* Ludwig Bergsträsser, ed. .Quellen und Forschungen zur hessischen Geschichte, 2. Darmstadt: Grossherzoglich hessischer Staatsverlag, 1914.

Elben, Otto. *Lebenserinnerungen 1823–1899.* Darstellungen aus der württembergischen Geschichte 22. Stuttgart: Kohlhammer, 1931.

Engels, Friedrich. *Revolution and Counter-Revolution in Germany.* Peking: Foreign Language Press, 1977.

Evans, Richard J. and W. R. Lee. *The German Family; Essays on the Social History of the Family in Nineteenth- and Twentieth-Century Germany.* London: Croom Helm Ltd., 1981.

Eyck, F. Gunther. "English and French Influences on German Liberalism before 1848." *Journal of the History of Ideas* 18 (1959): 313–34.

Eyck, Frank. *The Frankfurt Parliament 1848–1849.* London: Macmillan, 1968.

Fetscher, Elmar B. *Die Konstanzer Seeblätter und die Pressezensur des Vormärz 1840/41.* Konstanzer Geschichts- und Rechtsquellen, 27. Sigmaringen: Jan Thorbecke Verlag, 1981.

Feuerbach, Ludwig. *Das Wesen des Christentums.* Stuttgart: Reclam, 1974.

Flaubert, Gustave. *L'éducation sentimentale; histoire d'un jeune homme.* Paris: Flammarion, 1985.

———. *Madame Bovary.* Paris: Flammarion, 1986.

Focko, Eulen. *Vom Gewerbefleiss zur Industrie.* Schriften zur Wirtschafts- und Sozialgeschichte, 11. Berlin: Duncker & Humblot, 1967.

Förderer, Albert. *Erinnerungen aus Rastatt 1849.* Dokumente zur Weltgeschichte. Offenburg: Lehrmittel Verlag, 1948.

Fout, John C. *German Women in the Nineteenth Century: a Social History.* New York Holmes & Meier, 1984.

Frahm, Friedrich. "Entstehungs- und Entwicklungsgeschichte der preussischen Verfassung (vom März 1848 bis zum Januar 1850)." *Forschungen zur brandenburgischen und preussischen Geschichte* 41/2 (1928): 248–301.

France. *Ministère des travaux publics, de l'agriculture et du commerce. Direction générale des ponts et chaussées.* Exposé général des études fâites pour le trace des chemins de fer de Paris en Belgique. Paris: Impr. royale 1837.

Franz, Eugen. *Bayerische Verfassungskämpfe.* Munich: Pfeiffer, 1926.

Frenzel, Karl. *Die berliner Märztage und andere Erinnerungen.* Leipzig: Reclam, 1912.

Frevert, Ute *Women in Germany Society; from Bourgeois Emancipation to Sexual Liberation.* New York: St. Martin's Press, 1989.

Freytag, Gustav. *Karl Mathy; Geschichte seines Lebens.* 2d ed. Leipzig: Hirzel, 1872.

Friedrich Wilhelm IV. in seiner Zeit. Beiträge eines Colloquiums. Otto Busch, ed. Einzelveröffentlichungen der Historischen Kommission zu Berlin, 63. Berlin: Colloquium-Verlag, 1987.

Friedensburg, Wilhelm. *Stephan Born* [Reprint] with *Das Volk.* .

Fröbel, Julius. *Die deutsche Auswanderung and ihre culturhistorische Bedeutung. Fünfzehn Briefe an den Herausgeber der Allgemeine Auswanderungs-Zeitung.* Leipzig: Franz Wagner, 1858.

————. *Ein Lebenslauf. Aufzeichnungen, Erinnerungen und Bekenntnisse.* Stuttgart: Cotta, 1890–1891.

Fünfzigjähriges Jubiläum der "Belleviller Zeitung" 1849–1899. [Belleville? 1899?]

Füssl, Wilhelm. *Professor in der Politik. Friedrich Julius Stahl (1802–1861). Das monarchische Prinzip und seine Umsetzung in der parlamentarische Praxis.* Schriftenreihe der Historischen Kommission bei der Bayerischen Akademie der Wissenschaften, 33. Göttingen: Vanderhoeck & Ruprecht, 1988.

Funke, Georg Ludwig Wilhelm. "Zur Lage der Heuerleute" [his *Über die gegenwartige Lage der Heuerleute im Fürstenthume Osnabrück* Bielefeld 1847] in Carl Jantke and Dietrich Hilger, eds., *Die Eigentumslosen,* pp.101–111.

Gagern, Heinrich von. *Das Leben des Generals Friedrich von Gagern.* 3 vols. Leipzig: Winter, 1856–58.

Gall, Lothar. *Bürgertum in Deutschland.* Berlin: Siedler Verlag, 1989.

Gallaher, John G. *The Students of Paris and the Revolution of 1848.* Carbondale: Southern Illinois University Press, 1950.

Gallo and Thibault. s.v. "Révolutions de 1848" *Grand Larousse* (1962) 9:240. *Die Gegenwart.* Vol.1. Leipzig: Brockhaus, 1848.

Geheime Gesellschaften. Heidelberg: Verlag Lambert Schneider, 1979.

Geiger, Ludwig, ed. *Bettine von Arnim und Friedrich Wilhelm IV. Ungedruckte Briefe und Aktenstücke.* Frankfurt am Main: Rütten & Loening, 1902.

Georg Büchner, Ludwig Weidig, Der hessische Landbote; Texte, Briefe, Prozessakten, kommentiert von Hans Magnus Enzensberger. Frankfurt am Main: Insel-Verlag, 1965.

Geppert, Ernst-Günther. *Die Herkunft, die Gründer, die Namen der Freimauerlogen in Deutschland seit 1737.* Bayreuth: Quatuor Coronati, 1976.

Gerhardt, Bruno. *Handbuch der deutschen Geschichte.* 9th ed. Herbert Grundmann ed. vol.3. Stuttgart: Union Verlag, 1970.

Gerlach, Leopold von. *Denkwürdigkeiten.* Berlin: Verlag von Wilhelm Hertz, 1891.

German Library Society of St. Clair County, Illinois. *Numeral-Katalog der deutschen Bibliothek von St. Clair County, Ill.* [Belleville? 1854?]

Germans to America, Guenter Moltmann ed. Stuttgart: Inst. for Foreign Cultural Relations, 1982.

Gesellschaftskritik im Werk Heinrich Heines. Hedwig Walwei-Wiegelmann, ed. Paderborn: Ferdinand Schöningh, 1974.

Giebel, Hans Rainer. *Strukturanalyse der Gesellschaft des Königreichs Bayern im Vormärz 1818–1848.* Munich, 1971.

Gille, Bertrand. *Histoire de la maison Rothschild.* Travaux de droit, d'économie, de sociologie et de sciences politiques 39, 56. Geneva: Droz, 1965–67.

Gioberti, Vincenzo. *Del primato morale e civile degli italiani.* Milan: Ed. Allegranza, 1944.

Godechot, Jacques, ed. *La presse ouvrière 1819–1850.* Bibliothèque de la révolution de 1848, 23 [n.p.] 1966.

[Goegg, Armand.] *Nachträgliche authentische Aufschlüsse über die badische Revolution von 1849, deren Entstehung, politischen und militärischen Verlauf.* "Spezial-Ausgabe für die Vereinigten Staaten." New York: Bickel, 1876.

Gossez, Rémi. "Diversité des antagonismes sociaux vers le milieu du XIXe siècle." *Revue économique* (May 1956): 439–482.

Gould, Roger V. *Insurgent Identities: Class, Community and Protest in Paris from 1848 to the Commune.* Chicago: University of Chicago Press, 1995.

Grab, Walter, ed. *Die Revolution von 1848/49; eine Dokumentation.* Munich: Nymphenburger Verlagshandlung, 1980.

Grauer, Karl Johannes. *Wilhelm I., König von Württemberg; ein Bild seines Lebens und seiner Zeit.* Stuttgart: Schwabenverlag, 1960.

Gray, Marion W. "From the Household Economy to 'Rational Agriculture'. The Establishment of Liberal Ideals in German Agricultural Thought" in *In Search of a Liberal Germany*, New York, St. Martin's Press, 1990, pp. 25–54

Grimm, Dieter. *Deutsche Verfassungsgeschichte 1776–1866. Vom Beginn des modernen Verfassungsstaats bis zur Auflösung des Deutschen Bundes.* Neue historische Bibliothek n.F.271. Frankfurt am Main: Suhrkamp Verlag, 1988.

Gruenerr, Wolf D. *Das bayerische Heer 1825 bis 1864.* Militärgeschichtliche Studien 14. Boppard am Rhein: Harald Bodtt Verlag, 1972.

Gutzkow, Karl. *Rückblick auf mein Leben.* Berlin: Hofmann & Co., 1875.

Haefelin, Jürg. *Wilhelm Weitling; Biographie und Theorie der zürcher Kommunisten-prozess von 1843.* Europäische Hochschulschriften ser.3, no.304. Bern: Peter Lang, 1986.

Hahn, Hans Henning. *Aussenpolitik in der Emigration. Die Exildiplomatie Adam Jerzy Czartoryskis 1830–1840.* Studien zur Geschichte des neunzehnten Jahrhunderts. Abhandlung der Forschungsabteilung des Historischen Seminars der Universität Köln, 10. Munich: R. Oldenbourg Verlag, 1978.

———— "Die Diplomatie des Hôtel Lambert 1831–1847." *Jahrbücher für Geschichte Osteuropas* n.F. 21 (1973): 345–374.

Hamerow, Theodore S. *Restoration, Revolution, Reaction; Economics and Politics in Germany, 1815–1871.* Princeton: Princeton Univ Press, 1958.

Handbuch der deutschen Burschenschaft. Torsten Locher and Hans-Martin Sass, eds. Bad Nauheim: Ludwig Wagner, 1964.

Hansen, Joseph. *Gustav von Mevissen; ein rheinisches Lebensbild 1815–1899.* 2 vols. Berlin: 1906.

————. *Preussen und Rheinland von 1815 bis 1915; hundert Jahre politischen Lebens am Rhein.* Bonn: Marcus & Weber, 1918.

Hartig, Franz von. *Genesis, or Details of the Late Austrian Revolution.* Published as an appendix to Walter Keating Kelly, *History of the House of Austria.* London: Henry G. Bohn, 1853.

Hausmann, Sebastian. *Die Grund-Entlastung in Bayern.* Strasbourg, 1892.

Haym, Rudolf. *Die deutsche Nationalversammlung bis zu den Septemberereignissen: Ein Bericht aus der Partei des rechten Centrum.* Frankfurt a. M.: Verlag von Carl Jügel, 1848.

Hecker, Friedrich. *Die Erhebung des Volkes in Baden für die deutsche Republik im Frühjahr 1848.* Basel: Schabelitz, 1848.

Heine, Heinrich. *Sämtliche Werke* Munich: Winkler Verlag, 1969–72.

Henderson, W. O. *The Zollverein.* Cambridge: Cambridge Univ. Press, 1939.

Hertz, Friedrich Otto. *The German Public Mind in the Nineteenth Century; A Social History of German Political Sentiments, Aspirations and Ideas.* Frank Eyck, ed. London: George Allen & Unwin, 1975.

Herzen, Aleksandr Ivanovich. *Letters from France and Italy 1847–1848.* Pitt series in Russian and East European studies, 25. Pittsburgh: University of Pittsburg Press, 1995.

———. *My Past and Thoughts.* New York: Alfred A. Knopf, 1973.

Herzog, Dagmar. "Liberalism, Religious Dissent, and Women's Rights. Louise Dittmar's Writings from the 1840s." In *In Search of a Liberal Germany; Studies in the History of German Liberalism from 1789 to the Present,* pp. 55–85. New York: Berg, 1990.

Heske, Franz. *German Forestry.* New Haven: Yale University Press, 1938.

Heuberger, Georg, ed. *The Rothschilds; a European Family.* Sigmaringen; Thorbeck-Boydell & Brewer, 1994.

Hildebrandt, Gunther. *Rastatt 1849.* Berlin: Deutscher Verlag der Wissenschaften, 1976.

Himka, John-Paul. *Galician Villagers and the Ukrainian National Movement in the Nineteenth Century.* New York: St. Martin's Press, 1988.

Histoire économique et sociale de la France par Pierre Léon et al.
vol. 3. L'avènement de l'ère industrielle 1789–années 1880. Paris:
Presses universitaires de France, 1976.

Holborn, Hajo. *A History of Modern Germany, 1840–1945.* New
York: Knopf, 1969.

Hubensteiner, Benno. *Bayerische Geschichte; Staat und Volk, Kunst
und Kultur.* 5th ed. Munich: Pflaum, 1967.

Huber, Ernst Rudolf. *Der Kampf um Einheit und Freiheit 1830 bis
1850. Deutsche Verfassungsgeschichte seit 1789,* vol..2.
Stuttgart, W. Kohlhammer Verlag 1960.

Huber, Max. *Ludwig I. von Bayern und die Ludwig-Maximilians-
Universität in München (1826–1832).* Würzburg: Triltsch,
1929.

Hübinger, Gangolf. *Georg Gottfried Gervinus; historisches Urteil
und politische Kritik.* Göttingen: Vandenhoeck & Ruprecht,
1984.

Hugo, Victor. *Choses vues; souvenirs, journaux, cahiers 1830–1846*
[n.p.] Gallimard, 1972

————. *Les feuilles d'automne* Oxford: Blackwell, 1944.

————. *Les Misérables.* Paris: Garnier, 1963.

*In Search of a Liberal Germany. Studies in Search of a Liberal
Germany; Studies in the History of German Liberalism from
1789 to the Present.* Konrad H. Jarausch and Larry Eugene
Jones, eds. New York: Berg, 1990.

Ippel, Edward, ed. *Briefwechsel zwischen Jacob und Wilhelm Grimm,
Dahlmann und Gervinus .* 2 vols.[1886] Walluf bei Wiesbaden:
Sändig, 1973.

Jacoby, Johann. *Briefwechsel 1816–1849.* Edmund Silberner, ed.
Veröffentlichungen des Instituts für Sozialgeschichte
Braunschweig. Hannover: Fackelträger Verlag, l974.

————. *Briefwechsel 1850–1877.* Edmund Silberner, ed.
Veröffentlichungen des Instituts für Sozialgeschichte
Braunschweig. Bonn: Verlag Neue Gesellschaft, 1978.

————. *Gesammelte Schriften und Reden.* 2 vols. Hamburg: Meissner,
1872.

————. *Vier Fragen, beantwortet von einem Ostpreussen.* Mannheim: Hoff, 1841.

Jantke, Carl and Dietrich Hilger, eds. *Die Eigentumslosen.* Freiburg: Verlag Karl Alber, 1965.

Jessen, Hans. *Die deutsche Revolution 1848/49 in Augenzeugenberichten.* Fribourg: Office du livre, 1968.

Jordan, Erich. *Die Entstehung der konservativen Partei und die preussischen Agrarverhältnisse von 1848.* Munich: Duncker & Humblot, 1914.

Jucho, Friedrich Sigmund. *Verhandlungen des deutschen Parlaments.* Officielle Ausgabe. Frankfurt am Main, Sauerländer's Verlag, 1848.

Käfer-Dittmar, Gabriele. *Louise Dittmar (1807–1884) Un-erhörte Zeitzeugnisse.* Darmstadter Schriften, 61. Darmstadt, Justus von Liebig Verlag, 1992.

Kähni, Otto. *Offenburg und die demokratische Volksbewegung 1848–1849.* Offenburg in Baden: Verlag Franz Huber, 1947.

Kaufmann, Wilhelm. *Die Deutschen im amerikanischen Bürgerkriege.* Munich: Oldenberg 1911.

Keller, Hans Gustav. *Das "Junge Europa" 1834–1836; eine Studie zur Geschichte der Völkerbundsidee und des nationalen Gedankens.* Zurich: Max Niehan, 1938.

————. *Die politischen Verlagsanstalten und Druckereien in der Schweiz 1840–1848.* Berner Untersuchungen zur allgemeinen Geschichte 8. Bern: Haupt, 1935.

Kerchnawe, Hugo. *Radetzky; eine militär-biographische Studie.* Prague: Volk und Reich Verlag, 1944.

Kersken, Hans. *Stadt und Universität Bonn in den Revolutionsjahren 1848–49.* Rheinisches Archiv, 19. Bonn: Röhrscheid Verlag, 1931.

Klaus, Hans-Christian. "Das preussische Königtum und Friedrich Wilhelm IV. aus der Sicht Ernst Ludwig von Gerlachs." In *Friedrich Wilhelm IV. in seiner Zeit; Beiträge eines Colloquiums,* pp.48-131. Einzelveröffentlichungen der Historischen Kommission zu Berlin, 62. Berlin: Colloquium Verlag, 1987.

Klein, Tim. *1848: Der Vorkampf deutscher Einheit und Freiheit. Erinnerungen, Urkunden, Berichte, Briefe.* Leipzig: Lange Wiesche, 1914.

Klemke, Ulrich. *"Eine Anzahl überflüssiger Menschen." Die Exilierung politischer Straftäter nach Übersee: Vormärz und Revolution 1848/49.* Europäische Hochschulschriften 591. Frankfurt am Main: Peter Lang, 1993.

Klessmann, Christoph. "Zur Sozialgeschichte der Reichsverfassungskampagne von 1849." *Historische Zeitschrift* 218/2 (April 1974): 283–337.

Kobschaetzky, Hans. *Streckenatlas der deutschen Eisenbahnen 1835–1892.* Düsselsorf: Alba, 1971.

Koch-Gontard, Clotilde. *Tagebuch über die konstituierende deutsche Nationalversammlung zu Frankfurt am Main (Mai bis Dezember 1848).* Georg Küntzel, ed. Frankfurt am Main: Englert und Schlosser, 1924.

Körner, Hermann Joseph Aloys. *Lebenskämpfe in der alten und neuen Welt. Eine Selbstbiographie.* vol. 2. New York: L. W. Schmidt, 1866.

Kolb, Georg Friedrich. *Lebenserinnerungen einer liberalen Demokraten, 1808–1884.* Ludwig Merckle, ed. Freiburg: Verlag Rombach, 1976.

Koselleck, Reinhart. *Preussen zwischen Reform und Revolution. Allgemeines Landrecht, Verwaltung und soziale Bewegung von 1791 bis 1848.* Industrielle Welt, 7. Stuttgart: Ernst Klett, 1975.

Kossmann, E. H. *The Low Countries, 1780–1940.* Oxford History of Modern Europe. Oxford: Clarendon Press, 1978.

Kozik, Jan. *The Ukrainian National Movement in Galicia: 1815–1849.* Edmonton: Canadian Institute of Ukrainian Studies, University of Alberta, 1986.

Kramer, Helmut. *Fraktionsbindungen in den deutschen Volksvertretungen 1819–1849.* Schriften zur Verfassungs-geschichte 7. Berlin: Duncker & Humblot, 1968.

Kraus, Hans-Christof, ed. *Konservative Politiker in Deutschland; eine Auswahl biographischer Porträts aus zwei Jahrhunderten.* Berlin: Duncker & Humblot, 1995.

Kretzschmar, Hellmut and Horst Schlechte, eds. *Französische und sächsische Gesandschaftsberichte aus Dresden und Paris, 1848–1849.* Berlin: Rütten & Loening, 1956.

Krischker, Gerhard C. *Bamberg in alten Ansichtskarten.* Frankfurt am Main: Flechsig Verlag, 1978.

Kristl, Wilhelm Lukas. *Lola, Ludwig und der General.* Pfaffenhofen: Verlag W. Ludwig, 1979.

Kukiel, Marian. *Csartoryski and European Unity 1770–1861.* Poland's Millenium Series of the Kosciuszko Foundation. Princeton: Princeton University Press, 1955.

Lamartine, Alphonse de. *Histoire de la révolution de 1848.* 3d ed. Paris: Perrotin, 1852.

Langewiesche, Dieter. *Die deutsche Revolution von 1848/49.* Wege der Forschung 164. Darmstadt: Wissenschaftliche Buchgesellschaft, 1983.

Laube, Heinrich *Das erste deutsche Parlament.* Selections, Karl H. Lange, ed. Der Geist Europas, 10. Wiesbaden: Metopen-Verlag, 1948.

Lautenschlager, Friedrich. *Volksstaat und Einherrschaft. Dokumente aus der badischen Revolution 1848/1849.* Baden: Reuss & Itta, 1920.

Le Forestier, René. *Maçonnerie féminine et loges académiques.* Bibliothèque de l'unicorne série française 10. Milan: Archê, 1979.

Lewald-Stahr, Fanny. *Erinnerungen aus dem Jahre 1848.* Selections, Dietrich Schaefer, ed. Sammlung Insel. Frankfurt am Main: Insel Verlag, 1969.

Liberalismus und Region; zur Geschichte des deutschen Liberalismus im 19. Jahrhundert. Lothar Gall and Dieter Langewiesche, eds. Historische Zeitschrift Beiheft 19. Munich: Oldenbourg Verlag, 1995.

Lill, Rudolf. *Die Beziehung der Kölner Wirren 1840–1842; vorwiegend nach Akten des vatikanischen Geheimarchivs.* Studien zur Kölner Kirchengeschichte, 6. Düsseldorf: L. Schjwann, 1962.

———. "Kirche und Revolution; zu den Anfängen der katholischen Bewegung im Jahrzehnt vor 1848." *Archiv für Sozialgeschichte* 18 (1978): 565–575.

Linnenkamp, Iris. *Leo von Klenze; Das Leuchtenberg-Palais in München.* Miscellanea bavarica monacensia, 159. Munich: Kommissionsverlag UNI-Druck, 1992.

Lipp, Carola et al. "Frauen bei Brotkrawallen, Strassentumulten und Katzenmusiken. Zum politischen Verhalten von Frauen 1847 und in der Revolution 1848/49." In *Transformationen der Arbeiterkultur,* pp. 49–63. 3. Arbeitstagung der Kommission "Arbeiterkultur" in der Deutschen Gesellschaft für Volkskunde in Marburg 3–6 Juni 1985. Marburg: Jonas Verlag 1985.

List, Friedrich. "Die Ackerverfassung, die Zwergwirtschaft und die Auswanderung," [from *Deutsche Vierteljahrs Schrift* 1842, Hft.4, 119–164] in Carl Jantke and Dietrich Hilger, eds., *Die Eigentumslosen*, pp. 112–156.

Lola Montes; the tragic story of a "liberated woman". Melbourne: Heritage, 1973.

Longerich, Peter, ed. *"Was ist des Deutschen Vaterland?" Dokumente zur Frage der deutschen Einheit 1800 bis 1990.* Munich: Piper, 1990.

Lonn, Ella. *Foreigners in the Union Army and Navy.* [Reprint] New York: Greenwood Press Publ., 1951.

Los Angeles County Museum. *Honoré Daumier; Exhibition of Prints, Drawings, Water Colors, Paintings and Sculpture November 1958.* Los Angeles, 1958.

Lougee, Robert W. *Midcentury Revolution, 1848. Society and Revolution in France and Germany.* Civilization and Society. Lexington: D. C. Heath and Co., 1972.

Ludz, Peter Christian. "Überlegungen zu einer soziologischen Analyse geheimer Gesellschaften des späten 18. und frühen 19. Jahrhunderts." In *Geheime Gesellschaften,* 5/1: 89–119.

Lüders, Gustav. *Die demokratische Bewegung in Berlin im Oktober 1848*. Abhandlungen zur mittleren und neueren Geschichte, ll. Berlin: Walter Rothschild, 1909.

Macartney, C. A. *The Habsburg Empire 1790–1918*. New York: Macmillan Company, 1969.

Mack Smith, Denis. *Mazzini*. New Haven: Yale University Press, 1994.

Männer der Revolution von 1848. Hrsg. vom Arbeitskreis Vorgeschichte und Geschichte der Revolution von 1848/49. Deutsche Akademie der Wissenschaften zu Berlin, Schriften des Zentralinstituts für Geschichte, Reihe 1: Allgemeine und deutsche Geschichte, 33. Berlin: Akademie-Verlag, 1970.

Mah, Harold. *The End of Philosophy; the Origin of "Ideology". Karl Marx and the Crisis of the Young Hegelians*. Berkeley and Los Angeles: University of California Press, 1987

Mann, Thomas. *Buddenbrooks*. H. T. Lowe-Porter tr. New York: Vintage Books, 1961.

———. *The Magic Mountain*. H. T. Lowe-Porter tr. New York: Vintage Books, 1969.

Marggraff, Hugo. *Die Kgl. bayerischen Staatseisenbahnen in geschichtlicher und statistischer Beziehung* Munich: Oldenbourg, 1894.

Markovitch, T. J. "La crise de 1847–1848 dans les industries parisiennes." *Revue d'histoire économique et sociale* 43 (1965): 256–260.

Marx, Karl and Friedrich Engels. *The Communist Manifesto*. New York: Washington Square Press, 1964.

Marx-Engels Reader 2d ed. Robert C. Tucker ed. New York: W. W. Norton, 1972.

Mathy, Ludwig, ed. *Aus dem Nachlass von Karl Mathy: Briefe aus den Jahren 1846*–1848. Leipzig: Hirzel, 1898.

Mauchenheim gt. Bechtolsheim, Hartmann. *Das Heiligen Römischen Reiches unmittelbar-freie Ritterschaft zu Franken, Ort Steigerwald, im 17. und 18. Jahrhundert*, pt.1. Würzburg: Kommissionsverlag Ferdinand Schirrningh, 1972.

May, Arthur J. *The Age of Metternich 1814–1848*. Rev. ed. New York: Holt, Rinehart and Winston, 1963.

McKay, Donald Cope. *The National Workshops: a Study in the French Revolution of 1848*. Harvard Historical Studies, 35. Cambridge: Harvard University Press, [1933] 1965.

McKay, John. "The House of Rothschild (Paris) as a Multinational Industrial Enterprise 1875–1914." In *Multinational Enterprise in Historical Perspective*, pp. 74–86. Cambridge: Cambridge University Press, 1986.

Meusch, Hans. *Die Handwerkerbewegung von 1848/49*. Eschwege, 1949.

Mieroslawski, Ludwig. *Berichte des Generals Mieroslawski über den Feldzug in Baden*. Bern: Verlag von Jenni, Sohn, 1849.

Mill, John Stuart. *On Liberty*. Stefan Collini ed. Cambridge texts in the history of political thought, 192. Cambridge: Cambridge University Press, 1989.

Modern Germany Reconsidered, 1870–1945. Gordon Martel, ed. London: Routledge, 1992.

Moleschott, Jakob. *Für meine Freunde. Lebenserinnerungen*. Giessen: Roth, 1894.

Mollier, Jean-Yves. "Belle-Ile-en-Mer, prison politique (1848–1858)." In *Maintien de l'ordre et polices en France et en Europe au XIXe siècle*, pp. 185–211. Société d' histoire de la révolution de 1848 et des révolutions du XIXe siècle. Paris: Créaphis, 1987.

Mommsen, Wilhelm. *Grösse und Versagen des deutschen Bürgertums: ein Beitrag zur Geschichte der Jahre 1848–1849*. Stuttgart: Deutsche Verlags-Anstalt, 1949.

Montanelli, Indro. *L'Italia carbonaro*. His *Storia d'Italia*, 26. Milan: Rizzoli, 1971.

Mooser, Josef. "Property and Wood Theft: Agrarian Capitalism and Social Conflict in Rural Society, 1800–50. A Westphalian Case Study." In *Peasants and Lords in Modern Germany*, pp. 52–80. Boston: Allen & Unwin, 1986.

Morazé, Charles. *The Triumph of the Middle Classes*. Garden City: Doubleday, 1968.

Morrall, J. B. "Lamennais: a Liberal Catholic." *History Today* 8 (1958): 821–828.

Münich, Friedrich. *Geschichte der Entwickelung der bayerischen Armee seit zwei Jahrhunderten.* Munich: Lindauer, 1864.

". . . *nach Amerika!" Auswanderung in die Vereinigten Staaten.* Aus den Schausammlungen des Museums für Hamburgische Geschichte, 5. Hamburg, 1976.

Neher, Walter. *Arnold Ruge als Politiker und politischer Schriftsteller. Ein Beitrag zur deutschen Geschichte des 19. Jahrhunderts.* Heidelberger Abhandlungen 64. Heidelberg: Carl Winters Universitätsbuchhandlung, 1933.

Nickel, Dietmar. *Die Revolution 1848/49 in Augsburg und Bayerisch-Schwaben.* Schwäbische Geschichtsquellen und Forschungen, 8. Augsburg: Seitz, 1965.

Nicolson, Harold. *The Congress of Vienna: a Study in Allied Unity, 1812–1822.* [1946] New York: Viking Press, 1966.

Nipperdey, Thomas. "Verein als soziale Struktur in Deutschland im späten 18. und frühen 19. Jahrhundert." In Hartmut Boockmann et al. *Geschichtswissenshaft und Vereinswesen im 19. Jahrhundert.* Veröffentlichungen des Max-Planck-Instituts für Geschichte, 1/1:1-44. Göttingen: Vanderhoeck & Ruprecht, 1972.

Noack, Richard. *Die Revolutionsbewegung von 1848/49 in der Saargegend.* Mitteilungen des Histor. Vereins für die Saargegend 18/2. Saarbrücken: Hofer AG, 1930.

Noyes, P. H. *Organization and Revolution. Working-class Associations in the German Revolutions of 1848–1849.* Princeton: Princeton University Press, 1966.

Obermann, Karl. *Die deutschen Arbeiter in der Revolution von 1848.* 2d ed. Berlin: Dietz Verlag, 1953.

———. *Einheit und Freiheit; Die deutsche Geschichte von 1815 bis 1849 in zeitgenössischen Dokumentation.* Berlin: Dietz Verlag, 1950.

———. "Karl d'Ester, Arzt und Revolutionär; seine Tätigkeit in den Jahren 1842–1849." In *Aus der Frühgeschichte der deutschen Arbeiterbewegung.* Deutsche Akademie der Wissenschaften zu

Berlin. Schriften des Instituts für Geschichte, series 1, vol. 1. Berlin: Akademie-Verlag, 1964.

Oesterreich Lexikon. Richard Bamberger et al. 2 vols. Vienna: Verlagsgemeinschaft Oesterreich Lexikon, 1995.

The Opening of an Era: 1848. François Fejtö ed. New York: Grosset & Dunlap, 1973.

Ostadal, Hubert. *Die Kammer der Reichsräte in Bayern von 1819 bis 1848.* Miscellanea Bavarica Monacensia, 12. Neue Schriftenreihe des Stadtarchivs, l. Munich, 1968.

Otto, Ulrich. *Die historisch-politischen Lieder und Karikaturen des Vormärz und der Revolution von 1848/1849.* Pahl-Rugenstein Hochschulschriften, Gesellschafts- und Naturwissenschaften, 100. Cologne: Pahl-Rugenstein Verlag, 1982.

Paine, Thomas. *The Rights of Man.* Everyman Library. London: J. M. Dent, 1993.

Paletschek, Sylvia. *Frauen und Dissens. Frauen im Deutschkatholizismus und in der freien Gemeinden 1841–1852.* Kritische Studien zur Geschichtswissenschaft, 89. Göttingen: Vanderhoeck & Ruprecht, 1990.

Paschen, Joachim. *Demokratische Vereine und preussischer Staat. Entwicklung und Unterdrückung der demokratischen Bewegung während der Revolution von 1848/49.* Studien zur modernen Geschichte, 22. Munich: R. Oldenbourg Verlag, 1977.

Pech, Stanley Z. *The Czech Revolution of 1848.* Chapel Hill: Univ. of North Carolina Press, 1969.

Pellico, Silvio. *Le mie prigioni.* Milan: U. Mursia, 1971.

Pevsner, Nikolaus. *An Outline of European Architecture.* Harmondsworth: Penguin Books, 1970.

Polisensky, Josef. *Aristocrats and the Crowd in the Revolutionary Year 1848; a Contribution to the History of Revolution and Counter-Revolution in Austria.* Albany: State University of New York Press, 1980.

Porsch, Johann Karl. "Aus einer Landgemeinde." [from his *Der Arme im Wohlstand oder vorteilhafteste Armenhülfe auf dem Lande durch Armenbeschäftigung* Nürnberg 1840] In Carl Jantke and Dietrich Hilger, eds. *Die Eigentumslosen* 149–156.

Prelinger, Catherine M. "Religious Dissent, Women's Rights, and the *Hamburger Hochschule fuer das weibliche Geschlecht* in mid-nineteenth Century Germany." *Church History* 45 (1976): 42–55.

Price, Arnold H. *The Evolution of the Zollverein*. Ann Arbor: Univ. of Michigan Press, 1949.

Pröhle, Heinrich. *Friedrich Ludwig Jahn's Leben, nebst Mittheilungen aus seinem literarischen Nachlasse*. 2. Aufl. Berlin: Verlag Franz Duncker, 1872.

Prutz, Robert. *Zehn Jahre: Geschichte der neuesten Zeit 1840–1850*. Leipzig: Verlagsbuchhandlung von J. J. Weber, 1850–1856.

Prittwitz, Karl Ludwig von. *Berlin 1848; Das Erinnerungswerk des Generalleutnants Karl Ludwig von Prittwitz und andere Quellen zur berliner Märzrevolution und zur Geschichte Preussens um die Mitte des 19. Jahrhunderts*. Gerd Heinrich, ed. New York, 1985.

Raabe, Wilhelm Karl. *Ausgewählte Werke*. Berlin: Aufbau-Verlag. 1966.

Radowitz, Josef Maria von. *Gesammelte Schriften*, vol.2. Berlin: Georg Reimer, 1852.

Ranke, Leopold von, ed.. *Aus dem Briefwechsel Friedrich Wilhelms IV. mit Bunsen*. Leipzig: Duncker & Humblot, 1873.

Rattelmueller, Paul Ernst. *Das bayerische Bürgermilitär*. Munich, 1969.

Raveaux, Franz. *Mittheilungen über die badische Revolution*. Frankfurt am Main: Literarische Anstalt J. Rütten, 1850.

Real, Willy. *Die Revolution in Baden 1848/49*. Stuttgart: Kohlhammer, 1983.

Reindl, Josef. *Der Deutsch-Österreichische Telegraphenverein und die Entwicklung des deutschen Telegraphenwesens 1850–1871. Eine Fallstudie zur administrativ-technischen*

Kooperation deutscher Staaten vor der Gründung des Deutschen Reiches. Münchner Studien zur neueren und neuesten Geschichte, 2. Frankfurt am Main: Peter Lang, 1993.

Reiter, Herbert. *Politisches Asyl im 19. Jahrhundert. Die deutschen politischen Flüchtlinge des Vormärz und der Revolution von 1848/49 in Europa und der USA.* Berlin: Duncker & Humblot, 1992.

Reith, Reinhold. *Der Aprilaufstand von 1848 in Konstanz. Zur biographischen Dimensionen von "Hochverrath und Aufruhr"; Versuch einer historischen Protestanalyse.* Konstanzer Geschichts- und Rechtsquellen, 28. Sigmaringen: Jan Thorbecke Verlag, 1982.

Repgen, Konrad. *Märzbewegung und Maiwahlen des Revolutionsjahres 1848 im Rheinland.* Bonner historische Forschungen, 4. Bonn: Ludwig Röhrscheid Verlag, 1955.

Répression et prison politiques en France et en Europe au XIXe siècle. Société d'histoire de la révolution de 1848 et des révolutions du XIXe siècle. Paris: Créaphis, 1990.

Révolutions du XIXe siècle. Paris: E.D.H.I.S., 1974. 12 vols.

Revolutionsbriefe 1848/49. Rolf Weber, ed. Leipzig: Verlag Philipp Reclam jun., 1973.

Riedel, Manfred. "Vom Biedermeier zum Maschinenzeitalter; Zur Kulturgeschichte der ersten Eisenbahnen in Deutschland." *Archiv für Kulturgeschichte* (1961): 100–123, 431.

Riehl, Wilhelm Heinrich. *Die bürgerliche Gesellschaft.* 4th ed. Stuttgart, 1856.

Robertson, Priscilla. *Revolutions of 1848; A Social History.* Princeton: Princeton Univ. Press [1952] 1971.

Rosamunda [pseud]. *Die Köchin ohne Fehl und Tadel.* Munich: Joseph Lindauer, 1844.

Rotteck, Karl von. *Gesammelte und nachgelassenen Schriften mit Biographie und Briefwechsel.* Pflorzheim: Dennig Finck, 1841. 3 vols.

Rousseau, Jean-Jacques. *The Essential Rousseau.* New York: New American Library, 1974.

Rudé, George. *The Crowd in History; a Study of Popular Distur-bances in France and England 1730–1848.* New Dimensions in History. New York: John Wiley & Sons, 1964.

Sachse, H. E. *Erinnerungen an die Entstehung und Entwicklung der Magdeburger freien Gemeinde. Eine Festschrift zur Jubelfeier des 25jährigen Bestehens derselben am 29. November 1872.* Magdeburg: Selbstverlag des Vorstandes der Magdeburger freien Gemeinde, 1873.

Schieder, Wolfgang. "Kirche und Revolution; sozialgeschichtliche Aspekte der Trierer Wallfahrt von 1844." *Archiv für Sozialgeschichte* 14 (1974): 419–454.

Schimpfende Weiber und patriotische Jungfrauen; Frauen im Vormärz und in der Revolution 1848/49. Carola Lipp, ed. Moos: Elster Verlag, 1987.

Schindler, Norbert. "Aufklärung und Geheimnis im Illuminatenorden." In *Geheime Gesellschaften,* 6/1.

Schlögl, Alois. *Bayerische Agrar.Wirtschaft seit Beginn des 19. Jahrhunderts.* Munich: Bayerische Landwirtschaftsverlag, 1954.

Schmidt, Gerhard. *Die Staatsreform in Sachsen in der ersten Hälfte des 19. Jahrhunderts.* Weimar, 1966.

Schmidt, Siegfried. *Robert Blum.* Weimar: Herman Böhlaus Nachfolger, 1970.

Schmoller, Gustav. *Zur Geschichte der deutschen Kleingewerbe im 19. Jahrhundert. Statistische und nationalökonomische Unter-suchungen.* Halle: Waisenhaus, 1870.

Schoeps, Hans-Joachim, ed. *Neue Quellen zur Geschichte Preussens im 19. Jahrhundert.* Berlin: Haude & Spenersche Verlags-buchhandlung, 1968.

Schröter, Alfred, and Walter Becker. *Die deutsche Maschinenbauindustrie in der industriellen Revolution.* Veröffentlichungen des Instituts für Wirtschafts-geschichte an der Hochschule für Ökonomie Berlin-Karlshorst, 2. Berlin: Akademie Verlag, 1962.

Schulte, Wilhelm. *Volk und Staat: Westfalen im Vormärz und in der Revolution 1848/49.* Regensberg, 1954.

————. "Zustände und Vorgänge in Iserlohn und Hagen 1841/49. Aufzeichnungen des Karl Sudhaus (1827–1915)." In *Fritz Kuhn zum Gedächtnis. Beiträge zur Geschichte Iserlohns,* pp. 105–122. Iserlohn, 1966.

Schurz, Carl. *Als Amerika jung war; Lebenserinnerungen aus den Jahren 1852–1859.* Ebenhausen bei München: Langewiesche-Brandt, 1941.

————. *Sturmjahre; Lebenserinnerungen 1829–1852.* Berlin: Verlag der Nation, 1973.

————. *Vormärz in Deutschland; Erinnerungen/Briefe.* Herbert Pönicke ed.. Munich: Nymphenburger Verlag, 1948.

Schwender, Jakob. *Der Steigerwald; ein Beitrag zur Geographie Frankens.* Inaug.- Diss. Stuttgart, 1908.

Schwentker, Wolfgang. *Konservative Vereine und Revolution in Preussen 1848/49. Die Konstituierung des Konservatismus als Partei.* Düsseldorf: Droste, 1988.

Sechs Stimmen über geheime Gesellschaften und Freimauerei. Leipzig: Herbig, 1824.

Seeley, J. R. *Life and Times of Stein, or Germany and Prussia in the Napoleonic Age.* Cambridge: University Press, 1878. 3 vols. Reprinted St. Clair Shores: Scholarly Press, 1972.

Seidel, Friedrich. *Das Armutsproblem im deutschen Vormärz bei Friedrich List.* Kölner Vorträge zu Sozial- und Wirtschaftsgeschichte, 13. Cologne:1971.

Seton-Watson, Hugh. *The Russian Empire 1801–1917.* Oxford History of Modern Europe. Oxford: Clarendon Press, 1988.

Seward, Desmond. *Metternich, the first European.* New York: Viking, 1991.

Seymour, Bruce. *Lola Montez; a Life.* New Haven: Yale University Press, 1996.

Seyppel, Marcel. *Die Demokratische Gesellschaft in Köln 1848/49. Städtische Gesellschaft und Parteienstehung während der bürgerlichen Revolution.* Kölner Schriften zu Geschichte und Kultur, 15. Cologne: Janus Verlags-gesellschaft, 1991.

Sheehan, James J. *German History 1770–1886.* Oxford, Clarendon Press, 1989

_____. *German Liberalism in the Nineteenth Century.* Atlantic Highlands: Humanities Press International inc., 1995.

Shiner, L. E. *The Secret Mirror: Literary Form and History in Tocqueville's Recollections.* Ithaca: Cornell University Press, 1988.

Sie machen uns langsam tot. Zeugnisse politischer Gefangener in Deutschland 1780–1980. Kurt Kreiler, ed. Darmstadt: Luchterhand, 1983.

Siemann, Wolfram. *Die deutsche Revolution 1848/49.* Neue historische Bibliothek. Frankfurt am Main: Suhrkamp, 1985.

_____, ed. *Der "Polizeiverein" zur Überwachung der Öffentlichkeit nach der Revolution von 1848/49.* Tübingen: Niemeyer Verlag, 1983.

Spangenberg, Ilse. *Hessen-Darmstadt und der deutsche Bund 1815–1848.* Darmstadt: Selbstverlag des Historischen Vereins für Hessen, 1969.

Sperber, Jonathan. *The European Revolutions, 1848–1851.* Cambridge: Cambridge University Press, 1994.

_____. "Festivals of National Unity in the German Revolution of 1848–1849." *Past and Present* 136 (1992): 114–138.

_____. *Popular Catholicism in Nineteenth-Century Germany.* Princeton: Princeton University Press, 1984.

_____. *Rhineland Radicals: The Democratic Movement and the Revolution of 1848–1849.* Princeton: Princeton University Press, 1991.

Spevack, Edmund. *Charles Follen's Search for Nationality and Freedom; Germany and America, 1796–1840.* Harvard Historical Studies, 124. Cambridge: Harvard University Press, 1997.

Stadelmann, Rudolph. *Social and Political History of the German 1848 Revolution.* Athens: Ohio University Press, 1975.

Stearns, Peter N. *1848: The Revolutionary Tide in Europe.* New York: Norton, 1974.

Stern, Daniel. *Histoire de la révolution de 1848.* Paris: Gustave Sandré, 1850–53.

————. *Mémoires, souvenirs et journaux de la contesse d'Agoult.* Paris: Mercure de France, 1990.

Steuernagel, Bella. *The Belleville Public Library 1836–1936.* Belleville [1936?]

Stiles, William H. *Austria in 1848–49.* New York: Harper & Brothers, 1852.

Stolberg-Wernigerode, Otto *Graf* zu. *Anton Graf zu Stolberg-Wernigerode; ein Freund und Ratgeber König Friedrich Wilhelms IV.* Munich: R. Oldenbourg, 1926.

Stromberg, Roland N. *An Intellectual History of Modern Europe.* 2d ed. Englewood Cliffs: : Prentice-Hall, 1975.

Struve, Gustav von. *Politische Briefe.* Mannheim: Bensheimer, 1846.

Swart, Koenraad W. *The Sense of Decadence in Nineteenth-Century France.* Archives internationales d'histoire des idées. The Hague: Martinus Nijhoff, 1964.

Thomas, Richard Hinton. *Liberalism, Nationalism and the German Intellectuals (1822–1847) An Analysis of the Academic and Scientific Conferences of the Period.* [Cambridge; W. Heffer & Sons, 1951] Westport: Greenwood Press, 1975.

Tilly, Charles, Louise Tilly and Richard Tilly. *The Rebellious Century, 1830–1930.* Cambridge: Harvard University Press, 1975.

Tilly, Richard. "Popular Disorders in Nineteenth-Century Germany." *Journal of Social History* 4 (1970–1971) 1–40.

Tocqueville, Alexis de. *Democracy in America* [Eng tr of 1848 edition] Everyman's Library 179. New York: Knopf [1945] 1972.

————. *The Recollections of Alexis de Tocqueville.* New York: Meridian Books, 1959.

Tolzmann, Don Heinrich, ed. *The German-American Forty-Eighters, 1848–1998.* Indianapolis: The Max Kade German-American Center at Indiana University Purdue University & Indiana German Heritage Society, 1998.

Traugott, Mark. *Armies of the Poor; Determinants of Working-class Participation in the Parisian Insurrection of June 1848.* Princeton: Princeton Univ. Press, 1985.

Ullmann, Wilhelm. *Die hessische Gewerbepolitik von der Zeit des Rheinbundes bis zur Einführung der Gewerbefreiheit im Jahre 1866, insbesondere das Handwerk und das Hausierwerbe.* Inaug.-Diss. Heidelberg. Darmstadt: Herbert, 1903.

Ursel, Ernst. *Die bayereische Herrscher von Ludwig I. bis Ludwig III. im Urteil der Presse nach ihrem Tode.* Berlin: Duncker & Humblot, 1974.

Valentin, Veit. *Geschichte der deutschen Revolution von 1848–1849.* [Cologne: Verlag Kiepenheuer & Witsch 1931] Aalen, Scientia Verlag, 1968. 2 vols.

———. *Das hambacher Nationalfest.* Vaduz: Topos Verlag, 1978.

———. *Die erste deutsche Nationalversammlung; eine geschichtliche Studie über die frankfurter Paulskirche.* Munich: Oldenbourg, 1919.

Veblen, Thorstein. *Imperial Germany and the Industrial Revolution.* New York: Augustus M. Kelley, 1964.

Veit-Brause, Irmline. *Die deutsch-französische Krise von 1840; Studien zur deutschen Einheitsbewegung.* Cologne, 1967.

Vico, Giambattista. *The New Science,* tr. from the 3rd ed. by Thomas Goddard Bergin Walker and Max Harold Fisch. Garden City: Doubleday and Co., 1961.

Vigier, Philippe. *La vie quotidienne en province et à Paris pendant les journées de 1848.* Paris: Hachette, 1982.

Das Volk [Reprint] Glashütten im Taunus: Auvermann, 1973.

Vollmer, Franz X. *Vormärz und Revolution 1848/49 in Baden; Strukturen, Elemente, Fragestellungen.* Frankfurt am Main: Verlag Moritz Diesterweg, 1979.

Von der Revolution zum Norddeutschen Bund. Politik und Ideengut der preussischen Hochkonservativen 1848–1866. Aus dem Nachlass von Ernst Ludwig von Gerlach. H. Diwald, ed. Göttingen, 1970.

Vormärz und Revolution 1840–1849. Hans Fenske, ed. Quellen zum politischen Denken der deutschen im 19. und 20. Jahrhundert, 4. Darmstadt: Wissenschaftliche Buchgesellschaft, 1976.

Walker, Mack. *German Home Towns; Community, State, and General Estate, 1648–1871*. Ithaca: Cornell University Press, 1971.

Walwei-Wiegelmann, Hedwig. *Gesellschaftskritik im Werk Heinrich Heines*. Paderborn: Ferdinand Schöningh, 1974.

Wassermann, Suzanne. *Les clubs de Barbès et de Blanqui en 1848*. Geneva: Mégariotis reprints [1913] 1978.

Wawrykowa, Maria. "Die studentische Bewegung in Deutschland im ersten Jahrzehnt nach dem wiener Kongress." *Bourgeoisie und bürgerliche Umwälzung in Deutschland 1789–1871*. Akademie der Wissenschaften der DDR. Schriften des Zentralinstituts für Geschichte 50, pp.49 ff.. Berlin: Akademie-Verlag, 1977.

Weber, Rolf. "Centralmärzverein (CMV) 1848–1849." In *Die bürgerliche Parteien in Deutschland. Handbuch der Geschichte der bürgerlichen Parteien und anderer bürgerlicher Interessenorganisationer vom Vormärz bis zum Jahre 1945*, pp. 227–235. Leipzig, VEB Bibliographisches Institut, 1968.

————. *Johann Jacoby*. Cologne: Pahl-Rugenstein, 1988.

————. *Die Revolution in Sachsen 1848/49. Entwicklung und Analyse ihrer Triebkräfte*. Deutsche Akademie der Wissenschaften zu Berlin. Schriften des Zentralinstituts für Geschichte. Series 2, vol.11. Berlin: Akademie-Verlag, 1970.

Weiland, C. F. *Das Königreich Bayern* 1859. [map and related printed sheet]

Weiss, Hildegard. *Stadt- und Landkreis Bamberg*. Historischer Atlas von Bayern. Franken. Series 1. no.2. Munich: Komm. für bayerische Landesgeschichte, 1974.

Wellauer, Maralyn A. *German Immigration to America in the Nineteenth Century*. Milwaukee: Roots Int, 1985.

Wernicke, Kurt. *Geschichte der revolutionären berliner Arbeiterbewegung 1830–1849*. Beiträge zur Geschichte der berliner Arbeiterbewegung: Sonderreihe: Geschichte der revolutionären berliner Arbeiterbewegung von den Anfängen bis zur Gegenwart. Berlin: Bezirksleitung Berlin der SED, 1978.

Westermann Lexikon der Geographie. [n.p]. Georg Westermann Verlag, 1968.

Wettengel, Michael. *Die Revolution von 1848/49 im Rhein-Main-Raum; Politische Vereine und Revolutionsalltag im Grossherzogtum Hessen, Herzogtum Nassau und in der freien Stadt Frankfurt.* Veröffentlichungen der Historischen Kommission für Nassau, 49. Wiesbaden, 1989.

Wild, Karl. *Staat und Wirtschaft in den Bistümern Würzburg und Bamberg: Eine Untersuchung über die organisatorische Tätigkeit des Bischofs Friedrich Karl von Schönborn 1729–1746.* Heidelberger Abhandlungen zur mittleren und neueren Geschichte, 15. Nendeln: Kraus Reprint, 1977.

Wilson, Edmund. *To the Finland Station; A Study in the Writing and Acting of History.* Garden City: Doubleday & Co., [1940] 1953.

Winkler, Arnold. "Metternich und der Schweiz." *Zeitschrift für schweizerische Geschichte* 7 (1927) 60–116; 127–163.

Wollstein, Günter. *Das "Grossdeutschland" der Paulskirche: Nationale Ziele in der bürgerlichen Revolution 1848/49.* Düsseldorf: Droste Verlag, 1977.

Wright, Gordon. "A Poet in Politics: Lamartine and the Revolution of 1848." *History Today* 8 (1958) 616–627.

Wurzbach, Constantin. *Ritter von Tannenberg. Biographisches Lexikon des Kaiserthums Österreich.* Wien, 1876.

Zechlin, Egmont. *Schwarz Rot Gold und Schwarz Weiss Rot in Geschichte und Gegenwart, mit Benützung unveröffentlicher Akten.* Einzelschriften zur Politik und Geschichte, 15. Berlin: Deutsche Verlagsgesellschaft für Politik und Geschichte, 1926.

Index

New German-American Studies
Neue Deutsch-Amerikanische Studien

This series features scholarly monographs, published in German or English, that deal with topics in the humanities or social sciences pertaining to the German-American experience.

Original monographs in the following areas are welcome: history, literature, language, politics, philosophy, religion, education, geography, art and architecture, music and musical life, the theater, and contemporary issues of general interest.

All inquiries should be directed to the Editor of the series. Manuscripts should be between two and four hundred pages in length and prepared in accordance with the Chicago Manual of Style.

For additional information, contact the editor:

Dr. Don Heinrich Tolzmann
Blegen Library
University of Cincinnati
PO Box 210113
Cincinnati, OH 45221